HTML Quick Reference

Structure Tags

`<!--.....-->`	Creates a comment
`<html>...</html>`	Encloses the entire HTML document
`<head>...</head>`	Encloses the head of the HTML document
`<isindex>`	Indicates the document is a gateway script that allows searches
`<meta>`	Provides general information about the document
`<style>...</style>`	Style information
`<script>...</script>`	Scripting language
`<noscript>...</noscript>`	Alternative content when scripting not supported
`<title>...</title>`	The title of the document
`<body>...</body>`	Encloses the body (text and tags) of the HTML document

Headings

`<h1>...</h1>`	Headings 1 through 6
`<h2>...</h2>`	
`<h3>...</h3>`	
`<h4>...</h4>`	
`<h5>...</h5>`	
`<h6>...</h6>`	

Paragraphs

`<p>...</p>`	A plain paragraph; `</p>` is optional

Links

`<a>...</a>`	Creates a link or anchor Includes common attributes
`href="..."`	The URL of the document to be linked to this one
`name="..."`	The name of the anchor
`target="..."`	Identifies the window or location to open the link in
`rel="..."`	Defines forward link types
`rev="..."`	Defines reverse link types
`accesskey="..."`	Determines the accessibility character
`shape="..."`	Is for use with object shapes

Links

`coords="..."`	Is for use with object shapes
`tabindex="..."`	Determines the tabbing order
`onClick`	Is an intrinsic event
`onMouseOver`	Is an intrinsic event
`onMouseOut`	Is an intrinsic event

Lists

`<ol>...</ol>`	An ordered (numbered) list
`<ul>...</ul>`	An unordered (bulleted) list
`<menu>...</menu>`	A menu list of items
`<dir>...</dir>`	A directory listing
`<li>`	A list item
`<dl>...</dl>`	A definition or glossary list
`<dt>`	A definition term
`<dd>`	The corresponding definition to a definition term

Character Formatting

`<em>...</em>`	Emphasis (usually italic)
`<strong>...</strong>`	Stronger emphasis (usually bold)
`<code>...</code>`	Code sample
`<kbd>...</kbd>`	Text to be typed
`<var>...</var>`	A variable or placeholder for some other value
`<samp>...</samp>`	Sample text
`<dfn>...<dfn>`	A definition of a term
`<cite>...</cite>`	A citation
`<b>...</b>`	Boldface text
`<i>...</i>`	Italic text
`<tt>...</tt>`	Typewriter font
`<u>...</u>`	Underlined text
`<pre>...</pre>`	Preformatted text

Other Elements

`<hr />`	A horizontal rule line
` `	A line break
`<blockquote>...</blockquote>`	Used for long quotes or citations
`<address>...</address>`	Signatures or general information about a document's author

Other Elements

`<font>...</font>`	Change the size and color of the font
`size="..."`	The size of the font, from 1 to 7
`color="..."`	The font color
`face="..."`	The font type
`<basefont>`	Sets the default size of the font for the current page
`size="..."`	The default size of the font, from 1 to 7

Images

`<img>`	Inserts an inline image into the document; includes common attributes
`ismap`	This image is a server-side imagemap
`usemap`	This image is a client-side imagemap
`src="..."`	The URL of the image
`alt="..."`	A text string that will be displayed in browsers that cannot support images
`align="..."`	Determines the alignment of the given image
`height="..."`	Is the suggested height in pixels
`width="..."`	Is the suggested width in pixels
`vspace="..."`	The space between the image and the text above or below it
`hspace="..."`	The space between the image and the text to its left or right

Frames

`<frameset>...</frameset>`	Defines a frameset
`rows="..."`	Number of rows in frame
`cols="..."`	Number of columns in frame
`onLoad`	Is an intrinsic event
`onUnload`	Is an intrinsic event
`<frame>`	Creates a frame
`name="..."`	Is the name of target frame
`src="..."`	Calls the frame content source
`frameborder="..."`	Determines the frame border
`marginwidth="..."`	Defines margin widths
`marginheight="..."`	Defines margin heights
`noresize="..."`	Determines ability to resize frames
`scrolling="..."`	Determines ability to scroll within frames

Frames

`<iframe>...</iframe>`	Defines an inline frame
`<noframes>...</noframes>`	Alternate content when frames not supported

Tables

`<table>...</table>`	Creates a table
`border="..."`	Width of the border in pixels
`cols="..."`	Number of columns
`cellspacing="..."`	Spacing between cells
`cellpadding="..."`	Spacing in cells
`width="..."`	Table width
`<caption>...</caption>`	The caption for the table
`<tr>...</tr>`	A table row
`align="..."`	The horizontal alignment of the contents of the cells within this row; possible values are LEFT, RIGHT, CENTER, and JUSTIFY
`valign="..."`	The vertical alignment of the contents of the cells within this row; possible values are TOP, MIDDLE, BOTTOM, and BASELINE
`<th>...</th>`	A table heading cell
`align="..."`	The horizontal alignment of the contents of the cell
`valign="..."`	The vertical alignment of the contents of the cell
`rowspan="..."`	The number of rows this cell will span
`colspan="..."`	The number of columns this cell will span
`nowrap`	Do not automatically wrap the contents of this cell
`<td>...</td>`	Defines a table data cell
`align="..."`	The horizontal alignment of the contents of the cell
`valign="..."`	The vertical alignment of the contents of the cell
`rowspan="..."`	The number of rows this cell will span
`colspan="..."`	The number of columns this cell will span
`nowrap`	Do not automatically wrap the contents of this cell

Acclaim for Laura Lemay's *Sams Teach Yourself Web Publishing with HTML*

"There are some good HTML primers on the Web itself, but if you're like me, you'll find it easier to learn by cracking a book. The best I've found is Laura Lemay's *[Sams] Teach Yourself Web Publishing with HTML.*"
—Marc Frons, *Business Week*

"Laura Lemay delivers on her title's promise. By following her clear sequence of explanations, examples, and exercises, even the absolute Web novice can create serviceable documents within a few days. Better, she moves quickly beyond mechanics to techniques and tools for designing maximally effective and attractive presentations in spite of the medium's limitations."
—Michael K. Stone, *Whole Earth Review*

"If you're going to read only one book on HTML, and want it to be as comprehensive as can be, then make it this one."
—Mitch Gitman, *Pittsburgh Post-Gazette*

"Of all the HTML books out right now, I think Lemay's is the best, and I recommend it."
—Nancy McGough, Infinite Ink

"If you are looking for an easy-to-read introduction to HTML, this book is for you. Lemay has a clear understanding of what works and what doesn't, and she conveys her thoughts in a concise, orderly fashion."
—Robert Stewart, *The Virtual Mirror*

"If you want to create a Web page, or even if you already have created one, and you want a *great* book to help you understand it all, check out Laura Lemay's *[Sams] Teach Yourself Web Publishing with HTML.* I've used mine so much I practically know it by heart!"
—Camille Tillman, Book Stacks Unlimited

"All in all, this is a quality 'do-it-yourself' book for beginners of HTML publishing. The ABCs of HTML are explained clearly, and the exercises are instructive and easy to follow."

 —Jim Duber, *Chorus*

"This is a very thorough book on HTML, and quite accurate. Laura Lemay is a good technical writer who explains things well. This is the book I wish I'd had when I started to learn HTML."

 —Bob Cunningham, University of Hawaii

"My best recommendation goes to this book by Laura Lemay, entitled *[Sams] Teach Yourself Web Publishing with HTML*. There is simply no better book available, and many that are much worse than this one. If you study it, you will know more than enough to create stunning Web pages of your own."

 —Bob Bickford

"If you want a good book that will help you understand how everything is really working, take a look at Sams Publishing's *Teach Yourself Web Publishing with HTML*. It is a very well-written book, and it includes all the information in an easy to understand format."

 —Ron Loewy, HyperAct, Inc.

"There's a superb new book about HTML called *[Sams] Teach Yourself Web Publishing with HTML*.... It is very thorough and well-laid out."

 —Michael MacDonald

"I think Lemay's first book can take some degree of credit for the growth of the Web itself. I wonder how many of the tens of thousands of home pages created in the past six months have been done by folks with dog-eared copies of *[Sams] Teach Yourself Web Publishing* within arm's reach.

 —Dave Elliott, The Web Academy

Laura Lemay

With revisions by Denise Tyler

SAMS
Teach Yourself
Web Publishing
with HTML 4
in 21 Days
SECOND EDITION

SAMS

A Division of Macmillan USA
201 West 103rd St., Indianapolis, Indiana, 46290 USA

Sams Teach Yourself Web Publishing with HTML 4 in 21 Days, Second Edition

Copyright © 2000 by Sams Publishing

International Standard Book Number: 0-672-31725-7

Library of Congress Catalog Card Number: 99-63541

Printed in the United States of America

First Printing: December 1999

01   00   4   3   2

Trademarks

Warning and Disclaimer

ACQUISITIONS EDITOR
Jeff Schultz

DEVELOPMENT EDITOR
Damon Jordon

MANAGING EDITOR
Charlotte Clapp

PROJECT EDITOR
George E. Nedeff

COPY EDITOR
Jill Bond

INDEXER
Christine Nelsen

PROOFREADER
Maryann Steinhart

TECHNICAL EDITOR
Will Kelly

INTERIOR DESIGNER
Gary Adair

COVER DESIGNER
Aren Howell

TEAM COORDINATOR
Amy Patton

COPY WRITER
Eric Borgert

PRODUCTION
Dan Harris
Mark Walchle

Overview

Contents

About the Authors

Laura Lemay is a technical writer, author, Web addict, and motorcycle enthusiast. One of the world's most popular authors on Web development topics, she is the author of *Sams Teach Yourself Web Publishing with HTML, Sams Teach Yourself Java in 21 Days,* and *Sams Teach Yourself Perl in 21 Days.* You can visit her home page at `http://www.lne.com/lemay/`.

Denise Tyler is a freelance author, graphics artist, animator, and Web designer who resides in Madison, Wisconsin. She is the author of several FrontPage books in the *Laura Lemay's Web Workshop* series, the most recent being the best-selling *Laura Lemay's Web Workshop: Microsoft FrontPage 98.* She was also a contributing author for *Tricks of the Game Programming Gurus,* and author of *Fractal Design Painter 3.1 Unleashed.*

Deidre Hayes is an information architect with a Web services group and author of *Sams Teach Yourself HTML 4 in 10 Minutes.*

Bob Correll is a freelance author specializing in HTML and Web development.

Dedication

For Ed, a constant source of inspiration and support in my attempts to follow my dreams.
—Denise

Acknowledgments

To Sams Publishing for letting me write the kind of HTML book I wanted to see.

To the Coca-Cola Company, for creating Diet Coke and selling so much of it to me.

To all the folks on the `comp.infosystems.www` newsgroups, the `www-talk` mailing list, and the Web conference on the WELL, for answering questions and putting up with my late-night rants.

To innumerable people who helped me with the writing of this book, including Lance Norskog, Ken Tidwell, Steve Krause, Tony Barreca, CJ Silverio, Peter Harrison, Bill Whedon, Jim Graham, Jim Race, Mark Meadows, and many others I'm sure I've forgotten.

And finally, to Eric Murray, the other half of `lne.com`, for moral support when I was convinced I couldn't possibly finish writing any of this book on time, for setting up all my UNIX and networking equipment and keeping it running, and for writing a whole lot of Perl code on very short notice.

—Laura Lemay

The more I write, the more people I have to thank. With this book comes a whole new wave of talented folks at Macmillan with which I've had the pleasure to work. These people consistently demonstrate endless amounts of talent, dedication, and knowledge that never fails to impress me. Thanks, especially, to Mark Taber for his expert guidance in my efforts to update Laura's ever-popular and successful book. In spite of hard drive crashes, doctor visits, and a faulty call-waiting connection that knocked me offline as I downloaded files, he continued to provide an endless amount of positive feedback and atta-girls.

Thanks also to my family and friends for understanding that I have to disappear every now and then to focus on my work; and to caffeine for keeping my eyes open late at night while I scrounged through code examples and prose.

I also thank Laura Lemay for writing this great book in the first place. As always, her inspiration and talented writing style helps bring everything in focus and makes learning fun.

—Denise Tyler

Tell Us What You Think!

As the reader of this book, *you* are our most important critic and commentator. We value your opinion and want to know what we're doing right, what we could do better, what areas you'd like to see us publish in, and any other words of wisdom you're willing to pass our way.

You can fax, email, or write me directly to let me know what you did or didn't like about this book—as well as what we can do to make our books stronger.

Please note that I cannot help you with technical problems related to the topic of this book, and that due to the high volume of mail I receive, I might not be able to reply to every message.

When you write, please be sure to include this book's title and authors as well as your name and phone or fax number. I will carefully review your comments and share them with the authors and editors who worked on the book.

Fax: 317-581-4770

Email: webdev_sams@mcp.com

Mail: Mark Taber
          Associate Publisher
          Sams Publishing
          201 West 103rd Street
          Indianapolis, IN 46290 USA

Introduction

So you've browsed the Web for a while, and you've seen the sort of stuff that people are putting up on the Internet. And you're noticing that more and more stuff is going up all the time, and that more and more people are becoming interested in it. "I want to do that," you think. "How can I do that?" If you have the time and you know where to look, you could find out everything you need to know from the information out on the Web. It's all there, it's all available, and it's all free. Or, you could read this book instead. Here, in one volume that you can keep by your desk to read, reference, and squish spiders with, is a wealth of information that you'll need to create your own Web pages—everything from how to write them, to how to link them together, to how to present and publish them on the Internet.

But wait, there's more. This book goes beyond the scope of other books on how to create Web pages, which just teach you the basic technical details such as how to produce a boldface word. In this book, you'll learn why you should be producing a particular effect and when you should use it, as well as how. In addition, this book provides hints, suggestions, and examples of how to structure your overall Web site, not just the words within each page. This book won't just teach you how to create a Web site—it'll teach you how to create a good Web site.

Also, unlike many other books on this subject, this book doesn't focus on any one computer system. Regardless of whether you're using a PC running Windows, a Macintosh, or some dialect of UNIX (or any other computer system), many of the concepts in this book will be valuable to you. And you'll be able to apply them to your Web pages regardless of your platform of choice.

Sound good? Glad you think so. I thought it was a good idea when I wrote it, and I hope you get as much out of this book reading it as I did writing it.

Who Should Read This Book

Is this book for you? That depends:

- If you've seen what's out on the Web, and you want to contribute your own content, this book is for you.

- If you work for a company that wants to create a Web "presence" and you're not sure where to start, this book is for you.

- If you're an information developer, such as a technical writer, and you want to learn how the Web can help you present your information online, this book is for you.

- If you're just curious about how the Web works, some parts of this book are for you, although you might be able to find what you need on the Web itself.

- If you've never seen the Web before but you've heard that it's really nifty and want to get set up using it, this book isn't for you. You'll need a more general book about getting set up and browsing the Web before moving on to actually producing Web documents yourself.

- You've done Web presentations before with text, images, and links. Maybe you've played with a table or two and set up a few simple forms. In this case, you may be able to skim the first half of the book, but the second half should still offer you a lot of helpful information.

What This Book Contains

This book is intended to be read and absorbed over the course of 21 days (although it may take you more or less time depending on how much you can absorb in a day). On each day you'll read one chapter, each of which describes concepts in an area of Web site design. The chapters are arranged in a logical order, taking you from the simplest tasks toward more advanced techniques.

Part 1 Getting Started
In Part 1, you get a general overview of the World Wide Web and what you can do with it, and then come up with a plan for your Web presentation. You'll also write your first *very* basic Web page.

Part 2 Creating Simple Web Pages
In Part 2, you learn about the HTML language and how to write simple documents and link them together using hypertext links. You'll also learn how to format the paragraphs and characters on your Web pages.

Part 3 Web Graphics
In Part 3, you learn how to use images and color in your Web pages. You'll also learn how to compile and create animated graphics, and how to create and use clickable imagemaps to link to other pages in your Web site.

Part 4 Doing More with HTML
In Part 4, you learn how to format Web pages by using Cascading Style Sheets (CSS), and how HTML and CSS work together to enhance the appearance of your Web pages. You'll also learn how to create and format tables, and how to design Web sites that use frames to display multiple pages in a single browser window.

Part 5   Multimedia, Forms, and Dynamic HTML

In Part 5, you learn how to enhance your Web pages with multimedia, sound, video, and other advanced presentation methods. You'll learn how to add Java, JavaScript, and Dynamic HTML to take your Web pages to a higher level of interactivity and presentation.

Part 6   Designing Effective Web Pages

In Part 6, you get some hints for creating a well-constructed Web site, and you explore some examples of Web sites to get an idea of what sort of work you can do. You'll also learn about some things to consider when you want to design pages that will reach the types of "real world" users that you want to reach.

Part 7   Going Live on the Web

In Part 7, you learn how to put your presentation up on the Web, including how to advertise the work you've done. Finally, you'll learn how to test and maintain your Web site.

What You Need Before You Start

There are seemingly hundreds of books on the market about how to get connected to the Internet, and lots of books about how to use the World Wide Web. This book isn't one of them. I'm assuming that if you're reading this book, you already have a working connection to the Internet, that you have a Web browser such as Netscape Navigator or Microsoft Internet Explorer available to you, and that you've used it at least a couple of times. You should also have at least a passing acquaintance with some other portions of the Internet such as electronic mail and Usenet news, because I may refer to them in general terms in this book. Although you won't need to explicitly use them to work through the content in this book, some parts of the Web may refer to these other concepts.

In other words, you need to have used the Web in order to provide content for the Web. If you have this one simple qualification, then read on!

Note

To really take advantage of all the concepts and examples in this book, you should seriously consider using a recent version of Netscape Navigator (version 4.0 or later) or Microsoft Internet Explorer (version 4.0 or later).

Conventions Used in This Book

This book uses special typefaces and other graphical elements to highlight different types of information.

Special Elements

Four types of "boxed" elements present pertinent information that relates to the topic being discussed: Note, Tip, Caution, and New Term. Each item has a special icon associated with it, as described here.

Note

> Notes highlight special details about the current topic.

Tip

> It's a good idea to read the tips because they present shortcuts or trouble-saving ideas for performing specific tasks.

Caution

> Don't skip the cautions. They supply you with information to help you avoid making decisions or performing actions that can cause you trouble.

NEW TERM Whenever I introduce a *new term*, I set it off with an icon like this one, and define it for you. I use italic for new terms.

HTML Input and Output Examples

Throughout the book, I present exercises and examples of HTML input and output. Here are the input and out icons.

INPUT An input icon identifies HTML code that you can type in yourself.

OUTPUT An output icon indicates what the HTML input produces in a Web browser such as Microsoft Internet Explorer.

Special Fonts

Several items are presented in a monospace font, which can be plain or italic. Here's what each one means:

`plain mono`   Applied to commands, filenames, file extensions, directory names, Internet addresses, URLs, and HTML input. For example, HTML tags such as `<TABLE>` and `<P>` appear in this font.

mono italic   Applied to placeholders, which are generic items for which something specific is substituted as part of a command or as part of computer output. For instance, the term represented by `filename` would be the real name of the file, such as `myfile.txt`.

Teach Yourself Web Publishing with HTML: The Web Site

To help you get the most out of this book, there is also a Web site. This site contains the source code and graphics for the examples used in this book plus updated information about where to find tools and hints to help you further develop and expand your Web presentations. The site is at `http://www.tywebpub.com/`. Check it out!

PART 1

Getting Started

DAY 1

The World of the World Wide Web

A journey of a thousand miles begins with a single step, and here you are at Day 1 of a journey that will show you how to write, design, and publish pages on the World Wide Web. Before beginning the actual journey, however, you should start simple, with the basics. You'll learn the following:

- What the World Wide Web is, and why it's really cool
- Web browsers: what they do, and a couple popular ones from which to choose
- What a Web server is and why you need one
- Some information about Uniform Resource Locators (URLs)

If you've spent even a small amount time exploring the Web, most, if not all, of this chapter will seem like old news. If so, feel free to skim this chapter and skip ahead to the next chapter, where you'll find an overview of points to think about when you design and organize your own Web documents.

What Is the World Wide Web?

I have a friend who likes to describe things using many meaningful words strung together in a chain so that it takes several minutes to sort out what he's just said.

If I were he, I'd describe the World Wide Web as a global, interactive, dynamic, cross-platform, distributed, graphical hypertext information system that runs over the Internet. Whew! Unless you understand each of these words and how they fit together, this description isn't going to make much sense. (My friend often doesn't make much sense, either.)

So let's look at all these words and see what they mean in the context of how you'll be using the Web as a publishing medium.

The Web Is a Hypertext Information System

If you've used any sort of basic online help system, you're already familiar with the primary concept behind the World Wide Web: *hypertext*.

The idea behind hypertext is that instead of reading text in a rigid, linear structure (such as a book), you can skip easily from one point to another. You can get more information, go back, jump to other topics, and navigate through the text based on what interests you at the time.

NEW TERM   *Hypertext* enables you to read and navigate text and visual information in a non-linear way, based on what you want to know next.

Online help systems, such as Windows Help on PCs or HyperCard help stacks on the Macintosh, use hypertext to present information. To get more information on a topic, you just click that topic. The topic might be a link that takes you to a new screen (or window or dialog box) that contains the new information. Perhaps you'll find links on words or phrases that take you to still other screens, and links on those screens that take you even farther away from your original topic. Figure 1.1 shows a simple diagram of how this kind of system works.

Imagine that your online help system is linked to another online help system on another application related to yours; for example, your drawing program's help is linked to your word processor's help. Your word processor's help is then linked to an encyclopedia, where you can look up any other concepts that you don't understand. The encyclopedia is hooked into a global index of magazine articles that enables you to get the most recent information on the topics the encyclopedia covers. The article index also then is linked to information about the writers of those articles and some pictures of their children (see Figure 1.2).

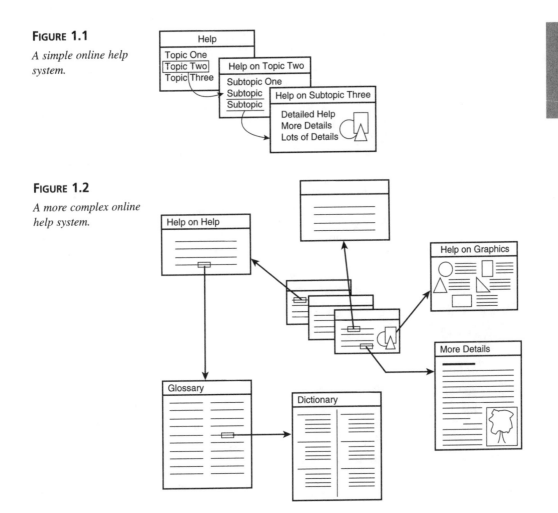

FIGURE 1.1

A simple online help system.

FIGURE 1.2

A more complex online help system.

If you had all these interlinked help systems available with every program you bought, you would rapidly run out of disk space. You also might question whether you needed all this information when all you wanted to know was how to do one simple task. All this information could be expensive, too.

If the information didn't take up much disk space, if it were freely available, and you could get it reasonably quickly any time you wanted, however, the system would be more interesting. In fact, the information system might very well end up being more interesting than the software you bought in the first place.

That's just what the World Wide Web is: more information than you could ever digest in a lifetime, linked together in various ways, out there on the net, available for you to browse whenever you want. It's big and deep and easy to get lost in, but it's also an immense amount of fun.

> **Note**
>
> Because Web technology is so good at organizing and presenting information, the business world has taken notice. Many large corporations and medium-sized businesses and organizations are using Web technology to manage projects, order materials, and distribute company information in a paperless environment. By locating their documents on a private, secure Web server, called an *intranet*, they take advantage of the technologies the World Wide Web has to offer, while keeping the information contained within the company.

The Web Is Graphical and Easy to Navigate

In the early days, using the Internet involved simple text-only connections. You had to navigate the Internet's various services by using typed commands and arcane tools. Although plenty of really exciting information was available on the net, it wasn't necessarily pretty to look at.

Then along came the first graphical Web *browser*—Mosaic—that paved the way for the Web to display both text and graphics in full color on the same page. This is one of the best parts of the Web, and arguably the reason it has become so popular. Now, Web browsers provide capabilities for graphics, sound, and video to be incorporated with the text, as well as even more for multimedia and embedded applications.

New Term   A *browser* is used to view and navigate Web pages and other information on the World Wide Web.

More important, you can easily navigate the interface to all these capabilities—just jump from link to link, from page to page, across sites and servers.

> **Note**
>
> If the Web incorporates so much more than text, why do I keep calling the Web a hypertext system? Well, if you're going to be absolutely technically correct about it, the Web is not a hypertext system—it's a hyper*media* system. But, on the other hand, you might argue that the Web began as a text-only system, and much of the content is still text-heavy, with extra bits of media added in as emphasis. Many very educated people are arguing these very points at this moment and presenting their arguments in papers and

1

> discursive rants as educated people like to do. Whatever. I prefer the term
> *hypertext*, and it's my book, so I'm going to use it. You know what I mean.

The Web Is Cross-Platform

If you can access the Internet, you can access the World Wide Web, regardless of
whether you're working on a low-end PC or a fancy expensive graphics workstation. You
can use a simple text-only modem connection, a small 14-inch black-and-white monitor,
or a 21-inch full-color super gamma-corrected graphics accelerated display system. And
more recently, people are accessing the Internet through their television sets, portable
hand-held PCs, and personal information managers. If you think Windows menus buttons
look better than Macintosh menus and buttons, or vice versa (or if you think both
Macintosh and Windows people are weenies), it doesn't matter. The World Wide Web is
not limited to any one kind of machine or developed by any one company. The Web is
entirely cross-platform.

NEW TERM *Cross-platform* means that you can access Web information equally well from
any computer hardware running any operating system using any display.

Note
> The whole idea that the Web is—and should be—cross-platform is strongly
> held to by purists. The reality, however, is somewhat different. With the
> introduction over the years of numerous special features, technologies, and
> media types, the Web has lost some of its capability to be truly cross-
> platform. As Web authors choose to use these nonstandard features, they
> willingly limit the potential audience for the content of their sites. For
> example, a site centered around a Java program essentially is unusable for
> someone using a browser that doesn't support Java, or for a user who may
> have turned off Java in his browser for quicker downloads. Similarly, some
> programs that extend the capabilities of a browser (known as *plug-ins*) are
> available only for one platform (either Windows, Macintosh, or UNIX).
> Choosing to use one of these plug-ins makes that portion of your site
> unavailable to users who either are on the wrong platform, or who don't
> want to bother to download and install the plug-in.

You gain access to the Web through an application called a *browser*, such as Netscape
Navigator or Microsoft Internet Explorer. You can find many browsers out there for most
existing computer systems. After you have a browser and a connection to the Internet,
you've got it made. You're on the Web. (I explain more about what the browser actually
does later in this chapter, in "Web Browsers.")

The Web Is Distributed

Information takes up a great deal of space, particularly when you include images and multimedia capabilities. To store all the information, graphics, and multimedia that the Web provides, you would need an untold amount of disk space, and managing it would be almost impossible. Imagine that you were interested in finding out more information about alpacas (a Peruvian mammal known for its wool), but when you selected a link in your online encyclopedia, your computer prompted you to insert CD-ROM #456 ALP through ALR. You could be there for a long time just looking for the right CD-ROM!

The Web is successful in providing so much information because that information is distributed globally across thousands of Web sites, each of which contributes the space for the information it publishes. You, as a consumer of that information, go to that site to view the information. When you're done, you go somewhere else, and your system reclaims the disk space. You don't have to install it, change disks, or do anything other than point your browser at that site.

NEW TERM   A *Web site* is a location on the Web that publishes some kind of information. When you view a Web page, your browser connects to that Web site to get that information.

Each Web site, and each page or bit of information on that site, has a unique address. This address is called a *Uniform Resource Locator*, or *URL*. When people tell you to visit a site at `http://www.coolsite.com/`, they've just given you a URL. You can use your browser (with the Open command, sometimes called Open Page or Go) to enter in the URL (or just copy and paste it).

NEW TERM   A *Uniform Resource Locator (URL)* is a pointer to a specific bit of information on the Internet.

Note   URLs are alternatively pronounced as if spelled out "You are Ells" or as an actual word ("earls"). Although I prefer the former pronunciation, I've heard the latter used equally as often.

You'll learn more about URLs later in this chapter in "Uniform Resource Locators (URLs)."

The Web Is Dynamic

Because information on the Web is contained on the site that published it, the people who published it in the first place can update it at any time.

If you're browsing that information, you don't have to install a new version of the help system, buy another book, or call technical support to get updated information. Just display your browser and check out what's there.

If you're publishing on the Web, you can make sure your information is up-to-date all the time. You don't have to spend a lot of time re-releasing updated documents. There is no cost of materials. You don't have to get bids on numbers of copies or quality of output. Color is free. And you won't get calls from hapless customers who have a version of the book that was obsolete four years ago.

Consider, for example, the development effort for a Web server called *Apache*. Apache is being developed and tested through a core of volunteers, has many of the features of the larger commercial servers, and is free. The Apache Web site at `http://www.apache.org/` is the central location for information about the Apache software, documentation, and the server software itself. Figure 1.3 shows Apache's home page. Because the site can be updated any time, new releases can be distributed quickly and easily. Changes and bug fixes to the documentation, which is all online, can be made directly to the files. New information and news can be published almost immediately.

FIGURE 1.3

The Apache Web site.

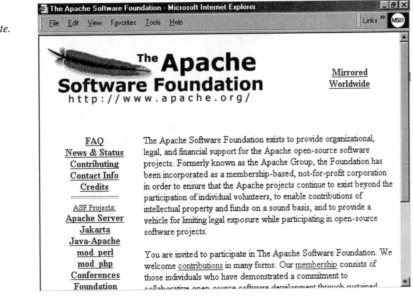

Note

The pictures throughout this book usually are taken from a Windows browser (Microsoft Internet Explorer, most often). The only reason for this

use is that I'm writing this book primarily on a Windows PC. If you're using a
Macintosh or UNIX system, don't feel left out. As I noted earlier, the glory of
the Web is that you see the same information regardless of the platform
you're using. So ignore the buttons and window borders, and focus on
what's inside the window.

For some sites, the capability to update the site on-the-fly, at any moment, is precisely
why the site exists. Figure 1.4 shows the home page for The Nando Times, an online
newspaper that is updated 24 hours a day to reflect new news as it happens. Because the
site is up and available all the time, it has an immediacy that neither hard-copy newspapers or most television news programs can match. Visit The Nando Times at
`http://www.nandotimes.com`.

FIGURE **1.4**

The Nando Times.

Web Browsers Can Access Many Forms of Internet Information

If you've read any of the innumerable books on how to use the Internet, you're aware of
the dozens of different ways to get at information on the net: FTP, Gopher, Usenet news,
WAIS databases, Telnet, and email. Before the Web became as popular as it is now, to
get to these different kinds of information, you had to use different tools for each one, all

of which had to be installed and all of which used different commands. Although all these choices made for a great market for *How to Use the Internet* books, they weren't really very easy to use.

Web browsers changed that. Although the Web itself is its own information system, with its own Internet protocol (the Hypertext Transfer Protocol, HTTP), Web browsers also can read files from other Internet services. And, even better, you can create links to information on those systems just as you would create links to information on Web pages. This process is all seamless and all available through a single application.

To point your browser to different kinds of information on the Internet, you use different kinds of URLs. Most URLs start with `http:`, which indicates a file at an actual Web site. To get to a file on the Web by using FTP, you would use a URL that looks something like `ftp://name_of_site/directory/filename`. You can also use an `ftp:` URL ending with a directory name, and your Web server will show you a list of the files, as shown in Figure 1.5. This particular figure shows a listing of files from Microsoft's Web site, at `ftp://ftp.microsoft.com/`.

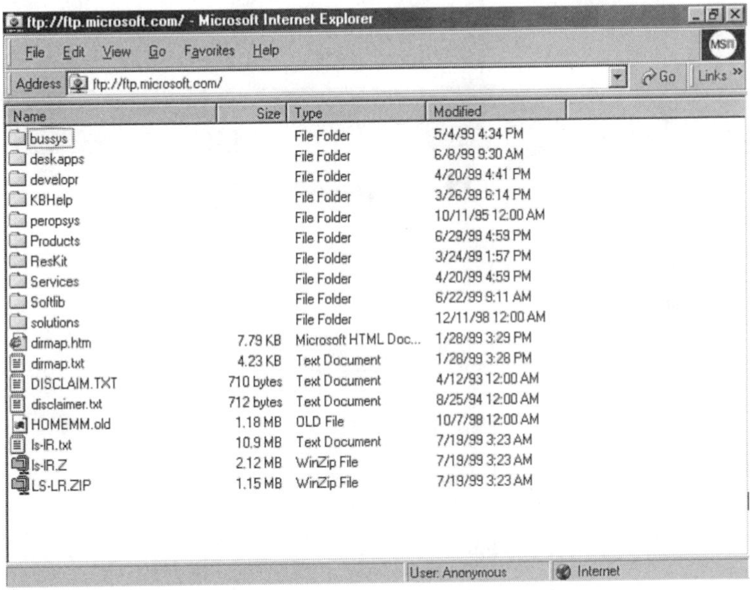

FIGURE 1.5

A listing of files and directories available at Microsoft's FTP site.

Gopher servers aren't as common these days as they were a few years ago, but if you needed to access Gopher resources from a Web browser, use a URL that looks something like this `gopher://name_of_gopher_server/`.

You'll learn more about different kinds of URLs tomorrow in Chapter 5, "All About Links."

The Web Is Interactive

Interactivity is the capability to "talk back" to the Web server. More traditional media, such as television, isn't interactive at all; all you do is sit and watch as shows are played at you. Other than changing the channel, you don't have much control over what you see. Add WebTV capability to it, however, and television becomes a new experience.

The Web is inherently interactive; the act of selecting a link and jumping to another Web page to go somewhere else on the Web is a form of interactivity. In addition to this simple interactivity, however, the Web also enables you to communicate with the publisher of the pages you're reading and with other readers of those pages.

For example, pages can be designed to contain interactive forms that readers can fill out. Forms can contain text-entry areas, radio buttons, or simple menus of items. When the form is "submitted," the information readers type is sent back to the server from which the pages originated. Figure 1.6 shows an example of an online form for a rather ridiculous census (a form you'll create later in this book).

FIGURE 1.6

The Surrealist census form.

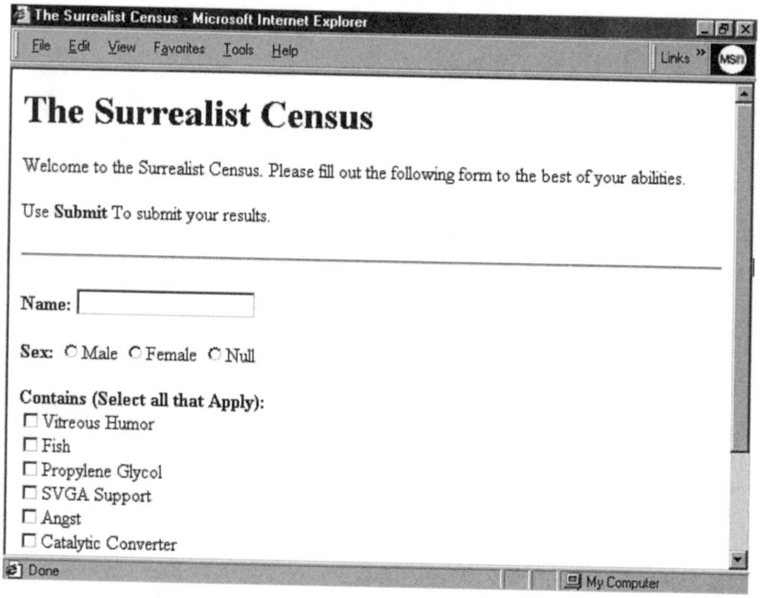

As a publisher of information on the Web, you can use forms for many different purposes, such as the following:

- To get feedback about your pages
- To get information from your readers (survey, voting, demographic, or any other kind of data). You then can collect statistics on that data, store it in a database, or do anything you want with it.
- To provide online order forms for products or services available on the Web
- To create "guestbooks" and conferencing systems that enable your readers to post their own information on your pages. These kinds of systems enable your readers to communicate not only with you, but also with other readers of your pages.

In addition to forms, which provide some of the most popular forms of interactivity on the Web, advanced features of Web technologies provide even more interactivity. Java and Shockwave, for example, enable you to include entire programs and games inside Web pages. Software can run on the Web to enable realtime chat sessions between your readers. Developments in 3D worlds also enable your readers to browse the Web as if they were wandering through real three-dimensional rooms and meeting other people. As time goes on, the Web becomes less of a medium for people passively sitting and digesting information (and becoming "Net potatoes") and more of a medium for reaching and communicating with other people all over the world.

Web Browsers

A Web browser, as mentioned earlier, is the program that you use to view pages and navigate the World Wide Web. Web browsers sometimes are called Web *clients* or other fancy names (Internet navigation tools), but *Web browser* is the most common term.

A wide array of Web browsers is available for just about every platform you can imagine, including graphical-user-interface–based systems (Macintosh and Windows, for example), and text-only systems for dial-up UNIX connections. Most browsers are freeware or shareware (try before you buy) or have a lenient licensing policy. Both Netscape Navigator and Microsoft Internet Explorer, for example, are available for free to both individuals and organizations. Usually, all you have to do to get a browser is download it from the Net (although downloading usually is easier if you already have a browser you can use to download the new one—sort of a chicken-and-the-egg situation).

If you get your Internet connection through a commercial online service such as America Online, you may have several browsers from which to choose. Try a couple and see what works best for you.

Currently, the most popular browsers for the World Wide Web are Microsoft Internet Explorer (sometimes called just Internet Explorer or "IE") and Netscape Navigator (often referred to simply as Netscape). Despite the fact that these browsers have the lion's share of the market, however, they are not the only browsers on the Web. This point will become important later, when you learn how to design Web pages and learn about the different capabilities of different browsers. Assuming that Internet Explorer and Netscape are the only browsers in use on the Web and designing your pages accordingly will limit the audience you can reach with the information you want to present.

Note

Choosing to develop for a specific browser, such as Netscape Navigator or Internet Explorer, is suitable when you know a limited audience using the targeted browser software will view your Web site. Developing this way is a common practice in corporations implementing intranets. In these situations, it is a fair assumption that all users in the organization will use the browser supplied to them and, accordingly, it is possible to design the Web component of the intranet to use the specific capabilities of the browser in question.

What the Browser Does

Any Web browser's job is twofold: given a pointer to a piece of information on the net (a URL), the browser has to be able to access that information or operate in some way based on the contents of that pointer. For hypertext Web documents, the browser must be able to communicate with the Web server. Because the Web also can manage information contained on FTP and Gopher servers, in Usenet news postings, in email, and so on, browsers often can communicate with those servers or protocols as well.

What the browser does most often, however, is deal with formatting and displaying Web documents. Each Web page is a file written in a language called *Hypertext Markup Language* (HTML) that includes the text of the page, its structure, and links to other documents, images, or other media. (You'll learn much more about HTML on Day 3 ("An Introduction to HTML"), Day 4 ("Begin with the Basics"), Day 5, ("All About Links,") and Day 6 ("More Text Formatting with HTML"), because you need to know it so that you can write your own Web pages.) The browser takes the information it gets from the Web server and formats and displays it for your system. Different browsers may format and display the same file differently, depending on the capabilities of that system and the default layout options for the browser itself.

Retrieving documents from the Web and formatting them for your system are the two tasks that make up the core of a browser's functionality. Depending on the browser you use and the features it includes, however, you also may be able to play multimedia files, view and interact with Java applets, read your mail, or use other advanced features that a particular browser offers.

An Overview of Two Popular Browsers

This section describes the two most popular browsers currently on the Web. They are in no way the only browsers available, and if the browser you're using isn't listed here, don't feel that you have to use one of these. Whichever browser you have is fine as long as it works for you.

You can use the browsers in this section only if you have a direct Internet connection or a dial-up SLIP or PPP Internet connection. Getting your machine connected to the Internet is beyond the scope of this book, but you can find plenty of books to help you do so.

If your connection to the Internet is through a commercial online service (AOL, CompuServe, or MSN), you may have a choice of several browsers including the ones in this section and browsers that your provider supplies.

Finally, if the only connection you have to the Internet is through a dial-up, text-only UNIX (or other) account, you are limited to using text-only browsers such as Lynx. You cannot view documents in color or view graphics online (although you usually can download them to your system and view them there).

Microsoft Internet Explorer

Microsoft's browser, Microsoft Internet Explorer, runs on Windows 3.1, Windows 95/98, Windows NT, Macintosh, and UNIX, and it is free for downloading from Microsoft's Web site (http://www.microsoft.com/ie/). No further license fee is required. In fact, if you're using Windows 98, you have Internet Explorer 4 already built in to your system. You can still install and use Netscape Navigator if you like, but if all you want to use is Internet Explorer you don't need to do anything more.

Microsoft has been the only browser developer that has met and exceeded Netscape's pace of development. Internet Explorer supports many of Netscape's features and adds a few of its own. In addition, Microsoft has made significant deals with several commercial online services, so its share of the browser market has grown significantly and is a direct challenge to Netscape for control of the browser market. Even with the large number of browsers available today, there are only two in widespread use: Microsoft's and Netscape's.

For more information about all versions of Internet Explorer, see its home page at http://www.microsoft.com/windows/ie/default.htm. Figure 1.7 shows Internet Explorer 5 running on Windows 98.

FIGURE 1.7

Microsoft Internet Explorer (Windows 98).

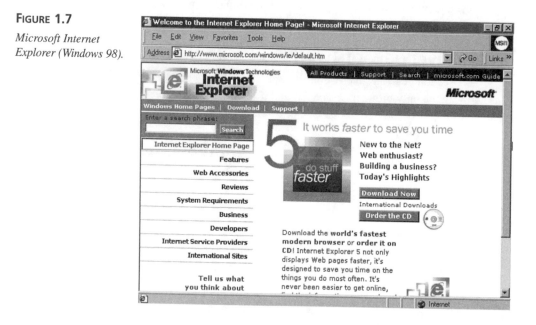

As with Netscape Navigator, Microsoft is fast at work on version 6 of its browser, due sometime near the release of Windows 2000. It promises to be faster and better integrated than any of its previous releases.

Note

With each release of their browsers, Microsoft and Netscape have tried to introduce more new, fancy features. The current releases are no exception. As you will see in Day 10 ("XHTML and Style Sheets"), these new features include style sheets for providing fine control over the appearance of documents. In Day 15 ("Using Dynamic HTML"), you'll learn more about Dynamic HTML, which encompasses everything from precise layout control to improved scripting of HTML pages.

Netscape Navigator

Another widely used browser in use on the Web today is Netscape Navigator, from Netscape Communications Corporation.

The most common way to obtain Netscape Navigator is as part of a suite of Internet tools called *Netscape Communicator*. In addition to Web browsing, this suite includes components for email and newsgroup reading (Netscape Messenger), Web page editing (Netscape Composer) and online collaboration (Netscape Conference). It's available for Windows, Macintosh, and for many different versions of UNIX running the X Window System. Figure 1.8 shows the Windows 95/98 version.

FIGURE 1.8

Netscape (for Windows 95/98).

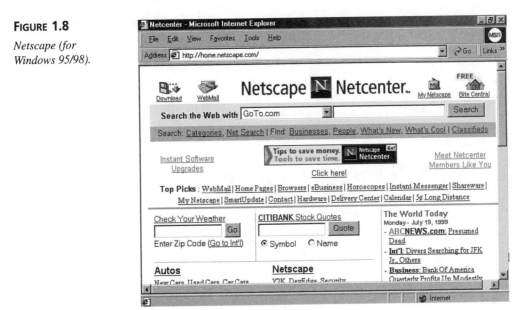

The good news is that you can download and use Netscape Communicator Standard Edition for free. The current version of Netscape is 4.7, which is available for downloading at Netscape's site at `http://home.netscape.com/`, or in boxes from your favorite computer software store. For an additional reasonable fee, you can purchase Netscape Communicator Professional, which adds calendar functions, central management features, and IBM host functions to the package.

Web Servers

To view and browse pages on the Web, all you need is a Web browser. To publish pages on the Web, most of the time you'll need a Web server.

NEW TERM A *Web server* is the program that runs on a Web site and is responsible for replying to Web browser requests for files. You need a Web server to publish documents on the Web.

When you use a browser to request a page on a Web site, that browser makes a Web connection to a server (using the HTTP protocol). The server accepts the connection, sends the contents of the files that were requested, and then closes the connection. The browser then formats the information it got from the server.

On the server side, many different browsers can connect to the same server to get the same information. The Web server is responsible for handling all these requests.

Web servers do more than just deposit files. They also are responsible for managing form input and for linking forms and browsers with programs such as databases running on the server.

Just as with browsers, many different servers are available for many different platforms, each with many different features and ranging in cost from free to very expensive. For now, all you need to know is what the server is there for; you'll learn more about Web servers on Day 19, "Putting Your Site Online."

Uniform Resource Locators (URLs)

As you learned earlier, a URL is a pointer to some bit of data on the Web, be it a Web document, a file on FTP or Gopher, a posting on Usenet, or an email address. The URL provides a universal, consistent method for finding and accessing information, not necessarily for you, but mostly for your Web browser. (If URLs were for you, they would be in a format that would make them easier to remember.)

In addition to typing URLs directly into your browser to go to a particular page, you also use URLs when you create a hypertext link within a document to another document. So, any way you look at it, URLs are important to how you and your browser get around on the Web.

URLs contain information about

- how to get to the information (which protocol to use—FTP, Gopher, HTTP).
- the Internet host name showing where to look (www.ncsa.uiuc.edu, ftp.apple.com, netcom16.netcom.com, and so on).
- the directory or other location on that site to find the file. You also can use special URLs for tasks such as sending mail to people (called Mailto URLs) and for using the Telnet program.

You'll learn all about URLs and what each part means in Day 5.

Summary

To publish on the Web, you have to understand the basic concepts that make up the parts of the Web. In this chapter, you learned three major concepts. First, you learned about a few of the more useful features of the Web for publishing information. Second, you learned about Web browsers and servers and how they interact to deliver Web pages. Third, you learned about what a URL is and why it's important to Web browsing and publishing.

Workshop

Each chapter in this book contains a workshop to help you review the topics you learned. The first section of this workshop lists some common questions about the Web. Next, you'll answer some questions that I'll ask you about the Web. The answers to the quiz appear in the next section. At the end of the chapter, you'll find some exercises that will help you retain the information you learned about the Web.

Q&A

Q Who runs the Web? Who controls all these protocols? Who's in charge of all this?

A No single entity "owns" or controls the World Wide Web. Given the enormous number of independent sites that supply information to the Web, for any single organization to set rules or guidelines would be impossible. Two groups of organizations, however, have a great influence over the look and feel and direction of the Web itself.

The first is the World Wide Web (W3) Consortium, based at Massachusetts Institute of Technology (MIT) in the United States and INRIA in Europe. The W3 Consortium is made up of individuals and organizations interested in supporting and defining the languages and protocols that make up the Web (HTTP, HTML, and so on). It also provides products (browsers, servers, and so on) that are freely available to anyone who wants to use them. The W3 Consortium is the closest anyone gets to setting the standards for and enforcing rules about the World Wide Web. You can visit the Consortium's home page at `http://www.w3.org/`.

The second group of organizations that influences the Web is the browser developers themselves, most notably Microsoft and Netscape Communications Corporation. The competition to be most popular and technically advanced browser on the Web can be fierce. Although both organizations claim to support and adhere to the guidelines proposed by the W3 Consortium, both also include their own new features in new versions of their software—features that often conflict with each other and with the work the W3 Consortium is doing.

Sometimes trying to keep track of all the new and rapidly changing developments feels like being in the middle of a war zone, with the W3 trying to mediate and prevent global thermonuclear war. As a Web designer, you're stuck in the middle, and you'll have to make choices about which browsers to support, and how to deal with the rapid changes. But that's what the rest of this book is for!

Q A lot of the magazine articles I've seen about the Web mention CERN, the European Particle Physics Lab, as having a significant role in Web development. You didn't mention them. Where do they stand in Web development?

A The Web was invented at CERN by Tim Berners-Lee, as I'm sure you know by now from all those magazine articles. And, for several years, CERN was the center for much of the development that went on. In late 1995, however, CERN passed its part in World Wide Web development to INRIA (the Institut National pour la Recherche en Informatique et Automatique) in France. INRIA today is the European leg of the W3 Consortium.

Quiz

1. What makes a hypertext information system so cool?
2. Do you need a special type of computer to access the Internet?
3. Besides a connection to the Internet, what else is required to view and navigate Web pages and other information on the World Wide Web? Why is it necessary?
4. What is a URL?
5. What is required to publish documents on the Web?

Answers

1. A hypertext information system enables you to skip easily from one point to another rather than text in a linear structure.
2. You don't need a special computer. You can access the Internet with any computer, from low-end PC to expensive UNIX workstation, using any operating system and any display. The Web is entirely cross-platform.
3. You must have a browser to view and navigate Web pages on the Web. In addition to retrieving Web documents, the most important function of the browser is to format and display Web documents and make them readable on your system.

4. A URL, or Uniform Resource Locator, is an *address* that points to a specific document or bit of information on the Internet.

5. Most of the time, you need access to a Web server. Web servers, which are programs that run on a Web site, reply to Web browser requests for files and send the requested pages to many different types of browsers. They also manage form input and handle database integration.

Exercises

1. Try navigating to each of the different types of URLs mentioned in this chapter (`http:`, `ftp:`, and `gopher:`).

2. To become a bit more aware of the vast number of browsers that are available, visit BROWSERS.COM, a part of the CNET Web site. The URL for BROWSERS.COM is `http://www.browsers.com`. Initially, you may find this information quite overwhelming—but the main point of this exercise is to show you that there are far more than two browsers out there, and they support a wide variety of features. You'll want to keep this URL handy as you learn more about HTML. Here, you will keep informed of the latest versions of all available browsers and the features they support.

DAY 2

Get Organized

When you write a book, a paper, an article, or even a memo, you usually don't just jump right in with the first sentence and then write it through to the end. The same goes with the visual arts—you don't normally start from the top left corner of the canvas or page and work your way down to the bottom right.

A better way to write or draw or design a work is to do some planning beforehand—to know what you're going to do and what you're trying to accomplish, and to have a general idea or rough sketch of the structure of the piece before you jump in and work on it.

Just as with more traditional modes of communication, the process of writing and designing Web pages takes some planning and thought before you start flinging text and graphics around and linking them wildly to each other. It's perhaps even more important to plan ahead with Web pages because trying to apply the rules of traditional writing or design to online hypertext often results in documents that are either difficult to understand and navigate online or that simply don't take advantage of the features that hypertext provides. Poorly organized Web pages also are difficult to revise or to expand.

In this chapter, I describe some of the things you should think about before you begin developing your Web pages. Specifically, you do the following:

- Learn the differences between a Web server, a Web site, a Web page, and a home page
- Think about the sort of information (content) you want to put on the Web
- Set the goals for the Web site
- Organize your content into main topics
- Come up with a general structure for pages and topics

After you have an overall idea of how you're going to construct your Web pages, you'll be ready to actually start writing and designing those pages in Day 4, "Begin with the Basics." If you're eager to get started, be patient! You will have more than enough HTML to learn over the next three days.

Anatomy of a Web Site

First, here's a look at some simple terminology I'll be using throughout this book. You need to know what the following terms mean and how they apply to the body of work you're developing for the Web:

- Web site: a collection of one or more Web pages.
- Web server: a computer on the Internet or on an intranet, which stores one or more Web sites.
- Web pages: a single element of a Web site, contained in one file on the disk.
- Home pages: the "entry" page in a Web site, which can link to additional pages in the same Web site.

A *Web site* consists of one or more Web pages linked together in a meaningful way, which, as a whole, describes a body of information or creates an overall consistent effect. (See Figure 2.1.)

NEW TERM A *Web site* is a collection of one or more Web pages.

Each Web site is stored on a Web server, which is the actual computer on the Web that stores the site. Throughout the first week or so of this book, you'll learn how to develop well-thought out and well-designed Web sites. Later, you'll learn how to publish your site on an actual Web server.

NEW TERM A *Web server* is a computer on the Internet containing one or more Web sites.

A *Web page* is an individual element of a Web site in the same way that a page is a single element of a book or a newspaper (although, unlike paper pages, Web pages can be of any length). Web pages sometimes are called *Web documents*. Both terms refer to the same thing: a Web page is a single disk file with a single filename that is retrieved from a server and formatted by a Web browser.

FIGURE 2.1

Web sites and pages.

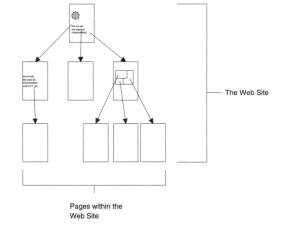

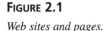 A *Web page* is a single element of a Web site and is contained in a single disk file.

The terms Web *server*, *site*, and *page* are pretty easy to grasp, but the term *home page* is a little more problematic because it can have several different meanings.

If you're reading and browsing the Web, you usually can think of the home page as the Web page that loads when you start up your browser or when you click the Home button. Each browser has its own default home page, which often is the same page for the site that developed the browser. (For example, the Netscape home page is at Netscape's Web site and the Internet Explorer home page is at Microsoft's Web site.)

Within your browser, you can change that default home page to start up any page you want—a common tactic I've seen many people use to create a simple page of links to other interesting places or pages that they often visit.

If you're publishing pages on the Web, however, the term *home page* has an entirely different meaning. The home page is the first or topmost page in your Web site. It's the entry point to the rest of the pages you've created and the first page your readers will see (see Figure 2.2).

A home page usually contains an overview of the content of the Web site available from that starting point—for example, in the form of a table of contents or a set of icons. If your content is small enough, you might include everything on that single home page—making your home page and your Web site the same thing.

FIGURE **2.2**

A home page.

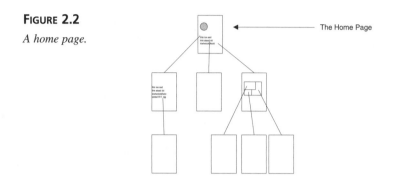

The Home Page

NEW TERM A *home page* is the entry or starting point for the rest of your Web site.

What Do You Want to Do on the Web?

This question may seem silly. You wouldn't have bought this book if you didn't already have some idea of what you want to put online. But maybe you don't really know what you want to put on the Web, or you have a vague idea but nothing concrete. Maybe it has suddenly become your job to put a page for your company on the Web, and someone handed you this book and said, "Here, this will help." Maybe you just want to do something similar to some other Web page you've seen and thought was particularly cool.

What you want to put on the Web is what I'll refer to throughout this book as your content. *Content* is a general term that can refer to text, graphics, media, interactive forms, and so on. If you tell someone what your Web pages are "about," you are describing your content.

NEW TERM Your *content* is the stuff you're putting on the Web. Information, fiction, images, art, programs, humor, diagrams, games—all this is content.

What sort of content can you put on the Web? Just about anything you want to. Here are some of the types of content that are popular on the Web right now:

- **Personal information**   You can create pages describing everything anyone could ever want to know about you and how incredibly marvelous you are—your hobbies, your résumé, your picture, things you've done.

- **Hobbies or special interests**   A Web page can contain information about a particular topic, hobby, or something you're interested in; for example, music, Star Trek, motorcycles, cult movies, hallucinogenic mushrooms, antique ink bottles, or upcoming jazz concerts in your city.

- **Publications**   Newspapers, magazines, and other publications lend themselves particularly well to the Web, and they have the advantage of being more immediate and easier to update than their print counterparts.

- **Company profiles**   You could offer information about what a company does, where it is located, job openings, data sheets, white papers, marketing collateral, product demonstrations, and whom to contact.

- **Online documentation**   The term *online documentation* can refer to everything from quick-reference cards to full reference documentation to interactive tutorials or training modules. Anything task-oriented (changing the oil in your car, making a soufflé, creating landscape portraits in oil, learning HTML) could be described as online documentation.

- **Shopping catalogs**   If your company offers items for sale, making your lists available on the Web is a quick and easy way to let your customers know what you have available and your prices. If prices change, you can just update your Web documents to reflect that new information.

- **Online stores**   You also can use the Web to actually sell items to customers through use of a "shopping basket." Users place into and remove items from their baskets as they browse the catalog. At the end, they can provide a credit card number and shipping information to place the order.

- **Polling and opinion gathering**   Interactivity and forms on the Web enable you to get feedback on nearly any topic from your readers, including opinion polls, suggestion boxes, comments on your Web pages or your products, and so on.

- **Online education**   The Web's interactivity and low cost of information delivery in many places make it an attractive medium for delivery of distance-learning programs. Already, numerous traditional universities, as well as new online schools and universities, have begun offering distance learning on the Web.

- **Anything else that comes to mind**   Hypertext fiction, online toys, media archives, collaborative art…anything!

The Web is limited only by what you want to do with it. In fact, if what you want to do with it isn't in this list, or seems especially wild or half-baked, that's an excellent reason to try it. The most interesting Web pages are the ones that stretch the boundaries of what the Web is supposed to be capable of.

If you really have no idea of what to put up on the Web, don't feel that you have to stop here, put this book away, and come up with something before continuing. Maybe by reading through this book you'll get some ideas (and this book will be useful even if you don't have ideas). I've personally found that the best way to come up with ideas is to spend an afternoon browsing on the Web and exploring what other people have done.

Set Your Goals

What do you want people to be able to accomplish on your Web site? Are your readers looking for specific information on how to do something? Are they going to read through each page in turn, going on only when they're done with the page they're reading? Are they just going to start at your home page and wander aimlessly around, exploring your "world" until they get bored and go somewhere else?

Suppose that you're creating a Web site that describes the company where you work. Some people reading that Web site might want to know about job openings. Others might want to know where the company actually is located. Still others may have heard that your company makes technical white papers available over the Net, and they want to download the most recent version of a particular paper. Each of these goals is valid, so you should list each one.

For a shopping catalog Web site, you might have only a few goals: to enable your readers to browse the items you have for sale by name or by price, and to order specific items after they're done browsing.

For a personal or special-interest Web site, you may have only a single goal: to enable your readers to browse and explore the information you've provided.

The goals do not have to be lofty ("this Web site will bring about world peace") or even make much sense to anyone except you. Still, coming up with goals for your Web documents prepares you to design, organize, and write your Web pages specifically to reach these goals. Goals also help you resist the urge to obscure your content with extra information.

If you're designing Web pages for someone else—for example, if you're creating the Web site for your company or if you've been hired as a consultant—having a set of goals for the site from your employer definitely is one of the most important pieces of information you should have before you create a single page. The ideas you have for the Web site might not be the ideas that other people have for it, and you might end up doing a lot of work that has to be thrown away.

Break Up Your Content into Main Topics

With your goals in mind, now try to organize your content into main topics or sections, chunking related information together under a single topic. Sometimes the goals you came up with in the preceding section and your list of topics will be closely related. For example, if you're putting together a Web page for a bookstore, the goal of being able to order books fits nicely under a topic called, appropriately, "Ordering Books."

You don't have to be exact at this point in development. Your goal here is just to try to come up with an idea of what, specifically, you'll be describing in your Web pages. You can organize the information better later, as you write the actual pages.

Suppose that you're designing a Web site about how to tune up your car. This example is simple because tune-ups consist of a concrete set of steps that fit neatly into topic headings. In this example, your topics might include the following:

- Change the oil and oil filter.
- Check and adjust engine timing.
- Check and adjust valve clearances.
- Check and replace the spark plugs.
- Check fluid levels, belts, and hoses.

Don't worry about the order of the steps or how you're going to get your readers to go from one section to another. Just list the points you want to describe in your Web site.

How about a less task-oriented example? Suppose that you want to create a set of Web pages about a particular rock band because you're a big fan, and you're sure other fans would benefit from your extensive knowledge. Your topics might be as follows:

- The history of the band
- Biographies of each of the band members
- A "discography"—all the albums and singles the band has released
- Selected lyrics
- Images of album covers
- Information about upcoming shows and future albums

You can come up with as many topics as you want, but try to keep each topic reasonably short. If a single topic seems too large, try to break it up into subtopics. If you have too many small topics, try to group them together into some sort of more general topic heading. For example, if you're creating an online encyclopedia of poisonous plants, having individual topics for each plant would be overkill. You can just as easily group each plant name under a letter of the alphabet (A, B, C, and so on) and use each letter as a topic. That's assuming, of course, that your readers will be looking up information in your encyclopedia alphabetically. If they want to look up poisonous plants by using some other method, you would have to come up with different topics.

Your goal is to have a set of topics that are roughly the same size and that group together related bits of information you have to present.

Ideas for Organization and Navigation

At this point, you should have a good idea of what you want to talk about and a list of topics. The next step is to actually start structuring the information you have into a set of Web pages. Before you do that, however, consider some "standard" structures that have been used in other help systems and online tools. This section describes some of these structures, their various features, and some important considerations, including the following:

- The kinds of information that work well for each structure
- How readers find their way through the content of each structure type to find what they need
- How to make sure readers can figure out where they are within your documents (context) and find their way back to a known position

Think, as you read this section, how your information might fit into one of these structures, or how you could combine these structures to create a new structure for your Web site.

Note

Many of the ideas I describe in this section were drawn from a book called *Designing and Writing Online Documentation* by William K. Horton (John Wiley & Sons, 1994). Although Horton's book was written primarily for technical writers and developers working specifically with online help systems, it's a great book for ideas on structuring documents and for dealing with hypertext information in general. If you start doing a lot of work with the Web, you might want to pick up this book; it provides a lot of insight beyond what I have to offer.

Hierarchies

Probably the easiest and most logical way to structure your Web documents is in a hierarchical or menu fashion, as illustrated in Figure 2.3. Hierarchies and menus lend themselves especially well to online and hypertext documents. Most online help systems, for example, are hierarchical. You start with a list or menu of major topics; selecting one leads you to a list of subtopics, which then leads you to a discussion about a particular topic. Different help systems have different levels, of course, but most follow this simple structure.

In a hierarchical organization, readers can easily know their position in the structure. Choices are to move up for more general information or down for more specific information. If you provide a link back to the top level, your readers can get back to some known position quickly and easily.

FIGURE 2.3

Hierarchical organization.

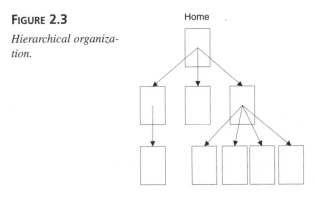

In hierarchies, the home page provides the most general overview to the content below it. The home page also defines the main links for the pages further down in the hierarchy.

For example, a Web site about gardening might have a home page with the topics shown in Figure 2.4.

FIGURE 2.4

A Gardening home page with a hierarchical structure.

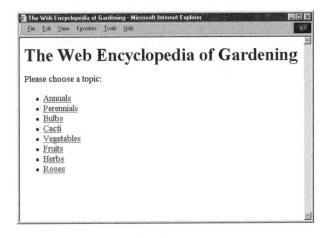

If you select Fruits, you then follow a link "down" to a page about fruits (see Figure 2.5). From there, you can go back to the home page, or you can select another link and go further down into more specific information about particular fruits.

Selecting Soft Fruits takes you to yet another menu-like page, where you have still more categories from which to choose (see Figure 2.6). From there, you can go up to Fruits, back to the home page, or down to one of the choices in this menu.

FIGURE 2.5

Your hierarchy takes you to the Fruits page.

Note that each level has a consistent interface (up, down, back to index), and that each level has a limited set of choices for basic navigation. Hierarchies are structured enough that the chance of getting lost is minimal. (This especially is true if you provide clues about where "Up" is; for example, a link that says "Up to Soft Fruits" as opposed to just "Up.")

Additionally, if you organize each level of the hierarchy and avoid overlap between topics (and the content you have lends itself to a hierarchical organization), using hierarchies can be an easy way to find particular bits of information. If that use is one of your goals for your readers, using a hierarchy may work particularly well.

Avoid including too many levels and too many choices, however, because you can easily annoy your readers. Having too many menu pages results in "voice-mail syndrome."

After having to choose from too many menus, readers may forget what it was they origi-nally wanted, and they're too annoyed to care. Try to keep your hierarchy two to three levels deep, combining information on the pages at the lowest levels (or endpoints) of the hierarchy if necessary.

Linear

Another way to organize your documents is to use a linear or sequential organization, much like printed documents are organized. In a linear structure, as illustrated in Figure 2.7, the home page is the title, or introduction, and each page follows sequentially from that structure. In a strict linear structure, links move from one page to another, typically forward and back. You also might want to include a link to "Home" that takes you quick-ly back to the first page.

FIGURE 2.7

Linear organization.

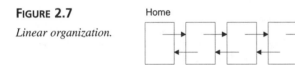

Context generally is easy to figure out in a linear structure simply because there are so few places to go.

A linear organization is very rigid and limits your readers' freedom to explore and your freedom to present information. Linear structures are good for putting material online when the information also has a very linear structure offline (such as short stories, step-by-step instructions, or computer-based training), or when you explicitly want to prevent your readers from skipping around.

For example, consider teaching someone how to make cheese by using the Web. Cheese-making is a complex process that involves several steps that must be followed in a specif-ic order.

Describing this process using Web pages lends itself to a linear structure rather well. When navigating a set of Web pages on this subject, you would start with the home page, which might have a summary or an overview of the steps to follow. Then, by using the link for "forward," move on to the first step, "Choosing the Right Milk"; to the next step, "Setting and Curdling the Milk"; all the way through to the last step, "Curing and Ripening the Cheese." If you need to review at any time, you could use the link for "back." Because the process is so linear, you would have little need for links that branch off from the main stem or links that join together different steps in the process.

Linear with Alternatives

You can soften the rigidity of a linear structure by enabling the readers to deviate from the main path. You could, for example, have a linear structure with alternatives that branch out from a single point (see Figure 2.8). The off-shoots can then rejoin the main branch at some point further down, or they can continue down their separate tracks until they each come to an "end."

FIGURE 2.8

Linear with alternatives.

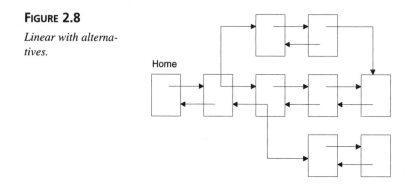

Home

Suppose that you have an installation procedure for a software package that is similar in most ways, regardless of the computer type, except for one step. At that point in the linear installation, you could branch out to cover each system, as shown in Figure 2.9.

FIGURE 2.9

Different steps for different systems.

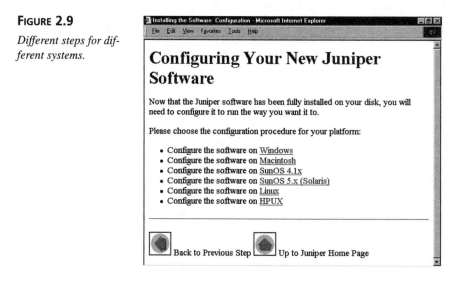

After the system-specific part of the installation, you then could link back to the original branch and continue with the generic installation.

In addition to branching from a linear structure, you also could provide links that enable readers to skip forward or backward in the chain if they need to review a particular step, or if they already understand some content (see Figure 2.10).

FIGURE 2.10

Skip ahead or back.

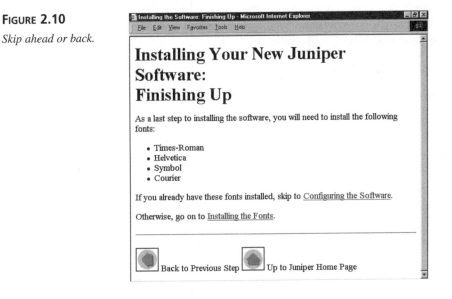

Combination of Linear and Hierarchical

A popular form of document organization on the Web is a combination of a linear structure and a hierarchical one, as shown in Figure 2.11. This structure occurs most often when very structured but linear documents are put online; the popular Frequently Asked Questions (FAQ) files use this structure.

FIGURE 2.11

Combination of linear and hierarchical organization.

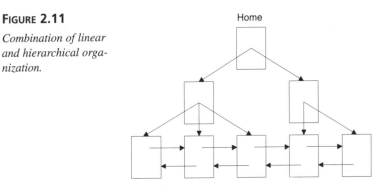

The combination of linear and hierarchical documents works well as long as you have appropriate clues regarding context. Because the readers can either move up and down or forward and backward, they can easily lose their mental positioning in the hierarchy when crossing hierarchical boundaries by moving forward or backward.

Suppose that you're putting the Shakespearean play *Macbeth* online as a set of Web pages. In addition to the simple linear structure that the play provides, you can create a hierarchical table of contents and summary of each act linked to appropriate places within the text, similar to what is shown in Figure 2.12.

FIGURE 2.12

Macbeth's hierarchy.

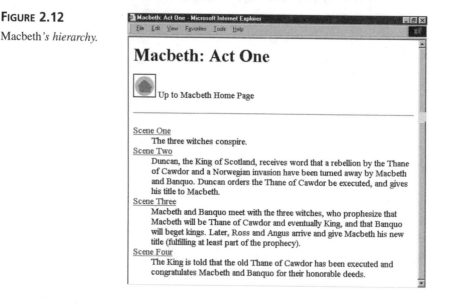

Because this structure is both linear and hierarchical, you provide links to go forward, backward, return to beginning, and up on each page of the script. But what is the context for going up?

If you've just come down into this page from an act summary, the context makes sense. "Up" means go back to the summary from which you just came.

But suppose that you go down from a summary and then go forward, crossing an act boundary (say from Act 1 to Act 2). Now what does "up" mean? The fact that you're moving up to a page you may not have seen before is disorienting given the nature of what you expect from a hierarchy. Up and down are supposed to be consistent.

Consider two possible solutions:

- Do not allow "forward" and "back" links across hierarchical boundaries. In this case, to read from Act 1 to Act 2 in *Macbeth*, you have to move up in the hierarchy and then back down into Act 2.

- Provide more context in the link text. Rather than just "Up" or an icon for the link that moves up in the hierarchy, include a description as to where the user is moving.

Web

A Web is a set of documents with little or no actual overall structure; the only thing tying each page together is a link (see Figure 2.13). Readers drift from document to document, following the links around.

FIGURE 2.13

A Web structure.

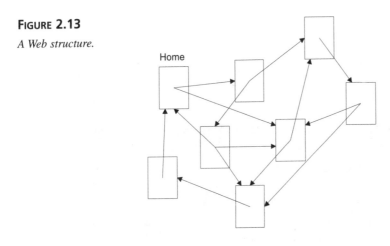

Web structures tend to be free-flowing and enable readers to wander aimlessly through the content. Web structures are excellent for content that is intended to be meandering or unrelated, or when you want to encourage browsing. The World Wide Web itself is, of course, a giant Web structure.

An example of content organized in a Web structure might be a set of virtual "rooms" created by using Web pages. If you've ever played an old text-adventure game like Zork or Dungeon, or if you've used a Multiuser Dungeon (MUD), you are familiar with this type of environment.

In the context of a Web site, the environment is organized so that each page is a specific location (and usually contains a description of that location). From that location, you can "move" in several different directions, exploring the environment much in the way you would move from room to room in a building in the real world (and getting lost just as easily). The initial home page, for example, might look something like the one shown in Figure 2.14.

From that page, you then can explore one of the links, for example, to go into the building, which takes you to the page shown in Figure 2.15.

FIGURE 2.14

The home page for a Web-based virtual environment.

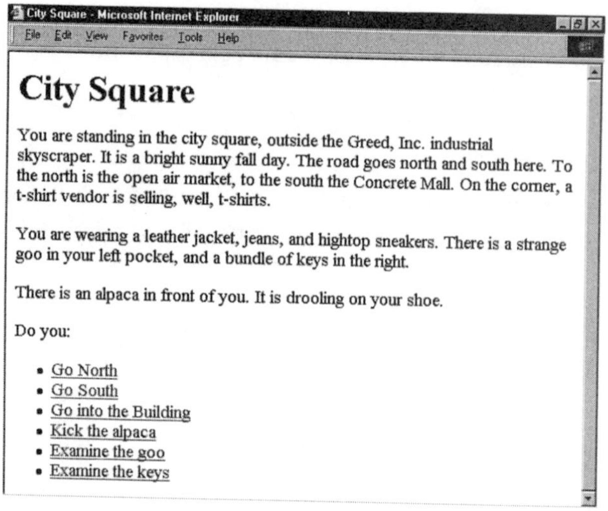
City Square - Microsoft Internet Explorer
File Edit View Favorites Tools Help
City Square
You are standing in the city square, outside the Greed, Inc. industrial skyscraper. It is a bright sunny fall day. The road goes north and south here. To the north is the open air market, to the south the Concrete Mall. On the corner, a t-shirt vendor is selling, well, t-shirts.
You are wearing a leather jacket, jeans, and hightop sneakers. There is a strange goo in your left pocket, and a bundle of keys in the right.
There is an alpaca in front of you. It is drooling on your shoe.
Do you:
Go North
Go South
Go into the Building
Kick the alpaca
Examine the goo
Examine the keys

FIGURE 2.15

Another page in the Web environment.

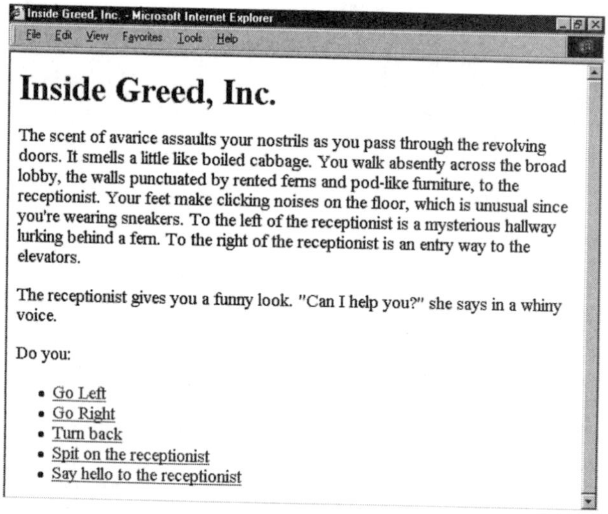
Inside Greed, Inc. - Microsoft Internet Explorer
File Edit View Favorites Tools Help
Inside Greed, Inc.
The scent of avarice assaults your nostrils as you pass through the revolving doors. It smells a little like boiled cabbage. You walk absently across the broad lobby, the walls punctuated by rented ferns and pod-like furniture, to the receptionist. Your feet make clicking noises on the floor, which is unusual since you're wearing sneakers. To the left of the receptionist is a mysterious hallway lurking behind a fern. To the right of the receptionist is an entry way to the elevators.
The receptionist gives you a funny look. "Can I help you?" she says in a whiny voice.
Do you:
Go Left
Go Right
Turn back
Spit on the receptionist
Say hello to the receptionist

Each room has a set of links to each "adjacent" room in the environment. By following the links, you can explore the rooms in the environment.

The problem with Web organizations is that you can get lost in them too easily—just as you might in the "world" you're exploring in the example. Without any overall structure to the content, figuring out the relationship between where you are, where you're going, and, often, where you've been is difficult. Context is difficult, and often the only way to find your way back out of a Web structure is to retrace your steps. Web structures can be extremely disorienting and immensely frustrating if you have a specific goal in mind.

To solve the problem of disorientation, you can use clues on each page. Here are two ideas:

- Provide a way out. "Return to Home Page" is an excellent link.
- Include a map of the overall structure on each page, with a "you are here" indication somewhere in the map. It doesn't have to be an actual visual map, but providing some sort of context will go a long way toward preventing your readers from getting lost.

Storyboarding Your Web Site

The next step in planning your Web site is to figure out what content goes on what page and to come up with some simple links for navigation between those pages.

If you're using one of the structures described in the preceding section, much of the organization may arise from that structure, in which case this section will be easy. If you want to combine different kinds of structures, however, or if you have a lot of content that needs to be linked together in sophisticated ways, sitting down and making a specific plan of what goes where will be incredibly useful later as you develop and link each individual page.

What Is Storyboarding and Why Do I Need It?

Storyboarding a Web site is a concept borrowed from filmmaking in which each scene and each individual camera shot is sketched and roughed out in the order in which it occurs in the movie. Storyboarding provides an overall structure and plan to the film that allows the director and staff to have a distinct idea of where each individual shot fits into the overall movie.

NEW TERM   *Storyboarding* is the process of creating a rough outline and sketch of what your Web site will look like before you actually write any pages. Storyboarding helps you visualize the entire Web site and how it will look when it's complete.

The storyboarding concept works quite well for developing Web pages. The storyboard provides an overall rough outline of what the Web site will look like when it's done, including which topics go on which pages, the primary links, and maybe even some conceptual idea of what sort of graphics you'll be using and where they will go. With that representation in hand, you can develop each page without trying to remember exactly where that page fits into the overall Web site and its often complex relationships to other pages.

In the case of really large sets of documents, a storyboard enables different people to develop different portions of the same Web site. With a clear storyboard, you can minimize duplication of work and reduce the amount of contextual information each person needs to remember.

For smaller or simpler Web sites, or Web sites with a simple logical structure, storyboarding may be unnecessary. For larger and more complex projects, however, the existence of a storyboard can save enormous amounts of time and frustration. If you can't keep all the parts of your content and their relationships in your head, consider creating a storyboard.

So what does a storyboard for a Web site look like? It can be as simple as a couple of sheets of paper. Each sheet can represent a page, with a list of topics each page will describe and some thoughts about the links that page will include. I've seen storyboards for very complex hypertext systems that involved a really large bulletin board, index cards, and string. Each index card had a topic written on it, and the links were represented by string tied on pins from card to card (see Figure 2.16).

FIGURE 2.16

A complex storyboard.

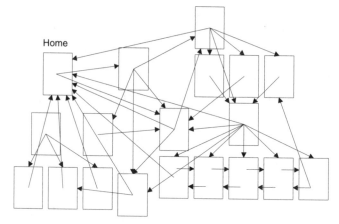

The point of a storyboard is that it organizes your Web pages in a way that works for you. If you like index cards and string, work with these tools. If a simple outline on paper or on the computer works better, use that instead.

Hints for Storyboarding

Some things to think about when developing your storyboard are as follows:

- **Which topics will go on each page?**

  A simple rule of thumb is to have each topic represented by a single page. If you have several topics, however, maintaining and linking them can be a daunting task. Consider combining smaller, related topics onto a single page instead. Don't go overboard and put everything on one page, however; your readers still have to download your document over the net. Having several medium-sized pages (such as the size of two to ten pages in your word processor) is better than having one monolithic page or hundreds of little tiny pages.

- **What are the primary forms of navigation between pages?**

  What links will you need for your readers to navigate from page to page? They are the main links in your document that enable your readers to accomplish the goals you defined in the first section. Links for forward, back, up, down, or home all fall under the category of primary navigation.

- **What alternative forms of navigation are you going to provide?**

  In addition to the simple navigation links, some Web sites contain extra information that is parallel to the main Web content, such as a glossary of terms, an alphabetical index of concepts, or a credits page. Consider these extra forms of information when designing your plan, and think about how you're going to link them into the main content.

- **What will you put on your home page?**

  Because the home page is the starting point for the rest of the information in your Web site, consider what sort of information you're going to put on the home page. A general summary of what's to come? A list of links to other topics?

- **Review your goals**

  As you design the framework for your Web site, keep your goals in mind, and make sure you are not obscuring your goals with extra information or content.

Note

> Several utilities and packages can assist you in storyboarding. Foremost among them are site management packages that can help you manage links in a site, view a graphical representation of the relationship of documents in your site, move documents around, and automatically update all relevant links in and to the documents.

Summary

Designing a Web site, like designing a book outline, a building plan, or a painting, can sometimes be a complex and involved process. Having a plan before beginning can help you keep the details straight and help you develop the finished product with fewer false starts. Today, you've learned how to put together a simple plan and structure for creating a set of Web pages, including the following:

- Deciding what sort of content to present
- Coming up with a set of goals for that content
- Deciding on a set of topics
- Organizing and storyboarding the Web site

With that plan in place, you now can move on to the next few chapters and learn the specifics of how to write individual Web pages, create links between them, and add graphics and media to enhance the Web site for your audience.

Workshop

The first section of the workshop lists some of the common questions people ask while planning a Web site, along with an answer to each. Following that, you'll have an opportunity to answer some quiz questions yourself. If you have problems answering any of the questions in the quiz, go to the next section where you'll find the answers. The exercises help you formulate some ideas for your own Web site.

Q&A

Q Getting organized seems like an awful lot of work. All I want to do is make something simple, and you're telling me I have to have goals and topics and storyboards.

A If you're doing something simple, then no, you won't need to do much, if any, of the stuff I recommend in this chapter. If you're talking about developing two or three interlinked pages or more, however, having a plan before you start really helps. If you just dive in, you may discover that keeping everything straight in your head is too difficult. And the result may not be what you expected, making it hard for people to get the information they need out of your Web site as well as making difficult for you to reorganize it so that it makes sense. Having a plan before you start can't hurt, and it may save you time in the long run.

Q You've talked a lot in this chapter about organizing topics and pages, but you've said nothing about the design and layout of individual pages.

A I discuss design and layout later in this book, after you've learned more about the sorts of layout HTML (the language used for Web pages) can do, and the stuff that it just can't do. You'll learn more about page layout and design in Day 16, "Writing and Designing Web Pages: Dos and Don'ts."

Q What if I don't like any of the basic structures you talked about in this chapter?

A Then design your own. As long as your readers can find what they want or do what you want them to do, no rules say you *must* use a hierarchy or a linear structure. I presented these structures only as potential ideas for organizing your Web pages.

Quiz

1. How would you briefly define the meaning of the terms *Web site*, *Web server*, and *Web pages*?
2. In terms of Web publishing, what is the meaning of the term *home page*?
3. After you set a goal or purpose for your Web site, what is the next step to designing your pages?
4. Regardless of the navigation structure you use in your Web site, there is one link that should typically appear on each of your Web pages. What is it?
5. What is the purpose of a storyboard?

Answers

1. A *Web site* is one or more Web pages linked together in a meaningful way. A *Web server* is the actual machine that stores the Web site. *Web pages* are the individual elements of the Web site, like a page is to a book.
2. A *home page*, in terms of Web publishing, is the entry point to the rest of the pages in your Web site (the first or topmost page).
3. After you set a goal or purpose for your Web site, you should try to organize your content into topics or sections.
4. You should try to include a link to your home page on each of the pages in your Web site. This way, users can always find their way back home if they get lost.
5. A storyboard provides an overall outline of what the Web site will look like when it's done. It helps organize your Web pages in a way that works for you. They are most beneficial for larger Web sites.

Exercises

1. As an exercise, come up with a list of several goals that your readers might have for your Web pages. The clearer your goals, the better.
2. After you set your goals, visit sites on the Web that cover topics similar to those you want to cover in your own Web site. As you examine the sites, ask yourself whether they are easy to navigate and have good content. Then make a list—what do you like about the sites? How would you make your Web site better?

PART 1

DAY 3

An Introduction to HTML

After finishing up the discussions about the World Wide Web and getting organized, with a large amount of text to read and concepts to digest, you're probably wondering when you're actually going to get to write a Web page. That is, after all, why you bought the book. Wait no longer! In this chapter, you'll get to create your very first (albeit brief) Web page, learn about HTML (the language for writing Web pages), and learn about the following:

- What HTML is and why you have to use it
- What you can and cannot do when you design HTML pages
- HTML tags: what they are and how to use them

What HTML Is—and What It Isn't

Take note of just one more thing before you dive into actually writing Web pages. You should know what HTML is, what it can do, and most importantly what it can't do.

HTML stands for *Hypertext Markup Language*. HTML is based on the *Standard Generalized Markup Language* (SGML), a much larger document-processing system. To write HTML pages, you won't need to know a whole lot about SGML, but knowing that one of the main features of SGML is that it describes the general *structure* of the content inside documents, not that content's actual *appearance* on the page or on the screen, does help. This concept might be a bit foreign to you if you're used to working with WYSIWYG (What You See Is What You Get) editors, so let's go over the information carefully.

HTML Describes the Structure of a Page

HTML, by virtue of its SGML heritage, is a language for describing the structure of a document, not its actual presentation. The idea here is that most documents have common elements—for example, titles, paragraphs, or lists. Before you start writing, therefore, you can identify and define the set of elements in that document and give them appropriate names (see Figure 3.1).

FIGURE 3.1

Document elements.

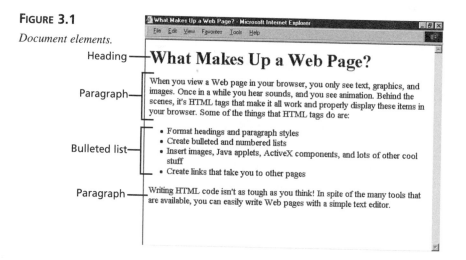

If you've worked with word processing programs that use style sheets (such as Microsoft Word) or paragraph catalogs (such as FrameMaker), you've done something similar; each section of text conforms to one of a set of styles that are predefined before you start working.

HTML defines a set of common styles for Web pages: headings, paragraphs, lists, and tables. It also defines character styles such as boldface and code examples. Each element has a name and is contained in what's called a *tag*. When you write a Web page in HTML, you label the different elements of your page with these tags that say "this is a heading" or "this is a list item."

HTML Does Not Describe Page Layout

When you're working with a word processor or page layout program, styles are not just named elements of a page—they also include formatting information such as the font size and style, indentation, underlining, and so on. So when you write some text that's supposed to be a heading, you can apply the Heading style to it, and the program automatically formats that paragraph for you in the correct style.

HTML doesn't go this far. For the most part, HTML doesn't say anything about how a page looks when it's viewed. HTML tags just indicate that an element is a heading or a list; they say nothing about how that heading or list is to be formatted. For example, consider an article you've written for a magazine and the layout person who formats your article; the layout person's job is to decide how big the heading should be and what font it should be in. The only thing you have to worry about is marking which section is supposed to be a heading.

Note

> Although HTML doesn't say much about how a page looks when it's viewed, cascading style sheets (abbreviated as CSS) enable you to apply advanced formatting to HTML tags. There are many changes in HTML 4.0 that favor the use of CSS tags. You'll begin to learn more about CSS in Day 4, "Begin with the Basics," and Day 10, "XHTML and Style Sheets."

Web browsers, in addition to providing the networking functions to retrieve pages from the Web, double as HTML formatters. When you read an HTML page into a browser such as Netscape or Internet Explorer, the browser interprets, or *parses*, the HTML tags and formats the text and images on the screen. The browser has mappings between the names of page elements and actual styles on the screen; for example, headings might be in a larger font than the text on the rest of the page. The browser also wraps all the text so that it fits into the current width of the window.

Different browsers, running on different platforms, may have different style mappings for each page element. Some browsers may use different font styles than others. So, for example, one browser might display italics as italics, whereas another might use reverse text or underlining on systems that don't have italic fonts. Or it might put a heading in all capital letters instead of a larger font.

What this means to you as a Web page designer is that the pages you create with HTML may look radically different from system to system and from browser to browser. The actual information and links inside those pages will still be there, but the onscreen appearance will change. You can design a Web page so that it looks perfect on your computer system, but when someone else reads it on a different system, it may look entirely different (and it may very well be entirely unreadable).

Why It Works This Way

If you're used to writing and designing on paper, this concept may seem almost perverse. No control over the layout of a page? The whole design can vary depending on where the page is viewed? This is awful! Why on earth would a system work like this?

Remember in Day 1, "The World of the World Wide Web," when I mentioned that one of the cool things about the Web is that it is cross-platform and that Web pages can be viewed on any computer system, on any size screen, with any graphics display? If the final goal of Web publishing is for your pages to be readable by anyone in the world, you can't count on your readers having the same computer systems, the same size screens, the same number of colors, or the same fonts that you have. The Web takes into account all these differences and allows all browsers and all computer systems to be on equal ground.

The Web, as a design medium, is not a new form of paper. The Web is an entirely different medium, with its own constraints and goals that are very different from working with paper. The most important rules of Web page design, as I'll keep harping on throughout this book, are the following:

Do	Don't
Do design your pages so they work in most browsers.	**Don't** design your pages based on what they look like on your computer system and on your browser.
Do focus on clear, well-structured content that is easy to read and understand.	

Throughout this book, I'll show you examples of HTML code and what they look like when displayed. In examples where browsers display code very differently, I'll give you a comparison of how a snippet of code looks in two very different browsers. Through these examples, you'll get an idea of how different the same page can look from browser to browser.

Note

Although this rule of designing by structure and not by appearance is the way to produce good HTML, when you surf the Web, you might be surprised that the vast majority of Web sites seem to have been designed with appearance in mind—usually appearance in a particular browser such as Netscape Navigator or Microsoft Internet Explorer. Don't be swayed by these designs. If you stick to the rules I suggest, in the end, your Web pages and Web sites will be all the more successful simply because more people can easily read and use them.

HTML Is a Markup Language

HTML is a *markup language*. Writing in a markup language means that you start with the text of your page and add special tags around words and paragraphs. The tags indicate the different parts of the page and produce different effects in the browser. You'll learn more about tags and how they're used in the next section.

HTML has a defined set of tags you can use. You can't make up your own tags to create new appearances or features. And, just to make sure that things are really confusing, different browsers support different sets of tags. To further explain this, take a brief look at the history of HTML.

3

A Brief History of HTML Tags

The base set of HTML tags, the lowest common denominator, is referred to as HTML 2.0. HTML 2.0 is the old standard for HTML (a written specification for it is developed and maintained by the W3 Consortium) and the set of tags that all browsers must support. In the next few chapters, you'll primarily learn to use tags that were first introduced in HTML 2.0.

The HTML 3.2 specification was developed in early 1996. Several software vendors, including IBM, Microsoft, Netscape Communications Corporation, Novell, SoftQuad, Spyglass, and Sun Microsystems, joined with the W3 consortium to develop this specification. Some of the primary additions to HTML 3.2 included features such as tables, applets, and text flow around images. HTML 3.2 also provided full backward-compatibility with the existing HTML 2.0 standard.

Note

The enhancements introduced in HTML 3.2 are covered later in this book. You'll learn more about tables in Day 11, "Tables." Day 13, "Multimedia: Adding Sounds, Videos, and More" tells you how to use Java applets.

HTML 4.0, first introduced in 1997, incorporated many new features that gave you greater control than HTML 2.0 and 3.2 in how you designed your pages. Like HTML 2.0

and 3.2, the W3 Consortium maintains the HTML 4.0 standard. While both Internet Explorer 4 and Netscape Navigator 4 support most HTML 4.0 features, users with browsers older than that won't be able to view HTML 4.0 features such as cascading style sheets and dynamic HTML.

Note

> Cascading style sheets and dynamic HTML are additional Web technologies that work in conjunction with HTML to give you additional control over the appearance of your Web pages. Style sheets are discussed further in Day 10, "XHTML and Style Sheets." See Day 15, "Using Dynamic HTML" for an introduction to the capabilities of dynamic HTML.

Framesets (originally introduced in Netscape 2.0) and floating frames (originally introduced in Internet Explorer 3.0) became an official part of the HTML 4.0 specification. Framesets are discussed in more detail in Day 12, "Frames and Linked Windows." We also see additional improvements to table formatting and rendering. By far, however, the most important change in HTML 4.0 was its increased integration with style sheets.

Note

> If you're interested in how HTML development is working and just exactly what's going on at the W3 Consortium, check out the pages for HTML at the consortium's site at `http://www.w3.org/pub/WWW/MarkUp/`.

In addition to the tags defined by the various levels of HTML, individual browser companies also implement browser-specific extensions to HTML. Netscape and Microsoft are particularly guilty of creating extensions, and they offer many new features unique to their browsers.

Confused yet? You're not alone. Even Web designers with years of experience and hundreds of pages under their belts have to struggle with the problem of which set of tags to choose to strike a balance between wide support for a design (using HTML 3.2- and 2.0-level tags) or having more flexibility in layout but less consistency across browsers (HTML 4.0 or specific browser extensions). Keeping track of all this information can be really confusing. Throughout this book, as I introduce each tag, I'll let you know which version of HTML the tag belongs to, how widely supported it is, and how to use it to best effect in a wide variety of browsers.

Bridging the Future with XHTML 1.0

The Internet is no longer limited to computer hardware and software. WebTV enables you to access the Internet, giving you more reason to become a couch potato. Personal Information Managers and palmtop computers enable you to access the Internet while you're on the road. Special interfaces and hardware allow disabled individuals to access the Internet. As we head toward the millennium, the Internet has become an effective means of communication and education for the masses.

Many of the newer portable technologies, however, pose problems for the old HTML specification. They simply don't have the processing power of a desktop computer, and are not as forgiving with sloppy code. The developers of the HTML specification have struggled to accommodate these ongoing changes, and the limitations of HTML have become evident. We are stretching and distorting the HTML specification far beyond its capabilities. As a result, there probably *won't* be an HTML 5.

The future of the Internet demands a markup language that is more extensible and portable than HTML. The direction is heading toward the use of XML (short for *Extensible Markup Language*), a subset of SGML that allows for custom tags to be processed. And here is where XHTML 1.0 comes in to play.

XHTML 1.0 is written in XML, and is the up-and-coming standard that will help Web designers prepare for the future. In case you're sitting here wondering why you're reading a book about HTML 4 instead of XHTML 1.0, allow me to offer a little bit of solace.

Technically, XHTML 1.0 and HTML 4 are *very* similar. The tags and attributes are virtually the same, but there are a few simple rules that have to be followed in order to adhere to the XHTML 1.0 specification. Throughout this book, I'll give you hints on how to deal with the different HTML tags to make sure that your pages are readable and still look good in all kinds of browsers.

What HTML Files Look Like

Pages written in HTML are plain text files (ASCII), which means they contain no platform- or program-specific information. Any editor that supports text (which should be just about any editor—more about this subject in "Programs to Help You Write HTML" later in this chapter) can read them. HTML files contain the following:

- The text of the page itself
- HTML tags that indicate page elements, structure, formatting, and hypertext links to other pages or to included media

Most HTML tags look something like the following:

```
<thetagname> affected text </thetagname>
```

The tag name itself (here, `thetagname`) is enclosed in brackets (`< >`). HTML tags generally have a beginning and an ending tag surrounding the text they affect. The beginning tag "turns on" a feature (such as headings, bold, and so on), and the ending tag turns it off. Closing tags have the tag name preceded by a slash (`/`). The opening tag (for example, `<p>` for paragraphs) and closing tag (for example, `</p>` for paragraphs) compose what is officially called an *HTML element*.

NEW TERM *HTML tags* are the information inside brackets (`< >`) that indicate features or elements of a page. The opening and closing tags compose *HTML elements*.

Caution Be aware of the difference between the forward slash (`/`) mentioned with relation to tags, and backslashes (`\`), which are used by DOS and Windows in directory references on hard drives (as in `C:\window` or other directory paths). If you accidentally use the backslash in place of a forward slash in HTML, the browser won't recognize the ending tags.

Not all HTML tags have a beginning and an end. Some tags are only one-sided, and still other tags are "containers" that hold extra information and text inside the brackets. XHTML 1.0, however, requires that *all* tags must have an end, or a closure. You'll learn the proper way to open and close the tags as the book progresses.

Another difference between HTML 4.0 and XHTML 1.0 relates to usage of lowercase tags and attributes. HTML tags are not case sensitive; that is, you can specify them in uppercase, lowercase, or in any mixture. So, `<HTML>` is the same as `<html>` is the same as `<HtMl>`. This is not the case for XHTML 1.0, where all tag and attribute names must be written in lowercase. To get you thinking in this mindset, the examples in this book will display all tag and attribute names in bold lowercase text.

Exercise 3.1: Creating Your First HTML Page

Now that you've seen what HTML looks like, it's your turn to create your own Web page. Start with a simple example so you can get a basic feel for HTML.

To get started writing HTML, you don't need a Web server, a Web provider, or even a connection to the Web itself. All you really need is something to create your HTML files and at least one browser to view them. You can write, link, and test whole suites of Web pages without even touching a network. In fact, that's what you're going to do for the majority of this book. I'll talk later about publishing everything on the Web so other people can see your work.

▼ First, you'll need a text editor. A text editor is a program that saves files in ASCII format. ASCII format is just plain text, with no font formatting or special characters. In Windows, Notepad, Microsoft Write, and DOS edit are good basic text editors (and free with your system). Shareware text editors are also available for various operating systems, including DOS, Windows 3.1, Windows 95/98, Windows NT, Macintosh, and Linux. If you point your Web browser to www.download.com and enter Text Editors as a search term, you will find many resources available to download.

If you have only a word processor, such as Microsoft Word, don't panic. You can still write pages in word processors just as you would in text editors, although doing so is more complicated. When you use the Save or Save As command, you'll see a menu of formats you can use to save the file. One of them should be Text Only, Text Only with Line Breaks, or DOS Text. All these options will save your file as plain ASCII text, just as if you were using a text editor. For HTML files, if you have a choice between DOS Text and just Text, use DOS Text, and use the Line Breaks option if you have it.

3

Note   If you do use a word processor for your HTML development, be very careful. Many recent word processors are including HTML modes or mechanisms for creating HTML or XML code. This feature can produce unusual results or files that simply don't behave as you expect. If you run into trouble with a word processor, try using a text editor and see whether it helps.

What about the plethora of free and commercial HTML editors that claim to help you write HTML more easily? Most of them are actually simple text editors with some buttons that stick the tags in for you. If you've got one of these editors, go ahead and use it. If you've got a fancier editor that claims to hide all the HTML for you, put it aside for the next couple of days and try using a plain text editor just for a little while. Appendix A, "Sources for Further Information," lists many URLs where you can download many free and commercial HTML editors that are available for different platforms. They appear in the section titled "HTML Editors and Convertors."

Open your text editor, and type the following code. You don't have to understand what any of it means at this point. You'll learn more about much of this today and tomorrow. This simple example is just to get you started.

```
<!DOCTYPE html PUBLIC "-//W3C//DTD XHTML 1.0 Transitional//EN"
  "http://www.w3.org/TR/xhtml1/DTD/transitional.dtd">
<html>
<head>
<title>My Sample HTML page</title>
</head>
```

▼
```
<body>
<h1>This is an HTML Page</h1>
</body>
</html>
```

Note

In this example, and in most other examples throughout this book, the HTML tags are printed darker than the rest of the text so you can easily spot them. When you type your own HTML files, all the text will be the same color (unless you are using a special HTML editing program that uses color to highlight tags).

After you create your HTML file, save it to your hard disk. Remember that if you're using a word processor, choose Save As and make sure you're saving it as text only. When you choose a name for the file, follow these two rules:

- The filename should have an extension of .html (.htm on DOS or Windows systems that have only three-character extensions)—for example, myfile.html, text.html, or index.htm. Most Web software will require your files to have these extensions, so get into the habit of doing it now.

▲
- Use small, simple names. Don't include spaces or special characters (bullets, accented characters)—just letters and numbers are fine.

Exercise 3.2: Viewing the Result

To Do
Now that you have an HTML file, start up your Web browser. You don't have to be connected to the network because you're not going to be opening pages at any other site. Your browser or network connection software may complain about the lack of a network connection, but usually it will give up and let you use it anyway.

▼

Tip

If you're using a Web browser from Windows 3.1, using that browser without a network is unfortunately more complicated than on other older systems. Many Windows 3.1 browsers (including some versions of Netscape) cannot run without a network, preventing you from looking at your local files without running up online charges. Try starting your browser while not online to see if this is the case. If your browser has this problem, you can try several workarounds. Depending on your network software, you might be able to start your network package (Trumpet or Chameleon) but not actually dial the network. This solution often is sufficient for many browsers.

If this solution doesn't work, you'll have to replace the file winsock.dll in your Windows directory with a "null sock"—a special file that makes your system think it's on a network when it's not. The book's Web support site

▼

▼

(see the inside back cover of the book for the URL) contains a `nullsock.dll` file you can use with your Windows browser. If you use Netscape, use `mozock.dll` instead.

First, put your original `winsock.dll` in a safe place; you'll need to put everything back the way it was to get back on to the Web. Next, rename the null sock file to `winsock.dll`, and copy it to your Windows directory. With the fake `winsock` file installed, you should be able to use your Windows browser without a network. (It may still give you errors, but it should work.)

To restore things back the way they were. Rename the fake `winsock.dll` file back to `nullsock.dll` or `mozock.dll`, and then copy the original `winsock.dll` back into the Windows directory.

After your browser is running, look for a menu item or button labeled Open Local, Open File, or maybe just Open. Choosing it will enable you to browse your local disk. The Open File command (or its equivalent) tells the browser to read an HTML file from your disk, parse it, and display it, just as if it were a page on the Web. By using your browser and the Open Local command, you can write and test your HTML files on your computer in the privacy of your own home.

If you don't see something similar to what is shown in Figure 3.2 (for example, if parts are missing or if everything looks like a heading), go back into your text editor and compare your file to the example. Make sure that all your tags have closing tags and that all your < characters are matched by > characters. You don't have to quit your browser to do so; just fix the file and save it again under the same name.

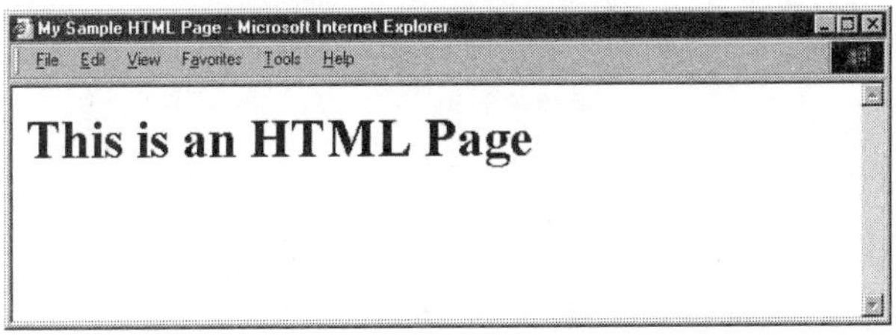

FIGURE 3.2

The sample HTML file.

This is an HTML Page

Next, go back to your browser. Locate and choose a menu item or button called Reload (for Netscape users) or Refresh (for Internet Explorer users). The browser will read the new version of your file, and voilà: you can edit and preview and edit and preview until you get the file right.

If you're getting the actual HTML text repeated in your browser rather than what's shown in Figure 3.2, make sure your HTML file has an `.html` or `.htm` extension. This file extension tells your browser that it is an HTML file. The extension is important.

▼

▼ If things are going really wrong—if you're getting a blank screen or you're getting some really strange characters—something is wrong with your original file. If you've been using a word processor to edit your files, try opening your saved HTML file in a plain text editor (again Notepad or SimpleText will work just fine). If the text editor can't read the file, or if the result is garbled, you haven't saved the original file in the right format. Go back into your original editor, and try saving the file as text only again. Then try
▲ viewing the file again in your browser until you get it right.

A Note About Formatting

When an HTML page is parsed by a browser, any formatting you may have done by hand—that is, any extra spaces, tabs, returns, and so on—are all ignored. The only thing that formats an HTML page is an HTML tag. If you spend hours carefully editing a plain text file to have nicely formatted paragraphs and columns of numbers but don't include any tags, when you read the page into an HTML browser, all the text will flow into one paragraph. All your work will have been in vain.

Note
> The one exception to this rule is a tag called <pre>. You'll learn about this tag in Day 6, "More Text Formatting with HTML."

The advantage of having all white space (spaces, tabs, returns) ignored is that you can put your tags wherever you want.

The following examples all produce the same output. Try them!

```
<h1>If music be the food of love, play on.</h1>
```

```
<h1>
If music be the food of love, play on.
</h1>
```

```
<h1>
If music be the food of love, play on.              </h1>
```

```
<h1>    If    music    be    the    food    of    love,
play    on. </h1 >
```

Programs to Help You Write HTML

You may be thinking that all this tag stuff is a real pain, especially if you didn't get that small example right the first time. (Don't fret about it; I didn't get that example right the first time, and I created it.) You have to remember all the tags, and you have to type them in right and close each one. What a hassle!

Many freeware and shareware programs are available for editing HTML files. Most of these programs essentially are text editors with extra menu items or buttons that insert the appropriate HTML tags into your text. HTML-based text editors are particularly nice for two reasons: you don't have to remember all the tags, and you don't have to take the time to type them all.

Many editors on the market purport to be WYSIWYG (short for "What You See is What You Get"). As you learned earlier today, there's really no such thing as WYSIWYG when you're dealing with HTML. "WYG" can vary wildly based on the browser someone is using to read your page.

With that said, as long as you're aware that the result of working in those editors can vary, using WYSIWYG editors can be a quick way to create simple HTML files. For professional Web development and for using many of the very advanced features, however, WYSIWYG editors usually fall short, and you'll need to go "under the hood" to play with the HTML code anyhow. Even if you intend to use a WYSIWYG editor for the bulk of your HTML work, I recommend you bear with me for the next couple of days and try these examples in text editors so that you get a feel for what HTML really is before you decide to move on to an editor that hides the tags.

In addition to HTML and WYSIWYG editors, you also can use converters, which take files from many popular word processing programs and convert them to HTML. With a simple set of templates, you can write your pages entirely in your favorite program and then convert the result when you're done.

In many cases, converters can be extremely useful, particularly for putting existing documents on the Web as fast as possible. However, converters suffer from many of the same problems as WYSIWYG editors: the result can vary from browser to browser, and many newer or advanced features aren't available in the converters. Also, most converter programs are fairly limited, not necessarily by their own features, but mostly by the limitations in HTML itself. No amount of fancy converting is going to make HTML do things that it can't yet do. If a particular capability doesn't exist in HTML, the converter cannot do anything to solve that problem. (In fact, the converter may end up doing strange things to your HTML files, causing you more work than if you just did all the formatting yourself.)

As previously mentioned, Appendix A lists many of the Web page editors that are currently available. For now, if you have a simple HTML editor, feel free to use it for the examples in this book. If all you have is a text editor, no problem; you'll just have to do a little more typing.

Summary

In today's chapter, you learned some basic points about what HTML is, and how you define a text document as a Web page. You learned a bit about the history of HTML and the reasons why the HTML specification has changed several times since the beginning. Using page structure tags, a title, and a heading, you created your first Web page. It wasn't so bad, was it? In tomorrow's lesson, you'll expand on this and will learn more about adding headings, text, and lists to your pages.

Workshop

Now that you've had an introduction to HTML, and a taste of creating your first very simple Web page, here's a workshop that will guide you toward more of what you'll be learning. A couple of questions and answers that relate to HTML formatting are followed by a brief quiz and answers about HTML. Exercises prompt you to examine the code of a more advanced page in your browser.

Q&A

Q Can I do *any* formatting of text in HTML?

A You can do some formatting to strings of characters; for example, making a word or two bold. Tags in HTML 3.2 (the predecessor to HTML 4.0) enabled you to change the font size and color of the text in your Web page (for readers using browsers that support the tags—including Netscape and Microsoft Internet Explorer), but these tags have given way to CSS formatting in HTML 4.0. You'll learn some formatting tricks in Day 6.

Q I'm using Windows. My word processor won't let me save a text file with an extension that's anything except `.txt`. If I type in `index.html`, my word processor saves the file as `index.html.txt`. What can I do?

A You can rename your files after you've saved them so that they have an `html` or `htm` extension, but having to do so can be annoying if you have a large number of files. Consider using a text editor or HTML editor for your Web pages.

Quiz

1. What does HTML stand for?
2. What is the primary function of HTML?
3. Why doesn't HTML control the layout of a page?
4. Which version of HTML provides the lowest common denominator of HTML tags?

5. What is the basic structure of an HTML tag?

Answers

1. HTML stands for Hypertext Markup Language.

2. HTML defines a set of common styles for Web pages (headings, paragraphs, lists, tables, character styles, and more).

3. HTML doesn't control the layout of a page because it is designed to be cross-platform. It takes the differences of many platforms into account and allows all browsers and all computer systems to be on equal ground.

4. The lowest common denominator for HTML tags is HTML 2.0, the oldest standard for HTML. This is the set of tags that *all* browsers *must* support. HTML 2.0 tags can be used anywhere.

5. Most HTML tags generally have a beginning and an ending tag, and surround the text that they affect. The tags are enclosed in brackets (<>). The beginning tag turns on a feature, and the ending tag, which is preceded by a forward slash (/), turns it off.

Exercises

1. Before you actually start writing a meatier HTML page, getting a feel for what an HTML page looks like certainly helps. Luckily, you can find plenty of source material to look at. Every page that comes over the wire to your browser is in HTML format. (You almost never see the codes in your browser; all you see is the final result.)

   Most Web browsers have a way of letting you see the HTML source of a Web page. If you're using Internet Explorer 4.0, for example, navigate to the Web page that you want to look at. Choose View, Source to display the source code in a text window. In Netscape Navigator/Communicator 4, choose View, Page Source.

Tip

In some browsers, you cannot directly view the source of a Web page, but you can save the current page as a file to your local disk. In a dialog box for saving the file, you might find a menu of formats—for example, Text, PostScript, or HTML. You can save the current page as HTML and then open that file in a text editor or word processor to see the HTML source.

Try going to a typical home page and then viewing its source. For example, Figure 3.3 shows the home page for Alta Vista, a popular search page at www.altavista.com/.

FIGURE 3.3

Alta Vista home page.

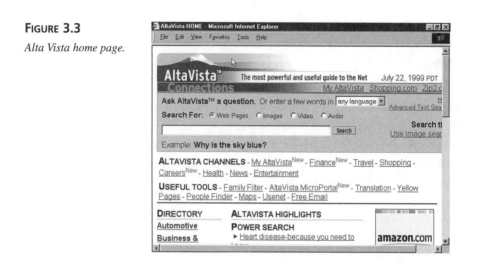

The HTML source of the Alta Vista home page looks something like Figure 3.4.

FIGURE 3.4

Some HTML source.

2. Try viewing the source of your own favorite Web pages. You should start seeing some similarities in the way pages are organized and get a feel for the kinds of tags that HTML uses. You can learn a lot about HTML by comparing the text onscreen with the source for that text.

PART 2

Creating Simple
Web Pages

DAY 4

Begin with the Basics

Yesterday, you learned about the World Wide Web, how to organize and plan your Web sites, and why you need to use HTML to create a Web page. You even created your first very simple Web page. Today, you'll learn about each of the basic HTML tags in more depth, and begin writing Web pages with headings, paragraphs, and several different types of lists. This chapter focuses on the following topics and HTML tags:

- Tags for overall page structure: `<html>`, `<head>`, and `<body>`
- Tags for titles, headings, and paragraphs: `<title>`, `<h1>`...`<h6>`, and `<p>`
- Tags for comments: `<!--......-->`
- Tags for lists: `<ol>`, `<ul>`, `<li>`, `<dt>`, and `<dd>`

Structuring Your HTML

HTML defines three tags that are used to describe the page's overall structure and provide some simple "header" information. These three tags—`<html>`, `<head>`, and `<body>`—identify your page to browsers or HTML tools. They also provide simple information about the page (such as its title or its author) before loading the entire thing. The page structure tags don't affect what the page looks like when it's displayed; they're only there to help tools that interpret or filter HTML files.

In the strict HTML definition, these tags are optional. If your page does not contain them, browsers usually can read the page anyway. These tags, however, *are* required elements in XHTML 1.0. Tools and browsers that need these tags also will come along. You should get into the habit of including the page structure tags now.

> **Note**
>
> Though not a page structure tag, the proposed XHTML 1.0 specification includes one additional requirement for your Web pages. The first line of each page must include a DOCTYPE identifier that defines the XHTML 1.0 version to which your page conforms, and the document type definition (DTD) that defines the specification. This is followed by the <html>, <head>, and <body> tags. In the following example, the XHTML 1.0 Strict document type appears before the page structure tags:
>
> ```
> <!DOCTYPE html PUBLIC "-//W3C//DTD XHTML 1.0 Strict//EN"
>      "http://www.w3.org/TR/xhtml1/DTD/strict.dtd">
> <html>
> <head>
> <title>Page Title</title>
> </head>
> <body>
> ...your page content...
> </body>
> </html>
> ```
>
> There are three types of HTML 4.0 document types specified in the XHTML 1.0 specification: Strict, Transitional, and Frameset. Refer to Day 10, "XHTML and Style Sheets," for more information about the DOCTYPE tag, and Day 18, "Designing for the Real World" for more information about the differences between Strict, Transitional, and Frameset document types.

The <html> Tag

The first page structure tag in every HTML page is the <html> tag. It indicates that the content of this file is in the HTML language. In the proposed XHTML 1.0 specification, the <html> tag should follow the DOCTYPE identifier (as mentioned in the previous note) as shown in the following example.

All the text and HTML commands in your HTML page should go within the beginning and ending HTML tags, like the following:

```
<!DOCTYPE html PUBLIC "-//W3C//DTD XHTML 1.0 Transitional//EN"
 "http://www.w3.org/TR/xhtml1/DTD/transitional.dtd">
<html>
```

```
...your page...
</html>
```

The <head> Tag

The <head> tag specifies that the lines within the beginning and ending points of the tag are the prologue to the rest of the file. Generally, only a few tags go into the <head> portion of the page (most notably, the page title, described later). You should never put any of the text of your page into the header.

Here's a typical example of how you properly use the <head> tag (you'll learn about <title> later):

```
<!DOCTYPE html PUBLIC "-//W3C//DTD XHTML 1.0 Transitional//EN"
 "http://www.w3.org/TR/xhtml1/DTD/transitional.dtd">
<html>
<head>
<title>This is the Title.</title>
</head>
...your page...
</html>
```

The <body> Tag

The remainder of your HTML page (represented in the following example as ...your page...) is enclosed within a <body> tag. This includes all the text and other content (links, pictures, and so on). In combination with the <html> and <head> tags, your code looks like the following:

```
<!DOCTYPE html PUBLIC "-//W3C//DTD XHTML 1.0 Transitional//EN"
 "http://www.w3.org/TR/xhtml1/DTD/transitional.dtd">
<html>
<head>
<title>This is the Title. It will be explained later on</title>
</head>
<body>
...your page...
</body>
</html>
```

You may notice here that each HTML tag is nested. That is, both <body> and </body> tags go inside both <html> tags; the same with both <head> tags. All HTML tags work this way, forming individual nested sections of text. You should be careful never to overlap tags; that is, to do something like the following:

```
<!DOCTYPE html PUBLIC "-//W3C//DTD XHTML 1.0 Transitional//EN"
 "http://www.w3.org/TR/xhtml1/DTD/transitional.dtd">
<html>
<head>
<body>
```

4

```
</head>
</body>
</html>
```

Whenever you close an HTML tag, make sure that you're closing the most recently opened tag. (You'll learn more about closing tags as you go on.)

> **Note**
>
> In HTML 4.0 and earlier, some tags are optionally closed. In other tags, closing tags are forbidden. In the proposed XHTML 1.0 specification, *all* tags *must* be closed. The why's, how's, and where's of how to close these tags will be discussed in more detail in Day 10, "XHTML and Style Sheets." However, in preparation for what you will learn there, the examples shown in this book will display the proper way to close tags so that older browsers will interpret proposed XHTML 1.0 closures correctly.

The Title

Each HTML page needs a title to indicate what the page describes. The title is used by your browser's bookmarks or hotlist program, and also by other programs that catalog Web pages. Use the `<title>` tag to give a page a title.

NEW TERM   The *title* indicates what your Web page is about and is used to refer to that page in bookmark or hotlist entries. Titles also appear in the title bar of graphical browsers such as Netscape Navigator and Microsoft Internet Explorer.

`<title>` tags always go inside the page header (the `<head>` tags) and describe the contents of the page, as follows:

```
<!DOCTYPE html PUBLIC "-//W3C//DTD XHTML 1.0 Transitional//EN"
 "http://www.w3.org/TR/xhtml1/DTD/transitional.dtd">
<html>
<head>
<title>The Lion, the Witch, and the Wardrobe</title>
</head>
<body>
...your page...
</body>
</html>
```

You can have only one title in the page, and that title can contain only plain text; that is, no other tags should appear inside the title.

When you choose a title, try to choose one that is both short and descriptive of the content on the page. Additionally, your title should be relevant out of context. If someone browsing on the Web follows a random link and ends up on this page, or if a person finds your title in a friend's browser history list, would he or she have any idea what this page is about? You may not intend the page to be used independently of the pages you specifically linked to it, but, because anyone can link to any page at any time, be prepared for that consequence and pick a helpful title.

Also, because most browsers put the title in the title bar of the window, you may have a limited number of words available. (Although the text within the `<title>` tag can be of any length, it may be cut off by the browser when it's displayed.) The following are some other examples of good titles:

```
<title>Poisonous Plants of North America</title>
<title>Image Editing: A Tutorial</title>
<title>Upcoming Cemetery Tours, Summer 1999</title>
<title>Installing the Software: Opening the CD Case</title>
<title>Laura Lemay's Awesome Home Page</title>
```

Here are some not-so-good titles:

```
<title>Part Two</title>
<title>An Example</title>
<title>Nigel Franklin Hobbes</title>
<title>Minutes of the Second Meeting of the Fourth Conference of the
Committee for the Preservation of English Roses, Day Four, After Lunch</title>
```

Figure 4.1 shows how a title looks in Internet Explorer.

INPUT   `<title>Poisonous Plants of North America</title>`

OUTPUT

FIGURE 4.1

The output in Internet Explorer.

Headings

You use headings to divide sections of text, just like this book is divided. ("Headings," at the beginning of this section, is a heading.) HTML defines six levels of headings. Heading tags look like the following:

```
<h1>Installing Your Safetee Lock</h1>
```

The numbers indicate heading levels (h1 through h6). The headings, when they're displayed, are not numbered. They are displayed either in larger or bolder text, are centered or underlined, or are capitalized—so that they stand out from regular text.

Think of the headings as items in an outline. If the text you're writing has a structure, use the headings to indicate that structure, as shown in the following code lines. (Notice that I've indented the headings in this example to better show the hierarchy. They don't have to be indented in your page; in fact, the indenting will be ignored by the browser.)

```
<h1>Mythology Through the Ages</h1>
  <h2>Common Mythological Themes</h2>
  <h2>Earliest Known Myths</h2>
  <h2>Origins of Mythology</h2>
    <h3>Mesopotamian Mythology</h3>
    <h3>Egyptian Mythology</h3>
      <h4>The Story of Isis and Osiris</h4>
      <h4>Horus and Set: The Battle of Good vs. Evil</h4>
      <h4>The Twelve Hours of the Underworld</h4>
      <h4>The River Styx</h4>
  <h2>History in Myth</h2>
```

Unlike titles, headings can be any length, including many lines of text. (Because headings are emphasized, however, having many lines of emphasized text may be tiring to read.)

A common practice is to use a first-level heading at the top of your page to either duplicate the title (which usually is displayed elsewhere), or to provide a shorter or less contextual form of the title. If you have a page that shows several examples of folding bed sheets, for example, part of a long presentation on how to fold bed sheets, the title might look something like the following:

```
<title>How to Fold Sheets: Some Examples</title>
```

The topmost heading, however, might just be as follows:

```
<h1>Examples</h1>
```

Don't use headings to display text in boldface type or to make certain parts of your page stand out more. Although the result may look cool on your browser, you don't know what it will look like when other people use their browsers to read your page. Other browsers may number headings or format them in a manner that you don't expect. Also, tools to create searchable indexes of Web pages may extract your headings to indicate the important parts of a page. By using headings for something other than an actual heading, you may be foiling those search programs and creating strange results.

Figure 4.2 shows various headings as they appear in Internet Explorer.

`INPUT`
```
<h1>Mythology Through the Ages</h1>
  <h2>Common Mythological Themes</h2>
  <h2>Earliest Known Myths</h2>
  <h2>Origins of Mythology</h2>
    <h3>Mesopotamian Mythology</h3>
    <h3>Egyptian Mythology</h3>
```

```
          <h4>The Story of Isis and Osiris</h4>
          <h4>Horus and Set: The Battle of Good vs. Evil</h4>
          <h4>The Twelve Hours of the Underworld</h4>
          <h4>The River Styx</h4>
    <h2>History in Myth</h2>
```

FIGURE 4.2

*The output in
Internet Explorer.*

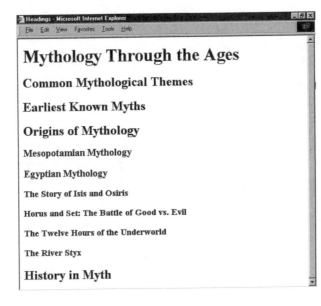

Paragraphs

Now that you have a page title and several headings, you can add some ordinary paragraphs to the page.

The first version of HTML specified the <p> tag as a one-sided tag. There was no corresponding </p>, and the <p> tag was used to indicate the end of a paragraph (a paragraph break), not the beginning. So paragraphs in the first version of HTML looked like the following:

```
Slowly and deliberately, Enigern approached the mighty dragon.
A rustle in the trees of the nearby forest distracted his attention
for a brief moment, a near fatal mistake for the brave knight.<p>
The dragon lunged at him, searing Enigern's armor with a rapid
blast of fiery breath. Enigern fell to the ground as the dragon
hovered over him. He quickly drew his sword and thrust it into the
dragon's chest.<p>
```

Most early browsers assumed that paragraphs would be formatted this way. When they came across a <p> tag, these older browsers started a new line and added some extra vertical space between the line just ended and the next one.

In the HTML 4.0 specification (as with HTML 3.2 and 2.0), and as supported by most current browsers, the paragraph tag is revised. In these versions of HTML, the paragraph tags are two-sided (<p>...</p>), but <p> indicates the beginning of the paragraph. Also, the closing tag (</p>) is optional. So the Enigern story would look like this in the current versions of HTML:

```
<p>Slowly and deliberately, Enigern approached the mighty dragon.
A rustle in the trees of the nearby forest distracted his attention
for a brief moment, a near fatal mistake for the brave knight.</p>
<p>The dragon lunged at him, searing Enigern's armor with a rapid
blast of fiery breath. Enigern fell to the ground as the dragon
hovered over him. He quickly drew his sword and thrust it into the
dragon's chest.</p>
```

Getting into the habit of using <p> at the start of a paragraph is a good idea; it will become important when you learn how to align text left, right, or centered. Older browsers will accept this form of paragraphs just fine. Although at one time it was optional to use the closing </p> tag, this will not be the case for XHTML 1.0, as all tags must be closed. For that reason, I'll use the closing </p> throughout this book.

Some people like to use extra <p> tags between paragraphs to spread out the text on the page. Once again, here's the cardinal reminder: design for content, not for appearance. Someone with a text-based browser or a small screen is not going to care much about the extra space you so carefully put in, and some browsers may even collapse multiple <p> tags into one, erasing all your careful formatting.

Figure 4.3 shows another paragraph about Enigern and the dragon in Internet Explorer.

INPUT
```
<p>The dragon fell to the ground, releasing an anguished cry and
seething in pain. The thrust of Enigern's sword proved fatal as
the dragon breathed its last breath. Now Enigern was free to
release Lady Aelfleada from her imprisonment in the dragon's lair. </p>
```

OUTPUT

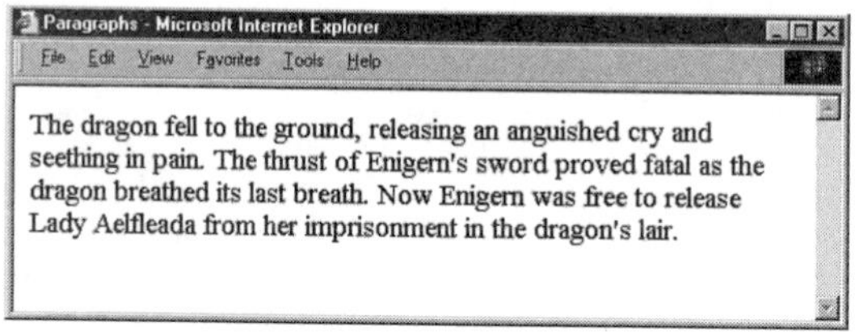

FIGURE 4.3

The output in Internet Explorer.

Lists, Lists, and More Lists

In addition to headings and paragraphs, probably the most common HTML element you'll use is the list. After this section, you'll not only know how to create a list in HTML, but also how to create several different types of lists—a list for every occasion!

HTML 4.0 defines these three types of lists:

- Numbered, or ordered lists, typically labeled with numbers
- Bulleted, or unordered lists, typically labeled with bullets or some other symbol
- Glossary lists, in which each item in the list has a term and a definition for that term, arranged so that the term somehow is highlighted or drawn out from the text

 Note You'll also notice a couple of deprecated list types in the HTML 4.0 specification: menu lists (<menu>) and directory lists (<dir>). These two list types are not frequently used, and support for them varies in browsers. Instead, use the <ul> (or bulleted list) tags in place of these deprecated list types.

 NEW TERM A *deprecated* tag or attribute is one that currently is still supported but that has been outdated by newer methods.

 Note Browsers generally continue to support deprecated elements for reasons of backward compatibility. There is still a need to learn about and use the deprecated elements if you expect that a portion of your audience will be using HTML 3.2-level browsers, such as Netscape Navigator 3 and earlier or Microsoft Internet Explorer 3 or earlier. Because deprecated elements may become obsolete in future versions of HTML, however, you should try to use the newer methods when possible.

Note The majority of tags and attributes that are deprecated in HTML 4.0 are done so in favor of using Cascading Style Sheet (CSS) properties and values, which you will learn more about in Day 10, "XHTML and Style Sheets."

List Tags

All the list tags have the following common elements:

- The entire list is surrounded by the appropriate opening and closing tag for the type of list (for example, <ul> and </ul>, or <ol> and </ol>).
- Each list item within the list has its own tag: <dt> and <dd> for the glossary lists, and <li> for all the other lists.

> **Note**
>
> The closing tags for `<dd>`, `<dt>`, and `<li>` are optional in HTML. To prepare yourself for XHTML 1.0, use closing tags of `</dd>`, `</dt>`, `</li>`.

Although the tags and the list items can appear in any arrangement in your HTML code, I prefer to arrange the HTML for producing lists so that the list tags are on their own lines, and each new item starts on a new line. This way, you can easily choose the whole list as well as the individual elements. In other words, I find the following arrangement

```
<p>Dante's Divine Comedy consists of three books:</p>
<ul>
<li>The Inferno</li>
<li>The Purgatorio</li>
<li>The Paradiso</li>
</ul>
```

easier to read than

```
<p>Dante's Divine Comedy consists of three books:</p>
<ul><li>The Inferno</li><li>The Purgatorio</li><li>The Paradiso</li></ul>
```

although both result in the same output in the browser.

Numbered Lists

Numbered lists are surrounded by the `<ol>`...`</ol>` tags (ol stands for Ordered List), and each item within the list begins with the `<li>` (List Item) tag.

> **Note**
>
> In HTML, the `<li>` tag is one-sided; you do not have to specify the closing tag because it is optional. The existence of the next `<li>` (or the closing `</ol>` or `</ul>` tag) indicates the end of that item in the list. However, to properly form your documents in XHTML 1.0, you must use a closing tag of `</li>`.

When the browser displays an ordered list, it numbers (and often indents) each of the elements sequentially. You do not have to perform the numbering yourself, and, if you add or delete items, the browser will renumber them the next time the page is loaded.

NEW TERM *Ordered lists* are lists in which each item is numbered.

Use numbered lists only when you want to indicate that the elements are ordered—that is, that they must appear or occur in that specific order. Ordered lists are good for steps to follow or instructions to the readers. If you just want to indicate that something has some number of elements that can appear in any order, use an unordered list instead.

So, the following, for example, is an ordered list of steps that tell you how to install a new operating system, with each list item a step in the set of procedures. The following input and output examples show this list. You can see how it appears in Internet Explorer in Figure 4.4.

INPUT

```
<p>Installing Your New Operating System</p>
<ol>
<li>Insert the CD-ROM into your CD-ROM drive.</li>
<li>Choose RUN.</li>
<li>Enter the drive letter of your CD-ROM (example: D:\),
followed by SETUP.EXE.</li>
<li>Follow the prompts in the setup program.</li>
<li>Reboot your computer after all files are installed.</li>
<li>Cross your fingers.</li>
</ol>
```

OUTPUT

FIGURE 4.4

The output in Internet Explorer.

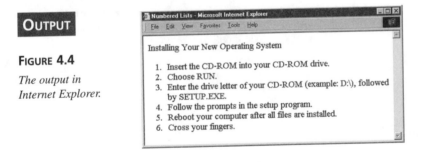

4

Customizing Ordered Lists with HTML 3.2

HTML 3.2 provided several attributes for ordered lists. They were used to customize how the browser renders the list. These attributes enabled you to control several features of ordered lists including which numbering scheme to use and from which number to start counting (if you don't want to start at 1). In HTML 4.0, the attributes mentioned in this section are deprecated in favor of using style sheet properties and values that accomplish the same task. To support HTML 3.2 browsers, however, you may have a need to use these attributes on occasion.

NEW TERM   *Attributes* are extra parts of HTML tags that contain options or other information about the tag itself.

You can customize ordered lists in two main ways: how they are numbered and the number with which the list starts. HTML 3.2 provides the type attribute that can take one of five values to define which type of numbering to use on the list:

- "1"   Specifies that standard Arabic numerals should be used to number the list (that is, 1, 2, 3, 4, and so on)

- "a"   Specifies that lowercase letters should be used to number the list (that is, a, b, c, d, and so on)

- "A"   Specifies that uppercase letters should be used to number the list (that is, A, B, C, D, and so on)

- "i"   Specifies that lowercase Roman numerals should be used to number the list (that is, i, ii, iii, iv, and so on)

- "I"   Specifies that uppercase Roman numerals should be used to number the list (that is, I, II, III, IV, and so on)

You can specify types of numbering in the <ol> tag, as follows: <ol type="a">. By default, type="1" is assumed.

Note

The nice thing about Web browsers is that they generally ignore attributes they don't understand. If a browser doesn't support the type attribute of the <ol> tag, for example, it will simply ignore it when it is encountered.

As an example, consider the following list:

```
<p>The Days of the Week in French:</p>
<ol>
<li>Lundi</li>
<li>Mardi</li>
<li>Mercredi</li>
<li>Jeudi</li>
<li>Vendredi</li>
<li>Samedi</li>
<li>Dimanche</li>
</ol>
```

If you were to add type="I" to the <ol> tag, as follows, it would appear in Internet Explorer as shown in Figure 4.5.

INPUT
```
<p>The Days of the Week in French:</p>
<ol type="I">
<li>Lundi</li>
<li>Mardi</li>
<li>Mercredi</li>
<li>Jeudi</li>
<li>Vendredi</li>
<li>Samedi</li>
<li>Dimanche</li>
</ol>
```

OUTPUT

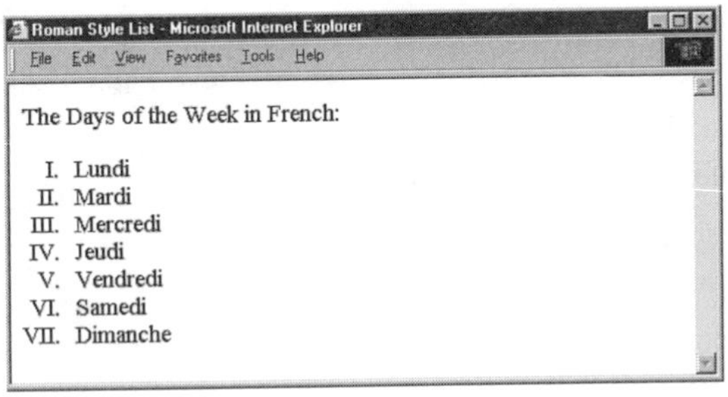

FIGURE **4.5**

The output in Internet Explorer.

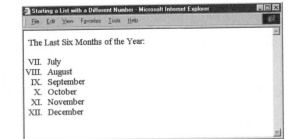

You also can apply the `type` attribute to the `<li>` tag, effectively changing the numbering type in the middle of the list. When the `type` attribute is used in the `<li>` tag, it affects the item in question and all entries following it in the list.

Using another attribute, `start`, you can specify which number or letter to start your list. The default starting point is 1, of course. You can change this number by using `start`. `<ol start="4">`, for example, would start the list at number 4, whereas `<ol type="a" start="3">` would start the numbering with *c* and move through the alphabet from there.

For example, you can list the last six months of the year, and start its numbering with the Roman numeral *VII* as follows. The results appear in Figure 4.6.

INPUT

```
<p>The Last Six Months of the Year:</p>
<ol type="I" start="7">
<li>July</li>
<li>August</li>
<li>September</li>
<li>October</li>
<li>November</li>
<li>December</li>
</ol>
```

OUTPUT

FIGURE **4.6**

The output in Internet Explorer.

As with the `type` attribute, you can change the value of an entry's number at any point in a list. You do so by using the `value` attribute in the `<li>` tag. Assigning a value in an `<li>` tag restarts numbering in the list starting with the affected entry.

4

Suppose that you wanted the last three items in a list of ingredients to be 10, 11, and 12 rather than 6, 7, and 8. You can reset the numbering at Eggs using the value attribute, as follows:

```
<p>Cheesecake ingredients:</p>
<ol type="I">
<li>Quark Cheese</li>
<li>Honey</li>
<li>Cocoa</li>
<li>Vanilla Extract</li>
<li>Flour</li>
<li value="10">Eggs</li>
<li>Walnuts</li>
<li>Margarine</li>
</ol>
```

Unordered Lists

In unordered lists, the elements can appear in any order. An unordered list looks just like an ordered list in HTML except that the list is indicated by using <ul>...</ul> tags rather than ol. The elements of the list are separated by <li>, just as with ordered lists.

Browsers usually format unordered lists by inserting bullets or some other symbolic marker; Lynx, a text browser, inserts an asterisk (*).

New Term   In *unordered lists,* the items are bulleted or marked with some other symbol.

The following input and output example shows an unordered list. Figure 4.7 shows the results in Internet Explorer.

INPUT
```
<p>Things I like to do in the morning:</p>
<ul>
<li>Drink a cup of coffee</li>
<li>Watch the sunrise</li>
<li>Listen to the birds sing</li>
<li>Hear the wind rustling through the trees</li>
<li>Curse the construction noises for spoiling the peaceful mood</li>
</ul>
```

OUTPUT

FIGURE 4.7

The output in Internet Explorer.

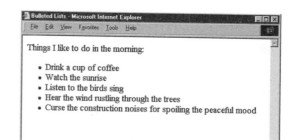

Customizing Unordered Lists in HTML 3.2

As with ordered lists, unordered lists can be customized with HTML 3.2 attributes (these are also deprecated in HTML 4.0). By default, most browsers (Netscape and Internet Explorer included) use bullets to delineate entries on unordered lists. Text browsers such as Lynx generally opt for an asterisk.

If you use the type attribute in the <ul> tag, some browsers can display other types of markers to delineate entries. According to the HTML 3.2 specification, the type attribute can take three possible values:

- "disc"   A disc or bullet; this style generally is the default.
- "square"   Obviously, a square rather than a disc.
- "circle"   As compared with the disc, which most browsers render as a filled circle, this value should generate an unfilled circle on compliant browsers.

In the following input and output example, you see a comparison of these three types as rendered in Internet Explorer (see Figure 4.8).

INPUT

```
<ul type="disc">
<li>DAT - Digital Audio Tapes</li>
<li>CD - Compact Discs</li>
<li>Cassettes</li>
</ul>
<ul type="square">
<li>DAT - Digital Audio Tapes</li>
<li>CD - Compact Discs</li>
<li>Cassettes</li>
</ul>
<ul type="circle">
<li>DAT - Digital Audio Tapes</li>
<li>CD - Compact Discs</li>
<li>Cassettes</li>
</ul>
```

4

OUTPUT

FIGURE 4.8

The output in Internet Explorer.

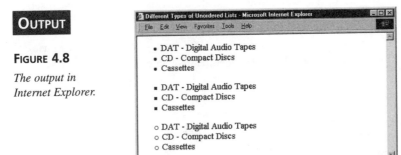

Just as you can change the numbering scheme in the middle of an ordered list, you can change the type of bullet mid-stream in a list by using the `type` attribute in the `<li>` tag. Again, this attribute is deprecated in HTML 4.0.

Glossary Lists

Glossary lists are slightly different from other lists. Each list item in a glossary list has two parts:

- A term
- The term's definition

Each part of the glossary list has its own tag: `<dt>` for the term ("definition term"), and `<dd>` for its definition ("definition definition"). `<dt>` and `<dd>` are both one-sided tags, and they usually occur in pairs, although most browsers can handle single terms or definitions. The entire glossary list is indicated by the tags `<dl>`...`</dl>` ("definition list").

NEW TERM In *glossary lists,* each list item has two parts: a term and a definition. Glossary lists are sometimes called definition lists.

The following is a glossary list example with a set of herbs and descriptions of how they grow:

```
<dl>
<dt>Basil</dt>
<dd>Annual. Can grow four feet high; the scent of its tiny white
flowers is heavenly.</dd>
<dt>Oregano</dt>
<dd>Perennial. Sends out underground runners and is difficult
to get rid of once established.</dd>
<dt>Coriander</dt>
<dd>Annual. Also called cilantro, coriander likes cooler
weather of spring and fall.</dd>
</dl>
```

Glossary lists usually are formatted in browsers with the terms and definitions on separate lines, and the left margins of the definitions are indented.

You don't have to use glossary lists for terms and definitions, of course. You can use them anywhere that the same sort of list is needed. Here's an example:

```
<dl>
<dt>Macbeth</dt>
<dd>I'll go no more. I am afraid to think of
what I have done; look on't again I dare not.</dd>
<dt>Lady Macbeth</dt>
<dd>Infirm of purpose! Give me the daggers.
The sleeping and the dead are as but pictures. 'Tis the eye
of childhood that fears a painted devil. If he do bleed, I'll
gild the faces of the grooms withal, for it must seem their
```

```
guilt. (Exit. Knocking within)</dd>
<dt>Macbeth</dt>
<dd>Whence is that knocking? How is't wit me when
every noise apalls me? What hands are here? Ha! They pluck out
mine eyes! Will all Neptune's ocean wash this blood clean from
my hand? No. This my hand will rather the multitudinous seas
incarnadine, making the green one red. (Enter Lady Macbeth)</dd>
<dt>Lady Macbeth</dt>
<dd>My hands are of your color, but I shame to
wear a heart so white.</dd>
</dl>
```

The following input and output example shows how a glossary list is formatted in Internet Explorer (see Figure 4.9).

INPUT

```
<dl>
<dt>Basil</dt>
<dd>Annual. Can grow four feet high; the scent
of its tiny white flowers is heavenly.</dd>
<dt>Oregano</dt>
<dd>Perennial. Sends out underground runners
and is difficult to get rid of once established.</dd>
<dt>Coriander</dt>
<dd>Annual. Also called cilantro, coriander
likes cooler weather of spring and fall.</dd>
</dl>
```

OUTPUT

FIGURE 4.9

The output in Internet Explorer.

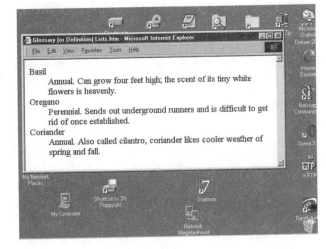

Nesting Lists

What happens if you put a list inside another list? Nesting lists is fine as far as HTML is concerned; just put the entire list structure inside another list as one of its elements. The nested list just becomes another element of the first list, and it is indented from the rest of the list. Lists like this work especially well for menu-like entities in which you want to show hierarchy (for example, in tables of contents) or as outlines.

Indenting nested lists in HTML code itself helps show their relationship to the final layout:

```
<ol>
    <ul>
    <li>WWW</li>
    <li>Organization</li>
    <li>Beginning HTML</li>
    <ul>
        <li>What HTML is</li>
        <li>How to Write HTML</li>
        <li>Doc structure</li>
        <li>Headings</li>
        <li>Paragraphs</li>
        <li>Comments</li>
    </ul>
<li>Links</li>
<li>More HTML</li>
</ol>
```

Many browsers format nested ordered lists and nested unordered lists differently from their enclosing lists. They might, for example, use a symbol other than a bullet for a nested list, or number the inner list with letters (a, b, c) rather than numbers. Don't assume that this will be the case, however, and refer back to "section 8, subsection b" in your text, because you cannot determine what the exact formatting will be in the final output.

The following input and output example shows a nested list and how it appears in Internet Explorer (see Figure 4.10).

INPUT

```
<h1>Peppers</h1>
<ul>
<li>Bell</li>
<li>Chile</li>
    <ul>
    <li>Serrano</li>
    <li>Jalapeno</li>
    <li>Habanero</li>
    <li>Anaheim</li>
    </ul>
<li>Szechuan</li>
<li>Cayenne</li>
</ul>
```

OUTPUT

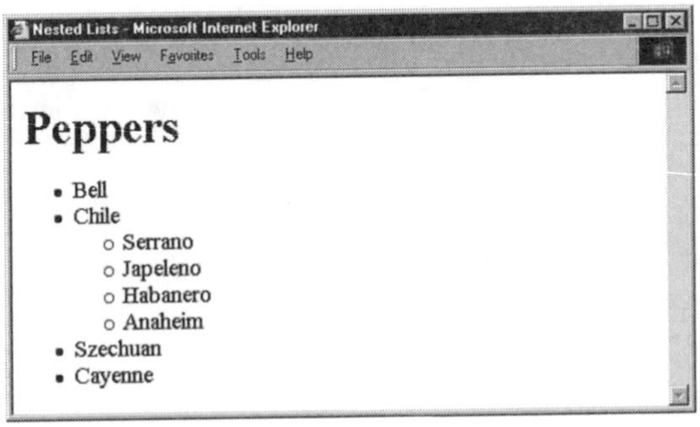

FIGURE 4.10

The output in Internet Explorer.

> **Nested Lists - Microsoft Internet Explorer**
> File   Edit   View   Favorites   Tools   Help
>
> # Peppers
>
> - Bell
> - Chile
>   - Serrano
>   - Japeleno
>   - Habanero
>   - Anaheim
> - Szechuan
> - Cayenne

Comments

You can put comments into HTML pages to describe the page itself or to provide some kind of indication of the status of the page. Some source code control programs can put page status into comments, for example. Text in comments is ignored when the HTML file is parsed; comments don't ever show up onscreen—that's why they're comments. Comments look like the following:

```
<!-- This is a comment -->
```

Each line of text should be individually commented. Not including other HTML tags within comments usually is a good idea. (Although this practice isn't strictly illegal, many browsers may get confused when they encounter HTML tags within comments and display them anyway.) As a good rule of thumb, don't include <, >, or -- inside an HTML comment.

Here are some examples:

```
<!-- Rewrite this section with less humor -->
<!-- Neil helped with this section -->
<!-- Go Tigers! -->
```

Exercise 4.1: Creating a Real HTML Page

At this point, you know enough to get started creating simple HTML pages. You understand what HTML is, you've been introduced to a handful of tags, and you've even tried browsing an HTML file. You haven't created any links yet, but you'll get to that soon enough, in the next chapter.

This exercise shows you how to create an HTML file that uses the tags you've learned about up to this point. It will give you a feel for what the tags look like when they're

▼ displayed onscreen and for the sorts of typical mistakes you're going to make. (Everyone makes them, and that's why using an HTML editor that does the typing for you is often helpful. The editor doesn't forget the closing tags, leave off the slash, or misspell the tag itself.)

So, create a simple example in that text editor of yours. Your example doesn't have to say much of anything; in fact, all it needs to include are the structure tags, a title, a couple of headings, and a paragraph or two, Here's an example:

```
<!DOCTYPE html PUBLIC "-//W3C//DTD XHTML 1.0 Transitional//EN"
 "http://www.w3.org/TR/xhtml1/DTD/transitional.dtd">
<html>
<head>
<title>Company Profile, Camembert Incorporated</title>
</head>
<body>
<h1>Camembert Incorporated</h1>
<p>"Many's the long night I dreamed of cheese -- toasted, mostly."
-- Robert Louis Stevenson</p>
<h2>What We Do</h2>
<p>We make cheese. Lots of cheese; more than eight tons of cheese
a year.</p>
<h2>Why We Do It</h2>
<p>We are paid an awful lot of money by people who like cheese.
So we make more.</p>
<h2>Our Favorite Cheeses</h2>
<ul>
<li>Brie</li>
<li>Havarti</li>
<li>Camembert</li>
<li>Mozzarella</li>
</ul>
</body>
</html>
```

Save the example to an HTML file, open it in your browser, and see how it came out.

If you have access to another browser on your computer or, even better, one on a different computer, I highly recommend opening the same HTML file there so that you can see the differences in appearance between browsers. Sometimes the differences can surprise you; lines that looked fine in one browser might look strange in another browser.

▼ Figure 4.11 shows what the cheese factory example looks like in Internet Explorer.

FIGURE 4.11

The cheese factory example in Internet Explorer.

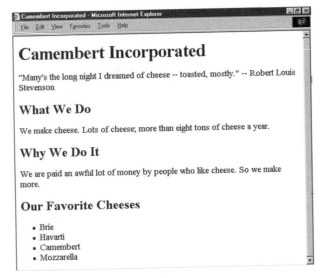

Summary

HTML, a text-only markup language used to describe hypertext pages on the World Wide Web, describes the structure of a page, not its appearance.

In this chapter, you learned what HTML is and how to write and preview simple HTML files. You also learned about the HTML tags shown in Table 4.1.

TABLE 4.1 HTML Tags from Day 4

Tag	Attribute	Use
`<html>` ... `</html>`		The entire HTML page.
`<head>` ... `</head>`		The head, or prologue, of the HTML page.
`<body>` ... `</body>`		All the other content in the HTML page.
`<title>` ... `</title>`		The title of the page.
`<h1>` ... `</h1>`		First-level heading.
`<h2>` ... `</h2>`		Second-level heading.
`<h3>` ... `</h3>`		Third-level heading.
`<h4>` ... `</h4>`		Fourth-level heading.
`<h5>` ... `</h5>`		Fifth-level heading.
`<h6>` ... `</h6>`		Sixth-level heading.

continues

TABLE 4.1   continued

Tag	Attribute	Use
`<p> ... </p>`		A paragraph.
`<ol>...</ol>`		An ordered (numbered) list. Each of the items in the list begins with `<li>`.
	`type`	Specify the numbering scheme to use in the list. This attribute is deprecated in HTML 4.0.
	`start`	Specify at which number to start the list. This attribute is deprecated in HTML 4.0.
`<ul>...</ul>`		An unordered (bulleted or otherwise-marked) list. Each of the items in the list begins with `<li>`.
	`type`	Specify the bulleting scheme to use in the list. This attribute is deprecated in HTML 4.0.
`<li>...</li>`		Individual list items in ordered, unordered, menu, or directory lists. Closing tag is optional in HTML, but required in XHTML 1.0.
	`type`	Reset the numbering or bulleting scheme from the current list element. Only applies to `<ul>` and `<ol>` lists. This attribute is deprecated in HTML 4.0.
	`value`	Reset the numbering in the middle of an ordered (`<ol>`) list. This attribute is deprecated in HTML 4.0.
`<dl>...</dl>`		A glossary or definition list. Items in the list consist of pairs of elements: a term and its definition.
`<dt>...</dt>`		The term part of an item in a glossary list. Closing tag is optional in HTML, but required in XHTML 1.0.
`<dd>...</dt>`		The definition part of an item in a glossary list. Closing tag is optional in HTML, but required in XHTML 1.0.
`<!-- ... -->`		A comment.

Workshop

You've learned a lot in this chapter, and the following workshop will help you remember some of the most important points. I've anticipated some of the questions you might have in the first section of the workshop.

Q&A

Q I've noticed in many Web pages that the page structure tags (`<html>`, `<head>`, `<body>`) aren't used. Do I really need to include them if pages work just fine without them?

A Most browsers will handle plain HTML without the page structure tags. But as we move forward to XHTML, where these page structure tags are important, it is mandatory that they appear in your pages. It's a good idea to get into the habit of using them now. Including the tags now will allow your pages to be read by more general SGML tools and to take advantage of features of future browsers. And, using these tags is the "correct" thing to do if you want your pages to conform to true HTML format.

Q My glossaries came out formatted really strangely! The terms are indented farther in than the definitions!

A Did you mix up the `<dd>` and `<dt>` tags? The `<dt>` tag is always used first (the definition term), and then the `<dd>` follows (the definition). I mix them up all the time. There are too many D tags in glossary lists.

Q I've seen HTML files that use `<li>` outside a list structure, alone on the page, like this:

```
<li>And then the duck said, "put it on my bill"</li>
```

A Most browsers will at least accept this tag outside a list tag and will format it either as a simple paragraph or as a non-indented bulleted item. According to the true HTML definition, however, using an `<li>` outside a list tag is illegal, so "good" HTML pages shouldn't do this. And, because you're striving to write good HTML (right?), you shouldn't write your lists this way either. Always put your list items inside lists where they belong.

Q You mentioned that some of the list tags and attributes have been deprecated in HTML 4.0. What should I use instead?

A In a way, it depends on your audience. For example, if your Web pages reside on a corporate intranet where you know for sure that everyone is using an HTML 4.0 browser that supports style sheets (CSS), you can use CSS properties and values in place of the deprecated tags. If your Web pages reside on the World Wide Web, however, where people using a wide variety of browsers and PC platforms are accessing your site, it may be to your advantage to continue using the deprecated tags to make your pages presentable in older browsers. You'll learn more about the pros and cons of each approach, and see some examples of how to replace deprecated tags, in Day 18.

4

Quiz

1. What three HTML tags are used to describe the overall structure of a Web page, and what do each of them define?
2. Where does the `<title>` tag go, and what is it used for?
3. How many different levels of headings does HTML support? What are their tags?
4. Why is it a good idea to use two-sided paragraph tags, even though the closing tag `</p>` is optional in HTML?
5. What two list types have been deprecated? What can you use in place of the deprecated list types?

Answers

1. The `<html>` tag indicates the file is in the HTML language. The `<head>` tag specifies that the lines within the beginning and ending points of the tag are the prologue to the rest of the file. The `<body>` tag encloses the remainder of your HTML page (text, links, pictures, and so on).
2. The `<title>` tag is used to indicate the title of a Web page in a browser's bookmarks, hotlist program, or other programs that catalog Web pages. This tag always goes inside the `<head>` tags.
3. HTML supports six levels of headings. Their tags are `<h1 ... /h1>` through `<h6 ... /h6>`.
4. The closing `</p>` tag becomes important when aligning text to the left, right, or center of a page. Closing tags also are required for XHTML 1.0.
5. The `<menu>` and `<dir>` list types have been deprecated in favor of using bulleted, or unordered, lists `<ul>`.

Exercises

1. Using the Camembert Incorporated page as an example, create a page that briefly describes topics that you would like to cover on your own Web site. You'll use this page to learn how to create your own links in the next chapter.
2. Create a second page that provides further information about one of the topics you listed in the first exercise. Include a couple of subheadings (such as those shown in Figure 4.2). If you feel really adventurous, complete the page's content and include lists where you think they enhance the page. This exercise also will help prepare you for the next chapter.

DAY 5

All About Links

After finishing the preceding chapter, you now have a couple of pages that have some headings, text, and lists in them. These pages are all well and good, but rather boring. The real fun starts when you learn how to create hypertext links and link your pages to the Web. In this chapter, you'll learn just that. Specifically, you'll learn about the following:

- All about the HTML link tag (<a>) and its various parts
- How to link to other pages on your local disk by using relative and absolute pathnames
- How to link to other pages on the Web by using URLs
- How to use links and anchors to link to specific places inside pages
- All about URLs: the various parts of the URL and the kinds of URLs you can use

Creating Links

To create a link in HTML, you need two things:

- The name of the file (or the URL of the file) to which you want to link

- The text that will serve as the "hot spot"—that is, the text that will be highlighted in the browser, which your readers can then select to follow the link

Only the text that serves as the "hot spot" is actually visible on your page. When your readers select the text that points to a link, the browser uses the first part as the place to which to "jump."

The Link Tag—<a>

To create a link in an HTML page, you use the HTML link tag <a>...</a>. The <a> tag often is called an anchor tag, as it also can be used to create anchors for links. (You'll learn more about creating anchors later in this chapter.) The most common use of the link tag, however, is to create links to other pages.

Unlike the simple tags you learned about in the preceding chapter, the <a> tag has some extra features: the opening tag, <a>, includes both the name of the tag ("a") and extra information about the link itself. The extra features are called *attributes* of the tag. (You first discovered attributes in Day 4, "Begin with the Basics," when you learned about lists.) So rather than the opening <a> tag having just a name inside brackets, it looks something like the following:

```
<a name="Up" href="menu.html" title="The Twelve Caesars">
```

The extra attributes (in this example, name, href, and title) describe the link itself. The attribute you'll probably use most often is the href attribute, which is short for "Hypertext REFerence." You use the href attribute to specify the name or URL of the file to which this link points.

Like most HTML tags, the link tag also has a closing tag, </a>. All the text between the opening and closing tags will become the actual link on the screen and be highlighted, underlined, or colored blue or red when the Web page is displayed. That's the text you or your readers will click (or select, in browsers that don't use mice) to jump to the place specified by the href attribute.

Figure 5.1 shows the parts of a typical link using the <a> tag, including the href, the text of the link, and the closing tag.

FIGURE 5.1

An HTML link using the <a> tag.

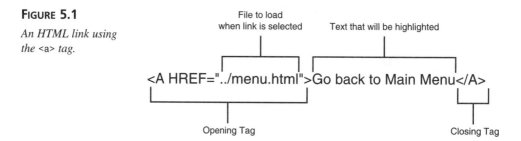

The following example shows a simple link and what it looks like in Internet Explorer (see Figure 5.2).

```
Go back to <a href="menu.html">Main Menu</a>
```

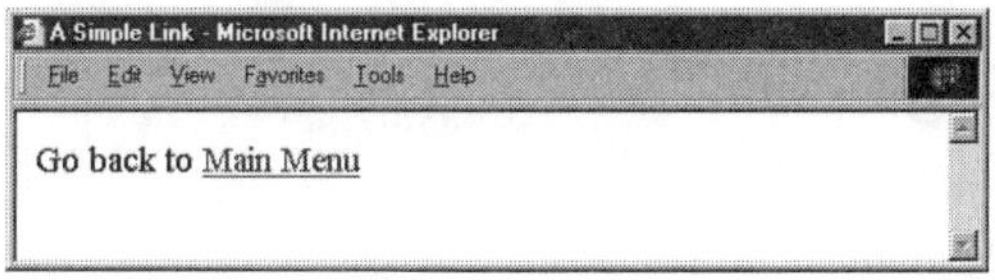

FIGURE 5.2

The output in Internet Explorer.

Exercise 5.1: Linking Two Pages

Now you can try a simple example, with two HTML pages on your local disk. You'll need your text editor and your Web browser for this exercise. Because both the pages you'll be fooling with are on your local disk, you don't need to be connected to the network. (Be patient; you'll get to do network stuff in the next section of this chapter.)

First, create two HTML pages, and save them in separate files. Here's the code for the two HTML files I created for this section, which I called menu.html and claudius.html. What your two pages look like or what they're called really doesn't matter, but make sure you put in your own filenames if you're following along with this example.

The following is the first file, called menu.html:

```
<!DOCTYPE html PUBLIC "-//W3C//DTD XHTML 1.0 Transitional//EN"
 "http://www.w3.org/TR/xhtml1/DTD/transitional.dtd">
<html>
<head>
<title>The Twelve Caesars</title>
</head>
<body>
<h1>"The Twelve Caesars" by Suetonius</h1>
<p>Seutonius (or Gaius Suetonius Tranquillus) was born circa A.D. 70
and died sometime after A.D. 130. He composed a history of the twelve
Caesars from Julius to Domitian (died A.D. 96). His work was a
significant contribution to the best-selling novel and television
series "I, Claudius." Suetonius' work includes biographies of the
following Roman emperors:</p>
<ul>
  <li>Julius Caesar</li>
  <li>Augustus</li>
  <li>Tiberius</li>
  <li>Gaius (Caligula)</li>
  <li>Claudius</li>
  <li>Nero</li>
  <li>Galba</li>
```

5

```
▼       <li>Otho</li>
        <li>Vitellius</li>
        <li>Vespasian</li>
        <li>Titus</li>
        <li>Domitian</li>
      </ul>
      </body>
      </html>
```

The list of menu items (Julius Caesar, Augustus, and so on) will be links to other pages. For now, just type them as regular text; you'll turn them into links later.

The following is the second file, `claudius.html`:

```
<!DOCTYPE html PUBLIC "-//W3C//DTD XHTML 1.0 Transitional//EN"
 "http://www.w3.org/TR/xhtml1/DTD/transitional.dtd">
<html>
<head>
<title>The Twelve Caesars: Claudius</title>
</head>
<body>
<h2>Claudius Becomes Emperor</h2>
<p>Claudius became Emperor at the age of 50. Fearing the attack of
Caligula's assassins, Claudius hid behind some curtains. After a guardsman
discovered him, Claudius dropped to the floor, and then found himself
declared Emperor.</p>
<h2>Claudius is Poisoned</h2>
<p>Most people think that Claudius was poisoned. Some think his wife
Agrippina poisoned a dish of mushrooms (his favorite food). His death
was revealed after arrangements had been made for her son, Nero, to
succeed as Emperor.</p>
<p>Go back to Main Menu</p>
</body>
</html>
```

Make sure that both of your files are in the same directory or folder. If you haven't called them `menu.html` and `claudius.html`, make sure that you take note of the names because you'll need them later.

First, create a link from the menu file to the feeding file. Edit the `menu.html` file, and put the cursor at the following line:

```
<li>Claudius</li>
```

Link tags do not define the format of the text itself, so leave in the list item tags and just add the link inside the item. First, put in the link tags themselves (the <a> and </a> tags) around the text that you want to use as the link:

```
<li><a>Claudius</a></li>
```

Now add the name of the file you want to link to as the href part of the opening link tag.
▼   Enclose the name of the file in quotation marks (straight quotes ("), not curly or

▼ typesetter's quotes (")), with an equal sign between `href` and the name. Note that upper-case and lowercase are different, so make sure you type the filename exactly as you saved it. (`Claudius.html` is not the same file as `claudius.html`; it has to be exactly the same case.) Here I've used `claudius.html`; if you used different files, use those different filenames.

```
<li><a href="claudius.html">Claudius</a></li>
```

Now, start your browser, select Open File (or its equivalent in your browser), and open the `menu.html` file. The paragraph you used as your link should now show up as a link that is in a different color, underlined, or otherwise highlighted. Figure 5.3 shows how it looked when I opened it in the Windows 98 version of Internet Explorer.

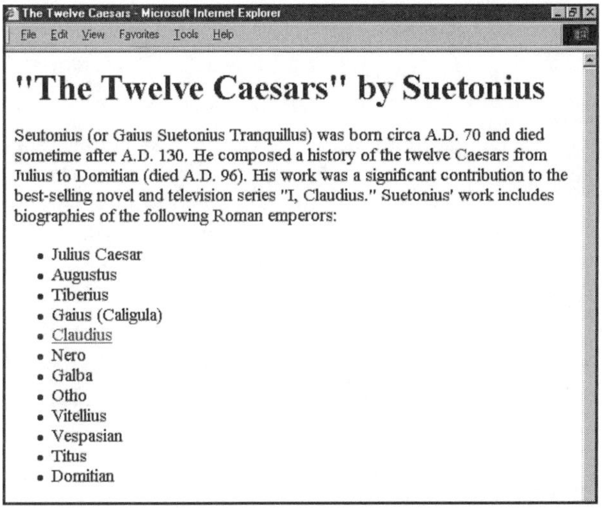

FIGURE 5.3

The `menu.html` *file with link.*

Now, when you click the link, your browser should load in and display the `claudius.html` page, as shown in Figure 5.4.

If your browser can't find the file when you choose the link, make sure that the name of the file in the `href` part of the link tag is the same as the name of the file on the disk, that uppercase and lowercase match, and that both of the files are in the same directory. Remember to close your link, using the `</a>` tag, at the end of the text that serves as the link. Also, make sure that you have quotation marks at the end of the filename (some-times you can easily forget) and that both quotation marks are ordinary straight quotes. All these things can confuse the browser and make it not find the file or display the link

▼ properly.

▼

FIGURE 5.4

The claudius.html *page.*

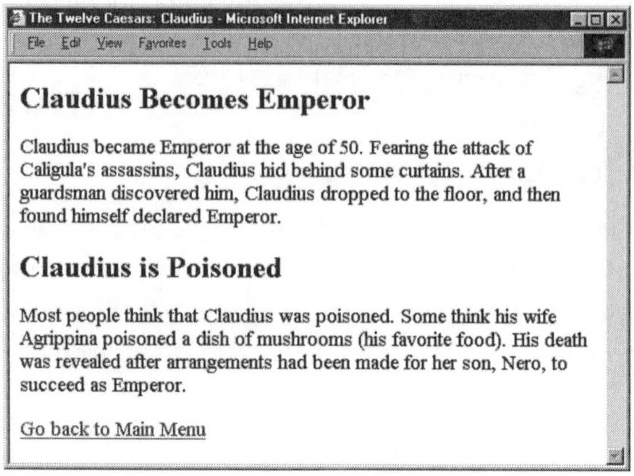

Claudius Becomes Emperor

Claudius became Emperor at the age of 50. Fearing the attack of Caligula's assassins, Claudius hid behind some curtains. After a guardsman discovered him, Claudius dropped to the floor, and then found himself declared Emperor.

Claudius is Poisoned

Most people think that Claudius was poisoned. Some think his wife Agrippina poisoned a dish of mushrooms (his favorite food). His death was revealed after arrangements had been made for her son, Nero, to succeed as Emperor.

Go back to Main Menu

> **Note**
>
> Don't get confused by this issue of case sensitivity. Tags in HTML are not case sensitive. But filenames refer to files on a Web server somewhere, and because Web servers often run on operating systems where filenames are case sensitive (such as UNIX), you should make sure the case of letters in filenames in your links is correct.

Now you can create a link from the feeding page back to the menu page. A paragraph at the end of the claudius.html page is intended for just this purpose:

`<p>Go back to Main Menu</p>`

Add the link tag with the appropriate href to that line, like the following, where menu.html is the original menu file:

`<p><a href="menu.html">Go back to Main Menu</a></p>`

> **Note**
>
> When you include tags inside other tags, make sure that the closing tag closes the tag that you most recently opened. That is, enter
>
> `<p> <a> ... </a> </p>`
>
> rather than
>
> `<p> <a> ... </p> </a>`
>
> Some browsers can become confused if you overlap tags in this way, so always make sure that you close the most recently opened tag first.

▼

▲ Now when you reload the "Claudius" file, the link will be active, and you can jump between the menu and the feeding file by selecting those links.

Linking Local Pages Using Relative and Absolute Pathnames

The example in the preceding section shows how to link together pages that are contained in the same folder or directory on your local disk (local pages). This section continues that thread, linking pages that are still on the local disk but may be contained in different directories or folders on that disk.

Note Folders and directories are the same, but they're called different names depending on whether you're on Macintosh, Windows, DOS, or UNIX. I'll simply call them directories from now on to make your life easier.

When you specify just the filename of a linked file within quotation marks, as you did earlier, the browser looks for that file in the same directory as the current file. This is true even if both the current file and the file being linked to are on a server somewhere else on the Internet; both files are contained in the same directory on that server. It is the simplest form of a relative pathname.

Relative pathnames also can include directory names, or they can point to the path you would take to navigate to that file if you started at the current directory or folder. A pathname might, for example, include directions to go up two directory levels and then go down two other directories to get to the file.

New Term *Relative pathnames* point to files based on their locations relative to the current file.

To specify relative pathnames in links, use UNIX-style pathnames regardless of the system you actually have. You therefore separate directory or folder names with forward slashes (/), and you use two dots to refer generically to the directory above the current one (..).

Table 5.1 shows some examples of relative pathnames and what they mean.

5

TABLE 5.1   Relative Pathnames

Pathname	Means
href="file.html"	file.html is located in the current directory.
href="files/file.html"	file.html is located in the directory (or folder) called files (and the files directory is located in the current directory).
href="files/morefiles/file.html"	file.html is located in the morefiles directory, which is located in the files directory, which is located in the current directory.
href="../file.html"	file.html is located in the directory one level up from the current directory (the "parent" directory).
href="../../files/file.html"	file.html is located two directory levels up, in the directory files.

If you're linking files on a personal computer (Macintosh or PC), and you want to link to a file on a different disk, use the name or letter of the disk as just another directory name in the relative path.

When you want to link to a file on a local drive on the Macintosh, the name of the disk is used just as it appears on the disk itself. Assume that you have a disk called Hard Disk 2, and your HTML files are contained in a folder called HTML Files. If you want to link to a file called jane.html in a folder called Public on a shared disk called Jane's Mac, you can use the following relative pathname:

href="../../Jane's Mac/Public/jane.html"

When linking to a file on a local drive on DOS, Windows 95/98 or Windows NT systems, you refer to the disks by letter, just as you would expect, but rather than using c:, d:, and so on, substitute a vertical bar (¦) for the colon (the colon has a special meaning in link pathnames), and don't forget to use forward slashes like you do with UNIX. So, if the current file is located in C:\FILES\HTML\, and you want to link to D:\FILES.NEW\HTML\MORE\INDEX.HTM, the relative pathname to that file is as follows:

href="../../d¦/files.new/html/more/index.htm"

In most instances, you'll never use the name of a disk in relative pathnames, but I've included it here for completeness. Most of the time, you'll link between files that are reasonably close (only one directory or folder away) in the same presentation.

Absolute Pathnames

You also can specify the link to another page on your local system by using an *absolute pathname*. Relative pathnames point to the page you want to link by describing its location relative to the current page. Absolute pathnames, on the other hand, point to the page by starting at the top level of your directory hierarchy and working downward through all the intervening directories to reach the file.

NEW TERM   *Absolute pathnames* point to files based on their absolute location on the file system.

Absolute pathnames always begin with a slash, which is the way they are differentiated from relative pathnames. Following the slash are all directories in the path from the top level to the file you are linking.

Note

"Top" has different meanings, depending on how you're publishing your HTML files. If you're just linking to files on your local disk, the top is the top of your file system (/ on UNIX, or the disk name on a Macintosh or PC). When you're publishing files using a Web server, the top may or may not be the top of your file system (and generally isn't). You'll learn more about absolute pathnames and Web servers in Day 19, "Putting Your Site Online."

Table 5.2 shows some examples of absolute pathnames and what they mean.

TABLE 5.2   Absolute Pathnames

Pathname	Means
`href="/u1/lemay/file.html"`	`file.html` is located in the directory `/u1/lemay` (typically on UNIX systems).
`href="/d¦/files/html/file.htm"`	`file.htm` is located on the `D:` disk in the directories `files/html` (on DOS systems).
`href="/Hard Disk 1/HTML Files/file.html"`	`file.html` is located on the disk `Hard Disk 1`, in the folder `HTML Files` (typically on Macintosh systems).

Should You Use Relative or Absolute Pathnames?

To link between your own pages, most of the time you should use relative pathnames rather than the absolute pathnames. Using absolute pathnames may seem easier for complicated links between a large number of pages, but absolute pathnames are not portable. If you specify your links as absolute pathnames, and you move your files elsewhere on the disk or rename a directory or a disk listed in that absolute path, all your links will break, and you'll have to edit all your HTML files laboriously and fix them all. Using absolute pathnames also makes moving your files to a Web server very difficult when you decide to actually make them available on the Web.

5

Specifying relative pathnames enables you to move your pages around on your own system and to move them to other systems with little or no file modifications to fix the links. Maintaining HTML pages with relative pathnames is much easier, so the extra work of setting them up initially is often well worth the effort.

Links to Other Documents on the Web

So now you have a whole set of pages on your local disk, all linked to each other. In some places in your pages, however, you want to refer to a page somewhere else on the Internet—for example, to "The First Caesars" page by Dr. Ellis Knox at Boise State University for more information on the early Roman Emperors. You also can use the link tag to link those other pages on the Internet, which I'll call remote pages.

NEW TERM   *Remote pages* are contained somewhere on the Web other than the system on which you're currently working.

The HTML code you use to link pages on the Web looks exactly the same as the code you use for links between local pages. You still use the <a> tag with an href attribute, and you include some text to serve as the link on your Web page. Rather than a filename or a path in the href, however, you use the URL of that page on the Web, as Figure 5.5 shows.

FIGURE 5.5

Link to remote files.

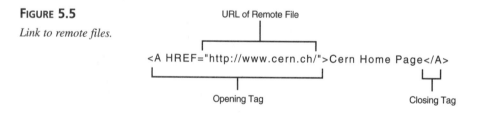

Exercise 5.2: Linking Your Caesar Pages to the Web

Go back to those two pages you linked together earlier in this chapter, the ones about the Caesars. The menu.html file contains several links to other local pages that provide information about 12 Roman Emperors.

Now suppose that you want to add a link to the bottom of the menu file to point to "The First Caesars" page by Dr. Ellis Knox at Boise State University, whose URL is http://history.idbsu.edu/westciv/julio-cl/index.html.

First, add the appropriate text for the link to your menu page, as follows:

```
<p><i>The First Caesars</i> page by Dr. Ellis Knox has more information on
these Emperors.</p>
```

▼ What if you don't know the URL of the home page for "The First Caesars" page (or the page to which you want to link), but you do know how to get to it by following several links on several different people's home pages? Not a problem. Use your browser to find the home page for the page to which you want to link. Figure 5.6 shows what "The First Caesars" page looks like in your browser.

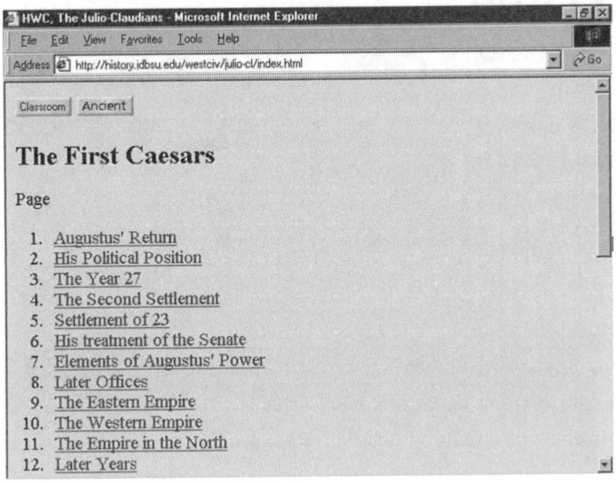

FIGURE 5.6

"The First Caesars" page.

Note

If you set up your system so that it does not connect to the network (as mentioned in Day 3, "An Introduction to HTML"), you might want to put it back now to follow along with this example.

Most browsers display the URL of the file they're currently looking at in a box somewhere near the top of the page. (In Internet Explorer 4.0 or 5.0, this box may be hidden; choose View, Toolbars, Address Bar to see it.) This way, you can easily link to other pages; all you have to do is use your browser to go to the page to which you want to link, copy the URL from the window, and paste it into the HTML page on which you're working. No typing!

After you have the URL of the page, you can construct a link tag in your menu file and paste the appropriate URL into the link, like this:

```
<p>"<a href="http://history.idbsu.edu/westciv/julio-cl/index.html"><i>The First
Caesars</i></a>"
page by Dr. Ellis Knox has more information on these Emperors.</p>
```

Of course, if you already know the URL of the page to which you want to link, you can
▼ just type it into the href part of the link. Keep in mind, however, that if you make a

▼ mistake, your browser won't be able to find the file on the other end. Most URLs are too complex for normal humans to be able to remember them; I prefer to copy and paste whenever I can to cut down on the chances of typing URLs incorrectly.

Figure 5.7 shows how the `menu.html` file, with the new link in it, looks when it is displayed in Internet Explorer.

FIGURE 5.7

"The First Caesars" link.

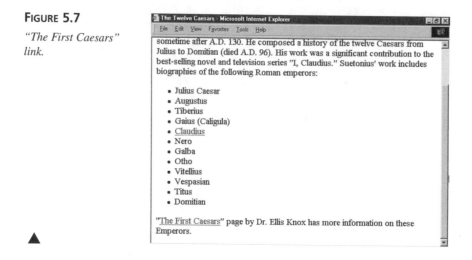

▲

Exercise 5.3: Creating a Link Menu

▼ To Do

Now that you've learned how to create lists and links, you can create a link menu. Link menus are links on your Web page that are arranged in list form or in some other short, easy-to-read, and easy-to-understand format. Link menus are terrific for pages that are organized in a hierarchy, for tables of contents, or for navigation among several pages. Web pages that consist of nothing but links often organize the links in menu form.

NEW TERM *Link menus* are short lists of links on Web pages that give your readers a quick, easy-to-scan overview of the choices they have to jump to from the current page.

The idea of a link menu is that you use short, descriptive terms as the links, with either no text following the link or with a further description following the link itself. Link menus look best in a bulleted or unordered list format, but you also can use glossary lists or just plain paragraphs. Link menus enable your readers to scan the list of links quickly and easily, a task that may be difficult if you bury your links in body text.

In this exercise, you'll create a Web page for a set of book reviews. This page will serve as the index to the reviews, so the link menu you'll create is essentially a menu of book
▼ names.

▼ Start with a simple page framework: a first-level head and some basic explanatory text:

```
<!DOCTYPE html PUBLIC "-//W3C//DTD XHTML 1.0 Transitional//EN"
 "http://www.w3.org/TR/xhtml1/DTD/transitional.dtd">
<html>
<head>
<title>Really Honest Book Reviews</title>
</head>
<body>
<h1>Really Honest Book Reviews</h1>
<p>I read a lot of books about many different subjects. Though I'm not a
book critic, and I don't do this for a living, I enjoy a really good read
every now and then. Here's a list of books that I've read recently:</p>
```

Now add the list that will become the links, without the link tags themselves. It's always easier to start with link text and then attach actual links afterward. For this list, you'll use a tag to create a bulleted list of individual books. The <ol> tag wouldn't be appropriate because the numbers would imply that you were ranking the books in some way. Here's the HTML list of books; Figure 5.8 shows the page in Internet Explorer as it currently looks with the introduction and the list.

```
<ul>
  <li><i>The Rainbow Returns</i> by E. Smith</li>
  <li><i>Seven Steps to Immeasurable Wealth</i> by R. U. Needy</li>
  <li><i>The Food-Lovers Guide to Weight Loss</i> by L. Goode</li>
  <li><i>The Silly Person's Guide to Seriousness</i> by M. Nott</li>
</ul>
</body>
</html>
```

FIGURE 5.8

A list of books.

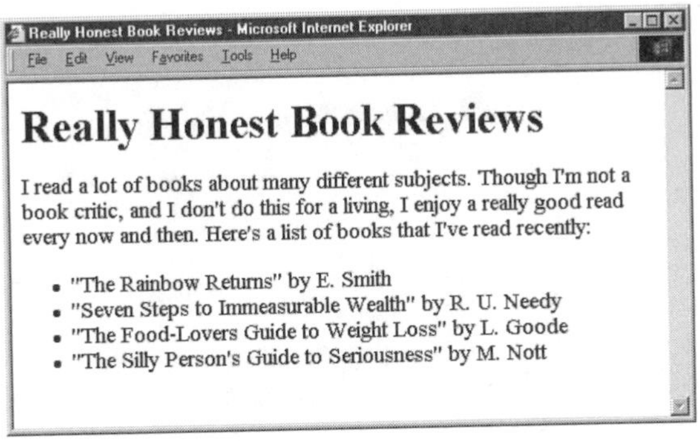

Now, modify each of the list items so that they include link tags. You'll need to keep the <li> tag in there because it indicates where the list items begin. Just add the <a> tags around the text itself. Here you'll link to filenames on the local disk in the same directo-
▼ ry as this file, with each individual file containing the review for the particular book:

```
▼   <ul>
      <li><a href="rainbow.html"><i>The Rainbow Returns</i> by E. Smith</a></li>
      <li><a href="wealth.html"><i>Seven Steps to Immeasurable Wealth</i> by R. U.
      Needy</a></li>
      <li><a href="food.html"><i>The Food-Lovers Guide to Weight Loss</i> by L.
      Goode</a></li>
      <li><a href="silly.html"><i>The Silly Person's Guide to Seriousness</i> by M.
      Nott</a></li>
    </ul>
```

The menu of books looks fine, although it's a little sparse. Your readers don't know any-thing about what each book is like (although some of the book names indicate the sub-ject matter) or whether the review is good or bad. An improvement would be to add some short explanatory text after the links to provide hints of what is on the other side of the link:

```
<ul>
  <li><a href="rainbow.html"><i>The Rainbow Returns</i> by E. Smith</a>. A
  fantasy story set in biblical times. Slow at times, but interesting.</li>
  <li><a href="wealth.html"><i>Seven Steps to Immeasurable Wealth</i> by R. U.
  Needy</a>. I'm still poor, but I'm happy! And that's the whole point.</li>
  <li><a href="food.html"><i>The Food-Lovers Guide to Weight Loss</i> by L.
  Goode
  </a>. At last! A diet book with recipes that taste good!</li>
  <li><a href="silly.html"><i>The Silly Person's Guide to Seriousness</i> by M.
  Nott</a>. Come on ... who wants to be serious?</li>
</ul>
```

The final list then looks like Figure 5.9.

FIGURE 5.9

The final menu listing.

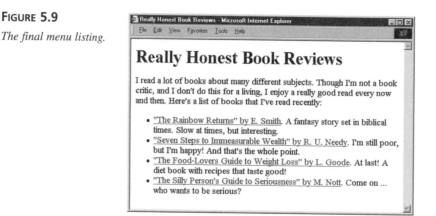

▲   You'll use link menus similar to this one throughout this book.

Linking to Specific Places Within Documents

The links you've created so far in this chapter have been from one point in a page to another page. But what if, rather than linking to that second page in general, you want to link to a specific place within that page—for example, to the fourth major section down?

You can do so in HTML by creating an anchor within the second page. The anchor creates a special element that you can link to inside the page. The link you create in the first page will contain both the name of the file to which you're linking and the name of that anchor. Then, when you follow the link with your browser, the browser will load the second page and then scroll down to the location of the anchor (Figure 5.10 shows an example).

FIGURE 5.10.

Links and anchors.

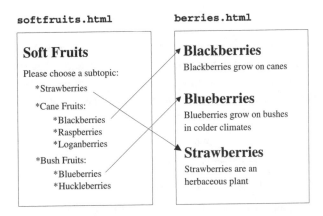

 Anchors are special places that you can link to inside documents. Links can then jump to those special places inside the page as opposed to jumping just to the top of the page.

You also can use links and anchors within the same page, so that if you select one of those links, you jump to different places within that same page.

Creating Links and Anchors

You create an anchor in nearly the same way that you create a link: by using the <a> tag. If you wondered why the link tag uses an <a> rather than an <l>, now you know: a actually stands for anchor.

When you specify links by using <a>, the link has two parts: the href attribute in the opening <a> tag, and the text between the opening and closing tags that serve as a hot spot for the link.

You create anchors in much the same way, but rather than using the `href` attribute in the `<a>` tag, you use the `name` attribute. The `name` attribute takes a keyword (or words) that will be used to name the anchor. Figure 5.11 shows the parts of the `<a>` tag when used to indicate an anchor.

FIGURE 5.11.

The `<a>` tag and anchors.

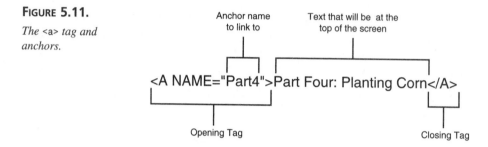

Anchors also require some amount of text between the opening and closing `<a>` tags, although they usually point to a single-character location. The text between the `<a>` tags is used by the browser when a link that is attached to this anchor is selected. The browser scrolls the page to the text within the anchor so that it is at the top of the screen. Some browsers also may highlight the text inside the `<a>` tags.

So, for example, to create an anchor at the section of a page labeled Part 4, you might add an anchor called `part4` to the heading, like the following:

```
<h1><a name="part4">Part Four: Grapefruit from Heaven</a></h1>
```

Unlike links, anchors do not show up in the final displayed page. Anchors are invisible until you follow a link that points to them.

To point to an anchor in a link, you use the same form of link that you would when linking to the whole page, with the filename or URL of the page in the `href` attribute. After the name of the page, however, include a hash sign (#) and the name of the anchor exactly as it appears in the `name` attribute of that anchor (including the same uppercase and lowercase characters!), like the following:

```
<a href="mybigdoc.html#part4">Go to Part 4</a>
```

This link tells the browser to load the page `mybigdoc.html` and then to scroll down to the anchor name `part4`. The text inside the anchor definition will appear at the top of the screen.

Exercise 5.4: Linking Sections Between Two Pages

Now do an example with two pages. These two pages are part of an online reference to classical music, in which each Web page contains all the references for a particular letter of the alphabet (`a.html`, `b.html`, and so on). The reference could have been organized such that each section is its own page. Organizing it that way, however, would have involved several pages to manage, as well as many pages the readers would have to load if they were exploring the reference. Bunching the related sections together under lettered groupings is more efficient in this case. (Day 16, "Writing and Designing Web Pages: Dos and Don'ts," goes into more detail about the trade-offs between short and long pages.)

The first page you'll look at is the one for "M," the first section that looks like the following in HTML:

```
<!DOCTYPE html PUBLIC "-//W3C//DTD XHTML 1.0 Transitional//EN"
  "http://www.w3.org/TR/xhtml1/DTD/transitional.dtd">
<html>
<head>
<title>Classical Music: M</title>
</head>
<body>
<h1>M</h1>
<h2>Madrigals</h2>
<ul>
   <li>William Byrd, <em>This Sweet and Merry Month of May</em></li>
   <li>William Byrd, <em>Though Amaryllis Dance</em></li>
   <li>Orlando Gibbons, <em>The Silver Swan</em></li>
   <li>Claudio Monteverdi, <em>Lamento d'Arianna</em></li>
   <li>Thomas Morley, <em>My Bonny Lass She Smileth</em></li>
   <li>Thomas Weelkes, <em>Thule, the Period of Cosmography</em></li>
   <li>John Wilbye, <em>Sweet Honey-Sucking Bees</em></li>
</ul>
<p>Secular vocal music in four, five and six parts, usually a capella.
15th-16th centuries.</p>
<p><em>See Also</em>
Byrd, Gibbons, Monteverdi, Morley, Weelkes, Wilbye</p>
</body>
</html>
```

5

Figure 5.12 shows how this section looks when it's displayed.

In the last line (the *See Also*), linking the composer names to their respective sections elsewhere in the reference would be useful. If you use the procedure you learned previously in this chapter, you can create a link here around the word Byrd to the page b.html. When your readers select the link to b.html, the browser drops them at the top of the Bs. These hapless readers then have to scroll down through all the composers whose names start with B (and there are many of them: Bach, Beethoven, Brahms, Bruckner) to get to Byrd—a lot of work for a system that claims to link information so you can find what you want quickly and easily.

What you want is to be able to link the word Byrd in m.html directly to the section for Byrd in b.html. Here's the relevant part of b.html you want to link. (I've deleted all the Bs before Byrd to make this file shorter for this example. Pretend they're still there.)

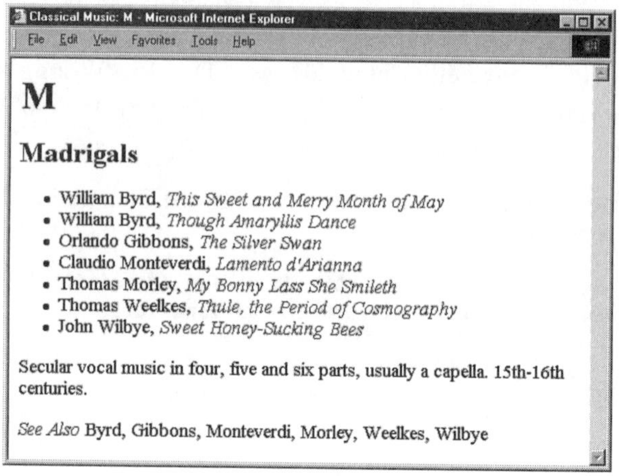
Classical Music: M - Microsoft Internet Explorer
File Edit View Favorites Tools Help
M
Madrigals
William Byrd, This Sweet and Merry Month of May
William Byrd, Though Amaryllis Dance
Orlando Gibbons, The Silver Swan
Claudio Monteverdi, Lamento d'Arianna
Thomas Morley, My Bonny Lass She Smileth
Thomas Weelkes, Thule, the Period of Cosmography
John Wilbye, Sweet Honey-Sucking Bees
Secular vocal music in four, five and six parts, usually a capella. 15th-16th centuries.
See Also Byrd, Gibbons, Monteverdi, Morley, Weelkes, Wilbye

FIGURE 5.12.
Part M of the Online Music Reference.

Note

In this example you will see the use of the <em> tag. This tag is used to specify text that should be emphasized. The emphasis usually is done by rendering the text italic in Netscape and Internet Explorer.

```
<!DOCTYPE html PUBLIC "-//W3C//DTD XHTML 1.0 Transitional//EN"
"http://www.w3.org/TR/xhtml1/DTD/transitional.dtd">
<html>
<head>
<title>Classical Music: B</title>
</head>
<body>
<h1>B</h1>
<!-- I've deleted all the Bs before Byrd to make things shorter -->
<h2><a name="Byrd">Byrd, William, 1543-1623</a></h2>
<ul>
  <li>Madrigals
    <ul>
      <li><em>This Sweet and Merry Month of May</em></li>
      <li><em>Though Amaryllis Dance</em></li>
      <li><em>Lullabye, My Sweet Little Baby</em></li>
    </ul>
  </li>
  <li>Masses
    <ul>
      <li><em>Mass for Five Voices</em></li>
      <li><em>Mass for Four Voices</em></li>
      <li><em>Mass for Three Voices</em></li>
    </ul>
```

```
    </li>
    <li>Motets
      <ul>
          <li><em>Ave verum corpus a 4</em></li>
      </ul>
    </li>
</ul>
<p><em>See Also</em> Madrigals, Masses, Motets</p>
</body>
</html>
```

You'll need to create an anchor at the section heading for `Byrd`. You then can link to that anchor from the *See Also*s in the file for M.

As I described earlier in this chapter, you need two elements for each anchor: an anchor name and the text inside the link to hold that anchor (which may be highlighted in some browsers). The latter is easy; the section heading itself works well, as it's the element to which you're actually linking.

You can choose any name you want for the anchor, but each anchor in the page must be unique. (If you have two or more anchors with the name `fred` in the same page, how would the browser know which one to choose when a link to that anchor is selected?) A good, unique anchor name for this example is simply `byrd` because `byrd` can appear only one place in the file, and this is it.

After you've decided on the two parts, you can create the anchor itself in your HTML file. Add the `<a>` tag to the `William Byrd` section heading, but be careful here. If you were working with normal text within a paragraph, you'd just surround the whole line with `<a>`. But when you're adding an anchor to a big section of text that also is contained within an element—such as a heading or paragraph—always put the anchor inside the element. In other words, enter

```
<h2><a name="byrd">Byrd, William, 1543-1623</a></h2>
```

but do not enter

```
<a name="byrd"><h2>Byrd, William, 1543-1623</h2></a>
```

The second example can confuse your browser. Is it an anchor, formatted just like the text before it, with mysteriously placed heading tags? Or is it a heading that also happens to be an anchor? If you use the right code in your HTML file, with the anchor inside the heading, you avoid the confusion.

You can easily forget about this solution—especially if you're like me and you create text first and then add links and anchors. Just surrounding everything with <a> tags makes sense. Think of the situation this way: If you're linking to just one word, and not

5

▼ to the entire element, you put the <a> tag inside the <h2>. Working with the whole line of text isn't any different. Keep this rule in mind, and you'll get less confused.

> **Note**
>
> If you're still confused, refer to Appendix B, "HTML 4.0 Quick Reference," which has a summary of all the HTML tags and rules for which tags can and cannot go inside each one.

So you've added your anchor to the heading, and its name is "byrd". Now go back to your m.html file, to the line with See Also:

```
<p><em>See Also</em>
 Byrd, Gibbons, Monteverdi, Morley, Weelkes, Wilbye</p>
```

You're going to create your link here around the word byrd, just as you would for any other link. But what's the URL? As you learned previously, pathnames to anchors look like the following:

page_name#anchor_name

If you're creating a link to the b.html page itself, the href is as follows:

```
<a href="b.html">
```

Because you're linking to a section inside that page, add the anchor name to link that section so that it looks like this:

```
<a href="b.html#byrd">
```

Note the small b in byrd. Anchor names and links are case sensitive; if you put #Byrd in your href, the link might not work properly. Make sure that the anchor name you use in the name attribute and the anchor name in the link after the # are identical.

> **Tip**
>
> A common mistake is to put a hash sign in both the anchor name and in the link to that anchor. You use the hash sign only to separate the page and the anchor in the link. Anchor names should never have hash signs in them.

So, with the new link to the new section, the See Also line looks like this:

```
<p><em>See Also</em>
 <a href="b.html#byrd">Byrd</a>,
 Gibbons, Monteverdi, Morley, Weelkes, Wilbye</p>
```

Of course, you can go ahead and add anchors and links to the other parts of the reference
▼ for the remaining composers.

▼   With all your links and anchors in place, test everything. Figure 5.13 shows the
    `Madrigals` section with the link to `Byrd` ready to be selected.

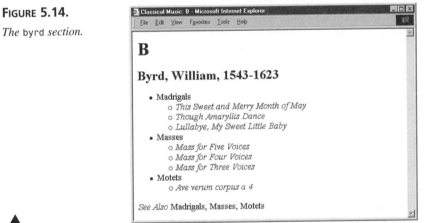

Figure 5.14 shows the screen that pops up when you select the `Byrd` link.

▲

Linking to Anchors in the Same Document

What if you have only one large page, and you want to link to sections within that page?
You can use anchors for it, too. For larger pages, using anchors can be an easy way to
jump around within sections. To link to sections, you just need to set up your anchors at
each section the way you usually do. Then, when you link to those anchors, leave off the
name of the page itself, but include the hash sign and the name of the anchor. So, if

you're linking to an anchor name called `section5` in the same page as the link, the link looks like the following:

```
Go to <a href="#section5">The Fifth Section</a>
```

When you leave off the page name, the browser assumes that you're linking with the current page and scrolls to the appropriate section. You'll get a chance to see this feature in action in Day 6, "More Text Formatting with HTML." There, you'll create a complete Web page that includes a table of contents at the beginning. From this table of contents, the reader can jump to different sections in the same Web page. The table of contents includes links to each section heading. In turn, other links at the end of each section enable the user to jump back to the table of contents or to the top of the page.

Anatomy of a URL

So far in this book, you've encountered URLs twice—in Day 1, "The World of the World Wide Web," as part of the introduction to the Web, and in this chapter, when you created links to remote pages. If you've ever done much exploring on the Web, you've encountered URLs as a matter of course. You couldn't start exploring without a URL.

As I mentioned in Day 1, URLs are Uniform Resource Locators. URLs are effectively street addresses for bits of information on the Internet. Most of the time, you can avoid trying to figure out which URL to put in your links by simply navigating to the bit of information you want with your browser, and then copying and pasting the long string of gobbledygook into your link. But understanding what a URL is all about and why it has to be so long and complex is often useful. Also, when you put your own information up on the Web, knowing something about URLs will be useful so that you can tell people where your Web page is.

In this section, you'll learn what the parts of a URL are, how you can use them to get to information on the Web, and the kinds of URLs you can use (HTTP, FTP, Mailto, and so on).

Parts of URLs

Most URLs contain (roughly) three parts: the protocol, the host name, and the directory or filename (see Figure 5.15).

The protocol is the way in which the page is accessed, that is, the type of protocol or program your browser will use to get the file. If the browser is using HTTP to get to the file, the protocol part is `http`. If the browser uses FTP, the protocol is `ftp`. If you're using Gopher, it's `gopher`, and so on. The protocol matches an information server that must be installed on the system for it to work. You can't use an FTP URL on a machine that does not have an FTP server installed, for example.

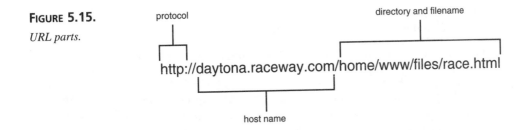

FIGURE 5.15.

URL parts.

The host name is the system on the Internet on which the information is stored, such as `www.netcom.com`, `ftp.apple.com`, or `www.aol.com`. You can have the same host name but have different URLs with different protocols, like the following:

```
http://mysystem.com
ftp://mysystem.com
gopher://mysystem.com
```

Same machine, three different information servers, and the browser will use different methods of connecting to that same machine. As long as all three servers are installed on that system and available, you won't have a problem.

The host name part of the URL may include a port number. The port number tells your browser to open a connection of the appropriate protocol on a specific network port other than the default port. The only time you'll need a port number in a URL is if the server handling the information has been explicitly installed on that port. (This issue is covered in Day 19.)

If a port number is necessary, it goes after the host name but before the directory, like the following:

```
http://my-public-access-unix.com:1550/pub/file
```

Finally, the directory is the location of the file or other form of information on the host. The directory can be an actual directory and filename, or it can be another indicator that the protocol uses to refer to the location of that information. (Gopher directories, for example, are not explicit directories.)

Special Characters in URLs

A *special character* in a URL is anything that is not an upper- or lowercase letter, a number (0–9), or the following symbols: dollar sign ($), dash (-), underscore (_), period (.), or plus sign (+). You might need to specify any other characters by using special URL escape codes to keep them from being interpreted as parts of the URL itself.

URL escape codes are indicated by a percent sign (%) and a two-character hexadecimal symbol from the ISO-Latin-1 character set (a superset of standard ASCII). For example, `%20` is a space, `%3f` is a question mark, and `%2f` is a slash.

5

Suppose that you have a directory named `All My Files`. Your first pass at a URL with this name in it might look like the following:

```
http://myhost.com/harddrive/All My Files/www/file.html
```

If you put this URL in quotation marks in a link tag, it might work (but only if you put it in quotation marks). Because the spaces are considered special characters to the URL, however, some browsers may have problems with them and not recognize the pathname correctly. For full compatibility with all browsers, use %20, as in the following:

```
http://myhost.com/harddrive/A¦¦%20My%20Files/www/file.html
```

Most of the time, if you make sure your file and directory names are short and use only alphanumeric characters, you won't need to include special characters in URLs. Keep this point in mind as you write your own pages.

HTML 4.0 and the <a> tag

HTML 4.0 includes some additional attributes for the <a> tag that are less common. These offer the following:

- `tabindex` Support for a tabbing order so that authors can define an order for anchors and links, and then the user can tab between them the way they do in a dialog box in Windows or the MacOS
- Support for event handlers such as those used in the Netscape JavaScript environment and Microsoft's Active Scripting Model (see `onfocus` and `onblur` in the list of intrinsic events in section "Common Attributes and Events" of Appendix B, "HTML 4.0 Quick Reference")

Kinds of URLs

Many kinds of URLs are defined by the Uniform Resource Locator specification. (See Appendix A, "Sources for Further Information," for a pointer to the most recent version.) This section describes some of the more popular URLs and some situations to look out for when using them.

HTTP

An HTTP URL is the most popular form of URL on the World Wide Web. HTTP, which stands for Hypertext Transfer Protocol, is the protocol that World Wide Web servers use to send HTML pages over the Net.

HTTP URLs follow this basic URL form:

```
http://www.foo.com/home/foo/
```

If the URL ends in a slash, the last part of the URL is considered a directory name. The file that you get using a URL of this type is the "default" file for that directory as defined by the HTTP server, usually a file called index.html. (If the Web page you're designing is the top-level file for all the files in a directory, calling it index.html is a good idea.)

You also can specify the filename directly in the URL. In this case, the file at the end of the URL is the one that is loaded, as in the following examples:

```
http://www.foo.com/home/foo/index.html
http://www.foo.com/home/foo/homepage.html
```

Using HTTP URLs like the following, where foo is a directory, is also usually acceptable:

```
http://www.foo.com/home/foo
```

In this case, because foo is a directory, this URL should have a slash at the end. Most Web servers can figure out that you meant this to be a directory and "redirect" to the appropriate file. Some older servers, however, may have difficulties resolving this URL, so you should always identify directories and files explicitly and make sure that a default file is available if you're indicating a directory.

Anonymous FTP

FTP URLs are used to point to files located on FTP servers—and usually anonymous FTP servers, that is, the ones that you can log in to using anonymous as the login ID and your email address as the password. FTP URLs also follow the "standard" URL form, as shown in the following examples:

```
ftp://ftp.foo.com/home/foo
ftp://ftp.foo.com/home/foo/homepage.html
```

Because you can retrieve either a file or a directory list with FTP, the restrictions on whether you need a trailing slash at the end of the URL are not the same as with HTTP. The first URL here retrieves a listing of all the files in the foo directory. The second URL retrieves and parses the file homepage.html in the foo directory.

5

Note

Navigating FTP servers by using a Web browser often can be much slower than navigating them by using FTP itself because the browser does not hold the connection open. Instead, it opens the connection, finds the file or directory listing, displays the listing, and then closes down the FTP connection. If you select a link to open a file or another directory in that listing, the browser will construct a new FTP URL from the items you selected, re-open the FTP connection by using the new URL, get the next directory or file, and close it again. For this reason, FTP URLs are best for when you know exactly

> which file you want to retrieve rather than for when you want to browse an archive.

Although your browser uses FTP to fetch the file, you still can get an HTML file from that server just as if it were an HTTP server, and it will parse and display just fine. Web browsers don't care how they get a hypertext file. As long as they can recognize the file as HTML, either by the servers telling them it's an HTML file (as with HTTP—you'll learn more about it later), or by the extension to the filename, the browsers will parse and display that file as an HTML file. If they don't recognize it as an HTML file, no big deal. The browsers can either display the file if they know what kind of file it is or just save the file to disk.

Non-Anonymous FTP

All the FTP URLs in the preceding section are used for anonymous FTP servers. You also can specify an FTP URL for named accounts on an FTP server, like the following:

```
ftp://username:password@ftp.foo.com/home/foo/homepage.html
```

In this form of the URL, the `username` part is your login ID on the server, and `password` is that account's password. Note that no attempt is made to hide the password in the URL. Be very careful that no one is watching you when you're using URLs of this form—and don't put them into links that someone else can find!

Mailto

The Mailto URL is used to send electronic mail. If the browser supports Mailto URLs, when a link that contains one is selected, the browser will prompt you for a subject and the body of the mail message, and send that message to the appropriate address when you're done.

Some browsers do not support Mailto and produce an error if a link with a Mailto URL is selected.

The Mailto URL is different from the standard URL form. It looks like the following:

```
mailto:internet_e-mail_address
```

Here's an example:

```
mailto:lemay@lne.com
```

> **Note**
>
> If your email address includes a percent sign (%), you'll have to use the escape character %25 instead. Percent signs are special characters to URLs.

Gopher

Gopher URLs use the standard URL file format up to and including the host name. After that, they use special Gopher protocols to encode the path to the particular file. The directory in Gopher does not indicate a directory pathname as HTTP and FTP URLs do and is too complex for this chapter.

Most of the time, you'll probably use a Gopher URL just to point to a Gopher server, which is easy. A URL of this sort looks like the following:

```
gopher://gopher.myhost.com/
```

If you really want to point directly to a specific file on a Gopher server, probably the best way to get the appropriate URL is not to try to build it yourself. Instead, navigate to the appropriate file or collection by using your browser, and then copy and paste the appropriate URL into your HTML page.

Usenet Newsgroups

Usenet news URLs have one of two forms:

```
news:name_of_newsgroup
news:message-id
```

The first form is used to read an entire newsgroup, such as `comp.infosystems.www.authoring.html` or `alt.gothic`. If your browser supports Usenet news URLs (either directly or through a newsreader), it will provide you with a list of available articles in that newsgroup.

The second form enables you to retrieve a specific news article. Each news article has a unique ID, called a message ID, which usually looks something like the following:

```
<lemayCt76Jq.CwG@netcom.com>
```

To use a message ID in a URL, remove the angle brackets and include the `news:` part:

```
news:lemayCt76Jq.CwG@netcom.com
```

Be aware that news articles do not exist forever—they "expire" and are deleted—so a message ID that was valid at one point may become invalid a short time later. If you want a permanent link to a news article, you should just copy the article to your Web presentation and link it as you would any other file.

5

Both forms of URL assume that you're reading news from an NNTP server. Both can be used only if you have defined an NNTP server somewhere in an environment variable or preferences file for your browser. Therefore, news URLs are most useful simply for reading specific news articles locally, not necessarily for using in links in pages.

> **Note**
>
> News URLs, like Mailto URLs, might not be supported by all browsers.

File

File URLs are intended to reference files contained on the local disk. In other words, they refer to files that are located on the same system as the browser. For local files, file URLs take one of these two forms: the first with an empty host name (see the three slashes rather than two?) or with the host name as `localhost`:

```
file:///dir1/dir2/file
file://localhost/dir1/dir2/file
```

Depending on your browser, one or the other will usually work.

File URLs are very similar to FTP URLs. In fact, if the host part of a file URL is not empty or `localhost`, your browser will try to find the given file by using FTP. Both of the following URLs result in the same file being loaded in the same way:

```
file://somesystem.com/pub/dir/foo/file.html
ftp://somesystem.com/pub/dir/foo/file.html
```

Probably the best use of file URLs is in startup pages for your browser (which are also called "home pages"). In this instance, because you will almost always be referring to a local file, using a file URL makes sense.

The problem with file URLs is that they reference local files, where "local" means on the same system as the browser that is pointing to the file—not the same system from which that the page was retrieved! If you use file URLs as links in your page, and then someone from elsewhere on the Internet encounters your page and tries to follow those links, that person's browser will attempt to find the file on his or her local disk (and generally will fail). Also, because file URLs use the absolute pathname to the file, if you use file URLs in your page, you cannot move that page elsewhere on the system or to any other system.

If your intention is to refer to files that are on the same file system or directory as the current page, use relative pathnames rather than file URLs. With relative pathnames for local files and other URLs for remote files, you should not need to use a file URL at all.

Summary

In this chapter, you learned all about links. Links turn the Web from a collection of unrelated pages into an enormous, interrelated information system (there are those big words again).

To create links, you use the `<a>...</a>` tag, called the link or anchor tag. The anchor tag has several attributes for indicating files to link to (the `href` attribute) and anchor names (the `name` attribute).

When linking pages that are all stored on the local disk, you can specify their pathnames in the `href` attribute as relative or absolute paths. For local links, relative pathnames are preferred because they enable you to move local pages more easily to another directory or to another system. If you use absolute pathnames, your links will break if you change anything in the hard-coded path.

If you want to link to a page on the Web (a remote page), the value of the `href` attribute is the URL of that page. You can easily copy the URL of the page you want to link. Just go to that page by using your favorite Web browser, and then copy and paste the URL from your browser into the appropriate place in your link tag.

To create links to specific parts of a page, first set an anchor at the point you want to link to, use the `<a>...</a>` tag as you would with a link, but rather than the `href` attribute, you use the `name` attribute to name the anchor. You then can link directly to that anchor name by using the name of the page, a hash sign (#), and the anchor name.

Finally, URLs (Uniform Resource Locators) are used to point to pages, files, and other information on the Internet. Depending on the type of information, URLs can contain several parts, but most contain a protocol type and location or address. URLs can be used to point to many kinds of information but are most commonly used to point to Web pages (`http`), FTP directories or files (`ftp`), information on Gopher servers (`gopher`), electronic mail addresses (`mailto`), or Usenet news (`news`).

Workshop

Congratulations, you learned a lot in this chapter! Now it's time for the chapter workshop. Many questions about links appear here. The quiz focuses on other items that are important for you to remember, followed by the quiz answers. In the chapter exercises, you'll take that list of items you created yesterday and link them to other pages.

Q&A

Q My links aren't being highlighted in blue or purple at all. They're still just plain text.

A Is the filename in a `name` attribute rather than in an `href`? Did you remember to close the quotation marks around the filename to which you're linking? Both of these errors can prevent links from showing up as links.

Q I put a URL into a link, and it shows up as highlighted in my browser, but when I click it, the browser says "unable to access page." If it can't find the page, why did it highlight the text?

A The browser highlights text within a link tag whether or not the link is valid. In fact, you don't even need to be online for links to show up as highlighted links, although you cannot get to them. The only way you can tell whether a link is valid is to select it and try to view the page to which the link points.

As to why the browser couldn't find the page you linked to—make sure you're connected to the network and that you entered the URL into the link correctly. Make sure you have both opening and closing quotation marks around the filename, and that those quotation marks are straight quotes. If your browser prints link destinations in the status bar when you move the mouse cursor over a link, watch that status bar and see whether the URL that appears is actually the URL you want.

Finally, try opening that URL directly in your browser and see whether that solution works. If directly opening the link doesn't work either, there might be several reasons why. The following are two common possibilities:

- The server is overloaded or is not on the Internet.

  Machines go down, as do network connections. If a particular URL doesn't work for you, perhaps something is wrong with the machine or the network. Or maybe the site is popular, and too many people are trying to access it at once. Try again later or during non-peak hours for that server. If you know the people who run the server, you can try sending them electronic mail or calling them.

- The URL itself is bad.

  Sometimes URLs become invalid. Because a URL is a form of absolute pathname, if the file to which it refers moves around, or if a machine or directory name gets changed, the URL won't be any good any more. Try contacting the person or site you got the URL from in the first place. See if that person has a more recent link.

Q Can I put any URL in a link?

A You bet. If you can get to a URL using your browser, you can put that URL in a link. Note, however, that some browsers support URLs that others don't. For example, Lynx is really good with Mailto URLs (URLs that allow you to send electronic mail to a person's email address). When you select a Mailto URL in Lynx, it prompts you for a subject and the body of the message. When you're done, it sends the mail.

Other browsers, on the other hand, may not handle Mailto URLs, and insist that a link containing the mailto URL is invalid. The URL itself may be fine, but the browser can't handle it.

Q Can I use images as links?

A Yup, in more ways than one, actually. You'll learn how to use images as links in Day 7, "Using Images, Color, and Background," and how to create what are called imagemaps in Day 9, "Creating and Using Imagemaps."

Q You've described only two attributes of the `<a>` tag: `href` and `name`. Aren't there others?

A Yes. The `<a>` tag has several attributes including `rel`, `rev`, `shape`, `accesskey`, and `title`. However, most of these attributes can be used only by tools that automatically generate links between pages, or by browsers that can manage links better than most of those now available. Because 99 percent of the people reading this book won't care about (or ever use) those links or browsers, I'm sticking to `href` and `name` and ignoring the other attributes.

If you're really interested, I've summarized the other attributes in Appendix B, and pointers to the various HTML specifications are listed in Appendix A, as well.

Q My links are not pointing to my anchors. When I follow a link, I'm always dropped at the top of the page rather than at the anchor. What's going on here?

A Are you specifying the anchor name in the link after the hash sign the same way that it appears in the anchor itself, with all the uppercase and lowercase letters identical? Anchors are case sensitive, so if your browser cannot find an anchor name with an exact match, the browser may try to select something else in the page that is closer. This is dependent on browser behavior, of course, but if your links and anchors aren't working, the problem usually is that your anchor names and your anchors do not match. Also, remember that anchor names don't contain hash signs—only the links to them do.

5

Q It sounds like file URLs aren't overly useful. Is there any reason I'd want to use them?

A I can think of two. The first one is if you have many users on a single system (for example, on a UNIX system), and you want to give those local users (but nobody else) access to files on that system. By using file URLs, you can point to files on the local system, and anyone on that system can get to them. Readers from outside the system won't have direct access to the disk and won't be able to get to those files.

A second good reason for using file URLs is that you actually want to point to a local disk. For example, you could create a CD-ROM full of information in HTML form and then create a link from a page on the Web to a file on the CD-ROM by using a file URL. In this case, because your presentation depends on a disk your readers must have, using a file URL makes sense.

Q Is there any way to indicate a subject in a Mailto URL?

A Not at the moment. According to the current Mailto URL definition, the only thing you can put in a Mailto URL is the address to mail to. If you really need a subject or something in the body of the message, consider using a form instead.

Quiz

1. What two things do you need to create a link in HTML?
2. What is a relative pathname? Why is it advantageous to use them?
3. What is an absolute pathname?
4. What is an anchor, and what is it used for?
5. Besides HTTP ("Web page") URLs, what other kinds are there?

Answers

1. To create a link in HTML, you need the name or URL of the file or page to which you want to link, and the text that your readers can select to follow the link.
2. A relative pathname points to a file, based on the location that is relative to the current file. Relative pathnames are portable, meaning that if you move your files elsewhere on a disk or rename a directory, the links require little or no modification.
3. An absolute pathname points to a page by starting at the top level of a directory hierarchy and working downward through all intervening directories to reach the file.
4. An anchor marks a place that you can link to inside a Web document. A link on the same page or on another page can then jump to that specific location instead of the top of the page.

5. Other types of URLs are FTP URLs (which point to files on FTP servers), File URLs (which point to a file contained on a local disk), Mailto URLs (which are used to send electronic mail), Gopher URLs (which point to files on a Gopher server), and Usenet URLs (which point to newsgroups or specific news articles in a newsgroup).

Exercises

1. Remember that list of topics that you created in the first exercise in the last chapter? Create a link to the page you created in the previous chapter's second exercise (the page that described one of the topics in more detail).

2. Now, open up the page that you created in the second exercise in the previous chapter, and create a link back to the first page. Also, find some pages on the World Wide Web that discuss the same topic and create links to those pages as well. Good luck!

5

DAY 6

More Text Formatting with HTML

In Days 4 and 5, you learned the basics of HTML, including several basic page elements and links. With that background, you're now ready to learn more about what HTML can do in terms of text formatting and layout. This chapter describes most of the remaining tags in HTML that you'll need to know to construct pages, including tags in standard HTML 2.0 through HTML 4.0, as well as HTML attributes in individual browsers. Today you'll learn how to do the following:

- Specify the appearance of individual characters (bold, italic, underlined)
- Include special characters (characters with accents, copyright and registration marks, and so on)
- Create preformatted text (text with spaces and tabs retained)
- Align text left, right, justified, and centered
- Change the font and font size
- Create other miscellaneous HTML text elements, including line breaks, rule lines, addresses, and quotations

In addition, you'll learn the differences between standard HTML and HTML extensions, and when to choose which tags to use in your pages. At the end of this chapter, you'll create a complete Web page that uses many of the tags presented in this chapter as well as the information from the preceding four chapters.

This chapter covers several tags and options, so you might find it a bit overwhelming. Don't worry about remembering everything now; just get a grasp of what sort of formatting you can do in HTML, and then you can look up the specific tags later.

Character Styles

When you use HTML tags for paragraphs, headings, or lists, those tags affect that block of text as a whole, changing the font, changing the spacing above and below the line, or adding characters (in the case of bulleted lists).

Character styles are tags that affect words or characters within other HTML entities and change the appearance of that text so that it is somehow different from the surrounding text—making it bold or underline, for example.

To change the appearance of a set of characters within text, you can use one of two kinds of tags: logical styles or physical styles.

Logical Styles

Logical style tags indicate how the given highlighted text is to be used, not how it is to be displayed. They are similar to the common element tags for paragraphs or headings. They don't indicate how the text is to be formatted, just how it is to be used in a document. Logical style tags might, for example, indicate a definition, a snippet of code, or an emphasized word.

NEW TERM *Logical style* tags indicate the way text is used (emphasis, citation, definition).

Using logical style tags, the browser determines the actual presentation of the text, be it in bold, italic, or any other change in appearance. You cannot guarantee that text highlighted using these tags will always be bold or always be italic (and, therefore, you should not depend on it, either).

Note

HTML 4.0 extends HTML's model of physical and logical styles by providing support for style sheets. With style sheets, page authors are able to define more precisely the appearance (including font family, style and size) of individual elements or entire classes of elements (such as all unordered lists) in a document. We'll cover style sheets in Chapters 10, "XHTML and Style Sheets" and 18, "Designing for the Real World."

Each character style tag has both opening and closing sides and affects the text within those two tags. The following are the eight logical style tags in standard HTML:

<em> This tag indicates that the characters are to be emphasized in some way; that is, they are formatted differently from the rest of the text. In graphical browsers, <em> is typically italic. For example,

```
<p>The anteater is the <em>strangest</em> looking animal,
isn't it?</p>
```

<strong> With this tag, the characters are to be more strongly emphasized than with <em>. <strong> text is highlighted differently from <em> text—for example, in bold. Consider the following:

```
<p>Take a <strong>left turn</strong> at <strong>Dee's Hop
Stop</strong></p>
```

<code> This tag indicates a code sample (a fixed-width font such as Courier in graphical displays). For example,

```
<p><code>#include "trans.h"</code></p>
```

<samp> This tag indicates sample text, similar to <code>, as in the following example:

```
<p>The URL for that page is <samp>http://www.cern.ch/
</samp></p>
```

<kbd> This tag indicates text intended to be typed by a user. Consider the following:

```
<p>Type the following command: <kbd>find . -name "prune"
-print</kbd></p>
```

<var> This tag indicates the name of a variable, or some entity to be replaced with an actual value. It often is displayed as italic or underline, as in the following:

```
<p><code>chown </code><var>your_name the_file
</var></p>
```

<dfn> This tag indicates a definition. <dfn> is used to highlight a word that will be defined or has just been defined, as in the following example:

```
<p>Styles that are named after how they are actually
used are called
<dfn>logical styles</dfn></p>
```

<cite> This tag indicates a short quote or citation, as in the following:

```
<p>Eggplant has been known to cause nausea in some
people<cite> (Lemay, 1994)</cite></p>
```

6

> **Note**
>
> Of the tags in this list, all except `<dfn>` are part of the official HTML 2.0 specification. `<dfn>` was added in the HTML 3.2 specification.

HTML 4.0 introduced two additional logical style tags that are most useful for audio browsers. A graphical browser, such as Netscape or Internet Explorer, will not display them any differently. When an audio browser reads content included within one of these tags, however, each letter is spoken individually. For example, FOX is pronounced "F-O-X" rather than "fox".

These tags also use opening and closing sides and affect the text within. Following are new tags:

`<abbr>`   This tag indicates the abbreviation of a word, as in the following:

```
<p>Use the standard two-letter state abbreviation
(such as <abbr>CA</abbr> for California)</p>
```

`<acronym>`   Similar to the `<abbr>` tag, `<acronym>` designates a word formed by combining the initial letters of several words, as in the following example:

```
<p>Jonathan learned his great problem-handling skills
from <acronym>STEPS</acronym> (Simply Tackle Each Problem
Seriously)</p>
```

Got all these tags memorized now? Good! There will be a pop quiz at the end of the chapter. The following code snippets demonstrate each of the logical style tags, and Figure 6.1 illustrates how all the tags are displayed in Internet Explorer.

INPUT
```
<p>The anteater is the <em>strangest</em> looking animal, isn't it?</p>
<p>Take a <strong>left turn</strong> at <strong>Dee's Hop Stop
</strong></p>
<p><code>#include "trans.h"</code></p>
<p>The URL for that page is <samp>http://www.cern.ch/</samp></p>
<p>Type the following command: <kbd>find . -name "prune" -print</kbd></p>
<p><code>chown </code><var>your_name the_file</var></p>
<p>Styles that are named after how they are used are called <dfn>logical
styles</dfn></p>
<p>Eggplant has been known to cause nausea in some
people<cite> (Lemay, 1994)</cite></p>
<p>Use the standard two-letter state abbreviation (such as
<abbr>CA</abbr> for California)</p>
<p>Jonathan learned his great problem-handling skills from
<acronym>STEPS</acronym> (Simply Tackle Each Problem Seriously)</p>
```

OUTPUT

FIGURE 6.1

The output in Internet Explorer.

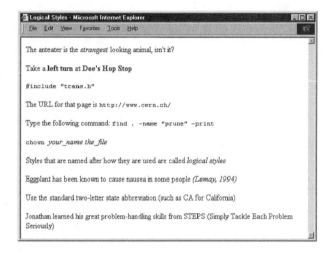

Physical Styles

In addition to the tags for style in the preceding section, you also can use a set of tags, physical style tags, to change the actual presentation style of the text—to make it bold, italic, or monospace.

NEW TERM *Physical style* tags indicate exactly the way text is to be formatted (bold, underline, and so on).

Like the character style tags, each formatting tag has a beginning and ending tag. Standard HTML 2.0 defined three physical style tags:

<b>	Bold
<i>	Italic
<tt>	Monospaced typewriter font

HTML 3.2 defined several additional physical style tags, including the following:

<u>	Underline (deprecated in HTML 4.0)
<s>	Strike-through (deprecated in HTML 4.0)
<big>	Bigger print than the surrounding text
<small>	Smaller print
<sub>	Subscript
<sup>	Superscript

6

If you use the physical style tags, particularly the HTML 3.2 tags, be forewarned that if a browser cannot handle one of the physical styles, it may substitute another style for the one you're using or ignore that formatting altogether. Although most of the latest browsers, such as Netscape Communicator and Internet Explorer 5, are happy with these tags, enough users are using older versions of these browsers that support these tags to varying degrees. On top of all this, in text-based browsers, such as Lynx, some of these tags can't be rendered visually and other workarounds will be used to get across the idea.

You can nest character tags—for example, use both bold and italic for a set of characters—like the following:

```
<b><i>Text that is both bold and italic</i></b>
```

The result on the screen, however, like all HTML tags, is browser dependent. You will not necessarily end up with text that is both bold and italic. You may end up with one style or the other.

Figure 6.2 shows some of the physical style tags and how they appear in Internet Explorer.

INPUT
```
<p>In Dante's <i>Inferno</i>, malaboge was the eighth circle of hell,
and held the malicious and fraudulent.</p>
<p>All entries must be received by <b>September 26, 1999</b>.</p>
<p>Type <tt>lpr -Pbirch myfile.txt</tt> to print that file.</p>
<p>Sign your name in the spot marked <u>Sign Here</u>:</p>
<p>People who wear orange shirts and plaid pants <s>have no taste</s>
are fashion-challenged.</p>
<p>RCP floor mats give you <big>big</big> savings over the
competition!</p>
<p>Then, from the corner of the room, he heard a <small>tiny voice
</small>.</p>
<p>In heavy trading today. Consolidated Orange Trucking
rose <sup>1</sup>/<sub>4</sub>
points on volume of 1,457,900 shares.</p>
```

FIGURE 6.2

The output in Internet Explorer.

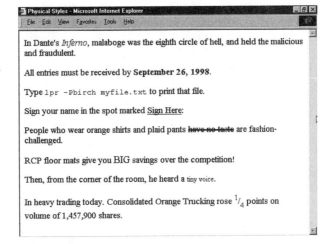

Preformatted Text

Most of the time, text in an HTML file is formatted based on the HTML tags used to mark up that text. As I mentioned in Chapter 3, "An Introduction to HTML," any extra white space (spaces, tabs, returns) that you put in your text are stripped out by the browser.

The one exception to this rule is the preformatted text tag <pre>. Any white space that you put into text surrounded by the <pre> and </pre> tags is retained in the final output. With the <pre> and </pre> tags, you can format the text the way you want it to look, and it will be presented that way.

The catch is that preformatted text usually is displayed (in graphical displays, at least) in a monospaced font such as Courier. Preformatted text is excellent for displays such as programming code examples, where you want to indent and format lines appropriately. Because you also can use the <pre> tag to align text by padding it with spaces, you can use it for simple tables. However, the fact that the tables are presented in a monospaced font may make them less than ideal. (You'll learn how to create real tables in Chapter 11, "Tables.") The following is an example of a table created with <pre>. Figure 6.3 shows how it looks in Internet Explorer.

6

INPUT `<pre>`

```
                    Diameter    Distance     Time to        Time to
            (miles)    from Sun     Orbit         Rotate
                       (millions
                       of miles)
    ---------------------------------------------------------------
    Mercury    3100        36       88 days       59 days
    Venus      7700        67       225 days      244 days
    Earth      7920        93       365 days      24 hrs
    Mars       4200        141      687 days      24 hrs 24 mins
    Jupiter    88640       483      11.9 years    9 hrs 50 mins
    Saturn     74500       886      29.5 years    10 hrs 39 mins
    Uranus     32000       1782     84 years      23 hrs
    Neptune    31000       2793     165 days      15 hrs 48 mins
    Pluto      1500        3670     248 years     6 days 7 hrs
```
`</pre>`

OUTPUT

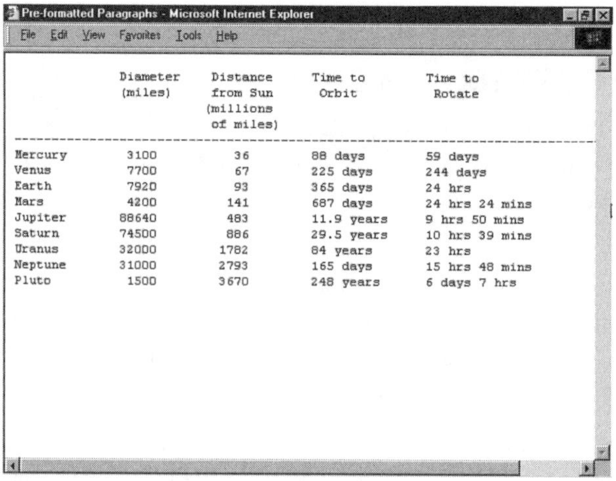

FIGURE 6.3

A table created using
<pre>, shown in
Internet Explorer.

When creating text for the <pre> tag, you can use link tags and character styles, but not element tags such as headings or paragraphs. You should break your lines by using a return and try to keep your lines at 60 characters or fewer. Some browsers may have limited horizontal space in which to display text. Because browsers usually will not reformat preformatted text to fit that space, you should make sure that you keep your text within the boundaries to prevent your readers from having to scroll from side to side.

Be careful with tabs in preformatted text. The actual number of characters for each tab stop varies from browser to browser. One browser may have tab stops at every fourth character, whereas another may have them at every eighth character. If your preformatted text relies on tabs at a certain number of spaces, consider using spaces rather than tabs.

The <pre> tag also is excellent for converting files that originally were in some sort of text-only form, such as mail messages or Usenet news postings, to HTML quickly and easily. Just surround the entire content of the article within <pre> tags, and you have instant HTML, as in the following example:

```
<pre>
To: lemay@lne.com
From: jokes@lne.com
Subject: Tales of the Move From Hell, pt. 1

I spent the day on the phone today with the entire household
services division of northern California, turning off services,
turning on services, transferring services and other such fun
things you have to do when you move.

It used to be you just called these people and got put on hold for
and interminable amount of time, maybe with some nice music, an
then you got a customer representative who was surly and hard of
hearing, but with some work you could actually get your phone
turned off.
</pre>
```

A creative use of the <pre> tag is to create ASCII art for your Web pages. The following HTML input and output example shows a simple ASCII art cow, as displayed in Figure 6.4 in Internet Explorer.

```
<pre>
       (   )
Moo   (oo)
       \/------\
        ||     | \
        ||---W||  *
        ||     ||
        ||     ||
</pre>
```

OUTPUT

FIGURE 6.4

The output in Internet Explorer.

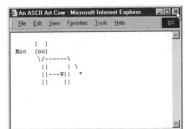

6

Horizontal Rules

The <hr> tag, which has no closing tag in HTML and no text associated with it, creates a horizontal line on the page. Rule lines are excellent for visually separating sections of a Web page—just before headings, for example, or to separate body text from a list of items.

> **Note**
>
> The <hr> tag has no closing tag in HTML. To convert this tag to XHTML, and to ensure compatibility with HTML browsers, add a space and forward slash to the end of the tag:
>
> **<hr />**
>
> If the horizontal line has attributes associated with it, the forward slash still appears at the end of the tag, as shown in the following examples:
>
> **<hr size="2" />**
> **<hr width="75%" />**
> **<hr align="center" size="4" width="200" />**

The following input and output example shows a rule line and a list as you would write it in XHTML 1.0. Figure 6.5 shows how they appear in Internet Explorer.

INPUT

```
<hr />
<h2>To Do on Friday</h2>
<ul>
<li>Do laundry</li>
<li>Send FedEx with pictures</li>
<li>Have lunch with Mollie</li>
<li>Read Email</li>
<li>Set up Ethernet</li>
</ul>
<hr />
```

OUTPUT

FIGURE 6.5

The output in Internet Explorer.

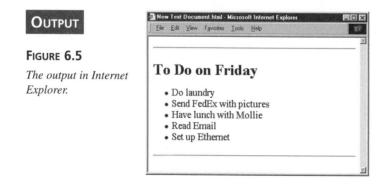

Attributes of the <hr> Tag

In HTML 2.0, the <hr> tag is just as you see it, with no closing tag or attributes. However, HTML 3.2 introduced several attributes to the <hr> tag that give you greater control over the appearance of the line drawn by <hr>. All these attributes have been deprecated in favor of style sheets in the HTML 4.0 specification.

> **Note**
>
> Although presentational attributes such as size, width, and align are still supported in HTML 4.0, style sheets are now the recommended way to control appearance.

The size attribute indicates the thickness, in pixels, of the rule line. The default is 2, and this also is the smallest thickness that you can make the rule line. Figure 6.6 shows some sample rule line thicknesses, created with the following code:

INPUT

```
<h2>2 Pixels</h2>
<hr size="2" />
<h2>4 Pixels</h2>
<hr size="4" />
<h2>8 Pixels</h2>
<hr size="8" />
<h2>16 Pixels</h2>
<hr size="16" />
```

OUTPUT

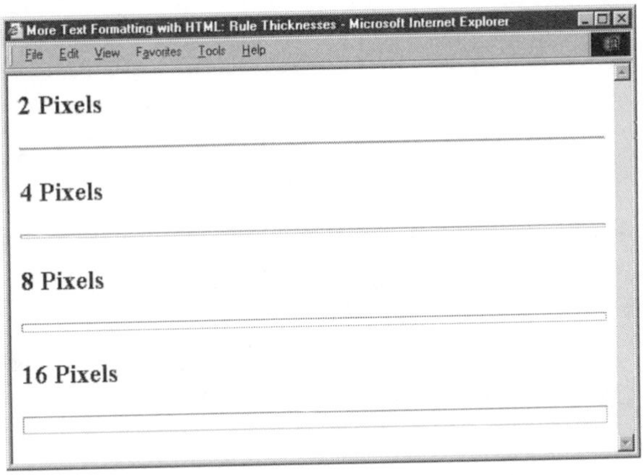

FIGURE 6.6

Examples of rule line thicknesses.

The width attribute indicates the horizontal width of the rule line. You can specify either the exact width, in pixels, or the value as a percentage of the screen width (for example, 30 percent or 50 percent), which changes if you resize the window. Figure 6.7 shows the result of the following code, which displays some sample rule line widths.

INPUT

```
<h2>100%</h2>
<hr />
<h2>75%</h2>
<hr width="75%" />
<h2>50%</h2>
<hr width="50%" />
<h2>25%</h2>
<hr width="25%" />
<h2>10%</h2>
<hr width="10%" />
```

OUTPUT

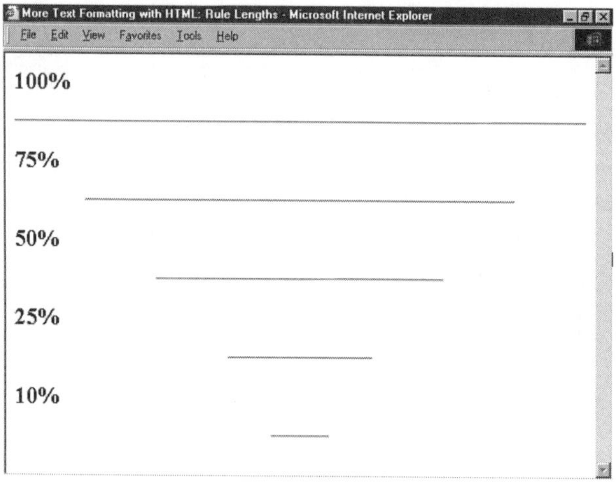

FIGURE 6.7

Examples of rule line widths.

If you specify a width smaller than the actual width of the screen, you also can specify the alignment of that rule line with the align attribute, making it flush left (align="left"), flush right (align="right"), or centered (align="center"). By default, rule lines are centered.

A popular trick used by Web designers who use these attributes is to create patterns with several small rule lines. The following example displays a design created with horizontal rules, and the result is shown in Figure 6.8.

INPUT

```
<hr align="center" size="4" width="200" />
<hr align="center" size="4" width="300" />
<hr align="center" size="4" width="400" />
<h1 align="center">NorthWestern Video</h1>
<hr align="center" size="4" width="400" />
<hr align="center" size="4" width="300" />
<hr align="center" size="4" width="200" />
<h2 align="center">Presents</h2>
```

OUTPUT

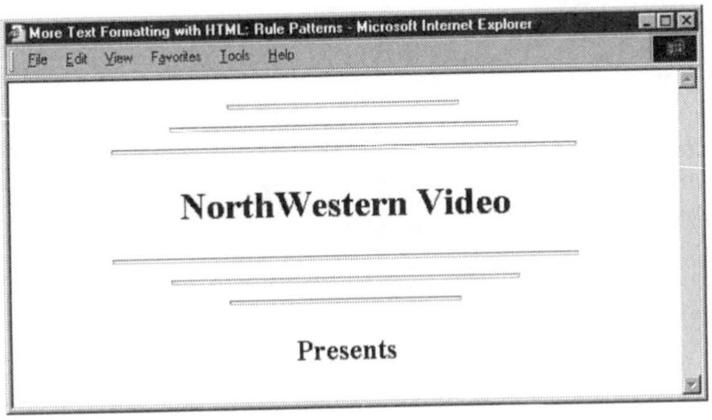

FIGURE 6.8

An example of patterns created with several small rule lines.

Finally, the noshade attribute shown in the following example causes the browser to draw the rule line as a plain line in most current browsers, without the three-dimensional shading, as shown in Figure 6.9.

Note

In HTML 4.0 and earlier versions, an attribute value is not necessary for noshade. The method you use to apply this attribute appears as follows:

```
<hr align="center" size="4" width="200" noshade>
```

In XHTML 1.0, however, a value is mandatory. The example that follows demonstrates how to apply the noshade attribute to the <hr> tag according to the proposed XHTML 1.0 specification.

INPUT

```
<hr align="center" size="4" width="200" noshade="noshade" />
<hr align="center" size="4" width="300" noshade="noshade" />
<hr align="center" size="4" width="400" noshade="noshade" />
<h1 align="center">NorthWestern Video</h1>
<hr align="center" size="4" width="400" noshade="noshade" />
<hr align="center" size="4" width="300" noshade="noshade" />
<hr align="center" size="4" width="200" noshade="noshade" />
<h2 align="center">Presents</h2>
```

6

OUTPUT

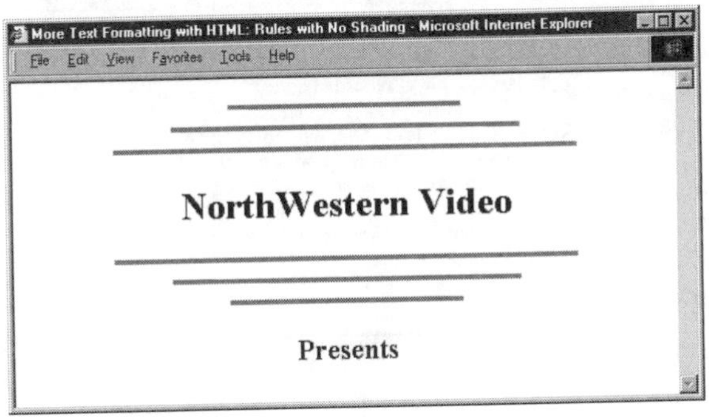

FIGURE 6.9

Rule lines without shading.

Line Break

The <br> tag breaks a line of text at the point where it appears. When a Web browser
encounters a <br> tag, it restarts the text after the tag at the left margin (whatever the
current left margin happens to be for the current element). You can use <br> within other
elements such as paragraphs or list items;
 will not add extra space above or below
the new line or change the font or style of the current entity. All it does is restart the text
at the next line.

Note

Like the <hr> tag, the <br> tag has no closing tag in HTML. To convert this
tag to XHTML, and to ensure compatibility with HTML browsers, add a space
and forward slash to the end of the tag and its attributes, as shown in the
following example:

```
And then is heard no more: it is a tale <br />
Told by an idiot, full of sound and fury, <br />
Signifying nothing.</p>
```

The following example shows a simple paragraph in which each line ends with a <br>.
Figures 6.10 shows how it appears in Internet Explorer.

INPUT

```
<p>Tomorrow, and tomorrow, and tomorrow,<br />
Creeps in this petty pace from day to day,<br />
To the last syllable of recorded time;<br />
And all our yesterdays have lighted fools<br />
The way to dusty death. Out, out, brief candle!<br />
Life's but a walking shadow; a poor player,<br />
That struts and frets his hour upon the stage,<br />
And then is heard no more: it is a tale <br />
Told by an idiot, full of sound and fury, <br />
Signifying nothing.</p>
```

OUTPUT

FIGURE 6.10

The output in Internet Explorer.

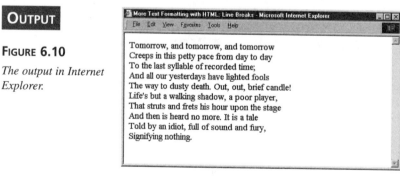

Note

clear is an attribute of the <br> tag. It is used with images that have text wrapped alongside them. You'll learn about this attribute in Chapter 7, "Using Images, Color, and Backgrounds."

Addresses

The address tag <address> is used for signature-like entities on Web pages. Address tags usually go at the bottom of each Web page and are used to indicate who wrote the Web page, who to contact for more information, the date, any copyright notices or other warnings, and anything else that seems appropriate. Addresses often are preceded with a rule line (<hr>), and the <br> tag can be used to separate the lines.

Without an address or some other method of "signing" your Web pages, finding out who wrote it, or who to contact for more information, becomes close to impossible. Signing each of your Web pages by using the <address> tag is an excellent way to make sure that, if people want to get in touch with you, they can.

The following simple input and output example shows an address. Figure 6.11 shows it in Internet Explorer.

INPUT

```
<hr />
<address>
Laura Lemay lemay@lne.com <br />
A service of Laura Lemay, Incorporated <br />
last revised Nov 11, 1999 <br />
Copyright Laura Lemay 1999 all rights reserved <br />
Void where prohibited. Keep hands and feet inside the vehicle at all
times.
</address>
```

OUTPUT

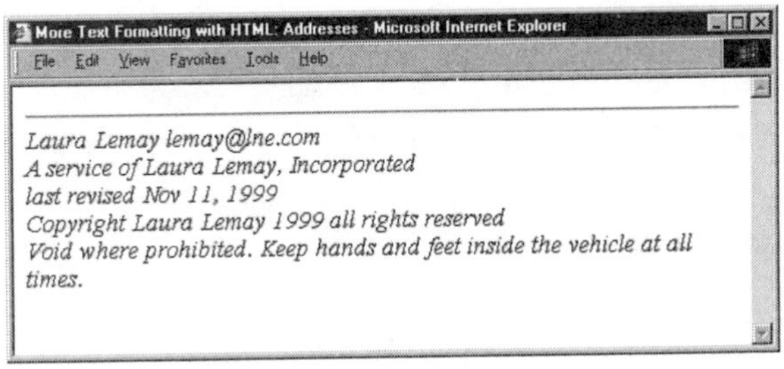

FIGURE 6.11

The output in Internet Explorer.

More Text Formatting with HTML: Addresses - Microsoft Internet Explorer

File   Edit   View   Favorites   Tools   Help

Laura Lemay lemay@lne.com
A service of Laura Lemay, Incorporated
last revised Nov 11, 1999
Copyright Laura Lemay 1999 all rights reserved
Void where prohibited. Keep hands and feet inside the vehicle at all times.

6

Quotations

The `<blockquote>` tag is used to create a quotation. (Unlike the `<cite>` tag, which high-lights small quotes, `<blockquote>` is used for longer quotations that should not be nested inside other paragraphs.) Quotations generally are set off from regular text by indentation or some other method. For example, the *Macbeth* soliloquy I used in the example for line breaks would have worked better as a `<blockquote>` than as a simple paragraph. Here's an input example:

INPUT

```
<blockquote>
"During the whole of a dull, dark, and soundless day in the autumn
of the year, when the clouds hung oppressively low in the heavens,
I had been passing alone, on horseback, through a singularly dreary
tract of country, and at length found myself, as the shades of evening
grew on, within view of the melancholy House of Usher."--Edgar Allen Poe
</blockquote>
```

As in paragraphs, you can separate lines in a `<blockquote>` using the line break tag `<br>`. The following input example shows a sample of this use.

INPUT

```
<blockquote>
Guns aren't lawful, <br />
nooses give.<br />
gas smells awful.<br />
You might as well live.<br />
--Dorothy Parker
</blockquote>
```

Figure 6.12 shows how the preceding input example appears in Internet Explorer.

OUTPUT

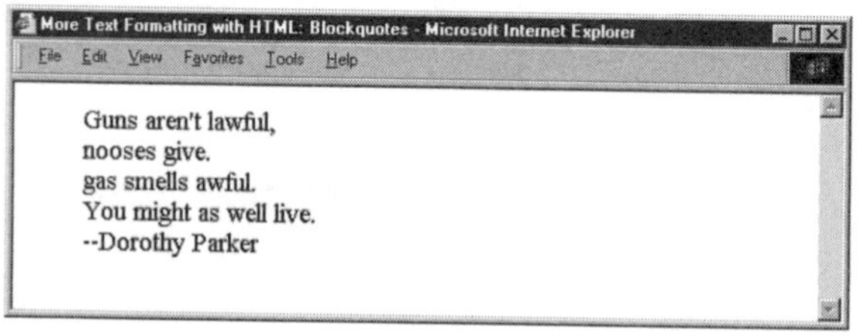

FIGURE 6.12

The output in Internet Explorer.

Special Characters

As you learned earlier in the week, HTML files are ASCII text and should contain no formatting or fancy characters. In fact, the only characters you should put in your HTML files are characters that are actually printed on your keyboard. If you have to hold down any key other than Shift or type an arcane combination of keys to produce a single char-acter, you can't use that character in your HTML file. That includes characters you may use every day, such as em dashes and curly quotes (and, if your word processor is set up to do automatic curly quotes, you should turn them off when you write your HTML files).

"But wait a minute," you say. "If I can type a character, like a bullet or an accented *a* on my keyboard using a special key sequence, include it in an HTML file, and my browser can display it just fine when I look at that file, what's the problem?"

The problem is that the internal encoding your computer does to produce that character (which allows it to show up properly in your HTML file and in your browser's display) most likely will not translate to other computers. Someone else on the Internet reading your HTML file with that funny character in it may very well end up with some other character, or garbage. Or, depending on how your page gets shipped over the Internet, the character may be lost before it ever gets to the computer where the file is being viewed.

> **Note**
>
> In technical jargon, the characters in HTML files must be from the standard (7-bit) ASCII character set and cannot include any characters from "extended" (8-bit) ASCII, as every platform has a different definition of the characters that are included in the upper ASCII range. HTML browsers interpret codes from upper ASCII as characters in the ISO-Latin-1 (ISO-8859-1) character set, a superset of ASCII.

So what can you do? HTML provides a reasonable solution. It defines a special set of codes, called character entities, that you can include in your HTML files to represent the characters you want to use. When interpreted by a browser, these character entities are displayed as the appropriate special characters for the given platform and font.

Character Entities for Special Characters

Character entities take one of two forms: named entities and numbered entities.

Named entities begin with an ampersand (&) and end with a semicolon (;). In between is the name of the character (or, more likely, a shorthand version of that name like `agrave` for an *a* with a grave accent or `reg` for a registered trademark sign). The names, unlike other HTML tags, are case sensitive, so you should make sure to type them exactly. Named entities look something like the following:

```
&agrave;
&quot;
&laquo;
&copy;
```

6

The numbered entities also begin with an ampersand and end with a semicolon, but rather than a name, they have a hash sign (#) and a number. The numbers correspond to character positions in the ISO-Latin-1 (ISO 8859-1) character. Every character for which you can type or use a named entity also has a numbered entity. Numbered entities look like the following:

```
&#130;
&#245;
```

You use either numbers or named entities in your HTML file by including them in the same place that the character they represent would go. So, to have the word *résumé* in your HTML file, you would use either

```
r&eacute;sum&eacute;
```

or

```
r&#233;sum&#233;
```

In Appendix B, "HTML 4.0 Quick Reference," I've included a table that lists the named entities currently supported by HTML. See that table for specific characters.

Note

HTML's use of the ISO-Latin-1 character set allows it to display most accented characters on most platforms, but it has limitations. For example, common characters such as bullets, em dashes, and curly quotes are simply not available in the ISO-Latin-1 character set. You therefore cannot use these characters at all in your HTML files. Also, many ISO-Latin-1 characters may be entirely unavailable in some browsers, depending on whether those characters exist on that platform and in the current font.

HTML 4.0 takes things a huge leap further by proposing that Unicode should be available as a character set for HTML documents. Unicode is a proposed standard character encoding system that, while backwards compatible with our familiar ASCII encoding, offers the capability to encode almost any of the world's characters—including those found in languages such as Chinese and Japanese. This will mean that documents can be easily created in any language, and that they also can contain multiple language. Browsers have already started supporting Unicode. Netscape Communicator, for example, supports Unicode, and, as long as the necessary fonts are available, it can render documents in many of the scripts provided by Unicode.

This is an important step because Unicode is emerging as a new *de facto* standard for character encoding. Java, for example, uses Unicode as its default character encoding, and Windows NT supports Unicode character encoding.

Character Entities for Reserved Characters

For the most part, character entities exist so that you can include special characters that are not part of the standard ASCII character set. Several exceptions do exist, however, for the few characters that have special meaning in HTML itself. You also must use entities for these characters.

Suppose that you want to include a line of code that looks something like the following in an HTML file:

```
<p><code>if x < 0 do print i</code></p>
```

Doesn't look unusual, does it? Unfortunately, HTML cannot display this line as written. Why? The problem is with the < (less-than) character. To an HTML browser, the less-than character means "this is the start of a tag." Because in this context the less-than character is not actually the start of a tag, your browser may get confused. You'll have the same problem with the greater-than character (>) because it means the end of a tag in HTML, and with the ampersand (&), meaning the beginning of a character escape. Written correctly for HTML, the preceding line of code would look like the following instead:

```
<p><code>if x &lt; 0 do print i</code></p>
```

HTML provides named escape codes for each of these characters, and one for the double quotation mark, as well, as shown in Table 6.1.

Table 6.1 Escape Codes for Characters Used by Tags

Entity	Result
&lt;	<
&gt;	>
&amp;	&
&quot;	"

The double quotation mark escape is the mysterious one. Technically, to produce correct HTML files, if you want to include a double quotation mark in text, you should use the escape sequence and not type the quotation mark character. However, I have not noticed any browsers having problems displaying the double quotation mark character when it is typed literally in an HTML file, nor have I seen many HTML files that use it. For the most part, you probably are safe using plain old " in your HTML files rather than the escape code.

6

Text Alignment

Text alignment is the capability to arrange a block of text, such as a heading or a paragraph, so that it is aligned against the left margin (left justification, the default), aligned against the right margin (right justification), or centered. Standard HTML 2.0 has no mechanisms for aligning text; the browser is responsible for determining the alignment of the text (which means most of the time it's left-justified).

HTML 3.2 introduced attributes for text and element alignment, and these attributes have been incorporated into all the major browsers. HTML 4.0 still supports alignment attributes, but the preferred method of controlling text alignment now is with style sheets.

Aligning Individual Elements

To align an individual heading or paragraph, use the `align` attribute to that HTML element. `align` has three values: `left`, `right`, or `center`. Consider the following examples:

```
<h1 align="center">Northridge Paints, Inc.</h1>
<p align="center">We don't just paint the town red.</p>

<h1 align="left">Serendipity Products</h1>
<h2 align="right"><a href="who.html">Who We Are</a></h2>
<h2 align="right"><a href="products.html">What We Do</a></h2>
<h2 align="right"><a href="contacts.html">How To Reach Us</a></h2>
```

The following input and output example shows simple alignment of several headings. Figure 6.13 shows the results in Internet Explorer.

INPUT

```
<h1 align="left">Serendipity Products</h1>
<h2 align="right"><a href="who.html">Who We Are</a></h2>
<h2 align="right"><a href="products.html">What We Do</a></h2>
<h2 align="right"><a href="contacts.html">How To Reach Us</a></h2>
```

OUTPUT

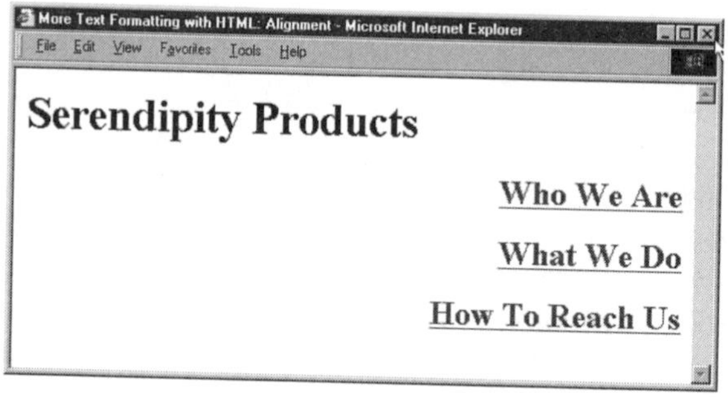

FIGURE 6.13

The output in Internet Explorer.

More Text Formatting with HTML: Alignment - Microsoft Internet Explorer

File   Edit   View   Favorites   Tools   Help

Serendipity Products

<u>Who We Are</u>

<u>What We Do</u>

<u>How To Reach Us</u>

Aligning Blocks of Elements

A slightly more flexible method of aligning text elements is to use the <div> tag. <div> stands for division. <div> includes several attributes, which are listed in Appendix B. Among these attributes is align (deprecated in HTML 4.0), which aligns elements to the left, right, or center just as it does for headings and paragraphs. Unlike using alignments in individual elements, however, <div> is used to surround a block of HTML tags of any kind, and it affects all the tags and text inside the opening and closing tags. Two advantages of div over the align attribute follow:

- div needs to be used only once, rather than include align repeatedly in several different tags.
- div can be used to align anything (headings, paragraphs, quotes, images, tables, and so on); the align attribute is available only on a limited number of tags.

To align a block of HTML code, surround that code by opening and closing <div> tags, and then include the align attribute in the opening tag. As in other tags, align can have the values left, right, or center, as shown in the following:

```
<h1 align="left">Serendipity Products</h1>
<div align="right">
<h2><a href="who.html">Who We Are</a></h2>
<h2><a href="products.html">What We Do</a></h2>
<h2><a href="contacts.html">How To Reach Us</a></h2>
</div>
```

All the HTML between the two <div> tags will be aligned according to the value of the align attribute. If individual align attributes appear in headings or paragraphs inside the div, those values will override the global div setting.

Note that <div> is not itself a paragraph type. You still need regular element tags (<p>, <h1>, <ul>, <blockquote>, and so on) inside the opening and closing <div> tags.

In addition to <div>, you also can use the centering tag <center>. The HTML 3.2 specification defines it as a short version of <div align="center">. The <center> tag acts identically to <div align="center">, centering all the HTML content inside the opening and closing tags. You put the <center> tag before the text you want centered and the </center> tag after you're done, like the following:

```
<center>
<h1>Northridge Paints, Inc.</h2>
<p>We don't just paint the town red.</p>
</center>
```

For consistency's sake, you're probably better off using <div> and align to achieve centering.

6

Fonts and Font Sizes

The <font> tag, part of HTML 3.2 but deprecated in HTML 4.0 (again, in favor of style sheets), is used to control the characteristics of a given set of characters not covered by the character styles. Originally, <font> was used only to control the font size of the characters it surrounds, but it was then extended to allow you to change the font itself and the color of those characters.

In this section, I'll discuss fonts and font sizes. You'll learn about changing the font color in Chapter 7.

Changing the Font Size

The most common use of the <font> tag is to change the size of the font for a character, word, phrase, or on any range of text. The <font>...</font> tags enclose the text, and the size attribute indicates the size to which the font is to be changed. The values of size are 1 to 7, with 3 being the default size. Consider the following example:

```
<p>Bored with your plain old font?
<font size="5">Change it.</font></p>
```

Figure 6.14 shows the typical font sizes for each value of size.

FIGURE 6.14

Font sizes in Internet Explorer.

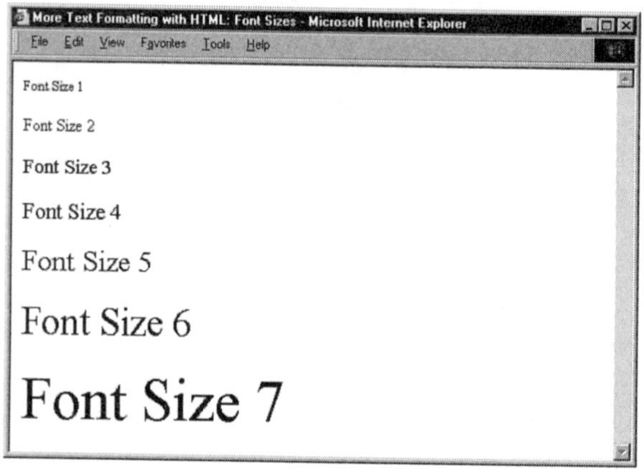

You can also specify the size in the <font> tag as a relative value by using the + or - characters in the value for size. Because the default size is 3, you can change relative font sizes in the range from to -3 to +4, as in the following:

```
<p>Change the <font size="+2">Font</font> size again.</p>
```

Here, the word Font (inside the <font> tags) will be two size levels larger than the default font when you view that example in a browser that supports this feature.

Relative font sizes actually are based on a value that you can define by using the <basefont>tag, another tag that is deprecated in the HTML 4.0 specification. The <basefont> tag also has the required attribute size. size can have a value of 1 to 7. All relative font changes in the document after the <basefont> tag will be relative to that value.

Try to avoid using the <font> tag to simulate the larger-font effect of the HTML content-based tags such as the heading tags (<h1>, <h2>, and so on) or to emphasize a particular word or phrase. If your documents are viewed in browsers that don't support this feature, you'll lose the font sizes, and your text will appear as if it were any other paragraph. If you stick to the content-based tags, however, a heading is a heading, regardless of where you view it. Try to limit your use of the <font> tag to small amounts of special effects.

Changing the Font Face

Netscape introduced the <font> tag to HTML with its 1.0 browser. Microsoft's Internet Explorer, playing the same game, extended the <font> tag to include the face attribute. The tag was made a part of HTML 3.2, but with HTML 4.0, the preferred method is to use style sheets to specify the fonts you use.

The face attribute takes as its value a set of font names, surrounded by quotation marks and separated by commas. When a browser that supports face interprets a page with face in it, it will search the system for the given font names one at a time. If it can't find the first one, it'll try the second, and then the third, and so on, until it finds a font that actually is installed on the system. If the browser cannot find any of the listed fonts, the default font will be used instead. So, for example, the following text would be rendered in Futura. If Futura is not available, the browser will try Helvetica; it then will fall back on the default if Helvetica is not available.

```
<p><font face="Futura,Helvetica">Sans Serif fonts are fonts without
the small "ticks" on the strokes of the characters. </font></p>
```

If you use the face attribute, keep in mind that currently some older browsers don't support it, so it may be unavailable to a large part of your audience. Also, many fonts have different names on different systems; for example, plain old Times is Times on some systems, Times Roman on others, and Times New Roman elsewhere. Because of the varying names of fonts and the lack of widespread support for the face attribute, changing the font name should be used only as an optional presentation-only feature rather than one to be relied on in your pages.

The Dreaded <blink>

You won't find the <blink> tag listed in Netscape's official documentation of its attributes. The capability to cause text to blink was included in Netscape as a hidden, undocumented feature or Easter egg. Still, many pages on the Web seem to use this feature.

The `<blink>...</blink>` tags cause the text between the opening and closing tags to have a blinking effect. Depending on the version of Netscape you're using, the text itself can vanish and come back at regular intervals, or an ugly gray or white block may appear and disappear behind the text. Blink usually is used to draw attention to a portion of the page.

The problem with blink is that it provides too much emphasis. Because it repeats, the blink continues to draw attention to that one spot and, in some cases, can be so distracting that it can make absorbing any of the other content of the page nearly impossible. The use of `<blink>` is greatly discouraged by most Web designers (including myself) because many people find it extremely intrusive, ugly, and annoying. Blink is the HTML equivalent of fingernails on a blackboard.

If you must use blink, use it sparingly (no more than a few words on a page). Also, be aware that in some versions of Netscape, blinking can be turned off. If you want to emphasize a word or phrase, you should use a more conventional way of doing so, in addition to (or in place of) blink, because you cannot guarantee that blink will be available, even if your readers are using Netscape to view your pages.

`<nobr>` and `<wbr>`

The `<nobr>...</nobr>` element is the opposite of the `<br>` tag. The text inside the `<nobr>` tags always remains on one line, even if it would have wrapped to two more lines without the `<nobr>`. The `<nobr>` tag is used for words or phrases that must be kept together on one line, but be careful: Long unbreakable lines can look really strange on your page, and if they are longer than the page width, they might extend beyond the right edge of the screen.

The `<wbr>` tag (word break) indicates an appropriate breaking point within a line (typically one inside a `<nobr>...</nobr>` sequence). Unlike `<br>`, which forces a break, `<wbr>` is used only where it is appropriate to do so. If the line will fit on the screen just fine, the `<wbr>` is ignored. In XHTML 1.0, add closure to the tag by using the syntax of `<wbr />`.

Neither `<nobr>` nor `<wbr>` are part of HTML 3.2 or HTML 4.0. They are extensions introduced by Netscape, but are supported in both Netscape Navigator 4 and Internet Explorer 4.

Exercise 6.1: Creating a Real HTML Page

To Do

Here's your chance to apply what you've learned and create a real Web page. No more disjointed or overly silly examples. The Web page you'll create in this section is a real one, suitable for use in the real world (or the real world of the Web, at least).

Your task for this example is to design and create a home page for a bookstore called The Bookworm, which specializes in old and rare books.

Plan the Page

In Chapter 2, "Get Organized," I mentioned that planning your Web page before writing it usually makes building and maintaining the elements easier. So, first consider the content you want to include on this page. The following are some ideas for topics for this page:

- The address and phone number of the bookstore
- A short description of the bookstore and why it is unique
- Recent titles and authors
- Upcoming events

Now, come up with some ideas for the content you're going to link to from this page. Each title in a list of recently acquired books seems like a logical candidate. You also can create links to more information about each book, its author and publisher, its pricing, maybe even its availability.

The Upcoming Events section might suggest a potential series of links, depending on how much you want to say about each event. If you have only a sentence or two about each one, describing them on this page might make more sense than linking them to another page. Why make your readers wait for each new page to load for just a couple of lines of text?

Other interesting links may arise in the text itself, but for now, starting with the basic link plan will be enough.

Begin with a Framework

Next, create the framework that all HTML files must include: the document structuring commands, a title, and some initial headings. Note that the title is descriptive but short; you can save the longer title for the <h1> element in the body of the text. The four <h2> subheadings help you define the four main sections you'll have on your Web page.

```
<!DOCTYPE html PUBLIC "-//W3C//DTD XHTML 1.0 Transitional//EN"
  "http://www.w3.org/TR/xhtml1/DTD/transitional.dtd">
<html>
```

6

```
<head>
<title>The Bookworm Bookshop</title>
</head>
<body>
<h1>The Bookworm: A Better Book Store</h1>
<h2>Contents</h2>
<h2>About the Bookworm Bookshop</h2>
<h2>Recent Titles (as of 11-Nov-99)</h2>
<h2>Upcoming Events</h2>
</body>
</html>
```

Each of the headings you've placed on your page will mark the beginning of a particular section on your page. You'll create an anchor at each of the topic headings, so that you can jump from section to section with ease. The anchor names are simple: top (for the main heading), contents (for the table of contents), and about, recent, and upcoming for the three subsections on the page. The revised code looks like the following with the anchors in place:

```
<!DOCTYPE html PUBLIC "-//W3C//DTD XHTML 1.0 Transitional//EN"
 "http://www.w3.org/TR/xhtml1/DTD/transitional.dtd">
<html>
<head>
<title>The Bookworm Bookshop</title>
</head>
<body>
<a name="top"><h1>The Bookworm: A Better Book Store</h1></a>
<a name="contents"><h2>Contents</h2></a>
<a name="about"><h2>About the Bookworm Bookshop</h2></a>
<a name="recent"><h2>Recent Titles (as of 11-Nov-99)</h2></a>
<a name="upcoming"><h2>Upcoming Events</h2></a>
</body>
</html>
```

Add Content

Now begin adding the content. Because you're undertaking a literary endeavor, starting the page with a nice quote about old books would be a nice touch. Since you're adding a quote, you can use the <blockquote> tag to make it stand out as such. Also, the name of the poem is a citation, so use <cite> there, too.

Insert the following code on the line after the level 1 heading:

```
<blockquote>
"Old books are best--how tale and rhyme<br />
Float with us down the stream of time!"<br />
- Clarence Urmy, <cite>Old Songs are Best</cite>
</blockquote>
```

▼ Immediately following the quote, add the address for the bookstore. This is a simple paragraph, with the lines separated by line breaks, like the following:

```
<p>The Bookworm Bookshop<br />
1345 Applewood Dr<br />
Springfield, CA 94325<br />
(415) 555-0034
</p>
```

Adding the Table of Contents

The page you are creating will take a lot of scrolling to get from the top of the page to the bottom. A nice enhancement is to add a small table of contents at the beginning of the page, which lists the sections in a bulleted list. If a reader clicks one of the links in the table of contents, he or she will automatically jump to the section that is of most interest to him or her. Because you already created the anchors, it's easy to see where the links will take you.

You already have the heading for the table of contents. You need to add the bulleted list and a horizontal rule. Then you create the links to the other sections on the page. The code looks like the following:

```
<a name="contents"><h2>Contents</h2></a>
<ul>
  <li><a href="#about">About the Bookworm Bookshop</a></li>
  <li><a href ="#recent">Recent Titles</a></li>
  <li><a href ="#upcoming">Upcoming Events</a></li>
</ul>
<hr />
```

Figure 6.15 shows an example of the introductory portion of the Bookworm Bookshop page as it appears in Internet Explorer.

FIGURE 6.15

The top section of the Bookworm Bookshop page.

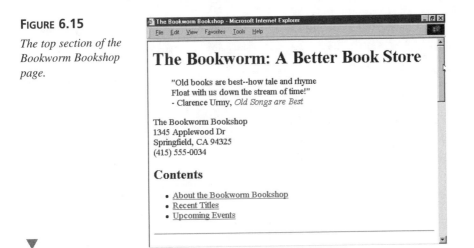

▼

▼ **Creating the Description of the Bookstore**

Now you come to the first descriptive subheading on the page, which you have already added. This section gives a description of the bookstore. After the heading (shown in the first line in the following example), I've arranged the description to include a list of features, to make the features stand out from the text better:

```
<a name="about"><h2>About the Bookworm Bookshop</h2></a>
<p>Since 1933, The Bookworm Bookshop has offered
rare and hard-to-find titles for the discerning reader.
The Bookworm offers:</p>
<ul>
<li>Friendly, knowledgeable, and courteous help</li>
<li>Free coffee and juice for our customers</li>
<li>A well-lit reading room so you can "try before you buy"</li>
<li>Four friendly cats: Esmerelda, Catherine, Dulcinea and Beatrice</li>
</ul>
```

Add a note about the hours the store is open, and emphasize the actual numbers:

```
<p>Our hours are <strong>10am to 9pm</strong> weekdays,
<strong>noon to 7</strong> on weekends.</p>
```

Then, end the section with links to the Table of Contents and the top of the page, followed by a horizontal rule to end the section:

```
<p><a href="#contents">Back to Contents</a> ¦ <a href="#top">Back to Top</a></p>
<hr />
```

Figure 6.16 shows you what the "About the Bookworm Bookshop" section looks like in Internet Explorer.

FIGURE 6.16

The About the Bookworm Bookshop section.

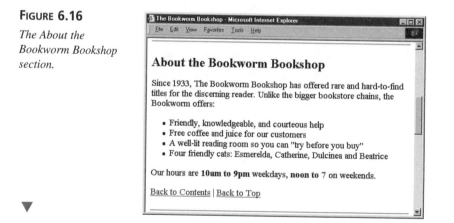

▼

▼ Creating the Recent Titles Section

The Recent Titles section itself is a classic link menu, as I described earlier in this section. Here you can put the list of titles in an unordered list, with the titles themselves as citations (by using the `<cite>` tag). End the section with another horizontal rule.

After the Recent Titles heading (shown in the first line in the following example), enter the following code:

```
<a name="recent"><h2>Recent Titles (as of 11-Nov-99)</h2></a>
<ul>
<li>Sandra Bellweather, <cite>Belladonna</cite></li>
<li>Jonathan Tin, <cite>20-Minute Meals for One</cite></li>
<li>Maxwell Burgess, <cite>Legion of Thunder</cite></li>
<li>Alison Caine, <cite>Banquo's Ghost</cite></li>
</ul>
<hr />
```

Now, add the anchor tags to create the links. How far should the link extend? Should it include the whole line (author and title), or just the title of the book? This decision is a matter of preference, but I like to link only as much as necessary to make sure the link stands out from the text. I prefer this approach to overwhelming the text. Here, I've linked only the titles of the books. At the same time, I've also added links to the Table of Contents and the top of the page:

```
<a name="recent"><h2>Recent Titles (as of 11-Nov-99)</h2></a>
<ul>
<li>Sandra Bellweather, <a href="belladonna.html">
<cite>Belladonna</cite></a></li>
<li>Johnathan Tin, <a href="20minmeals.html">
<cite>20-Minute Meals for One</cite></a></li>
<li>Maxwell Burgess, <a href="legion.html">
<cite>Legion of Thunder</cite></a></li>
<li>Alison Caine, <a href="banquo.html">
<cite>Banquo's Ghost</cite></a></li>
</ul>
<p><a href="#contents">Back to Contents</a> ¦ <a href="#top">Back to Top</a></p>
<hr />
```

Note that I've put the `<cite>` tag inside the link tag `<a>`. I could have just as easily put it outside the anchor tag; character style tags can go just about anywhere. But as I mentioned once before, be careful not to overlap tags. Your browser may not be able to understand what is going on. In other words, don't do the following:

```
<a href="banquo.html"><cite>Banquo's Ghost</a></cite>
```

Take a look at how the Recent Titles section appears in Internet Explorer. An example is
▼ shown in Figure 6.17.

6

FIGURE 6.17

*The Recent Titles
section.*

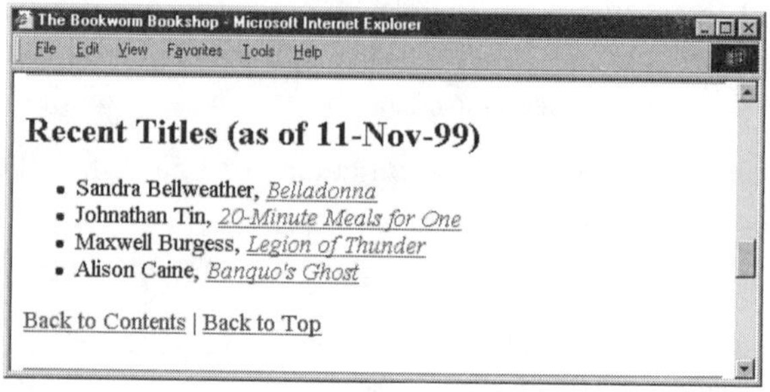

Completing the Upcoming Events Section

Next, move on to the Upcoming Events section. In the planning stages, you weren't sure
whether this would be another link menu or whether the content would work better
solely on this page. Again, this decision is a matter of preference. Here, because the
amount of extra information is minimal, creating links for just a couple of sentences
doesn't make much sense. So, for this section, create a menu list (by using the <ul> tag)
that results in short paragraphs (bulleted in some browsers). I've boldfaced a few phrases
near the beginning of each paragraph. These phrases emphasize a summary of the event
itself so that each paragraph can be scanned quickly and ignored if the readers aren't
interested.

As in the previous sections, you end the section with links to the top and to the contents,
followed by a horizontal rule.

```
<a name="upcoming"><h2>Upcoming Events</h2></a>
<ul>
<li><b>The Wednesday Evening Book Review</b> meets, appropriately, on
Wednesday evenings at 7 pm for coffee and a round-table discussion.
Call the Bookworm for information on joining the group.</li>
<li><b>The Children's Hour</b> happens every Saturday at 1 pm and includes
reading, games, and other activities. Cookies and milk are served.</li>
<li><b>Carole Fenney</b> will be at the Bookworm on Friday, September 17,
to read from her book of poems <cite>Spiders in the Web.</cite></li>
<li><b>The Bookworm will be closed</b> October 1 to remove a family
of bats that has nested in the tower. We like the company, but not
the mess they leave behind!</li>
</ul>
<p><a href="#contents">Back to Contents</a> ¦ <a href="#top">Back to
Top</a></p>
<hr />
```

Sign the Page

To finish, sign what you have so that your readers know who did the work. Here, I've
separated the signature from the text with a rule line. I've also included the most recent

▼ revision date, my name as the *Webmaster* (cute Web jargon meaning the person in charge of a Web site), and a basic copyright (with a copyright symbol indicated by the numeric escape ©):

```
<hr />
<address>
Last Updated: 11-Nov-99<br />
Webmaster: Laura Lemay lemay@bookworm.com<br />
&#169; copyright 1999 the Bookworm<br />
</address>
```

Figure 6.18 shows the bottom portion of the page, which includes the Upcoming Events section and the page signature as they look in Internet Explorer.

FIGURE 6.18

The Upcoming Events section and the page signature.

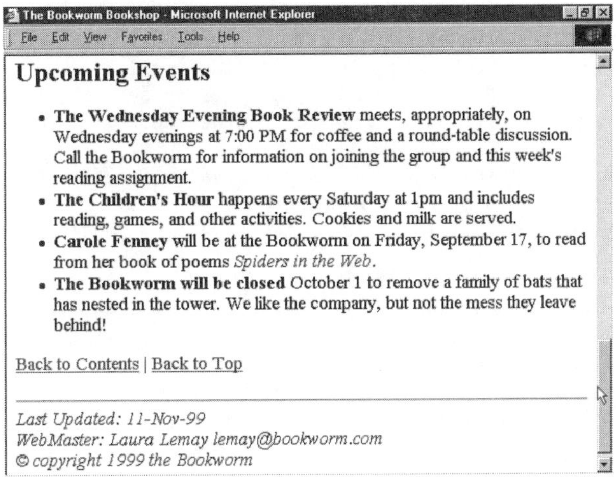

Review What You've Got

Here's the HTML code for the page so far:

```
<!DOCTYPE html PUBLIC "-//W3C//DTD XHTML 1.0 Transitional//EN"
  "http://www.w3.org/TR/xhtml1/DTD/transitional.dtd">
<html>
<head>
<title>The Bookworm Bookshop</title>
</head>
<body>
<a name="top"><h1>The Bookworm: A Better Book Store</h1></a>
<blockquote>
"Old books are best--how tale and rhyme<br />
Float with us down the stream of time!"<br />
- Clarence Urmy, <cite>Old Songs are Best</cite>
</blockquote>
```
▼ `<p>The Bookworm Bookshop<br />`

```
1345 Applewood Dr<br />
Springfield, CA 94325<br />
(415) 555-0034
</p>
<a name="contents"><h2>Contents</h2></a>
<ul>
  <li><a href="#about">About the Bookworm Bookshop</a></li>
  <li><a href ="#recent">Recent Titles</a></li>
  <li><a href ="#upcoming">Upcoming Events</a></li>
</ul>
<hr />
<a name="about"><h2>About the Bookworm Bookshop</h2></a>
<p>Since 1933, the Bookworm Bookshop has offered
rare and hard-to-find titles for the discerning reader.
The Bookworm offers:</p>
<ul>
  <li>Friendly, knowledgeable, and courteous help</li>
  <li>Free coffee and juice for our customers</li>
  <li>A well-lit reading room so you can "try before you buy"</li>
  <li>Four friendly cats: Esmerelda, Catherine, Dulcinea and Beatrice</li>
</ul>
<p>Our hours are <strong>10am to 9pm</strong> weekdays,
<strong>noon to 7</strong> on weekends.</p>
<p><a href="#contents">Back to Contents</a> ¦ <a href="#top">Back to
Top</a></p>
<hr />
<a name="recent"><h2>Recent Titles (as of 11-Nov-99)</h2></a>
<ul>
  <li>Sandra Bellweather, <a href="belladonna.html">
    <cite>Belladonna</cite></a></li>
  <li>Johnathan Tin, <a href="20minmeals.html">
    <cite>20-Minute Meals for One</cite></a></li>
  <li>Maxwell Burgess, <a href="legion.html">
    <cite>Legion of Thunder</cite></a></li>
  <li>Alison Caine, <a href="banquo.html">
    <cite>Banquo's Ghost</cite></a></li>
</ul>
<p><a href="#contents">Back to Contents</a> ¦ <a href="#top">Back to
Top</a></p>
<hr />
<a name="upcoming"><h2>Upcoming Events</h2></a>
<ul>
  <li><b>The Wednesday Evening Book Review</b> meets, appropriately, on
      Wednesday evenings at 7 pm for coffee and a round-table discussion.
      Call the Bookworm for information on joining the group.</li>
  <li><b>The Children's Hour</b> happens every Saturday at 1 pm and includes
      reading, games, and other activities. Cookies and milk are served.</li>
  <li><b>Carole Fenney</b> will be at the Bookworm on Friday, September 17,
      to read from her book of poems <cite>Spiders in the Web.</cite></li>
  <li><b>The Bookworm will be closed</b> October 1 to remove a family
      of bats that has nested in the tower. We like the company, but not
      the mess they leave behind!</li>
```

```
</ul>
<p><a href="#contents">Back to Contents</a> ¦ <a href="#top">Back to
Top</a></p>
<hr />
<address>
Last Updated: 11-Nov-99<br />
WebMaster: Laura Lemay lemay@bookworm.com<br />
&#169; copyright 1999 the Bookworm<br />
</address>
</body>
</html>
```

So, now you have some headings, some text, some topics, and some links, which form the basis for an excellent Web page. At this point, with most of the content in place, consider what else you might want to create links for or what other features you might want to add to this page.

For example, in the introductory section, a note was made of the four cats owned by the bookstore. Although you didn't plan for them in the original organization, you could easily create Web pages describing each cat (and showing pictures), and then link them back to this page, one link (and one page) per cat.

Is describing the cats important? As the designer of the page, that's up to you to decide. You could link all kinds of things from this page if you have interesting reasons to link them (and something to link to). Link the bookstore's address to the local Chamber of Commerce. Link the quote to an online encyclopedia of quotes. Link the note about free coffee to the Coffee Home Page.

I'll talk more about good things to link (and how not to get carried away when you link) in Chapter 16, "Writing and Designing Web Pages: Dos and Don'ts." My reason for bringing up this point here is that after you have some content in place in your Web pages, opportunities for extending the pages and linking to other places may arise, opportunities you didn't think of when you created your original plan. So, when you're just about finished with a page, stop and review what you have, both in the plan and in your Web page.

For the purposes of this example, stop here and stick with the links you've got. You're close enough to being done that I don't want to make this chapter longer than it already is!

Test the Result

Now that all the code is in place, you can preview the results in a browser. Figures 6.15 through 6.18 show how it looks in Internet Explorer. Actually, these figures show how the page looks after you fix the spelling errors and forgotten closing tags and other

6

▼ strange bugs that always seem to creep into an HTML file the first time you create it. These problems always seems to happen no matter how good you get at creating Web pages. If you use an HTML editor or some other help tool, your job will be easier, but you'll always seem to find mistakes. That's what previewing is for—so you can catch the problems before you actually make the document available to other people.

Get Fancy

Everything I've included on the page up to this point has been plain-vanilla HTML 2.0, so it's readable in all browsers and will look pretty much the same in all browsers. After you get the page to this point, however, you can add additional formatting tags and attributes that won't change the page for many readers, but might make it look a little fancier in browsers that do support these attributes.

So what attributes do you want to use? I chose two:

- Centering the title of the page, the quote, and the bookstore's address
- Making a slight font size change to the address itself

To center the topmost part of the page, you can use the `<div>` tag around the heading, the quote, and the bookshop's address, as in the following:

```
<div align="center">
<a name="top"><h1>The Bookworm: A Better Book Store</h1></a>
<blockquote>
"Old books are best--how tale and rhyme<br />
Float with us down the stream of time!"<br />
- Clarence Urmy, <cite>Old Songs are Best</cite>
</blockquote>
<p>The Bookworm Bookshop<br />
1345 Applewood Dr<br />
Springfield, CA 94325<br />
(415) 555-0034
</p>
</div>
```

To change the font size of the address, add a `<font>` tag around the lines for the address:

```
<p><font size="+1">The Bookworm Bookshop<br />
1345 Applewood Dr<br />
Springfield, CA 94325<br />
(415) 555-0034
</font></p>
```

Figure 6.19 shows the final result, with attributes, in Internet Explorer. Note that neither of these changes affects the readability of the page in browsers that don't support `<div>`
▼ or `<font>`; the page still works just fine without them. It just looks different.

FIGURE **6.19**

The final Bookworm home page, with additional attributes.

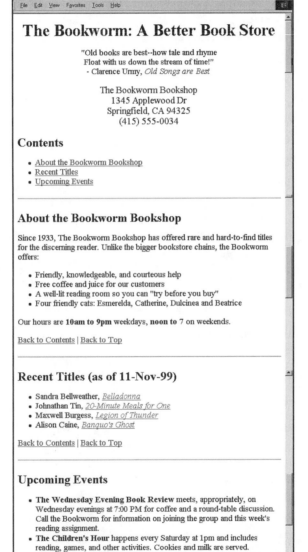

▼   When should you use text-formatting attributes? The general rule that I like to follow is
    to use these tags only when using them will not interfere with other, generally older,
    browsers. Similarly, while HTML 4.0 officially encourages Web page authors to use style
    sheets rather than text formatting tags such as `font` and attributes such as `align`, only the
    most recent generation of browsers support style sheets. So, for the time being, if you
    want to spiff up the appearance of your text, you'll need to continue to use these tags and
    attributes.

    You'll learn more about formatting tags and attributes as well as how to design well with
▲   them in Chapter 16.

Summary

Tags, tags, and more tags! In this chapter, you learned about most of the remaining tags
in the HTML language for presenting text and quite of a few of the tags for additional
text formatting and presentation. You also put together a real-life HTML home page. You
could stop now and create quite presentable Web pages. But more cool stuff is to come,
so don't put down the book yet.

Table 6.2 presents a quick summary of all the tags and attributes you've learned about in
this chapter that are included in the HTML 4.0 specification.

Table 6.2   HTML Tags from Chapter 6

Tag	Attribute	Use
`<address>...</address>`		A "signature" for each Web page; typically occurs near the bottom of each document and contains contact or copyright information.
`<b>...</b>`		Bold text.
`<big>...</big>`		Text in a larger font than the text around it.
`<blink>...</blink>`		Causes the enclosed text to have a blinking effect (Netscape only).
`<blockquote>...</blockquote>`		A quotation longer than a few words.
`<cite>...</cite>`		A citation.
`<code>...</code>`		A code sample.
`<dfn>...</dfn>`		A definition, or a term about to be defined.
`<em>...</em>`		Emphasized text.

Tag	Attribute	Use
`<i>...</i>`		Italic text.
`<kbd>...</kbd>`		Text to be typed in by the user.
`<pre>...</pre>`		Preformatted text; all spaces, tabs, and returns are retained. Text also is printed in a monospaced font.
`<s>...</s>`		Strikethrough text. (Deprecated in HTML 4.0.)
`<samp>...</samp>`		Sample text.
`<small>...</small>`		Text in a smaller font than the text around it.
`<strong>...</strong>`		Strongly emphasized text.
`<sub>...</sub>`		Subscript text.
`<sup>...</sup>`		Superscript text.
`<tt>...</tt>`		Text in typewriter font (a monospaced font such as Courier).
`<u>...</u>`		Underlined text.
`<var>...</var>`		A variable name.
`<hr>`		A horizontal rule line at the given position in the text. There is no closing tag in HTML for `<hr>`; for XHTML, add a space and forward slash (/) at the end of the tag and its attributes (for example: `<hr size="2" width="75%" />`)
	`size`	The thickness of the rule, in pixels. (Deprecated in HTML 4.0.)
	`width`	The width of the rule, either in exact pixels or as a percentage of page width (for example, 50 percent). (Deprecated in HTML 4.0.)
	`align`	The alignment of the rule on the page. Possible values are `left`, `right`, and `center`. (Deprecated in HTML 4.0.)
	`noshade`	Displays the rule without three-dimensional shading. (Deprecated in HTML 4.0.)

continues

6

Table 6.2 continued

Tag	Attribute	Use
` `		A line break; starts the next character onto the next line (but does not create a new paragraph or list item). There is no closing tag in HTML for ` `; for XHTML, add a space and forward slash (`/`) at the end of the tag and its attributes (for example: `<br clear="left" />`).
`<nobr>...</nobr>`		Does not wrap the enclosed text (non-standard; supported by Netscape and Internet Explorer).
`<wbr>`		Wraps the text at this point only if necessary (non-standard; supported by Netscape and Internet Explorer). Add a space and forward slash at the end of the tag for XHTML 1.0.
`<p>`, `<h1-6>`	`align="left"`	Left-justifies the text within that paragraph or heading. (Deprecated in HTML 4.0.)
	`align="right"`	Right-justifies the text within that paragraph or heading. (Deprecated in HTML 4.0.)
	`align="center"`	Centers the text within that paragraph or heading. (Deprecated in HTML 4.0.)
`<div>...</div>`	`align="left"`	Left-justifies all the content between the opening and closing tags. (Deprecated in HTML 4.0.)
	`align="right"`	Right-justifies all the content between the opening and closing tags. (Deprecated in HTML 4.0.)
	`align="center"`	Centers all the content between the opening and closing tags. (Deprecated in HTML 4.0.)
`<center>...</center>`		Centers all the content between the opening and closing tags. (Deprecated in HTML 4.0.)

Tag	Attribute	Use
`<font>...</font>`	`size`	The size of the font to change to, either from 1 to 7 (default is 3) or as a relative number using `+N` or `-N`. Relative font sizes are based on the value of `<basefont>`. (Deprecated in HTML 4.0.)
	`face`	The name of the font to change to, as a list of fonts to choose from. (Deprecated in HTML 4.0.)
`<basefont>`	`size`	The default font size on which relative font size changes are based. (Deprecated in HTML 4.0.) There is no closing tag in HTML for `<basefont>`; for XHTML, add a space and forward slash (`/`) at the end of the tag and its attributes (for example: `<basefont size="-1" />`.

Workshop

Here you are at the close of another chapter (a long one!) and facing yet another workshop. You covered a lot of ground today, so I'll try to keep the questions easy. There are a couple of exercises that focus on building some additional pages for your Web site. Ready?

Q&A

Q If line breaks appear in HTML, can I also do page breaks?

A HTML doesn't have a page break tag. Consider what the term "page" means in a Web document. If each document on the Web is a single "page," the only way to produce a page break is to split your HTML document into separate files and link them.

Even within a single document, browsers have no concept of a page; each HTML document simply scrolls by continuously. If you consider a single screen a page, you still cannot have what results in a page break in HTML. The screen size in each browser is different, and is based on not only the browser itself but the size of the monitor on which it runs, the number of lines defined, the font being currently used, and other factors that you cannot control from HTML.

6

When you're designing your Web pages, don't get too hung up on the concept of a "page" the way it exists in paper documents. Remember, HTML's strength is its flexibility for multiple kinds of systems and formats. Think instead in terms of creating small chunks of information and how they link together to form a complete presentation.

Q How can I include em dashes or curly quotes (typesetter's quotes) in my HTML files?

A You can't. Neither em dashes nor curly quotes are defined as part of the ISO-Latin-1 character set, and therefore those characters are not available in HTML at the moment. HTML 4.0 promises to fix the promise with its support for Unicode, which provides access to a much richer character set.

Q "Blink is the HTML equivalent of fingernails on a blackboard"? Isn't that a little harsh?

A I couldn't resist. :)

Many people absolutely detest `blink` and will tell you so at a moment's notice, with a passion usually reserved for politics and religion. Some people might ignore your pages simply because you use blink. Why alienate your audience and distract from your content for the sake of a cheesy effect?

Quiz

1. What are the differences between logical character styles and physical character styles?

2. What are some things that the `<pre>` (preformatted text) tag can be used for?

3. What is the most common use of the `<address>` tag?

4. Older versions of HTML provided ways to align and center text on a Web page. What is the recommended way to accomplish these tasks in HTML 4.0?

5. Without looking at Table 6.2, list all eight logical style tags and what they're used for. Explain why you should use the logical tags instead of the physical tags.

Answers

1. Logical styles indicate how the highlighted text is used (citation, definition, code, and so on). Physical styles indicate how the highlighted text is displayed (bold, italic, or monospaced, for example).

2. Preformatted text can be used for text-based tables, code examples, ASCII art, and any other Web page content that requires extra spaces to align characters.

3. The <address> tag is most commonly used for signature-like entities on a Web page. These include the author of the Web page, contact information, dates, copyright notices, or warnings. Address information usually appears at the bottom of a Web page.

4. Alignment and centering of text can be accomplished with style sheets, which is the recommended approach in HTML 4.0.

5. The eight logical styles are: <em> (for emphasized text), <strong> (for bold text), <code> (for programming code), <samp> (similar to <code>), <kbd> (to indicate user keyboard input), <var> (for variable names), <dfn> (for definitions), and <cite> (for short quotes or citations). Logical tags rely on the browser to format their appearance.

Exercises

1. Now that you've had a taste of building your first really thorough Web page, take a stab at your own home page. What can you include that would entice people to dig in deeper into your pages? Don't forget to include links to other pages on your site.

2. Here's a silly exercise to get your creative juices flowing. You have invented a product that *guarantees* that no sock will lose its partner in the washer or dryer. Design a page that touts the advantages of this product, and why no home should be without it! Use different character styles to accentuate or highlight the most important points on the page.

6

PART 3

Web Graphics

DAY 7

Using Images, Color, and Backgrounds

If you've been struggling to keep up with all the HTML tags I've been flinging at you over the last couple of days, you can breathe easier: This section's chapters will be easier. In fact, today you're going to learn very few new HTML tags. The focus for this section is on adding images and color to your Web pages. In this chapter, you'll learn about the HTML codes for adding images, color, and backgrounds. In particular, you'll learn the following:

- The kinds of images you can use in Web pages
- How to include images on your Web page, either alone or alongside text
- How to use images as clickable links
- How to use external images as a substitute for or in addition to inline images
- How to provide alternatives for browsers that cannot view images
- How to use image dimensions and scaling, and how to provide image previews

- How to change the font and background colors in your Web page
- How to use images for tiled page backgrounds
- How (and when) to use images in your Web pages

After this chapter, you'll know all you need to know about adding images to your Web pages.

Images on the Web

Images for Web pages fall into two general classes: inline images and external images. Inline images appear directly on a Web page among the text and links. They are loaded automatically when you load the page itself—assuming, of course, that you have a graphical browser and that you have automatic image loading turned on. External images are not directly displayed when you load a page. They are downloaded only at the request of your readers, usually on the other side of a link. You don't need a graphical browser to view external images; you can download an image file just fine using a text-only browser and then use an image editor or viewer to see that image later. You'll learn how to use both inline and external images in this chapter.

NEW TERM *Inline* images appear on a Web page along with text and links and are automatically loaded when the page itself is retrieved.

NEW TERM *External* images are stored separate from the Web page and are loaded only on demand, for example, as the result of a link.

Regardless of whether you're using inline or external images, those images must be in a specific format. For inline images, that image has to be in one of two formats: GIF or JPEG. GIF is the more popular standard, and more browsers can view inline GIF files than JPEG files. Support for JPEG is becoming more widespread but is still not as popular as GIF, so sticking with GIF is the safest method of making sure your images can be viewed by the widest possible audience. You'll learn more about external images and the formats you can use for them later in this chapter.

For this chapter, assume that you already have an image you want to put on your Web page. How do you get it into GIF or JPEG format so that your page can view it? Most image-editing programs such as Adobe Photoshop (http://www.adobe.com/), Paint Shop Pro (http://www.jasc.com/), or CorelDRAW (http://www.corel.com/) provide ways to convert between image formats. You may have to look under an option for Save As or Export in order to find it. Freeware and shareware programs that do nothing but convert between image formats are also available for most platforms. Many shareware and demo versions of image editing software are available to choose from at http://www.download.com (search for *image editors* using the software platform of your choice).

> **Note** You'll learn more about image editing programs in Day 8, "Creating Animated Graphics."

To save files in GIF format, look for an option called CompuServe GIF, GIF87, GIF89, or just plain GIF. Any of them will work. If you're saving your files as JPEG, usually the option will be simply JPEG.

Remember how your HTML files had to have an .html or .htm extension for them to work properly? Image files have extensions, too. For GIF files, the extension is .gif. For JPEG files, the extension is either .jpg or .jpeg; either will work fine.

> **Note** Some image editors will try to save files with extensions in all caps (.GIF, .JPEG). Although they are the correct extensions, image names, like HTML filenames, are case sensitive, so GIF is not the same extension as gif. The case of the extension isn't important when you're testing on your local system, but it will be when you move your files to the server. So use lowercase if you possibly can.

Inline Images in HTML: The `<img>` Tag

After you have an image in GIF or JPEG format ready to go, you can include it in your Web page. Inline images are indicated in HTML by using the `<img>` tag. The `<img>` tag, like the `<hr>` and `<br>` tags, has no closing tag in HTML. For XHTML, you add an extra space and forward slash to the end of the tag and its attributes.

The `<img>` tag has many different attributes that allow different ways of presenting and handling inline images. Many of these attributes are part of HTML 3.2 or HTML 4.0 and may not be available in some older browsers. Still others have been deprecated in favor of using style sheets with the HTML 4.0 and XHTML 1.0 specifications.

The most important attribute to the `<img>` tag is src. The src attribute indicates the filename or URL of the image you want to include, in quotation marks. The pathname to the file uses the same pathname rules as the href attribute in links. So, for a GIF file named image.gif in the same directory as this file, you can use the following tag:

```
<img src="image.gif" />
```

For an image file one directory up from the current directory, use this tag:

```
<img src="../image.gif" />
```

And so on, using the same rules as for page names in the href part of the `<a>` tag.

7

Adding an Image Alternative

Images can turn a simple text-only Web page into a glorious visual feast. But what happens if someone is reading your Web page from a text-only browser, or what if he or she has image loading turned off so that all your carefully crafted graphics appear as plain generic icons? All of a sudden, that glorious visual feast doesn't look as nice. And, worse, if you haven't taken these possibilities into consideration while designing your Web page, that portion of your audience might not be able to read or use your work.

You can come up with a simple solution to one of these problems. By using the alt attribute of the <img> tag, you can substitute something meaningful in place of the image on browsers that cannot display the image.

Usually in text-only browsers, such as Lynx, graphics that are specified using the <img> tag in the original file are "displayed" as the word IMAGE with square brackets around it like this: [IMAGE]. If the image itself is a link to something else, that link is preserved.

The alt attribute in the <img> tag provides a more meaningful text alternative to the blank [IMAGE] for your readers who are using text-only Web browsers, or who have their graphics turned off in their browsers. The alt attribute contains a string with the text you want to substitute for the graphic:

```
<img src="myimage.gif" alt="[a picture of a cat]" />
```

Most browsers will interpret the string you include in the alt attribute as a literal string; that is, if you include any HTML tags in that string, they will be printed as typed instead of being parsed and displayed as HTML code. You therefore can't use whole blocks of HTML code as a replacement for an image—just a few words or phrases.

I bring up image alternatives early in this chapter for good reason. Alternatives to images are optional in earlier versions of HTML, but mandatory in HTML 4.0 Strict and XHTML 1.0 specifications. Therefore, it's a good idea to start using them now.

Exercise 7.1: Adding Images

Try a simple example. Here's the Web page for a local haunted house that is open every year at Halloween. Using all the excellent advice I've given you in the preceding six chapters, you should be able to create a page like this one fairly easily. Here's the HTML code for this HTML file, and Figure 7.1 shows how it looks so far.

```
<!DOCTYPE html PUBLIC "-//W3C//DTD XHTML 1.0 Transitional//EN"
"http://www.w3.org/TR/xhtml1/DTD/transitional.dtd">
<html>
<head>
<title>Welcome to the Halloween House of Terror</title>
</head>
```

To Do

```
<body>
<h1>Welcome to The Halloween House of Terror!!</h1>
<hr />
<p>Voted the most frightening haunted house three years in a row,
the <strong>Halloween House of Terror</strong> provides the
ultimate in Halloween thrills. Over <strong>20 rooms of thrills
and excitement</strong> to make your blood run cold and your hair
stand on end!</p>
<p>The Halloween House of Terror is open from <em>October 20 to
November 1st</em>, with a gala celebration on Halloween night.
Our hours are:</p>
<ul>
<li>Mon-Fri 5PM-midnight</li>
<li>Sat &amp; Sun 5PM-3AM</li>
<li><strong>Halloween Night (31-Oct)</strong>: 3PM-???</li>
</ul>
<p>The Halloween House of Terror is located at:<br />
The Old Waterfall Shopping Center<br />
1020 Mirabella Ave<br />
Springfield, CA 94532</p>
</body>
</html>
```

FIGURE 7.1

The Halloween House home page.

So far, so good. Now, you can add an image to the page. Suppose that you happen to have an image of a haunted house kicking around on your hard drive; it would look excellent at the top of this Web page. The image, called house.jpg, is in JPG format. It is located in the same directory as the halloween.html page, so it's ready to go into the Web page.

Now, suppose that you want to add this image to this page on its own line so that the heading appears just below it. To do so, add an <img> tag to the file inside its own

7

▼ paragraph, just before the heading. (Images, like links, don't define their own text elements, so the <img> tag has to go inside a paragraph or heading element.)

```
<p><img src="house.jpg" alt="House of Terror" /></p>
<h1>Welcome to The Halloween House of Terror!!</h1>
```

And now, when you reload the halloween.html page, your browser should include the haunted house image in the page, as shown in Figure 7.2.

FIGURE 7.2

The Halloween House home page with the haunted house.

If the image doesn't load (if your browser displays a funny-looking icon in its place), first make sure you've specified the name of the file properly in the HTML file. Image filenames are case sensitive, so all the uppercase and lowercase letters have to be the same.

If checking the case doesn't work, double-check the image file to make sure that it is indeed a GIF or JPEG image and that it has the proper file extension.

Finally, make sure that you have image loading turned on in your browser. (The option is called Auto Load Images in Netscape and Show Pictures in Internet Explorer.)

If one image is good, two would be really good, right? Try adding another <img> tag next to the first one, as follows, and see what happens:

```
<p><img src="house.jpg" alt="House of Terror" />
<img src="house.jpg" alt="House of Terror" /></p>
<h1>Welcome to The Halloween House of Terror!!</h1>
```

▼   Figure 7.3 shows how the page looks in Internet Explorer, with both images adjacent to
    each other, as you would expect.

FIGURE 7.3

Multiple images.

And that's all there is to adding images! No matter what the image or how large or small
▲   it is, you now know how to include it on a Web page.

Images and Text

In the preceding exercise, you put an inline image on a page in its own separate paragraph, with text below the image. You also can include an image inside a line of text. (In
fact, this is what the phrase "inline image" actually means—in a line of text.)

To include images inside a line of text, just add the `<img>` tag at the appropriate point,
inside an element tag (`<h1>`, `<p>`, `<address>`, and so on), as in the following line.
Figure 7.4 shows the difference that putting the image inline with the heading makes.
(I've also shortened the heading itself and changed it to `<h2>` so that it all fits on one
line.)

```
<h2><img src="house.jpg" alt="House of Terror" />The Halloween House of
Terror!!</h2>
```

The image doesn't have to be large, and it doesn't have to be at the beginning of the text.
You can include an image anywhere in a block of text, like the following:

7

FIGURE 7.4

The Halloween House page with an image inside the heading.

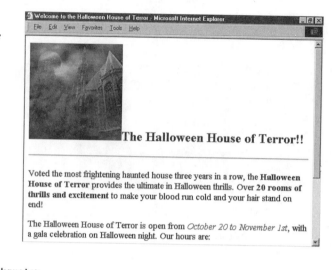

INPUT

```
<blockquote>
Love, from whom the world
<img src="world.gif" alt="World" />begun,<br />
Hath the secret of the sun.
<img src="sun.gif" alt="Sun" /><br />
Love can tell, and love alone, Whence the million stars
<img src="star.gif" alt="Star" /> were strewn<br />
Why each atom <img src="atom.gif" alt="Atom" />
knows its own.<br />
—Robert Bridges
</blockquote>
```

Figure 7.5 shows how this block looks.

OUTPUT

FIGURE 7.5

Images can go anywhere in text.

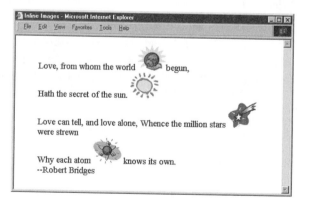

Text and Image Alignment

Notice that with these examples of including images in text the image appears so that the bottom of the image and the bottom of the text match up. The <img> tag also includes an align attribute, which enables you to align the image upward or downward with the surrounding text or other images in the line.

> **Note**
>
> The align attribute for the <img> tag is deprecated in HTML 4.0 in favor of using style sheet attributes. You'll learn more about style sheets in Day 10, "XHTML and Style Sheets."

Standard HTML 2.0 defined three basic values for align:

align="top"   Aligns the top of the image with the topmost part of the line (which may be the top of the text or the top of another image)

align="middle"   Aligns the center of the image with the middle of the line (usually the baseline of the line of text, not the actual middle of the line)

align="bottom"   Aligns the bottom of the image with the bottom of the line of text

HTML 3.2 provided two other values: left and right. These values are discussed in the next section, "Wrapping Text Next to Images."

Figure 7.6 shows the Robert Bridges poem from the previous section with the world image unaligned, the sun image aligned to the top of the line, the star image aligned to the middle, and the atom aligned to the bottom of the text.

INPUT

```
<blockquote>
Love, from whom the world
<img src="world.gif" alt="World" />begun,<br />
Hath the secret of the sun.
<img src="sun.gif" alt="Sun" align="top" /><br />
Love can tell, and love alone, Whence the million stars
<img src="star.gif" alt="Star" align="middle" />
were strewn<br />
Why each atom
<img src="atom.gif" alt="Atom" align="bottom" />
knows its own.<br />
</blockquote>
```

7

OUTPUT

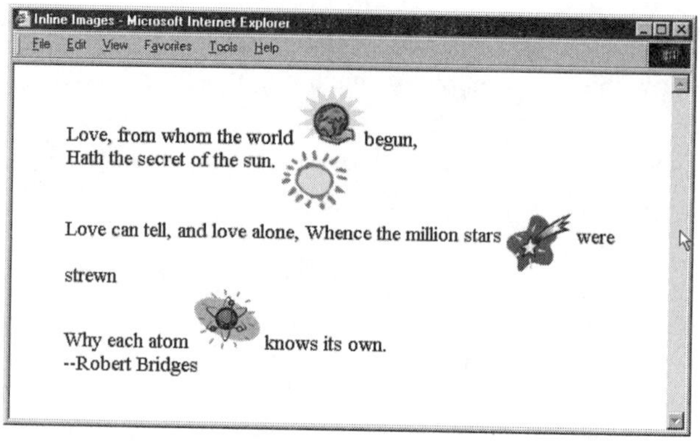

FIGURE 7.6

Images unaligned, aligned top, aligned middle, and aligned bottom.

In addition to the preceding values, several other non-standard values for `align` provide greater control over precisely where the image will be aligned within the line. The following values are all supported by Netscape Navigator (and, to some extent, Internet Explorer) but are not part of HTML 3.2 or 4.0. The following four attributes are not approved in the proposed specification for XHTML 1.0, and your page will not verify as XHTML 1.0 compliant if they are used:

`align="texttop"`	Aligns the top of the image with the top of the tallest text in the line (whereas `align="top"` aligns the image with the topmost item in the line).
`align="absmiddle"`	Aligns the middle of the image with the middle of the largest item in the line. (`align="middle"` usually aligns the middle of the image with the baseline of the text, not its actual middle.)
`align="baseline"`	Aligns the bottom of the image with the baseline of the text. `align="baseline"` is the same as `align="bottom"`, but `align="baseline"` is a more descriptive name.
`align="absbottom"`	Aligns the bottom of the image with the lowest item in the line (which may be below the baseline of the text).

The following code example shows these alignment options at work. Figure 7.7 shows examples of all the options as they appear in Netscape Navigator. In each case, the line on the left side and the text are aligned to each other, and the position of the arrow varies.

INPUT

```
<h2>Middle of Text and Line aligned, arrow varies:</h2>
<img src="line.gif" alt="Line" />
Align: Top
<img src="uparrow.gif" alt="Up" align="top" />
Align: Text Top
<img src="uparrow.gif" alt="Up" align="texttop" />
```

```
<h2>Top of Text and Line aligned, arrow varies:</h2>
<img src="line.gif" alt="Line" />
Align: Absolute Middle
<img src="forward.gif" alt="Next" align="absmiddle" />
Align: Middle
<img src="forward.gif" alt="Next" align="middle" />
<h2>Top of Text and Line aligned, arrow varies:</h2>
<img src="line.gif" alt="Line" />
Align: Baseline / Bottom
<img src="down.gif" alt="Down" align="baseline" />
Align: Absolute Bottom
<img src="down.gif" alt="Down" align="absbottom" />
```

OUTPUT

FIGURE 7.7

Alignment options in Netscape Navigator.

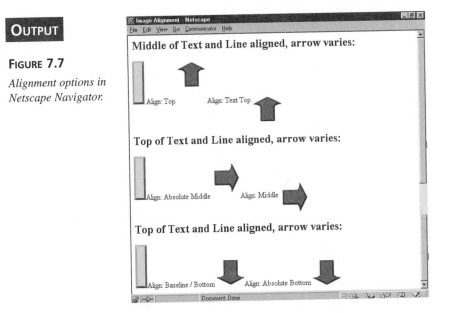

Wrapping Text Next to Images

Including an image inside a line works fine if you have only one line of text. One aspect of inline images I have sneakily avoided mentioning up to this point is that in HTML 2.0 this alignment worked only with a single line of text. If you had multiple lines of text, and you included an image in the middle of it, all the text around the image (except for the one line) appears above and below that image.

What if you want to wrap multiple lines of text next to an image so you have text surrounding all sides? Using HTML 2.0, you couldn't. You were restricted to just a single line of text on either side of the image, which limited the kinds of designs you could do.

7

To get around this HTML 2.0 limitation, Netscape defined two new values for the `align` attribute of the `<img>` tag: `left` and `right`. These new values were incorporated into HTML 3.2 and are now supported by many browsers other than Netscape.

`align="left"` and `align="right"`

`align="left"` aligns an image to the left margin, and `align="right"` aligns an image to the right margin. Using these attributes, however, also causes any text following the image to be displayed in the space to the right or left of that image, depending on the margin alignment. Figure 7.8 shows an image with some text aligned next to it.

INPUT
```
<img src="tulips.gif" alt="Tulips" align="left" />
<h1>Mystery Tulip Murderer Strikes</h1>
<p>Someone, or something, is killing the tulips of New South
Haverford, Virginia. Residents of this small town are shocked and
dismayed by the senseless vandalism that has struck their tiny
town.</p>
<p>New South Haverford is known for its extravagant displays of
tulips in the springtime, and a good portion of its tourist trade
relies on the people who come from as far as New Hampshire to see
what has been estimated as up to two hundred thousand tulips that
bloom in April and May.</p>
<p>Or at least the tourists had been flocking to New South
Haverford until last week, when over the course of three days the
flower of each and every tulip in the town was neatly clipped off
while the town slept.</p>
```

OUTPUT

FIGURE 7.8

Text and images aligned.

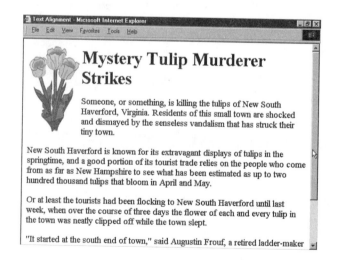

You can put any HTML text (paragraphs, lists, headings, other images) after an aligned image, and the text will be wrapped into the space between the image and the margin (or you also can have images on both margins and put the text between them). The browser fills in the space with text to the bottom of the image and then continues filling in the text beneath the image.

Stopping Text Wrapping

What if you want to stop filling in the space and start the next line underneath the image? A normal line break won't do it; it will just break the line to the current margin alongside the image. A new paragraph also will continue wrapping the text alongside the image. To stop wrapping text next to an image, use a line break tag (<br>) with the attribute clear. With the clear attribute, you can break the line so that the next line of text begins after the end of the image (all the way to the margin).

The clear attribute can have one of three values:

left　　Break to an empty left margin, for left-aligned images

right　　Break to an empty right margin, for right-aligned images

all　　Break to a line clear to both margins

Note The clear attribute for the <br> tag is deprecated in HTML 4.0, in favor of using style sheet attributes.

The following code snippet, for example, shows a picture of a tulip with some text wrapped next to it. A line break with clear="left" breaks the text wrapping after the heading and restarts the text after the image. Figure 7.9 shows the result in Internet Explorer.

INPUT

```
<!DOCTYPE html PUBLIC "-//W3C//DTD XHTML 1.0 Transitional//EN"
"http://www.w3.org/TR/xhtml1/DTD/transitional.dtd">
</head>
<body>
<img src="tulips.gif" alt="Tulips" align="left" />
<h1>Mystery Tulip Murderer Strikes</h1>
<br clear="left" />
<p>Someone, or something, is killing the tulips of New South
Haverford, Virginia. Residents of this small town are shocked and
dismayed by the senseless vandalism that has struck their tiny
town.</p>
<p>New South Haverford is known for its extravagant displays of
tulips in the springtime, and a good portion of its tourist trade
relies on the people who come from as far as New Hampshire to see
what has been estimated as up to two hundred thousand tulips that
bloom in April and May.</p>
<p>Or at least the tourists had been flocking to New South
Haverford until last week, when over the course of three days the
flower of each and every tulip in the town was neatly clipped off
while the town slept.</p>
```

7

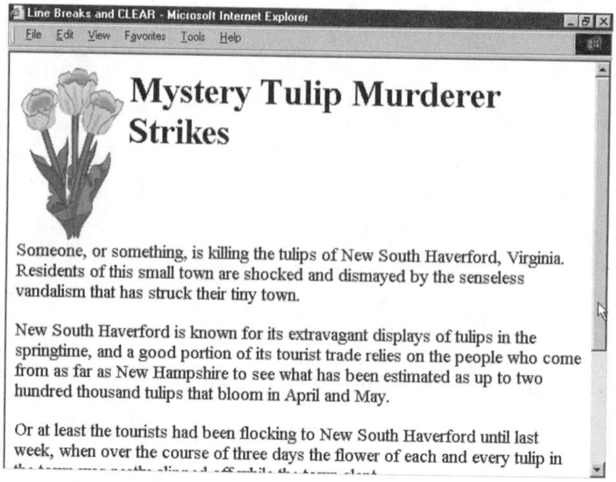

FIGURE 7.9.

Line break to a clear margin.

Adjusting the Space Around Images

With the capability to wrap text around an image, you also might want to adjust the amount of space around that image. The vspace and hspace attributes (introduced in HTML 3.2) enable you to make these adjustments. Both take values in pixels; vspace controls the space above and below the image, and hspace controls the space to the left and the right.

Note

The vspace and hspace attributes for the <img> tag are deprecated in HTML 4.0 in favor of using style sheet attributes.

The following HTML code, displayed in Figure 7.10, illustrates two examples. The upper example shows default horizontal and vertical spacing around the image, while the lower example shows the effect produced by the hspace and vspace attributes. Both images use the align="left" attribute so that the text wraps along the left side of the image. However, in the bottom example, the text aligns with the extra space above the top of the image (added with the vspace attribute).

INPUT

```
<img src="eggplant.gif" alt="Eggplant" align="left" />
<p>This is an eggplant. We intend to stay a good ways away from
it, because we really don't like eggplant very much.</p>
<br clear="left" />
<hr />
<img src="eggplant.gif" alt="Eggplant" vspace="50" hspace="50"
align="left" />
<p>This is an eggplant. We intend to stay a good ways away from
it, because we really don't like eggplant very much.</p>
```

OUTPUT

FIGURE 7.10

Upper example with-out image spacing, and lower example with image spacing.

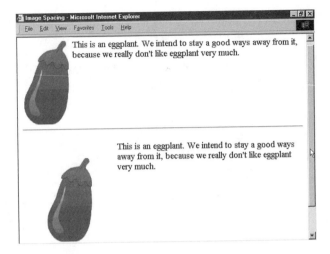

Images and Links

Can an image serve as a link? Sure, it can! If you include an `<img>` tag inside the open-ing and closing parts of a link tag (`<a>`), that image serves as a clickable hot spot for the link itself:

```
<a href="index.html"><img src="uparrow.gif" alt="Up" /></a>
```

If you include both an image and text in the anchor, the image and the text become hot spots pointing to the same page:

```
<a href="index.html"><img src="uparrow.gif" alt="Up" />Up to Index</a>
```

By default in HTML 2.0, images that also are hot spots for links appear with borders around them to distinguish them from ordinary non-clickable images. Figure 7.11 shows an example of this. The butterfly image is a non-clickable image, so it does not have a border around it. The up arrow, which takes the reader back to the home page, has a bor-der around it because it is a link.

You can change the width of the border around the image by using the `border` attribute to `<img>`. The `border` attribute was a Netscape extension that became part of HTML 3.2, but it has been deprecated in HTML 4.0 in favor of style sheets. This attribute takes a number, which is the width of the border in pixels. `border="0"` hides the border entirely.

Be careful when setting `border` to `0` (zero) for images with links. The border provides a visual indication that the image also is a link. By removing that border, you make it diffi-cult for the readers to know which are plain images and which are hot spots without them having to move the mouse around to find them. If you must use borderless image links, make sure that your design provides some indication that the image is selectable

7

and isn't just a plain image. For example, you might design your images so they actually look like buttons, as shown in Figure 7.12.

FIGURE 7.11

Images used as links have a border around them.

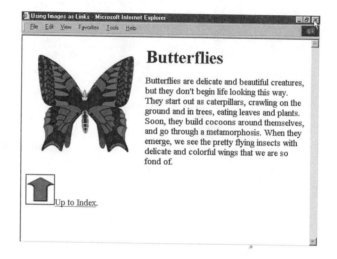

FIGURE 7.12

Images that look like buttons.

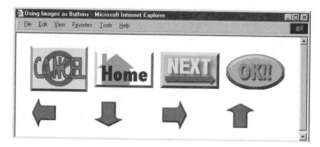

Exercise 7.2: Using Navigation Icons

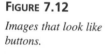

Now you can create a simple example of using images as links. When you have a set of related Web pages among which the navigation takes place in a consistent way (for example, moving forward, or back, up, home, and so on), providing a menu of navigation options at the top or bottom of each page makes sense so your readers know exactly how to find their way through your pages.

This example shows you how to create a set of icons that are used to navigate through a linear set of pages. You have three icons in GIF format: one for forward, one for back, and a third to enable the readers to jump to a global index of the entire page structure.

First, you'll write the HTML structure to support the icons. Here, the page itself isn't very important, so you can just include a shell page. Figure 7.13 shows how the page looks at the beginning.

INPUT

```
<!DOCTYPE html PUBLIC "-//W3C//DTD XHTML 1.0 Transitional//EN"
"http://www.w3.org/TR/xhtml1/DTD/transitional.dtd">
<html>
<head>
<title>Motorcycle Maintenance: Removing Spark Plugs</title>
<h1>Removing Spark Plugs</h1>
<p>(include some info about spark plugs here)</p>
<hr />
</body>
</html>
```

OUTPUT

FIGURE 7.13

The basic page, no icons.

Now, at the bottom of the page, add your images using `<img>` tags. Figure 7.14 shows the result.

INPUT

```
<img src="next.gif" alt="Next" />
<img src="back.gif" alt="Back" />
<img src="uparrow.gif" alt="Up" />
```

OUTPUT

FIGURE 7.14

The basic page with icons.

Now, add the anchors to the images to activate them. Figure 7.15 shows the result of this addition.

INPUT

```
<a href="replacing.html"><img src="next.gif" alt="Next" /></a>
<a href="ready.html"><img src="back.gif" alt="Back" /></a>
<a href="index.html"><img src="uparrow.gif" alt="Up" /></a>
```

7

FIGURE 7.15

The basic page with iconic links.

When you click the icons now, the browser jumps to the page in the link just as it would have if you had used text links.

Speaking of text, are the icons usable enough as they are? How about adding some text describing exactly what is on the other side of the link? You can add the text inside or outside the anchor, depending on whether you want the text to be a hot spot for the link as well. Here, include it outside the link so that only the icon serves as the hot spot. You also can align the bottoms of the text and the icons using the `align` attribute of the `<img>` tag. Finally, because the extra text causes the icons to move onto two lines, arrange each one on its own line instead. See Figure 7.16 for the final menu.

INPUT

```
<hr />
<p><a href="replacing.html"><img src="next.gif" alt="Next" /></a>
On to "Gapping the New Plugs"<br />
<a href="ready.html"><img src="back.gif" alt="Back" /></a>
Back to "When You Should Replace your Spark Plugs"<br />
<a href="index.html"><img src="uparrow.gif" alt="Up" /></a>
Up To Index
</p>
```

OUTPUT

FIGURE 7.16

The basic page with iconic links and text.

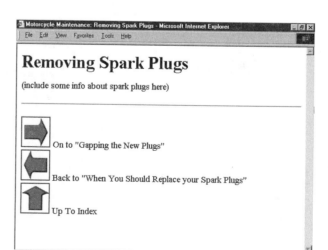

Using External Images

Unlike inline images, external images don't actually appear on your Web page; instead, they're stored separate from the page and linked from that page in much the same way that other HTML pages are.

The reason external images are worth mentioning in this chapter is that external images often can serve a complementary role to inline images. For example

- Most Web browsers support inline GIF images, and many of them support inline JPEG images as well. However, most browsers support a much wider array of image formats through the use of external image files and helper applications. So, by using external images, you can use many other image formats besides GIF and JPEG—for example, BMP (Windows bitmaps) or PICT (Macintosh bitmaps).

- Text-only browsers can't display images inline with Web pages, but you can download external images with a text-only browser and view them with an image-editing or viewing program.

- You can combine a small inline image on your Web page that loads quickly with a larger, more detailed external image. This way, if readers want to see more, they can choose to load the image themselves.

To use external images, you create the image as you would an inline image and then save it with an appropriate filename. As with other files on the Web, the file extension is important. Depending on the image format, use one of the extensions listed in Table 7.1.

TABLE 7.1 Image Formats and Extensions

Format	Extension
GIF	.gif
JPEG	.jpg, .jpeg
XBM	.xbm
TIFF	.tiff, .tif
BMP	.bmp
PNG	.png
PICT	.pict

After you have an external image, all you have to do is create a link to it, the same way you would create a link to another HTML page, like the following:

```
<p>I grew some really huge <a href="bigtomatoes.jpeg"
alt="Tomatoes">tomatoes</a> in
my garden last year</p>
```

7

For this next exercise, you'll use inline and external images together.

Exercise 7.3: Linking to External GIF and JPEG Files

A common practice in Web pages is to provide a small GIF or JPEG image (a "thumbnail") inline on the page itself. You then can link the thumbnail image to its larger external counterpart. Using this approach has two major advantages over including the entire image inline:

- It keeps the size of the Web page small so that the page can be downloaded quickly.
- It gives your readers a "taste" of the image so they can choose to download the entire image if they want to see more or get a better view.

In this simple example, you'll set up a link between a small image and an external, larger version of that same image. The large image is a rendering of a castle near a river, called `castle.jpg`. It is shown in Figure 7.17.

FIGURE 7.17

The large castle image.

First, create a thumbnail version of the castle image in your favorite image editor. Paint Shop Pro is a good shareware program for Windows, while Adobe Photoshop is pretty much the standard for professional-level designers on both the Macintosh and Windows PCs. The thumbnail can be a scaled version of the original file, a clip of that file (just the castle rather than the whole scene, for example), or anything else you want to indicate the larger image.

Here, I've created a scaled version of the larger image to serve as the inline image. (I've called it `sm-castle.jpg`.) Unlike the large version of the file, which is 24K, the small picture is only 3K. By using the `<img>` tag, you can put your thumbnail image directly on a nearly content-free Web page:

```
<!DOCTYPE html PUBLIC "-//W3C//DTD XHTML 1.0 Transitional//EN"
"http://www.w3.org/TR/xhtml1/DTD/transitional.dtd"><html>
<head>
<title>Castle at Sunrise</title>
```

```
▼   </head>
    <body>
    <h1>Castle at Sunrise</h1>
    <img src="sm-castle.jpg" alt="Castle Thumbnail" />
    </body>
    </html>
```

Now, by using a link tag, you can link the small icon to the bigger picture by enclosing the <img> tag inside an <a> tag:

```
<a href="castle.jpg"><img src="sm-castle.jpg" alt="Castle Thumbnail" /></a>
```

The final result of the page is shown in Figure 7.18. Now, if you click the small castle image, the larger image will be downloaded and viewed either by the browser itself or by the helper application defined for JPEG files for that browser.

FIGURE 7.18

The Castle at Sunrise home page with link.

An alternative to linking the small image directly to the larger image is to provide the external image in several different formats and then create plain text links to the various different external versions. (You might want to take this approach for readers who have software for one format but not another.) In this part of the example, you'll link to a GIF version of that same castle file.

To create the GIF version of the castle, you need to use your image editor or converter again to convert the original photograph. Here, I've called it castle.gif.

To provide both GIF and JPEG forms of the castle, you'll convert the link on the image into a simple link menu to the JPEG and GIF files, providing some information about file size. The result is shown in Figure 7.19.

INPUT

```
    <p><img src="sm-castle.jpg" alt="Castle Thumbnail" /></p>
    <ul>
    <li>Castle at Sunrise (<a href="castle.jpg">25K JPEG
    file</a>)</li>
    <li>Castle at Sunrise (<a href="castle.gif">49K GIF
    file</a>)</li>
▼   </ul>
```

7

▼

FIGURE 7.19

The Castle at Sunrise link menu.

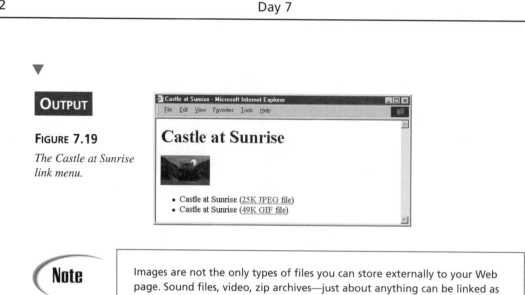

▲

> **Note**
>
> Images are not the only types of files you can store externally to your Web page. Sound files, video, zip archives—just about anything can be linked as external files. You'll learn more about other alternatives in Day 13, "Multimedia: Adding Sounds, Videos, and More."

Other Neat Tricks with Images

Now that you've learned about inline and external images, images as links, and how to wrap text around images, you know the majority of what most people do with images in Web pages. But you can play with a few newer tricks, and they are what this section is all about.

All the attributes in this section were originally Netscape extensions. They were later incorporated into HTML 3.2, but most have been deprecated in its successor, HTML 4.0.

Image Dimensions and Scaling

Two attributes of the `<img>` tag, `height` and `width`, specify the height and width of the image in pixels. Both became part of the HTML 3.2 specification, but they are deprecated in HTML 4.0 in favor of style sheets.

If you use the actual height and width of the image in these values (which you can find out in most image-editing programs), your Web pages will appear to load and display much faster in some browsers than if you do not include these values.

Why? Normally, when a browser parses the HTML code in your file, it has to load and test each image to get its width and height before proceeding so that it can format the text appropriately. Therefore, the browser loads and formats some of your text, waits for the image to load, formats around the image when it gets the dimensions, and then moves on for the rest of the page. If the width and height are already specified in the

HTML code itself, the browser can just make a space of the appropriate size for the image and keep formatting all the text around it. This way, your readers can continue reading the text while the images are loading rather than having to wait. And, because width and height are ignored in other browsers, there's no reason not to use them for all your images. They neither harm nor affect the image in browsers that don't support them.

Tip

If you test your page with images in it in Netscape Navigator 4, try choosing View, Document Info. You'll get a window that lists all the images in your page. By selecting each image in turn, you'll get information about that image—including its size, which you then can copy into your HTML file.

If the values for width and height are different from the actual width and height of the image, your browser will automatically scale the image to fit those dimensions. Because smaller images take up less disk space than larger images and therefore take less time to transfer over the network, you can use this sneaky method to get away with using large images on your pages without the additional increase in load time: Just create a smaller version, and then scale it to the dimensions you want on your Web page. Note, however, that the pixels also will be scaled, so the bigger version may end up looking grainy or blocky. Experiment with different sizes and scaling factors to get the right effect.

Note

Don't perform reverse scaling—creating a large image and then using width and height to scale it down. Smaller file sizes are better because they take less time to load. If you're just going to display a small image, make it smaller to begin with.

More About Image Borders

You learned about the border attribute to the <img> tag as part of the section on links, where setting border to a number or to zero determined the width of the image border (or hid it entirely).

Normally, plain images don't have borders; only images that hold links do. You can use the border attribute with plain images, however, to draw a border around the image, like the following:

```
<p><img src="eggplant.gif" alt="Eggplant" align="left" border="5"
width="102" height="178" />
This is an eggplant. We intend to stay a good ways away from it,
because we really don't like eggplant very much.</p>
```

7

Figure 7.20 shows an example of an image with a border around it.

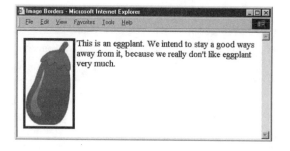

Image Previews

One completely optional HTML extension (supported by both Netscape and Internet Explorer 4) is the use of the lowsrc attribute to <img>, which provides a sort of preview for the actual image on the page. You use lowsrc just like you use src, with a pathname to another image file, as follows:

```
<img src="wall.gif" lowsrc="wallsmall.gif" />
```

When a browser that supports lowsrc encounters a lowsrc tag, it loads the lowsrc image first, in the first pass for the overall page layout. Then, after all the layout and lowsrc images are done loading and displaying, the image specified in src is loaded and fades in to replace the lowsrc image.

Why would you want this type of preview? The image in lowsrc usually is a smaller or lower resolution preview of the actual image, one that can load very quickly and give the readers an idea of the overall effect of the page. (Make sure your lowsrc image is indeed a smaller image; otherwise, there's no point to including it.) Then, after all the layout is done, the readers can scroll around and read the text while the better images are quietly loaded in the background.

Using lowsrc is entirely optional; it's simply ignored in older browsers.

Using Color

One way to add color to your Web pages is to add images; images can provide a splash of color among the black and gray and white. Several HTML attributes, however, enable you also to change the colors of the page itself, including changing the background color of the page, changing the color of the text and links on that page, and to add "spot color" to individual characters on that page.

In this section, you'll learn how to make all these changes in HTML 3.2. However, as is the case with most of the presentational attributes we've covered thus far, color attributes also are deprecated in HTML 4.0 in favor of style sheets. You'll learn more about the style sheet approach in Day 10.

Naming Colors

Before you can change the color of any part of an HTML page, you have to know what color you're going to change it to. You can specify colors using the color extensions to HTML in two ways:

- Using a hexadecimal number representing that color
- Using one of a set of predefined color names

The most flexible and most widely supported method of indicating color involves finding out the numeric value of the color you want to use. Most image-editing programs have what's called a *color picker*—some way of choosing a single color from a range of available colors. Most color pickers, in turn, will tell you the value of that color in RGB form, as three numbers (one for red, one for green, and one for blue—that's what RGB stands for). Each number is usually 0 to 255, with 0 0 0 being black and 255 255 255 being white.

After you have your colors as three numbers from 0 to 255, you have to convert those numbers into hexadecimal. You can use any scientific calculator that converts between ASCII and hex to get these numbers. A slew of freeware and shareware color pickers for HTML are available as well, including HTML Color Reference and ColorFinder for Windows, and ColorMeister and ColorSelect for the Macintosh. Alternatively, you can use rgb.html, a form that will do the conversion for you, which you'll learn how to implement later in this book. For now, you can try out the rgb.html form at http://www.lne.com/rgb.html, which will give you the hex for any three numbers. So, for example, the RGB values 0 0 0 convert to 00 00 00, and the RGB values 255 255 255 convert to ff ff ff.

The final hex number you need is all three numbers put together with a hash sign (#) at the beginning, like the following:

```
#000000
#de04e4
#ffff00
```

Netscape and Internet Explorer support a much easier way of indicating colors. Rather than using arcane numbering schemes, you just choose a color name such as Black, White, Green, Maroon, Olive, Navy, Purple, Gray, Red, Yellow, Blue, Teal, Lime, Aqua, Fuchsia, or Silver.

Although color names are easier to remember and to figure out than the numbers, they do offer less flexibility in the kinds of colors you can use, and names are not as widely

7

supported in browsers as the color numbers. Keep in mind that if you do use color names, you may lose the colors in most other browsers.

After you have a color name or number in hand, you can apply that color to various parts of your HTML page.

Changing the Background Color

To change the color of the background on a page, decide what color you want and then add an attribute called bgcolor to the <body> tag. The <body> tag, in case you've forgotten, is the tag that surrounds all the content of your HTML file. <head> contains the title, and <body> contains almost everything else. bgcolor is an HTML extension introduced by Netscape in the 1.1 version of the browser and incorporated into HTML 3.2.

To use color numbers for backgrounds, you enter the value of the bgcolor attribute of the <body> tag (the hexadecimal number you found in the preceding section) in quotation marks. They look like the following:

```
<body bgcolor="#ffffff">
<body bgcolor="#934ce8">
```

To use color names, simply use the name of the color as the value to bgcolor:

```
<body bgcolor="white">
<body bgcolor="green">
```

Note

Some browsers enable you to indicate color numbers without the leading hash sign (#). Although this method may seem more convenient, given that it is incompatible with many other browsers, the inclusion of the one extra character does not seem like that much of a hardship.

Changing Text Colors

When you can change the background colors, also changing the color of the text itself makes sense. More HTML attributes enable you to change the color of the text globally in your pages.

To change the text and link colors, you'll need your color names or numbers just as you did for changing the backgrounds. With a color in hand, you then can add any of the following attributes to the <body> tag with either a color number or color name as their values:

text   Controls the color of all the page's body text that isn't a link, including headings, body text, text inside tables, and so on.

link   Controls the color of normal, unfollowed links in the page (the ones that are usually blue by default).

vlink   Controls the color of links you have visited (the ones that usually are purple or red by default).

alink   Controls the color of a link that has had the mouse button pressed on it but not released (an activated link). They are often red by default.

Remember the haunted house image that you inserted on a page in the beginning of this chapter? The page would be decidedly more spooky with a black background, and orange text would be so much more appropriate for the holiday. To create a page with an orange background, black text, and deep red unfollowed links, you might use the following <body> tag:

```
<body bgcolor="#ff9933" text="#000000" link="#800000">
```

Using the following color names for the background and unfollowed links would produce the same effect:

```
<body bgcolor="orange" text="black" link="#800000">
```

Both these links would produce a page that looks something like the one shown in Figure 7.21.

Spot Color

When you change the text colors in a page by using attributes to the <body> tag, that change affects all the text on the page. Spot color is the capability to change the color of individual characters inside your page, which you can use instead of or in addition to a global text color.

Yesterday you learned about using the HTML tag <font> for setting the font size and font name. A third attribute to <font>, color, enables you to change the color of individual words or phrases. The value of color is either a color name or number:

```
<p>When we go out tonight, we're going to paint the town
<font color="#ff0000">RED</font>.
```

You can, of course, use font spot colors in addition to font names and sizes.

7

FIGURE 7.21

Background and text colors.

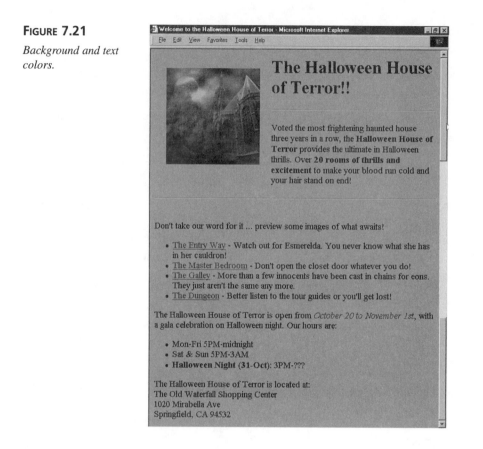

Image Backgrounds

One last topic for this chapter is the ability to use an image as a background for your pages rather than simply a solid colored background. When you use an image for a background, that image is "tiled"; that is, the image is repeated in rows to fill the browser window.

To create a tiled background, you'll need an image to serve as the tile. Usually, when you create an image for tiling, you need to make sure that the pattern flows smoothly from one tile to the next. You can usually do some careful editing of the image in your favorite image-editing program to make sure the edges line up. The goal is to have the edges meet cleanly so that you don't have a "seam" between the tiles after you've laid them end to end. (See Figure 7.22 for an example of tiles that don't line up very well.) You also can try clip art packages for wallpaper or tile patterns that often are designed specifically to be tiled in this fashion.

FIGURE 7.22

Tiled images with "seams."

When you have an image that can be cleanly tiled, all you need to create a tiled image background is the background attribute, part of the <body> tag. The value of background is a filename or URL that points to your image file, as in the following example:

```
<body background="tiles.gif">
<body background="backgrounds/rosemarble.gif">
```

Figure 7.23 shows the result of a simple tiled background.

FIGURE 7.23

A tiled background in Internet Explorer.

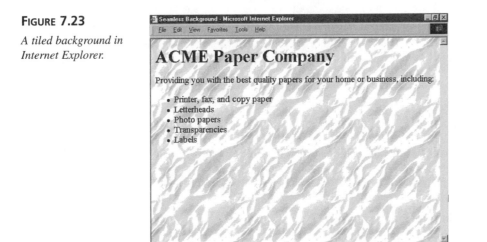

Internet Explorer offers a twist on the tiled background design: a fixed tile pattern called a *watermark*. The idea here is that when you scroll a page, rather than everything on the page including the background scrolling by, only the page foreground (text and images)

7

scrolls. The tiles in the background stay rooted in one place. To create this effect, use the `bgproperties="fixed"` attribute to the `<body>` tag, as follows:

```
<body background="backgrounds/rosemarble.gif" bgproperties="fixed">
```

Hints for Better Use of Images

The use of images in Web pages causes one of the bigger arguments among users and providers of Web pages today. For everyone who wants to design Web pages with more, bigger, and brighter images to take full advantage of the graphical capabilities of the Web, someone on a slow network connection is begging for fewer images so that his browser doesn't take three hours to load a page.

As a designer of Web pages, you should consider both of these points of view. Balance the fun of creating a highly visual, colorful Web page with the need to get your information to everyone you want to have it—and that includes people who may not have access to your images at all.

This section offers some hints and compromises you can make in the design of your Web pages so that you can make everyone happy (or everyone unhappy, depending on how you look at it).

Do You Really Need This Image?

For each image you put inline on your Web page, consider why you are putting it there. What does the image add to the design? Does it provide information that could be presented in the text instead? Is it just there because you like how it looks?

Try not to clutter your Web page with pretty but otherwise unnecessary images. A simple Web page with only a few iconic images often is more effective than a page that opens with an enormous graphic and continues the trend with flashy 3D buttons, drop-shadow bullets, and psychedelic line separators.

Keep Your Images Small

A smaller image takes less time to transfer over the Internet; therefore, using smaller images makes your Web page load faster and causes less frustration for people trying to read it over a slow link. What could be easier?

To create small images, you can reduce their actual physical dimensions onscreen. You also can create smaller file sizes for your images by reducing the number of colors in an image. Your goal is to reduce the file size of the image so that it transfers faster, but a four-inch by four-inch black-and-white image (two colors) may be smaller in file size than a ½-inch by ½-inch full-color photographic image. With most image-processing programs, you can reduce the number of colors and touch up the result so that it looks good even with fewer colors.

A good rule to follow is that you should try to keep your inline images somewhere under 20K. That size may seem small, but a single 20K file takes nearly 10 seconds to download over a 28.8Kbps connection. Multiply that number by the number of images on your Web page, and the page may take a substantial amount of time to load (even if you're using a browser that can load multiple images at once; the pipe is only so wide). Will people care about what you have in your Web page if they have had to go off and have lunch while it's loading?

Reuse Images as Often as Possible

In addition to keeping individual images small, try to reuse the same images as often as you can, on single pages and across multiple pages. For example, if you have images as bullets, use the same image for all the bullets rather than different ones. Reusing images has two significant advantages over using different images:

- Reusing images provides a consistency to your design across pages, part of creating an overall "look" for your site.
- Even more important, reusing images means that your browser has to download the image only once. After the browser has the image in memory, it can simply draw the image multiple times without having to make a larger number of connections back to the server.

To reuse an image, you don't have to do anything special; just make sure you refer to each image with the same URL each time you use it. The browser will take care of the rest.

Provide Alternatives to Images

If you're not using the `alt` attribute in your images, you should be. The `alt` attribute is extremely useful for making your Web page readable by text-only browsers. But what about people who turn off images in their browser because they have a slow link to the Internet? Most browsers do not use the value of `alt` in this case. And sometimes `alt` isn't enough; because you can specify text only inside an `alt` string, you can't substitute HTML code for the image.

To get around all these problems while still keeping your nifty graphical Web page, consider creating alternative text-only versions of your Web pages and putting links to them on the full-graphics versions of the same Web page, like the following:

```
<p>A <a href="TextVersion.html">text-only</a>
version of this page is available.</p>
```

7

The link to the text-only page takes up only one small paragraph on the "real" Web page, but it makes the information much more accessible. Providing this version is a courtesy that readers with slow connections will thank you for, and it still enables you to load up your "main" Web page with as many images as you like for those people who have fast connections.

Summary

One of the major features that makes the World Wide Web stand out from other forms of Internet information is that pages on the Web can contain full-color images. It was arguably the existence of those images that allowed the Web to catch on so quickly and to become so popular in so short a time.

To place images on your Web pages, you learned that those images must be in GIF or JPEG format (GIF is more widely supported) and small enough that they can be quickly downloaded over a potentially slow link. In this chapter, you also learned that the HTML tag <img> enables you to put an image on the Web page, either inline with text or on a line by itself. The <img> tag has three primary attributes supported in standard HTML:

src	The location and filename of the image to include.
align	How to position the image vertically with its surrounding text. align can have one of three values: top, middle, or bottom. (Deprecated in HTML 4.0 in favor of style sheets.)
alt	A text string to substitute for the image in text-only browsers.

You can include images inside a link tag (<a>) and have those images serve as hot spots for the links, same as text.

In addition to the standard attributes, several other attributes to the <img> tag provide greater control over images and layout of Web pages. You learned how to use these HTML 3.2 attributes in this chapter, but most of them have been deprecated in HTML 4.0 in favor of style sheets. They include the following:

align="left" align="right"	Place the image against the appropriate margin, allowing all following text to flow into the space alongside the image.
clear	A Netscape extension to , clear allows you to stop wrapping text alongside an image. clear can have three values: left, right, and all.
align="texttop" align="absmiddle" align="baseline" align="absbottom"	Allow greater control over the alignment of an inline image and the text surrounding it

vspace hspace	Define the amount of space between an image and the text surrounding it.
border	Defines the width of the border around an image (with or without a link). border="0" hides the border altogether.
lowsrc	Defines an alternative, lower-resolution image that is loaded before the image indicated by src.

In addition to images, you also can add color to the background and to the text of a page using attributes to the <body> tag, or add color to individual characters using the color attribute to <font>. Finally, you also learned that you can add patterned or tiled backgrounds to images by using the background attribute to <body> with an image for the tile.

Workshop

Now that you know how to add images and color to your pages, you can really get creative with your Web pages. This workshop will help you remember some of the most important points about using images and color in your pages so that your Web pages will be compatible with HTML 3.2 and HTML 4.0 browsers. If you want to strictly design your pages around the HTML 4.0 specification, you'll need to forfeit many of the presentation options you learned in this chapter in favor of style sheets.

Q&A

Q What is the difference between a GIF image and a JPEG image? Is there any rule of thumb that defines when you should use one format over the other?

A As a rule, use GIF files when images contain 256 or fewer colors. Some good examples are cartoon art, clip art, black-and-white images, or images with many solid color areas. You'll also need to use GIF files if you want your images to contain transparent areas, or if you want to create an animation that does not require a special plug-in or browser helper. Remember to use your image editing software to reduce the number of colors in the image palettes where possible, because this also reduces the size of the file.

JPEG images are best for photographic quality or high-resolution 3D rendered graphics, because they can display true-color images to great effect. Most image editing programs enable you to specify how much to compress a JPEG image. The size of the file decreases the more an image is compressed; however, compression also deteriorates the quality and appearance of the image if you go overboard. You

7

have to find just the right balance between quality and file size, and this can differ from image to image.

Q How can I create thumbnails of my images so that I can link them to larger external images?

A You'll have to do that with some type of image-editing program (such as Adobe Photoshop or Paint Shop Pro); the Web won't do it for you. Just open up the image, and scale it down to the right size.

Q What about those images that let you see through portions of them to display the page background? They look like they sort of float on the page. How do I create those?

A That is another task that you accomplish with an image editing program. These types of images are known as *transparent GIFs*, and you can only achieve this effect with a GIF image. I'll show you how to create a transparent GIF in the next chapter, "Creating Animated Graphics."

Q Can I put HTML tags in the string for the `alt` attribute?

A That would be nice, wouldn't it? Unfortunately, you can't. All you can do is put an ordinary string in there. Keep it simple, and you should be fine.

Q You discussed a technique for including `lowsrc` images on a page that are loaded in before regular images are. I've seen an effect on Web pages where an image seems to load in as a really blurry image and then become clearer as time goes on. Is that a `lowsrc` effect?

A No, actually, that effect is something called an interlaced GIF. Only one image is there; it just displays as it's loading differently from regular GIFs. You'll learn more about interlaced GIFs in the next chapter.

`lowsrc` images load just like regular images (with no special visual effect).

Q I've seen some Web pages where you can click different places in an image and get different link results, such as a map of the United States where each state has a different page. How do you do this in HTML?

A You use something called an imagemap, which is an advanced form of Web page development. There are two types of imagemaps—client-side imagemaps and server-side imagemaps. I describe both types in Day 9, "Creating and Using Imagemaps."

Quiz

1. Describe the two classes of images that are used in Web pages.

2. What is the most important attribute of the `<img>` tag? What does it do?

3. If you see a funny-looking icon rather than an image when you view your page in a browser, the image is not loading. What are some of the reasons this could happen?

4. As a rule, when a person views a Web page in a browser, what distinguishes a clickable image (one that is used as a link) from a non-clickable image?

5. Why is it important to use the `alt` attribute to display a text alternative for an image? When is it most important to do so?

Answers to Quiz

1. Inline images appear directly on a Web page, among the text and links. External images are downloaded at the request of your readers, usually as a result of clicking a link.

2. The most important attribute of the `<img>` tag is the `src` attribute. It indicates the filename or URL of the image you want to include on your page.

3. There are several things that cause an image not to load. The URL may be incorrect; the filename might not be correct (they are case sensitive); it might have the wrong file extension or be the wrong type of file; or image loading might be turned off in your browser.

4. By default, clickable images (those used for links) are surrounded by a border, whereas non-clickable images are not.

5. It is a good idea to use text alternatives with images because some people use text-only browsers or have graphics turned off in their browsers. It is most important to use text alternatives for images used as links.

Exercises

1. Create or find some images that you can use as navigation icons or buttons on one or more pages in your Web site. Remember that it is always advantageous to use images more than once. Create a simple navigation bar that you can use on the top or bottom of your page.

2. Create or find some images that you can use to enhance the appearance of your Web pages. Images such as small banners (for page titles), bullets, horizontal rules, and background images are always handy to keep around. After you find some that you like, try to create background, text, and link colors that are compatible with them.

7

DAY 8

Creating Animated Graphics

You've probably had enough of coding for a while, so here's a chapter that will give you a break from typing and let you learn how to move pixels around! Animated graphics add spark and emphasis to Web pages, and they are not as difficult to create as you might think. With the right software tools, you can create your own original animations for your Web pages. In this chapter, I'll teach you some of the basics of how to do just that. Get ready to learn the following:

- Examine individual frames of an animated GIF to learn what makes them look like they are moving
- When and where to use animation on your Web pages
- How to create a transparent GIF file and how to choose a transparent color
- Learn about image editing and GIF creation tools that help you create your own animated GIF files
- Review software features that are very useful in an image editing package
- Learn how to compile and reduce the size of an animated GIF file
- Create your own frames for your first animation

What Is an Animation?

Imagine that you have a pile of pictures stacked, one on top of the other. Each picture is slightly different than the one that precedes it, and they are arranged in a specific sequence. When you flip the pages, you see the illusion of movement. The speed of the animation varies, depending on how fast you flip the pictures.

Basically, any animation file (whether it is an animated GIF, Windows AVI file, Quick Time movie, or an MPEG file) really is nothing more than a virtual picture flip book. Several images, usually of the same size, are arranged in a specific order by use of software that in one way or another generates a script. The script is "built in" to the animation file and defines parameters such as how fast the images flip (the speed of the animation), how one image should overlay the next one, and so on. Rather than having to load each individual image one at a time, what you have is a single file, consisting of multiple frames that play in a sequence somewhat like a movie.

You might be familiar with the dancing baby that has taken the Internet by storm. In fact, the dancing baby has turned into quite a celebrity. After surfing the Web, the creator of the hit TV show *Ally McBeal* found the dancing baby and featured it on the show. "Baby Cha" came into being through the combined efforts of Viewpoint Datalabs (the creators of the baby model) and Kinetix, a division of Autodesk (creators of 3D Studio Max and its Character Studio plug-in). If you haven't yet seen Baby Cha, by all means check out the Kinetix Web site for some delightful examples of how animation can really draw attention to a site. All the animations are in Video for Windows AVI format (be sure your browser supports them), and some of the files take a while to download; however, they are *well* worth the wait. Check them out at `http://www.ktx.com/cs/html/babycha.html`.

In Figure 8.1, you see a Baby Cha counterpart. This dancing chimp also was created with 3D Studio Max and Character Studio—the same software that was used to bring Baby Cha to life. Here, I show 30 frames for my dancing chimp (I rendered every fifth frame so that I could fit the entire sequence in one screen shot). They all are shown in sequence, beginning with the top-left image and ending with the bottom-right image. Notice that each frame of the animation is slightly different. When the frames are viewed in sequence, you see the chimp spinning around and jumping while he raises and lowers his left arm.

By playing these images in a sequence, it creates the illusion of movement. When you create animation, the frames don't always have to change smoothly as they do in this example. You also can display a series of still images, such as photographs or banner advertisements, in a timed sequence. This creates something similar to a slide show or presentation.

FIGURE 8.1

Thirty animation frames of a dancing chimp.

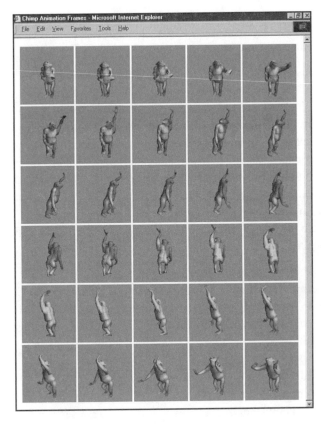

8

When and Where to Use Animation

Baby Cha and the dancing chimp are cute, but not very practical. So what can you really use animation for on a Web page?

The general rule of thumb is to use animation to draw attention to something. Too much animation detracts from a page. The reader won't know where to look first, and attention might be drawn away from the important text on your page. Use animation sparingly and appropriately. Above all, don't pile a whole slew of animations on a single page, because it will take forever for your page to load.

Following are some common uses of animation:

- **Banner advertisements**. Some people find these annoying and sometimes avoid them. If your Web site is sponsored by an organization, however, or if you want to draw attention to your own products and capabilities, banner advertisements are a fairly standard way to do it.

- **Animated bullets**. Animated bullets are nice for brief lists, but try to keep them subtle. If the list contains too many items (over 10), a busy animated bullet can be very distracting.

- **Horizontal rules**. Many times, you'll see thin lines of animated gradients that are used as horizontal rules. You also can create much more clever rules—a line of piano keys, musical notes playing on a staff, Cupid shooting an arrow, two people hitting a tennis ball back and forth, a shark fin swimming from left to right and back again, or anything else that fits the theme of a Web page. Try to keep the width and height of the animation fairly reasonable, however, or the file size will get too large.

- **Animated logos**. An animated logo on a home page can draw attention to your company or product name. If your logo is large, you can split it into several different sections, creating an animated graphic in one of the sections. You then can use borderless tables to fit the sections together so that they appear on your page as one graphic.

- **Icons**. Animations can be quite effective in drawing attention to important information on your page. Place an animated envelope or mailbox near your email address, a flashing "New!" icon near a worthy piece of news, a ringing telephone near your phone number, a burning fire near a hot link, and so on.

Creating Transparent GIF Files

You've no doubt seen Web page images that appear as if they are floating on the page. Rather than an image that appears as a square or a rectangle, a transparent GIF appears to be irregularly shaped and allows the background to show through.

You also can apply transparency to animated GIF files, depending on the software you use to create or compile your GIF files. Some GIF animation compilers enable you to define a transparent color when you compile your animation, and others don't. Based on this, you can use one of two different approaches to creating transparent GIF animations:

- If your GIF animation program enables you to choose a transparent color, globally or on a frame-by-frame basis, you can add the transparency before you save the animation.

- If your GIF animation does not enable you to select transparent colors, you'll need to choose a transparent color for each of the still images in your image editing software. Save each individual frame as a transparent GIF and import it into your GIF animation program. It takes a little bit longer to create your animation this way, but it still works.

Choosing a Transparent Color

Here's how a transparent GIF works. You typically use images that have a solid background color behind the areas that you want to stay visible on your Web page. You designate this solid background color as the "transparent" color for your image. If you are designing your animation for a Web page that uses a background image, create or choose GIF files with a background color that is close in color. If your page background is a black sky with stars, for example, use a solid black background for your transparent GIF. If your Web page background is soft and pastel in appearance, create or choose GIF images on a white or light-colored background.

Why is this important? Many image-editing programs use *antialiasing* to soften the appearance of diagonal or curved lines. If you put your black line against a medium or dark background, you'll see outlines and pixels that look wildly out of place. So it's best to start with a background that is similar in color or tone to the page on which you're going to put the graphic.

 Antialiasing is the name of a process that softens the harsh appearance of sharp contrasts in colors. It achieves this by blending pixels that are intermediate in color between the two original contrasting colors. If, for example, you have a black line on a white background, the image editor softens the appearance of a line by inserting shades of gray against the line.

In Figure 8.2, you see an example of antialiasing in action. The cartoon in this image was created against a white background. You might notice some strange pixels and *ghosting* around the image on the black portion of the page (left side), while the same transparent GIF file looks fine on the white side on the right. This is an extreme example, but it illustrates how antialiasing can affect a transparent GIF file.

FIGURE 8.2

Antialiasing can sometimes cause ghosting around a transparent GIF.

If you are creating your own images for transparent GIFs, be sure not to use the background color in any other portion that you do not want to be transparent. There is a reason for this. Any instance of the color you select as transparent will *be* transparent. If any portions of your image also contain that color, your nice artwork will appear to have holes in it that you don't want to be there.

What do you do if you want to *use* the same color that you've selected as transparent within your image? Suppose that you're creating a cartoon on a white background, but you want to use white in the eyes of a character. The solution is simple. Use pure white (Red 255, Green 255, Blue 255) as the background color, and use an *almost* white color (Red 255, Green 255, Blue 250, for example) for your eyes. The colors look very nearly the same, but to the image editing program, color 255,255,255 is different than color 255,255,250. Your character's eyes will be safe.

Programs to Help You Compile Animated GIFs

Assume that you have selected or created a series of images that you want to include in your animation frames. The next step is to compile the individual images into one single animated file. There is a wide variety of utilities that help you create animated GIFs for the Web. Animated GIFs have become so popular that several commercial and shareware graphics programs now include built-in support for creating them. Paint Shop Pro 5.0 and ULead PhotoImpact, both very popular Windows 95/98 image editors, are among those that include GIF animation builders. Both applications are described in more detail later in this chapter in "Tools to Help You Create Your Pictures."

Even presentation programs, such as Microsoft PowerPoint, enable you to create and save presentations as animated GIF files that can be used as banner advertisements.

Although most image editing programs allow you to create GIF files, not all of them enable you to create *animated* GIF files. Conversely, there are programs that help you create animated GIF files but do not create the images themselves. If you have your heart set on a graphics program that doesn't save animated GIFs, have no fear. Here are a couple of standalone programs that help you compile animated GIF files.

GIF Construction Set (Windows Platform)

One of the most popular shareware GIF builders for the Windows platform (available in Windows 3.1 and Windows 95/NT versions) is GIF Construction Set by Alchemy Mindworks. This reasonably priced shareware utility features an Animation wizard that makes construction of animated GIFs a breeze. You build your GIF files through

8

drag-and-drop file selection. Slick features enable you to manage your palette, select transparent colors, add effect transitions and timing, convert AVI video clips to animated GIFs, and much, much more.

You can download the Windows 3.1 and Windows 95/NT versions of GIF Construction Set from Alchemy Mindwork's Web site at `http://www.mindworkshop.com/alchemy/gifcon.html`. The site offers many demos and examples as well.

GifBuilder (Macintosh Platform)

A very popular program for the Macintosh is GifBuilder, by Yves Piquet. GifBuilder is a freeware scriptable utility that enables you to input graphics in several different formats. You can modify existing animated GIFs or import a collection of GIF, TIFF, PICT, or Photoshop (PSD) files. GifBuilder also enables you to input several other animation formats, such as QuickTime movies, PICS files, Adobe Premiere FilmStrip 1.0 files, or the layers of an RGB or grayscale Adobe Photoshop 3.0 file. The current version is 0.5, and it features frame icons in the Frames window, filters, transitions, animation cropping, and more.

The home page for GifBuilder is located at `http://iawww.epfl.ch/Staff/Yves.Piguet/clip2gif-home/GifBuilder.html`. There are links to tutorials included on the Web page.

Exercise 8.1: Compiling an Animation

To Do

The following exercise compiles 10 images of a bouncing ball animation. The filenames are `ball01.tga` through `ball10.tga`. Later in this chapter, I'll show you how these images were created.

I am using ULead PhotoImpact GIF Animator to compile my GIF animation. If you're using another Windows graphics editor but don't have a GIF animator, you can download a trial version of the ULead PhotoImpact GIF Animator from ULead's Web Utilities Web site (`http://www.webutilities.com/ga/ga_main.htm`).

The commands and terminology might be different in the software you use, but the concepts will be pretty much the same. Each GIF animation compiler basically asks you which images you want to insert, the order in which to insert them, time delays between each frame, and so on. If your software has a wizard or helper that steps you through the process, so much the better.

To compile a GIF animation using ULead's GIF Animator, follow these steps:

1. If you downloaded the trial version of the ULead GIF Animator, choose Start, Programs, ULead GIF Animator 3.0a, GIF Animator. When the Startup Wizard screen appears, select the File, Animation Wizard command.

▼   2. In the first screen, you choose the files to include in your animation. Click the Add
        Image button and locate the drive and folder into which you saved your image
        files. Click the *last* filename (ball10.tga) and then shift-click the *first* filename
        (ball01.tga) to select all the frames. Then click Open to place them in the list.
        (For some reason, when you click the first file and Shift-click the last file, the first
        and last files end up in the opposite positions. This is an example of why it's
        important to save your files in a numerical sequence. If you forget to reverse the
        order, you can always drag and drop the filenames in the list to change the order.)

     3. Click Next to advance to the next screen. You're asked if the animation is text ori-
        ented or photo oriented. Depending on your response, it decides whether to apply
        dithering to the image. Dithering is used to simulate colors that don't appear in the
        palette and is most effective when an image contains more than 256 colors. Choose
        Photo Oriented (Dither) and then click Next to continue.

     4. In the Frame Duration screen, you specify how long each image should appear
        before the next one replaces it. You can specify the speed by delay time in hun-
        dredths of a second or by the number of frames per second. If you adjust one
        value, the other changes in relation to it. A small preview of the speed, which
        increments numbers at the speed you select, gives you an idea of how quickly the
        images flip. After you find a value you like (I chose a speed of 15 hundredths of a
        second, which equates to 7 frames per second), click Next to continue.

     5. That's it! The Animation Wizard gives you some information about how it will cre-
        ate the animation. All that is left is to click the Finish button. After the Animation
        Wizard builds your animation file, you see the file appear in your window, as
        shown in Figure 8.3.

FIGURE 8.3

*All the animation files
are combined into a
single file.*

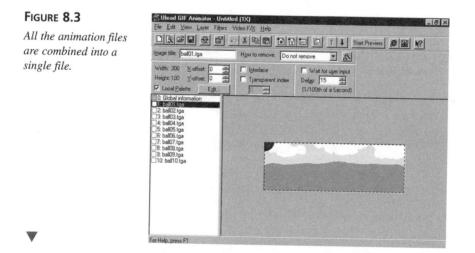

▼

6. To preview the animation, click the Start Preview button in the top toolbar. Press Click Preview to end the preview.

▲

8

Now you know some very basic steps of creating and compiling an animated GIF file. Each GIF animation compiler has its own additional features that are worth looking into. If you've taken the time to download ULead GIF Animator, you can add text transitions, color transitions, special effects, and much more. Because all these effects are rather unique to each program, I'll leave the studying and experimenting up to you.

Before you save your file in ULead GIF Animator, I have to explain *optimization,* because you'll be prompted to answer some questions before the GIF animator saves your file.

Optimization reduces the size of your animation file so that it doesn't take so long to download. Although not all GIF animators provide the same type of optimization wizard, the concepts behind what this wizard does are very helpful and important to learn. These concepts will demonstrate some of the ways you can trim the size of an animation file. And for the demonstration, I'll show you a more complicated animation.

Economizing Animation Size

Remember the dancing chimp you saw at the beginning of the chapter? I made some decisions about file size even before I rendered the individual frames. I was concerned about how large the file was going to be and how long it would take people to download the animation before they could see it appear on my Web page.

The first consideration I made when creating the chimp animation was the physical dimensions of the file. I knew the download time would be much less if the file was small, so I experimented with different sizes until I decided on a 115×120 pixel animation. Smaller dimensions resulted in images that hardly looked like a chimp.

The second consideration was the number of frames to include in the animation. Again, it took experimentation to decide on a good number. The chimp was created in an animation software package that is geared toward video production. The standard speed of videotape in the U.S. is approximately 30 frames per second; however, 30 frames per second is not at all practical for the Internet because the download times would be horrendous. Ten to fifteen frames per second is a far more reasonable speed, but sometimes you can get away with even less. So, I decided to reduce the number of frames to 6 per second and rendered every fifth frame of the animation.

Now, however, I need to adjust the speed of the animated GIF file to compensate for the reduction of frames. Thirty frames per second equates to a display time of approximately 3.33 hundredths of a second per frame. If I multiply that by 5 (because I rendered every fifth frame), this means that I have to set each frame to somewhere around 16 hundredths of a second per frame to make the chimp dance at the right speed.

So far, I've economized the chimp in two ways: the dimensions of the file and the number of frames in the animation. The next way I can trim the file size down is to look at color reduction. Normally, a GIF image contains 256 colors unless you specify otherwise. You can, however, reduce the number of colors in the palette, which reduces the size of the file. Table 8.1 shows what palette optimization does to the download times on the chimp (based on a 28.8Kbps modem). These file sizes were achieved by selecting the option to not dither the palette in the chimp image, which generally results in a smaller file.

TABLE 8.1   Reducing the Number of Colors in the Chimp Palette

Number of Colors	File Size	Download Time at 28.8
256-color palette	54,654 bytes	23 seconds
Reduced to 128 colors	50,290 bytes	17 seconds
Reduced to 64 colors	41,637 bytes	15 seconds
Reduced to 32 colors	34,772 bytes	13 seconds
Reduced to 16 colors	28,324 bytes	10 seconds

At 16 colors, my chimp still looks somewhat respectable, but there are some little sparkles that appear around him in some of the frames. So, I've decided that the 32-color version is a good trade between appearance and download time. By reducing the number of colors in the palette, I've shaved off nearly 20K in file size, and 10 seconds of download time at 28.8 Kbps. Not bad! And as you can see in Figure 8.4, the chimp still looks like a chimp.

FIGURE 8.4

Decreasing the chimp animation to 32 colors reduces the file size by nearly 30Kb, and the appearance is still acceptable.

Exercise 8.2: Optimizing an Animation

▼ To Do

Right now, each of the frames in your bouncing ball animation has a true-color palette, because you compiled your animation with 24-bit Targa (TGA) files. It's highly doubtful that you have 256 colors in your simple animation, so you can decrease the download time considerably by reducing the number of colors in the palette.

Look at what optimization of colors does to the size of your 10-frame 300×100 animation. Look at Table 8.2 and check out the differences in the total file sizes when you reduce the number of colors in the palette. The download times shown in the table are based on a 28.8Kbps modem.

TABLE 8.2 Results of Bouncing Ball Color Palette Reduction

Number of Colors	File Size	Download Time at 28.8
256-color palette	9,476 bytes	3 seconds
Reduced to 128 colors	8,765 bytes	3 seconds
Reduced to 64 colors	8,418 bytes	2 seconds
Reduced to 32 colors	6,971 bytes	2 seconds
Reduced to 16 colors	5,552 bytes	1 second

A two-second download time reduction might not seem like much, but when you have several graphics on a page, every little byte counts. Sixteen colors is perfectly acceptable for your bouncing ball. The 32-color version is a bit better, but is the difference in the quality really worth the extra 1.5Kb in file size? You have to be the judge, and it depends on how important the animation is to your page. Animations that are photographic quality and contain many subtle color changes will not look so wonderful if too much color reduction is applied. In these cases, the only options you have to make the file size smaller is to reduce the number of frames or to reduce the dimensions of the animation.

To optimize the number of colors in your animation, follow these steps in ULead GIF Animator:

1. Choose File, Optimization Wizard, or press F11. The first screen of the Optimization Wizard appears.

2. You are asked whether you want to create a Super Palette for your animation. It generally is a good idea to do so, because this selects the best possible colors from all the frames in your animation. Cases when you don't want to do this are when you have drastic color changes (flashing lights, stark transitions, and so on). Generally, file sizes are smaller when you use the Super Palette. Click Next after you choose Yes to create a Super Palette.

3. The Optimization Wizard asks how many colors you want to include in the Super Palette. Type **32** in the Number of Colors field. Then, choose the Yes option to dither the colors in the Super Palette for photo-oriented images. Choose Next to advance to the next screen.

4. Two options that affect the size of your animation appear on the next screen. The first option asks whether you want to remove redundant pixels. If a pixel is the same color in one frame as it was in the previous one, why not reuse it rather than redrawing it? Choose Yes (default selection) to remove the redundant pixels.

   Next, the wizard asks whether you want to remove comment blocks. You can add comments such as name, notes, and so on to your GIF file, but it increases its size. Choose Yes (default selection) to remove them if you don't really need them.

   Click Next to advance to the next screen.

5. The wizard displays your choices so that you can review them. After you're satisfied with your selections, click Finish to optimize the animation. The screen shown in Figure 8.5 displays the savings and the download times for you. You can preview the animation by clicking the Preview button. Close the Preview window (if you've selected it) by clicking the upper-right X button.

6. After you preview the results, click the Save As button in the GIF Optimization screen. Save the animation as `bouncing-32.gif`.

FIGURE 8.5.

The wizard displays the results of the optimization and shows you the savings.

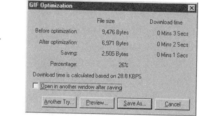

Tools to Help You Create Your Pictures

Baby Cha and the dancing chimp are examples of what you can achieve with state-of-the-art animation software today. Don't despair, however. You don't *really* need expensive software to create animations for your Web pages. Several very respectable image editors are available as reasonably priced shareware. You can download them from the Internet and evaluate their features before you purchase them. If you prefer retail software and the advantages of a nice user manual, there are several retail packages that are powerful and reasonably priced as well.

Earlier, I mentioned that one of the more popular image editing tools for the Windows 95/98 and Windows NT platforms is Paint Shop Pro 5.0. This powerful shareware/retail graphics program also includes an animated GIF compiler called Animation Shop that steps you through the process of creating animated GIF files quite easily. Its features are very similar to the ULead GIF Animator that I used earlier in this chapter to create my animated GIF file. You can download the most current shareware version of Paint Shop Pro (and Animation Studio) from `http://www.jasc.com/psp5.html`.

ULead PhotoImpact (`http://www.ulead.com/pi/runme.htm`) is a retail graphics editor that also includes many image editing and animation capabilities. I've already shown you its companion program, the GIF Animator, in this chapter. You can download a 30-day trial version of both from ULead's Web site.

CNET includes on its Web site a great resource for product demos and shareware downloads in all different categories. Its Download.com site (shown in Figure 8.6) offers easy access to information on just about every type of software program you can imagine. Some are time-limited or save-disabled demos of retail software, while others are shareware applications that you can try fully before you buy. You can easily tell at a glance which are the most popular by the number of downloads, but most products also include a comprehensive list of features that you can review before clicking the download button.

FIGURE 8.6

CNET's Download.com provides a wealth of resources for image editing and animation software.

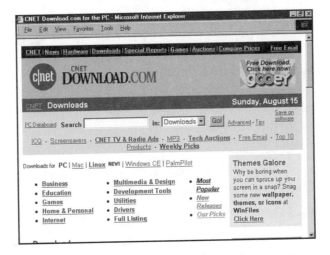

For animation, image editing, or multimedia authoring tools, check out the Multimedia and Design category at Download.com for the platform of your choice (PC or Macintosh). PC programs can be found at
`http://www.download.com/pc/fdoor/0,322,0,00.html?st.dl.mfd.platforms.fd`.

Macintosh users can find programs of interest at
`http://www.download.com/mac/fdoor/0,322,0,00.html?st.dl.fd.platforms.fd`.

Alternatively, you can visit CNET's shareware download areas at `http://www.`
`shareware.com/` or the Web Building area at `http://home.cnet.com/category/`
`0-3880.html`. Shareware.com enables you to search through more than 250,000 different
shareware titles for the shareware of your choice, while the Web Building area focuses
on software that is more related to the Web.

Useful Software Features

All graphics programs are not created equal, and there are so many of them that often it
is hard to decide which ones are the best. There are, however, some features that are
advantageous, especially when creating animations for the Web. Following are a few recommendations for what your software should include:

- The capability to open, create, and save images in a wide variety of file formats.
  Most importantly, you want to be able to create and save GIF and JPEG images for
  Web pages.

- The capability to reduce the number of colors in a 256-color GIF image. Saving an
  image that has only three or four colors with a 256-color palette wastes a *lot* of
  bytes, as you learned earlier in this chapter.

- The capability to work with selections, objects, and layers. Selections enable you
  to work with a portion of an image without affecting the remaining part of the
  image. Objects "float" in an image, enabling you to easily reposition or resize
  them as necessary to fit the composition. Layers enable you to place objects in
  front of or behind each other.

- The capability to save an image with transparent regions. This is important if you
  want to create transparent GIF files that appear as though they are floating on your
  Web page. It's even better if your GIF animation compiler also has this feature.

After you find an image editor you like, the remaining ingredients are a bit trickier—you
need an eye for movement, a reasonable amount of patience, and a lot of creativity.

Exercise 8.3: Creating the Bouncing Ball Animation Frames

▲ To Do

I've chosen ULead PhotoImpact to create the example in this chapter. If you are using a
different graphics program, don't worry. The concepts I discuss here are fairly common.
Though it might be a bit challenging if the software is new to you, you should be able to
muddle your way through a similar example with your own image editor. My intent is to
spark ideas and software features you should look for in an image editing package. If
your graphics program supports selections and gradient fills, the bouncing ball animation
should be fairly easy to reproduce.

It's easiest to begin any animation with the portions that remain the same from frame to
frame. To start the bouncing ball animation, create a 300×100-pixel true-color image

▼ with a white background. (You have access to all the available effects while working in true-color mode in any image editing program). Then, using the Paint tool (third button from the bottom in the left toolbar), draw the sky and the ground as shown in Figure 8.7.

Most image editing programs enable you to adjust the size of the brush that you paint with. In PhotoImpact, you can adjust the size of the brush and select your color from the control bar near the top of your screen, where indicated in Figure 8.7. There is a multiple undo feature that enables you to delete one or more actions if you don't like what you've done. Just choose Edit, Undo Before. The most recent action appears at the top of the list.

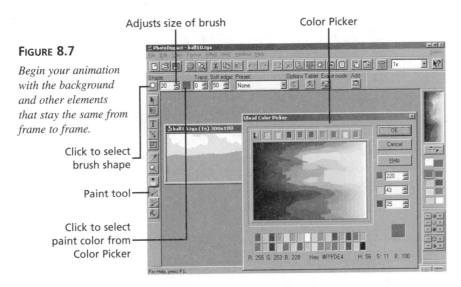

FIGURE 8.7

Begin your animation with the background and other elements that stay the same from frame to frame.

Adjusts size of brush

Color Picker

Click to select brush shape

Paint tool

Click to select paint color from Color Picker

Easy enough so far? The next step is to create the ball. For this, you'll create a circle and fill it with a color gradient. This is another feature that is very common to most image editors. Fortunately, PhotoImpact makes it easy for you. Create a second true-color image that measures 40×40 pixels. The background color doesn't matter because it will eventually be transparent, but leave it at white. Choose the Selection tool, and change the shape of the selection to Circle. To create a circular selection, begin at the top-left corner of the small image. Drag your mouse or stylus toward the bottom-right corner until the small image is filled with a circle. Then release the mouse. You'll see a blue and red marquee that surrounds the circle. This indicates that the area you selected is active (see Figure 8.8).

Now you need to fill the circle with the gradient. This process probably will be different if you are using another image editor. You typically find gradient fills as an option for the Paint Bucket or Fill command. In PhotoImpact, choose the Elliptical Gradient Fill from

▼ the toolbox (you'll need to click and hold the Fill tool to open the flyout menu and select

▼   the Elliptical Gradient Fill from there). Select Two-Color fill method and choose Red and Black for the gradient colors.

FIGURE 8.8

Create a circular selection in a second smaller image.

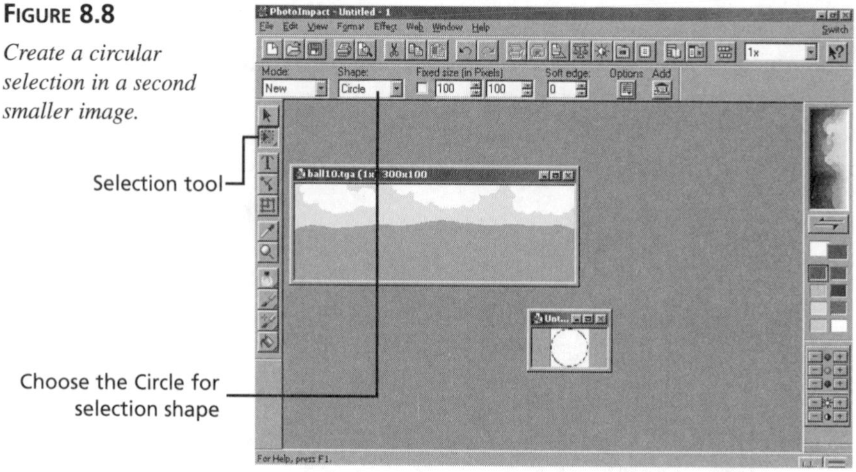

Selection tool—

Choose the Circle for selection shape

Now, position the Fill tool where you want the bright red highlight to appear on the ball. For example, place the highlight above and right of the center. Then, click and drag until the outline for the gradient fill surrounds the ball completely, as shown in Figure 8.9. After you release the mouse, you'll have a nice three-dimensional ball!

Choose Two-Color fill method   Outer color for gradient (Black)

FIGURE 8.9

Create a Sunburst gradient to fill the circular selection.

Inner color for gradient (Red)

Elliptical Gradient Fill tool

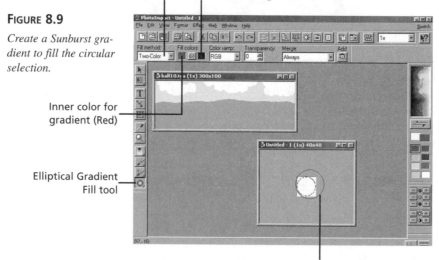

▼

Surround ball with circle that defines the gradient

8

▼ Now you place the ball into the background, which is really easy to do. With the filled circle still selected, use Ctrl+C to copy the circular selection into your Clipboard. Switch to the background image (click its title bar to make it active) and use Ctrl+V to paste the ball into the background, as an object. Choose the Pick tool from the toolbox and position the ball, as shown in Figure 8.10.

FIGURE 8.10

Copy the ball and paste it into the background image.

Pick tool

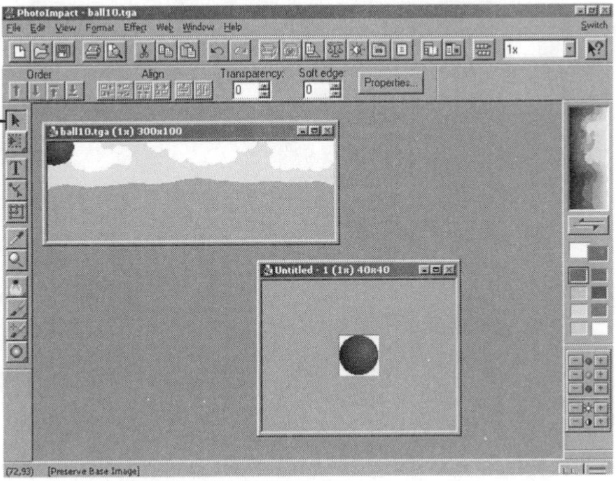

When I create an animation, I usually like to save each frame in true-color format and let the GIF animation program choose the best palette of colors for all the frames. This might not always be possible, however. If you want to add transparent areas to an animation, for example, some programs force you to reduce the image to 256 colors before selecting a transparent color and saving it as a GIF file.

Your bouncing ball animation does not contain transparent areas, and palettes tend to be more reliable when you start with true-color images. To save the first frame, choose File, Save As. From the Save As Type field, choose TGA (Targa File Format), as shown in Figure 8.11. Save the file with a name that you can easily remember (such as ball01.tga), and be sure to end the filename with enough digits to accommodate the total number of frames you want to create. To create a 10-frame animation, for example, name the first file ball01.tga, and number each subsequent file in order until you end with ball10.tga.

Note

When you save your images in PhotoImpact, you'll receive a warning that the floating object will be merged with the background. It's fine to choose Yes to continue, because as long as you keep your original file open while you create the remaining frames, the ball will remain floating. If you want

▼

▼

> to save a copy of your image with the ball still floating, just in case, save a
> frame in UFO (ULead File for Objects) format, or the native format that is
> applicable to your image editor if it supports floating objects.

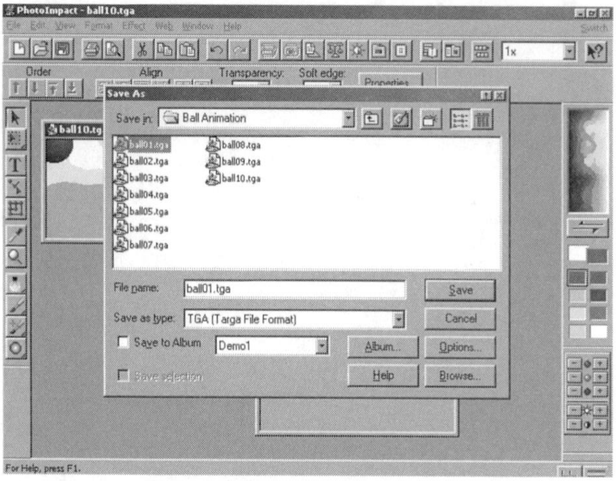

FIGURE 8.11

*Save the first frame of
the animation with a
filename that ends with
a number.*

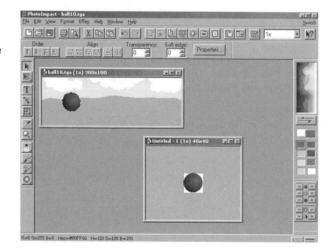

For the next frame, use the Pick tool to reposition the ball downward and toward the
right, as shown in Figure 8.12. Save this frame as `ball02.tga`.

FIGURE 8.12

*For the next frame,
reposition the ball with
the Pick tool and save
the file under a new
name.*

Get the idea? As you advance from frame to frame, you reposition the ball to simulate a
▼   bouncing movement, up and down from left to right. Create the remaining frames of

▼ your animation in this manner and number them sequentially until you make the ball bounce off the right side of the background. For the last frame, delete the ball from your image using the Delete key and save the final TGA file. Figure 8.13 shows some additional frames that I created for this animation. I'm displaying them at half size so that you can easily see how each frame looks in relation to the other.

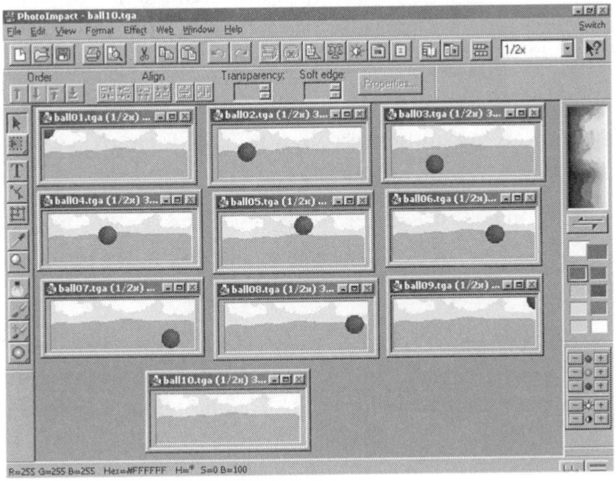

FIGURE 8.13

Create the remaining frames in a similar manner, saving each file with a sequential filename.

▲

Summary

Hopefully, you've had a nice relaxing break while doing the exercises in this chapter. The simple examples should teach you some very basic concepts that will help you progress further. If you can't create a perfect animation the first time, don't be discouraged—it takes a bit of practice. Just keep at it, and eventually you'll get there. Also, study the features and capabilities of the software you select. Each program has its own bag of tricks that help make graphics and animation creation easy for you.

Workshop

This workshop covers the most important points in creating animations for the Web, and you also have a couple more exercises that will take you to the next step in animation.

Q&A

Q I'd like my animated GIF file to pause at the end and then start from the beginning again. How do I do this?

A Most animated GIF compilers allow you to adjust the display times of each frame individually. Simply select the last frame in your animation and increase the display time for that frame. To pause it for one second, for example, enter 100 hundredths of a second. The other frames will still play at their original speed, and when you reach the last frame, it is displayed for one second before the animation begins again.

Q Can I create an animated background for my Web page?

A You can, but it's not really a good idea. Although animated clouds or twinkling stars seem like neat ideas for backgrounds, they will distract people from the information on your page. Remember what's most important on your page and use animation to enhance it where appropriate.

Q How do I create animations in other file formats, such as Video for Windows (AVI), Quick Time, or MPEG?

A The development process is pretty much the same. You'll still need to create each individual frame of your animation, but you'll need to obtain a software program that saves animations in the formats you desire.

Quiz

1. How does an animated GIF differ from a regular GIF file?
2. What is the easiest way to begin an animation?
3. Name three ways that you can reduce the download time of an animation file.
4. Why is it a good idea to save your individual frames with filenames that are numbered sequentially?
5. What is the best use of animation on a Web page?

Answers

1. An animated GIF file contains multiple images that are compiled into one. They play in sequence to give the illusion of movement.
2. The easiest way to begin an animation is by drawing the portions of the image that will stay the same from frame to frame.
3. You can reduce the size of an animation file by reducing its dimensions, decreasing the number of frames in an animation, or reducing the number of colors in the animation.
4. Some animation programs will change the order of frames when you select more than one at a time. By numbering your frames in order, you can tell at a glance if this has happened.
5. Animations are best used to draw attention to an important piece of information on a Web page.

Exercises

1. Now that you've learned how to add some movement, try a slightly more challenging example. Create a simple face. Make the eyes blink, and change the expression from a frown to a smile.

2. Create a text banner. Animate the text by changing color, position, or both from frame to frame.

8

DAY 9

Creating and Using Imagemaps

Imagemaps are a special kind of clickable image. Usually, when you embed an image inside a link, clicking anywhere on that image takes you to one single location. Using imagemaps, you can go to different locations, depending on where inside the image you click. In this chapter, you'll learn all about imagemaps and how to create them, including the following:

- What an imagemap is
- Creating server-side imagemaps
- Creating client-side imagemaps
- Supporting both types of imagemaps

What Is an Imagemap?

In Chapter 7, "Using Images, Color, and Backgrounds," you learned how to create an image that doubles as a link simply by including the `<img>` tag inside a link (`<a>`) tag. In this way, the entire image becomes a link. You then can click the image, the background, or the border, and get the same effect.

In imagemaps, different parts of the image activate different links. By using imagemaps, you can create a visual hyperlinked map that links you to pages describing the regions you click, as in Figure 9.1. You also can create visual metaphors for the information you're presenting: a set of books on a shelf or a photograph in which each person in the picture is individually described.

FIGURE 9.1

Imagemaps: different places, different links.

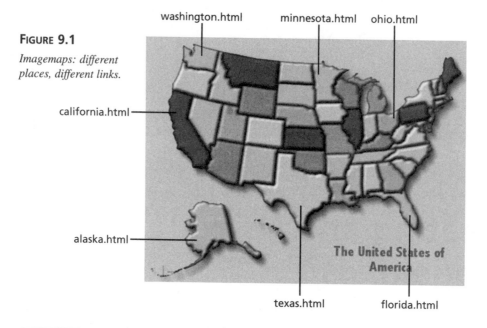

NEW TERM *Imagemaps* are special images containing different areas that point to different link locations. The place on the image where you click the mouse determines the place on the site to which you go.

There are two kinds of imagemaps: *server-side* imagemaps and *client-side* imagemaps. Server-side imagemaps were used in the earlier days of the Web, but they posed some problems for Web authors that will be discussed in this chapter. Today, client-side imagemaps, which are processed by browsers, are used more frequently and offer many advantages over older, server-side imagemaps.

NEW TERM *Server-side imagemaps* are implemented using an image displayed by the client and a program that runs on the server.

Client-side imagemaps work in the same ways as server-side imagemaps, except no program runs on the server. All the processing of coordinates and pointers to different locations occurs in the browser.

Although server-side imagemaps are not used as frequently as they used to be, learning about both types of image maps can be advantageous. If you want to provide backward-compatibility for imagemaps, you'll need to learn both methods, which this chapter discusses.

Server-Side Imagemaps

When imagemaps first appeared on the Web, they were created with special programs that ran on the server. Such imagemaps are referred to as *server-side* imagemaps.

When a browser activates a link on a server-side imagemap, it calls a special imagemap program stored on a Web server. In addition to calling the imagemap program, the browser also sends the program the x,y coordinates of the position, on the image, where the mouse was clicked. The imagemap program then looks up a special map file that matches regions in the image to URLs, performs some calculations to determine which page to load, and then loads the page.

Server-side imagemaps were one of the earliest Web features. They are supported by most, if not all, graphical browsers. There are, however, problems associated with server-side imagemaps, as the following list explains:

- Normally, when you move your cursor over a hyperlink, the URL to which the link points appears in the Web browser's status bar. Because the Web browser has no idea where the parts of a server-side imagemap point, however, all you see when you place your cursor over a server-side imagemap is the URL of the imagemap program itself (not very helpful), or that URL and a set of x,y coordinates (still not very helpful).

- You cannot use or test server-side imagemaps with local files. Imagemaps require the use of a Web server to run the imagemap program and process the x,y coordinates.

- Because a special program must be run by the server every time a user clicks a page that contains imagemaps, imagemaps are much slower to respond to mouse clicks than normal links or images as links. Consequently, the imagemaps seem to take forever to respond to requests for a new page.

Client-Side Imagemaps

Although server-side imagemaps have been in common use for some time, the problems associated with them have led to the development of a new type of imagemap called a *client-side* imagemap. Client-side imagemaps remove all the difficulties of server-side imagemaps by eliminating the need for a special imagemap program on the server. Instead, they manage all the image-map processing locally on the Web browser itself (the "client"). As a result, most Web designers are now using this method instead.

> **Note**
> Client-side imagemaps are supported by the latest Web browsers, including Netscape (2.0 and later) and Internet Explorer (3.0 and later). The proposal for client-side imagemaps made its way into the HTML 3.2 specification and also is part of HTML 4.0.

Now you know the basic differences between server-side and client-side imagemaps. Later in this chapter, you'll learn how to create and use each type.

Imagemaps and Text-Only Browsers

Because of the inherently graphical nature of imagemaps, they can work only in graphical browsers. In fact, if you try to view a document with an imagemap in a text-only browser such as Lynx, you don't even get an indication that the image exists—unless, of course, the image contains an `alt` attribute. Even with the `alt` attribute, however, you won't be able to navigate the presentation with a text browser or when images are turned off in a graphical browser. If you decide to create a Web page that contains an imagemap, it's doubly important that you also create a text-only equivalent so that readers who don't see the imagemap can use your page. The use of imagemaps can effectively lock out readers using text-only browsers; have sympathy and allow them at least some method for viewing your content.

Creating Server-Side Imagemaps

Although server-side imagemaps have their disadvantages, it is still helpful to know how to create them. Unfortunately, because some Web servers have different ways of creating server-side imagemaps, explaining how to create them presents its own wrinkles. The methods even vary among servers on the same platform. The W3C (CERN) httpd server and NCSA HTTPd server, for example, have incompatible methods of implementing image files. All servers, however, use the same basic ingredients for imagemaps, as in the following:

- Special HTML code to indicate that an image is a map
- A map file on the server that indicates regions on the image and the Web pages to which they point
- An image-mapping CGI script that links it all together

This section explains how to construct server-side, clickable images in general, but its examples focus on the NCSA HTTP-style servers such as NCSA and Apache. If you need more information for your server, see the documentation that comes with that server, or get help from your Web administrator.

Getting an Image

To create an imagemap, you'll need an image (of course). The image that serves as the map is most useful if it has several discrete visual areas that can be individually selected—for example, images with several symbolic elements or images that can be easily broken down into polygons. Photographs make difficult imagemaps because their various "elements" tend to blend together or are of unusual shapes. Figures 9.2 and 9.3 show examples of good and poor images for imagemaps.

9

FIGURE 9.2

A good image for an imagemap.

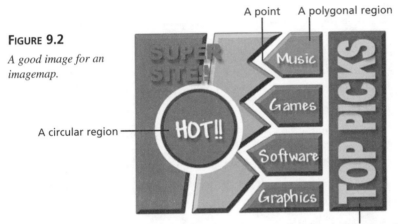

FIGURE 9.3

A not-so-good image for an imagemap.

Determining Your Coordinates

The heart of the server-side imagemap is a *map file*. Creating a map file involves sketching out the regions in your image that are clickable, determining the coordinates that define those regions, and deciding on the HTML pages to which they should point.

> **Note**
>
> The format of the map file depends on the image-mapping program you're using on your server. This section discusses imagemaps on the NCSA HTTP server and the map files it uses by default. If you're using a different server, you might have several image-mapping programs with several map formats from which to choose. If you're in this situation, check with your Web administrator or read your server documentation carefully.

You can create a map file either by sketching regions and manually noting the coordinates or by using an imagemap-making program. The latter method is easier because the program automatically generates a map file based on the regions you draw with the mouse.

The Mapedit program for Windows and WebMap for the Macintosh can help you create map files in NCSA format. If you use a UNIX-based system, there is a version of Mapedit available via FTP. (See Appendix A, "Sources of Further Information," for a full list of related FTP sites.) In addition, many of the latest WYSIWYG editors for HTML pages provide facilities for generating imagemaps.

Table 9.1 provides a list of current tools for generating imagemaps.

Table 9.1   Imagemap Creation Software

Name	Platform	URL
Imaptool	Linux/X-Windows	http://www.sci.fi/~uucee/ownprojects/
LiveImage	Windows	http://www.mediatec.com/
Mapedit	Windows/UNIX/Mac	http://www.boutell.com/mapedit/
Poor Person's Image Mapper	X Window	http://www.pangloss.com/seidel/ClrHlpr/ imagemap.html

If you need your map file in a different format, you can always use these programs to create a basic map and then convert the coordinates into the map file format your server needs.

If you must create your map files by hand, here's how to do it. First, make a sketch of the regions you want to make active on your image. Figure 9.4 shows an example of the three types of shapes that you can specify in an imagemap: circles, rectangles, and polygons.

FIGURE 9.4

Sketching map-able regions.

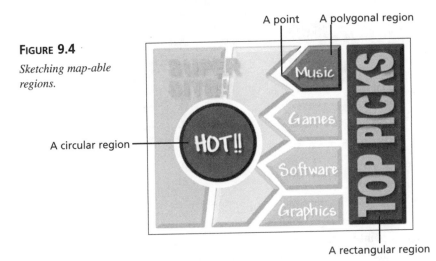

9

You next need to determine the coordinates for the endpoints of those regions—this process is pretty much the same whether you are creating server-side or client-side imagemaps. Most image-editing programs have an option that displays the coordinates of the current mouse position. Use this feature to note the appropriate coordinates. (All the mapping programs mentioned previously will create a map file for you, but for now, following the steps manually will help you better understand the processes involved.)

Defining a Polygon

Figure 9.5 shows the (x,y) coordinates of a polygonal region. These values are based on their positions from the upper-left corner of the image, which is coordinate (0,0). The first number in the coordinate pair indicates the x value and defines the number of pixels from the extreme left of the image. The second number in the pair indicates the y measurement and defines the number of pixels from the top of the image.

Note

The 0,0 origin is in the upper-left corner of the image, and positive y is down.

FIGURE 9.5

Getting the coordinates for a polygon.

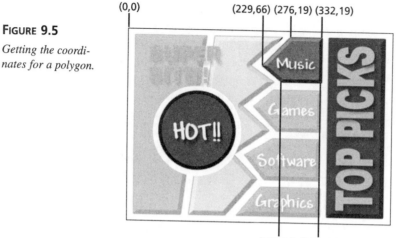

Defining a Circle

Figure 9.6 shows how to get the coordinates for circle regions. Here, you note the coordinates for the center point of the circle and the radius, in pixels. The center point of the circle is defined as the (x,y) coordinate from the upper-left corner of the image.

FIGURE 9.6

Getting the coordinates for a circle.

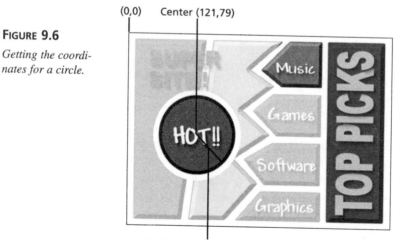

Defining a Rectangle

Figure 9.7 shows how to obtain coordinates for rectangle regions. Here, note the (x,y) coordinates for the upper-left and lower-right corners of the rectangle.

FIGURE 9.7

Getting the coordinates for a rectangle.

9

Defining a Point

Older browsers also enabled you to define points in an imagemap. Points enable you to specify that a given mouse click will activate the nearest point if it doesn't land directly on a region. Points are useful for photographs or other images with nondiscrete elements, or for a finer granularity than just "everything not in a region." For points, simply note the (x,y) coordinates from the upper-left corner of the image.

Creating and Saving Your Map File

After you map all the clickable regions in your image, you're more than halfway there. The next step is to come up with a set of URLs to link to for each region or point that is selected. You can have multiple regions pointing to the same URL, but each region must have only one link.

With all your regions, coordinates, and URLs noted, you now can write a map file for your server. The syntax for NCSA HTTP map files looks like the following:

```
default URL
circle URL x,y radius
rect URL x,y x,y
poly URL x1,y1 x2,y2 ... xN,yN
point URL x,y
```

The map files for your particular server's image-map program might look different than this, but the essential parts are there. Substitute the values for the coordinates you noted previously in each of the *x* or *y* positions (or *x1*, *y1*, and so on). Note that the *radius* (in the `circle` line) is the radius for the circle region.

The order of regions in the map file is relevant: The farther up a region is in the file, the higher precedence it has for mouse clicks. If part of the region that occurs on overlapping regions is selected, the first region listed in the map file is the one that is activated.

Finally, the map file includes a "default" region with no coordinates, just a URL. The default is used when a mouse click that is not inside a region is selected; it provides a catch-all for the parts of the image that do not point to a specific link. (Note that if you use an NCSA HTTPd map file and you include default, you shouldn't include any points. The existence of point elements precludes that of default.)

If you plug the coordinates shown in Figures 9.5 through 9.7 into the NCSA HTTPd map file, the coordinates and URLs might look as follows:

```
poly http://www.foo.com/mysite/music.html 229,66 276,19, 332,19 333,94, 263,94
circle http://www.foo.com/mysite/hotlinks.html 121,79 66
rect http://www.foo.com/mysite/toppicks.html 342,19 440,318
```

The URLs you specify for either format must be either full URLs (starting with http, ftp, or some other protocol) or the full pathnames to the files you are linking—that is, everything you could include after the hostname in a URL. You cannot specify relative pathnames in the imagemap file.

Here's another sample of an NCSA HTTPd map file:

```
circle /www/mapping.html 10,15 20
circle /www/mapping.html 346,23 59
poly /www/test/orange.html 192,3 192,170 115,217
rect /www/pencil.html 57,57 100,210
point /www/pencil.html 100,100
point /www/orange.html 200,200
```

Creating the map file is the hardest part of making an imagemap. After you write a map file for your image, you'll need to install the map file on your server. Save your map file with a descriptive name, such as myimage.map). Where you install the map file on your server isn't important, but I like to put my map files in a central directory called maps, at the top level of my Web files.

Installing the Server-Side Imagemap Program

In addition to the imagemap file that you just learned about, you'll have to install a server-side imagemap program on your server. These usually are placed into a special directory called cgi-bin, which has been specially set up to store programs and scripts for your server. Most servers have an image program set up by default, and if you're using someone else's server, that program most likely will be available to you as well. The program to look for is often called htimage or imagemap.

Caution
Be careful with the NCSA server and the imagemap program. Older versions of imagemap were more difficult to work with and required an extra configuration file; the program that comes with the 1.5 version of the server works much better. If you aren't running the most recent version of the NCSA server, you can get the new imagemap program from http://hoohoo.ncsa.uiuc.edu/docs/tutorials/imagemap.txt.

9

Linking It All Together

Now you have an image, a map file that describes the coordinates of the clickable regions and their destinations, and a server-side imagemap program. Now you can hook it all up.

Insert the image on a Web page. In this page, you'll use the <a> and <img> tags together to create the effect of the clickable image. Following is an example using NCSA's imagemap program:

```
<a href="/cgi-bin/imagemap/maps/myimage.map">
<img src="image.gif" ismap></a>
```

Notice several things about this link. First, the link to the image-map script (imagemap) is indicated the way you would expect, but then the path to the map file is appended to the end of it. The path to the map file should be a full pathname from the root of your Web directory (everything after the hostname in your URL), in this case cgi-bin/imagemap/maps/myimage.map.

The second part of the HTML code that creates a server-side map is the ismap attribute to the <img> tag. This is a simple attribute with no value that tells the browser to send individual mouse-click coordinates to the imagemap program on the server side for processing.

And now, with all three parts of the server-side imagemap in place (the map file, the imagemap program, and the special HTML code), the imagemap should work. You should be able to load your HTML file into your browser and use the imagemap to go to different pages on your server by selecting different parts of the map.

Note
If you're running the NCSA HTTPd server and you don't have the newest version of imagemap, you'll get the error Cannot Open Configuration file when you try to select portions of your image. If you get these errors, check with your Web administrator.

Exercise 9.1: A Clickable Jukebox

Imagemaps can get pretty hairy. The map files are prone to error if you don't have your areas clearly outlined and everything installed in the right place. In this exercise, you'll take an image and create a map file for it using the NCSA server map file format (see Figure 9.8). This way, you can get a feel for what the map files look like and how to create them.

FIGURE 9.8

The jukebox image.

First, you define the regions that will be clickable on this image. You might notice there are six rectangular "buttons" with music categories on them, a center area that looks like a house (which is perfect for the polygon tool), and a circle with a question mark inside. Figure 9.9 shows examples of the type of regions it makes sense to create on the image.

FIGURE 9.9

The jukebox with areas defined.

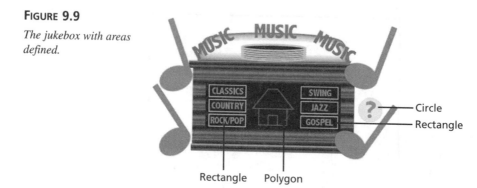

Now that you have an idea of where the various regions are on your image, you'll need to find the exact coordinates of the areas as they appear in your image. To find those coordinates, you can use a mapping program such as Mapedit or WebMap (highly recommended), or you can do it manually. If you try it manually, most image-editing programs should have a way of displaying the x and y coordinates of the image when you move the mouse over it.

▼ PhotoImpact 4.0, which I mentioned in Chapter 8, "Creating Animated Graphics," displays the position of the cursor at the bottom-left corner in the status bar. PhotoImpact 4.0 also comes with an imagemap assistant. You simply use the Rectangle, Circle, or Polygon selection tools to create a rectangular, circular, or polygonal selection around the area you want to define. You then choose Web, Image Map Tag, and you can view the coordinate information, specify a URL, and choose the type of imagemap you want to create. PhotoImpact displays the proper code for NCSA and CERN server-side imagemaps as well as for client-side imagemaps. Figure 9.10 shows an example of the Imagemap Assistant in PhotoImpact.

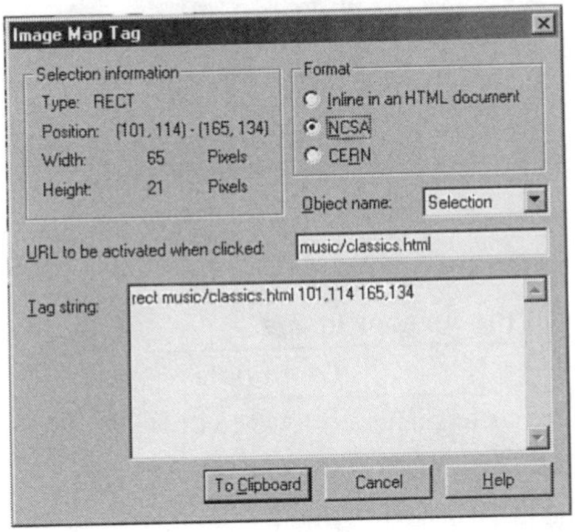

FIGURE 9.10

The Image Map Tag dialog box in PhotoImpact 4.0.

> **Tip**
>
> You don't have an image-editing program? Here's a trick if you use Netscape as your browser: Create an HTML file with the image inside a link pointing to a fake file and include the `ismap` attribute inside the `<img>` tag. You don't actually need a real link; anything will do. The HTML code might look something like the following:
>
> `<a href="nothing"><img src="myimage.gif" ismap></a>`
>
> Now, if you load that HTML file into your browser, the image will be displayed as if it were an imagemap, and when you move your mouse over it, the x and y coordinates will appear in the status line of the browser. Using this trick, you can find the coordinates for the map file of any point on that image.

With regions and a list of coordinates, you just need the Web pages to jump to when the appropriate area is selected. These can be any documents, or they can be scripts; you can
▼ use anything you can call from a browser as a jump destination. For this example, I've

▼ created several documents and have stored them inside the `music` directory on my Web server. These are the pages you'll define as the end-points of the jumps when the clickable images are selected. Figure 9.11 identifies each of the eight clickable areas in the imagemap. Table 9.2 shows the coordinates of each and the URL to which each clickable area navigates when it is clicked.

FIGURE 9.11

Eight hotspots, numbered as identified in Table 9.2.

Table 9.2   Clickable Areas in the Jukebox Image

Number	Type	URL	Coordinates
1	rect	music/classics.html	101,113 165,134
2	rect	music/country.html	101,139 165,159
3	rect	music/rockpop.html	101,163 165,183
4	poly	music/home.html	175,152 203,118
			220,118 247,152
			237,153 237,181
			186,181 186,153
5	rect	music/swing.html	259,113 323,134
6	rect	music/jazz.html	259,139 323,159
7	rect	music/gospel.html	259,163 323,183
8	circle	music/help.html	379,152 21

Now, create the entry in the map file for the Classics rectangle, with the coordinates and the file to link to when that area is clicked. In NCSA map file, the information looks like the following:

▼ `rect /music/classics.html 101,113 165,134`

▼ Note that the URLs in the map file must be absolute pathnames from the top of the Web root (not from the top of the file system). They cannot be relative URLs from the map file; imagemaps don't work like that. In this case, my `music` directory is at the Web root, and the `classics.html` file is in that directory; so, the URL for the purposes of the map file is `/music/classics.html`.

You now can create identical entries for the other areas in the image (Country, Rock/Pop, Home, Swing, Jazz, Gospel, and Help). Don't forget to include a default line in the map file to map mouse clicks that don't hit any clickable areas (here, a file called `notaspot.html`). After you finish, the entire map file looks like the following:

```
default /music/notaspot.html
rect /music/classics.html 101,113 165,134
rect /music/country.html 101,139 165,159
rect /music/rockpop.html 101,163 165,183
poly /music/home.html 175,152 203,118 220,118 247,152 237,153
   237,181 186,181 186,153
rect /music/swing.html 259,113 323,134
rect /music/jazz.html 259,139 323,159
rect /music/gospel.html 259,163 323,183
circle /music/help.html 379,152 21
```

Save your map file to your map directory on the server (or wherever you keep your maps). Use a filename such as `jukebox.map`. Finally, create a Web page that includes the jukebox image, the `ismap` attribute in the `<img>` tag, and the link to the image mapping program. Following is an example that uses the imagemap program on my server:

```
<a href="http://www.lne.com/cgi-bin/imagemap/maps/jukebox.map">
<img src="jukebox.gif" ismap></a>
```

▲ That's it! With everything connected, clicking the image should load the page for that part of the image.

Figure 9.12 shows the completed Web page. Notice that I also have included equivalent text links beneath the imagemap. These are added in case those who visit your page are using text-only browsers, or have their images turned off. The complete code for the Web page is as follows:

INPUT

```
<!DOCTYPE html PUBLIC "-//W3C//DTD XHTML 1.0 Transitional//EN"
"http://www.w3.org/TR/xhtml1/DTD/transitional.dtd">
<html>
<head>
<title>The Really Cool Music Page</title>
</head>
<body bgcolor="#ffffff">
<div align="center">
<h1>The Really Cool Music Page</h1>
<p>Select the type of music you want to hear.<br />
```

```
You'll go to a list of songs that you can select from.</p>
<p><a href="http://www.lne.com/cgi-bin/imagemap/maps/jukebox.map">
<img src="jukebox.gif" alt="Juke Box" ismap width="425" height="242" />
</a>
</p>
<p><a href="code/music/home.html">Home</a> |
<a href="code/music/classics.html">Classics</a> |
<a href="code/music/country.html">Country</a> |
<a href="code/music/rockpop.html">Rock/Pop</a> |
<a href="code/music/swing.html">Swing</a> |
<a href="code/music/jazz.html">Jazz</a> |
<a href="code/music/gospel.html">Gospel</a> |
<a href="code/music/help.html">Help</a></p>
</div>
</body>
</html>
```

FIGURE 9.12

A completed Jukebox Web page with server-side imagemap.

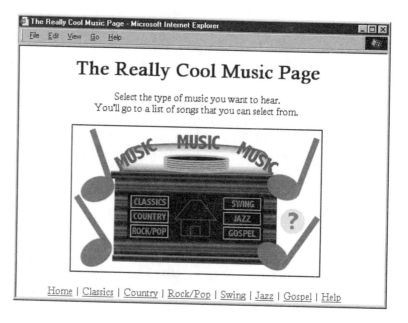

Creating Client-Side Imagemaps

Now that you know how to create imagemaps the old way, take a look at the new way. As mentioned previously, client-side imagemaps offer several improvements over server-side imagemaps. The most significant improvement is that you don't need to include a server-side imagemap program on your server. Newer Web browsers process the imagemap locally on users' computers.

When you create a client-side imagemap, many of the steps for finding the coordinates of each area on the map are exactly the same as they are for creating server-side imagemaps. Unlike a server-side imagemap, however, which uses a separate file to store the coordinates and references for each hyperlink, client-side imagemaps store all the mapping information as part of an HTML document.

The `<map>` and `<area>` Tags

To include a client-side imagemap inside an HTML document, you use the `<map>` tag, which looks like the following:

```
<map name="mapname"> coordinates and links  </map>
```

The value assigned to the `name` attribute is the name of this map definition. This is the name that will be used later to associate the clickable image with its corresponding coordinates and hyperlink references—so, if you have multiple imagemaps on the same page, you can have multiple `<map>` tags with different names.

Between the `<map>` and the `</map>` tags, you enter the coordinates for each area in the imagemap and the destinations of those regions using the same values and links you determined in the section on server-side imagemaps. This time, however, the coordinates are defined inside yet another new tag: the `<area>` tag. To define the polygon area from Exercise 9.1, for example, you would write the following:

```
<area shape="poly" coords="175,152, 203,118, 220,118,
    247,152, 237,153, 237,181, 186,181, 186,153"
    href="music/home.html">
```

The type of shape to be used for the region is declared by the `shape` attribute, which can have the values `rect`, `poly`, and `circle`. The coordinates for each shape are noted using the `coords` attribute. So, for example, the `coords` attribute for the `poly` shape is the following, where each *x,y* combination represents a point on the polygon:

```
<area shape="poly" coords="x1,y1,x2,y2,x3,y3,...,xN,yN" href="URL">
```

For `rect` shapes, *x1,y1* is the upper-left corner of the rectangle, and *x2,y2* is the lower-right corner:

```
<area shape="rect" coords="x1,y1,x2,y2" href="URL">
```

For `circle` shapes, *x,y* represents the center of a circular region of size *radius*:

```
<area shape="circle" coords="x,y,radius" href="URL">
```

Another attribute you need to define for each `<area>` tag is the `href` attribute. You can assign `href` any URL you usually would associate with an `<a>` link, including relative pathnames. In addition, you can assign `href` a value of `"nohref"` to define regions of the image that don't contain links to a new page.

Note

> When using client-side imagemaps with frames, you also can include the
> target attribute inside an `<area>` tag to open a new page in a specific win-
> dow, as in this example:
>
> ```
> <area shape="rect" coords="x1,y1,x2,y2" href="URL" target=
> "window_name">
> ```

You need to include one more attribute in HTML 4.0. In Chapter 7, you learned how to
assign alternate text to images. In HTML 4.0, the `alt` attribute is an additional requirement for the `<area>` tag. The `alt` attribute displays a short description for a clickable
area on a client-side imagemap when you pass your cursor over it. Using the Home polygon from the jukebox image, the `alt` attribute appears as shown in the last line of the following example:

```
<area shape="poly" coords="175,152, 203,118, 220,118,
   247,152, 237,153, 237,181, 186,181, 186,153"
   href="music/home.html"
   alt="Home Page for Music Section">
```

The usemap Attribute

After you define your client-side imagemap using the `<map>` tag, you put the image on
your Web page. To do this, you use a special form of the `<img>` tag that includes an
attribute called usemap. (This is different from the `ismap` for server-side imagemaps.)
usemap looks like the following, where *mapname* is the name of a map defined by the
`<map name="mapname">` tag:

```
<img src="image.gif" usemap="#mapname">
```

Note

> Unlike server-side imagemaps, you do not need to enclose the `<img>` tag
> inside an `<a>` tag in client-side imagemaps. Instead, the usemap attribute tells
> the Web browser that the `<img>` contains a clickable imagemap.

Tip

> The value assigned to usemap is a standard URL. This is why *mapname* has a
> pound (#) symbol in front of it. As with links to anchors inside a Web page,
> the pound symbol tells the browser to look for *mapname* in the current Web
> page.If you have a very complex imagemap, however, you can store it in a
> separate HTML file and reference it using a standard URL.

Exercise 9.2: The Clickable Jukebox Exercise Revisited

To conclude this discussion of imagemaps, take a look at how the imagemap example discussed in Exercise 9.1 would be written using client-side imagemaps. Because you already have the coordinates and the destination, all you really need to do is convert the server-side map file into client-side HTML.

For the jukebox image, the <map> tag and its associated <area> tag and attributes for the Classics link look like the following:

```
<map name="jukebox">
<area shape="rect" coords="101,113, 165,134"
   href="/music/classics.html"
   alt="Classical Music and Composers">
</map>
```

The <img> tag that refers to the map coordinates also is different. It uses usemap instead of ismap and doesn't have a link around it, as follows:

```
<img src="jukebox.gif" usemap="#jukebox">
```

Finally, put the whole lot together and test it. Here's a sample HTML file that contains both the <map> tag and the image that uses it. To create The Really Cool Music Page with a client-side imagemap, the complete code looks as follows. Figure 9.13 shows the client-side version of the imagemap in Netscape.

INPUT

```
<!DOCTYPE html PUBLIC "-//W3C//DTD XHTML 1.0 Transitional//EN"
"http://www.w3.org/TR/xhtml1/DTD/transitional.dtd">
<html>
<head>
<title>The Really Cool Music Page</title>
</head>
<body bgcolor="#ffffff">
<div align="center">
<h1>The Really Cool Music Page</h1>
<p>Select the type of music you want to hear.<br />
 You'll go to a list of songs that you can select from.</p>
<p>
<img src="jukebox.gif" alt="Juke Box" usemap="#jukebox" />
<map name="jukebox">
<area shape="rect" coords="101,113, 165,134"
   href="/music/classics.html"
   alt="Classical Music and Composers" />
<area shape="rect" coords="101,139, 165,159"
   href="/music/country.html"
   alt="Country and Folk Music" />
<area shape="rect" coords="101,163, 165,183"
   href="/music/rockpop.html"
   alt="Rock and Pop from 50's On" />
```

▲ To Do

9

▼

▼

```
<area shape="poly" coords="175,152, 203,118, 220,118, 247,152,
    237,153, 237,181, 186,181, 186,153"
    href="code/music/home.html"
    alt="Home Page for Music Section" />
<area shape="rect" coords="259,113, 323,134"
    href="/music/swing.html"
    alt="Swing and Big Band Music" />
<area shape="rect" coords="259,139, 323,159"
    href="/music/jazz.html"
    alt="Jazz and Free Style" />
<area shape="rect" coords="259,163, 323,183"
    href="/music/gospel.html"
    alt="Gospel and Inspirational Music" />
<area shape="circle" coords="379,152, 21"
    href="/music/help.html"
    alt="Help" />
</map></p>
<p>
<a href="code/music/home.html">Home</a> |
<a href="code/music/classics.html">Classics</a> |
<a href="code/music/country.html">Country</a> |
<a href="code/music/rockpop.html">Rock/Pop</a> |
<a href="code/music/swing.html">Swing</a> |
<a href="code/music/jazz.html">Jazz</a> |
<a href="code/music/gospel.html">Gospel</a> |
<a href="code/music/help.html">Help</a>
</p>
</div>
</body>
</html>
```

OUTPUT

FIGURE 9.13

*The finished Really
Cool Music Page with
client-side imagemap.*

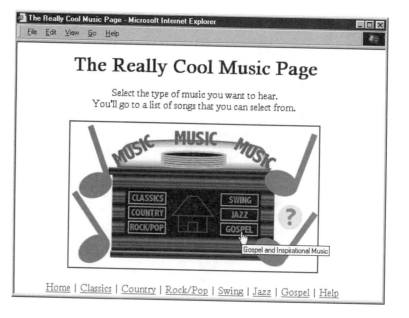

▲

Building Web Pages That Support Both Types of Imagemaps

Although client-side imagemaps are faster and easier to implement than server-side imagemaps, they're not supported by all browsers. A few older browsers that won't work with client-side imagemaps are still in use, although their numbers are decreasing. If you want to play it safe, you can create imagemaps that work in these older browsers as well as in the newer browsers. For the time being, it's a good idea to also create a server-side equivalent. Then, modify your HTML files so that they support both forms of imagemaps. This way, your pages will work equally well with both imagemap formats while taking advantage of the newer client-side capabilities in browsers that support them.

To create an imagemap that uses client-side support if available, but falls back to server-side support when needed, take the following standard server-side definition for the Really Cool Music Page example:

```
<a href="http://www.lne.com/cgi-bin/imagemap/maps/jukebox.map">
<img src="jukebox.gif" ismap>
</a>
```

Add the client-side imagemap details as part of the `<img src="jukebox.gif" ismap>` text, as in the following:

```
<a href="http://www.lne.com/cgi-bin/imagemap/maps/jukebox.map">
<img src="jukebox.gif" usemap="#jukebox" ismap>
</a>
```

You will, of course, need to install the `jukebox.map` file on your server and to include the "jukebox" `<map>` tag definition somewhere in your HTML document.

Summary

In this chapter, you learned how to add imagemaps to your Web pages. You now should know the difference between server-side and client-side imagemaps, and which ones are available in which browsers. You also learned how to find regions and the coordinates that defined them and to create map files for client-side imagemaps. You now should know how to connect clickable images, map files, and imagemap programs on the appropriate servers.

It's been a very full chapter, so to help refresh your memory, Table 9.3 presents a summary of the tags and attributes you learned about in this chapter.

Table 9.3   HTML Tags Presented in This Chapter

Tag	Attribute	Use
<map>		Defines a map for a client-side imagemap.
	name	Used to define the map's name.
	usemap	Used to associate an image with a client-side imagemap specified by <map name="*mapname*">.
<area>		The individual regions within a <map> element.
	shape	Indicates the type of region. Possible values are rect, poly, and circle.
	coords	Indicates the point bounding the region.
	href	Indicates the URL of the region.
	nohref	An attribute of the <area> tag that indicates a region that has no action when clicked (or one that has no associated URL).
	alt	Displays alternate text for a clickable area. (Now a requirement for HTML 4.0.)

Workshop

As always, at the end of a chapter, you go through a workshop to review what you've learned. And you've covered a lot in this chapter! A few common questions and answers that pertain to imagemaps (server-side and client-side) are included. The quiz questions will help you remember the advantages and disadvantages of each type of imagemap. Finally, a couple of examples are here to help you experiment with imagemaps on your own.

Q&A

Q Do I need a server to create imagemaps? I want to create and test all this offline, in the same way I did for my regular HTML files.

A If you're using client-side imagemaps, you can create and test them all on your local system (assuming, of course, that your map destinations all point to files in your local presentation as well). If you're using server-side imagemaps, however, because you need the imagemap program on the server, you'll have to be connected to the server for all of this to work.

Q My server-side imagemaps aren't working. What's wrong?

A The following are a couple things you can look for:

- Make sure that the URLs in your map file are absolute pathnames, from the top of your root Web directory to the location of the file where you want to link. You cannot use relative pathnames in the map file. If absolute paths aren't working, try full URLs (starting with http).

- Make sure that when you append the path of the map file to the imagemap program, you also use an absolute pathname (as it appears in your URL).

- If you're using NCSA, make sure that you're using the newest version of imagemap. Requests to the new imagemap script should not look for configuration files.

Q My client-side imagemaps aren't working. What's wrong?

A The following are a couple suggestions:

- Make sure the pathnames or URLs in your <area> tags point to real files.

- Make sure the map name in the <map> file and the name of the map in the usemap attribute in the <img> tag match. Only the latter should have a pound sign in front of it.

Quiz

1. What is an imagemap?

2. What are the two types of imagemaps, and what are the advantages and disadvantages of each?

3. Why is it a good idea to also provide text versions of links that you create on an imagemap?

4. True or false: You can use a relative URL when you specify a URL destination in an imagemap file.

5. What three things do you need to create a server-side imagemap? Which of these do you not need for a client-side imagemap?

Answers

1. An imagemap is a special image that contains different areas that point to different locations.

2. Server-side imagemaps are supported by more browsers, but because the hotspots are processed by the server, the browser has no idea where each hotspot points to. They cannot be tested with local files. They also are slower to respond to mouse clicks.

Client-side imagemaps remove the need for a special program on the server and are faster because the processing is done in the Web browser. This method is being used by most Web designers. Not all browsers support client-side imagemaps (although this is becoming less of an issue as older browsers decrease in use).

3. It is a good idea to include text versions of imagemap links in case there are users who visit your page with text-only browsers or with images turned off in their browser. This way, they can still follow the links on the Web page and visit other areas of your Web site.

4. False. URLs in a map file must be absolute pathnames from the top of the Web root. The URLs cannot be relative from the map file.

5. To create a server-side imagemap, you need an image, an imagemap file, and an imagemap program that resides on the server. You do not need a map file or a server-side imagemap program when you create a client-side imagemap. Instead, the information that defines the imagemap is included directly in the Web page itself and is processed by a compatible Web browser.

Exercises

1. Create and test a simple client-side imagemap that links to pages that reside in different subdirectories in a Web site, or to other sites on the World Wide Web.

2. Create and test a client-side imagemap for your own home page, or for the entry page in one of the main sections in your Web site. Remember to include alternatives for those who are using older or text-only browsers. If you really feel adventurous, create and test the server-side alternative.

PART 4

Doing More with HTML

XHTML and Style Sheets

In the last three days, you've seen several references to HTML tags that I've frequently referred to as "deprecated in HTML 4.0 in favor of *style sheets*." Well, it's time to solve this mystery and show you where things are heading. Today, you'll look at the World Wide Web Consortium's approach to formatting and design. As you learned in Day 3, "An Introduction to HTML," HTML is a markup language intended to describe the structure of a page, not the layout. HTML was never intended to describe the way a page looks (specifying fonts, colors, and spacing); it was intended only to describe the elements that make up the page (headings, text, images, and so on). The extensions to the original HTML tags (<font>, <color>, <margin>, and so on) have enabled Web authors to go beyond the original intentions.

To bring back the structure of HTML and still allow authors to have the design control they have been seeking, the World Wide Web Consortium has introduced *Cascading Style Sheets* (or CSS) and XHTML (eXtensible HyperText Markup Language).

In the pages to come, you'll learn the following:

- The differences between HTML and XHTML
- The concept behind cascading style sheets
- A brief history of style sheets
- How to create and implement external, embedded, and inline styles
- Commonly used style sheet properties and values
- How to control page layout, fonts, and colors with CSS properties

What is XHTML and Why Use It?

The World Wide Web Consortium (W3C) calls XHTML "a reformulation of HTML 4.0 as an XML 1.0 application." I call it good news for new Web authors. As the Internet grows, more and more companies will begin entering the marketplace with new Internet document viewers (such as browsers and other applications). It is very likely that in the very near future something completely unexpected will take the place of today's browsers and you'll want to make sure that your pages will still be readable. XHTML is intended to help ensure that they are. It does this by placing some specific requirements on your documents.

The <DOCTYPE> Identifier

You'll remember that all HTML pages must include certain elements: `<html>`, `<head>`, `<body>`, and their ending tags as in the following example:

```
<html>
<head>
<title>Basic HTML Pages</title></head>
<body>
The simplest HTML pages contain 3 tags.
</body>
</html>
```

XHTML adds one more required element: the `<DOCTYPE>` identifier. This tag identifies the type of HTML document you are authoring as transitional, strict, or a frameset.

- Use the transitional version of the `<DOCTYPE>` tag when your document uses a style sheet to perform most document formatting, but includes some HTML formatting attributes, such as color and size, that enable the document to be viewed by older browsers.

```
<!DOCTYPE html PUBLIC "-//W3C//DTD XHTML 1.0 Transitional//EN"
 "http://www.w3.org/TR/xhtml1/DTD/transitional.dtd">
<html>…</html>
```

- Use the strict version of the <DOCTYPE> tag when your document uses a style sheet to perform all document formatting. Only a browser that supports Cascading Style Sheets, such as Internet Explorer 4 and Netscape Navigator 4, will be able to view this type of document.

```
<!DOCTYPE html PUBLIC "-//W3C//DTD XHTML 1.0 Strict//EN"
 "http://www.w3.org/TR/xhtml1/DTD/strict.dtd">
<html>…</html>
```

- Use the frameset version of the <DOCTYPE> tag when your document uses a frameset. You will learn how to create frameset documents in Day 12.

```
<!DOCTYPE html PUBLIC "-//W3C//DTD XHTML 1.0 Frameset//EN"
 "http://www.w3.org/TR/xhtml1/DTD/frameset.dtd">
<html>…</html>
```

Note

> The examples and exercises in this book comply with the transitional XHTML standards.

10

XHTML Syntax

HTML is a very forgiving markup language. It knows, for example, that although you forgot to close your <li> (list item) tag within a <ol> (ordered, or numbered list), when you added the next <li> tag you wanted the last one to close. To HTML, the following example (which uses the correct syntax)

```
<ol>
<li start="3">One ring-y, ding-y</li>
<li>Two ring-y, ding-ys</li>
</ol>
```

is the same as

```
<OL>
<LI START="3">One ring-y, ding-y
<LI>Two ring-y, ding-ys</LI>
</OL>
```

and the same as

```
<ol>
<Li start="3">One ring-y, ding-y</Li>
<LI>Two ring-y, ding-ys</li>
</Ol>
```

To XHTML, all these examples are different. Find out why in the following text:

- **Use lowercase tags and attributes**. To XHTML, <LI>, <li>, and <Li> are all separate tags that should be treated differently. You should write all HTML tags and attributes in lowercase letters to avoid confusing document viewers.

- **Place attribute values in quotes**. Make sure that you enclose all your attribute values in quotes. The quotes help the browser recognize the contents as a value rather than a command.

- **Terminate all nonempty elements**. As mentioned earlier, in HTML you could forget to close a tag and the browser would still be able to render your document correctly. XHTML requires you to close *all* tags. So how do you close the <br>, line break, and <hr>, horizontal rule, tags that do not have a closing tag? Just include the closing slash (/) in the tag as shown in the following example:

```
<!DOCTYPE html PUBLIC "-//W3C//DTD XHTML 1.0 Strict//EN"
 "http://www.w3.org/TR/xhtml1/DTD/strict.dtd">
<html>
<head>
<title>Line Breaks and Horizontal Rules</title></head>
<body>
<hr />                <!-- Opens and closes the hr tag -->
The first line<br /> <!-- Opens and closes the br tag -->
The second line
<hr />                <!-- Opens and closes the hr tag -->
</body>
</html>
```

- **Use nested tags and don't overlap**. HTML didn't make a distinction between following the two examples, but XHMTL does. XHTML requires you to close nested tags in the order that you opened them. The first example shows the correct XHTML syntax; the second is incorrect.

```
<b>This text is bold.<i>This is bold and italicized.</i></b><i>This is just
italicized.</i>
```

```
<b>This text is bold.<i>This is bold and italicized.</b>This is just
italicized.</i>
```

The Concept of Style Sheets

Now that you know how to write your HTML documents using the proper syntax for XHTML and you know how to use the <DOCTYPE> identifier to describe the type of HTML document you are authoring, the concept of style sheets should be simple. First, the author creates a standard Web page, using standard HTML tags (the same as in the past). This standard Web page is designed to stand on its own—that is, it is designed so that it can be displayed properly in browsers that do not support style sheets. Following is a simple example:

```
<!DOCTYPE html PUBLIC "-//W3C//DTD XHTML 1.0 Strict//EN"
 "http://www.w3.org/TR/xhtml1/DTD/strict.dtd">
<html>
<head>
<title>Using Style Sheets</title></head>
<body>
<h1> Using Style Sheets </h1>
<p> In this simple example, the heading will be blue, and the
   paragraph will be rendered in a different font. </p>
</body>
</html>
```

The Web page in the preceding example doesn't contain any attributes that define its appearance. As the code suggests, the author wants a blue heading and a different font for the paragraphs. To accomplish this, the author creates *style rules* that format the content on the Web page in the manner that he or she chooses.

Style rules combine HTML tags (such as h1 or p) with properties (such as color: blue) to format each HTML tag. In the case of style sheets, an HTML tag is used as a *selector*. The property and value of the selector are combined into what is called a *declaration*. Style rules can define the layout of a tag, as well as other typographic and design properties. Following are some examples of style rules:

```
h1 { color: blue }
p { font-family: Arial, Helvetica, sans-serif; color: black }
```

New Term A CSS *style rule* consists of two parts: a *selector*, which can be an HTML tag such as h1 or p, and a *declaration*, which defines the *property* and *value* of the selector—for example, color: magenta, where color is the property and magenta is the value.

In the first line of the preceding example, the style rule renders the heading h1 on the page in blue text. In the second line, all paragraph text on the page (p tag) will be rendered in Arial, Helvetica, or another sans-serif font and will be colored black.

Now that the Web author has designed the page content (the standard Web page) and the style rules that define its appearance, the author attaches the style rules to the standard HTML document using one of three methods: through the use of an external style sheet, an embedded style sheet (as the following example shows), or an inline style. You'll learn more about these approaches later today, in "Approaches to Style Sheets."

10

The following example shows how our simple HTML example is formatted with an embedded style sheet:

```
<!DOCTYPE html PUBLIC "-//W3C//DTD XHTML 1.0 Strict//EN"
 "http://www.w3.org/TR/xhtml1/DTD/strict.dtd">
<html>
<head>
<title>Using Style Sheets</title>
<style type="text/css">
<!--
h1 { color: blue }
p { font-family: Arial, Helvetica, sans-serif; color: black }
-->
</style>
</head>
<body>
<h1>Using Style Sheets</h1>
<p> In this simple example, the heading will be blue, and the
    paragraph will be rendered in a different font. </p>
</body>
</html>
```

In the preceding example of an embedded style sheet, the author has separated the styles from the standard HTML document. The code that defines the appearance of the Web page appears within the opening `<style>` and closing `</style>` tags. Browsers that don't support style sheets can still render the document as a standard HTML document, while those that do support style sheets render the content on the page as defined by the style rules.

Some Background on Style Sheets

The first implementation of Cascading Style Sheets, known as CSS1, enables you to specify everything from typefaces for different HTML elements to font colors, background colors and graphics, margins, spacing, type style, and much more. Browsers that support this type of style sheet, which include Netscape Navigator 4 and later and Internet Explorer 4 and later, apply the style definitions to the final appearance of the document.

The next generation of style sheets, CSS2, became a formal recommendation in May 1998. Many CSS2 tags are supported in the latest versions of both Internet Explorer and

Netscape Navigator. In the very near future, style sheets will enable you to accomplish even more exciting things on the Web. With CSS2, XHTML, and compliant browsers, you'll be able to generate Web pages that target different types of media. For example, you'll be able to design aural style sheets that speak page elements to a user while using spatial audio and surround-sound properties. You'll also be able to split Web pages into multiple pages, much as you do in a word processor or page layout program. You'll be able to control page breaks, widows, orphans…. Exciting stuff, indeed!

This brings up yet another advantage to style sheet technology. Style sheets will allow Web documents to be viewed in nonstandard ways, such as through audio players for the visually impaired or through other means where standard browser technology is inaccessible. The standard HTML document can still be rendered in a useful way without being affected by the superfluous, and often confusing, HTML extension tags intended to provide the nonstandard layouts in a browser.

Just as browsers support HTML differently, cascading style sheets meet the same fate. Netscape has created its own alternative version of style sheets. Netscape Navigator has an alternative for layers, which positions objects on a page while still supporting the emerging standard. It also has its own JavaScript style sheets while continuing to support Cascading Style Sheets.

Because this is a new technology, it sounds like (and *is*) a confusing situation. As is the case with all new technologies, however, things will settle down and the VHS of style sheets will emerge while the Betamax falls to the side. In the meantime, you need to be aware that those browsers that handle CSS technology handle it differently.

In the remainder of today, you'll gain an introduction to what style sheets do. Note that properties you'll learn about today are only a sampling of those that are available in CSS1 and CSS2. To adequately cover this topic goes far beyond the scope of this book and would undoubtedly double its size. Still, the concepts you learn today will help you achieve a basic understanding of the power of style sheet properties and values. Further online resources are listed at the end of this day.

The Bookworm Bookshop Revisited

Rather than continue with a bunch of theory all at once, I'll take you through some CSS properties that relate to each other while you apply them to an HTML Web page. In Day 6, you learned about various text and font formatting commands in a page that displayed information about The Bookworm Bookshop. Now, you'll learn how to apply cascading style sheet properties and values to the page and give the Web page an entirely new appearance.

To refresh your memory, here's a version of The Bookworm Bookshop Web page as it was coded before you added the fancy items at the end of Day 6. Open or create this page, as you'll be converting it to a style sheet in the exercises today. Save the file as bookwrm.html. Figure 10.1 shows the upper portion of this page, which is fairly representative of the types of items that appear throughout the entire page.

INPUT

```
<!DOCTYPE html PUBLIC "-//W3C//DTD XHTML 1.0 Strict//EN"
  "http://www.w3.org/TR/xhtml1/DTD/strict.dtd">
<html>
<head>
<title>The Bookworm Bookshop</title>
</head>
<body>
<a name="top"><h1>The Bookworm: A Better Book Store</h1></a>
<blockquote>
"Old books are best--how tale and rhyme<br />
Float with us down the stream of time!"<br />
- Clarence Urmy, <cite>Old Songs are Best</cite>
</blockquote>
<p>The Bookworm Bookshop<br />
1345 Applewood Dr<br />
Springfield, CA 94325<br />
(415) 555-0034
</p>
<a name="contents"><h2>Contents</h2></a>
<ul>
  <li><a href="#about">About the Bookworm Bookshop</a></li>
  <li><a href ="#recent">Recent Titles</a></li>
  <li><a href ="#upcoming">Upcoming Events</a></li>
</ul>
<hr />
<a name="about"><h2>About the Bookworm Bookshop</h2></a>
<p>Since 1933, The Bookworm Bookshop has offered
rare and hard-to-find titles for the discerning reader.
The Bookworm offers:</p>
<ul>
<li>Friendly, knowledgeable, and courteous help
<li>Free coffee and juice for our customers
<li>A well-lit reading room so you can "try before you buy"
<li>Four friendly cats: Esmerelda, Catherine, Dulcinea and Beatrice
</ul>
```

```
<p>Our hours are <strong>10am to 9pm</strong> weekdays,
<strong>noon to 7</strong> on weekends.</p>
<p><a href="#contents">Back to Contents</a> ¦ <a href="#top">Back to
Top</a></p>
<hr>
<a name="recent"><h2>Recent Titles (as of 11-Nov-99)</h2></a>
<ul>
<li>Sandra Bellweather, <a href="belladonna.html">
<cite>Belladonna</cite></a>
<li>Johnathan Tin, <a href="20minmeals.html">
<cite>20-Minute Meals for One</cite></a>
<li>Maxwell Burgess, <a href="legion.html">
<cite>Legion of Thunder</cite></a>
<li>Alison Caine, <a href="banquo.html">
<cite>Banquo's Ghost</cite></a>
</ul>
<p><a href="#contents">Back to Contents</a> ¦ <a href="#top">Back to
Top</a></p>
<hr>
<a name="upcoming"><h2>Upcoming Events</h2></a>
<ul>
<li><b>The Wednesday Evening Book Review</b> meets, appropriately, on
Wednesday evenings at
7:00 pm for coffee and a round-table discussion. Call the Bookworm for
information on joining
the group and this week's reading assignment.
<li><b>The Children's Hour</b> happens every Saturday at 1pm and
includes reading,
games, and other activities. Cookies and milk are served.
  <li><b>Carole Fenney</b> will be at the Bookworm on Friday, September
17, to read
    from her book of poems <cite>Spiders in the Web.</cite>
  <li><b>The Bookworm will be closed</b> October 1 to remove a family
of bats that has nested in the tower. We like the company, but not
the mess they leave behind!
</ul>
<p><a href="#contents">Back to Contents</a> ¦ <a href="#top">Back to
Top</a></p>
<hr>
<address>
Last Updated: 11-Nov-99<br>
WebMaster: Laura Lemay lemay@bookworm.com<br>
&#169; copyright 1999 the Bookworm<br>
</address>
</body>
</html>
```

10

OUTPUT

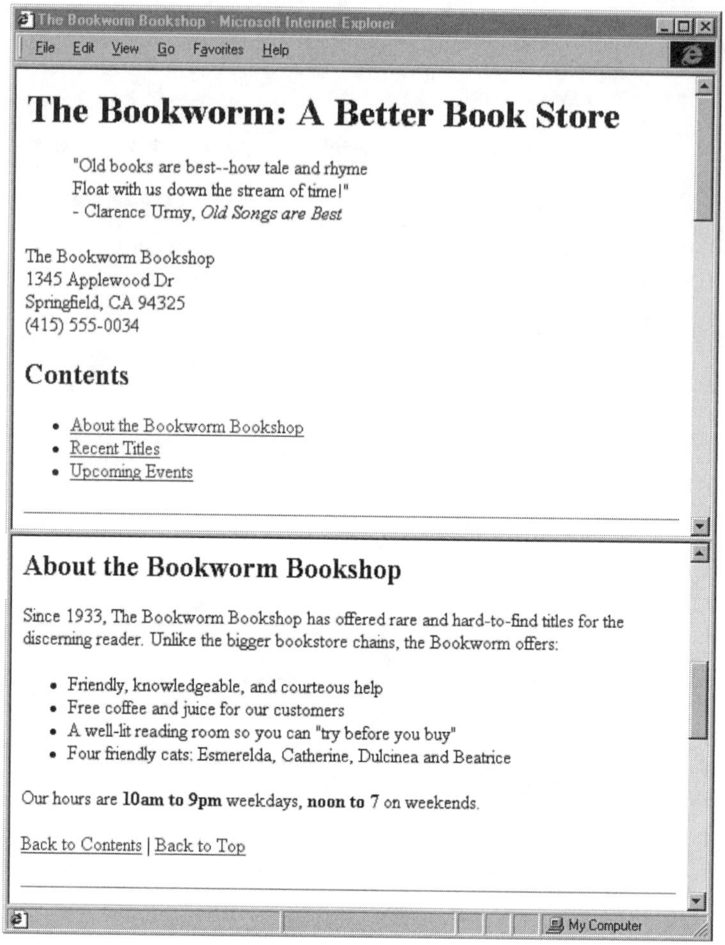

FIGURE 10.1

*The Bookworm
Bookshop as a
standalone HTML
Web page.*

What Figure 10.1 shows is a Web page that will readily stand on its own in a browser
that doesn't support style sheets. Granted, it's not exceptionally fancy. Perhaps we can
spice it up with color, different fonts, page margins, and so on. These are the types of
things style sheets excel at.

Approaches to Style Sheets

So how do you apply CSS technology to this standard Web page? There are basically
three ways that you can apply CSS rules to HTML elements. The wonder of the whole
style sheets concept is that it is flexible. The HTML tags and attributes used to apply

style rules to HTML documents don't tie authors and browser makers to a single type of style sheet.

Instead, the W3C has defined a set of tags and attributes that can be used to apply style definitions, discussed later, to any document or HTML tag. These tags enable you to work with style rules in three ways: external style sheets, embedded style sheets, and inline styles. The following sections cover the first two methods. You'll become more familiar with inline styles later in the day.

External Style Sheets

External style sheets keep the style rules in a separate file, apart from the HTML Web documents. The advantage of using external style sheets is that you can apply the same style rules to more than one document in your Web site. This enables you to create pages that have a consistent appearance. External style sheets also provide the advantage of enabling you to quickly change the appearance of your Web pages in the future. By defining your styles in a single document and linking them to multiple pages, you only need to edit the style sheet to change the presentation style of all pages linked to it.

Like an HTML document, a style sheet document is nothing more than an ASCII text document with a special extension. Although a Web page is saved with an .htm or .html extension, an external style sheet is saved with a .css extension. It defines all the common style rules that are shared in your Web documents. Then, using the <link> tag, you link the external style sheet to each HTML Web page.

I'll get into the particulars of creating the .css file in the following exercise. For now, suppose that you have created a style sheet and saved it in the same directory as your Bookworm Bookshop Web page. You use a filename of mystyle.css. The following code demonstrates how you attach the external style sheet into the header of the Bookworm Bookshop Web page:

```
<!DOCTYPE html PUBLIC "-//W3C//DTD XHTML 1.0 Strict//EN"
 "http://www.w3.org/TR/xhtml1/DTD/strict.dtd">
<html>
<head>
<title>The Bookworm Bookshop</title>
<link rel="stylesheet" href="mystyle.css">
</head>
<body>
```

The <link> tag associates the external style sheet file (mystyle.css) with the current HTML document. By applying the same code in each page of the site, a consistent style can be determined by the site manager and applied to documents created by any author in an organization.

10

The `rel` attribute of the `<link>` tag (discussed in Day 5, "All About Links") performs an important function. To effectively use the `<link>` tag, you need an understanding of persistent, default, and alternate styles. Following are the basics:

- *Persistent styles* are always applied regardless of users' local selections.
- *Default styles* are applied when a page is loaded, but can be disabled by the user in favor of an alternate style.
- *Alternate styles* are provided as options for the user to choose (as opposed to the default style).

The `rel` attribute controls some of this process. When you specify `rel="stylesheet"`, as in the previous code example, it forces the use of persistent styles and applies the styles in your style sheet, regardless of the user's local selections.

By adding a `title` attribute, the style becomes a default style. An example of this follows:

```
<link rel="stylesheet" title="mainstyle" href="mystyle.css">
```

Changing `rel="stylesheet"` to `rel="alternate stylesheet"` creates an alternate style sheet with a different title.

In this way, you can create a persistent style that contains those definitions that have to be applied, regardless of what choices a user makes, as well as provide a default and one or more alternatives that supplement the persistent style.

Exercise 10.1: Creating and Linking an External Style Sheet

If you haven't already done so, reopen or create the Bookworm Bookshop Web page from Day 6 and save it as `bookwrm.html`. The original code is shown in "The Bookworm Bookshop Revisited" section earlier today. To attach an external style sheet (which you will create shortly) to the page, enter the following line of code in the document head, immediately following the page title:

```
<link rel="stylesheet" href="mystyle.css">
```

The entire header looks like the following:

```
<!DOCTYPE html PUBLIC "-//W3C//DTD XHTML 1.0 Strict//EN"
 "http://www.w3.org/TR/xhtml1/DTD/strict.dtd">
<html>
<head>
<title>The Bookworm Bookshop</title>
<link rel="stylesheet" href="mystyle.css">
</head>
```

▼ Resave the page with the new header information. Now, you have linked a style sheet to the page, but you need to create the style sheet. Unless you define a few styles in a style sheet, you won't be able to tell whether your style sheet works correctly after it is linked. So in the next part of the exercise, you'll create a second document that contains a few basic styles.

The following example might not make sense to you at this point, but you'll learn what it all means as the day progresses. To explain briefly, here is what the following code accomplishes:

- It creates a style sheet that changes the background of a Web page to light aqua.
- The body text is rendered in Arial, Helvetica, or another sans-serif font, depending on the fonts the user has on his or her system.
- The body text color will be very dark aqua.

Link colors also are changed to the following:

- Unvisited links will be magenta.
- Visited links will be deep brown.
- Active links will be red.
- When the mouse hovers over a link, the link text will be bright gold.

Create a new text document and enter the code shown in the following example. The one thing to watch out for when you enter the following code is that the style rules are enclosed in curly braces (`{}`) rather than parentheses. Also, you most often see a single space between the style rules and the opening and closing braces—for example, `h1 { color: blue }`. After you enter the following text, save the page in the same directory as your Bookworm Bookshop page. Use the filename `mystyle.css`, which is the same filename you referenced in the header of the Bookworm Bookshop Web page. Following is the code to enter:

```
body { background-color: #ccffff; font-family: Arial, Helvetica, sans-serif;
color: #330066 }
    a:link { color: #ff00ff }
    a:visited { color: #660000 }
    a:hover { color: #ffcc00 }
    a:active { color: #ff0000 }
```

The first style rule in the preceding example specifies the background color of the Web
▼ page (light aqua, or #ccffff in this case). The text on the page will be rendered in Arial,

10

Helvetica, or another sans-serif font that resides on the reader's hard drive. The color of the text on the page will be deep blue (#330066):

```
body { background-color: #ccffff; font-family: Arial, Helvetica, sans-serif;
color: #330066 }
```

The next four lines of code define four pseudo-classes that format the link colors. Unvisited links (the same as the link= attribute in HTML) are formatted with the a:link pseudo-class. Visited links (HTML's vlink= attribute) are defined with the a:visited pseudo-class. Active links (the alink= attribute in HTML) are defined with a:active. The a:hover pseudo-class (which has no HTML equivalent) defines the color of the link when a pointer hovers over it:

```
a:link { color: #ff00ff }
a:visited { color: #660000 }
a:hover { color: #ffcc00 }
a:active { color: #ff0000 }
```

In just a moment, you'll see that, with only a few lines of code and an external style sheet, you've created a Web page with an entirely different appearance. Open the book-wrm.html page in a Web browser that supports cascading style sheets, such as Internet Explorer 4 or Netscape Navigator 4. You should now see something that looks something like Figure 10.2 (in part).

Embedded Style Sheets

Embedded style sheets are standard HTML Web pages that have style rules included *within* them. Suppose that you want your home page to appear on a black background with really bright, huge text and vivid link colors. The remaining pages in your Web are more subdued (to make it easier on your visitor's eyes) and have lighter background colors. It doesn't make much sense to make an external style sheet for one home page. (Why create two pages when you can create one?) So, you use an embedded style sheet for the home page and an external style sheet for the others.

"But wait a moment," you say. "Isn't the whole point of style sheets to keep the style rules separate?" In effect, they still are. The style rules appear in the header of the document, before your HTML content begins. The rules are still isolated from the content. The following shows the header of the Bookworm Bookshop home page as it might appear with embedded styles. In this case, you assign colors for body text, background, and link colors.

FIGURE 10.2

The Bookworm Bookshop with attached external style sheet.

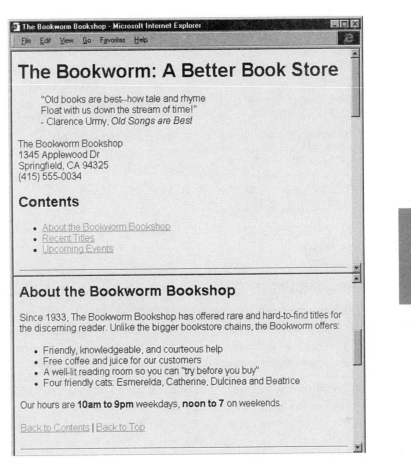

To create an embedded style sheet, you begin your Web page with the following header information as you normally would:

```
<!DOCTYPE html PUBLIC "-//W3C//DTD XHTML 1.0 Strict//EN"
 "http://www.w3.org/TR/xhtml1/DTD/strict.dtd">
<html>
<head>
<title>The Bookworm Bookshop</title>
```

Next, you begin the area where you insert your style rules, which are enclosed within opening and closing <style> tags. The type attribute of the style tag defines the page as one that uses embedded styles, as follows:

```
<style type="text/css">
```

You follow the opening `style` tag with your style rules. The example that follows is similar to that which was used for the external style sheet discussed earlier today.

Note that in the case of embedded style sheets, the style rules are enclosed within comment tags (`<!--` and `-->`). If you don't enclose them in this manner, older browsers that don't recognize the `style` tag might render your style rules on your Web page:

```
<!--
    body { color: #000000; background-color: #ffffff }
    a:active { color: #666699 }
    a:hover { color: #3366ff }
    a:link { color: #0066ff }
    a:visited { color: #9966cc }
-->
```

You complete the header of the page by closing the `style` and `head` tags as follows:

```
</style>
</head>
```

Exercise 10.2: Creating an Embedded Style Sheet

Reopen the Bookworm Bookshop HTML Web page which you saved as `bookwrm.html`. Using a different filename such as `bookback.html`, save a backup copy of this file before you make the following changes. In this exercise, you'll convert the `bookwrm.html` into a Web page that uses embedded styles.

You want to identify this Web page as one that includes embedded styles. For this, you need to modify the page header slightly. Remember that embedded style sheet code is enclosed between opening and closing `<style>` tags and that the style definitions are enclosed in curly brackets. First, remove the following line that references the external style sheet from the Web page:

```
<link rel="stylesheet" href="mystyle.css">
```

Next, edit the header so that it includes the code that defines it as one that uses an embedded style sheet. Add the `<style>` and comment tags as shown in following example. The new header should look like the following:

```
<!DOCTYPE html PUBLIC "-//W3C//DTD XHTML 1.0 Strict//EN"
 "http://www.w3.org/TR/xhtml1/DTD/strict.dtd">
<html>
<head>
<title>The Bookworm Bookshop</title>
<style type="text/css">
<!--
-->
</style>
</head>
```

▼ To illustrate the styles you define in the embedded style sheet, we'll make a slight modification to the styles you defined in the previous example. Rather than a light blue background, make it light green by changing the background color to #ccffcc. The text and link properties remain the same.

This time, however, the style rules go *inside* your Bookworm Bookshop HTML Web page, in between the <!-- and --> comment tags.

Enter the following style rules between the comment tags in your page header:

```
body { background-color: #ccffcc; font-family: Arial, Helvetica, sans-serif;
color: #330066 }
    a:link { color: #cc9900 }
    a:visited { color: #660000 }
    a:hover { color: #ffcc00 }
    a:active { color: #ff0000 }
```

In total, your page header now looks as shown in the following code example:

```
<!DOCTYPE html PUBLIC "-//W3C//DTD XHTML 1.0 Strict//EN"
 "http://www.w3.org/TR/xhtml1/DTD/strict.dtd">
<html>
<head>
<title>The Bookworm Bookshop</title>
<style type="text/css">
<!--
body { background-color: #ccffcc; font-family: Arial, Helvetica, sans-serif;
color: #330066 }
    a:link { color: #cc9900 }
    a:visited { color: #660000 }
    a:hover { color: #ffcc00 }
    a:active { color: #ff0000 }
-->
</style>
</head>
```

Resave the page as bookwrm.html and open it in your style sheet-compatible browser. The page now has a light green background. Otherwise, it looks quite the same as the external style sheet version shown in Figure 10.2.

For comparison's sake, open the same Web page in a browser that does not support cascading style sheets. In Figure 10.3, you see a portion of the same page as it is rendered in NCSA Mosaic 3.0. As you can see, all the information is still there because the HTML code stands on its own. The colors and fonts that you added in the style sheet, however,
▼ aren't rendered in this browser.

▼

FIGURE 10.3

The Bookworm Bookshop page displayed in a browser that does not support cascading style sheets.

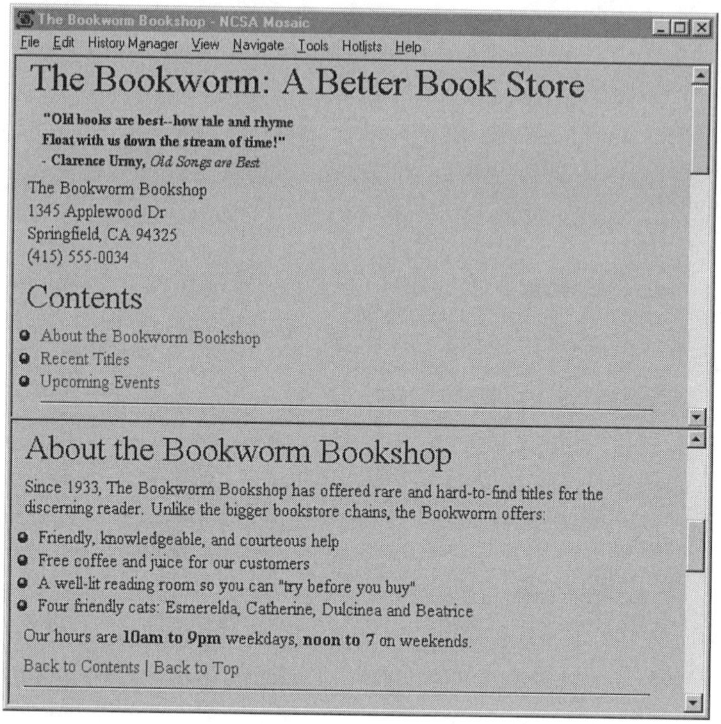

▲

About Cascading

Just what does it mean that this particular brand of style sheets is cascading? Clearly, there are no cascading waterfalls involved.

Cascading refers to the capability for style information from more than one source to be combined. As you've learned already, you can apply style rules to a page in a variety of ways. External style sheets can be linked to one or more pages, applying the same style rules to all. Embedded style sheets apply style rules to a single page. *Inline styles*, which you'll learn about later today, apply style rules to page elements. You can combine all three approaches within a single page, if you want.

The cascading part of the picture comes into play because there is an ordered sequence to the style sheets: rules in later sheets take precedence over earlier ones. Simply defined, here is what happens when external, embedded, and inline styles are applied to the same page:

- The styles defined in an external style sheet are applied to the page first.

- The styles defined in the embedded style sheet are applied second and override the styles in the first where applicable.
- The inline styles override both the external and embedded style sheets where applicable.

Commonly Used Style Sheet Properties and Values

Now you will look at some of the main properties and how to use them. There are far too many to cover in a single section of a single day. If you need more information, you can find the complete specification of Cascading Style Sheets Level 1 (CSS1) on the Web at `http://www.w3.org/TR/REC-CSS1`. This recommendation is dated January 11, 1999.

Recommendations for CSS2 also appear on the Web at `http://www.w3.org/TR/REC-CSS2/`. The most current version of this document is dated May 12, 1998. These documents, although fairly technical, tell you precisely what each property does and what is legal and illegal to code into your pages, and also give several examples that help you create pages compatible with old and new browsers.

In the previous examples, you've only scratched the surface at what style rules can accomplish. CSS1 and CSS2 provide many tags that enable you to control the appearance of just about every aspect of a Web page. Because CSS technology is still evolving, however, browsers support some CSS properties better and more reliably than other properties. That's the way of the Web.

While I demonstrate how to use some of these properties, be forewarned that you may see some unexpected surprises and variances in each CSS-compatible browser. Always test, test, *test* to make sure you get acceptable results.

Controlling Page Layout CSS Properties

In Exercises 10.1 and 10.2, you added some simple style rules that affected the fonts and colors on your Web page. These were accomplished through the `background-color`, `font-family`, and `color` properties that you applied to the body of the Web page. The colors for the links were applied by first defining four pseudo-classes for the `<a>` tag: `a:link` (for the link color), `a:visited` (for the visited links), `a:hover` (for the color of the link when the mouse hovers over it), and `a:active` (for the active link color).

There is much more that you can do to affect how the text appears on the page as well. You can control margins and padding with a style sheet much as you can in a page layout or word processing software package. Table 10.1 highlights some of the most frequently used properties.

10

Table 10.1 Useful Page Layout Properties

Property	Description
margin-top	Sets the top margin of an element. Values are entered in numerical lengths, percentages, or auto.
margin-right	Sets the right margin of an element. Acceptable values are the same as margin-top.
margin-bottom	Sets the bottom margin of an element. Acceptable values are the same as margin-top.
margin-left	Sets the left margin of an element. Acceptable values are the same as margin-top.
margin	A shorthand property that sets margin-top, margin-right, margin-bottom, and margin-left at the same location in the style sheet. Acceptable values are expressed in numerical lengths, percentages, or auto.
padding-top	Sets the space between the top border and the content of an element. Values are entered in numerical lengths, percentages, or auto.
padding-right	Sets the space between the right border and the content of an element. Acceptable values are the same as padding-top.
padding-bottom	Sets the space between the bottom border and the content of an element. Acceptable values are the same as padding-top.
padding-left	Sets the space between the left border and the content of an element. Acceptable values are the same as padding-top.
padding	A shorthand property that sets padding-top, padding-right, padding-bottom, and padding-left in the same location in the style sheet. Acceptable values are expressed as numerical lengths, percentages, or auto.

Margins and padding are expressed in numerical length followed by a *length unit*, a *percentage value*, or by assigning a value called auto.

NEW TERM *Length units* are expressed in relative or absolute values. Relative length units include em (the size of the relevant font), ex (the x-height of the relevant font), or px (pixels, relative to the device that the page is being viewed upon). Absolute values include pt (points), in (inches), cm (centimeters), mm (millimeters), and pc (picas).

Percentage values are always relative to another value, such as a length. You specify percentages by an optional + or - sign, immediately followed by a number, immediately followed by a percent sign.

You might notice that Table 10.1 makes mention of the term *shorthand property*. Several properties utilize many attributes to define their appearance. You can combine several values together with a shorthand property. For example, you can specify top, right, bottom, and left margins in a single property called margin. The same applies to the four individual padding settings in relation to the padding property.

Both margin and padding can accept from one to four values as follows:

One value	Applies to all sides.
Two values	The first value applies to the top and bottom; and the second applies to the left and right.
Three values	The first value applies to the top; the second value applies to the left and right; and the third value applies to the bottom.
Four values	Applies to the top, right, bottom, and left, respectively.

Exercise 10.3: Applying Margins and Padding to a Page

In this exercise, you'll apply some margin and padding settings to the Bookworm Bookshop page. You'll add the following style definitions to the style sheet:

- Twenty-pixel margins at the top and bottom of the page, and 30-pixel margins at the left and right of the page
- Fifteen-pixel padding at the top and bottom of each heading

To add the margin and padding settings to your Web page, add the following code to either the external style sheet (mystyle.css) or to the Web page that has the embedded style sheet properties defined within it (bookwrm.html). If you didn't save a backup copy of the Web page that uses the external style sheet, the embedded version is your only choice, so I'll continue using that page in my examples.

To accomplish this, you can use the margin shorthand property with two values to specify the top/bottom and left/right margin settings for the <body> tag and assign tpadding-top and padding-bottom properties to the <h1> and <h2> tags. A revised version of your style definitions looks as follows (I've rearranged the style definitions for the <body> tag in this example, so that you can see each CSS style rule more clearly):

```
<!--
body { background-color: #ccffcc;
       font-family: Arial, Helvetica, sans-serif;
       color: #330066;
       margin: 50px 70px }
   a:link { color: #cc9900 }
   a:visited { color: #660000 }
   a:hover { color: #ffcc00 }
   a:active { color: #ff0000 }
```

▲ To Do

```
▼   h1 { padding-top: 10px;
          padding-bottom: 5px }
    h2 { padding-top: 5px;
          padding-bottom: 3px }
    -->
```

After you save the new version of your style sheet, open it in a CSS-compatible browser and view the results. Figure 10.4 shows the new page margins and the additional padding ▲ on the upper portion of the Web page.

Backgrounds, Colors, and Images

As you learned in Day 7, "Using Images, Colors, and Backgrounds," you have basic control over the background appearance of a document in HTML. You can use bgcolor to set a background color of a document or background to set a background image. With tables, some browsers expanded on this by enabling page authors to apply backgrounds to individual cells in a table.

In CSS you have even more control. There are six properties for controlling background. Also, because style sheets are applied on an element-by-element basis, you can have more than one background in a page. The six properties are outlined in Table 10.2.

Table 10.2   Background Properties in CSS

Property	Description
color	Sets the foreground color for an element (most often, this applies to the text that appears in an element). The color value can be one of 16 color names or one of several variations of an RGB triplet.
background-color	Sets a background color for an element. The color value can be one of 16 color names, one of several variations of an RGB triplet, or transparent.
background-image	Assigns the background image. The value should be the URL of an image or none.
background-repeat	Determines whether the background image is repeated (tiled) and if so, how it is repeated. Possible values are repeat (repeat horizontally and vertically), repeat-x (repeat horizontally), repeat-y (repeat vertically), and no-repeat (no repetition of the image).
background-attachment	Determines whether the background image remains stationary (is attached to the document) or scrolls with the document. Possible values are scroll and fixed.
background-position	Sets the initial position of a background image. Possible values are described in the text following this table.
background	A shorthand property that sets one or more of the preceding properties in a single location in the style sheet.

FIGURE 10.4

Margin and padding settings applied to the Bookworm Bookshop page.

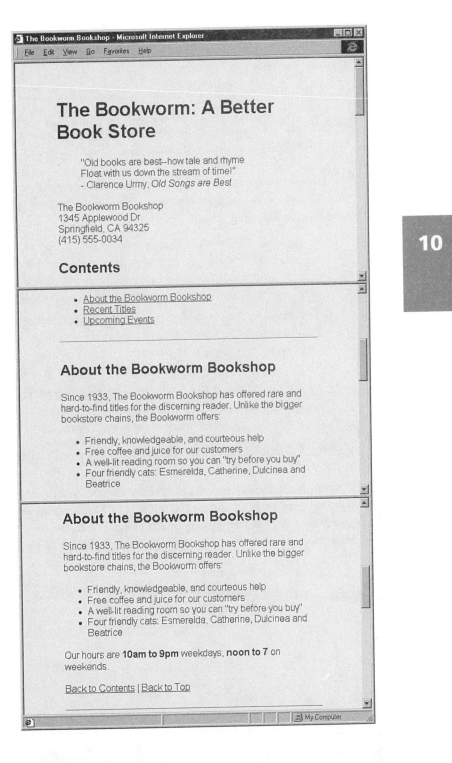

When you apply a background image to a Web document, the W3C recommends that you also set a background color as well. This way, if a background image is unavailable to a user, he or she can still view a colored background.

Note   You can find a list of the color names and RGB triplets that are applicable to style sheets in Appendix C, "Cascading Style Sheet (CSS) Quick Reference."

The background-position property requires further comment, because it is a little complex. This property accepts two values that are separated by a space. They are specified in one of the following ways:

- *By keyword.* The keyword top, center, or bottom identifies the vertical position of the background; the keyword left, center, or right identifies the horizontal position. To position the center of the image at the horizontal and vertical centers of a Web page, for example, you specify the values center center.
- *By length unit.* The values are given in x,y coordinates, with x being the horizontal axis (distance from the left side of the page) and y being the vertical axis (distance from the top of the page). A position of 20 25 positions the upper-left corner of the image 20 pixels to the left and 25 pixels from the top of the page or element.
- *By percentage value.* The default positioning of the background-position property is 0% 0%. This value is equal to the upper-left corner of the element. A value of 100% 100% positions the image at the bottom right.

Exercise 10.4: Applying Backgrounds and Colors to Elements with CSS

You've already added some color to the Bookworm Web page through the use of CSS tags, but there's more to come. The following CSS code adds a background image to your Web page. The background-image property specifies the URL of the background image and tells the browser to tile the background image as shown in Figure 10.5.

Note   The background.gif file referenced in the following example is available on the Web support site for this book, http://www.tywebpub.com/.

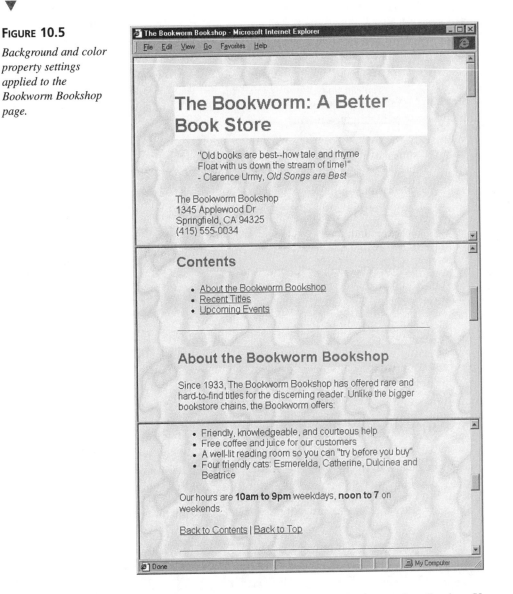

FIGURE 10.5

Background and color property settings applied to the Bookworm Bookshop page.

The Web page isn't the only thing to which you can apply backgrounds and colors. You also can apply different colors and backgrounds to the elements on the Web page. The following CSS code also adds some different colors to the headings on the page for an interesting effect. You'll change the color of the level 1 and level 2 headings to brown.

▼

The level 1 heading will be rendered over a light yellow background (signified by the color #ffffcc), and the level 2 headings will be rendered over a light green background color (signified by the color #ccffcc).

To clarify the new style rules that you should insert on your page, the next few examples show the new additions with a gray shading. Revise your style definition to include the following lines highlighted in gray:

```
<!--
body { background-color: #ccffcc;
       font-family: Arial, Helvetica, sans-serif;
       color: #330066;
       margin: 50px 70px;
       background-image: url(background.gif);
       background-repeat: repeat }
   a:link { color: #cc9900 }
   a:visited { color: #660000 }
   a:hover { color: #ffcc00 }
   a:active { color: #ff0000 }
h1 { color: #996633;
     padding-top: 10px;
     padding-bottom: 5px;
     background-color: #ffffcc }
h2 { color: #996633;
     padding-top: 5px;
     padding-bottom: 3px;
     background-color: #ccffcc }
-->
```

▲

Setting Border Appearance

Cascading Style Sheets provide numerous properties for controlling the borders of elements in a page. In HTML, you had borders on only a few objects, such as images and table cells, but with CSS you can theoretically apply a border to any page element.

Table 10.3 displays the properties for controlling border appearance.

Table 10.3   Border Properties in CSS

Property	Description
border-style	Sets the style of all four borders of an element. Values are the same as those indicated for border-bottom-style. You can set borders individually with border-bottom-style, border-left-style, border-right-style, or border-top-style. Values are none, dotted, dashed, solid, double, groove, ridge, inset, and outset.

Property	Description
border-color	Sets the color for all four borders of an element. You can set border colors individually set with border-bottom-color, border-left-color, border-right-color, or border-top-color. The color value can be one of 16 color names, one of several variations of an RGB triplet, or transparent.
border-width	Sets the width of all four borders. You can set border widths individually with border-bottom-width, border-left-width, border-right-width, and border-top-width. Values are thin, medium, thick, or a length value.
border	A shorthand property that sets the same width, color, and style on all four borders of an element. You can set width, color, and style for individual borders with border-bottom, border-left, border-right, or border-top.

Exercise 10.5. Applying Borders to Elements with CSS

The following code shows borders that are applied to the headings on the page. This makes the headings look somewhat like banner images. The border-color, border-style, and border-width properties have been applied to each of the headings. The top and left borders of each heading type will have a different color than the bottom and right borders. You can accomplish this by specifying two values for the border-color property. The borders on the level 1 heading give the appearance that it is facing outward from the Web page, while the level 2 headings seem to face inward. You can accomplish this by applying the border-style: outset and border style: inset properties and attributes to the respective tags.

To add the colors to the borders around the headings, add the code highlighted in gray to the CSS section in your Bookworm Bookshop Web page:

```
<!--
body { background-color: #ccffcc;
       font-family: Arial, Helvetica, sans-serif;
       color: #330066;
       margin: 50px 70px;
       background-image: url(background.gif);
       background-repeat: repeat }
a:link { color: #cc9900 }
a:visited { color: #660000 }
a:hover { color: #ffcc00 }
a:active { color: #ff0000 }
h1 { color: #996633;
     padding-top: 10px;
     padding-bottom: 5px;
```

```
▼         background-color: #ffffcc;
          border-color: #cccc33 #cc9933;
          border-style: outset;
          border-width: thin }
       h2 { color: #996633;
          padding-top: 5px;
          padding-bottom: 3px;
          background-color: #ccffcc;
          border-color: #99cc33 #996633;
          border-style: inset;
          border-width: thin }
       -->
```

When you preview your Web page in a CSS-compatible browser, it should look similar to Figure 10.6 in Internet Explorer 4. Netscape Navigator 4 renders the borders and backgrounds a little bit differently. Whereas Internet Explorer's borders appear somewhat bolder, Netscape's are thinner and slightly offset from the background color.

Font Appearance and Style

Cascading Style Sheets have a strong collection of properties for defining font appearance. In fact, with Cascading Style Sheets, page authors have more control than they had with the simplistic `<font>` tag in HTML.

Table 10.4 outlines the main properties for controlling font appearance.

Table 10.4   CSS Font Properties

Property	Description
font-family	Sets font face. Specify a typeface name (such as Arial, Times, or Palatino) or one of five generic font names: `serif`, `sans-serif`, `cursive`, `fantasy`, or `monospace`.
font-size	Sets the font size in absolute, relative, or percentage terms.
font-style	Sets the font style as `oblique`, `italic`, or `normal`.
font-weight	Sets the font weight as `normal`, `bold`, `bolder`, or `lighter`.
font-variant	Sets the font to `small-caps` or `normal`.
font	A shorthand property that sets `font-weight`, `font-size`, `font-style`, `font-family`, and `line-height` in the same location in the style sheet. The `line-height` property is explained in "Text Alignment Properties in CSS," which follows this section.

FIGURE **10.6**

Border property settings in Internet Explorer 4.0.

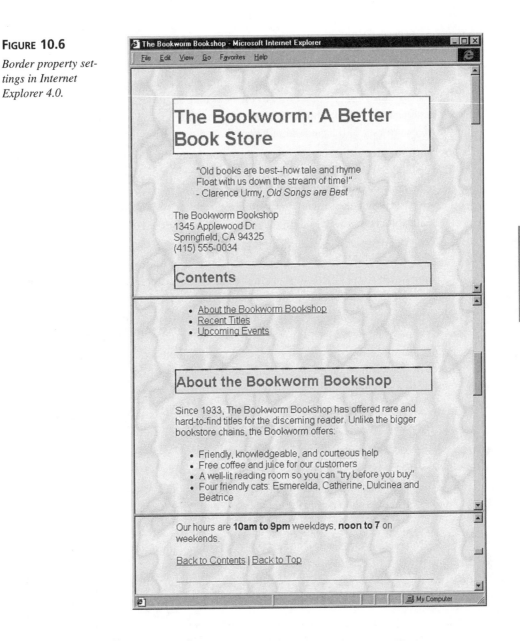

10

Following are a few things worth noting in this list:

- When you set the font family, using `font-family`, you can provide a comma-separated list of font names. If the system the browser is running doesn't have the first specified font, it moves on to the next font on the list. The W3C advises that a generic family name should be the last name in the list. The reason for this is that every browser will have a default font for a given generic family.

- When using generic family names, be careful when using cursive or fantasy. The appearance of these two family names are highly dependent on the fonts that the reader has installed on his or her hard drive. Serif, sans-serif, and monospace fonts are typically installed with an operating system or Web browser, while cursive and fantasy fonts might not be.

- When setting font size using `font-size`, absolute sizes are defined via a keyword such as `xx-small`, `x-small`, `small`, `medium`, `large`, `x-large`, or `xx-large`. These values map to specific font sizes in the browser. Relative sizes are relative to the font size of the parent element and can be defined as larger or smaller.

- Font weights are set on a scale of numerical values: `100`, `200`, `300`, `400`, `500`, `600`, `700`, `800`, and `900`. The `font-weight` property can take either one of the values `normal`, `bold`, `bolder`, or `lighter`, or one of the numbers. `normal` maps to `400`, and `bold` maps to `700` on the numerical scale. `bolder` and `lighter` set the weight relative to a parent element.

The following code example demonstrates some of these font properties. Figure 10.7 shows the result.

INPUT

```
<!DOCTYPE html PUBLIC "-//W3C//DTD XHTML 1.0 Strict//EN"
  "http://www.w3.org/TR/xhtml1/DTD/strict.dtd">
<html>
<head>
<title>CSS Font Properties</title>
<style type="text/css">
<!--
body { background-color: #ffffff }
-->
</style>
<p><span style="font-family: Arial">font-family: Arial</span> <br />
  <span style="font-family: fantasy">font-family: fantasy</span> </p>
<hr />
<span style="font-size: small">font-size: small</span>
<span style="font-size: medium">font-size: medium</span>
<span style="font-size: xx-large"> font-size: xx-large</span>
<hr />
<span style="font-style: italic">font-style: italic</span>
<hr />
```

```
<span style="font-weight: 100">font-weight: 100</span>
<br />
<span style="font-weight: 500">font-weight: 500</span>
<br />
<span style="font-weight: 900">font-weight: 900</span>
<hr />
<span style="font-variant: normal">font-variant: normal</span>
<br />
<span style="font-variant: small-caps">font-variant: small-caps</span>
</body>
</html>
```

OUTPUT

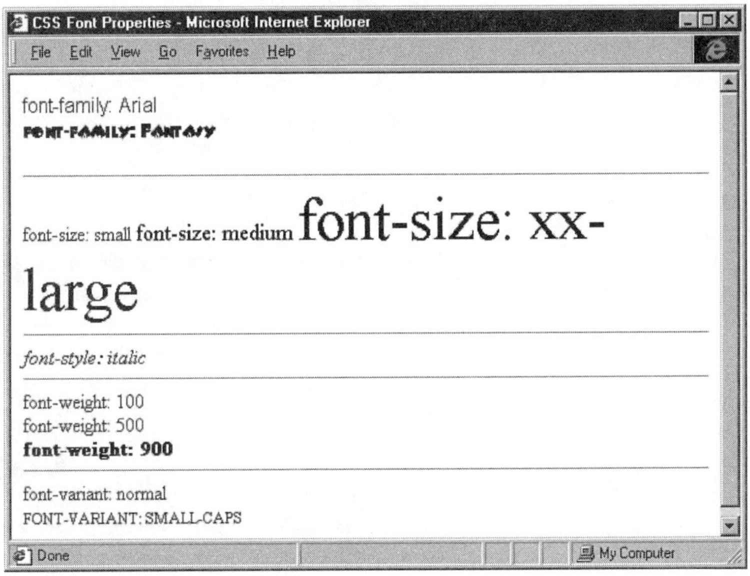

FIGURE 10.7

Various font properties.

Text Alignment Properties in CSS

In addition to the font properties, CSS includes numerous properties that enable page authors to align text. These properties allow the type of fine typographic control that is achieved in word processors and desktop publishing applications, which, until the development of CSS, were not available to the Web.

The main text alignment properties are outlined in Table 10.5.

Table 10.5 Text Alignment Properties in CSS

Property	Description
word-spacing	Sets space to add to the default space between words. Possible values are an absolute length or normal (the default). Currently not supported in either Internet Explorer 4.0 or Netscape Navigator 4.0.
letter-spacing	Sets space to add to the default space between letters. Possible values are an absolute length or normal (the default). Currently supported in Internet Explorer 4.0, but not in Netscape Navigator 4.0.
line-height	Sets the distance between the baseline of two line. A numerical value means the line height is the font size multiplied by the number. For example, line-height: 2 creates line spacing that is twice the size of the font. Absolute lengths can be defined for line height as well. For example, line-height: 15px spaces the lines 15 pixels apart. Percentage values are based on the height of the element. line-height: 200% is the same as specifying a numerical value of line-height: 2. You also can use normal, which sets the height to the default. Currently supported in Netscape Navigator 4.0.
vertical-align	Sets the vertical alignment for an element relative to the parent element, the line the element is part of, or the line height of the line the element is contained in. Values of baseline, middle, sub, super, text-top, and text-bottom are relative to the parent element. top and bottom are relative to the line itself. A percentage raises the baseline of the element above the baseline of the parent. Currently supported in Internet Explorer 4.0.
text-align	Sets the alignment of text within an element to left, center, right, or justify. The text-align: justify property is currently supported by Netscape Navigator 4.0, but is not supported in Internet Explorer 4.0.
text-decoration	Sets the font decoration as underline, overline, line-through, or blink. The first three values are supported in both Internet Explorer 4.0 and Netscape Navigator 4.0, while blink is only supported by Netscape.
text-indent	Sets the indentation of the first line of formatted text in an element. The value can either be an absolute length or a percentage of the element width. Percentages are based on the width of the element and work best in most cases. Currently supported by Netscape Navigator 4.0, but not Internet Explorer 4.0.
white-space	Indicates how whitespace inside an element should be handled. Possible values are normal (whitespace is collapsed as with standard HTML), pre (just like the <PRE> tag), and nowrap (need to use to wrap).

As the preceding table shows, these CSS properties are supported differently within Internet Explorer 4.0 and Netscape Navigator 4.0. Some properties are supported in one browser, but not the other, and others are supported in both browsers. So if you're getting confused about what's what, it might not be your coding!

The following example includes many of the text properties and applies them to different text elements. Notice how differently the same code is treated within the two major browsers. Here, you'll see why it's a good idea to check your pages in multiple browsers. Figures 10.8 and 10.9 show how Internet Explorer 4 and Netscape 4 render these properties differently.

```
<!DOCTYPE html PUBLIC "-//W3C//DTD XHTML 1.0 Strict//EN"
 "http://www.w3.org/TR/xhtml1/DTD/strict.dtd">
<html>
<head>
<title>CSS Text Properties</title>
<style type="text/css">
<!--
body { background-color: #ffffff }
-->
</style>
<p><span style="word-spacing: normal"> word-spacing: normal </span> <br />
  <span style="word-spacing: 25px"> word-spacing: 25px </span>
</p>
<hr />
<span style="letter-spacing: normal">letter-spacing: normal<br />
</span>
<span style="letter-spacing: 10px">letter-spacing: 10px</span>
<hr />
<span style="line-height: normal">line-height: normal</span>
<br />
<span style="line-height: 10px">line-height: 15px</span>
<br />
<span style="line-height: 150%">line-height: 150%</span>
<hr />
<span style="vertical-align: middle">vertical-align: middle</span>
<span style="vertical-align: sub">sub</span>
<span style="vertical-align: super">super</span>
<hr />
<span style="text-align: left">text-align: left<br />
</span>
<span style="text-align: center">text-align: center<br />
</span>
<span style="text-align: right">text-align: right<br />
</span>
<hr />
<span style="text-decoration: underline">text-decoration: underline</span><br />
<span style="text-decoration: overline">text-decoration: overline</span><br />
```

```
<span style="text-decoration: line-through">text-decoration: line-
through</span><br />
<span style="text-decoration: blink">text-decoration: blink</span>
<hr />
<span style="text-indent: 20px">text-indent: 20px</span><br />
<span style="text-indent: 40px">text-indent: 40px</span><br />
<span style="text-indent: 60px">text-indent: 60px</span><br />
</body>
</html>
```

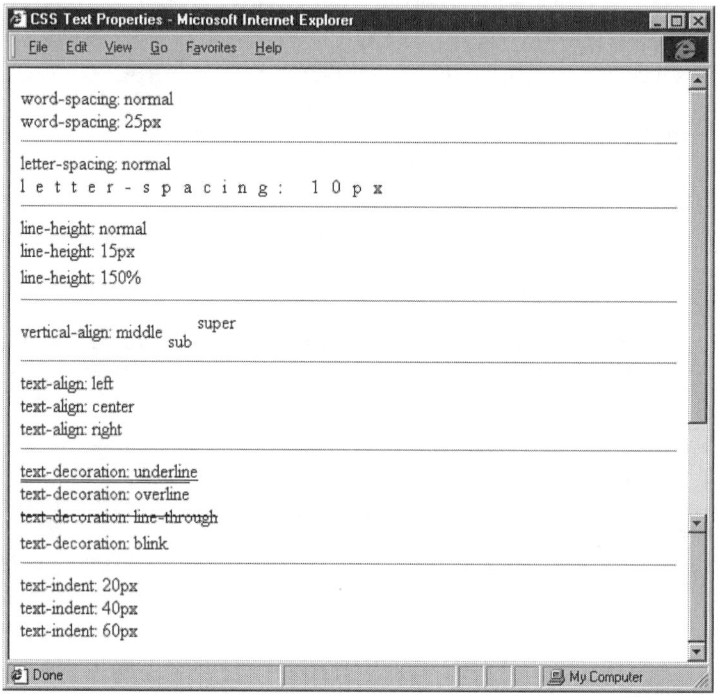

FIGURE 10.8

Various text properties in Internet Explorer 4.

Inline Styles

Before you apply font and text properties to the Bookworm Bookshop page, I'll tell you about the third method of application: *inline styles*. This method of application enables you to attach a style rule to a Web page element rather than across an entire page. If you have a heading or a paragraph that you want to emphasize with a different color or alignment, for example, and only want to use that emphasis on one page in one place, that's a case for an inline style.

HTML includes several attributes that enable you to attach style rules to HTML tags. The main attributes that apply are the style and class attributes. The <span> tag is another that also relates to style sheets. All these are discussed next.

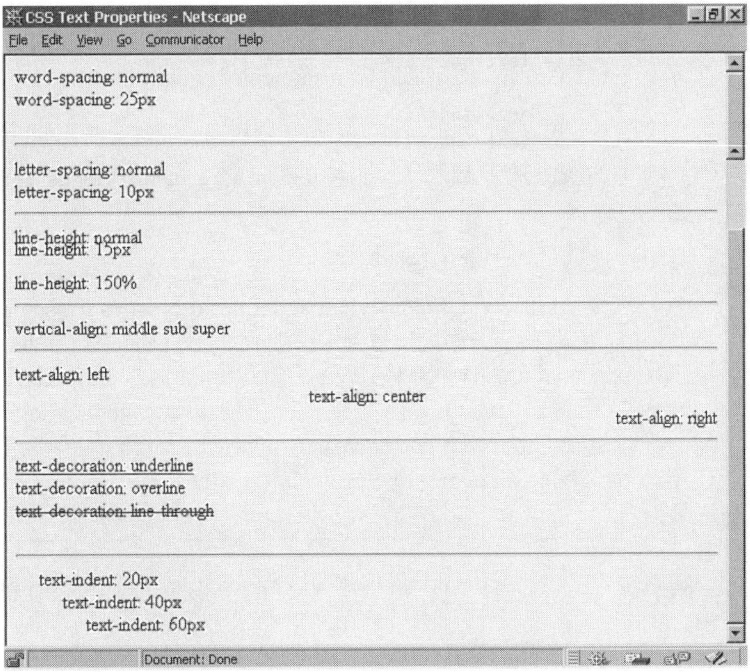

FIGURE 10.9

Various text properties in Netscape 4.

The `style` Attribute

Earlier in "Embedded Style Sheets," you were introduced to the `<style>` *tag*, which attached an external style sheet to a standard HTML Web *page*. The `style` *attribute* enables you to attach a style rule to a single *element* on a Web page.

Whereas external and embedded style sheets keep the style definitions separate from the HTML content, the `style` attribute is applied within the code of the Web document itself.

Note

You can assign the `style` attribute to any HTML tag *except* the following: `<base>`, `<basefont>`, `<head>`, `<html>`, `<meta>`, `<param>`, `<script>`, `<style>`, and `<title>`.

Suppose that you want to change the color of a single paragraph on your Web page using a style rule. Normally, the color of the text on your page is black, and the text is not emphasized in any way. You want one paragraph on your page to be rendered in a bold, red font.

The values you specify for the `style` attribute (the color `red` and the `bold` emphasis) are enclosed in quotes. The style rules that define these attributes (`color: red` and `font-weight: bold`) are separated by a semicolon within the quotes.

The following code demonstrates the `style` attribute as it is applied to a paragraph:

```
<p style="color: red; font-weight: bold">I want this paragraph to be bold and
red.</p>
```

The `class` Attribute

A *class* is a broadly defined style that defines properties for some or all elements in a document. Classes are defined in an external style sheet, or in the header of a standard Web page that uses embedded styles. Then, the `class` attribute assigns the special class to one or more elements on a Web page. The advantage of using this method over the previous method is that you can easily apply the same style rule to several elements on a Web page without having to repeatedly type the rule.

> **Note**
>
> You can assign the `class` attribute to any HTML tag *except* the following: `<base>`, `<basefont>`, `<head>`, `<html>`, `<meta>`, `<param>`, `<script>`, `<style>`, and `<title>`.

The following CSS code example demonstrates two paragraph style rules. The first rule specifies the properties for the "normal" paragraphs on the page. The second rule defines a special class for some of the paragraphs on the page. This special class is called `p.bigger`, with p being the paragraph tag designation and `bigger` being the class name:

```
<!DOCTYPE html PUBLIC "-//W3C//DTD XHTML 1.0 Strict//EN"
 "http://www.w3.org/TR/xhtml1/DTD/strict.dtd">
<html>
<head>
<title>Need New Glasses</title>
<style type="text/css">
<!--
p { font-family: Arial, Helvetica, sans-serif; color: black }
p.bigger { font-family: Arial, Helvetica, sans-serif; font-size: larger }
-->
</style>
</head>
```

Now that you've defined the special `bigger` class in your style sheet, you attach the style to the paragraphs in the page that you want to make bigger. To apply the `bigger` class to a specific paragraph, the syntax for the `class` attribute is as follows:

```
<p class="class-name">.
```

To further demonstrate this, the following shows the remaining code on this simple Web page. The first paragraph is normal, and the second paragraph uses the bigger style. Figure 10.11 displays the results:

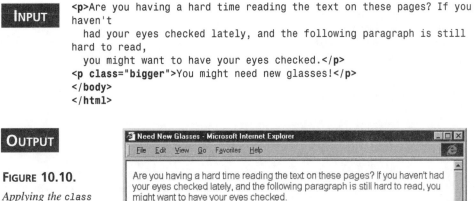

INPUT

```
<p>Are you having a hard time reading the text on these pages? If you haven't
   had your eyes checked lately, and the following paragraph is still
hard to read,
   you might want to have your eyes checked.</p>
<p class="bigger">You might need new glasses!</p>
</body>
</html>
```

OUTPUT

FIGURE 10.10.

Applying the class *property to a page element.*

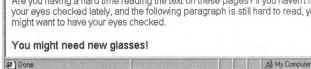

10

The <span> Tag

The exercise that follows makes extensive use of the <span> property. This property provides a way to apply a style to a portion of text without a structural role (which, therefore, isn't contained within a specific HTML structural tag). You can even use this property to apply a style to the first letter or word of a document. Because <span> itself has no effect on the text, only the style will affect the text's appearance.

Exercise 10.6. Applying Font and Text Properties with CSS

▼ To Do

For the final exercise today, you'll apply some font formatting properties to the previous examples. Note that the following examples use the fantasy generic family font name. Typically, these types of fonts are installed with page layout or graphics software. If you don't have a fantasy type font on your computer, substitute all instances of fantasy in the following code with fixed. The first portion of your bookwrm.html page looks like the following example:

```
<!DOCTYPE html PUBLIC "-//W3C//DTD XHTML 1.0 Strict//EN"
 "http://www.w3.org/TR/xhtml1/DTD/strict.dtd">
<html>
<head>
<title>The Bookworm Bookshop</title>
<style type="text/css">
<!--
```
▼

```
body { background-color: #ccffcc;
        font-family: Arial, Helvetica, sans-serif;
        color: #330066;
        margin: 50px 70px;
        background-image: url(background.gif);
        background-repeat: repeat }
a:link { color: #cc9900 }
a:visited { color: #660000 }
a:hover { color: #ffcc00 }
a:active { color: #ff0000 }
h1 { color: #996633;
     padding-top: 10px;
     padding-bottom: 5px;
     background-color: #ffffcc;
     border-color: #cccc33 #cc9933;
     border-width: thin;
     border: thin outset;
```

At this point, you want to add a style rule that changes the font for h1 to fantasy (or fixed, if you don't have a fantasy font) and align it to the center with the text-align property, as in the following:

```
font-family: "fantasy";
text-align: center }
```

The existing code continues as follows:

```
h2 { color: #996633;
     padding-top: 5px;
     padding-bottom: 3px;
     background-color: #ccffcc;
     border-color: #99cc33 #996633;
     border-width: thin;
     border: thin inset;
```

Apply the fantasy (or fixed) font family name to the second-level heading as well and align it to the center:

```
font-family: "fantasy";
text-align: center }
```

The code that you presently have in your bookwrm.html file finishes up with a block-quote style rule, which appears as follows:

```
blockquote { font-family: "Book Antiqua";
     line-height: 12pt;
     font-weight: normal;
     font-variant: normal;
     color: #996633;
     word-spacing: 2em;
     text-align: center }
```

▼ After the blockquote section, you add a class called `fantasy` (or `fixed`, if you don't have a fantasy font installed on your computer). You use this class to change some of the inline page elements to the fantasy (or fixed) font as well. To create the class, enter the following code, replacing all instances of `fantasy` with `fixed`, if necessary:

```
.fantasy { text-align: left;
    font-family: "fantasy";
    font-size: 16pt; color: #996600}
```

And the style section ends as usual with the following:

```
-->
</style>
</head>
```

You're not quite done! You still have to apply the inline styles to the HTML portion of your Web page. There are two parts of the Web page to which you should apply an inline style. The name of the bookstore appears in a couple of locations on the Web page, and you want to change them to the fantasy (or fixed) style. The following two sections of code demonstrate where the changes should go. Here's the first section:

```
<p><span class="fantasy">The Bookworm Bookshop</span><br />
1345 Applewood Dr<br />
Springfield, CA 94325<br />
(415) 555-0034
</p>
```

And here's the second section:

```
<p>Since 1933, <span class="fantasy">The Bookworm Bookshop</span>
  has offered rare and hard-to-find titles for the discerning
  reader. The Bookworm offers:</p>
```

Following is a complete listing of the final code on the Web page, with Figure 10.11 showing the result of the upper portion of the page in Internet Explorer:

```
<!DOCTYPE html PUBLIC "-//W3C//DTD XHTML 1.0 Strict//EN"
 "http://www.w3.org/TR/xhtml1/DTD/strict.dtd">
<html>
<head>
<title>The Bookworm Bookshop</title>
<style type="text/css">
<!--
body { background-color: #ccffcc;
       font-family: Arial, Helvetica, sans-serif;
       color: #330066;
       margin: 50px 70px;
       background-image: url(background.gif);
       background-repeat: repeat }
a:link { color: #cc9900 }
a:visited { color: #660000 }
▼ a:hover { color: #ffcc00 }
```

10

```
a:active { color: #ff0000 }
h1 { color: #996633;
     padding-top: 10px;
     padding-bottom: 5px;
     background-color: #ffffcc;
     border-color: #cccc33 #cc9933;
     border-width: thin;
     border: thin outset;
     font-family: "fantasy";
     text-align: center }
h2 { color: #996633;
     padding-top: 5px;
     padding-bottom: 3px;
     background-color: #ccffcc;
     border-color: #99cc33 #996633;
     border-width: thin;
     border: thin inset;
     font-family: "fantasy";
     text-align: center }
blockquote { font-family: "Book Antiqua";
     line-height: 12pt;
     font-weight: normal;
     font-variant: normal;
     color: #996633;
     word-spacing: 2em;
     text-align: center }
.fantasy { text-align: left;
     font-family: "fantasy";
     font-size: 16pt; color: #996600}
-->
</style>
</head>
<body>
<a name="top"><h1>The Bookworm: A Better Book Store</h1></a>
<blockquote>
"Old books are best--how tale and rhyme<br />
Float with us down the stream of time!"<br />
- Clarence Urmy, <cite>Old Songs are Best</cite>
</blockquote>
<p><span class="fantasy">The Bookworm Bookshop</span><br />
1345 Applewood Dr<br />
Springfield, CA 94325<br />
(415) 555-0034
</p>
<a name="contents"><h2>Contents</h2></a>
<ul>
  <li><a href="#about">About the Bookworm Bookshop</a></li>
  <li><a href ="#recent">Recent Titles</a></li>
  <li><a href ="#upcoming">Upcoming Events</a></li>
</ul>
<hr />
<a name="about"><h2>About the Bookworm Bookshop</h2></a>
```

```
<p>Since 1933, <span class="fantasy">The Bookworm Bookshop</span>
  has offered rare and hard-to-find titles for the discerning
  reader. The Bookworm offers:</p>
<ul>
<li>Friendly, knowledgeable, and courteous help</li>
<li>Free coffee and juice for our customers</li>
<li>A well-lit reading room so you can "try before you buy"</li>
<li>Four friendly cats: Esmerelda, Catherine, Dulcinea and Beatrice</li>
</ul>
<p>Our hours are <strong>10am to 9pm</strong> weekdays,
<strong>noon to 7</strong> on weekends.</p>
<p><a href="#contents">Back to Contents</a> ¦ <a href="#top">Back to Top</a></p>
<hr />
<a name="recent"><h2>Recent Titles (as of 11-Nov-99)</h2></a>
<ul>
<li>Sandra Bellweather, <a href="belladonna.html">
<cite>Belladonna</cite></a></li>
<li>Johnathan Tin, <a href="20minmeals.html">
<cite>20-Minute Meals for One</cite></a></li>
<li>Maxwell Burgess, <a href="legion.html">
<cite>Legion of Thunder</cite></a></li>
<li>Alison Caine, <a href="banquo.html">
<cite>Banquo's Ghost</cite></a></li>
</ul>
<p><a href="#contents">Back to Contents</a> ¦ <a href="#top">Back to Top</a></p>
<hr />
<a name="upcoming"><h2>Upcoming Events</h2></a>
<ul>
<li><b>The Wednesday Evening Book Review</b> meets, appropriately, on Wednesday
evenings at
7:00 pm for coffee and a round-table discussion. Call the Bookworm for
information on joining
the group and this week's reading assignment. </li>
<li><b>The Children's Hour</b> happens every Saturday at 1pm and includes
reading,
games, and other activities. Cookies and milk are served. </li>
  <li><b>Carole Fenney</b> will be at the Bookworm on Friday, September 17, to
read
    from her book of poems <cite>Spiders in the Web.</cite></li>
  <li><b>The Bookworm will be closed</b> October 1 to remove a family
of bats that has nested in the tower. We like the company, but not
the mess they leave behind! </li>
</ul>
<p><a href="#contents">Back to Contents</a> ¦ <a href="#top">Back to Top</a></p>
<hr />
<address>
Last Updated: 11-Nov-99<br />
WebMaster: Laura Lemay lemay@bookworm.com<br />
&#169; copyright 1999 the Bookworm<br />
</address>
</body>
</html>
```

10

OUTPUT

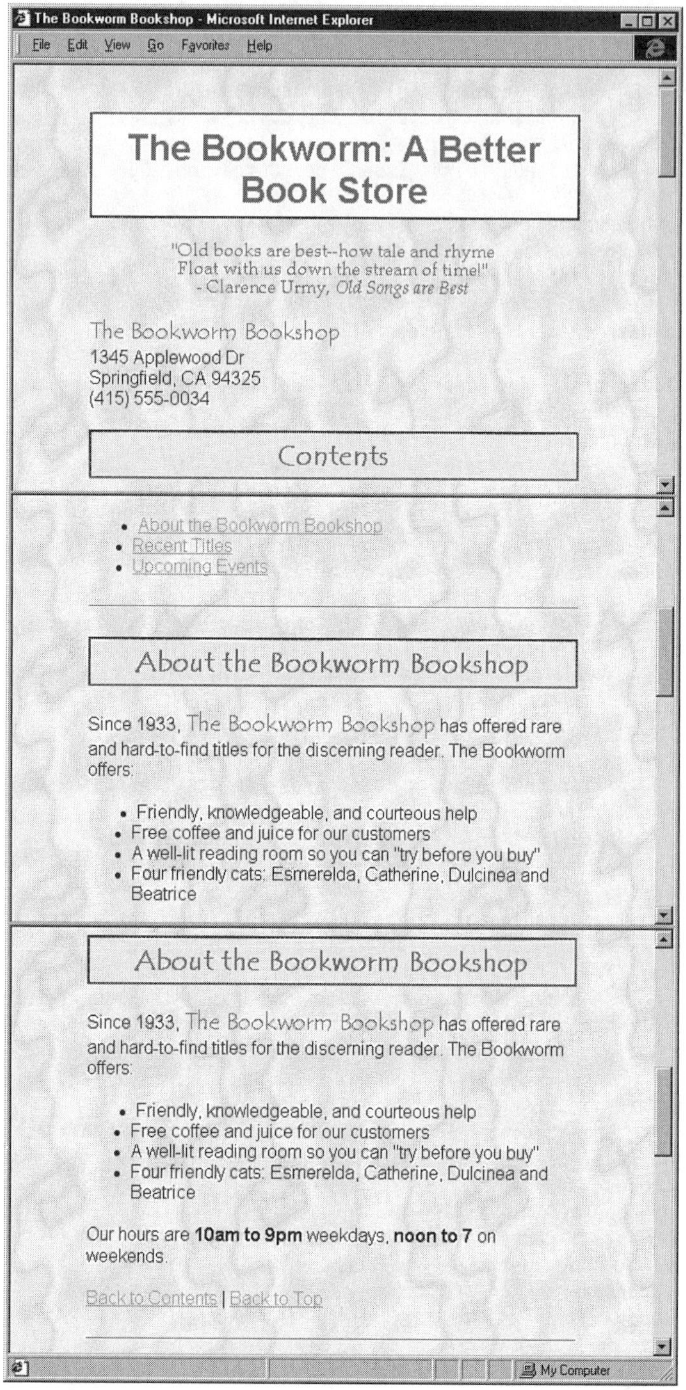

FIGURE 10.11

The Bookworm Bookshop with font and text styles added.

> **Note**
>
> If you viewed this example in Netscape Navigator, you probably noticed that the `<span>` tag is treated the same as the `<br />` tag. It moves any text that follows the tag to the next line. Knowing this, you'll probably want to avoid placing the `<span>` tag in the middle of a paragraph as we did here.

Sources of Information About Cascading Style Sheets

This section has only touched the surface of CSS. This mostly is because it is too large of a topic and because no browser really implements CSS well enough to dive deep into the possibilities.

If you want more information on Cascading Style Sheets, you can find it at the W3C Web site, where a specification of CSS is kept. The address for the Cascading Style Sheets page is `http://www.w3.org/Style/CSS/`.

Following are some other useful sources of information, as well:

- *Webreview.com*. Includes a Cascading Style Sheet guide on the site. A useful portion of this guide highlights the various ways that browsers implement CSS tags. `http://webreview.com/pub/guides/style/style.html`

- *Cascading Style Sheets*. This thorough reference from the Web Design Group gives great insight and information about the style sheet properties introduced in CSS Level 1. `http://www.htmlhelp.com/reference/css/`

- *W3C's CSS Home Page*. Start here for an extensive list of links to examples, history, and upcoming trends that relate to style sheets and other Web technologies. `http://www.w3.org/Style/`

10

Workshop

It's the close of a very long and jam-packed day. If you want to really drill in what you've learned, here's another workshop that will get you started. These questions and quiz will help you remember some of the important things you've learned about Cascading Style Sheets.

Q&A

Q. How do I decide which type of style sheets to use? Having to make this choice just confuses me.

A. Don't worry. You are not the only one who is confused by this choice. Basically, there are several approaches. If you are using styles to add some unique visual effects that aren't critical to your presentation, then you can choose the flavor with which you are most comfortable. If you want the widest possible audience to be able to view the styles, you are best off using Cascading Style Sheets because of the broader browser support at the moment.

Q. I am confused by these background color and image properties. Why don't I just use tables and apply background images and colors to specific cells?

A. You are absolutely correct that you can achieve some similar results using tables. The thing is this: Table tags have some problems. First, they are not strictly structural mark-up tags, so they cannot be rendered correctly in some browsers such as Lynx and spoken-word browsers for the blind. This means that the text within the table can come out in the wrong order and will appear awful in these browsers. By using style sheets to achieve some of the same results, you can focus on strict structural mark-up of your document, which ensures that even on a browser not supporting style sheets, the document is at least clear and useable.

Quiz

1. What is the difference between the strict and transitional HTML document types?
2. What is a CSS style rule?
3. What are the three main ways that you can apply cascading style sheet rules to HTML elements?
4. When you want to apply the same styles to multiple Web pages, which method is best to use? What special file extension is required?
5. True or False: You can use external, embedded, and inline styles in the same Web page.

Answers

1. The strict HTML document type uses a style sheet to define all the document's formatting, including colors and emphasis. The transitional HTML document uses a style sheet, but also incorporates HTML attributes to enable older browsers to see the document's formatting.

2. A CSS style rule defines a style that is to be applied to an HTML element. It consists of a selector (which can be an HTML tag), followed by a declaration that defines the property and value of the selector.

3. Cascading Style Sheet rules can be applied to HTML elements through the use of external style sheets, embedded style sheets, and inline styles.

4. External style sheets are best to use when you want to apply styles to more than one page. The external style sheet is saved with a .css file extension.

5. True. The properties you define in the embedded style sheet take precedence over those in the external style sheet. Likewise, the properties you define in the inline styles take precedence over the external and embedded styles.

Exercises

1. Create a simple Web page and apply some style rules of your own. Create your first example as an external style sheet that you can apply to more than one page.

2. Revise the example you created in the previous exercise to use an embedded style sheet. If you really feel adventurous, keep the external style sheet linked to the Web page. Add some new styles that override the styles in the external style sheet to see what happens!

10

DAY 11

Tables

So far in this book, you've used plain vanilla HTML to build and position the elements on your pages. Although you can get the point across using paragraphs and lists, there is another way to present information and content on your pages. By using tables, you can lay out any page content into rows and columns, with or without borders. And, the content you include within your tables isn't restricted to text. Because you can include *any* type of HTML content within a table (images, links, forms, and more), tables provide more control in the way your pages appear.

Tables first were officially introduced in HTML 3.2. Since then, they've had an enormous influence on Web page design and construction. HTML 4.0 includes changes that improve the manner in which tables are loaded and displayed in browsers. Now, authors can specify tables that display incrementally or that are more accessible to users that browse the Web with nonvisual browsers. Additional elements create tables with fixed headers and footers that render larger tables across several pages (such as for printouts).

Today, you'll learn all about tables, including the following:

- The state of table development on the Web
- Defining tables in HTML
- Creating captions, rows, and heading and data cells
- Modifying cell alignment
- Creating cells that span multiple rows or columns
- Adding color to tables
- How to use (or not use) tables in your Web documents

A Note About the Table Definition

When they were first introduced by Netscape in early 1995, tables almost immediately revolutionized Web page design—not just because they could be used for presenting data in a tabular form, but also because they gave a Web page designer much better control over page layout and the placement of various HTML elements on a page.

Now, in HTML 4.0, table specifications include many features that are customizable in style sheets, which you learned about in Day 10, "XHTML and Style Sheets." Although the HTML 4.0 specification is finalized, browser developers such as Microsoft and Netscape continue to push the envelope with new table features as they implement them in their browsers.

As you design your tables, keep in mind that they are still changing; although it's unlikely that anything you design now will break in the future, there probably will be changes still to come. With that one small warning in mind, let's jump right in.

Creating Tables

To create tables in HTML, you define the parts of your table and which bits of HTML go where. You then add HTML table code around those parts. Following that, you refine the appearance of the table with alignments, borders, and colored cells. In this section, you'll learn how to create a basic table with headings, data, and a caption.

One more note, however. Creating tables by hand in HTML is no fun. The code for tables was not necessarily designed to be easily written by hand. As such, it can be confusing. You'll do a lot of experimenting, testing, and going back and forth between your browser and your code to get a table to work out right. HTML editors can help a great deal with this, as can working initially in a word processor's table editor or a spreadsheet to get an idea of what goes where. But I suggest doing at least your first bunch of tables the hard way so you can get an idea how HTML tables work.

Table Parts

Before getting into the actual HTML code to create a table, let's look at the following terms so we both know what we're talking about:

- The *caption* indicates what the table is about, for example, "Voting Statistics, 1950–1994," or "Toy Distribution Per Room at 1564 Elm St." Captions are optional.

- The *table headings* label the rows, columns, or both. Table headings usually are in a larger or emphasized font that is different from the rest of the table. Table headings also are optional.

- *Table cells* are the individual squares in the table. A cell can contain normal table data or a table heading.

- *Table data* is the values in the table itself. The combination of the table headings and table data makes up the sum of the table.

Figure 11.1 shows a typical table and its parts.

FIGURE 11.1

The parts of a table.

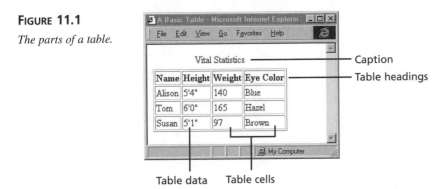

11

The `<table>` Element

To create a table in HTML, you use the `<table>...</table>` element to enclose the code for an optional caption, and then add the contents of the table itself:

```
<table>
...table caption (optional) and contents...
</table>
```

To demonstrate what the HTML code for a complete table looks like, here's an example of the code that created the table shown in Figure 11.1. Don't be concerned if you don't know what this all means right now. For now, notice that the table starts with a `<table>` tag and its attributes, and ends with a `</table>` tag:

```
<table border="1">
<caption>Vital Statistics</caption>
  <tr>
    <th>Name</th>
    <th>Height</th>
    <th>Weight</th>
    <th>Eye Color</th>
  </tr>
  <tr>
    <td>Alison</td>
    <td>5'4"</td>
    <td>140</td>
    <td>Blue</td>
  </tr>
  <tr>
    <td>Tom</td>
    <td>6'0"</td>
    <td>165</td>
    <td>Hazel</td>
  </tr>
  <tr>
    <td>Susan</td>
    <td>5'1"</td>
    <td>97</td>
    <td>Brown</td>
  </tr>
</table>
```

Rows and Cells

Now that you've been introduced to the `<table>` element, we'll move on to the rows and cells. Inside the `<table>`...`</table>` element, you define the actual contents of the table. Tables are specified in HTML row by row, and each row definition contains definitions for all the cells in that row. So, to define a table, you start by defining a top row and each cell in turn, left to right, and then you define a second row and its cells, and so on. The columns are automatically calculated based on how many cells there are in each row.

Each table row starts with the `<tr>` tag and ends with the appropriate closing `</tr>`. Your table can have as many rows as you want to and as many cells in each row as you need for your columns, but you should make sure that each row has the same number of cells so the columns line up.

The cells within each table row are indicated by one of two elements:

- `<th>`...`</th>` elements are used for heading cells. Headings are generally displayed in a different way than table cells, such as in a boldface font, and should be closed with a tag of `</th>`.
- `<td>`...`</td>` elements are used for data cells. td stands for Table Data. The `<td>` tag should be closed with a tag of `</td>`.

Note

> In early definitions of tables, the closing tags `</tr>`, `</th>`, and `</td>` were required for each row and cell. Since then, the table definition has been refined such that each of these closing tags is optional. However, many browsers that support tables still expect the closing tags to be there, and the tables might even break if you don't include the closing tags. Until tables become more consistently implemented across browsers, it's probably a good idea to continue using the closing tags even though they are optional—after all, using them is still correct, so there are no compelling reasons to leave them out.

In the table example you've been following along with so far, the heading cells appear in the top row and are defined with the following code:

```
<tr>
  <th>Name</th>
  <th>Height</th>
  <th>Weight</th>
  <th>Eye Color</th>
</tr>
```

This is followed by three rows of data cells, which are coded as follows:

```
<tr>
  <td>Alison</td>
  <td>5'4"</td>
  <td>140</td>
  <td>Blue</td>
</tr>
<tr>
  <td>Tom</td>
  <td>6'0"</td>
  <td>165</td>
  <td>Blue</td>
</tr>
<tr>
  <td>Susan</td>
  <td>5'1"</td>
```

11

```
  <td>97</td>
  <td>Brown</td>
</tr>
```

As you've seen, you can place the headings along the top edge by defining the <th> ele-ments inside the first row. Let's make a slight modification to the table. You'll put the headings along the left edge of the table instead. To accomplish this, put each <th> in the first cell in each row, and follow it with the data that pertains to each heading. The new code looks like the following:

```
<tr>
  <th>Name</th>
  <td>Alison</td>
  <td>Tom</td>
  <td>Susan</td>
</tr>
<tr>
  <th>Height</th>
  <td>5'4"</td>
  <td>6'0"</td>
  <td>5'1"</td>
</tr>
<tr>
  <th>Weight</th>
  <td>140</td>
  <td>165</td>
  <td>97</td>
</tr>
<tr>
  <th>Eye Color</th>
  <td>Blue</td>
  <td>Blue</td>
  <td>Brown</td>
</tr>
```

Figure 11.2 shows the results of this table.

OUTPUT

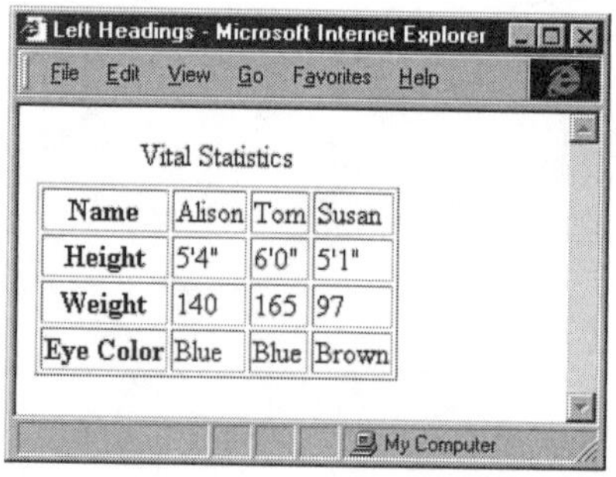

FIGURE 11.2

Small tables and headings.

Left Headings - Microsoft Internet Explorer

File   Edit   View   Go   Favorites   Help

Vital Statistics

Name	Alison	Tom	Susan
Height	5'4"	6'0"	5'1"
Weight	140	165	97
Eye Color	Blue	Blue	Brown

My Computer

Empty Cells

Both table heading cells and data cells can contain any text, HTML code, or both, including links, lists, forms, and other tables. But what if you want a cell with nothing in it? That's easy. Just define a cell with a `<th>` or `<td>` element with nothing inside it:

```
<table border="1">
<tr>
    <td></td>
    <td>10</td>
    <td>20</td>
</tr>
</table>
```

Some browsers display empty cells of this sort as if they don't exist at all. If you want to force a *truly* empty cell, you can add a line break with no other text in that cell by itself:

```
<table border="1">
<tr>
    <td><br /></td>
    <td>10</td>
    <td>20</td>
</tr>
</table>
```

Figure 11.3 shows examples of both types of empty cells: the empty cell, and the really empty cell with the line break added.

FIGURE 11.3

Empty and really empty cells.

An empty cell ——

The empty cell, really empty ——

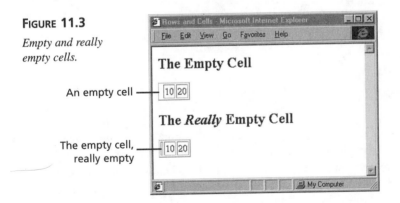

Captions

Table captions tell your reader what the table is for. The `<caption>` element, created just for this purpose, labels table captions as captions. Although you could just as easily use a regular paragraph or a heading as a caption for your table, tools that process HTML files can extract `<caption>` elements into a separate file, automatically number them, or treat them in special ways simply because they are captions.

If you don't want a caption, you don't have to include one; captions are optional. If you just want a table and don't care about a label, leave the caption off.

The `<caption>` element goes inside the `<table>` element just before the table rows, and it contains the title of the table. It closes with the `</caption>` tag.

```
<table>
<caption>Vital Statistics</caption>
<tr>
```

Exercise 11.1: Create a Simple Table

Now that you know the basics of how to create a table, try a simple example. For this example, you'll create a table that indicates the colors you get when you mix the three primary colors together.

Figure 11.4 shows the table you're going to re-create in this example.

FIGURE 11.4

The simple color table.

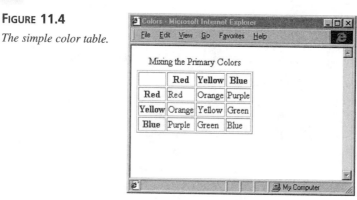

Here's a quick hint for laying out tables. Because HTML defines tables on a row-by-row basis, it sometimes can be difficult to keep track of the columns, particularly with very complex tables. Before you start actually writing HTML code, it's useful to make a sketch of your table so that you know what are the heads and the values of each cell. You might find that it's easiest to use a word processor with a table editor (such as Microsoft Word) or a spreadsheet to lay out your tables. Then, when you have the layout and the cell values, you can write the HTML code for that table.

▼ Start with a simple HTML framework for the page that contains a table. Like all HTML files, you can create this file in any text editor:

```
<html>
<head>
<title>Colors</title>
</head>
<body>
<table border="1">
...add table rows and cells here...
</table>
</body>
</html>
```

Now start adding table rows inside the opening and closing `<table>` tags (where the line "add table rows and cells here" was in the framework). The first row is the three headings along the top of the table. The table row is indicated by `<tr>`, and each cell by a `<th>` tag:

```
<tr>
    <th>Red</th>
    <th>Yellow</th>
    <th>Blue</th>
</tr>
```

Note You can format the HTML code any way you want; as with all HTML, the browser ignores most extra spaces and returns. I like to format it like this, with the contents of the individual rows indented and the cell elements on separate lines, so that I can pick out the rows and columns more easily.

Now add the second row. The first cell in the second row is the Red heading on the left side of the table, so it will be the first cell in this row, followed by the cells for the table data:

```
<tr>
    <th>Red</th>
    <td>Red</td>
    <td>Orange</td>
    <td>Purple</td>
▼   </tr>
```

▼   Continue by adding the remaining two rows in the table, with the Yellow and Blue headings. Here's what you have so far for the entire table:

```
<table border="1">
<tr>
    <th>Red</th>
    <th>Yellow</th>
    <th>Blue</th>
</tr>
<tr>
    <th>Red</th>
    <td>Red</td>
    <td>Orange</td>
    <td>Purple</td>
</tr>
<tr>
    <th>Yellow</th>
    <td>Orange</td>
    <td>Yellow</td>
    <td>Green</td>
</tr>
<tr>
    <th>Blue</th>
    <td>Purple</td>
    <td>Green</td>
    <td>Blue</td>
</tr>
</table>
```

Finally, add a simple caption. The `<caption>` element goes just after the `<table border>` tag and just before the first `<tr>` tag:

```
<table border="1">
<caption>Mixing the Primary Colors</caption>
<tr>
```

Now, with a first draft of the code in place, test the HTML file in your favorite browser that supports tables. Figure 11.5 shows how it looks in Internet Explorer.

Oops! What happened with that top row? The headings are all messed up. The answer, of course, is that you need an empty cell at the beginning of that first row to space the headings out over the proper columns. HTML isn't smart enough to match it all up for you (this is exactly the sort of error you're going to find the first time you test your tables).

Add an empty table heading cell to that first row (here, the line `<th><br /></th>`):

```
<tr>
    <th><br /></th>
    <th>Red</th>
    <th>Yellow</th>
    <th>Blue</th>
▼   </tr>
```

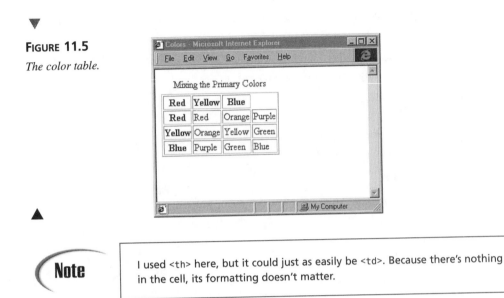

FIGURE 11.5

The color table.

> **Note**
>
> I used <th> here, but it could just as easily be <td>. Because there's nothing in the cell, its formatting doesn't matter.

If you try it again, you should get the right result with all the headings over the right columns, as the original example in Figure 11.4 shows.

Sizing Tables, Borders, and Cells

With the basics out of the way, now you'll look at some of the attributes that can change the overall appearance of your tables. The attributes you'll learn about in this section control the width of your tables and cells, the amount of spacing between cell content and rows and columns, and the width of the borders.

Setting Table Widths

The table in the preceding example relied on the browser itself to decide how wide the table and column widths were going to be. In many cases, this is the best way to make sure your tables are viewable on different browsers with different screen sizes and widths; simply let the browser decide.

In other cases, however, you might want to have more control over how wide your tables and columns are, particularly if the defaults the browser comes up with are really strange. In this section you'll learn a couple ways to do just this.

The width attribute of the <table> element defines how wide the table will be on the page. width can have a value that is either the exact width of the table (in pixels) or a percentage (such as 50 percent or 75 percent) of the current screen width, which can therefore change if the window is resized. If `width` is specified, the width of the columns within the table can be compressed or expanded to fit the required width.

To make a table fit a 100 percent screen width, you add the `width` attribute to the table, as shown in the following line of code. The result is shown in Figure 11.6.

```
<table border="1" width="100%">
```

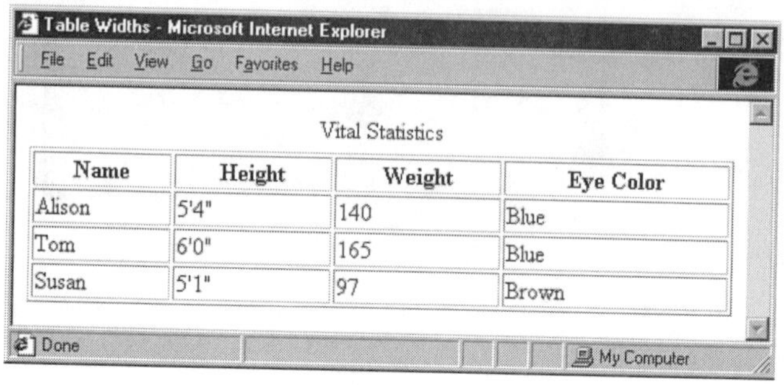

FIGURE 11.6

Table widths in Internet Explorer.

> **Note**
>
> Trying to make the table too narrow for the data it contains might be impossible, in which case the browser tries to get as close as it can to your desired width.

It's always a better idea to specify your table widths as percentages rather than as specific pixel widths. Because you don't know how wide the browser window will be, using percentages allows your table to be reformatted to whatever width the browser is. Using specific pixel widths might cause your table to run off the page.

Changing Table Borders

The `border` attribute, which appears immediately inside the opening `<table>` tag, is the most common attribute of the `<table>` element. With it, you specify whether border lines are displayed around the table, and if so, how wide the borders should be.

The `border` attribute has undergone some changes since it first appeared in HTML:

- In HTML 2.0, you used `<table border>` to draw a border around the table. The border could be rendered as fancy in a graphical browser or just a series of dashes and pipes (¦) in a text-based browser.
- Starting with HTML 3.2 and later, the correct usage of the `border` attribute is a little different: it indicates the width of a border in pixels. `<table border="1">` creates a 1-pixel wide border, `<table border="2">` a 2-pixel wide border, and so on.

HTML 3.2 and later browsers are expected to display the old HTML 2.0 form of `<table border>`, with no value, with a 1-pixel border (as if you specified `<table border="1">`.

- To create a border that has no width and is not displayed, you specify `<table border="0">`. Borderless tables are useful when you want to use the table structure for layout purposes, but you don't necessarily want the outline of an actual table on the page. HTML 3.2 and later browsers are expected to not display a border (the same as `<table border="0">`) if you leave out the border attribute entirely.

You can change the width of the border drawn around the table. If border has a numeric value, the border around the outside of the table is drawn with that pixel width. The default is `border="1"`; `border="0"` suppresses the border (just as if you had omitted the border attribute altogether).

Figure 11.7 shows a table that has a border width of 10 pixels. The table and border definition looks like this: 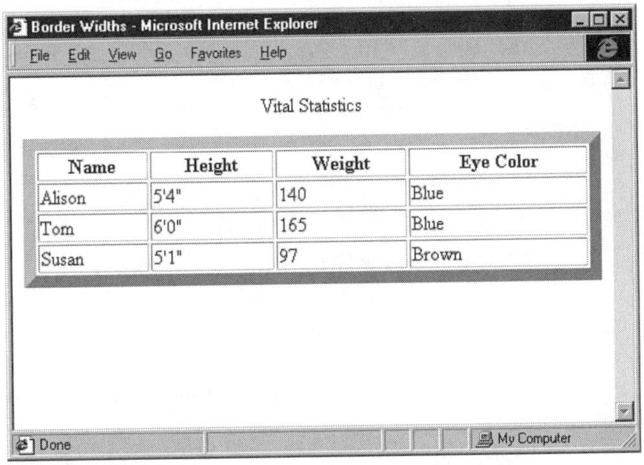

```
<table border="10" width="100%">
```

FIGURE 11.7

Border widths.

11

Cell Padding

The cell padding attribute defines the amount of space between the edges of the cells and the content of a cell. By default, many browsers draw tables with a cell padding of 1 pixel. You can add more space by adding the `cellpadding` attribute to the `<table>` element, with a value in pixels for the amount of cell padding you want.

Here's the revised code for your `<table>` element, which increases the cell padding to 10 pixels. The result is shown in Figure 11.8:

```
<table border="10" width="100%" cellpadding="10">
```

Cell padding
increases space
between cell
contents and its
borders

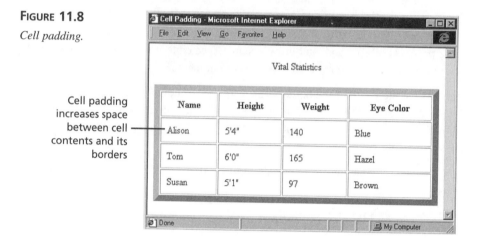

The `cellpadding` attribute with a value of 0 causes the edges of the cells to touch the edges of the cell's contents (which doesn't look very good).

Cell Spacing

Cell spacing is similar to cell padding except that it affects the amount of space between cells—that is, the width of the shaded lines that separate the cells. The `cellspacing` attribute in the `<table>` element affects the spacing for the table. Cell spacing is 2 by default.

Cell spacing also includes the outline around the table, which is just inside the table's border (as set by the `border` attribute). Experiment with it, and you can see the difference. For example, Figure 11.9 shows our table with cell spacing of 8 and a border of 4, as shown in the following code:

```
<table border="4" width="100%" cellpadding="10" cellspacing="8">
```

FIGURE 11.9

Cell spacing (and borders).

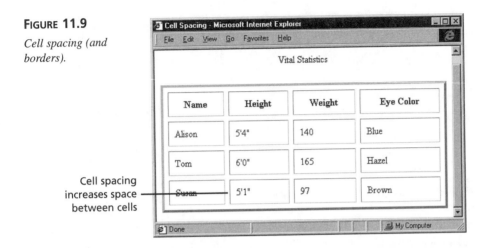

Cell spacing
increases space ————
between cells

Column Widths

You also can use the `width` attribute on individual cells (`<th>` or `<td>`) to indicate the width of individual columns. As with table widths, discussed earlier today, you can make the `width` attribute in cells an exact pixel width or a percentage (which is taken as a percentage of the full table width). As with table widths, using percentages rather than specific pixel widths is a better idea because it allows your table to be displayed regardless of the window size.

Column widths are useful when you want to have multiple columns of identical widths, regardless of their contents (for example, for some forms of page layout).

Figure 11.10 shows your original table from Figure 11.1. This time, however, the table spans 100 percent of the screen's width. The first column is 40 percent of the table width and the remaining three columns are 20 percent each.

To accomplish this, the column widths are applied to the heading cells as follows:

```
<table border="1" width="100%">
<caption>Vital Statistics</caption>
<tr>
    <th width="40%">Name</th>
    <th width="20%">Height</th>
    <th width="20%">Weight</th>
    <th width="20%">Eye Color</th>
</tr>
```

11

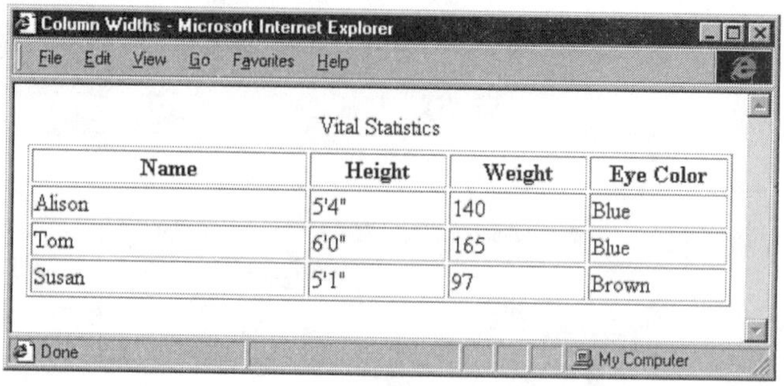

FIGURE **11.10**

Column widths.

What happens if you have a table that spans 80 percent of the screen, and it includes the same header cells (40 percent, 20 percent, 20 percent, and 20 percent) as in the preceding example? Revise the code slightly, changing the width of the entire table to 80 percent as shown in the following example. When you open the new table in your browser, you'll see that the table now spans 80 percent of the width of your screen. The four columns still span 40 percent, 20 percent, 20 percent and 20 percent of the *table*. To be more specific, the columns span 32 percent, 16 percent, 16 percent, and 16 percent of the entire screen width.

```
<table border="1" width="80%">
<caption>Vital Statistics</caption>
<tr>
    <th width="40%">Name</th>
    <th width="20%">Height</th>
    <th width="20%">Weight</th>
    <th width="20%">Eye Color</th>
  </tr>
```

Setting Breaks in Text

Often, the easiest way to make small changes to how a table is laid out is by using line breaks (
 elements). Line breaks are particularly useful if you have a table in which most of the cells are small and only one or two cells have longer data. As long as the screen width can handle it, the browser generally just creates really long rows, which looks rather funny in some tables. For example, the last row in the table shown in Figure 11.11 is coded as follows:

```
<tr>
    <td>TC</td>
    <td>7</td>
    <td>Suspicious except when hungry, then friendly</td>
  </tr>
```

FIGURE 11.11

A table with one long row.

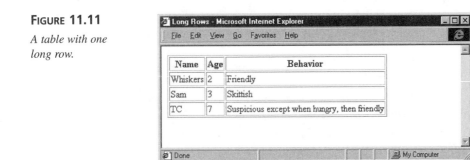

By putting in line breaks, you can wrap that row in a shorter column so that it looks more like the table shown in Figure 11.12. The following shows how the revised code looks for the last row:

```
<tr>
    <td>TC</td>
    <td>7</td>
    <td>Suspicious except<br />
        when hungry, <br />
        then friendly</td>
</tr>
```

FIGURE 11.12

The long row fixed with <br />.

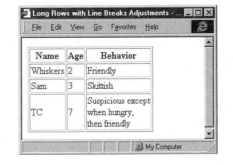

On the other hand, you might have a table in which a cell is being wrapped for which you want all the data on one line. (This can be particularly important for things such as form elements within table cells where you want the label and the input field to stay together.) In this instance, you can add the nowrap attribute to the <th> or <td> elements, and the browser keeps all the data in that cell on one line. Note that you can always add <br /> elements by hand to that same cell and get line breaks exactly where you want them.

> **Note**
>
> The `nowrap` attribute has been deprecated in HTML 4.0 in favor of using style sheet properties.

Be careful when you hard-code table cells with line breaks and `nowrap` attributes. Remember, your table might be viewed in many different screen widths. Try resizing the window in which your table is being viewed and see whether your table can still hold up under different widths with all your careful formatting in place. For the most part, you should try to let the browser itself format your table and make minor adjustments only when necessary.

Table and Cell Color and Alignment

After you have your basic table layout with rows, headings, and data, you can start refining how that table looks. You can refine tables in a couple of ways. One way to improve and enhance the appearance of tables is to add color to borders and cells.

Changing Table and Cell Background Colors

To change the background color of a table, a row, or a cell inside a row, use the `bgcolor` attribute of the `<table>`, `<tr>`, `<th>` or `<td>` elements. Just like in `<body>`, the value of `bgcolor` is a color specified as a hexadecimal triplet or, in many browsers including Internet Explorer and Netscape Navigator, one of the 16 color names: Black, White, Green, Maroon, Olive, Navy, Purple, Gray, Red, Yellow, Blue, Teal, Lime, Aqua, Fuchsia, or Silver. The `bgcolor` attribute is now part of the HTML 4.0 specification, but it has been deprecated in favor of style sheets.

Each background color overrides the background color of its enclosing element. So, for example, a table background overrides the page background, a row background overrides the table's, and any cell colors override all other colors. If you nest tables inside cells, that nested table has the background color of the cell that encloses it.

Also, if you change the color of a cell, don't forget to change the color of the text inside it so that you can still read it. If you want your pages to be compatible with browsers older than Internet Explorer 4.0 and Netscape Navigator 4.0, use `<font color...>`. For browsers that support cascading style sheets, such as Internet Explorer 4.0 (or later) or Netscape 4.0 (or later), use the CSS `color` property.

> **Note**
>
> In order for table cells to show up with background colors, they have to have some sort of contents. Simply putting a `<br />` element in empty cells works fine.

Here's an example of changing the background and cell colors in a table. I've created a checkerboard by using an HTML table. The table itself is white, with alternating cells in black. The checkers (here, red and black circles) are images.

> **Note**
>
> Speaking of using images in tables, it generally doesn't matter in the final output where white space appears in your original HTML code. In Netscape, however, there's one exception to the rule, and it applies when you are placing images in table cells. Suppose that you've formatted your code with the `<img>` tag on a separate line, like the following:
>
> ```
> <td>
>     <img src="check.gif">
> </td>
> ```
>
> With this code, the return between the `<td>` and the `<img>` tag is significant; your image will not be properly placed within the cell (this particularly shows up in centered cells). This quirk of the Netscape browser remains the case even in the latest release of Netscape Navigator. To correct the problem, just put the `<td>` and the `<img>` on the same line like the following:
>
> ```
> <td><img src="check.gif"></td>
> ```

I've applied the rule mentioned in the previous note in the following example. The result in Internet Explorer is shown in Figure 11.13.

```
<html>
<head>
<title>Checkerboard</title>
</head>
<body>
<table bgcolor="#ffffff" width="50%">
<tr align="center">
<td bgcolor="#000000" width="33%"><img src="redcircle.gif" alt="Red Circle"
width="75" height="75"></td>
<td width="33%"><img src="redcircle.gif" alt="Red Circle" width="75"
height="75"></td>
```

11

```
<td bgcolor="#000000" width="33%"><img src="redcircle.gif" alt="Red Circle"
width="75" height="75"></td>
</tr>

<tr align="center">
<td><img src="blackcircle.gif" alt="Black Circle" width="75" height="75"></td>
<td bgcolor="#000000"><br />
</td>
<td><img src="blackcircle.gif" alt="Black Circle" width="75" height="75"></td>
</tr>

<tr align="center">
<td bgcolor="#000000"><br />
</td>
<td><img src="blackcircle.gif" alt="Black Circle" width="75" height="75"><br />
</td>
<td bgcolor="#000000"><br />
</td>
</tr>
</table>
</body>
</html>
```

FIGURE 11.13

Table cell colors.

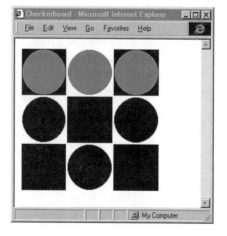

Changing Border Colors

Internet Explorer also enables you to change the colors of the elements of the table's
border by using the bordercolor, bordercolorlight, and bordercolordark attributes.
Each of these attributes takes either a color number or name and can be used in <table>,
<td>, or <th>. Like background colors, the border colors each override the colors of the
enclosing element. All three require the enclosing <table> tag to have the border
attribute set.

These extensions are only (currently) supported in Internet Explorer with the exception of bordercolor, which is supported in Netscape Navigator 4. All of these have been deprecated in favor of style sheets.

- bordercolor sets the color of the border, overriding the 3D look of the default border.
- bordercolordark sets the dark component of 3D-look borders, and places the dark color on the right and bottom sides of the table border.
- bordercolorlight sets the light component of 3D-look borders, and places the light color on the left and top sides of the table border.

Figure 11.14 shows an example of the table with a border of 10 pixels. To demonstrate the Internet Explorer attributes, bordercolordark and bordercolorlight have been added to give the thicker border a 3D look. The first line of the code has been changed as follows:

```
<table border="10" bordercolorlight="Red" bordercolordark="Black"
bgcolor="#ffffff" width="50%">
```

This line of code is getting a little long, isn't it? You might find it easier to read if you put each attribute on a separate line, as the following example shows. It still works the same. Just remember that the closing bracket (>) must appear only after the final attribute.

```
<table border="10"
    bordercolorlight="Red"
    bordercolordark="Black"
    bgcolor="#ffffff"
    width="50%">
```

11

FIGURE 11.14

Table border colors.

Table border —

Light border color —

Dark border color

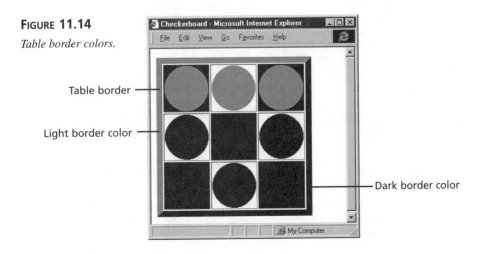

Aligning Your Table Content

Another enhancement that you can make to your tables is by making adjustments to how the content in the tables and cells is aligned. The `align` attribute aligns content horizontally, while the `valign` attribute aligns content vertically. Both of these attributes were introduced in HTML 3.2, but have been deprecated in HTML 4.0. The following sections describe how to use these attributes in tables.

Table Alignment

By default, tables are displayed on a line by themselves along the left side of the page, with any text above or below the table. However, you can use the `align` attribute to align tables along the left or right margins and wrap text alongside them the same way you can with images.

`align="left"` aligns the table along the left margin, and all text following that table is wrapped in the space between that table and the right side of the page. `align="right"` does the same thing, with the table aligned to the right side of the page.

In the example shown in Figure 11.15, a table that spans 70 percent of the width of the page is aligned to the left with the following code:

```
<table border="1" align="left" width="70%">
```

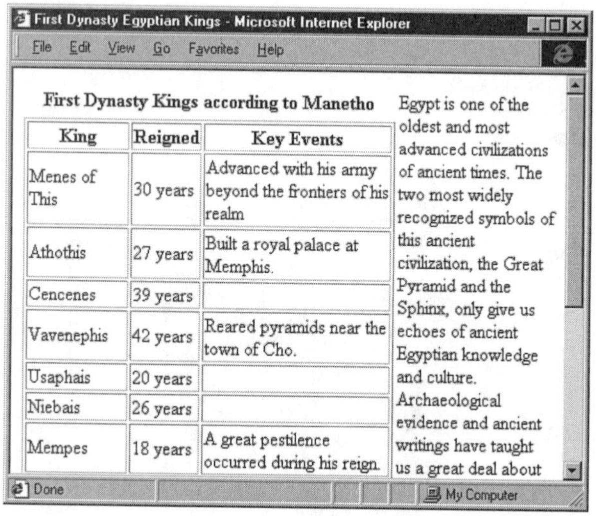

FIGURE 11.15

A table with text alongside it.

As with images, to stop wrapping text alongside an image, you can use the line break element with the `clear` attribute.

Centering tables is slightly more difficult. Up until the recent release of Internet Explorer 4 and Netscape Navigator 4, no browsers supported `align="center"` on tables. However, you could use the `<center>` or `<div align="center">` elements (both of which you learned about in Day 6, "More Text Formatting with HTML") to center tables on the page. Now, with the latest versions of both browsers, `<table align="center">` is correctly supported. As with other formatting attributes, however, the align attribute has been deprecated in HTML 4.0.

Cell Alignment

After you have your rows and cells in place inside your table and the table properly aligned on the page, you can align the data within each cell for the best effect, based on what your table contains. Several options allow you to align the data within your cells both horizontally and vertically. Figure 11.16 shows a table (a real HTML one!) of the various alignment options.

FIGURE 11.16

Cell alignment.

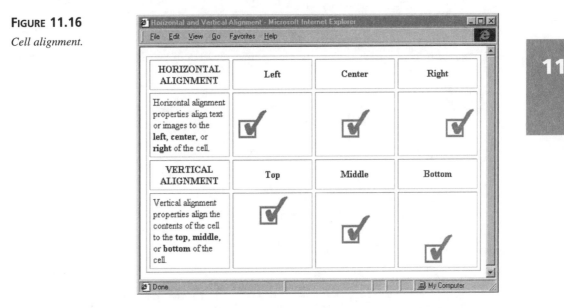

Horizontal alignment (the `align` attribute) defines whether the data within a cell is aligned with the left cell margin (`left`), the right cell margin (`right`), or centered within the two (`center`).

Vertical alignment (the `valign` attribute) defines the vertical alignment of the data within the cell, meaning whether the data is flush with the top of the cell (`top`), flush with the bottom of the cell (`bottom`), or vertically centered within the cell (`middle`). Netscape

Navigator also implements valign="baseline", which is similar to valign="top", except that it aligns the baseline of the first line of text in each cell (depending on the contents of the cell, this might or might not produce a different result than align="top").

By default, heading cells are centered both horizontally and vertically, and data cells are centered vertically but aligned flush left.

You can override the defaults for an entire row by adding the align or valign attributes to the <tr> element, as in the following:

```
<tr align="center" valign="top">
```

You can override the row alignment for individual cells by adding align to the <td> or <th> elements:

```
<tr align="center" valign="top">
    <td>14</td>
    <td>16</td>
    <td align=left>No Data</td>
    <td>15</td>
</tr>
```

The following input and output example shows the various cell alignments and how they look in Internet Explorer (see Figure 11.17).

INPUT

```
<html>
<head>
<title>Cell Alignments</title>
</head>
<body>
<table border="1">
<tr>
<th width="25%"><br /></th>
<th width="25%">Left</th>
<th width="25%">Centered</th>
<th width="25%">Right</th>
</tr>

<tr>
<th>Top</th>
<td align="left" valign="top"><img src="button.gif" alt="Button"
width="15" height="13"></td>
<td align="center" valign="top"><img src="button.gif" alt="Button"
width="15" height="13"></td>
<td align="right" valign="top"><img src="button.gif" alt="Button"
width="15" height="13"></td>
</tr>

<tr>
<th>Centered</th>
```

```
<td align="left" valign="middle"><img src="button.gif" alt="Button"
width="15" height="13"></td>
<td align="center" valign="middle"><img src="button.gif" alt="Button"
width="15" height="13"></td>
<td align="right" valign="middle"><img src="button.gif" alt="Button"
width="15" height="13"></td>
</tr>

<tr>
<th>Bottom</th>
<td align="left" valign="bottom"><img src="button.gif" alt="Button"
width="15" height="13"></td>
<td align="center" valign="bottom"><img src="button.gif" alt="Button"
width="15" height="13"></td>
<td align="right" valign="bottom"><img src="button.gif" alt="Button"
width="15" height="13"></td>
</tr>
</table>
</body>
</html>
```

OUTPUT

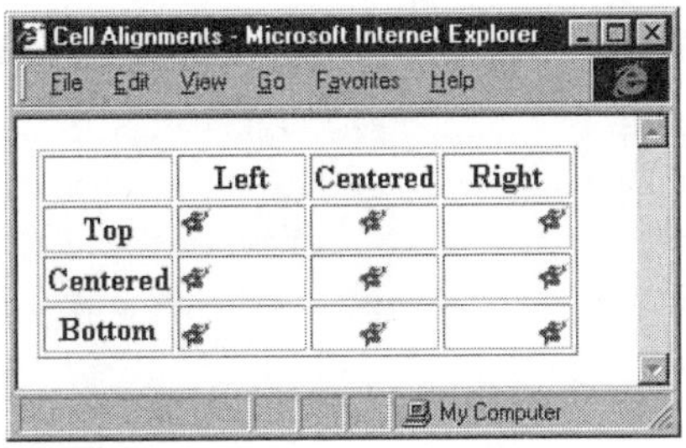

FIGURE 11.17

Alignment options.

11

Caption Alignment

The optional align attribute to the caption determines the alignment of the caption. Depending on which browser you're using, however, you have different choices for what align means.

In most browsers, align can have one of two values: top and bottom. This is the correct HTML standardized use of the align attribute. By default, the caption is placed at the top of the table (align="top"). You can use the align="bottom" attribute to the caption if you want to put the caption at the bottom of the table, like the following:

```
<table>
<caption align="bottom">Torque Limits for Various Fruits</caption>
```

In Internet Explorer, however, captions are different. With Internet Explorer, you use the valign attribute to put the caption at the top or the bottom, and align has three different values: left, right, and center, which align the caption horizontally.

To achieve similar results in Netscape Navigator, use `align="bottom"` or `align="top"`, and then use the `<div>` element with its `align` attribute to align the caption text to the left, right, or center. This also works in Internet Explorer 4.

If you want to place the caption at the bottom of the table, aligned to the right, in Internet Explorer, for example, you can use the following:

```
<caption valign="bottom" align="right">This is a caption</caption>
```

or you can use the `<div>` element, as in the following, which also works in Netscape Navigator:

```
<caption align="bottom"><div align="right">This is a caption</div></caption>
```

In general, unless you have a very short table, you should leave the caption in its default position—centered at the top of the table—so your readers will see the caption first and know what they are about to read, instead of seeing it after they're already done reading the table (at which point they've usually figured out what it's about anyway).

Spanning Multiple Rows or Columns

The tables you've created up to this point all had one value per cell or had the occasional empty cell. You also can create cells that span multiple rows or columns within the table. Those spanned cells then can hold headings that have subheadings in the next row or column, or you can create other special effects within the table layout. Figure 11.18 shows a table with spanned columns and rows.

FIGURE 11.18

Tables with spans.

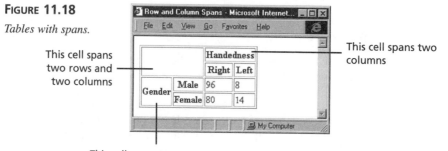

This cell spans two rows and two columns

This cell spans two columns

This cell spans two rows

To create a cell that spans multiple rows or columns, you add the `rowspan` or `colspan` attribute to the `<th>` or `<td>` elements, along with the number of rows or columns you want the cell to span. The data within that cell then fills the entire width or length of the combined cells, as in the following example:

```html
<html>
<head>
<title>Row and Column Spans</title>
</head>
<body>
<table border="1">
<tr>
<th colspan="2">Gender</th>
</tr>

<tr>
<th>Male</th>
<th>Female</th>
</tr>

<tr>
<td>15</td>
<td>23</td>
</tr>
</table>
</body>
</html>
```

Figure 11.19 shows how this table might appear when displayed.

FIGURE 11.19

Column spans.

Note that if a cell spans multiple rows, you don't have to redefine that cell as empty in the next row or rows. Just ignore it and move to the next cell in the row; the span will fill in the spot for you.

Cells always span downward and to the right. To create a cell that spans several columns, you add the `colspan` attribute to the leftmost cell in the span; for cells that span rows, you add `rowspan` to the topmost cell.

The following input and output example shows a cell that spans multiple rows (the cell with the word "Piston" in it). Figure 11.20 shows the result in Internet Explorer.

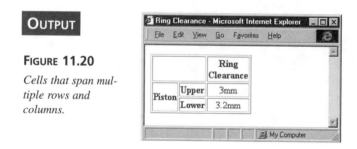

INPUT

```html
<html>
<head>
<title>Ring Clearance</title>
</head>
<body>
<table border="1">
<tr>
<th colspan="2"> </th>
<th>Ring<br />
 Clearance</th>
</tr>

<tr align="center">
<th rowspan="2">Piston</th>
<th>Upper</th>
<td>3mm</td>
</tr>

<tr align="center">
<th>Lower</th>
<td>3.2mm</td>
</tr>
</table>
</body>
</html>
```

OUTPUT

FIGURE 11.20

Cells that span multiple rows and columns.

Exercise 11.2: A Table of Service Specifications

Had enough of tables yet? Let's do another example that takes advantage of everything you've learned here: tables that use colors, headings, normal cells, alignments, and column and row spans. This is a very complex table, so we'll go step by step, row by row, to build it.

Figure 11.21 shows the table, which indicates service and adjustment specifications from the service manual for a car.

FIGURE 11.21

The really complex service specification table.

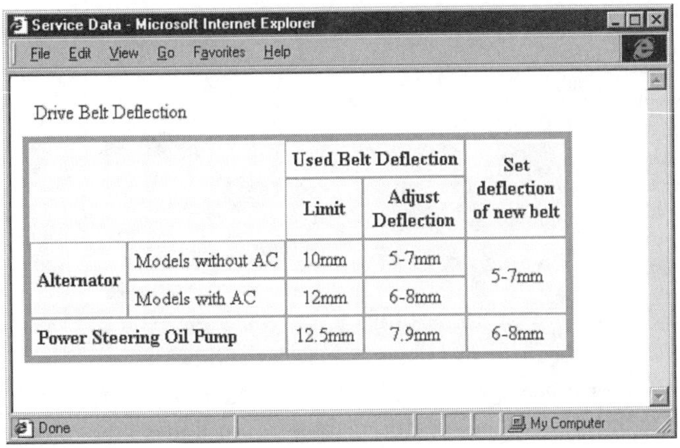

There are actually five rows and columns in this table. Do you see them? Some of them span columns and rows. Figure 11.22 shows the same table with a grid drawn over it so that you can see where the rows and columns are.

FIGURE 11.22

Five columns, five rows.

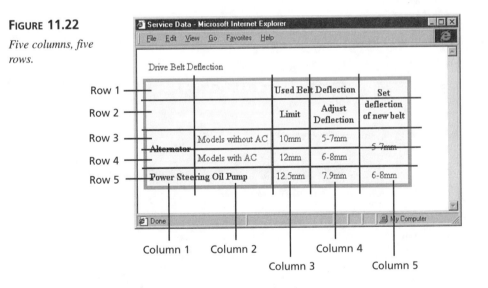

With tables such as this one that use many spans, it's helpful to draw this sort of grid to figure out where the spans are and in which row they belong. Remember, spans start at the topmost row and the leftmost column.

▼ Ready? Start with the framework, just as you have for the other tables today:

```
<html>
<head>
<title>Service Data</title>
</head>
<body>
<table border="1">
<caption>Drive Belt Deflection</caption>
</table>
</body>
</html>
```

To enhance the appearance of the table, you'll make all of the cells light yellow (#ffffcc) by using the bgcolor attribute. The border will be increased in size to 5 pixels, and you'll color it deep gold (#cc9900) by using the bordercolor attribute that is compatible with both Netscape and Internet Explorer. You'll make the rules between cells appear more solid by using a cellspacing setting of 0, and increase the white space between the cell contents and the borders of the cells by specifying a cellpadding setting of 5. The new table definition now looks like the following:

```
<table border="5"
   bgcolor="#ffffcc"
   bordercolor="#cc9900"
   cellspacing="0"
   cellpadding="5">
```

Now create the first row. With the grid on your picture, you can see that the first cell is empty and spans two rows and two columns (see Figure 11.23). Therefore, the HTML for that cell would be as follows:

```
<tr>
<th rowspan="2" colspan="2"></th>
```

FIGURE 11.23

The first cell.

The first cell (spans two columns and two rows)

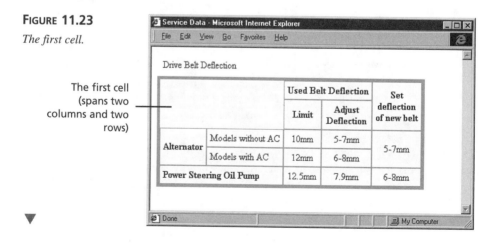

▼ The second cell in the row is the Used Belt Deflection heading cell, which spans two columns (for the two cells beneath it). The code for that cell is as follows:

```
<th colspan="2">Used Belt Deflection</th>
```

Now that you have two cells that span two columns each, there's only the one left in this row; however, this one, like the first one, spans the row beneath it:

```
<th rowspan="2">Set deflection of new belt</th>
</tr>
```

Now go on to the second row. This isn't the one that starts with the Alternator heading. Remember that the first cell in the previous row has a `rowspan` and a `colspan` of two, meaning that it bleeds down to this row and takes up two cells. You don't need to redefine it for this row; you just move on to the next cell in the grid. The first cell in this row is the Limit heading cell, and the second cell is the Adjust Deflection heading cell:

```
<tr>
    <th>Limit</th>
    <th>Adjust Deflection</th>
</tr>
```

What about the last cell? Just like the first cell, the cell in the row above this one had a `rowspan` of two, which takes up the space in this row. The only values you need for this row are the ones you already defined.

Are you with me so far? Now is a great time to try this out in your browser to make sure that everything is lining up. It will look kind of funny because you haven't really put anything on the left side of the table yet, but it's worth a try. Figure 11.24 shows what you've got so far.

11

FIGURE 11.24

The table so far.

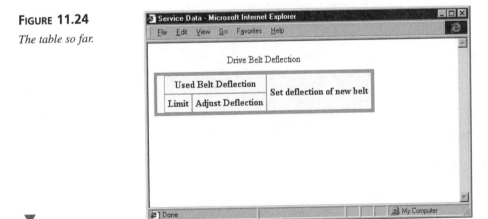

▼

▼ Next row! Check your grid if you need to. Here, the first cell is the heading for Alternator, and it spans this row and the one below it. Are you getting the hang of this yet?

```
<tr>
    <th rowspan="2">Alternator</th>
```

The next three cells are pretty easy because they don't span anything. Here are their definitions:

```
<td>Models without AC</td>
<td>10mm</td>
<td>5-7mm</td>
```

The last cell in this row is just like the first one:

```
<td rowspan="2">5-7mm</td>
</tr>
```

You're up to row number four. In this one, because of the rowspans from the previous row, there are only three cells to define: the cell for Models with AC, and the two cells for the numbers:

```
<tr>
    <td>Models with AC</td>
    <td>12mm</td>
    <td>6-8mm</td>
</tr>
```

Note

In this table, I've made the Alternator cell a heading cell and the AC cells plain data. This is mostly an aesthetic decision on my part; I could just as easily have made all three into headings.

Now for the final row—this one should be easy. The first cell (Power Steering Oil Pump) spans two columns (the one with Alternator in it and the with/without AC column). The remaining three are just one cell each:

```
<tr>
    <th colspan="2">Power Steering Oil Pump</th>
    <td>12.5mm</td>
    <td>7.9mm</td>
    <td>6-8mm</td>
</tr>
```

That's it. You're done laying out the rows and columns. That was the hard part; the rest is just fine-tuning. Try looking at it again to make sure there are no strange errors (see
▼ Figure 11.25).

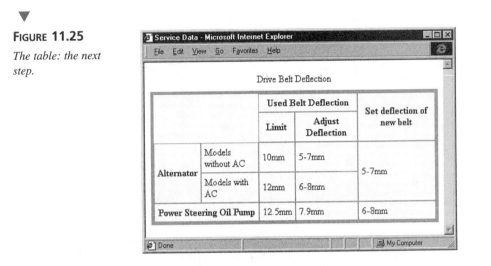

Now that you have all the rows and cells laid out, adjust the alignments within the cells. The numbers, at least, should be centered. Because they make up the majority of the table, make centered the default alignment for each row:

```
<tr align="center">
```

The labels along the left side of the table (Alternator, Models with/without AC, and Power Steering Oil Pump) look funny if they're centered, however, so left-align them using the following code:

```
<th rowspan="2" align="left">Alternator</th>
<td align="left">Models without AC</td>
<td align="left">Models with AC</td>

<th colspan="2" align="left">Power Steering Oil Pump</th>
```

I've put some line breaks in the longer headings so that the columns are a little narrower. Because the text in the headings is pretty short to start with, I don't have to worry too much about the table looking funny if it gets too narrow. Here are the lines I modified:

```
<th rowspan="2">Set<br />deflection<br />of new belt</th>
<th>Adjust<br />Deflection</th>
```

For one final step, you'll align the caption to the left side of the table:

```
<caption align="left">Drive Belt Deflection</caption>
```

Voilà—the final table, with everything properly laid out and aligned! Figure 11.26 shows the final result.

▼

FIGURE 11.26

*The final Drive Belt
Deflection table.*

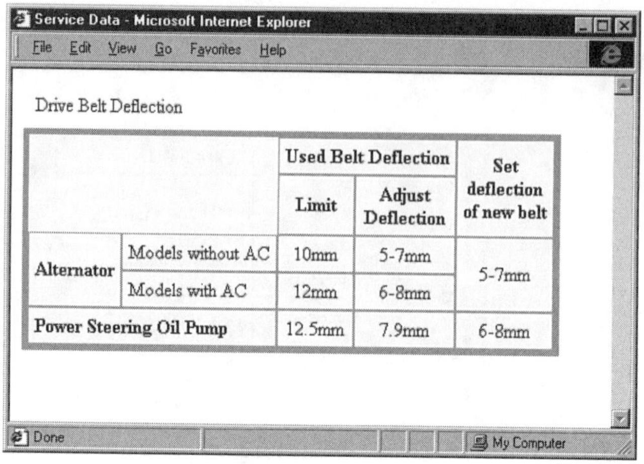

▲

> **Note**
>
> If you got lost at any time, the best thing you can do is pull out your handy text editor and try it yourself, following along tag by tag. After you've done it a couple of times, it becomes easier.

Here's the full text for the table example:

```
<html>
<head>
<title>Service Data</title>
</head>
<body>
<table border="5"
   bgcolor="#ffffcc"
   bordercolor="#cc9900"
   cellspacing="0"
   cellpadding="5">
<caption align="left">Drive Belt Deflection</caption>
<tr>
    <th rowspan="2" colspan="2"></th>
    <th colspan="2">Used Belt Deflection</th>
    <th rowspan="2">Set<br />deflection<br />of new belt</th>
</tr>
<tr>
    <th>Limit</th>
    <th>Adjust<br />Deflection</th>
</tr>
<tr align="center">
    <th rowspan="2" align="left">Alternator</th>
    <td align="left">Models without AC</td>
    <td>10mm</td>
```

```
    <td>5-7mm</td>
    <td rowspan="2">5-7mm</td>
</tr>
<tr align="center">
    <td align="left">Models with AC</td>
    <td>12mm</td>
    <td>6-8mm</td>
</tr>
<tr align="center">
    <th colspan="2" align="left">Power Steering Oil Pump</th>
    <td>12.5mm</td>
    <td>7.9mm</td>
    <td>6-8mm</td>
</tr>
</table>
</body>
</html>
```

More Advanced Table Enhancements

Believe it or not, after all the work you've done, you're *finally* getting into the table elements that were introduced in HTML 4.0. There are many improvements in the way that you define table columns and rows, which I'll cover in the following sections.

Grouping and Aligning Columns

One of the table enhancements offered in HTML 4.0 is the capability to render tables incrementally, rather than having to wait for all of the data in the table to load. This is accomplished, in part, by defining the columns of the table with the <colgroup> and <col> elements. These elements enable the Web page author to create structural divisions of table columns, which then can be visually enhanced through the use of style sheet properties.

The <colgroup>...</colgroup> element is used to enclose one or more columns in a group. The closing </colgroup> tag is optional. This element has two attributes:

- span defines the number of columns that the column group spans. Its value must be an integer greater than 0. If span is not defined, the <colgroup> element defaults to a column group that contains one column. If the <colgroup> element contains one or more <col> elements (described later), however, the span attribute is ignored.

- width defines the width for each column in the column group. Widths can be defined in pixels, percentages, and relative values. You also can specify a special width value of "0*" (zero followed by an asterisk). This value specifies that the width of the each column in the group should be the minimum amount necessary to hold the contents of each cell in the column. If you specify the "0*" value, however, browsers will be unable to render the table incrementally.

11

Suppose that you have a table that measures 450 pixels in width and contains six columns. You want each of the six columns to be 75 pixels wide. The code looks something like the following:

```
<table border="1" width="450">
<colgroup span="6" width="75">
</colgroup>
```

Now you want to change the columns. Using the same 450-pixel-wide table, you make the first two columns 25 pixels wide, and the last four columns 100 pixels wide. This requires two <colgroup> elements, as follows:

```
<table border="1" width="450">
<colgroup span="2" width="25">
</colgroup>
<colgroup span="4" width="100">
</colgroup>
```

What if you don't want all of the columns in a column group to be the same width or have the same appearance? This is where the <col> element comes into play. Where <colgroup> defines the structure of table columns, <col> defines their attributes. To use this element, begin the column definition with a <col> tag. The end tag is forbidden in this case.

Going back to your 450-pixel-wide table, you now want to format the two columns in the first group at 75 pixels each. In the second column group, you have columns at 50, 75, 75, and 100 pixels, respectively. Here's how you format the second column group with the <col> tag:

```
<table border="1" width="450">
<colgroup span="2" width="75">
</colgroup>
<colgroup>
   <col span="1" width="50">
   <col span="2" width="75">
   <col span="1" width="100">
</colgroup>
```

Now apply this to some *real* code. The following example shows a table that displays science and mathematics class schedules. Start by defining a table that has a 1-pixel-wide border and spans 100 percent of the browser window width.

Next, you define the column groups in the table. You want the first column group to display the names of the classes. The second column group consists of two columns that display the room number that the class takes place in, as well as the time that the class is held. The align and valign attributes you learned about earlier today have not been deprecated in HTML 4.0 for the <col> and <colgroup> elements, so you'll take advantage of them here. The first column group consists of one column of cells that spans 20 percent of the entire width of the table. The contents of the cell are aligned vertically toward the top and centered horizontally. The second column group consists of two columns, each spanning 40 percent of the width of the table. Their contents are vertically aligned to the top of the cells.

Finally, you enter the table data, no different than you have already done. Here's what the complete code looks like for the class schedule, and the results are shown in Figure 11.27 in Internet Explorer:

INPUT

```
<html>
<head>
<title>Grouping Columns</title>
</head>
<body>
<table border="1" width="100%" summary="Grouping Columns">
<caption><b>Science and Mathematic Class Schedules</b></caption>

<colgroup width="20%" align="center" valign="top"></colgroup>

<colgroup span="2" width="40%" valign="top"></colgroup>

<tr>
<th>Class</th>
<th>Room</th>
<th>Time</th>
</tr>

<tr>
<td>Biology</td>
<td>Science Wing, Room 102</td>
<td>8:00 AM to 9:45 AM</td>
</tr>

<tr>
<td>Science</td>
<td>Science Wing, Room 110</td>
<td>9:50 AM to 11:30 AM</td>
</tr>

<tr>
<td>Physics</td>
<td>Science Wing, Room 107</td>
<td>1:00 PM to 2:45 PM</td>
</tr>

<tr>
<td>Geometry</td>
<td>Mathematics Wing, Room 236</td>
```

11

```
<td>8:00 AM to 9:45 AM</td>
</tr>

<tr>
<td>Algebra</td>
<td>Mathematics Wing, Room 239</td>
<td>9:50 AM to 11:30 AM</td>
</tr>

<tr>
<td>Trigonometry</td>
<td>Mathematics Wing, Room 245</td>
<td>1:00 PM to 2:45 PM</td>
</tr>
</table>
</body>
</html>
```

OUTPUT

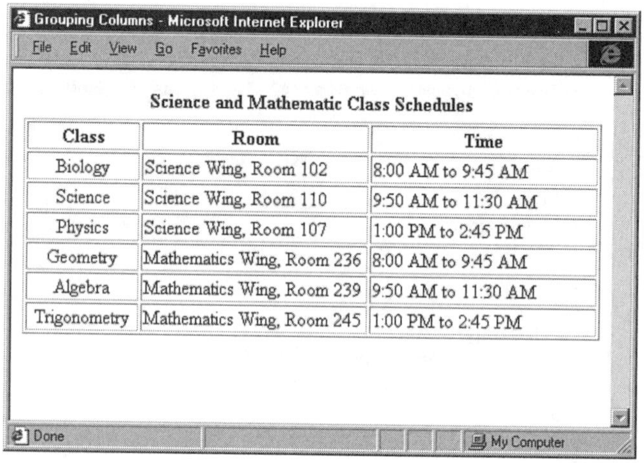

FIGURE 11.27

The class schedule with formatted column groups.

Grouping and Aligning Rows

Now that you know how to group and format columns the new way, let's turn to the rows. You can group the rows of a table into three sections: table head, table foot, and table body. There are advantages for doing so when your pages are viewed in an HTML 4.0-compliant browser. First, this allows the body of the table to scroll independently of the head and foot of the table. Additionally, if a table that contains row upon row of data is printed out in hard copy to your printer, the head and foot of the table will repeat on the top and bottom of each page in the table printout. You also can apply cascading style sheet properties to emphasize the table head and table foot, and give the body of the table a different appearance.

The table head, foot, and body sections are defined by the <thead>, <tfoot>, and <tbody> elements, respectively. Each of these elements must contain the same number of columns.

The <thead>...</thead>element defines the head of the table, which should contain information about the columns in the body of the table. This typically is the same type of information that you've been placing within header cells so far today. The starting <thead> tag is always required when you want to include a head section in your table, but the closing </thead> tag is optional.

The head of the table appears right after the <table> element or after <colgroup> elements as the following example shows, and must include at least one row group defined by the <tr> element. It is formatted as follows:

```
<table border="1" width="100%">
<caption><b>Science and Mathematic Class Schedules</b></caption>
<colgroup width="20%" align="center" valign="top">
  <colgroup span="2" width="40%" valign="top">
<thead>
  <tr>
    <th>Class</th>
    <th>Room</th>
    <th>Time</th>
  </tr>
</thead>
```

The <tfoot>...</tfoot> element defines the foot of the table. The starting <tfoot> tag is always required when defining the foot of a table, but the closing </tfoot> tag is optional. The foot of the table appears immediately after the head of the table (if one is present), or after the <table> element (if a table head is not present). It must contain at least one row group, defined by the <tr> element. A good example of information that you could place in a table footer is a row that totals columns of numbers in a table.

You must define the foot of the table before the table body. The reason is because the browser has to render the foot before it receives all the data in the table body. For the purposes of this example, we'll include the same information in the table head and the table foot. The code looks like this:

```
<tfoot>
  <tr>
   <th>Class</th>
   <th>Room</th>
   <th>Time</th>
  </tr>
</tfoot>
```

11

After you define the head and foot of the table, you define the rows in the table body. A table can contain more than one body, and each body can contain one or more rows of data. Are you confused, and wondering how this works and where you'd use it? I'll show you one example of why this is rather cool in a little bit.

The <tbody>...</tbody> element defines one or more table bodies in your table. The <tbody> start tag is required if at least one of the following is true:

- The table contains head or foot sections
- The table contains more than one table body

The following example shows two table bodies, each consisting of three rows of three cells each. The body appears after the table foot, as follows:

```
<tbody>
   <tr>
    <td>Biology</td>
    <td>Science Wing, Room 102</td>
    <td>8:00 AM to 9:45 AM</td>
   </tr>
   <tr>
    <td>Science</td>
    <td>Science Wing, Room 110</td>
    <td>9:50 AM to 11:30 AM</td>
   </tr>
   <tr>
    <td>Physics</td>
    <td>Science Wing, Room 107</td>
    <td>1:00 PM to 2:45 PM</td>
   </tr>
</tbody>
<tbody>
   <tr>
    <td>Geometry</td>
    <td>Mathematics Wing, Room 236</td>
    <td>8:00 AM to 9:45 AM</td>
   </tr>
   <tr>
    <td>Algebra</td>
    <td>Mathematics Wing, Room 239</td>
    <td>9:50 AM to 11:30 AM</td>
   </tr>
   <tr>
    <td>Trigonometry</td>
    <td>Mathematics Wing, Room 245</td>
    <td>1:00 PM to 2:45 PM</td>
   </tr>
</tbody>
</table>
```

Put all the preceding together and you get a table that looks like that shown in Figure 11.28.

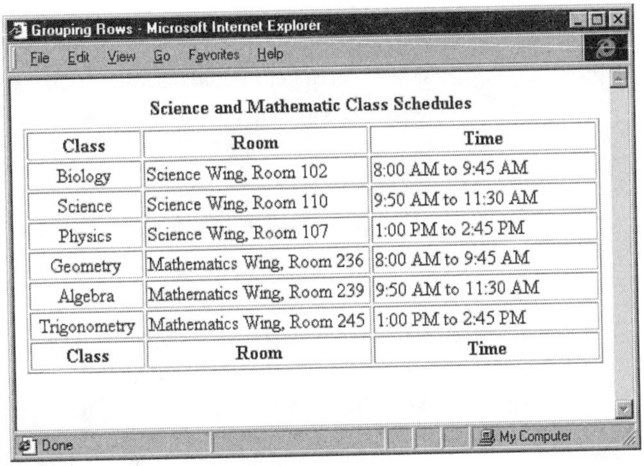

FIGURE **11.28**

The class schedule with a head, two bodies, and a foot.

The `frame` and `rules` Attributes

If you look at the preceding example, it's not really clear where the column groups and row groups appear. A simple way to see where they lie is to use the `frame` and `rules` attributes of the `table` element.

The `frame` attribute affects how the external border of the table is rendered. You can specify one of several different values to define which sides of the external border are visible:

`void`	The default value. No sides of the external border are visible.
`above`	Renders only the top side of the border.
`below`	Renders only the bottom side of the border.
`hsides`	Renders the top and bottom sides of the border.
`lhs`	Renders the left-hand side of the border.
`rhs`	Renders the right-hand side of the border.
`vsides`	Renders the right and left sides of the border.
`box`	Renders all four sides of the border.
`border`	Renders all four sides of the border.

The rules attribute is somewhat similar to the frame attribute, except that it defines the rules that appear in between the cells within a table. The following values apply to the rules attribute:

none	The default value. No rules are drawn around any of the cells.
groups	Rules will appear between row groups as defined by `<thead>`, `<tfoot>`, and `<tbody>`, and between column groups as defined by `<colgroup>` and `<col>`.
rows	Rules will appear only between rows.
cols	Rules will appear only between columns.
all	Rules will appear between all rows and columns.

Now make your column groups and your row groups stand out more. You'll draw a border around the Class Schedule table, but will only place the border along the top and bottom of the table by applying frame="hsides" to the `<table>` tag.

Inside the table, you'll separate the head and foot from the two table bodies (one body for the Science subjects and one body for the Math subjects). You'll also separate the Subject column group and the Room/Time column group. All this is accomplished by using rules="groups" with the `<table>` element.

You only need to modify one line in your code to accomplish all this now. The revised table definition looks as follows, and Figure 11.29 shows the results in Internet Explorer. 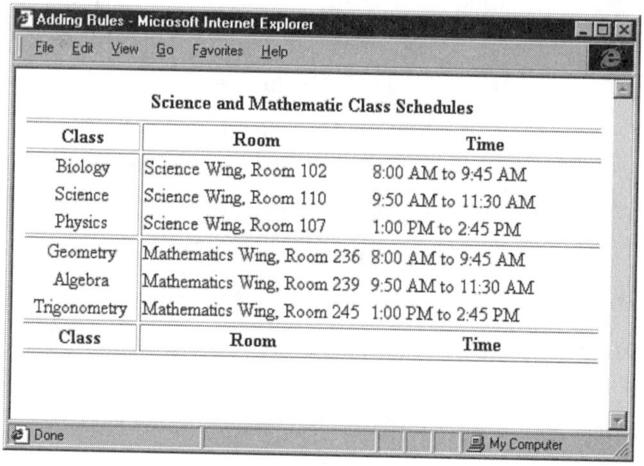

```
<table border="1" width="100%" frame="hsides" rules="groups">
```

FIGURE 11.29

The class schedule with rules added.

Other Table Elements and Attributes

Table 11.1 presents some of the additional elements and attributes that pertain to tables.

Table 11.1 Other Table Elements and Attributes

Attribute	Applied to Element	Use
char	See "Use" Column	Specifies a character to be used as an axis to align the contents of a cell. For example, you can use it to align a decimal point in numerical values. Can be applied to colgroup, col, tbody, thead, tfoot, tr, td and th elements.
charoff	See "Use" Column	Specifies the amount of offset applied to the first occurrence of the alignment character that is specified in the char attribute. Applies to colgroup, col, tbody, thead, tfoot, tr, td, and th elements.
summary	<table>	Provides a more detailed description of the contents of the table and is primarily used with nonvisual browsers.

11

Summary

Today, you've learned quite a lot about tables. Tables enable you to arrange your information in rows and columns so that your readers can scan the table quickly and get to the information they need.

While working with tables today, you've learned about headings and data, captions, defining rows and cells, aligning information within cells, and creating cells that span multiple rows or columns. With these features, you can create tables for most purposes.

As you're constructing tables, it's helpful to keep the following steps in mind:

- Sketch your table, indicating where the rows and columns fall. Mark which cells span multiple rows and columns.
- Start with a basic framework and lay out the rows, headings, and data row by row and cell by cell in HTML. Include row and column spans as necessary. Test frequently in a browser to make sure it's all working correctly.
- Modify the alignment in the rows to reflect the alignment of the majority of the cells.

- Modify the alignment for individual cells.
- Adjust line breaks, if necessary.
- Make other refinements such as cell spacing, padding, or color.
- Test your table in multiple browsers. Different browsers can have different ideas of how to lay out your table or be more accepting of errors in your HTML code.

Table 11.2 presents a quick summary of the HTML elements that you've learned about today, and which remain current in HTML 4.0. Attributes that apply to each element are listed in Table 11.3.

Table 11.2 Current HTML 4.0 Table Elements

Tag	Use
`<table>...</table>`	Indicates a table.
`<caption>...</caption>`	Creates an optional caption for the table.
`<colgroup>...</colgroup>`	Encloses one or more columns in a group.
`<col>`	Used to define the attributes of a column in a table.
`<thead>...</thead>`	Creates a row group that defines the heading of the table. A table can contain only one heading.
`<tfoot>...</tfoot>`	Creates a row group that defines the footer of the table. A table can contain only one footer. Must be specified before the body of the table is rendered.
`<tbody>...</tbody>`	Defines one or more row groups to include in the body of the table. Tables can contain more than one body section.
`<tr>...</tr>`	Defines a table row, which can contain heading and data cells.
`<th>...</th>`	Defines a table cell that contains a heading. Heading cells are usually indicated by boldface and centered both horizontally and vertically within the cell.
`<td>...</td>`	Defines a table cell containing data. Table cells are in a regular font, and are left-aligned and vertically centered within the cell.

Because several of the table attributes apply to more than one of the preceding elements, I'm listing them separately. Table 11.3 presents a quick summary of the HTML attributes you learned about today, and which remain current in HTML 4.0.

Table 11.3   Current HTML 4.0 Table Attributes

Attribute	Applied to Element	Use
align	`<tr>`	Possible values are `left`, `center`, and `right`, which indicate the horizontal alignment of the cells within that row (overriding the default alignment of heading and table cells).
	`<th>` or `<td>`	Overrides both the row's alignment and any default cell alignment. Possible values are `left`, `center`, and `right`.
	`<thead>`,`<tbody>`,`<tfoot>`	Used to set alignment of the contents in table head, body, or foot cells. Possible values are `left`, `center`, and `right`.
	`<col>`	Used to set alignment of all cells in a column. Possible values are `left`, `center`, and `right`.
	`<colgroup>`	Used to set alignment of all cells in a column group. Possible values are `left`, `center`, and `right`.
	`<table>`	Deprecated in HTML 4.0. Possible values are `left`, `center` and `right`. `align="center"` and are not supported in HTML 3.2 and older browsers. Determines the alignment of the table and indicates that text following the table will be wrapped alongside it.
	`<caption>`	Deprecated in HTML 4.0. Indicates which side of the table the caption will be placed. The possible values for most browsers are `top` and `bottom`. HTML 4.0 browsers also support `left` and `right`. In Internet Explorer, the possible values are `left`, `right`, and `center`, and indicate the horizontal alignment of the caption.

continues

11

Table 11.3 continued

Attribute	Applied to Element	Use
bgcolor	All	(HTML 3.2, deprecated in HTML 4.0) Changes the background color of that table element. Cell colors override row colors, which override table colors. The value can be a hexadecimal color number or a color name.
border	<table>	Indicates whether the table will be drawn with a border. The default is no border. If border has a value, that value is the width of the shaded border around the table.
bordercolor	<table>	(Internet Explorer and Netscape extension) Can be used with any of the table elements to change the color of the border around that elements. The value can be a hexadecimal color number or a color name.
bordercolorlight	<table>	(Internet Explorer extension) Same as bordercolor, except it affects only the light component of a 3D-look border.
bordercolordark	<table>	(Internet Explorer extension) Same as bordercolor, except it affects only the dark component of a 3D-look border.
cellspacing	<table>	Defines the amount of space between the cells in the table.
cellpadding	<table>	Defines the amount of space between the edges of the cell and its contents.
char		Specifies a character to be used as an axis to align the contents of a cell (for example, a decimal point in numerical values). Can be applied to colgroup, col, tbody, thead, tfoot, tr, td, and th elements.
charoff		Specifies the amount of offset to be applied to the first occurrence of the alignment character specified by the char attribute. Applies to the same elements previously listed in char.

Attribute	Applied to Element	Use
frame	\<table\>	Defines which sides of the frame that surrounds a table are visible. Possible values are void, above, below, hsides, lhs, rhs, vsides, box, and border.
height	\<th\> or \<td\>	Deprecated in HTML 4.0. Indicates the height of the cell in pixel or percentage values.
nowrap	\<th\> or \<td\>	Deprecated in HTML 4.0. Prevents the browser from wrapping the contents of the cell.
rules	\<table\>	Defines which rules (division lines) will appear between cells in a table. Possible values are none, groups, rows, cols, and all.
width	\<table\>	Indicates the width of the table, in exact pixel values or as a percentage of page width (for example, 50 percent).
span	\<colgroup\>	Defines the number of columns in a column group. Must be an integer greater than 0.
	\<col\>	Defines the number of columns which a cell spans. Must be an integer greater than 0.
width	\<colgroup\>	Defines the width of all cells in a column group.
	\<col\>	Defines the width of all cells in one column.
colspan	\<th\> or \<td\>	Indicates the number of cells to the right of this one that this cell will span.
rowspan	\<th\> or \<td\>	Indicates the number of cells below this one that this cell will span.
valign	\<tr\>	Indicates the vertical alignment of the cells within that row (overriding the defaults). Possible values are top, middle, and bottom.

11

continues

Table 11.3 continued

Attribute	Applied to Element	Use
	`<th>` or `<td>`	Overrides both the row's vertical alignment and the default cell alignment. Possible values are `top`, `middle`, and `bottom`. In Netscape, `valign` can also have the value `baseline`.
	`<thead>`,`<tfoot>`,`<tbody>`	Defines vertical alignment of cells in the table head, table foot, or table body.
	`<colgroup>`	Defines the vertical alignment of all cells in a column group.
	`<col>`	Defines the vertical alignment of all cells in a single column.
`width`	`<th>` or `<td>`	Deprecated in HTML 4.0. Indicates width of the cell, in exact pixel values or as a percentage of table width (for example, 50 percent).

Workshop

Q&A

Q Tables are a real hassle to lay out, especially when you get into row and column spans. That last example was awful.

A You're right. Tables are a tremendous pain to lay out by hand like this. However, if you're using writing editors and tools to generate HTML code, having the table defined like this makes more sense because you can programmatically just write out each row in turn. Sooner or later, we'll all be working in HTML editors anyhow, so you won't have to do this by hand for long.

Q My tables work fine in Netscape Navigator, but they're all garbled in many other browsers. What did I do wrong?

A Did you remember to close all your `<tr>`, `<th>`, and `<td>` elements? Make sure you've put in the matching `</tr>`, `</th>`, and `</td>` tags, respectively. The closing tags might be legally optional, but often other browsers need those tags to understand table layout.

Q Can you nest tables, putting a table inside a single table cell?

A Sure! As I mentioned earlier, you can put any HTML code you want to inside a table cell, and that includes other tables.

Q Why does most of the world use `align` for positioning a caption at the top or bottom of a page, but Internet Explorer does something totally different?

A I don't know. And, worse, Microsoft claims it got that definition for Internet Explorer from HTML 3.0, but no version of HTML 3.0 or the tables specification in HTML 3.2 has it defined in that way. HTML 4.0 proposes to add left and right aligning to this attribute, but Internet Explorer added this alignment before HTML even mentioned the possibility.

Quiz

1. What are the basic parts of a table, and which tags identify them?
2. Which attribute is the most common attribute of the table tag, and what does it do?
3. What attributes define the amount of space between the edges of the cells and their content, and the amount of space between cells?
4. Which attributes are used to create cells that span more than one column or row?
5. Which elements are used to define the head, body, and foot of a table?

Answers

1. The basic parts of a table (the `<table>` tag>` are the border (defined with the `border` attribute), the caption (defined with the `<caption>` tag), header cells (`<th>`), data cells (`<td>`), and table rows (`<tr>`).
2. The `border` attribute is the most common attribute for the table tag. It specifies whether border lines are displayed around the table, and how wide the borders should be.
3. `cellpadding` defines the amount of space between the edges of the cell and their contents. `cellspacing` defines the amount of space between the cells.
4. The `rowspan` attribute creates a cell that spans multiple rows. The `colspan` attribute creates a cell that spans multiple columns.
5. `<thead>`, `<tbody>`, and `<tfoot>` define the head, body, and foot of a table, respectively.

11

Exercises

1. Here's a brain-teaser for you. Try to create a nested table (a table within a table). Create a simple table that contains three rows and four columns. Inside the cell that appears at the second column in the second row, create a second table that contains two rows and two columns.

2. Modify the table shown in Figure 11.28 so that the rules in the table only appear between vertical cells.

DAY **12**

Frames and Linked Windows

Imagine this scenario: you navigate to a very large Web site that has multiple levels of Web pages in it. The deeper you get into the site, the more lost you become, and the more difficult it is to find your way back to the beginning. You wish there somehow was an easier way to find your way around. Good news: with frames, you can develop Web sites that help your visitors find their way around more easily. Frames divide the browser window into multiple sections, each having the capability to display a different Web page within it.

Today, you'll learn all about the following topics:

- What frames are, what they give you in terms of layout, and who supports them
- How to work with linked windows
- How to work with frames
- How to create complex framesets

What Are Frames and Who Supports Them?

With the exception of cascading style sheet properties, the majority of the features and tags discussed in the preceding days will, as a rule, work on just about any Web browser. The appearance of the page might not be exactly what you expect, but at the very least, people with older Web browsers can still view the text and links contained on the page.

In this day, you'll learn about the tags that you use to create *frames*. Due to the nature of these tags, Web pages that use frames simply won't display on older browsers. This fact made frames one of the most hotly debated topics of the "Netscape versus The Rest" debate. Frames were originally introduced in Netscape Navigator 2.0. Microsoft Internet Explorer 3.0 followed suit, but added another twist. In addition to the support of frames as designed by Netscape, Internet Explorer supported *inline frames* (also called floating frames).

Although the two major players in the browser war supported frames, they were not an official part of the HTML 3.2 specification. As a result, few other HTML 3.2 browsers offered frames support. However, Web page authors began to use frames in increasing numbers because frames offered ways to develop enhanced navigation systems for Web sites. As a result, HTML 4.0 now includes both types of frames (Netscape's frames and Internet Explorer's inline frames) as official parts of its specification.

The capabilities provided by the use of frames bring an entirely different level of layout control than what you've learned thus far in this book. Consider, for example, the example shown in Figure 12.1.

FIGURE 12.1

A sample Web page with frames.

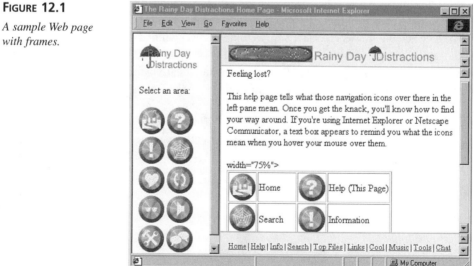

In this screen, you see information that previously would have taken many separate screen loads. In addition, because the information displayed on the page is separated into individual areas or frames, the contents of a single frame can be updated without the contents of any other frame being affected. If you click any of the hotlinks associated with the images in the left frame, for example, the contents of the large frame on the right are automatically updated to display the details about the subject you select. When this update occurs, the contents of the left frame and the bottom frame are not affected.

Working with Linked Windows

Before looking at how frames are added to a page, you need to learn about an attribute of the <a> tag. This attribute, called target, takes the following form:

```
target="window_name"
```

Usually, when you click a hyperlink, the contents of the page to which you're linking replaces the current page in the browser window. In a frameset environment, however, there technically is no reason why the contents of the new page can't be displayed in a new window, while leaving the contents of the original page onscreen in its own window.

The target attribute enables you to tell the Web browser to display the information pointed to by a hyperlink in a window called *window_name*. You can basically call the new window anything you want, with the only proviso being that you not use names that start with an underscore (_). These names are reserved for a set of special target values that you'll learn about later in the section "Magic target Names."

When you use the target attribute inside an <a> tag, a frames-compatible browser first checks to see whether a window with the name *window_name* exists. If it does, the document pointed to by the hyperlink replaces the current contents of *window_name*. On the other hand, if no window called *window_name* currently exists, a new browser window opens with the name *window_name*. The document pointed to by the hyperlink then is loaded into the newly created window.

Exercise 12.1: Working with Windows

Framesets rely on the target attribute to load pages into specific frames in a frameset. Each of the hyperlinks in the following exercise uses the target attribute to open a Web page in a different browser window. The concepts you learn here will help you understand later how targeted hyperlinks work in a frameset.

In this exercise, you'll create four separate HTML documents that use hyperlinks, including the target attribute. You use these hyperlinks to open two new windows called yellow_page and blue_page, as shown in Figure 12.2. The top window is the original

▼ Web browser window (the red page), `yellow_page` is on the bottom left, and `blue_page` is on the bottom right.

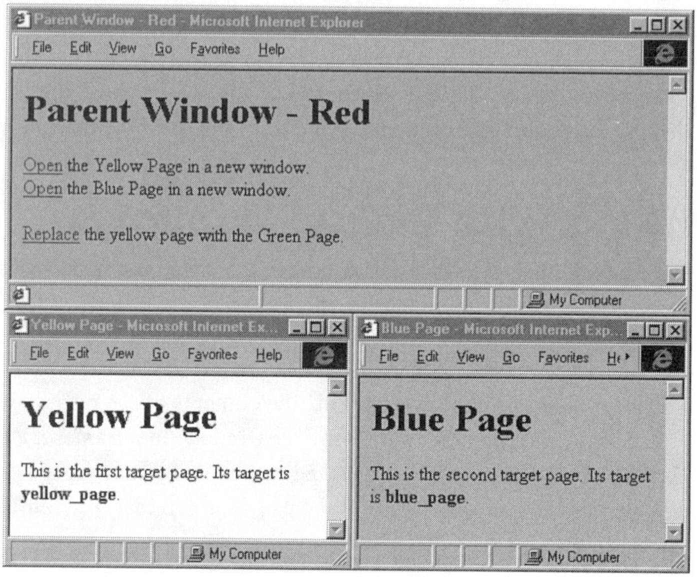

FIGURE 12.2

You can make hyperlinks to open new windows for each of the pages to which they point.

First, create the document to be displayed by the main Web browser window, shown in Figure 12.3, by opening your text editor of choice and entering the following lines of code:

INPUT

```
<html>
<head>
<title>Parent Window - Red</title>
</head>
<body bgcolor="#ff9999">
<h1>Parent Window - Red</h1>
<p><a href="yellow.html" target="yellow_page">Open</a> the Yellow Page
in a new window. <br>
  <a href="blue.html" target="blue_page">Open</a> the Blue Page in a new
  window. </p>
<p><a href="green.html" target="yellow_page">Replace</a> the yellow page
with the  Green Page.</p>
</body>
</html>
```

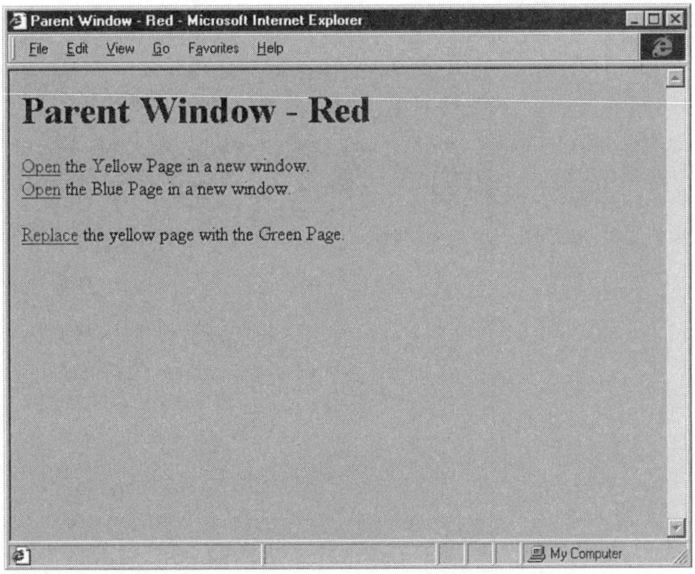

FIGURE 12.3

The Parent window (the red page).

> **Parent Window - Red - Microsoft Internet Explorer**
>
> File Edit View Go Favorites Help
>
> # Parent Window - Red
>
> Open the Yellow Page in a new window.
> Open the Blue Page in a new window.
>
> Replace the yellow page with the Green Page.
>
> My Computer

This creates a light red page that links to the other three pages. Save this HTML source as parent.html.

Next, create a document called yellow.html that looks like the page shown in Figure 12.4, by entering the following code:

```
<html>
<head>
<title>Yellow Page</title>
</head>
<body bgcolor="#ffffcc">
<h1>Yellow Page</h1>
<p>This is the first target page. Its target is <b>yellow_page</b></p>
</body>
</html>
```

12

FIGURE 12.4

yellow.html *displayed in the Web browser window named* yellow_page.

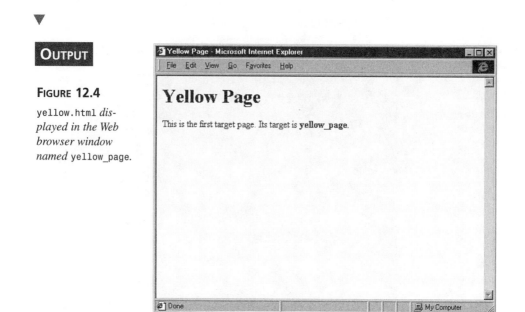

After saving yellow.html, create another document called blue.html that looks like the page shown in Figure 12.5. Do so by entering the following code:

```
<html>
<head>
<title>Blue Page</title>
</head>
<body bgcolor="#99ccff">
<h1>Blue Page</h1>
<p>This is the second target page. Its target is <b>blue_page</b>.</p>
</body>
</html>
```

OUTPUT

FIGURE 12.5

`blue.html` *displayed in the Web browser window named* `blue_window`.

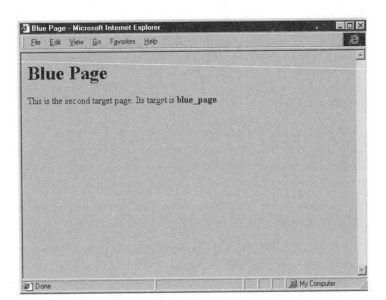

Next, create a fourth document, called `green.html`, which looks like the following:

INPUT

```html
<html>
<head>
<title>Green Page</title>
</head>
<body bgcolor="#ccffcc">
<h1>Green Page</h1>
<p>This is the third target page. Its target is <b>yellow_page</b>. It
should replace the yellow page in the browser.</p>
</body>
</html>
```

To complete the exercise, load `parent.html` (the red page) into your Web browser. Click the first hyperlink to open the yellow page in a second browser window. This happens because the first hyperlink contained a statement of `target="yellow_page"`, as the following code from `parent.html` demonstrates:

```html
<p><a href="yellow.html" target="yellow_page">Open</a> the Yellow Page in a
   new window.<br />
```

12

▼   Now, return to the red page and click the second link. The blue page opens in a third
    browser window. Note that the new windows probably won't be laid out like the ones
    shown in Figure 12.2; they'll usually overlap each other. The following
    `target="blue_page"` statement in the `parent.html` page is what causes the new window
    to open:

```
<a href="blue.html" target="blue_page">Open</a> the Blue Page in a new
  window.</p>
```

The previous two examples opened each of the Web pages in a new browser window.
The third link, however, uses the `target="yellow_page"` statement to open the green
page in the window named `yellow_page`. You accomplish this using the following code
in `parent.html`:

```
<p><a href="green.html" target="yellow_page">Replace</a> the yellow page
  with the Green Page.</p>
```

Because you already opened the `yellow_page` window when you clicked the link for the
yellow page, the green page should replace the page that is already in it. To verify this,
click the third hyperlink on the red page. You'll replace the contents of the yellow page
(with the `yellow_page` target name) with the green page (`green.html`), as shown in
Figure 12.6.

OUTPUT

FIGURE 12.6

`green.html` *dis-
played in the Web
browser window
named* `yellow_page`.

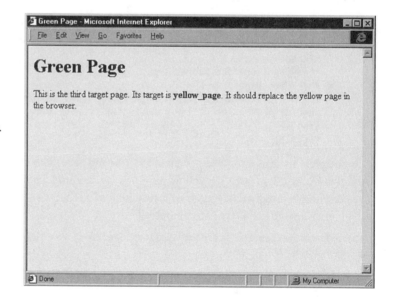

▲

The <base> Tag

When using the target attribute with links, you'll sometimes encounter a situation in which all or most of the hyperlinks on a Web page point to the same window—especially when using frames, as you'll discover in the following section.

In such cases, rather than including a target attribute for each <a> tag, you can use another tag, <base>, to define a global target for all the links of a Web page. The <base> tag takes the following form:

```
<base target="window_name">
```

If you include the <base> tag in the <head>...</head> block of a document, every <a> tag that does not have a corresponding target attribute will display the document it points to in the window specified by <base target="window_name">. For example, if you had included the tag <base target="yellow_page"> in the HTML source for parent.html, the three hyperlinks could have been written the following way:

```
<html>
<head>
<title>Parent Window - Red</title>
<base target="yellow_page">  <!-- add base target="value" here -->
</head>
<body bgcolor="#ff9999">
<h1>Parent Window - Red</h1>
<p>
<a href="yellow.html">Open</a> <!-- no need to include a target -->
  the Yellow Page in a new window.<br />
<a href="blue.html" target="blue_page">Open</a> the Blue Page in a new
  window. </p>
<p><a href="green.html">Replace</a> <!-- no need to include a target -->
the yellow page with the Green Page.</p>
</body>
</html>
```

In this case, yellow.html and green.html load into the default window assigned by the <base> tag (yellow_page); blue.html overrides the default by defining its own target window of blue_page.

You also can override the window assigned with the <base> tag by using one of two special window names. If you use target="_blank" in a hyperlink, a new browser window that does not have a name associated with it opens. Alternatively, if you use target="_self", the current window is used rather than the one defined by the <base> tag.

12

> **Note**
>
> A point to remember: if you don't provide a `target` using the `<base>` tag, and you don't indicate a target in a link's `<a>` tag, then the link will load the new document in the same frame as the link.

Working with Frames

The introduction of frames in Netscape 2.0 heralded a new era for Web publishers. With frames, you can create Web pages that look and feel entirely different from other Web pages—pages that have tables of contents, banners, footnotes, and sidebars, just to name a few common features that frames can give you.

At the same time, frames change what a "page" means to the browser and to the readers. Unlike all the preceding examples, which use a single HTML page to display a screen of information, when you create Web sites using frames, a single screen actually consists of a number of separate HTML documents that interact with each other. Figure 12.7 shows how a minimum of five separate documents is needed to create the screen shown earlier in Figure 12.1.

FIGURE 12.7

You must create separate HTML documents for each frame.

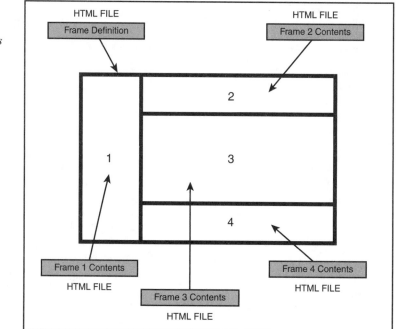

The first HTML document you need to create is called the *frameset document*. In this document, you enter the HTML code that describes the layout of each frame. In the preceding example, the document has three frames.

The frameset document also includes the names of the HTML documents that will appear in each of the frames. Each of the three remaining HTML documents (the ones that load in the frames) contains normal HTML tags that define the physical contents of each separate frame area. These documents are referenced by the frameset document.

> **NEW TERM** The *frameset document* is the page that contains the layout of each frame and the names of the HTML documents that will fill that frame.

The `<frameset>` Tag

To create a frameset document, you begin with the `<frameset>` tag. When used in an HTML document, the `<frameset>` tag replaces the `<body>` tag, as shown in the following:

```
<html>
<head>
<title>Page Title</title>
</head>
<frameset>
    ... your frameset goes here ...
</frameset>
</html>
```

It is important that you understand up front how a frameset document differs from a normal HTML document. If you include a `<frameset>` tag in an HTML document, you cannot also include a `<body>` tag. Basically, the two tags are mutually exclusive. In addition, no other formatting tags, hyperlinks, or document text should be included in a frameset document, except in one special case (the `<noframes>` tag) which you'll learn about in the section called, appropriately, "The `<noframes>` Tag" later today. The `<frameset>` tags contain only the definitions for the frames in this document—what's called the page's *frameset*.

The HTML 4.0 specification supports the `<frameset>` tag along with two possible attributes: `cols` and `rows`.

> **NEW TERM** A *frameset* is a group of frames that is defined within a frameset document through the use of the `<frameset>` tags.

The `cols` Attribute

When you define a `<frameset>` tag, you must include one of two attributes as part of the tag definition. The first of these attributes is the `cols` attribute, which takes the following form:

```
<frameset cols="column width, column width, ...">
```

12

The `cols` attribute tells the browser to split the screen into a number of vertical frames whose widths are defined by *column width* values separated by commas. You define the width of each frame in one of three ways: explicitly in pixels, as a percentage of the total width of the `<frameset>`, or with an asterisk (`*`). When you use the `*`, the frames-compatible browser uses as much space as possible for the specified frame.

When included in a complete frame definition, the following `<frameset>` tag creates a screen with three vertical frames, as shown in Figure 12.8. The line shown with a gray background in the following example creates a left frame 100 pixels wide, a middle column of 50 percent of the width of the screen, and a right column that uses all the remaining space:

INPUT

```
<html>
<head>
<title>Three Columns</title>
</head>
<frameset cols="100,50%,*">
    <frame src="leftcol.html">
    <frame src="midcol.html">
    <frame src="rightcol.html">
</frameset>
</html>
```

OUTPUT

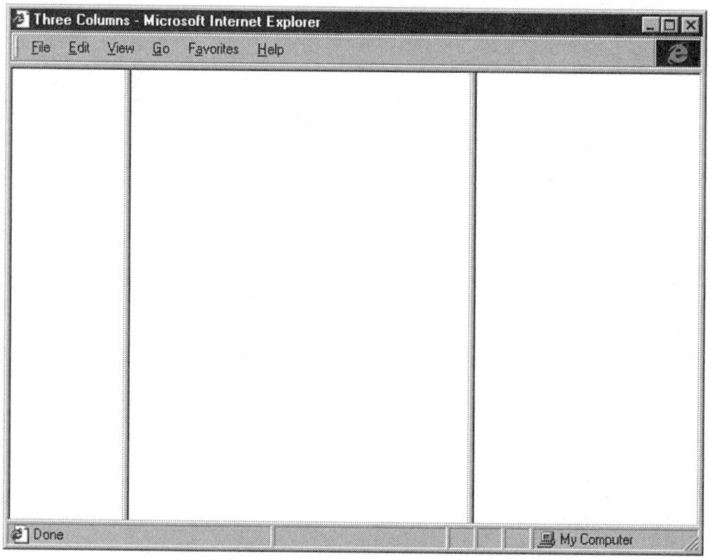

FIGURE 12.8

The cols *attribute defines the number of vertical frames or columns in a frameset.*

Note

Because you're designing Web pages that will be used on various screen sizes, you should use absolute frame sizes sparingly. Whenever you do use an absolute size, ensure that one of the other frames is defined using an * to take up all the remaining screen space.

Tip

To define a frameset with three equal-width columns, use `cols="*,*,*"`. This way, you won't have to mess around with percentages because frames-compatible browsers automatically assign an equal amount of space to each frame assigned an * width.

The rows Attribute

The rows attribute works the same as the cols attribute, except that it splits the screen into horizontal frames rather than vertical ones. To split the screen into two equal-height frames, for example, as shown in Figure 12.9, you would write the following:

INPUT

```html
<html>
<head>
<title>Two Rows</title>
</head>
<frameset rows="50%,50%">
    <frame src="toprow.html">
    <frame src="botrow.html">
</frameset>
</html>
```

Alternatively, you could use the following line:

INPUT

```html
<frameset rows="*,*">
```

12

OUTPUT

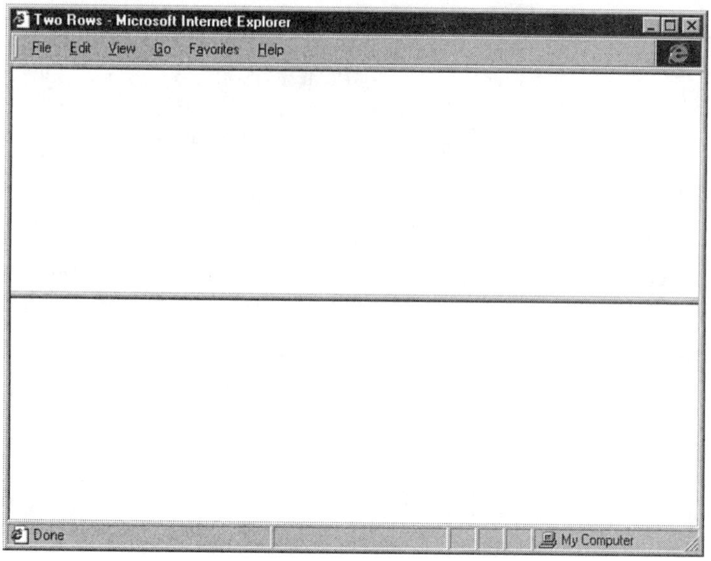

FIGURE 12.9

The rows *attribute defines the number of horizontal frames or rows in a frameset.*

Note

If you try either of the preceding examples for yourself, you'll find that the `<frameset>` tag does not appear to work. You get this result because currently no contents are defined for the rows or columns in the frameset. To define the contents, you need to use the `<frame>` tag, which is discussed in the next section.

The `<frame>` Tag

After you have your basic frameset laid out, you need to associate an HTML document with each frame. To do so, you use the `<frame>` tag, which takes the following form:

```
<frame src="document URL">
```

For each frame defined in the `<frameset>` tag, you must include a corresponding `<frame>` tag, as shown in the following:

INPUT

```
<html>
<head>
<title>The frame Tag</title>
</head>
<frameset rows="*,*,*">
    <frame src="document1.html">
    <frame src="document2.html">
    <frame src="document3.html">
</frameset>
</html>
```

In this example, a frameset with three equal-height horizontal frames is defined (see Figure 12.10). The contents of document1.html are displayed in the first frame; the contents of document2.html in the second frame; and the contents of document3.html in the third frame.

FIGURE 12.10

You use the <frame> tag to define the contents of each frame.

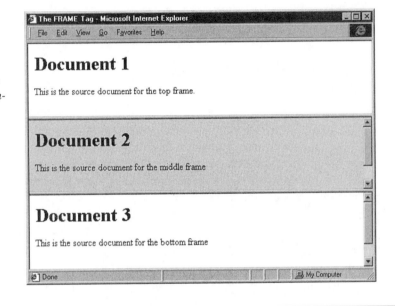

Tip

When creating frameset documents, you might find it helpful to indent the <frame> tags so that they're separated from the <frameset> tags in your HTML document. Doing so has no effect on the appearance of the resulting Web pages but does tend to make the HTML source easier to read.

12

The <noframes> Tag

What happens if a browser that does not support frames navigates to a frameset document? Nothing. You get only a blank page. Fortunately, there is a way around this problem.

A special tag block called <noframes> enables you to include additional HTML code as part of the frameset document. The code you enclose within the <noframes> element is not displayed in frames-compatible browsers, but is displayed in browsers that don't support frames. The <noframes> tag takes the following form:

```
<html>
<head>
<title>Frameset with No Frames Content</title>
</head>
<frameset>
 your frameset goes here.
<noframes>
   Include any text, hyperlinks, and tags you want to here.
</noframes>
</frameset>
</html>
```

Browsers that support frames will not display the text you include inside the <noframes> block, but when the page is loaded into a Web browser that does not support frames, the text is displayed. Using the frames' content and tags inside <noframes>, you can create pages that work well with both kinds of browsers. Later today, you'll add some <noframes> content to a frameset.

Changing Frame Borders

Notice that all the frames in today's lesson have thick borders separating them. In the original frames implementation in Netscape 2.0, you could do little about this situation. With the introduction of Netscape 3.0 and Internet Explorer 3.0, however, additional attributes of the <frame> and <frameset> tags give you some control over the color and width of frame borders.

Start with the <frame> tag. By using two attributes, bordercolor and frameborder, you can turn borders on and off and specify their color. You can assign bordercolor any valid color value, either as a name or a hexadecimal triplet. frameborder takes two possible values: 1 (to display borders) or 0 (to turn off the display of borders).

Note If you turn off the border, frames-compatible browsers will not display its default three-dimensional border, but a space will still be left for the border.

Note HTML 4.0 currently only lists the frameborder attribute. The bordercolor attribute qualifies as an extension.

The following code, for example, adds a deep red (defined by #cc3333) border around the middle frame in the frameset:

```html
<html>
<head>
<title>The frame Tag</title>
</head>
<frameset rows="*,*,*">
   <frame src="document1.html">
   <frame frameborder="1" bordercolor="#cc3333" src="document2.html">
   <frame src="document3.html">
</frameset>
</html>
```

Although HTML 4.0 doesn't provide either of these attributes for the `<frameset>` tag, you can use both of them to define default values for the entire frameset in Netscape and Microsoft Internet Explorer.

Of course, there is room for confusion when colored borders are defined. In the following frameset definition, for example, a conflict arises because the two frames share a single common border, but each frame is defined to have a different border color, by using the `bordercolor` attribute:

```html
<html>
<head>
<title>Conflicting Borders</title>
</head>
<frameset frameborder="0" rows="*,*,*">
   <frame frameborder="1" bordercolor="yellow" src="document1.html">
   <frame bordercolor="#cc3333" src="document2.html">
   <frame src="document3.html">
</frameset>
</html>
```

In addition, the frameset is defined as having no borders, but the first frame is supposed to have a border. How do you resolve this problem? You can apply three simple rules in these situations:

- Attributes in the outermost frameset have the lowest priority.
- Attributes are overridden by attributes in a nested `<frameset>` tag.
- Any `bordercolor` attribute in the current frame overrides previous ones in `<frameset>` tags.

Additional Attributes

Table 12.1 shows a few extra attributes for the `<frame>` tag. These attributes can give you additional control over how the user interacts with your frames. Other attributes control margins or spacing between frames and whether scrollbars appear when required.

12

Table 12.1 Control Attributes for the `<frame>` Tag

Attribute	Value	Description
frameborder	1	Displays borders around each frame (default).
frameborder	0	Creates borderless frames.
longdesc	*URL*	Specifies a URL that provides a longer description of the contents of the frameset. Primarily used with nonvisual browsers.
marginheight	*pixels*	To adjust the margin that appears above and below a document within a frame, set the marginheight to the number indicated by *pixels*.
marginwidth	*pixels*	The marginwidth attribute enables you to adjust the margin on the left and right sides of a frame to the number indicated by *pixels*.
name	*string*	Assigns a name to the frame, for targeting purposes.
noresize		By default, the users can move the position of borders around each frame on the current screen by grabbing the border and moving it with the mouse. To lock the borders of a frame and prevent them from being moved, use the noresize attribute.
scrolling	auto	(Default). If the contents of a frame take up more space than the area available to the frame, frames-compatible browsers automatically add scrollbars to either the side or the bottom of the frame so that the users can scroll through the document.
scrolling	no	Setting the value of scrolling to no disables the use of scrollbars for the current frame. (Note that if you set scrolling="no", but the document contains more text than can fit inside the frame, the users will not be able to scroll the additional text into view.)
scrolling	yes	If you set scrolling to yes, the scrollbars are included in the frame, regardless of whether they are required.
src	*URL*	Specifies the URL of the initial source document that appears in a frame when the frameset first opens in the browser.

Creating Complex Framesets

The framesets you've learned about so far represent the most basic types of frames that can be displayed. In day-to-day use, however, you'll rarely use these basic frame designs. In all but the simplest sites, you'll most likely want to use more complex framesets.

Therefore, to help you understand the possible combinations of frames, links, images, and documents that can be used by a Web site, this section explores the topic of complex framesets.

Exercise 12.2: Creating the Content Pages for Your Frameset

Most commonly, framesets provide navigation bars that help your readers navigate through your site much more easily. By far, the most common place to present the navigation bars is in the left side of the browser window. Each time the reader clicks a link in the left navigation frame, the content in the main frame displays the page he or she has selected. The (very silly) frameset that you create in this exercise demonstrates this technique. Although not a really practical example, it's simple and fun and demonstrates the very same techniques you would use for a navigation bar.

Normally, when you design a Web page that uses frames, you design the frameset before you go through all the trouble of designing the content that goes within it. The reason for this is because you'll want to know how big your frames are going to be before you start designing graphics and other page content to place within them.

I'm doing things a little backward here, but for good reason. It may help you to better understand how things fit together if you see "real" content in the frames as you design the frameset. For this reason, I'll have you design the content first.

The following content pages don't include any of the frameset tags discussed so far. There are eight pages in all, so I promise that I'll keep the code for these pages really brief so that you can create them quickly. Ready?

> **Tip**
>
> When you lay out the basic structure of a frameset, you normally don't want to be bothered with details such as the actual contents of the frames. Your frameset, however, will not display properly when it is loaded into a frames-compatible browser for testing unless you define `<frame>` tags that include valid documents. In cases where you want to design a frameset before you create the content, you can create a small empty HTML document called `dummy.html` and use it for all your frame testing.

The frameset that you create in Exercises 12.3 through 12.7 consists of three frames. The layout of the frameset will look as shown in Figure 12.11. The frameset page loads first and instructs the browser to divide the browser window into three frames. Next, it loads the three pages that display in the top, left, and main frames. Finally, if a user browses to the frameset without a frames-compatible browser, an alternate page will display.

12

FIGURE 12.11

You will create a frameset that consists of three frames: top, left, and main.

The top frame always displays the same Web page named away.html. The choices.html page that displays in the frame on the left side contains a list of links to six different pages named reason1.html through reason6.html. Each of these six pages will load into the main frame on the bottom-right portion of the frameset.

Start with the code that creates the page for the top frame. This page will always display in the frameset (but it won't if any links are clicked). You can easily include any information you want displayed permanently as readers browse through your site. Real-world examples for content for this frame could be the name of your Web site, a site logo, a link to your email address, or other similar content. Type the following code and save it to your hard drive as away.html; Figure 12.12 shows an example of the page.

```html
<html>
<head>
<title>I'm Away from My Desk Because</title>
</head>
<body bgcolor="#cc6600" text="#ffcc33">
<h3>I'm Away from My Desk, because .... </h3>
</body>
</html>
```

FIGURE 12.12

The top frame in the frameset.

▼

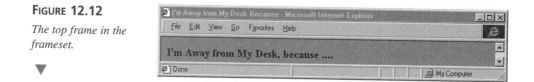

▼ Next, you'll create the left frame in the frameset. Typically, in a real-world example, this is the frame used for text or image navigation bars that take your readers to several different key pages in your site. A personal site, for example, might have a navigation bar that takes its readers to a home page, a guest book, a links page, an interests page, and other sections of interest. A corporate or business site could contain links to a products section, a customer support section, a frequently asked questions section, an employment section, and so on.

The contents page in the following example works exactly the same way that a real-world navigation bar does. It displays one of the six pages in the main frame of the frameset when the appropriate link is selected. The contents page contains links to six pages, `reason1.html` through `reason6.html`, which you'll create next.

After you enter the following code in a new page, save it to your hard drive in the same directory as the first page and name it `choice.html`; your page should look as shown in Figure 12.13 when you open it in a browser.

```
<html>
<head>
<title>Reason I'm Out</title>
</head>
<body bgcolor="#006699" text="#ffcc66" link="#ffffff" vlink="#66ccff"
alink="#ff6666">
<p>Select a reason:</p>
<hr />
<p><a href="reason1.html">Reason 1</a></p>
<p><a href="reason2.html">Reason 2</a></p>
<p><a href="reason3.html">Reason 3</a></p>
<p><a href="reason4.html">Reason 4</a></p>
<p><a href="reason5.html">Reason 5</a></p>
<p><a href="reason6.html">Reason 6</a></p>
</body>
</html>
```

Now to create the six pages that will appear in the main frame when the reader selects one of the links in the contents frame. The main frame is designed to display pages that you normally would display in a full browser window. One thing to remember, however, is that if you are going to display your pages in a frameset that has a left navigation bar, you'll have to size your graphics and page content smaller than if you displayed them in
▼ a full browser window.

12

FIGURE 12.13

The left frame in the frameset.

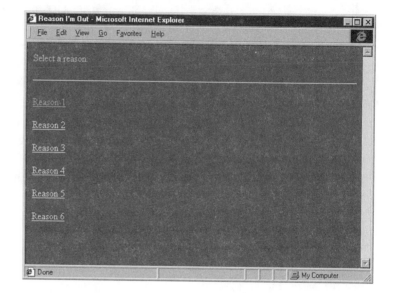

To keep the page examples relatively easy, I've created the pages so that each has the same basic appearance. This means that the code for each of these pages is pretty much the same. The only items that change from page to page are the following:

- The title of the page.

- The image that appears on each page. The images are uhoh.jpg, flirty.jpg, grumpy.jpg, happy.jpg, scared.jpg, and duh.jpg. All these images are available on the Web support site for this book, http://www.tywebpub.com/.

- The text that describes what each image means.

To create the first of the six pages that will appear in the main frame, type the following code into a new page and save it as reason1.html; Figure 12.14 shows an example of what each page generally should look like in Internet Explorer.

```
<html>
<head>
<title>Reason 1 - Forgot My Lunch</title>
</head>
<body bgcolor="#ffffff">
<h2><img src="uhoh.jpg" width="275" height="275" align="left">I forgot my lunch
  at home.</h2>
</body>
</html>
```

FIGURE 12.14

The first of the six pages that display in the main frame.

You code the remaining five pages for the main frame similarly. Modify the code you just created to build the second of the six main pages. The only differences from the previous code (`reason1.html`) are shown with a gray background. Save the new page as `reason2.html`. The complete code appears as follows:

```html
<html>
<head>
<title>Reason 2 - By the Water Cooler</title>
</head>
<body bgcolor="#ffffff">
<h2><img src="flirty.jpg" width="275" height="275" align="left">I'm flirting by
   the water cooler.</h2>
</body>
</html>
```

For the third page, modify the code again and save the new page as `reason3.html`. The complete code appears as follows:

```html
<html>
<head>
<title>Reason 3 - Don't Ask!</title>
</head>
<body bgcolor="#ffffff">
<h2><img src="grumpy.jpg" width="275" height="275" align="left">None of
   your business!</h2>
</body>
</html>
```

12

▼ Here's the fourth page (reason4.html):

```
<head>
<title>Reason 4 - Out to Lunch</title>
</head>
<body bgcolor="#ffffff">
<h2><img src="happy.jpg" width="275" height="275" align="left">I'm out
   to lunch.</h2>
</body>
</html>
```

The fifth page (reason5.html) looks like the following:

```
<head>
<title>Reason 5 - Boss's Office</title>
</head>
<body bgcolor="#ffffff">
<h2><img src="scared.jpg" width="275" height="275" align="left">The boss
   called me into his office.</h2>
</body>
</html>
```

The last main page (reason6.html) appears as follows:

```
<head>
<title>Reason 6 - I Don't Work Here Anymore</title>
</head>
<body bgcolor="#ffffff">
<h2><img src="duh.jpg" width="275" height="275" align="left">I just
   got fired.</h2>
</body>
</html>
```

Now you have the six pages that will appear in the main frame of the frameset. You're
▲ finally ready to build the frameset.

Exercise 12.3: Combining rows and cols

To remind you of the basic layout of the frameset that you'll create, Figure 12.15 is
another look at our complete page. It provides a good basis for a simple example that
explores how you can combine framesets to create complex designs.

> **Tip**
>
> When designing complex frame layouts, a *storyboard* is an invaluable tool.
> The storyboard helps you block out the structure of a frameset, and also can
> be invaluable when you're adding hyperlinks, as you will see in Exercise
> 12.5, "Using Named Frames and Hyperlinks."

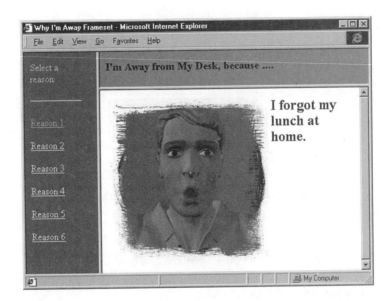

FIGURE 12.15

The frameset with three frames: top, left, and main.

In Figure 12.15, the right section of the screen is split into two horizontal frames, and the third frame, at the left of the page, spans the entire height of the screen. To create a frameset document that describes this layout, open your text editor and enter the following basic HTML structural details:

```
<html>
<head>
<title>Why I'm Away Frameset</title>
</head>
<frameset>
</frameset>
</html>
```

Next, you must decide whether you need to use a `rows` or `cols` attribute in your base `<frameset>`. To do so, look at your storyboard—in this case, Figure 12.15—and work out whether any frame areas extend right across the screen or from the top to the bottom of the screen. If any frames extend from the top to the bottom, as in this example, you need to start with a `cols` frameset; otherwise, you need to start with a `rows` frameset. On the other hand, if no frames extend completely across the screen in either direction, you should start with a `cols` frameset.

To put it more simply, here are three easy-to-remember rules:

- Left to right, use `rows`
- Top to bottom, use `cols`
- Can't decide, use `cols`

12

> **Note**
>
> The reasoning behind the use of the "Left to right, use `rows`" rule relates to how frames-compatible browsers create frames. Each separate `<frameset>` definition can split the screen (or a frame) either vertically or horizontally, but not both ways. For this reason, you need to define your framesets in a logical order to ensure that you achieve the layout you want.

In Figure 12.15, the left frame extends across the screen from top to bottom. As a result, by using the rules mentioned previously, you need to start with a `cols` frameset. To define the base frameset, write the following:

```
<frameset cols="125,*">
  <frame src="choice.html" <!-- this loads the choices page into the left frame
-->
  <frame src="dummy.html" <!-- this line is only temporary -->
</frameset>
```

Writing this code splits the screen into two sections. The first line defines a small frame at the left of the screen that is 125 pixels wide and a large frame at the right of the screen that uses the rest of the available space.

As mentioned earlier today, the frameset document itself does not describe the contents of each frame. The documents indicated by the `src` attribute of the `<frame>` actually contain the text, images, and tags displayed by the frameset. You can see an example of this tag in the second and third lines in the preceding code. The second line specifies the URL of the Web page that displays in the left frame (the `choice.html` page that you created earlier in this day). The third line would display a Web page named `dummy.html` (if you created one, that is), but we are just using this as a placeholder for the next exercise.

Exercise 12.4: Nesting Framesets

The next step in the process is to split the right frame area into two horizontal frames. You achieve this effect by placing a second `<frameset>` block inside the base `<frameset>` block. When one `<frameset>` block is nested inside another, the nested block must replace one of the `<frame>` tags in the outside frameset. In this case, you'll replace the line that loads the temporary `dummy.html` page (which doesn't really exist).

To split the right frame into two frame areas, you replace the dummy `<frame>` tag with an embedded `<frameset>` block. Doing so embeds the new frameset inside the area defined for the `<frame>` tag it replaces. Inside the `<frameset>` tag for this new block, you then need to define a `rows` attribute, as shown in the following complete example of the code:

```
<html>
<head>
<title>Why I'm Away Frameset</title>
</head>
<frameset cols="125,*">
  <frame src="choice.html" <!-- this loads the choices page into the left frame
-->
  <frameset rows="60,*">        <!-- the frame for column 2 -->
    <frame src="away.html">     <!-- has been replaced -->
    <frame src="reason1.html">  <!-- with an embedded -->
  </frameset>                   <!-- frameset block -->
</frameset>
```

The embedded rows frameset defines two rows, the first being 60 percent of the height of the embedded frame area and the second taking up all the remaining space in the embedded frame area. In addition, two <frame> tags are embedded inside the <frameset> block to define the contents of each column. The top frame loads away.html, and the bottom frame loads reason1.html.

> **Note**
>
> When used inside an embedded frameset, any percentage sizes are based on a percentage of the total area of the embedded frame and not as a percentage of the total screen.

Save the finished HTML document to your hard drive, assigning it a name of frame-set.html. Test it by using a frames-compliant browser. Also, if you happen to have a copy of a non–frames-compliant Web browser, try loading the document into it. (You should not see anything when you use the alternative browsers.)

Exercise 12.5: Using Named Frames and Hyperlinks

If you were to load your frameset.html page into a frames-compatible browser at this stage, you would see a screen similar to the one shown in Figure 12.15. Some of the text sizes and spacing might be slightly different, but the general picture would be the same.

Although it looks right, it doesn't yet work right. If you were to click any of the hyperlinks in the left frame, you would most likely get some very strange results. To be more specific, the frames-compatible browser would attempt to load the contents of the file you select into the left frame, when what you really want it to do is load each document into the larger right frame.

Earlier today, you learned about the target attribute, which loads different pages in a different browser window. To make the frameset work the way it should, you need to use a slight variation on the target attribute. Rather than the target pointing to a new window, you want it to point to one of the frames in the current frameset.

12

To Do

▼ You can achieve this by first giving each frame in your frameset a frame name, or window name. To do so, you include a `name` attribute inside the `<frame>` tag, which takes the following form:

```
<frame src="document URL" name="frame name">
```

Therefore, to assign a name to each of the frames in the `frameset.html` document, you add the `name` attribute to each of the `<frame>` tags. I've indicated the additions in bold text in the following example. Your frameset page now looks like the following:

```
<html>
<head>
<title>Why I'm Away Frameset</title>
</head>
<frameset cols="125,*">
  <frame src="choice.html" name="left"> <!-- this loads the choices page into
the left frame -->
  <frameset rows="60,*">        <!-- the frame for column 2 -->
    <frame src="away.html" name="top">    <!-- has been replaced -->
    <frame src="reason1.html" name="main"> <!-- with an embedded -->
  </frameset>                        <!-- frameset block -->
</frameset>
```

This source code names the left frame `"left"`, the top-right frame `"top"`, and the bottom-right frame `"main"`. Next, resave the updated `frameset.html` file, and you're just
▲ about finished with the example.

Exercise 12.6: Linking Documents to Individual Frames

Naming the frames is only half the battle. Now you have to fix the links in the `choice.html` page so that they load the target pages in the `main` frame rather than the `left` frame.

▼ You might recall from the beginning of the day that the `target` attribute was used with the `<a>` tag to force a document to load into a specific window. You use the same attribute to control into which frame a document is loaded.

Here is what you'll accomplish in this exercise. You want to load a page in the `main` frame (bottom-right) whenever you click a hyperlink in the `left` frame. Because you've already assigned the bottom-right frame a window name of `"main"`, all you need to do is add `target="main"` to each tag in the `choice.html` document. The following snippet of HTML source demonstrates how to make this change:

```
<p><a href="reason1.html" target="main">Reason 1</a></p>
<p><a href="reason2.html" target="main">Reason 2</a></p>
<p><a href="reason3.html" target="main">Reason 3</a></p>
<p><a href="reason4.html" target="main">Reason 4</a></p>
<p><a href="reason5.html" target="main">Reason 5</a></p>
▼ <p><a href="reason6.html" target="main">Reason 6</a></p>
```

▼   Alternatively, because every tag in the choice.html document points to the same frame, you also could use the <base target="*value*"> tag. In this case, you don't need to include target="main" inside each <a> tag. Instead, you place the following inside the <head>...</head> block of the document:

<base target="main">

With all the changes and new documents created, you now should be able to load frameset.html into your frames-compatible browser and view all your HTML reference documents by selecting from the choices in the left frame.

> **Tip**
>
> To get the layout exactly right, you might need to go back and adjust the size of the rows and columns as defined in the <frameset> tags after you get all your links working properly. Remember, the final appearance of a frameset is still determined by the size of the screen and the operating system used by people viewing the documents.

▲

Exercise 12.7: Adding Your noframes Content

Although you have a frameset that works perfectly now, there's another feature you need to add to your frameset. Remember, there are some people who might navigate to your frames page who don't use frames-compatible browsers. The following addition to the frameset page creates some content that they will see when they open the frameset.

Once again, open the frameset.html page. At this point, your code looks like the following:

```
<html>
<head>
<title>Why I'm Away Frameset</title>
</head>
<frameset cols="125,*">
  <frame src="choice.html" name="left"> <!-- this loads the choices page into
the left frame -->
  <frameset rows="60,*">         <!-- the frame for column 2 -->
    <frame src="away.html" name="top">    <!-- has been replaced -->
    <frame src="reason1.html" name="main"> <!-- with an embedded -->
  </frameset>                    <!-- frameset block -->
</frameset>
</html>
```

12

▼ Immediately after the last `</frameset>` tag, and before the final `</html>` tag, insert the
following `<noframes>`...`</noframes>` element and content:

```
<noframes>
   <body bgcolor="#ffffff">
<h1>I'm Away from My Desk, because ...</h1>
<ul>
  <li>Reason 1 - <a href="reason1.html">I forgot my lunch at home.</a></li>
  <li>Reason 2 - <a href="reason2.html">I'm flirting by the water
cooler.</a></li>
  <li>Reason 3 - <a href="reason3.html">None of your business.</a></li>
  <li>Reason 4 - <a href="reason4.html">I'm out to lunch.</a></li>
  <li>Reason 5 - <a href="reason5.html">The boss just called me in his
office.</a></li>
  <li>Reason 6 - <a href="reason6.html">I just got fired.</a></li>
</ul>
</body>
</noframes>
```

When a user who is not using a frames-compatible browser navigates to the frameset, he
or she will see the page that is similar to the one shown in Figure 12.16.

FIGURE 12.16

*This page displays
when users view the
frameset with a brows-
er that is not frames-
compatible.*

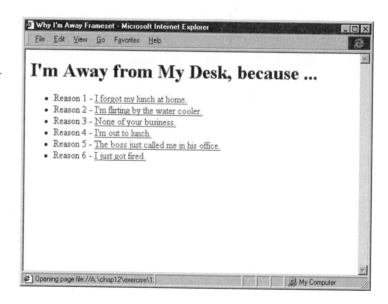

▲

Magic target Names

Now that you've learned what the `target` attribute does in a frameset, you should know
that there are some special target names you can apply to a frameset.

You can assign four special values to a `target` attribute, two of which (`_blank` and `_self`) you've already encountered. Netscape calls these values Magic `target` names. Table 12.2 lists the Magic `target` names and describes their use.

Table 12.2 Magic `target` Names

`target` *Name*	*Description*
`target="_blank"`	Forces the document referenced by the `<a>` tag to be loaded into a new unnamed window.
`target="_self"`	Causes the document referenced by the `<a>` tag to be loaded into the window or frame that held the `<a>` tag. This can be useful if the `<base>` tag sets the target to another frame but a specific link needs to load in the current frame.
`target="_parent"`	Forces the link to load into the `<frameset>` parent of the current document. If, however, the current document has no parent, `target="_self"` will be used.
`target="_top"`	Forces the link to load into the full Web browser window, replacing the current `<frameset>` entirely. If, however, the current document is already at the top, `target="_self"` will be used. More often than not, when you create links to other sites on the Web, you don't want them to open within your frameset. Adding target="top" to the link will prevent this from occurring.

Floating Frames

With Internet Explorer 3.0, Microsoft introduced a novel variation on frames: floating frames. This concept, which is a part of HTML 4.0, is somewhat different from the original frames idea Netscape introduced.

Floating frames have their advantages and disadvantages. The advantage is that you can position a floating frame anywhere on a Web page, just like you can an image, a table, or any other Web page element. This offers a lot of layout possibilities that you can't get with the standard framesets you've learned about so far today.

Note

The authors of the HTML 4.0 frames specification have included floating frames with some hesitation. According to the specification, you can use the `<object>` tag to achieve the same effect as floating frames, so the inclusion of this type of frame is questionable. Still, the tag is included in the HTML 4.0 specification, and Internet Explorer 3 and later supports the technology. Learning to use floating frames is worthwhile.

12

There are precautions in using floating frames, however. First, Internet Explorer 3.0 and later releases appear to be the only browsers that support them at the present time. Before you design pages that include floating frames, you should be aware of another caveat.

Standard framesets enable you to specify alternate content that can be viewed if a person navigates to a frameset without using a frames-compatible browser. Unfortunately, you don't have this option with the <iframe> element. If you include a floating frame on your Web page, and a user navigates to it with a browser that doesn't support them, he or she will see absolutely nothing at all in the area where the frame should be. Therefore, you might not want to use floating frames at all, unless you are certain that your entire audience will be using Internet Explorer 3.0 or later.

With that warning out of the way, here's a brief run-through of how you create floating frames. You define floating frames by using the <iframe> tag. Like images, these frames appear inline in the middle of the body of an HTML document (hence the "I" in <iframe>). The <iframe> tag enables you to insert an HTML document in a frame any-where in another HTML document.

Table 12.3 shows <iframe> takes the key attributes—all of which, except for those indi-cated as Internet Explorer extensions, appear currently in HTML 4.0:

Table 12.3   Key Attributes

Attribute	Description
width	Specifies the width in pixels of the floating frame that will hold the HTML document.
height	Specifies the height in pixels of the floating frame that will hold the HTML document.
src	Specifies the URL of the HTML document to be displayed in the frame.
name	Specifies the name of the frame for the purpose of linking and targeting.
frameborder	Indicates whether the frame should display a border. A value of 1 indicates the presence of a border, and a value of 0 indicates no border should be displayed.
marginwidth	Specifies the width of the margin in pixels.
marginheight	Specifies the height in pixels of the margin.
noresize	Indicates that the frame should not be resizable by the user (Internet Explorer extension).
scrolling	As with the <frame> tag, indicates whether the inline frame should include scrollbars. (This attribute can take the values yes, no, or auto; the default is auto.)

Attribute	Description
vspace	Specifies the height of the margin (Internet Explorer extension).
hspace	Specifies the width of the margin (Internet Explorer extension).
align:	As with the `<img>` tag, specifies the positioning of the frame with respect to the text line in which it occurs. Possible values include `left`, `middle`, `right`, `top`, and `bottom` with the last being the default value. `absbottom`, `absmiddle`, `baseline`, and `texttop` are available as Internet Explorer extensions.

Because you know how to use both regular frames and inline images, using the `<iframe>` tag is fairly easy. The following code displays one way that you can use the Away from My Desk pages in conjunction with a floating frame. In this example, you begin by creating a page with a red background. The links the user clicks appear on a single line, centered above the floating frame. I've arranged each of the links on separate lines in the code for clarity.

Following the links (which target the floating frame named `"reason"`), the code for the floating frame appears within a centered `<div>` element. As the following code shows, the floating frame will be centered on the page and will measure 450 pixels wide and 315 pixels high; Figure 12.17 shows the result.

```
<html>
<head>
<title>I'm Away From My Desk</title>
</head>
<body bgcolor="#ffcc99">
<h2>I'm away from my desk because ...</h2>
<p align="center">
    <a href="reason1.html" target="reason">Reason 1</a> |
    <a href="reason2.html" target="reason">Reason 2</a> |
    <a href="reason3.html" target="reason">Reason 3</a> |
    <a href="reason4.html" target="reason">Reason 4</a> |
    <a href="reason5.html" target="reason">Reason 5</a> |
    <a href="reason6.html" target="reason">Reason 6</a> </p>
<div align="center">
<iframe name="reason"
    src="reason1.html"
    width="450"
    height="315">
</div>
</body>
</html>
```

12

Figure **12.17**

*An inline (or floating)
frame.*

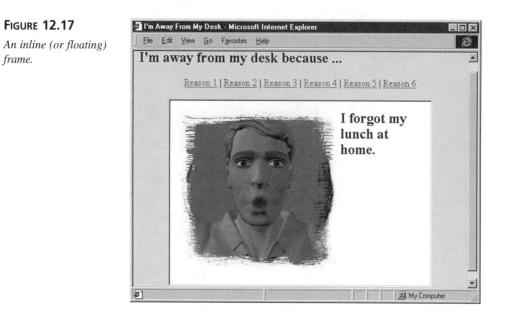

Summary

If your head is hurting after reading this today, you're probably not alone. Although the basic concepts behind the use of frames are relatively straightforward, their implementation is somewhat harder to come to grips with. As a result, the best way to learn about frames is by experimenting with them.

Today, you learned how to link a document to a new or an existing window. In addition, you learned how to create framesets and link them together by using the tags listed in Table 12.4.

Table 12.4   New Tags Discussed in Day 12

Tag	Attribute	Description
`<base target="window">`		Sets the global link window for a document.
`<frameset>`		Defines the basic structure of a frameset.
	`cols`	Defines the number of frame columns and their width in a frameset.
	`rows`	Defines the number of frame rows and their height in a frameset.
	`frameborder`	Indicates whether the frameset displays borders between frames.
	`bordercolor`	Defines the color of borders in a frameset.

Tag	Attribute	Description
`<frame>`		Defines the contents of a frame within a frameset.
	`src`	Indicates the URL of the document to be displayed inside the frame.
	`marginwidth`	Indicates the size in pixels of the margin on each side of a frame.
	`marginheight`	Indicates the size in pixels of the margin above and below the contents of a frame.
	`scrolling`	Enables or disables the display of scrollbars for a frame. Values are `yes`, `no`, and `auto`.
	`noresize`	Prevents the users from resizing frames.
	`frameborder`	Indicates whether the frameset displays borders between frames.
	`bordercolor`	Defines the color of borders in a frameset.
	`longdesc`	Specifies an URL that provides a longer description of the contents of the frameset. Used with nonvisual browsers.
	`name`	Assigns a name to the frame, for targeting purposes.
`<iframe>`		Defines an inline or floating frame.
	`src`	Indicates the URL of the document to be displayed in the frame.
	`name`	Indicates the name of the frame for the purpose of linking and targeting.
	`width`	Indicates the width of the frame in pixels.
	`height`	Indicates the height of the frame in pixels.
	`marginwidth`	Indicates the width of the margin in pixels.
	`marginheight`	Indicates the height of the margin in pixels.
	`scrolling`	Enables or disables the display of scrollbars in the frame. Values are `yes`, `no`, and `auto`.
	`frameborder`	Enables or disables the display of a border around the frame. Values are `1` or `0`.
	`vspace`	Indicates the height of the margin in pixels.
	`hspace`	Indicates the width of the margin in pixels.

12

continues

Table 12.4   continued

Tag	Attribute	Description
	align	Specifies the alignment of the frame relative to the current line of text. Values are left, right, middle, top, and bottom (also absbottom, absmiddle, texttop, and baseline in Internet Explorer).
\<noframes\>		Defines text to be displayed by Web browsers that don't support the use of frames.

If you've made it this far through the book, you should give yourself a pat on the back. With the knowledge you've gained in the last week, you've done just about everything you can do while still working along on a single computer. You're now ready to place your Web pages onto the Internet itself and add more interactive features to those pages such as forms, image maps, and embedded animations. And tomorrow, along with what you learned in Day 8, you'll start doing just that.

Workshop

As if you haven't had enough already, here's a refresher course. As always, there are questions, a quiz, and exercises that will help you remember some of the most important points.

Q&A

Q. Is there any limit to how many levels of \<frameset\> tags I can nest within a single screen?

A. No, there isn't a limit. Practically speaking, however, when you get below about four levels, the size of the window space available starts to become unusable.

Q. What would happen if I included a reference to a frameset document within a \<frame\> tag?

A. Netscape handles such a reference correctly, by treating the nested frameset document as a nested \<frameset\>. In fact, this technique is used regularly to reduce the complexity of nested frames.

One limitation does exist, however. You cannot include a reference to the current frameset document in one of its own frames. This situation, called recursion, causes an infinite loop. Netscape Communications has included built-in protection to guard against this type of referencing.

Quiz

1. What are the differences between a *frameset document*, a *frameset*, a *frame*, and a *page*?

2. When you create links to pages that are supposed to load into a frameset, what attribute makes the pages appear in the right frame? (*Hint: it applies to the* <a> *element.*)

3. When a Web page includes the <frameset> element, what element cannot be used at the beginning of the HTML document?

4. What two attributes of the <frameset> tag divide the browser window into multiple sections?

5. What attribute of the <frame> tag defines the HTML document that first loads into a frameset?

Answers

1. A *frameset document* is the HTML document that contains the definition of the frameset. A *frameset* is the portion of the frameset document that is defined by the <frameset> tag, which instructs the browser to divide the window into multiple sections. A *frame* is one of the sections, or windows, within a frameset. The *page* is the Web document that loads within a frame.

2. The target attribute of the <a> tag directs linked pages to load into the appropriate frame.

3. When a Web page includes the <frameset> element, it cannot include the <body> element at the beginning of the page. They are mutually exclusive.

4. The cols and rows attributes of the <frameset> tag divide the browser window into multiple frames.

5. The src attribute of the <frame> tag defines the HTML document that first loads into the frameset.

12

Exercises

1. Create a frameset that divides the browser window into three sections, as follows:

   - The left section of the frameset will be a column that spans the entire height of the browser window and will take up one-third of the width of the browser window. Name this frame `contents`.

   - Divide the right section of the frameset into two rows, each taking half the height of the browser window. Name the top section `top` and the bottom section `bottom`.

2. For the preceding frameset, create a page that you will use for a table of contents in the left frame. Create two links on this page, one that loads a page in the top frame and another that loads a page in the bottom frame.

PART 5

Multimedia, Forms, and Dynamic HTML

DAY 13

Multimedia: Adding Sounds, Videos, and More

Learning how to integrate multimedia into your Web pages is as simple as creating hyperlinks to sound or video files. Presto! You have added multimedia to your Web site. That's not the whole story, of course. Aside from linking to multimedia files, you also can embed them in your Web pages. Unfortunately, embedding them can be a little tricky. While you only need to learn a few HTML elements, the multimedia-related HTML elements suffer from what seems like schizophrenia. They either are implemented differently in Microsoft Internet Explorer and Netscape Navigator, not supported at all in one or the other of the two browsers, or are a part of the HTML standard to which no one seems to be paying attention. In addition, there are quite a few competing audio and video formats available today. It's almost impossible to learn the ins and outs of each one before more appear with the promise of being the "be all and end all" of multimedia.

Even with recent advances in communications speed (the current average is 56Kbps for most home modems), improved sound and video compression/decompression technologies (MP3 audio files come to mind), and powerful audio and video adapter cards, the Web is not the sound and video showcase that multimedia proponents dream of—not yet anyway.

Part of the problem of coming to grips with this fact is the incongruity between what we know today's computers are capable of and what we think the Web should deliver. Pop in a CD or DVD disk in your drive and, blammo, 3D graphics, stereo surround-sound, and full-screen 30-frames-per-second digital video jump out and assault your auditory and visual senses without letting up until you slump over in a blathering heap of multimedia overload. Contrast that with most multimedia on the Web and you can be sorely disappointed. Low-quality sound, small video sizes, and long download times are par for the course.

Things are getting better. Witness the advent of MP3 audio file and Macromedia Flash animations and their increasing popularity. Each offers a low-bandwidth high-quality multimedia option; however, there is a price to pay for the progress being made. Namely, as Web users, we are being deluged with audio and video formats each requiring special plug-ins or helper applications. As a Web developer, you have to purchase expensive audio/video equipment and software in order to create your own multimedia content.

Having said all this, I will try to strike a balance in this lesson between showing you the techniques you can immediately use and the technologies that require you to devote a significant amount of time and energy in order apply. You will learn to accomplish the following:

- Create links to audio and video files so that visitors can download or play them
- Use the `embed` and `object` elements to include sound and video files in Web pages
- Learn how to embed QuickTime, Shockwave, Flash, and RealAudio or RealVideo files into your Web pages
- Use some of the unique multimedia capabilities of Microsoft Internet Explorer
- Recognize the most popular multimedia file types and the plug-ins or helper applications they require

Understanding How to Present Sound and Video

Despite all the complexity surrounding multimedia files and the number of formats available, it all boils down to choosing a method to integrate them into your Web pages. You can choose to create hyperlinks to those files or embed them directly into your Web pages. Linking to files is relatively foolproof but embedding them can be problematic.

A linked sound or video file, no matter what type of sound or video file it is, has a hyperlink to the source file within the Web page. When you click on a linked sound or video file, one of three possible events occur. First, you can download the file and save it to your computer. This method enables you to listen or view at a later time your file in whatever application you choose. Secondly, the file can download and automatically launch a helper application or plug-in to play. This occurs when the file is a recognized type, and a suitable player or plug-in is configured to play the file. Thirdly, if the file is recognized as streaming audio or video, a player is launched as a separate process that will begin to play the file as it downloads.

Embedded sound and video are integrated into the Web browser itself and are played with the help of plug-ins or helper applications. Embedded sound and video offer fewer options for the user because the file is integrated into the Web page itself. Most often, a helper-application or plug-in interface is created in the Web browser's window to play the file.

Without much further ado, let's get your elbows dirty and add some sound and video to Web pages.

The Old Standby: Linking

The sure-fire way to include multimedia files in your Web pages is to provide a hyperlink to them, which is supported by all versions of all browsers. People can decide whether they want to download the file and either listen to or view it at their convenience.

A common technique is to link to the file and provide a thumbnail preview of the media clip, a description, and the file size. This is considered a common courtesy so that people can estimate the download time. You also should provide links to any players required so that people can download the appropriate player, should they need it.

If I have a QuickTime video that I want to share, for example, I might fashion the code as the following:

```
<div align="center">
<h1>Apollo 17 Videos</h1>
<p><a href="Apollo_17_Flag.qt">Astronauts placing the flag on the Moon</a><br>
[2.75Mb]</p>
<img src="Apollo_17_Flag.gif" align="texttop" width="160" height="120" />
<p>Apple <a href="http://www.apple.com/quicktime">QuickTime</a> is required
to view this movie.
<a href="http://www.apple.com/quicktime"><img src="getquicktime4.gif" border="0"
align="absmiddle" width="88" height"31" /></a></p>
</div>
```

13

Figure 13.1 shows the resulting Web page.

FIGURE 13.1

Linking to files is easy and effective.

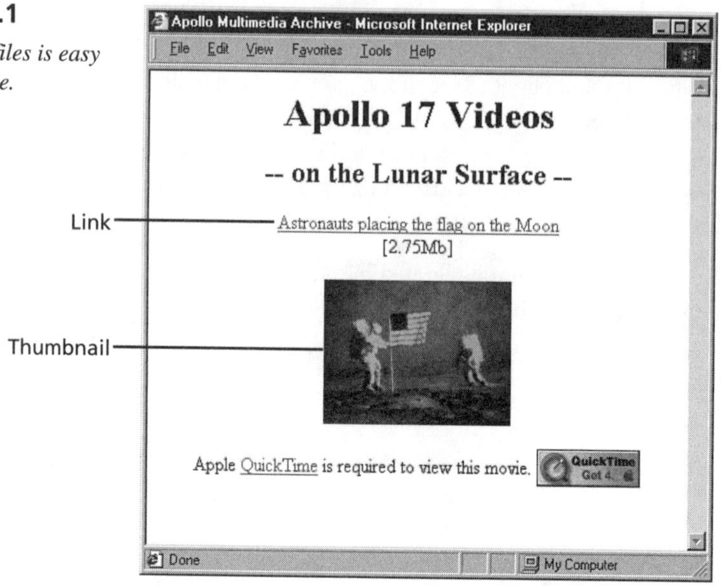

It also is considered good form to provide multiple types of media to download, should your visitors have a preference.

```
<html>
<head><title>Apollo Multimedia Archive</title></head>
<body>
<div align="center">
<h1>Apollo 17 Videos</h1>
<p>Astronauts placing the flag on the Moon</p>
<table border="0">
    <tr>
        <td rowspan="3"><img src="Apollo_17_Flag.gif" width="160" height="120"
/></td>
        <td><a href="Apollo_17_Flag.qt">QuickTime</a> [2.75Mb]</td>
    </tr>
    <tr>
        <td><a href="Apollo_17_Flag.mpg">MPEG</a> [2.45Mb]</td>
    </tr>
    <tr>
        <td><a href="Apollo_17_Flag.avi">AVI</a> [3.11Mb]</td>
    </tr>
</table>
<br />
<a href="http://www.apple.com/quicktime">
<img src="getquicktime4.gif" width="88" height"31" border="0"
```

```
alt="Get QuickTime" vspace="7" /></a>
<br>
<a href="http://microsoft.com/windows/mediaplayer/download/default.asp">
<img src="getmedia_white.gif" width="65" height="57" border="0"
alt="Get Windows Media Player" vspace="7" /></a>
<br />
</div>
</body>
</html>
```

Figure 13.2 shows the resulting Web page.

FIGURE 13.2

When linking sound and video, provide multiple formats if possible.

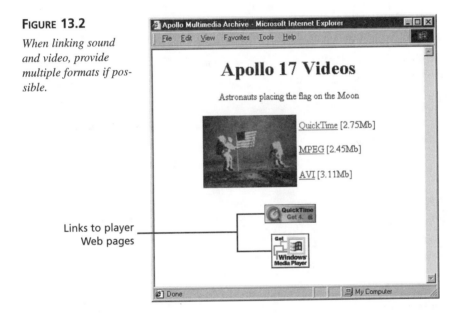

Links to player Web pages

Exercise 13.1: Creating a Family History Media Archive

One of the common types of pages available on the Web is a *media archive*. A media archive is a Web page that serves no purpose other than to provide quick access to images or other media files for viewing and downloading.

Before the Web became popular, media such as images, sounds, and video were stored in FTP or Gopher archives. The text-only nature of these sorts of archives makes it difficult for people to find what they're looking for, as the filename usually is the only description they have of the content of the file. Even reasonably descriptive filenames, such as the-trees-last-fall.gif or ave-maria.wav, aren't very useful when you're talking about images or sounds. Although they may describe the files, the only way people actually can sample them is to go through the process of downloading the entire file and playing it.

▲ To Do

13

▼   By using inline images as thumbnails and splitting up sound and video files into small "sample" clips with larger files, you can create a media archive on the Web that is far more usable than any of the text-only archives.

Note   Keep in mind that this sort of archive, with its heavy use of inline graphics and large media files, is optimally useful in graphical browsers attached to fast networks.

In this exercise, you'll create a simple example of a media archive with several GIF and JPEG images, WAV sounds, and a mixture of MPEG and AVI video.

By using your favorite image editor, you can create thumbnails of each of your pictures to serve as the inline icons and then insert <img> links in the appropriate spots in your archive file.

First, start with the framework for the archive, and then add a table for the thumbnail images, as in the following:

INPUT
```
<!DOCTYPE html PUBLIC "-//W3C//DTD XHTML 1.0 Transitional//EN"
"http://www.w3.org/TR/xhtml1/DTD/transitional.dtd">

<html>
<head>
<title>My Family History</title>
</head>
<body>
<h1>My Family Media Archive</h1>

<div align="center">
<table border="0">
<tr>
    <td width="80"><h2>Images</h2></td>
    <td><p>Select an image to view it in a larger size</p></td>
</tr>
<tr>
    <td width="80">A bunch of family members in the early 1950s.</td>
    <td><img src="groupoldsmall.gif" height="103" width="150" alt="An old
group photo" /></td>
</tr>
<tr>

    <td width="80">Aunts Betsy and Phyllis sitting on the porch.</td>
    <td><img src="auntssmall.gif" height="96" width="150" alt="Two aunts
on a porch" /></td>
</tr>
```
▼

```
<tr>
    <td width="80">Don when he was a child.</td>
    <td><img src="donoldsmall.gif" height="100" width="61" alt="Young
Don" /></td>
</tr>
</table>
</div>

</body>
</html>
```

Note that I include values for the `alt` attribute to the `<img>` tag, which will be substituted for the images in browsers that cannot view these images. Although you may not intend for your Web page to be seen by non-graphical browsers, at least offering a clue to people who stumble onto it is polite. This way, everyone can access the media files you're offering on this page.

Figure 13.3 shows how the page looks so far.

FIGURE 13.3

The Web page with the image archive almost completed.

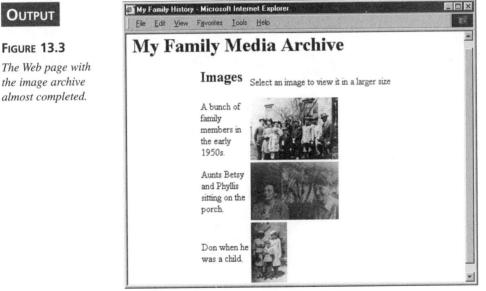

The next step is to create the hyperlinks to each image that point to the larger file. By clicking them, people can choose either to view these files or download them to their computers.

13

▼

```
...
<tr>
    <td width="80">A bunch of family members in the early 1950s.</td>
    <td><a href="groupoldlarge.jpg">
    <img src="groupoldsmall.gif" height="103" width="150"
     alt="An old group photo"/></a></td>
</tr>
<tr>
    <td width="80">Aunts Betsy and Phyllis sitting on the porch.</td>
    <td><a href="auntslarge.jpg"><img src="auntssmall.gif" height="96"
width="150"
    alt="Two aunts on a porch"/></a></td>
</tr>
<tr>
    <td width="80">Don when he was a child.</td>
    <td><a href="donoldlarge.jpg"><img src="donoldsmall.gif" height="100"
width="61"
     alt="Young Don" /></a></td>
</tr>
```

Figure 13.4 shows the result.

FIGURE 13.4

The image now linked to larger images. Thumbnail images form links

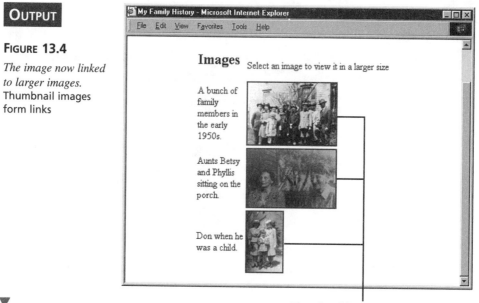

Thumbnail images form links

▼

▼ If I leave the archive like this, it looks nice, but I'm breaking one of my own rules: I haven't noted how large each file is. Here, you have several choices for formatting, but the easiest is to simply add the file size after the description of each picture, as follows:

INPUT

```
<tr>
    <td width="80">A bunch of family members in the early 1950s.
[103k]</td>
    <td><a href="groupoldlarge.jpg"><img src="groupoldsmall.gif"
height="103" width="150"
    alt="An old group photo"/></a></td>
</tr>
<tr>
    <td width="80">Aunts Betsy and Phyllis sitting on the porch.
[83k]</td>
    <td><a href="auntslarge.jpg"><img src="auntssmall.gif" height="96"
width="150"
    alt="Two aunts on a porch"/></a></td>
</tr>
<tr>
    <td width="80">Don when he was a child. [284k]</td>
    <td><a href="donoldlarge.jpg"><img src="donoldsmall.gif" height="100"
width="61"
     alt="Young Don" /></a></td>
</tr>
```

Figure 13.5 shows this result.

OUTPUT

FIGURE 13.5

Adding file sizes to the description of each image enables people determine how long it will take to load the image.

File sizes

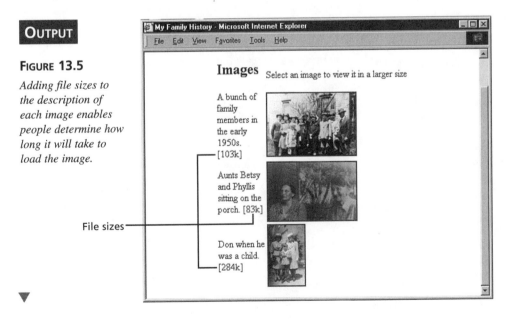

13

▼ Now, moving on to the sound and video sections. There are two approaches to formatting these sections. You can add the material in the same table that contains the images or you can create two new tables—either way is fine. For this exercise, you are going to create new tables virtually identical to the table that held the images.

Start by adding three sound and two video files. Because the sound files can't be reduced to a simple thumbnail image, you need to describe them better in the text in the archive; however, you usually can use your video player to copy one frame of the clip and provide that as a thumbnail. Following is the code for the sound portion of your archive:

INPUT

```
<div align="center">
<table border="0">
<tr>
    <td width="150"><h2>Sound Bites</h2></td>
    <td><p>Select a sound bite to download or listen to it.</p></td>
</tr>
<tr>
    <td width="150">An oral family history describing how we survived the
tornado of 1903. [1192k]</td>
    <td><a href="tornado.wav"><img src="soundicon.gif" height="29"
width="33"></a></td>
</tr>
<tr>

    <td width="150">Don describing his first job. [1004k]</td>
    <td><a href="donjob.wav"><img src="soundicon.gif" height="29"
width="33"></a></a></td>
</tr>
<tr>
    <td width="150">Grandma Jo telling how she came to America.
[2459k]</td>
    <td><a href="jo.wav"><img src="soundicon.gif" height="29"
width="33"></a></a></td>
</tr>
</table>
</div>
```

▼ Figure 13.6 shows how the linked sounds look on the Web page.

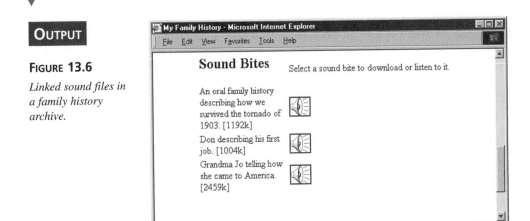

OUTPUT

FIGURE 13.6

Linked sound files in a family history archive.

Finally, add the video clip section just as you have the previous two. It's getting easier!

INPUT

```
<div align="center">
<table border="0">
<tr>
    <td width="100"><h2>Video Clips</h2></td>
    <td><p>Select a video clip to download it.</p></td>
</tr>
<tr>
    <td width="100">A video of a family wedding. [2492k]</td>
    <td><a href="wedding.mpeg"><img src="wedding.gif" height="120"
width="180"></a></td>
</tr>
<tr>

    <td width="100">Don and Mary talking. [3614k]</td>
    <td><a href="donandmary.mpeg"><img src="donandmary.gif" height="120"
width="180"></a></td>
</tr>
</table>
</div>
```

Figure 13.7 shows how the linked videos with thumbnails look on the Web page.

13

FIGURE 13.7

The video section of our multimedia archive.

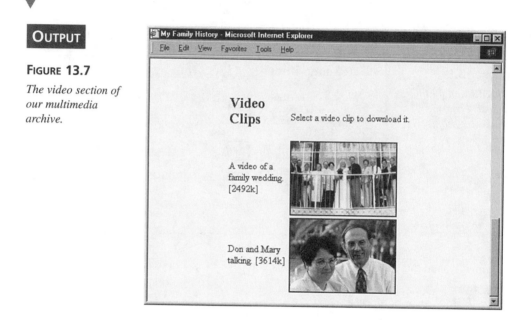

Et voilá, your media archive. Creating one is simple with the combination of inline images and external files. With the use of the `alt` attribute, you can even use it reasonably well in text-only browsers.

Embedding Sound and Video

Embedding sound and video is achieved through the `embed` or `object` elements. Remember, the principle behind embedding sound or video is to include it in a Web page so that it can be played as part of the page.

The `embed` element has been around for some time and is supported by both Internet Explorer and Netscape Navigator. It was created so that file types requiring plug-ins (multimedia primarily) to play could be added to Web pages. Despite this support, `embed` is not sanctioned by the World Wide Web Consortium (W3C) and can't be found in the official HTML standard. Of course, because both major browsers support the element, you can safely ignore the W3C for the time being.

The "competing" element, `object`, is officially sanctioned by the W3C, although browser support (mainly Navigator) is somewhat buggy at this time. The `object` element is supposed to provide a generic solution for embedding in Web pages all sorts of file types, from images to Java Applets to sound and video files. It is hoped that by standardizing a "one-size-fits-all" element, you will be able to include more types of files as well as have an element ready for any future multimedia types.

Using the embed Element

Despite the fact that embed isn't in the HTML standard, Microsoft or Netscape continue supporting embed in their latest Web browsers, and there are plenty of Web pages that make use of embed.

The syntax for using embed is simple:

```
<embed attributes />
```

Note the closing tag, which is optional.

Unfortunately, despite the fact that both Internet Explorer and Navigator support embed, they share only a handful of common attributes. The flip side to that coin is that each Web browser ignores the attributes it doesn't understand, allowing you to include as many different attributes as you like. Because of this, it is best to rely on a set of attributes that will work in all cases, and use them religiously, including the others for "added value."

Let's explore the attributes you absolutely need to use the embed element.

```
<embed src="a01607av.avi" height="120" width="160" />
```

The src attribute indicates the path and name of the media file you want to embed in the Web page, while the height and width attributes set a region of the browser window aside to display the media file.

Internet Explorer and Netscape Navigator handle the height and width a bit differently. In Internet Explorer 5, the media controls of the appropriate plug-in are always displayed while Navigator seems not to want to ever display them. This causes a huge problem in that setting the height and width attribute for Internet Explorer includes the space devoted to those controls. Setting the height and width to the exact size of the video display causes the video to become "crunched" because the controls take up some of this valuable real estate. One would think that increasing the height and width would solve this problem by increasing the space and allowing the controls and the video to be displayed at their proper sizes. Because of the Netscape Navigator implementation, however, that doesn't work. Netscape Navigator expands the video to the full size of the height and width attributes and ignores the controls entirely, resulting in a video that is stretched and distorted.

Figure 13.8 and 13.9 show the problem using this code:

```
<embed src="a01607av.avi" type="video/x-msvideo" height="120" width="180" />
```

13

FIGURE **13.8**

*Internet Explorer dis-
plays the controls and
sizes the overall box
accordingly.*

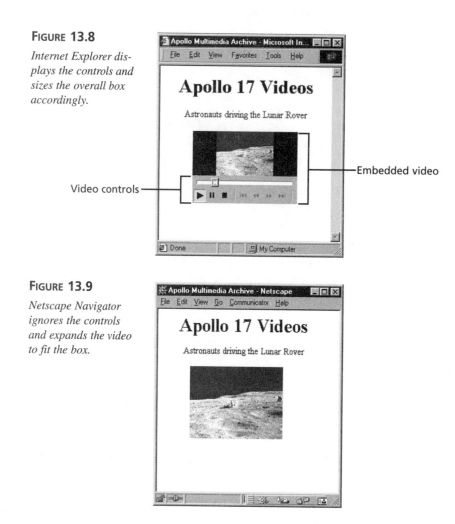

Video controls

Embedded video

FIGURE **13.9**

*Netscape Navigator
ignores the controls
and expands the video
to fit the box.*

Not using the `height` and `width` attributes and allowing the browsers to handle this will work, but only in Internet Explorer. Netscape Navigator displays a small window for the plug-in, cutting off much of the video.

So what's a person to do? Apart from throwing your hands up in complete frustration, writing letters to each company telling them how mad you are, or tossing your computer out the window, if embedding video is important to you, then you can do one of the following two things:

• Pick your poison and ignore how it looks in the other browser.

• Use scripting to "sniff" for the browser type and base your use of `embed` on the visitor's Web browser.

- Use both the object and embed elements for certain file types to provide cross-browser support.

Table 13.1 summarizes the embed attributes supported by Internet Explorer.

Table 13.1 embed Attributes Used in Internet Explorer

Attribute	Description
align	Aligns the element in relation to the Web page. Allowable values are absbottom, absmiddle, baseline, bottom, left, middle, right, texttop, and top.
alt	Provides alternate text.
class	Sets or retrieves the class of the element.
height	The height of the element.
hspace	The horizontal margin around the element.
id	The ID of the element.
name	The name of the element.
src	The source of the media file.
style	Style Sheet declaration.
title	The title of the element.
units	Sets or retrieves the height or width units. Pixels are the default unit of measurement.
vspace	The vertical margin around the element.
width	The width of the element.

Table 13.2 summarizes the embed attributes supported by Netscape Navigator.

Table 13.2 embed Attributes Used in Netscape Navigator

Attribute	Description
src	The file location.
type	The MIME type of the embedded media.
pluginspage	A URL pointing to a Web page that has instructions for installing the required plug-in.
pluginurl	A URL to a Java Archive (JAR) file.
align	Aligns the element in relation to the Web page. Allowable values are left, right, top, and bottom.
border	The width of a border drawn around the element.

13

continues

Table 13.2   continued

Attribute	Description
frameborder	Does not draw a border around the element when set to no.
height	The height of the element.
width	The width of the element.
units	The units used to measure the height and width. Pixels are the default unit of measurement.
hidden	Hides the element when set to true and displays it when set to false, which is the default value.
hspace	The horizontal margin around the element.
vspace	The vertical margin around the element.
name	The name of the plug-in required to play the file.
palette	For use in Windows only. foreground makes the plug-in use the foreground palette, while background (the default) makes the plug-in use the background palette.

In addition to these attributes, additional attributes may be available for specific plug-ins, such as the Macromedia Flash Player.

Finally, you can include the noembed element to provide support for visitors who do not have a Web browser that can display plug-ins.

```
<noembed>This Web page requires a web browser that can display
objects.</noembed>
<embed src="a01607av.avi" height="120" width="160" />
```

Using the object Element

According to the World Wide Web consortium, you should use the object element when embedding sound and video (among other things) in Web pages. This can be problematic, as Netscape Navigator does not fully support object and Internet Explorer is sometime quirky about it.

To use the object element, start with the opening object tag and attributes, as follows:

```
<object data="movie.mpeg" type="application/mpeg">
```

The data attribute indicates the source file for your sound or video, and type is the MIME type of the file.

Next, include any content you want to display, such as a caption, and close the object element with the closing tag, as in the following:

```
<object data="movie.mpeg" type="video/mpeg">
My homemade movie.
</object>
```

You also can cascade objects so that if one cannot be displayed, the browser keeps trying down the list.

```
<object data="movie.mpeg" type="video/mpeg">
    <object data="moviesplash.gif" type="image/gif">
    </object>
My homemade movie.
</object>
```

object also uses the param element to initialize any parameters the embedded file may require. The param element is included in the body of the object element and has no closing tag, as in the following:

```
<object data="movie.mpeg" type="video/mpeg">
    <param name="height" value="120" valuetype="data">
    <param name="width" value="160" valuetype="data">
My homemade movie.
</object>
```

The preceding code sets the height and width of the embedded object to 120×160 pixels. Parameters supplied by the param element are dependent on the type of object you are trying to embed.

Combining embed and object

As you will see in the next few sections, you can often use embed and object simultaneously to provide support for Netscape Navigator and Internet Explorer. To do this, create the object element with any required parameters (the param element), and include the embed element before you enter the closing object tag. The following generic code snippet illustrates how:

```
<object classid="value" codebase="value" height="480" width="512" name="myname">
<param name="src" value="source location" />
<embed src="filename" height="480" width="512" name="myname" />
</object>
```

When Internet Explorer loads the Web page, it will read the object element and use that to embed the multimedia file in the page, ignoring the embed element entirely. Netscape Navigator will use the embed element.

Embedding Flash Animations

Macromedia Flash may be one of the easier types of content to embed in a Web page because you publish the files within the Flash application. Figure 13.10 shows the Macromedia Flash interface used to create Flash files.

13

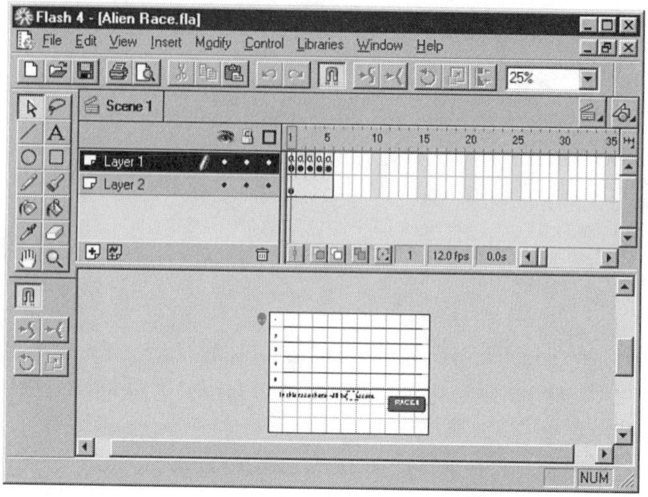

FIGURE 13.10

*Use Macromedia
Flash to create your
Flash files and save
them in Web pages.*

FIGURE 13.10

*Use Macromedia
Flash to create your
Flash files and save
them in Web pages.*

Flash uses HTML templates that are modified by setting the publishing preferences. The
following shows the default template:

```
<OBJECT classid="clsid:D27CDB6E-AE6D-11cf-96B8-444553540000"
 codebase="http://active.macromedia.com/flash2/cabs/swflash.cab#version=4,0,0,0"
 ID=$TI WIDTH=$WI HEIGHT=$HE>
 $PO
<EMBED $PE WIDTH=$WI HEIGHT=$HE
 TYPE="application/x-shockwave-flash"
PLUGINSPAGE="http://www.macromedia.com/shockwave/download/index.cgi?P1_Prod_Vers
ion=ShockwaveFlash">
</EMBED>
</OBJECT>
```

Notice that Flash uses both the object and embed elements to embed the animation in a
Web page. The dollar signs ($) are variables that Flash replaces with your custom prefer-
ences when you publish your file. You can modify the HTML settings through a convenient dialog box shown in Figure 13.11.

Embedding Shockwave Animations

Unless you are using Macromedia Dreamweaver, which automatically inserts the proper
HTML code into your Web page, you will have to input the code manually to embed a
Shockwave file.

To embed a Shockwave file, use a combination of the object element (for Microsoft
support) and the embed element (for Netscape support). You should use both to ensure
maximum compatibility.

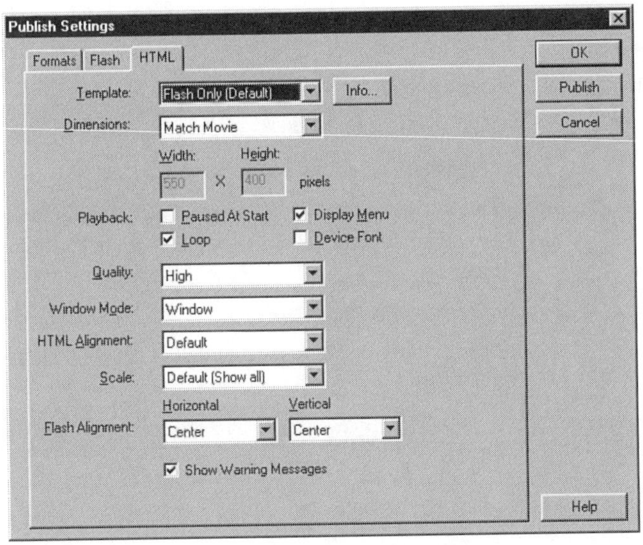

FIGURE 13.11

Flash enables you to publish your animations using an HTML template that is customizable from this dialog box.

For most Shockwave applications, you can enter the code as shown and simply substitute your own values for the location and size of the movie. Other embedded objects may require different information. You should always consult any information from the object retailer or developer for the exact parameters.

The source code for embedding Shockwave files takes the following general form:

```
<OBJECT CLASSID="clsid:166B1BCA-3F9C-11CF-8075-44553540000"
CODEBASE="http://download.macromedia.com/pub/shockwave/cabs/director/sw.cab#vers
ion=7,0,0,0" WIDTH="512" HEIGHT="480" NAME="MovieName">
<PARAM NAME="SRC" VALUE="MYMOVIE.DCR">
<EMBED SRC="MYMOVIE.DCR" HEIGHT=480 WIDTH=512 NAME="MovieName">
</OBJECT>
```

Table 13.3 lists the attributes you can use in the `object` element.

13

Table 13.3 `object` Attributes

Attributes	Description
classid	The universal class identifier for the Shockwave ActiveX Control. It must be set to the following value: `clsid:166B1BCA-3F9C-11CF-8075-444553540000`

codebase	Specifies the download location of the Shockwave control, if not currently installed. It must be set to the following value:
	
	`http://download.macromedia.com/pub/shockwave/cabs/`
	`➥director/sw.cab#version=7,0,0`

continues

Table 13.3   continued

Attributes	Description
width	The width of the Shockwave file (in pixels).
height	The height of the Shockwave file (in pixels).
name	The name of the Shockwave movie (text).
src	This attribute is used in a param element within the object element. The name should be src and the value points to the URL of the movie. Following is the code: `<param name="src" value="URL">`
bgcolor	The background color of box that holds the movie before it appears (hexadecimal number).
swmodifyreport	If true, it removes the src URL from Shockwave statistics collection (true).

Table 13.4 lists the embed attributes.

Table 13.4   embed Attributes

Attribute	Description
width	The width of the Shockwave file (in pixels).
height	The height of the Shockwave file (in pixels).
name	The name of the Shockwave movie (text).
src	The location and name of the movie (URL).
pluginspage	Applies to Netscape Navigator only. The URL of the Shockwave Plug-in. The value should be as follows: `http://www.macromedia.com/shockwave`
bgcolor	The background color of box that holds the movie before it appears (hexadecimal number).
swmodifyreport	If true, it removes the src URL from Shockwave statistics collection (true).

Shockwave files are created in Macromedia Director (see Figure 13.12).

Embedding RealAudio and RealVideo

RealNetworks RealAudio and RealVideo files also use object and embed. Following is the syntax for including the files:

```
<object id="RVOCX" classid="clsid:CFCDAA03-8BE4-11cf-B84B-0020AFBBCCFA"
width="300" height="134">
Optional parameters
```

```
<embed src="source" width="value" height="value" />
<noembed><a href="download page">Play with RealPlayer.</a></noembed>
</object>
```

FIGURE 13.12

Macromedia Director 7 can save movies as Shockwave files.

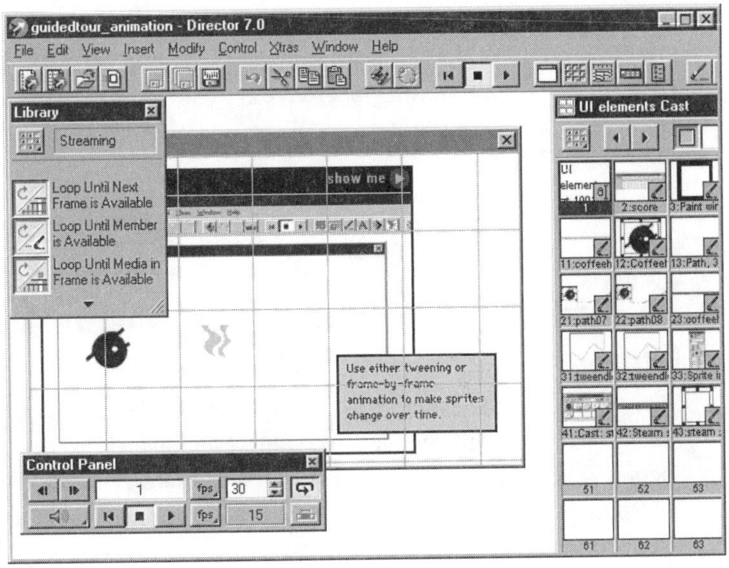

Table 13.5 lists the available attributes for embed and the parameters (<param name="name" value="value" />) for the object element.

Table 13.5 embed Attributes and object Parameters

Attribute/Parameter	Description
autostart	Sets automatic playback (true or false).
backgroundcolor	Sets background color (hexadecimal color value or name).
center	Centers clip in window (true or false).
console	Links multiple controls (yes, name, _master, or _unique).
controls	Adds RealPlayer controls (control name).
height	Sets window or control height (in pixels or percentage).
loop	Loops clips indefinitely (true or false).
maintainaspect	Preserves image aspect ratio (true or false).
nojava	Prevents the Java Virtual Machine from starting (true or false).
nolabels	Suppresses presentation information (true or false).
nologo	Suppresses RealLogo (true or false).

continues

13

Table 13.5   continued

Attribute/Parameter	Description
numloop	Loops clip a given number of times (number).
region	Ties clip to SMIL region (SMIL region).
shuffle	Randomizes playback (true or false).
src	Specifies source clip (URL).
width	Sets window or control width (in pixels or percentage).

You also can use the Web Page Wizard in RealProducer Plus to automatically create Web pages with embedded RealMedia.

Multimedia Techniques Using Microsoft Internet Explorer

Microsoft Internet Explorer offers a few unique capabilities worth mentioning: background sounds and inline video. Note, however, that while Netscape Navigator does not support either of these two techniques, you can safely include them in your Web pages. Navigator will ignore background sounds and you can code inline video in such a way that Navigator will display a static image in place of a video.

Including Background Sounds

Internet Explorer has an element that loads and plays audio files in the background. These sound files load when the page loads into the reader's Web browser and play without the user having to do anything special like starting the audio playback manually. Because no visual effect is created, there will be no indication that a sound is playing unless the users have a sound card and the volume is turned up. To add an embedded background sound to a page, use the bgsound element:

```
<bgsound src="ElevatorMusic.wav" />
```

Use the loop attribute to repeat the sound multiple times. If the value of loop is a number, the sound is played that number of times. If loop is –1 or infinite, the sound will repeat continually, until the reader leaves the page.

```
<bgsound src="ElevatorMusic.wav" loop="-1" />
```

Explorer supports three different formats for inline sounds: Sun's popular AU format, Windows WAV files, and MIDI files with a MID extension.

As with the inline video extensions, covered in the following section, the bgsound element is not supported in Netscape's browsers.

Inline Video with `dynsrc`

You can integrate video clips (AVI or MPEG) into Web pages displayed in Microsoft Internet Explorer 4 and above by using the `dynsrc` attribute in the `img` element, as in the following simple syntax:

```
<img dynsrc="a01607av.avi" loop="2" start="fileopen" />
```

In the previous line of code, Internet Explorer will play the video clip indicated by the `dynsrc` attribute two times after the Web page finishes loading. The `loop` attribute specifies the number of times to play the video clip, with one time being the default value. To play the clip indefinitely, use -1 instead. The `start` attribute defines when the video clip starts playing. You can choose from `fileopen`, which is the default, or `mouseover`, which plays the video when a person moves their mouse over the video.

Because you're using the `img` element, you can use other `img` attributes, such as `alt`, `align`, `border`, `height`, `width`, and so on, to format the video clip.

To make this compatible with Netscape Navigator, you should use the `src` attribute to designate a static GIF or JPG image that will be displayed in place of the video. That code would look like the following:

```
<img src="a01607av.gif" dynsrc="a01607av.avi" loop="2" start="fileopen" />
```

Internet Explorer will ignore the value of the `src` attribute as long as the video supplied by `dynsrc` is valid.

Exercise 13.2: Embedding a QuickTime Movie

For your second exercise, you'll try your hand at embedding a QuickTime movie in a Web page. QuickTime movies are a format created by Apple and are relatively popular, especially with Macintosh users.

According to Apple, you should use the `embed` element to embed QuickTime movies in your Web pages. This is a good example of a company that sponsors a multimedia file type creating additional attributes for you to use.

For starters, create or open a Web page template similar to the following:

```
<!DOCTYPE html PUBLIC "-//W3C//DTD XHTML 1.0 Transitional//EN"
"http://www.w3.org/TR/xhtml1/DTD/transitional.dtd">

<html>
<head>
<title></title>
</head>
<body>

</body>
</html>
```

▼ To Do

13

▼ From here, title the page and add a `div` element that you will use to center everything on the page.

Next, add a heading that appropriately describes the video and a title for the video.

```
<div align="center">
<h1>Apollo 17 Videos</h1>
<p>Astronauts placing the flag on the Moon</p>

</div>
```

Now it's time to add the video itself. Begin with the `embed` element (place it under the video title), and enter the source and size of the video. Remember, those attributes are required.

```
<embed src="Apollo_17_Flag.qt"
       width="160"
       height="136"
```

For this exercise, you will add an assortment of attributes (described in more detail later). Add them under the `height` of the video. Don't forget to close the `embed` tag at the end of your final attribute.

```
       autoplay="false"
       controller="true"
       kioskmode="true
       dontflattenwhensaving
       pluginspage="http://www.apple.com/quicktime/download/" />
```

OK, to see whether this works, test it using your Web browser. When you are satisfied, add a final piece to the page that will show people where to get the QuickTime plug-in, if they need it. Because this is the last element on the page, remember to close the `div` with the end tag.

```
<p>Apple <a href="http://www.apple.com/quicktime">QuickTime</a> is required to
view this movie. <a href="http://www.apple.com/quicktime"><img
src="getquicktime4.gif" border="0" align="absmiddle" width="88" height="31"
/></A></P>
```

When it's all put together, the source code for your Web page looks like the following:

```
<!DOCTYPE html PUBLIC "-//W3C//DTD XHTML 1.0 Transitional//EN"
"http://www.w3.org/TR/xhtml1/DTD/transitional.dtd">

<html>
<head>
<title>Apollo Multimedia Archive</title>
</head>
<body>
```

▼ `<div align="center">`

```
<h1>Apollo 17 Videos</h1>
<p>Astronauts placing the flag on the Moon</p>
<embed src="Apollo_17_Flag.qt"
       width="160"
       height="136"
       autoplay="false"
       controller="true"
       kioskmode="true
       dontflattenwhensaving
       pluginspage="http://www.apple.com/quicktime/download/" />

<p>Apple <a href="http://www.apple.com/quicktime">QuickTime</a> is required to
view this movie. <a href="http://www.apple.com/quicktime"><img
src="getquicktime4.gif" border="0" align="absmiddle" width="88" height="31"
/></A></P>
</div>

</body>
</html>
```

Figure 13.13 shows the result in Internet Explorer.

FIGURE 13.13

Embedded QuickTime movies use special attributes created by Apple.

Embedded video

Player controls

Links to download QuickTime

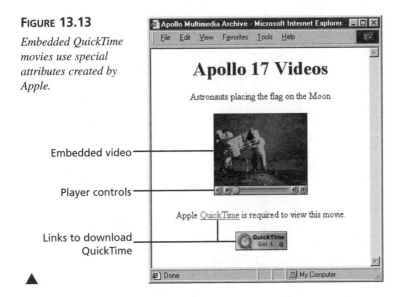

Table 13.6 summarizes the attributes that QuickTime 4 supports.

13

Table 13.6 Attributes Supported by QuickTime 4

Attribute	Description
autoplay	When `true`, plays the movie when the plug-in estimates the clip can be played without waiting for more data (`true` or `false`).
bgcolor	Specifies the background color of any space not taken up by the movie. QuickTime 4 accepts the 16 HTML color names defined by the W3C (hexadecimal color value).
cache	When `true`, the browser caches movies, resulting in the browser replaying a movie from its cache rather than downloading again. Supported by Netscape Navigator 3 and later only (`true` or `false`).
controller	When `true`, makes the movie controller visible. Sixteen pixels should be added to the height of the movie when the controller is shown and the `height` attribute is used (`true` or `false`).
correction	Applicable to QuickTime VR only (`none` or `full`).
dontflattenwhensaving	Saves the move without flattening (no value).
endtime	Defines the last frame of the movie (time in hours:minutes:seconds: frames).
fov	The initial field of view angle for QuickTime VR movies (integer between 8 and 64).
height	Required. Defines the height of the region in which to display the movie. If the movie controller is visible, add 16 to the movie height to reach the total height required (in pixels).
hidden	Hides the movie, and really is only useful for background sound (no value).
hotspotn	Enables hotspots in a VR panorama where *n* is the hotspot ID (URL).
href	Links to another Web page or movie (URL).
kioskmode	When `true`, no pop-up menu is available for the movie and you cannot save it by dragging and dropping it (`true` or `false`).
loop	When `true`, the movie plays in an infinite loop. When set to `palindrome`, the movie will play alternately forward and backward (`true`, `false`, or `palindrome`).
movieid	A numeric ID (integer).
moviename	The movie name (text).
node	Sets the initial node for multinode QuickTime VR movies (integer).
pan	Sets the initial pan angle for QuickTime VR movies (integer from 0 to 360 degrees).

Attribute	Description
playeveryframe	When set to `true`, audio tracks are turned off and every frame of the movie is required to play, even if that forces a slower frame rate (`true` or `false`).
pluginspage	The URL to the QuickTime download page. You should set this to `http://www.apple.com/quicktime/download/`.
qtnextn	Identifies the URL for a movie to load and play when the current movie finishes. The number *n* can be an integer from 1 to 255 and defines the index of the URL in the playlist. The number *nn* is the index of the next `qtnext` URL to load (URL or `gotonn`).
qtsrc	Forces a Web browser to use the QuickTime plug-in. The URL overrides any value in the `src` attribute (URL).
qtsrcchokespeed	Specifies the data rate of a movie, regardless of the actual connection speed (number).
scale	`tofit` scales the movie to the dimensions set by the `height` and `width` attributes. `aspect` scales it to fit this box while maintaining the original aspect ratio of the movie. A number scales the movie by that ratio (`tofit`, `aspect`, or a number).
src	Sets the URL of the movie (URL).
starttime	Sets the first frame of the movie (time in hours:minutes:seconds:frames).
target	Launches the QuickTime Player to play the movie. The `href` attribute must be set to the movie in order for this to work (`quicktimeplayer`).
targetn	Used with `hotspot` and `href`. Sets the target for links that use the `hotspot` or `href` attribute. The number *n* corresponds to the `hotspot` number (name of a valid HTML frame).
targetcache	Caches the movie that is targeted by another movie (`true` or `false`).
tilt	Sets the initial tilt angle for QuickTime VR movies (integer).
type	Defines the MIME type of the movie. If the movie is visible and has `width` and `height` values, `type` must be included. This attribute is supported by Netscape Navigator 2 or later only (MIME type).
volume	Sets the initial audio volume. The default is 100 (integer from 0 to 100).
width	Sets the width of the display area for the movie (in pixels).

13

Sound and Video File Types

I challenge anyone to come up with a complete list of the audio and video formats currently in use on the Web today! There are so many that it defies a comprehensive inspection of the different multimedia files, their extensions, and MIME types. So, I'll just try to cover the most popular, or at least the ones you might be inclined to include in your Web pages.

Before I list them, however, it would be useful for you to understand what factors to consider when choosing a media type. By this, I mean sound or video quality, the size of the final file, how many plug-ins or players are compatible with the file type, and how readily availability the file type is.

The quality of sound and video files depends primarily on the original sampling rate, number of bits used per sample, and the number of channels.

The sampling rate is the number of times per second the sound or video is sampled, or measured. This value is represented in thousands of cycles per second, or kilohertz (KHz). Imagine yourself walking through a room and only being able to open your eyes once every five seconds. Do you see how that might be dangerous? Now imagine yourself opening and closing your eyes every second. You get a much better picture of what is around you and a closer approximation of reality. It's the same with sampling rates: The faster the sample, the closer the sound or video will represent the original recording. The only problem with this is that when you increase the number of times you sample per second, the amount of data quickly becomes voluminous.

The number of bits you use determines the fidelity of the sound. An 8-bit sample, for example, can measure 256 discrete values while 16-bit samples measure more than 65,000 values. The more bits you use, the closer you come to the actual pitch of a sound or the color in a video clip.

The number of channels refers primarily to audio files, where you can have mono (one-channel) recordings, stereo (two-channel), and even more. Having more channels enriches the sound and makes for a more enjoyable experience, but again, at the price of file size.

Five audio file types are in common use on the Web today, each with its own unique advantages and drawbacks.

- Audio Interchange File Format (AIFF) files are uncompressed audio files and are most commonly used in the Macintosh community. The file sizes can be very large.

- Musical Instrument Digital Interface (MIDI) are synthesized rather than recorded sound. The file sizes are small; however, because you can't play back recorded sound, MIDI plays a niche role.

- μ-law (usually pronounced wu-law, also called Basic Sound) is the oldest form of audio on the Internet; however, its sound quality prevents it from being very attractive today. The good news is that the file sizes are small.

- Motion Picture Experts Group (MPEG) Audio offers three types (or layers) of sound files and is very popular because of MPEG's widespread acceptance as an audio and video format. The most recently successful type is MP3 audio, which offers almost CD-quality sound in a very small file size.

- Waveform (WAVE) files originally were created by Microsoft and IBM, and mostly are used on Windows computers.

Table 13.7 summarizes the popular audio formats.

Table 13.7   Common Audio File Formats

Name	Extension(s)	MIME Type
AIFF	AIFF, AIF, AIFC	audio/aiff
μ-law	AU, SND	audio/basic
MIDI	MID, RMI	audio/mid
Waveform (WAVE)	WAV	audio/wav
MPEG Audio	MP2, MP3	audio/x-mpeg

The common video types available are AVI, MPEG, and QuickTime, and are described in the following list:

- AVI, which stands for *Audio/Video Interleaved*, is a very popular Microsoft Windows video format. It is most compatible with Windows computers; however, in the last few years, it has become more accepted in other computing circles.

- MPEG video perhaps is the middleman between AVI and QuickTime and, as such, is very successful.

- QuickTime video is created by Macintosh and, much like AVI, finds the most support in circles that use the operating system of its creator. QuickTime has gained acceptance outside of the Macintosh community, however, so don't be afraid to use it.

Table 13.8 summarizes these video formats.

13

Table 13.8 Common Video File Formats

Name	Extension(s)	MIME Type
Audio/Video Interleaved	AVI	video/x-msvideo
MPEG	MPEG, MPG	video/mpeg
QuickTime	MOV, QT	video/quicktime

Of Plug-Ins and Players

Of all the advances made recently to support more inline multimedia and animation on the Web, plug-ins, over the longer term, will likely have the most significant effect.

Plug-ins are sort of like "built-in" helper applications for your browser. Rather than existing entirely separate from the browser, however, they "plug-in" to your browser (hence, the name) and work internally in conjunction with your browser, adding new capabilities to the browser itself. A video plug-in allows video files to be played directly inline with the browser. Similarly, a spreadsheet plug-in allows editable spreadsheets to be included as elements in a Web page. The plug-ins can enable links back to the browser as well. So, the spreadsheet, for example, could theoretically contain links that could be activated and followed from inside the plug-in.

Netscape introduced the concept of plug-ins with the 2.0 version of its browser, and maintains a current list of them on its site. Several plug-ins are available for many forms of sound and video; in fact, Netscape 4.7 includes sound and video plug-ins already installed, supporting formats such as AU, AIFF, WAV, MIDI, AVI, and QuickTime.

As you learned earlier today, the problem with plug-ins is that if you use them in your Web pages, all your readers will need to have browsers that support plug-ins (such as Netscape or Microsoft Internet Explorer). They must also have the correct plug-in installed and available. (Readers who don't have your plug-in will get empty space or broken icons on your page where the media should be.) To further complicate the matter, many plug-ins are available only for some platforms. For some forms of media, you also might need to configure your server to deliver the new media with the correct type of content.

Windows Media Player

The Windows Media Player, available at www.microsoft.com/windows/mediaplayer, is included as part of the Windows operating system and can play many multimedia file types. Version 6.4, shown in Figure 13.14, currently is shipping with Windows 98 and soon Windows 2000. Users of older versions of Windows (95 and NT 4), however, can download the latest version for free.

FIGURE **13.14**

The Windows Media Player can play AVIs and other popular media formats.

Although version 6.4 is optimized for Microsoft Internet Explorer 4 and above, versions for previous versions of Internet Explorer and other non-Microsoft browsers are available. In addition, a Macintosh version also is available.

Version 6.4 of the Media Player can play the following file types: ASF, WAV, AVI, MOV, MPEG, MIDI, IVF, AIF, VOD, AU, MP3, ID3.

Macromedia Flash

Developed by Macromedia, the Flash player is a popular plug-in that enables you to stream low-bandwidth animations (created with Macromedia Flash) into your Web pages. Flash animations are extremely compact in comparison to "traditional" bitmap animations. The Flash player offers the advantage of streaming the animations as your browser receives them, rather than having to wait for the entire animation to download. For further information, visit the Macromedia Flash Web site at http://www.macromedia.com/flash.

Macromedia Shockwave

Shockwave is a plug-in that enables Macromedia Director movies to be played as inline media on a Web page. Macromedia Director is an extremely popular tool among professional multimedia developers for creating multimedia presentations, including synchronized sound and video as well as interactivity. (In fact, many of the CD-ROMs you can buy today were developed by using Macromedia Director.) If you're used to working with Director, Shockwave provides an easy way to put Director presentations on the Web. Or, if you're looking to do serious multimedia work on the Web or anywhere else, Director is definitely a tool to check out. You can find additional information on Macromedia Shockwave at http://www.macromedia.com/shockwave.

13

QuickTime 4 by Apple

Apple QuickTime 4 is both a file format and a player. The player, available from Apple at www.apple.com/quicktime, plays Apple's QuickTime movies (QT, MOV) and is available for both Macintosh and Windows platforms (see Figure 13.15).

FIGURE 13.15

Use the QuickTime 4 player to play saved or streaming QuickTime movies.

When you install the player, plug-ins for both Internet Explorer and Netscape Navigator are installed.

In addition to playing QuickTime movies, QuickTimeVR (for virtual reality) also is supported. These aren't movies, per se, but interactive 3D video that enables you to move, pan, and zoom to areas of interest in the presentation.

RealNetworks Grab Bag

RealNetworks has two popular players available today for both Windows and Macintosh computers: RealPlayer G2 and RealJukebox (see Figure 13.16).

RealPlayer G2 plays streaming RealAudio and RealVideo files of the following variety:

- RM, RA, RAM—RealAudio/RealVideo streamed content
- RT—Real Text streamed text formats
- RP—RealPix streamed GIF and JPG images
- GIF, JPG—Standalone JPG and GIF images
- MP3—MPEG Layer 3 audio format
- SWF—RealFlash and Shockwave Flash animation
- SMIL, SMI—SMIL-formatted (multiple data type layout) files

- .VIV, .VIVO—Vivo video files
- .MPG, .MPEG—Standard MPEG Layer 1 video and Layer 2 audio formats
- WAV, AU, AIFF—Legacy sound files
- QT, MOV—QuickTime video (uncompressed)
- AVI—Audio/Video Interleave video (Microsoft)
- ASF—Active Streaming Format (Microsoft)
- MID—MIDI sound files

FIGURE 13.16

Use RealPlayer G2 to check out streaming audio and video.

RealNetworks also produces a product called RealJukebox, which is a player that enables you to record and play CDs, download and play music off the Internet, and manage your music collection (see Figure 13.17). File types RealJukebox can encode include RealAudio files as well as MP3, and WAV. RealJukebox can play all the files in the preceding list, as well as Liquid Audio (LQT), A2B, and EMMS files. New formats are scheduled to be added periodically.

Other Plug-Ins

While there isn't enough space to completely cover all the available audio and video plug-ins, following is a short list of some other popular plug-ins.

- mBED, by mBED Software (http://www.mbed.com), is available as a Netscape plug-in as well as an OCX version for Internet Explorer. This plug-in enables you to display animation, sounds, interactive buttons, and synchronized Real Audio.
- Sizzler, by Totally Hip Software (http://www.totallyhip.com/Products/Products.html), enables simultaneous viewing and interaction with Web pages while it streams animation to your browser. You can easily convert popular animations to Sizzler format.

13

- Crescendo, by LiveUpdate (`http://www.liveupdate.com/crescendo.html`), uses a CD-like control panel with transport controls and a digital counter to stream MIDI music into a Web page.
- Beatnik, by Headspace (`http://www.headspace.com`), plays Rich Music Format (RMF) and other sound file formats (`MIDI`, `MOD`, `WAV`, `AIFF`, and `AU`) within Web browsers. The sound comes through in high-fidelity and quality that is comparable to high-end soundcards, and sounds the same across multiple platforms.

FIGURE 13.17

RealJukebox playing a downloaded MP3 audio file.

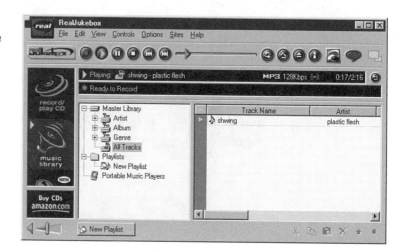

Summary

Well, today's lesson was certainly an eye- and ear-full! You learned that there are only two ways to include audio and video files in your Web pages: linking to them and embedding them.

External media files cannot be read directly by your Web browser. Instead, if you link to an external file, your browser starts up a "helper" application to view or play these files. You also learned how external media works, how to use sound and video files as external media, and some hints for designing by using external media files.

Much of this lesson focused on examples of embedding media files directly into the Web browser. You can use the `embed` element, or a combination of `embed` and `object`.

Table 13.9 shows a summary of the tags you learned about today.

Table 13.9 Tags for Inline Media

Tag	Attribute	Use
`<a>`	href	Links to a a sound or video file exactly as you link to any other type of file.
`<embed>`		Embeds objects into Web pages.
`<object>...<object>`		Embeds objects into Web pages.
`<param>...</param>`		Specifies parameters to be passed to the embedded object. Used in the `object` element.
`<img>`	dynsrc	Includes a sound or video file instead of an image. If the file cannot be found or played, the normal image (in `src`) is shown. Used by Internet Explorer only.
`<bgsound>`		Plays a background sound. Used by Internet Explorer only.

Workshop

The following workshop includes questions you might ask about including sound and video in Web pages, a quiz to test your knowledge, and two quick exercises.

Q&A

Q Help! I'm confused. What do I do?

A Remember that you can use at least one absolutely sure-fire method to include sound and video in your Web ages: link to them. While that may not be as sexy as embedding them in the Web browser window, you know the Web page will work. Of course, the person visiting your site must still have the appropriate application to play the file, but you can help them out by providing links to any required players or plug-ins.

Q Should I be worried about Web browser and HTML compatibility when it comes to audio and video?

A Unfortunately, yes. Most other HTML elements and techniques are standardized to the point that you can be confident that your code will work across most popular Web browsers. Embedding audio and video is a completely different ballgame. My best advice is for you to study up on the different ways to include sound and video, the differences in how the Web browsers embed these files, and then test your Web paged relentlessly in both Microsoft Internet Explorer and Netscape Navigator.

13

Q What are the differences between AVI, MPEG, and QuickTime movies?

A The underlying differences are beyond the scope of this lesson, but it has to do with how the audio and video data is encoded, compressed, and stored in the resulting files. Each file type uses different methods that are all unique. The practical difference is that each one may require a different player to be heard/viewed properly.

Q Should I bother using the techniques solely compatible with Internet Explorer, such as `dynrsrc`?

A My advice is not to bother with them because you may be ignoring (and hence alienating) a good portion of your audience. If you are in an environment that is "IE-only," you can feel free to use them. Ultimately, the choice is up to you.

Quiz

1. What are the differences between a helper application (also called a player) and a plug-in?

2. In what ways can you insert multimedia into your Web pages?

3. What are the advantages and disadvantages of using plug-ins?

4. What is streaming multimedia?

Answers

1. Helper applications run externally to your Web browser and open files that your browser does not support. The browser downloads a file and then passes it on to an external helper application that reads and plays the file. Plug-ins work within the browser to read and play files.

2. You can link to them or embed them.

3. The advantage to using plug-ins is that they enable you to insert many different types of content into your pages. The disadvantage to using them is that you can't guarantee that everyone will have them or want to take the time to download them to experience your site. Some people use browsers that don't support them, and not all plug-ins are universally supported across Web browsers and operating systems.

4. Streaming multimedia doesn't wait to be completely downloaded before it can begin playing.

Exercises

1. Tour the Web and visit sites that use multimedia. See how others include it in their Web sites. Try visiting the same site using Internet Explorer and Netscape Navigator. Is there a difference? What prompts you to download a plug-in?

2. Explore the plug-ins page at Netscape's site (`http://home.netscape.com/plugins/index.html`) to learn more about the wide range of available plug-ins, and which platforms are supported by each of them.

13

Designing Forms

Up to this point, you have learned almost everything you need to know to create functional, attractive, and somewhat interactive Web pages. If you think about it, however, the pages you've created thus far have an information flow that is one-way. Your HTML documents, images, sounds, and video have been traveling, with no return ticket, to the people viewing them in their Web browsers.

Today's lesson is about creating HTML forms in order to collect information from people visiting your Web site. Forms enable you to gather just about any kind of information for immediate processing by a server-side script or for later analysis using other applications. If you've spent much time browsing the Web, you undoubtedly have run across forms of various flavors. Many forms exist: simple forms that perform searches, forms that log you in to Web sites, forms that enable you to order products online, and so on. They all share one thing in common: accepting input from a Web page visitor.

If you're one to worry about compatibility, you can set your mind at ease. HTML forms have been around virtually since the beginning of the HTML language, and are widely supported by all leading Web browsers. I'll make sure to point out any possible compatibility problems along the way.

Don't be intimidated by forms! While they may look complex, they actually are very easy to code. The hardest part is formatting them. In today's lesson, the following topics are covered, which will enable you to create any type of form possible with HTML:

- How HTML forms interact with server-side scripts to provide interactivity
- Creating simple forms to get the hang of it.
- Learning all the types of form controls you can use to create radio buttons, check boxes, and more
- Using more advanced form controls to amaze your friends and coworkers
- Form planning so that your data matches any server-side scripts you use

Understanding Form and Function

Right off the bat, you need to understand a few things about forms. First, a form is part of a Web page that you create using HTML elements. Each form contains a form element that has special controls, such as buttons, text fields, check boxes, submit buttons, and menus. These controls make up the user interface for the form (that is, the pieces of the form users see on the Web page). When people fill out forms, they are interacting with the controls of the forms. In addition, you can use many other HTML elements within forms to create legends, provide additional information, add structure, and so on. These elements are not part of the form itself, but can enhance your form's look or improve its usability.

NEW TERM   An *HTML form* allows you to gather information from a person visiting your Web page. You can take the information you collect and send it to a script residing on your Web server to manipulate or store it.

When a person fills out an HTML form, he or she enters information or makes choices using the form controls. The final step is submitting it, at which time several things happen. First, the form identifies the controls within the form that contain data and builds a form data set to contain it. Next, the data set is encoded and sent to the Web server to be processed.

It is very important that you understand the implications of this final step. The data, after all, is what you are after! This is the reason you've chosen to create a form in the first place. After a user clicks the Submit button, the process ceases to be one of pure HTML and becomes reliant upon scripts (called *Common Gateway Interface*, or *CGI* scripts, most often written in a scripting language called Perl) that are resident on the Web server. In other words, for your form to be successful, you must already have a script on the server that will take the data and store it or manipulate it in some manner.

There are a few important exceptions to this rule. First, a form may redirect a person to another Web page, based on his or her input, or the form sends an email containing the form data to an email address. The second exception is useful and is an easy way for you to test forms. Rather than using a script, you can simply instruct the form to email the contents to you. One final exception is that forms sometimes are used in Dynamic HTML because they trap user events, such as clicking the mouse. A form in a Dynamic Web page may not be used to collect data, but could be used to create buttons from which the user can choose to perform some action.

Exercise 14.1: Creating a Simple Form that Accepts a Name and Password

Okay, let's get right to it and create a simple form that illustrates the concepts just presented.

I've created a Web page that prompts the user to enter a name and a password to continue. Take a peek down at Figure 14.1 to see the Web page.

Start by opening up your favorite HTML editor (mine is Notepad) and creating a Web page template. Begin by entering the standard HTML header information, include the body element, and then close the body and html elements to form a template from which to work. If you already have a template similar to this, just load it into your HTML editor.

> **Note**
>
> I tend to use Transitional HTML and note that in the <!doctype> declaration. This gives me the flexibility of adding deprecated HTML elements if I choose, without having to worry about validation errors.

```
<!DOCTYPE html PUBLIC "-//W3C//DTD XHTML 1.0 Transitional//EN"
"http://www.w3.org/TR/xhtml1/DTD/transitional.dtd">
<html>
<head>
<title>myTitle</title>
</head>
<body>


</body>
</html>
```

Next, add your title so that people will understand the purpose of the Web page.

```
<title>Enter the Wabbit Hole</title>
```

To Do

14

▼ Within the `body` of the Web page, add a `form` element. I have added both the opening and closing tags, with an empty line in between so that I don't forget to close the `form` when I'm finished.

```
<form action="http://www.fakeurl.com/cgi-bin/entrance.cgi" method="post">

</form>
```

Before continuing, you need to know more about the `form` element and the attributes you see within the opening tag. Obviously, `<form` begins the element and indicates that you are creating an HTML form. The `action` attribute, which is required, specifies the URL to the server-side script (including the file name) that will process the form when it is submitted. It is very important that the script with the name you have entered is present on your Web server at the location the URL specifies.

Note

> Prior to "going live" with forms, you should contact your ISP and ask them whether you can use the scripts they have or add your own. You also need to determine the URL that points to the directory in which the scripts reside on the server. Some ISPs rigidly control scripts for security purposes and will not allow you to create or add scripts to the server. If that is the case, and you really need to implement forms on your Web pages, you should consider searching for a new ISP.

The next attribute is `method`, which can accept one of two possible values: `post` or `get`. These values define how form data is submitted to your Web server. The `post` method includes the form data in the body of the form and sends it to the Web server. The `get` method appends the data to the URL specified in the `action` attribute and most often is used in searches.

Now add some form controls and information to make it easy for a visitor to understand how to fill out the form. Within the `form` element, begin by adding a helpful description of the data to be entered by the user, and then add a `text` form control. This prompts them to enter their name in a text-entry field. Don't worry about positioning just yet because later you will put all the form controls into a table.

```
<form action="http://www.fakeurl.com/cgi-bin/entrance.cgi" method="post">
Your wascawy name:<input type="text" name="username" />
</form>
```

Next, add another bit of helpful text and a password control.

```
<form action="http://www.fakeurl.com/cgi-bin/entrance.cgi" method="post">
Your wascawy name:<input type="text" name="username" />
Your just as wascawy password:<input type="password" name="userpassword" />
</form>
```
▼

▼ Notice that both of these form controls are part of the `input` element. The `type` attribute defines which type of control will be created. In this case, you have a text control and a password control. Each type of control looks differently when it appears in a Web browser (such as a text-entry field, button, or check box), accepts a different type of user input (such as entering text or the click of a button), and is suitable for different purposes. Each control also receives a name that distinguishes it and its data from the other form controls. You can use whatever `name` you like, as long as it is unique. (Normally control names must all be different; however, exceptions to this are explained later in this lesson).

Finally, add a `submit` button so that the user can send the information he or she entered into the form. Add a `reset` button that clears the form in case the user made a mistake or wants to start over.

```
<form action="http://www.fakeurl.com/cgi-bin/entrance.cgi" method="post">
Your wascawy name:<input type="text" name="username" />
Your just as wascawy password:<input type="password" name="userpassword" />
<input type="submit" value="Enter" />
<input type="reset" value="Oops!" />
</form>
```

The `submit` and `reset` buttons are another type of `input` element. Notice that I've included the `value` attribute with each. In this case, the `value` attribute modifies the text that is shown in the button and displayed in the Web browser. You can choose not to use the `value` attribute with these buttons. If so, the Web browser will display default text for these two types of buttons.

Note

When naming form controls and labeling buttons, you should strive for clarity and meaning. If a form is frustrating or hard to figure out, the person you want to provide the information most likely will leave your site for greener pastures!

At this point, you have created the form and it is ready to rumble; however, if you load it into your Web browser, you'll see that it doesn't look all that appealing. It's time to add a few graphical elements to make the page look better, and arrange the elements of the form into a nicely aligned table.

I've created three graphics to place at the top of the page and used a `table` to arrange them.

```
<table border="0">
    <tr>
        <td><img src="sign.gif" width="174" height="200" /></td>
```

14

```
        <td align="center"><img src="arrow.gif" width="85" height="100" /><br>
        <img src="hole.gif" width="143" height="58" /></td>
    </tr>
</table>
```

Next, create another `table` and that contains four rows and two columns. You're going to put your `form` in the table to position all the elements.

```
<table border="0">
<tr>
    <td></td>
    <td></td>
</tr>
<tr>
    <td></td>
    <td></td>
</tr>
<tr>
    <td></td>
    <td></td>
<tr>
    <td></td>
    <td></td>
</tr>
</table>
```

Now, add the form elements by inserting the opening `form` tag after the opening `table` tag. Insert the form controls into the rows and columns of the table, as I have shown, making sure not to forget the closing `form` tag.

Notice that I've left the third row of the `table` blank—that's because I'm cheating! After I completed the source code for this example, I wanted a bit more space between the `password` field and the buttons. After a bit of experimentation, I also aligned the text prompts to the right, set each column to take up 50 percent of the total width of the table, and centered the buttons in their respective columns.

```
<table border="0">
    <form action="http://www.fakeurl.com/cgi-bin/entrance.cgi" method="post">
    <tr>
        <td align="right" width="50%">Your wascawy name:</td>
        <td width="50%"><input type="text" name="username" /></td>
    </tr>
    <tr>
        <td align="right">Your just as wascawy password:</td>
        <td><input type="password" name="userpassword" /></td>
    </tr>
    <tr>
        <td></td>
        <td></td>
    </tr>
```

```
▼        <tr>
             <td align="center"><input type="submit" value="Enter" /></td>
             <td align="center"><input type="reset" value="Oops!" /></td>
         </tr>
         </form>
     </table>
```

This looks like it stands a chance of working, so now put all the source code together. A few final notes are warranted. First, I wrapped everything up in a div element, and set the align attribute to center in order to center everything on the page. Note on the page where the opening and closing div tags are located. To add some extra space between the graphics and the form, I also included a line break using the br element.

INPUT

```
<!DOCTYPE html PUBLIC "-//W3C//DTD XHTML 1.0 Transitional//EN"
"http://www.w3.org/TR/xhtml1/DTD/transitional.dtd">
<html>
<head>
<title>Enter the Wabbit Hole</title>
</head>
<body>
<div align="center">
<table border="0">
    <tr>
        <td><img src="sign.gif" width="174" height="200" /></td>
        <td align="center"><img src="arrow.gif" width="85" height="100"
/><br>
        <img src="hole.gif" width="143" height="58" /></td>
    </tr>
</table>
<br>
<table border="0">
    <form action="http://www.fakeurl.com/cgi-bin/entrance.cgi"
method="post">
    <tr>
        <td align="right" width="50%">Your wascawy name:</td>
        <td width="50%"><input type="text" name="username" /></td>
    </tr>
    <tr>
        <td align="right">Your just as wascawy password:</td>
        <td><input type="password" name="userpassword" /></td>
    </tr>
    <tr>
        <td></td> <!-- Comment: left blank to add space -->
        <td></td> <!-- Comment: left blank to add space -->
    </tr>
    <tr>
        <td align="center"><input type="submit" value="Enter" /></td>
        <td align="center"><input type="reset" value="Oops!" /></td>
    </tr>
    </form>
```

14

```
</table>
</div>
</body>
</html>
```

That took a little work, but I think the final product shown in Figure 14.1 looks good.

OUTPUT

FIGURE 14.1

A simple HTML form with four form controls provides access to the Secret Wabbit Hole.

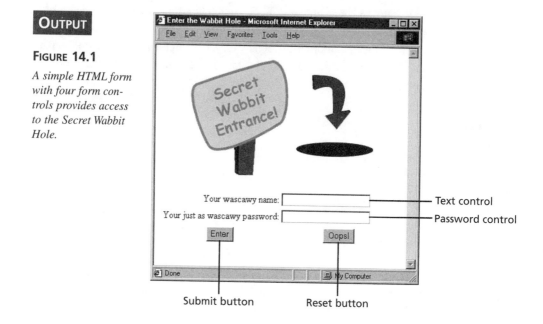

To complete the exercise, I tested the form to see whether it returned the data I wanted. Following is what the data set looks like:

```
username=Elmer&userpassword=hunter
```

It is pretty measly, but you can see that each form element name contains data that I entered into the form and is nicely tied to that data. Using a script, you will find it easy to parse this output, manipulate it, and achieve your overall purpose.

Essential Elements of a Form

After completing the first exercise, you should have picked up a few things: how to use the form element, including simple form controls, and using the submit and reset buttons. This section fully explains and expands upon them. The discussion is divided into two major areas: the form element and the controls created by the input element. After this discussion, you'll walk through a more complicated exercise.

Using the `form` Element to Create Forms

Because the `form` element is the basis for all forms created in Web pages, it is important that you understand how to use it.

First, `forms` are considered *block-level elements*. To understand this, you need to know about the other basic HTML content model: *inline elements*. You apply inline elements, such as `<b>` and `<u>`, to text or individual characters to modify their appearance. As such, they contain the text they modify, such as `<b>I Love this game!</b>`, and can contain other nested inline elements. `<b>I <i>Love</i> this game!</b>` is perfectly valid HTML.

Block-level elements are larger organizational structures (such as the `form` and `table` elements). They can include contain Web page content, inline, as well as other block-level HTML elements. If you display the following HTML in a Web browser, the existence of the nested inline element does not start a new line.

```
<b>Nesting <i>inline</i> elements does not cause a line-break.</b>
```

However, block-level elements such as `form` start a new line in the Web browser. The upshot of all of this is that if you are concerned about the layout of your page, the opening tag of the `form` element will cause a new line to be created. Consider the following code fragment:

NEW TERM   *Inline elements* such as `<b>...</b>` can contain text and other inline elements. *Block-level elements* such as `<div>...</div>` can contain content, other block-level elements, and inline elements. Most block-level elements are displayed on a new line while inline elements do not start a new line.

```
<p>Oatmeal <form action="http://www.fakeurl.com/cgi-bin/register.cgi"
method="post">
lovers wishing to view our private stock of recipes need to enter your name
and password.</p>
```

Placing the `form` tag in its current location causes a new line to be created after `Oatmeal`, resulting in the inappropriate visual effect shown in Figure 14.2.

To sum up thus far, the `form` element causes a new line to be created and the `form` can contain content, inline, and other block-level elements. The one exception to this is that you cannot nest forms—only one form at a time, please!

The syntax for creating the `form` element is fairly straightforward. You most often will use only two attributes—`action` and *method*—of which `action` is mandatory, as in the following code snippet.

```
<form action="someaction" method="get or post">
content, form controls, and other HTML elements
</form>
```

14

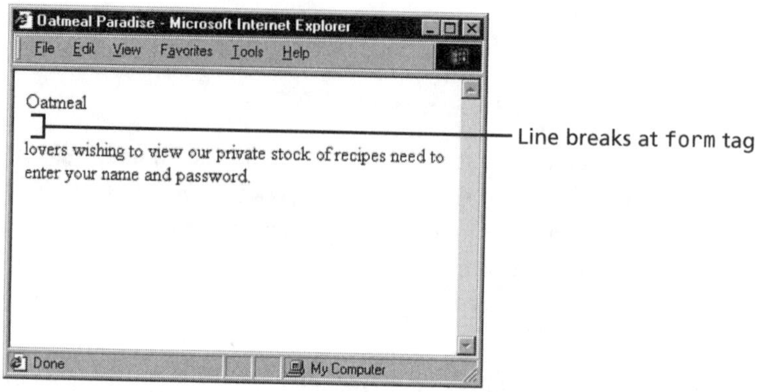

FIGURE 14.2

Placing a form *element within an inline element, such as the paragraph <p>, causes a line break.*

Line breaks at form tag

action defines the action taken when the form is submitted, and generally contains a URL to a CGI script on the Web server. Here again, remember that the script must be in the exact location you specify and working properly for the form to successfully be submitted. Although most forms send their data to scripts, you also can make the action link to another Web page or a mailto link. The latter is formed as follows:

```
<form action="mailto:somebody@isp.com" method="post">
```

This attaches the form data set to an email, which then is sent to the email address listed in the action attribute.

> **Tip**
>
> To test your forms, I recommend using mailto to send yourself the results of your test form. Doing this enables you to debug your form and ensures that you are getting the correct data prior to linking up with a script.

The method attribute can be one of only two possible values: get or post. These values define how the form data provided by the action attribute will be sent to the script. Forms that use get append the form data to the action URL with a question mark, and then send the entire kit-and-caboodle to the modified URL. Sites with search engines normally use this method. If I had a text control named searchstring and had entered Orangutans in the field, the resulting URL might look the following:

```
http://www.fakeurl.com/cgi-bin/search?searchstring=Orangutans
```

Although the method attribute is not required, the default value of get will be used if you omit it.

The other possible value is post. Rather than appending the form data to a URL and sending the combined URL-data string to the server, post simply sends the form data to the location specified by the action attribute.

That about does it for the `form` element, but you've really only just begun. Did you notice that the `form` element, by itself, doesn't do much more than indicate which type of action to take when the form is submitted? To actually gather information, you're going to need items called form controls.

Creating Form Controls with the `input` Element

Now it's time to learn how to create the elements that gather information within a form. The `input` element enables you to create many different types of controls.

NEW TERM *Form controls* are special HTML elements used in a `form` that allow you to gather information from a person viewing your Web page. The information is collected into a data set that is sent to the location of the `action` attribute when the form is submitted.

The `input` element consists of an opening tag with attributes, no other content, and no closing tag.

```
<input attributes />
```

The key point here is choosing the right attributes that will create the type of form control you need. The most important of these is `type`, which defines the control. For all controls, except submit and reset buttons, the `name` attribute is required. The `name` attribute names the control so that data can be assigned to the form control name when sent to the server. The rest of this section describes the different types of controls you can create using the `input` element.

Creating Text Controls

Text controls enable you to gather information from a user in small quantities. This creates a single-line text input field in which users can type information, such as their name or a search term. Unlike other controls, such as radio buttons (that have only two states—on and off) or menu items (that are predefined), text controls give visitors complete freedom to enter any text they desire.

Text controls always are part of an `input` element, which is included in the `form` element. Begin by creating an `input` element and choose `text` as the value for the `type` attribute. Make sure to name your control so that the server script will be able to process the value. Figure 14.3 shows a text control that offers helpful text that describes what you want the user to enter in the control.

```
<p>Enter the name of your pet: <input type="text" name="petname" /></p>
```

You can modify the appearance of text controls by using the `size` attribute. Entering a number sets the width of the text control in characters, as in the following:

```
<input type="text" name="petname" size="15" />
```

14

FIGURE 14.3

Text controls create a single-line text entry field.

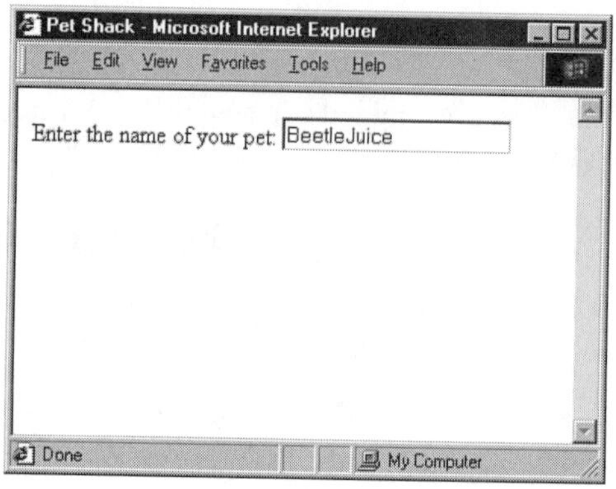

To limit the number of characters a user can enter, add the `maxlength` attribute to the text control. This sets the maximum number of characters the user can enter. If users attempt to enter more text, their Web browser will stop accepting input for that particular control.

```
<input type="text" name="petname" size="15" maxlength="15" />
```

To display text in the text control prior to the user entering information, use the `value` attribute. The `value` attribute can act as a prompt or reminder to the user to enter data, as in the following:

```
<input type="text" name="petname" size="15" maxlength="15" value="Enter Pet
Name" />
```

In this case, `Enter Pet Name` appears in the control when the form is drawn in the Web browser. It remains there until the user modifies it.

> **Tip**
>
> When using the `value` attribute, using a value that is larger than the size of the text control can confuse the user because the text will appear to be cut off. Try to use only enough information to make your point. Ensure that any `value` is less than or equal to the number of characters you specified in `maxlength`.

To make text controls read-only, include the `readonly` attribute, as in the following:

```
<input type="text" name="year" value="1999" readonly />
```

This prevents users from entering text in the text control. It also is useful to establish a constant default for a text control when the form is submitted.

Creating Password Controls

The password control is very similar to the text control in that users enter only a small amount of text in the form. This, however, is a special case because the password control uses asterisks to mask the user's input.

> **Tip**
>
> You don't have to limit your use of the password control to just passwords. You can use it for any sensitive material that you feel needs to be hidden when the user enters the information into the form.

To create a password control, create an input element and assign password to the type attribute. To limit the size of the password control and the maximum number of characters a user can enter, you can use the length and maxlength attributes, as in the following code:

```
<p>Enter your password: <input type="password" name="userpassword"
➥size="8" maxlength="8" /></p>
```

Figure 14.4 shows a password control with some helpful text that describes to the user the purpose of the control.

FIGURE 14.4

Create masked text input fields with password controls.

Note that you do not need to include the value attribute because the value you enter is masked when drawn into the user's Web browser.

14

> **Caution**
>
> Any information sent by a password control is not masked or encrypted in any way; therefore, this is not a secure means of transmitting sensitive information. Although the users can't read what they are typing, the password control has no other inherent security measures.

Creating Submit Buttons

You use the submit button to transmit form data for processing by a server-side script or other program. Entering submit as the type of control creates a submit button that contains the default caption of Submit Query. To change the text shown in the button, use the value attribute and enter your own description, as in the following.

```
<input type="submit" value="Send Form Data" />
```

> **Note**
>
> You can have more than one submit button per form.

Creating Reset Buttons

You use reset buttons to clear the contents of the form and set all the form controls to their initial default values. In most cases, this is the value you specify using the value attribute when you create each control. As with the submit button, you can change the default caption of reset to one of your own choosing by using the value attribute, as in the following:

```
<input type="reset" value="Clear Form" />
```

Creating Check Box Controls

Check boxes enable you to create a control that can be toggled between checked and unchecked, reflecting an on or off state (see Figure 14.5). To create a check box, use the input element and enter checkbox as the type of control. Be sure to include the name attribute so that the script will know to which control the data is assigned, as in the following:

```
<p>Check to receive SPAM e-mail <input type="checkbox" name="spam" /></p>
```

FIGURE 14.5

Check box controls create boxes users check.

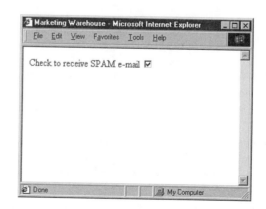

To initially display the check box as checked, include the `checked` attribute, as in the following:

```
<input type="checkbox" name="year" checked />
```

You can group check boxes together and assign the same control name. This allows multiple values to be chosen and applied to one property.

```
<p>Check all symptoms that you are experiencing:<BR />
Nausea <input type="checkbox" name="symptoms" value="nausea" /><br />
Light-headedness <input type="checkbox" name="symptoms" value="lightheadedness"
/><br />
Fever <input type="checkbox" name="symptoms" value="fever" /><br />
Headache <input type="checkbox" name="symptoms" value="headache" /><br />
</p>
```

When this form is submitted to a script for processing, each check box that is checked returns a value associated with the name of the check box.

Creating Radio Buttons

Radio buttons are almost identical to check boxes, but appear differently in the Web browser. Rather than a box that can be checked or unchecked, a small circular (sometimes diamond shaped) button is drawn and filled when the user selects it (see Figure 14.6). You create radio buttons in an `input` element by entering `radio` as the type of control. The `value` attribute, which is mandatory, assigns data to the radio button. When the `form` is submitted, the `value` is sent to the server if the radio button is selected.

```
<p>Do you agree? <input type="radio" name="agree" value="Yes" /></p>
```

FIGURE 14.6

Radio buttons are useful for yes or no questions or choosing one item from a list.

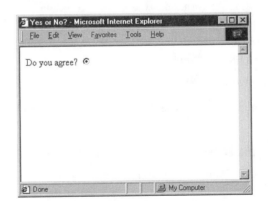

When two or more radio buttons share the same control name, they form a mutually exclusive data set. In other words, only one radio button can be selected. In the following code snippet, both radio buttons have the name of `sex`, which means that the user can

14

select only one. If a user selected Male, realized it was a mistake, and then selected
Female, the Male radio button automatically would then be unselected.

```
<input type="radio" name="sex" value="Male" />
<input type="radio" name="sex" value="Female" />
```

Creating Graphical Buttons

Using image as the type of input control creates a submit button decorated with the
image you choose using the src attribute, as in the following:

```
<input type="image" src="submit.gif" name="submitformbtn" />
```

Figure 14.7 shows a custom button created with an image.

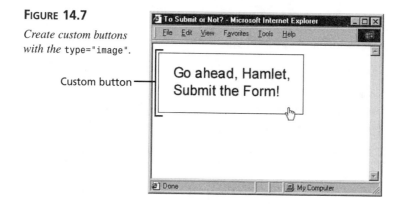

FIGURE 14.7

*Create custom buttons
with the* type="image".

Custom button

In addition to submitting the form data, the x and y coordinates of the point the user
clicked are transmitted to the server. The data is submitted as *name*.x = *x coord* and
name.y = *y coord*, where *name* is the name of the control. Using the preceding code, a
result might look like the following:

```
submitoformbtn.x=150&submitformbtn.y=200
```

You can omit the name, if you choose. In doing so, the coordinates returned would just
be x = and y =.

Creating Push Buttons

In addition to creating submit, reset, and image buttons, you also can create push buttons
that cause client-side scripts to execute when they are enabled. Figure 14.8 shows a button that has a client-side script as the action to take when it is pressed. Use the following
code to create a push button:

```
<input type="button" name="verify" value="verify" onclick="verifydata()" />
```

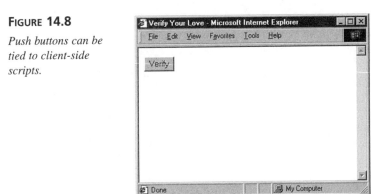

FIGURE 14.8

Push buttons can be tied to client-side scripts.

In this example, a button that runs a script function called `verifydata` when it is clicked is created. You indicate the name that appears in the button with the `value` attribute of `Verify Data`.

Buttons created using this method are more limited than those created by using the `button` element. Don't confuse the two!

Hiding Controls with `hidden`

Hidden controls are special controls that are hidden from and cannot be modified by the user. When the user submits the form, the value assigned to the hidden control is sent along with the other data.

```
<input type="hidden" name="surveynumber" value="1402" />
```

I have seen this technique used most often with surveys where a way to identify the data is required. In this case, I have created a hidden form control named `surveynumber` with a value of `1402`. When the form is submitted for processing, I can identify the form based on this information. When I change the survey tomorrow, I can change the `value` to a different number.

Upload Files with the `file` Select Control

The file select control enables you to enable a person to upload a file along with the form. Figure 14.9 shows a file select control.

```
<p>Please select a file for upload: <input type="file" name="fileupload" /></p>
```

Users can enter a file name (with the path) or choose to browse the contents of their hard drive in order to identify a file to upload. If you use the `value` attribute, you theoretically can specify an initial file name to appear; however, this does not seem to be supported by Microsoft Internet Explorer 5 or Netscape Navigator 4.5.

```
<input type="file" name="fileupload" value="myresume.doc" />
```

14

FIGURE 14.9

Uploading files is easy with the file select control.

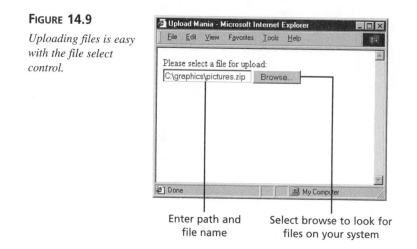

Enter path and
file name

Select browse to look for
files on your system

Exercise 14.2: Creating a Form with Several Types of `input` Controls

It's time for another exercise. For this exercise, you'll work with all the types of controls presented in this section.

To start, open the template you created in Exercise 14.1, and create three `form` templates. You will use the first form for a survey, the second to gain access to a member's area of a fictitious Mime Academy, and the third to search the site. Refer to the following code:

```
<form action="http://www.fakeurl.com/cgi-bin/survey.cgi method="post"
</form>
<form action="http://www.fakeurl.com/cgi-bin/members.cgi method="post"
</form>
<form action="http://www.fakeurl.com/cgi-bin/search.cgi method="get"
</form>
```

Notice that you will be using different scripts for each form, and that the third uses the `get` method.

Now it's time to add form controls to each form. For the survey, you will want to ask a few simple multiple-choice questions. For the first question, use check boxes and assign the same name to them all. Place the text prompt before the `input` element so that it shows up in the browser window to the left of the check box. The following code shows you how:

```
<form action="http://www.fakeurl.com/cgi-bin/survey.cgi method="post"
Take today's survey
I like miming because: (check all that apply)
It's fun<input type="checkbox" name="whyilikeit" value="fun" />
```

```
I meet interesting people<input type="checkbox" name="whyilikeit" value="people"
/>
It's who I am<input type="checkbox" name="whyilikeit" value="personality" />
The money<input type="checkbox" name="whyilikeit" value="money" />
```

The second question for this form is another multiple-choice question, but you only want to accept one answer. For this, use radio buttons that have the same assigned name. Rather than placing the text prompts before the button, place the text prompts after so that they will show up to the right of the buttons. Doing this ensures that the buttons are lined up.

```
The most difficult thing about being a mime is:
<input type="radio" name="difficult" value="makeup" />Putting on the makeup
<input type="radio" name="difficult" value="unitard" />Wearing a spandex unitard
<input type="radio" name="difficult" value="nottalking" />Not talking
```

Next, enter a file select element that enables users to select and upload a file when they submit the survey. Add submit and reset buttons. Finally, in order to track the survey, add a hidden control that is hard-coded to return the value of 061300. By using this hidden control, you can track all survey responses by date and change the control every day. After you add the hidden control, enter the closing form tag.

```
Upload a picture of yourself miming!
<input type="file" name="picture" />
<input type="submit" value="submit" />
<input type="reset" value="reset" />
<input type="hidden" name="surveynumber" value="091899" />
</form>
```

The second and third forms are much easier. The second form involves adding text and password controls for a person's user name and password, and finishes with a submit button. Limit the maximum number of characters that can be entered to 20 and 10 respectively, and then limit the password field 10 characters, as in the following:

```
<form action="http://www.fakeurl.com/cgi-bin/members.cgi method="post">
Enter our Member's Only area!
Username:<input type="text" name="username" maxlength="20" />
Password:<input type="password" name="userpassword" size="10" maxlength="10" />
<input type="submit" value="Submit" />
</form>
```

The final form is simply a text control and an image button. The image button acts as a submit button. It contains a graphic that I've created in place of the normal button face.

```
<form action="http://www.fakeurl.com/cgi-bin/search.cgi method="get">
Search our database<input type="text" name="searchstring" />
<input type="image" src="searchbtn.gif" name="searchbtn" />
</form>
```

14

▼ The forms, form controls, and other information are complete; however, in order for them to look good in an HTML document, you will need to format them.

Note | I have found that formatting my forms after I create them enables me to concentrate on each aspect separately, which produces better results.

The visual appearance of the page divides nicely into five elements: three forms, a title graphic that will appear at the top of the Web page, and another graphic to add interest.

To organize your items on the page, first center the title graphic at the top of the page by using the following code:

```
<!DOCTYPE html PUBLIC "-//W3C//DTD XHTML 1.0 Transitional//EN"
"http://www.w3.org/TR/xhtml1/DTD/transitional.dtd">
<html>
<head>
<title>Anne's Mime Academy</title>
</head>
<body>
<div align="center">
    <img src="welcome.gif" height="35" width="300" />
</div>
```

Moving on to the graphic and forms, notice that two forms are rather short and one is long. Think of the remainder of the page as having two columns in which you can place the two smaller forms, including seating the "interest" graphic on one side and the longer form on the other. How are you going to do this? Tables!

Start by creating a master table that contains two columns and three rows. In the following code, I've commented the role that each row and column of the table will play:

```
<table border="0">
<tr>
    <td></td> <!-- Row 1, Column 1: for the interest graphic -->
    <td></td> <!-- Row 1, Column 2: use for nested table holding the first form
-->
</tr>
<tr>
    <td></td> <!-- Row 2, Column 1: for another nested table and the second form
-->
    <td></td> <!-- Row 2, Column 2: first form continues -->
</tr>
<tr>
    <td></td> <!-- Row 3, Column 1: for the third nested table and third form --
>
    <td></td> <!-- Row 3, Column 2: first form continues -->
</tr>
▼ </table>
```

▼ Now use the following code to add the nested tables:

```
<table border="0">
<tr>
    <td></td> <!-- Row 1, Column 1: for the interest graphic -->
    <td><!-- Row 1, Column 2: use for nested table holding the first form -->
    <table border="0">
        <tr>
            <td></td>
            <td></td>
        </tr>
        <!-- add 12 more table rows here like the previous one -->
    </table>
    </td>
</tr>
<tr>
    <td><!-- Row 2, Column 1: use for nested table holding the second form -->
    <table border="0">
        <tr>
            <td></td>
            <td></td>
        </tr>
        <tr>
            <td></td>
            <td></td>
        </tr>
        <tr>
            <td></td>
            <td></td>
        </tr>
        <tr>
            <td></td>
            <td></td>
        </tr>
    </table>
    </td>
    <td></td> <!-- Row 2, Column 2: first form continues -->
</tr>
<tr>
    <td><!-- Row 3, Column 1: for the third nested table and third form -->
    <table border="0">
        <tr>
            <td></td>
            <td></td>
        </tr>
        <tr>
            <td></td>
            <td></td>
        </tr>
        </form>
    </table>
</tr>
▼ </table>
```

14

▼ Now add all the graphic and form elements to their appropriate locations in the tables and put the entire thing together.

INPUT

```
<!DOCTYPE html PUBLIC "-//W3C//DTD XHTML 1.0 Transitional//EN"
"http://www.w3.org/TR/xhtml1/DTD/transitional.dtd">
<html>
<head>
<title>Anne's Mime Academy</title>
</head>
<body>
<div align="center">
    <img src="welcome.gif" height="35" width="300" />
</div>
<table border="0">
<tr>
    <td align="center"><img src="anne.gif" height="146" width="200"
/></td>
    <td rowspan="3">
    <table border="0" bgcolor="#ffcc33">
        <form action="http://www.fakeurl.com/cgi-bin/survey.cgi"
method="post">
        <tr>
            <td align="center" colspan="2">Take today's survey</td>
            <td></td>
        </tr>
        <tr>
            <td colspan="2">I like miming because: (check all that
apply)</td>
            <td></td>
        </tr>
        <tr>
            <td> </td>
            <td>It's fun<input type="checkbox" name="whyilikeit"
value="fun" /></td>
        </tr>
        <tr>
            <td> </td>
            <td>I meet interesting people<input type="checkbox"
        name="whyilikeit" value="people" /></td>
        </tr>
        <tr>
            <td> </td>
            <td>It's who I am<input type="checkbox" name="whyilikeit"
        value="personality" /></td>
        </tr>
```

▼

```
        <tr>
            <td> </td>
            <td>The money<input type="checkbox" name="whyilikeit"
value="money" /></td>
        </tr>
        <tr>
            <td colspan="2">The most difficult thing about being a mime
is:</td>
            <td></td>
        </tr>
        <tr>
            <td> </td>
            <td><input type="radio" name="difficult" value="makeup" />
        Putting on the makeup</td>
        </tr>
        <tr>
            <td> </td>
            <td><input type="radio" name="difficult" value="unitard" />
        Wearing a spandex unitard</td>
</tr>
        <tr>
            <td> </td>
            <td><input type="radio" name="difficult" value="nottalking"
/>Not talking</td>
        </tr>
        <tr>
            <td colspan="2">Upload a picture of yourself miming!</td>
            <td></td>
        </tr>
        <tr>
            <td></td>
            <td><input type="file" name="picture" /></td>
        </tr>
        <tr>
            <td colspan="2" align="center"><input type="submit"
value="submit" />
        <input type="reset" value="reset" /></td>
            <td></td>
        </tr>
        <input type="hidden" name="surveynumber" value="091899" />
        </form>
    </table>
    </td>
</tr>
```

14

```html
<tr>
    <td valign="top">
    <table border="0" bgcolor="#ffff99" width="100%">
        <form action="http://www.fakeurl.com/cgi-bin/members.cgi"
method="post">
        <tr>
            <td align="center" colspan="2">Enter our Member's Only
area!</td>
            <td></td>
        </tr>
        <tr>
            <td>Username:</td>
            <td><input type="text" name="username" maxlength="20" /></td>
        </tr>
        <tr>
            <td>Password:</td>
            <td><input type="password" name="userpassword" size="10"
maxlength="10" /></td>
        </tr>
        <tr>
            <td align="center" colspan="2"><input type="submit"
value="submit" /></td>
            <td></td>
        </tr>
        </form>
    </table>
    </td>
</tr>
<tr>
    <td>
    <table border="0" width="100%" bgcolor="#ffcccc">
        <form action="http://www.fakeurl.com/cgi-bin/search.cgi"
method="get">
        <tr>
            <td>Search our database</td>
            <td><input type="text" name="searchstring" /></td>
        </tr>
        <tr>
            <td align="center" colspan="2"><input type="image"
        src="searchbtn.gif" name="searchbtn" /></td>
            <td></td>
        </tr>
        </form>
    </table>
    </td>
</tr>
</table>
</body>
</html>
```

▼   Figure 14.10 shows the completed Web page, complete with multiple forms and controls.

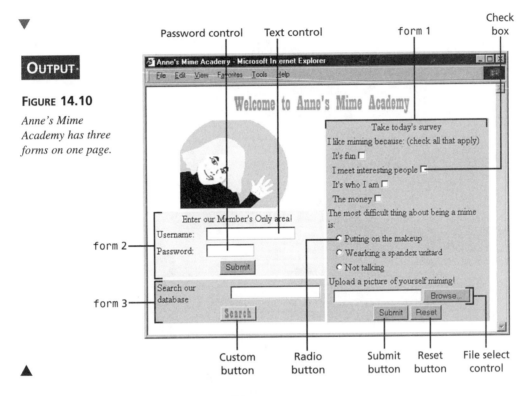

FIGURE 14.10

Anne's Mime Academy has three forms on one page.

Password control   Text control   form 1   Check box

form 2

form 3

Custom button   Radio button   Submit button   Reset button   File select control

Using Other Control Elements

In addition to form controls you can create using the input element, there are three that are elements in and of themselves.

Using the button Element

A button you create using the button element is similar to the buttons you create with the input element, except that these buttons can contain content within the opening and closing tags that actually appear on the buttons.

Note

The button element (as opposed to the input element of type="button") is not supported by Netscape Navigator.

14

You can create three different types of buttons: submit, reset, and custom. To create them, start by entering the opening tag of the button element, followed by the name attribute. The name attribute names the control. Next, enter the type attribute and choose the type of button you want to create. After that, close the opening tag and enter the text you want to appear in the button, and then finish things off with a closing button tag. The following code snippet creates the three types of buttons. Figure 14.11 shows three button elements, each with a different purpose. Note that I've used two line break tags, <br>, to give the buttons some room.

```
<button name="mysubmitbutton" type="submit"><b>Submit</b> Form</button><br /><br
/>
<button name="myresetbutton" type="reset"><u>Clear</u> Form Contents</button><br
/><br />
<button name="mycustombutton" type="button">Verify <code>Data</code></button>
```

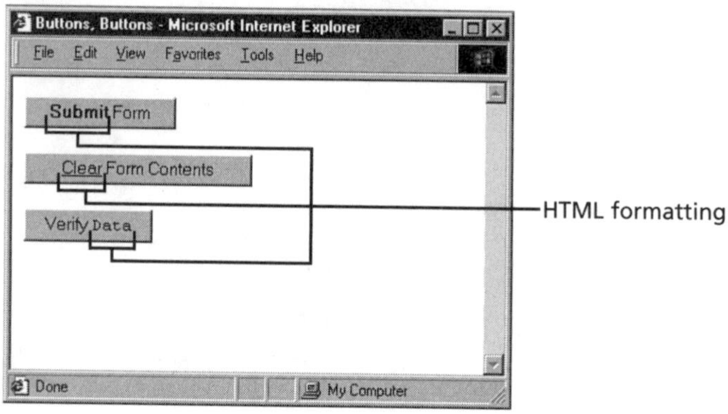

FIGURE 14.11

The button *element enables you to include content and HTML elements inside buttons.*

HTML formatting

Because you can include other HTML element within a button element, the following example is perfectly acceptable:

```
<button name="myresetbutton" type="reset"><b>Clear</b> Form Contents</button>
```

Using the <b> element within the button boldfaces the word Clear.

You also can include images that are displayed as your button. Just enter the <img> element within the contents of the button, as in the following:

```
<button name="mysubmitbutton" type="submit">
➥<img src="customimage.gif" width="50" height="10" /></button>
```

Create Large Text-Entry fields with textarea

The textarea element creates a large text-entry field where people can enter as much information as you allow. To create a textarea control, begin with the opening tag with the element name and then enter the rows and cols attributes before you close the tag. These mandatory attributes define the textarea region by rows and columns. You also can enter a helpful message that will appear in the text-entry field as an initial value. Following this, be sure to include the closing textarea tag. Figure 14.12 shows a textarea element in action.

```
<p>Please comment on our customer service.
<textarea name="question4" rows="10" cols="60">
Enter your answer here
</textarea>
</p>
```

FIGURE 14.12

Use textarea *to create large text-entry areas.*

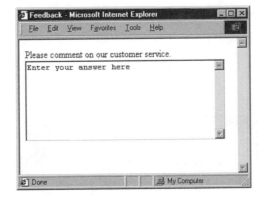

Note

You might be asking, "Where is the isindex element?" The isindex element creates a single-line text entry field much like the text control of the input element, and has been deprecated by the W3C. The syntax is <isindex prompt="Prompt for user input">. While writing this chapter, I tested this in the latest versions of Internet Explorer and Navigator and found that they no longer support isindex, so covering it in detail is not necessary.

Creating Menus with `select` and `option`

The select element creates a menu of choices from which the user can choose, much like the menus found in most software applications. By itself, select doesn't do much more than define how the menu will appear, either as a pull-down menu or scrollable menu. You must include at least one option or optgroup element to create the menus.

To create a pull-down select element with menu choices represented by option elements, start by entering the opening tag followed by a control name:

```
<select name="location">
```

Next, enter your menu items using the option element.

```
<select name="location">
    <option>Indiana</option>
    <option>Fuji</option>
    <option>Timbuktu</option>
    <option>Alaska</option>
```

14

Finally, close the `select` element with the end tag.

```
<p>Please pick a travel destination:
<select name="location">
    <option>Indiana</option>
    <option>Fuji</option>
    <option>Timbuktu</option>
    <option>Alaska</option>
</select>
</p>
```

Figure 14.13 shows a `select` control that creates a pull-down menu that offers four options.

FIGURE 14.13

You can use select *form controls to create pull-down menus.*

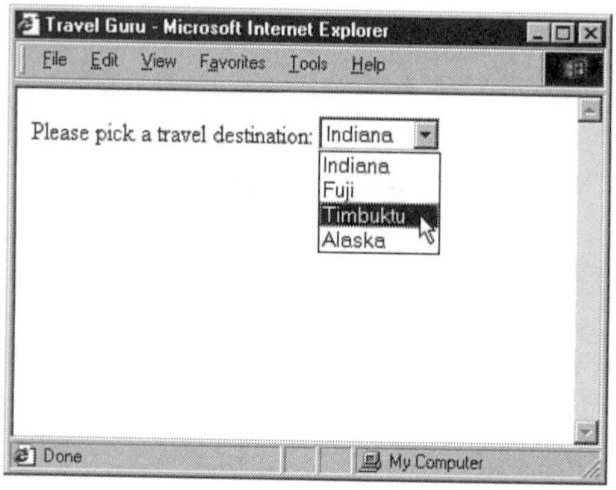

To create a scrollable list of items, just include the `size` attribute in the opening `select` tag, as in the following.

```
<select name="location" size="2">
```

Figure 14.14 shows the same `select` element as Figure 14.13, except that the `size` attribute is set to 2. Notice that it now turns into a scrollable menu.

FIGURE 14.14

You also can create scrollable lists using the select *element.*

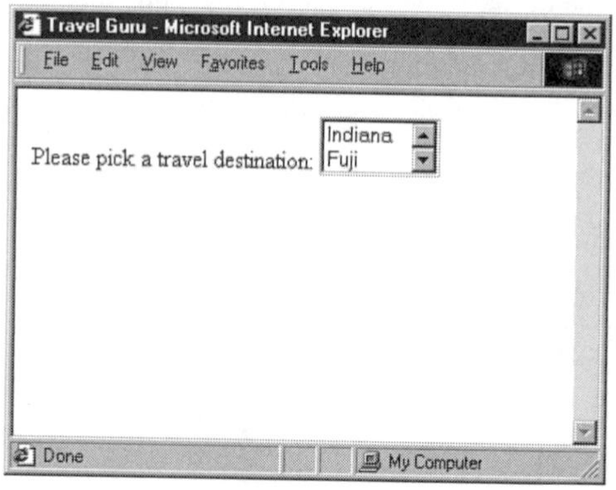

The select element restricts the display area of the scroll menu to two items. Users will need to scroll to see more options.

To send back to the server data other than what is displayed, you can use the value attribute in conjunction with your option elements. This is useful if you are processing the data and want a numerical value or other coded value associated with the menu choice. The following code, for example, causes bw499 to be sent back for Courses instead of Basket Weaving 499.

```
<select name="courses">
    <option value="p101">Programming 101</option>
    <option value="e312">Ecomomics 312</option>
    <option value="pe221">Physical Education 221</option>
    <option value="bw499">Basket Weaving 499</option>
</select>
```

To preselect options, include the selected attribute in an option element, as in the following:

```
<select name="courses">
    <option value="p101">Programming 101</option>
    <option value="e312">Ecomomics 312</option>
    <option value="pe221" SELECTED>Physical Education 221</option>
    <option value="bw499">Basket Weaving 499</option>
</select>
```

This causes the menu to display Physical Education 221 as an initial value.

Thus far, you have created menus in which a user can select only one choice. You can easily change that to multiple choices by including the multiple attribute in the select element, as in the following:

```
<select name="courses" multiple>
```

Note A user can choose multiple options Shift+clicking (for Windows) or Ctrl+clicking or Command+clicking (for Macintosh).

To finish off the creating menus discussion, I want to touch briefly on the optgroup element. Theoretically, this element organizes option components into groups and cascades the menus.

You should place optgroup elements in select elements. The optgroup elements also should contain option elements, as in the following.

14

```
<select name="futility">
    <optgroup label="Mild">
        <option>Swimming upstream</option>
        <option>Shaving with no shaving cream</option>
    </optgroup>
    <optgroup label="Extreme">
        <option>Sqeezing blood from turnips</option>
        <option>Crying over spilled milk</option>
    </optgroup>
</select>
```

Note

Note that the optgroup element is not currently supported by the latest versions of Internet Explorer or Netscape Navigator.

Adding Extras

You've created all the form controls that will accept user input. Now it's time to add functionality and make the controls a bit friendlier.

Displaying Control `labels`

The `label` element displays helpful information for a form control. You should tie the `for` attribute to the control it labels. To create a label, begin with the opening `label` tag and then enter the `for` attribute. The value for this attribute, when present, must match the `id` attribute for the control it is labeling. Next, enter text that will serve as the label, and then close the element with the end `label` tag, as in the following.

```
<label for="control4">Who is your favorite NFL Quarterback?</label>
<input type="text" name="favqb" id="control4" />
```

Note

Although the `label` element is not supported by Netscape Navigator, the contents within the opening and closing `label` tags are displayed.

Figure 14.15 shows this text control with a label assigned to it.

If you define your form control within the `label` element, as shown in the following code, you can omit the `for` attribute:

```
<label>User name: <input type="text" name="username" /></label>
```

FIGURE **14.15**

You can assign labels
*to any form control.
Note that they are
displayed with the
control.*

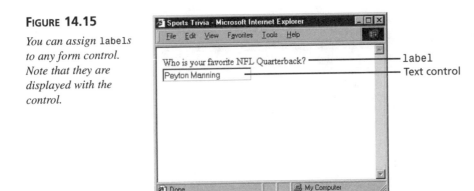

FIGURE **14.15**

You can assign labels
*to any form control.
Note that they are
displayed with the
control.*

Grouping Controls with `fieldset` and `legend`

The `fieldset` element organizes form controls into groupings that appear in the Web browser. The `legend` element displays a caption for the `fieldset`. To create a `fieldset` element, start with the opening `fieldset` tag, followed by the `legend` element, as in the following code:

```
<fieldset>
    <legend>Oatmeal Varieties</legend>
```

Note   Netscape Navigator does not support `fieldset` or `legend`.

Notice that the legend contains text; however, it also could contain inline HTML elements for formatting the text. Next, enter your form controls and finish things off with the closing `fieldset` tag. Figure 14.16 shows the result.

```
<fieldset>
    <legend>Oatmeal Varieties</legend>
    <label>Apple Cinnamon<input type="radio" name="applecinnamon" /></label><br
/>
    <label>Nutty Crunch<input type="radio" name="nuttycrunch" /></label><br />
    <label>Brown Sugar<input type="radio" name="brownsugar" /></label>
</fieldset>
```

14

FIGURE 14.16

The fieldset *and* legend *elements enable you to organize your forms.*

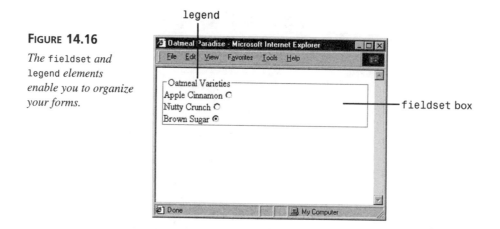

fieldset box

Changing the Default Tabbed Navigation

Using the keyboard to navigate some computer applications makes filling out forms much easier. Tabbed navigation enables users to press the Tab key to move from one form control to the next, in the order that you specify in your form.

> **Note**
>
> Although Netscape Navigator enables you to tab through form controls, you cannot change the order of tabbed navigation with the tabindex attribute.

To enable tabbed navigation, incorporate the tabindex attribute in all the form controls that you want to include this feature. Beginning with 1, order your form controls from start to finish. Controls that have duplicate tabindex values will be accessed in the order they appear in the HTML document. Following is an example of adding the attribute to one control:

```
<p>Enter your name: <input type="text" name="username" tabindex="1" /></p>
```

Using Access Keys

Access keys also make your forms easier to navigate. They assign a character to an element that moves the focus to that element when the users presses a key. To add an access key to a check box, use the following code:

```
<p>What are your interests?</p>
<p>Sports<input type="checkbox" name="sports" accesskey="S"></p>
<p>Music<input type="checkbox" name="music" accesskey="M"></p>
<p>Television<input type="checkbox" name="tv" accesskey="T"></p>
```

Note Unfortunately, Netscape Navigator does not support the use of accesskey. While Internet Explorer does support it, users must press Alt in conjunction with the key in order for it to work. Other operating systems and Web browsers may require a different method.

Creating `disabled` and `readonly` Controls

You sometimes might want to display a form control without enabling your visitors to use the control or enter new information. To disable a control, add the `disabled` attribute to the form control, as in the following:

```
<p>What is the meaning of life?
<textarea name="question42" disabled>
Enter your answer here.
</textarea>
</p>
```

When displayed in a Web browser, the control will appear a light shade of gray, or dimmed, to indicate that it is unavailable. To create a read-only control, use the `readonly` attribute, as in the following example:

```
<p>This month: <input type="text" name="month" value="September" readonly /></p>
```

A read-only control appears normal; however, when visitors attempt to enter new information (or, in the case of buttons or check boxes, select them) they will find that they cannot change the value. Figure 14.17 shows both a disabled control and a read-only control.

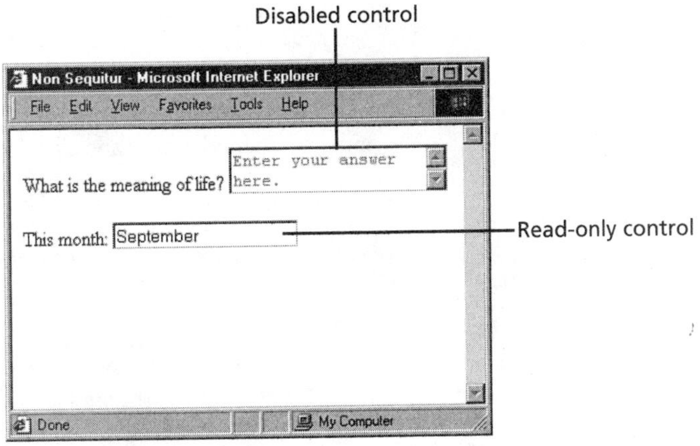

FIGURE 14.17

Disabled controls are dimmed, while read-only controls appear normally—they just can't be changed.

Disabled control

Read-only control

14

> **Note**
>
> Netscape Navigator does not support the `disabled` or `readonly` attributes.

Exercise 14.3: Creating a Form with Advanced Form Control

▼ To Do

Your final exercise for this chapter incorporates the form controls in the previous two sections into one large form in a Matchmaker Web page.

You begin with one large form. Open your template HTML document and create a `form` in the body of the document.

You'll want two major sections in this page: one section that asks questions about the visitor, and the other section that asks what the visitor is looking for in another person. This is perfectly suited for `fieldset` elements.

Create the first `fieldset` element now. Begin with the `form` tag and add a `fieldset` element and `legend`, as in the following:

```
<form action="http://www.fakeurl.com/cgi-bin/match.cgi" method="post">
<fieldset>
    <legend>Tell us about yourself.</legend>
```

Add a `label` for a `select` element, add the `select` element, and enter all the `options`. While you're at it, assign `tabindexes` and `accesskeys` as you go along.

```
    <label for="control1">I have a funny bone that...</label>
     <select name="humor" id="control1" tabindex="1" accesskey="h">
       <option value="-1">Please pick one</option>
       <option value="-1">--------------</option>
       <option value="0">has been removed.</option>
       <option value="1">is my skull.</option>
       <option value="2">is ticklish.</option>
     </select>
```

That wasn't too difficult. Now enter the second `label` and `select` element, as in the following:

```
    <label for="control2">I like to take long walks...</label>
    <select name="walks" id="control2" tabindex="2" accesskey="w">
       <option value="-1">Please pick one</option>
       <option value="-1">-------------</option>
       <option value="Fields">in the corn fields at our farm.</option>
       <option value="Streets">on the streets of my city.</option>
       <option value="Beach">down the hall in my dorm.</option>
       <option value="Apartment">to the refrigerator.</option>
    </select>
```

▼

▼ Complete the `fieldset` by adding a final `label` and a `textarea` control. Be sure to include the closing `fieldset` tag.

```
    <label for="control3">Why should we care?</label>
    <textarea name="mycomments" id="control3" rows="5" cols="30"
tabindex="3"></textarea>
</fieldset>
```

You are almost halfway done. Use the following code to create a second `fieldset` that contains questions about what the visitor is looking for in another person.

```
<fieldset>
    <legend>What are you looking for?</legend>
    <label for="control4">I want...</label>
    <select name="romance" id="control4" size="4" tabindex="4" accesskey="R">
        <option>somebody to watch movies with.</option>
        <option>a serious relationship.</option>
        <option>a Hot-N-Steamy romance.</option>
        <option>someone to clean the catbox.</option>
    </select>
    <label for="control5">Describe your perfect partner.</label>
    <textarea name="lookingfor" id="control5" rows="5" cols="30"
tabindex="5"></textarea>
</fieldset>
```

With your two `fieldsets` complete, add a disabled control and a read-only control to make sure you've covered all your bases.

```
Check if you want to join our club.<input type="checkbox"
➥name="single" checked disabled />
Do you agree to pay us for this service?<input type="text"
➥name="pay" value="yes" readonly />
```

Now add the submit and reset buttons and close the `form` element. Notice that I'm including special graphics for the buttons by using the `button` element.

```
<button name="submit" type="submit" tabindex="6">
<img src="submit.gif" width="60" height="30" />
</button>
<button name="reset" type="reset" tabindex="7">
<img src="reset.gif" width="60" height="30" />
</button>
</form>
```

Now that your form is complete, you can add a title graphic at the top of the page and insert most of your form controls into a `table`. The complete code listing shows the final results.

INPUT

```
<!DOCTYPE html PUBLIC "-//W3C//DTD XHTML 1.0 Transitional//EN"
"http://www.w3.org/TR/xhtml1/DTD/transitional.dtd">
<html>
<head>
```

14

```
<title>Matchmaker Matchmaker</title>
</head>
<body>
<div align="center">
<img src="title.gif" width="300" height="35" />
</div>
<form action="http://www.fakeurl.com/cgi-bin/match.cgi" method="post">
<table border="0" width="100%">
    <tr valign="top">
        <td width="50%">
            <table border="0">
            <tr>
            <td align="center">
            <fieldset>
            <legend>Tell us about yourself.</legend>
            <label for="control1">I have a funny bone that...</label><br
/>
            <select name="humor" id="control1" tabindex="1"
accesskey="H">
                <option value="-1">Please pick one</option>
                <option value="-1">--------------</option>
                <option value="0">has been removed.</option>
                <option value="1">is my skull.</option>
                <option value="2">is ticklish.</option>
            </select>
            <br />
            <label for="control2">I like to take long walks...</label>
            <select name="walks" id="control2" tabindex="2"
accesskey="W">
                <option value="-1">Please pick one</option>
                <option value="-1">-------------</option>
                <option value="Fields">in the corn fields at our
farm.</option>
                <option value="Streets">on the streets of my
city.</option>
                <option value="Beach">down the hall in my dorm.</option>
                <option value="Apartment">to the refrigerator.</option>
            </select>
            <br />
            <label for="control3">Why should we care?</label>
            <br />
            <textarea name="mycomments" id="control3" rows="5" cols="30"
        tabindex="3"></textarea>
            </fieldset>
            </td>
            </tr>
            </table>
        </td>
        <td width="50%">
            <table border="0">
            <tr>
```

```
                    <td align="center">
                    <fieldset>
                    <legend>What are you looking for?</legend>
                    <label for="control4">I want...</label>
                    <br />
                    <select name="romance" id="control4" size="4" tabindex="4"
        accesskey="R">
                        <option>somebody to watch movies with.</option>
                        <option>a serious relationship.</option>
                        <option>a Hot-N-Steamy romance.</option>
                        <option>someone to clean the catbox.</option>
                    </select>
                    <br />
                    <label for="control5">Describe your perfect partner.</label>
                    <textarea name="lookingfor" id="control5" rows="5" cols="30"
            tabindex="5"></textarea>
                    </fieldset>
                    </td>
                    </tr>
                    </table>
            </td>
        </tr>
        <tr>
            <td colspan="2">Check if you want to join our club.<input
type="checkbox"
        name="single" checked disabled /></td>
            <td></td>
        </tr>
        <tr>
            <td colspan="2">Do you agree to pay us for this service?<input
        type="text" name="pay" value="Yes" readonly /></td>
            <td></td>
        </tr>
    </table>
    <div align="center">
    <table border="0">
        <tr>
            <td><button name="submit" type="submit" tabindex="6"><img
src="submit.gif"
        width="60" height="30" /></button></td>
            <td><button name="reset" type="reset" tabindex="7"><img
src="reset.gif"
        width="60" height="30" /></button></td>
        </tr>
    </table>
    </div>
    </form>
    </body>
    </html>
```

▼   Figure 14.18 shows the final product of this exercise.

14

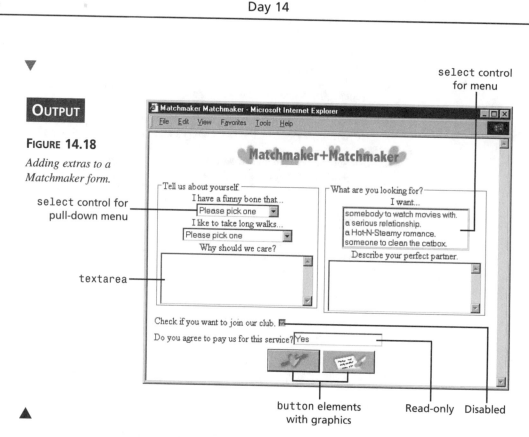

FIGURE 14.18

Adding extras to a Matchmaker form.

select control for pull-down menu

select control for menu

textarea

button elements with graphics

Read-only   Disabled

Planning Your Forms

Before you start creating complex forms for your Web pages, you should do some planning that will save you time and trouble in the long run.

First, decide what information you need to collect. That may sound obvious, but the time to think about this is when you aren't worried about the mechanics of creating the form.

Next, review this information and match each item with a type of form control. Ask yourself which type of control is most suited to the type of questions you are asking. If you need a yes or no answer, radio buttons or check boxes work great, while the textarea element is overkill. Try to make life easier for the person filling out the form by making the type of control fit the question. This way, analyzing the information using a script, if necessary, will be much easier.

You also need to coordinate with the person writing the CGI script to match with variables in the script the names you are going to assign to each control. There isn't much point in naming every control before collaborating with the script author—after all, you will need all the names to match. You also can create look-up tables that contain expansive descriptions and allowable values of each form control.

Finally, you might want to consider validating form input through scripting. If you check the user's input in a client-side script (used *in* the Web page), you can ensure the data you receive when the form is submitted is what you want. You can assign script functions to each form element, including the submit button, using intrinsic events such as onsubmit.

Summary

As you can see, the wonderful world of forms is full of different types of form controls with a person visiting your Web site can interact. This truly is a way to make your Web pages interactive.

Do be cautious, however. Web surfers that are constantly bombarded with forms of one sort or another are likely to get tired of typing and move on to another site. You need to give them a reason for playing!

Table 14.1 summarizes the HTML tags used in this chapter. Remember these points and you can't go wrong:

- Use the form element to create your forms
- Always assign an action to a form
- Create form controls with the input element or the other form control elements
- Test your forms extensively

Table 14.1 HTML Tags from Day 14

Tag	Use
<form>	Creates an HTML form. You can have multiple forms within a document, but you cannot nest the forms.
action	An attribute of <form> that indicates the server-side script (with a URL path) that will process the form data.
method	An attribute of <form> that defines how the form data is sent to the server. Possible values are get and post.
<input>	A <form> element that creates controls for user input.

continues

14

Table 14.1 continued

Tag	Use
type	An attribute of `<input>` that indicates the type of form control. Possible values are `text`, `password`, `submit`, `reset`, `checkbox`, `radio`, `image`, `button`, `hidden`, and `file`, and are shown in the following list:

	`text`	Creates a single-line text entry field.
	`password`	Creates a single-line text entry field that masks user input.
	`submit`	Creates a submit button that sends the form data to a server-side script.
	`reset`	Creates a reset button that resets all form controls to their initial values.
	`checkbox`	Creates a check box.
	`radio`	Creates a radio button.
	`image`	Creates a button from an image.
	`button`	Creates a push button. The three types are submit, reset, and push, with no default action.
	`hidden`	Creates a hidden form control that cannot be seen by the user.
	`file`	Creates a file upload control that enables users to select a file with the form data to upload to the server.

Tag	Use
`<button>`	Creates a button that can have HTML content.
`<textarea>`	A text-entry field with multiple lines.
`<select>`	A menu or scrolling list of items. Individual items are indicated by the `<option>` tag.
`<option>`	Individual items within a `<select>` element.
`<label>`	Creates a label associated with a form control.
`<fieldset>`	Organizes form controls into groups.
`<legend>`	Displays a caption for a `fieldset` element.

Workshop

If you've made it this far, I'm sure you still have a few questions, so I've included a few that I think are interesting. Afterward, test your retention by taking the quiz, and then expand your knowledge by tackling the exercises.

Q&A

Q I want to design a form that later on will be easy to analyze with a spreadsheet or database. How do I design my form to make this easier?

A First, make sure you have a default value for every form control in your form. That will fix the number of data entries and make importing it into a spreadsheet much easier. Don't be afraid to use values that can be manipulated programmatically. For example, I might make every Yes answer to my form a 1 and every No a 0 by using the `value` attributes. Then, when I import the data into my spreadsheet, I can chart and graph responses with 1s and 0s rather than text. You can use many other tricks, such as using lookup tables in your scripts to decode form responses. Experiment with what works best for you and your scripts.

Q I want to create a form and test it, but I don't have the script ready. Is there any way I can make sure the form is sending the right information with a working script?

A I run into this situation all the time! Fortunately, getting around it actually is very easy.

Within the opening `form` tag, modify the `action` attribute and make it a `mailto` link to your email address, as in the following:

```
<FORM ACTION="mailto:youremailaddress@isp.com" METHOD="post>
```

Now you can complete your test form and submit it without having a script ready. When you submit your form, it will be emailed to you as an attachment. Simply open the attachment in a text editor and voilá! Your form data is present.

Q I've heard that HTML 4.01 is under discussion. Will there be any changes to forms?

A HTML 4.01 currently is a Proposed Recommendation before the World Wide Web Consortium and forms have no major changes proposed. Following are those under consideration:

Adding the `name` attribute to the `form` element. This change would be for backward compatibility, enabling you to use the attribute to refer to the form in scripts.

Removing the reference to and example of the `mailto` value of the `action` attribute for the `form` element. It is unclear whether this would eliminate support for this action. The text of the Recommendation indicates that all actions are left up to the Web browser to implement.

Adding the missing `ismap` attribute to the `input` element to provide support for server-side image maps.

14

Adding an explanatory note for the select element, saying that when no option in chosen for a select element, no data is sent to the server for that element when the form is submitted.

Quiz

1. How many forms can you have on a Web page?
2. How do you create form controls such as radio buttons and check boxes?
3. Are passwords sent using a password control secure?
4. Explain the benefit of using hidden form controls.
5. What other technology do forms rely on?

Answers

1. Theoretically, you are limited only to the amount of memory on the client computer; however, you cannot nest forms. Another interesting tidbit is that each form control takes memory. I've run into situations in which I've used all the free memory of a computer by including too many form controls.

2. These form controls are created with the input element and have no life of their own, otherwise.

3. No!

4. Hidden form controls are more for you than the person filling out the form. By using unique value attributes, you can distinguish between different forms that may be sent to the same script or sent at different times.

5. In order for you to process the data forms, they must be paired with a server-side script through the action attribute. These scripts are written in Perl or other scripting languages.

Exercises

1. Check with your Internet Service Provider to see whether they have available scripts that you can use to process your forms. If you can use them, ask how the data is processed and which names you should use in your form controls. If you need to use forms and your ISP won't allow you to use their scripts, you should start looking elsewhere for a place to host your Web site.

2. Think of and visit some sites that might use forms, such as www.fedex.com. Look at which form controls they use, how they arrange them, and peek at the source to see the HTML code.

DAY 15

Using Dynamic HTML

In yesterday's lesson, you learned how to create powerful HTML forms that enable you to gather information from people visiting your Web site. Forms, in one "form" or another, have been around since the virtual birth of HTML and are pretty compatible among browsers. You didn't really need to worry too much about who could or couldn't see your site correctly.

Today's lesson departs from the relatively smooth waters of forms and sets sail toward the rough seas of Dynamic HTML. Batten down the hatches!

Dynamic HTML offers you something unique: the capability to make changes in Web pages on-the-fly. Using conventional HTML, Web pages are loaded by a browser and just sit there until you click a link or interact with forms. That's pretty simple, but can be static and boring.

People have improved upon static Web pages by using a variety of technologies outside the realm of HTML. CGI has been a longtime method of providing interactivity in Web pages. You can embed Shockwave and Flash to create animation and interactivity, and use Java applets or ActiveX controls to provide application-like functions; however, these methods rely on browser plug-ins or virtual machines (which can be messy), and can lead to longer download times.

Dynamic HTML is different. *DHTML*, as it is commonly known, enables you to create Web pages that look, feel, and act a lot like the other programs you use on your computer—using the Web browser as an interface, having to rely on external programming solutions. Can you see the promise of that?

I hope you do, because you'll need that enthusiasm to come to grips with the darker side of DHTML. This side is sometimes, quite frankly, a mess. If you want to appeal to the largest possible audience (within realistic limitations), you must account for differences in Web browsers and how they implement a variety of Web technologies including HTML, Cascading Style Sheets, and scripting.

Today is a "full plate" of information, so let's get right to it. In this lesson, you will learn about the following:

- Defining Dynamic HTML and the technologies that make it possible
- The basics of JavaScript
- Understanding what Document Object Models are
- Creating cross-browser routines with DHTML, such as sniffing for browsers and DOM references
- Creating expandable menus and a neat tic-tac-toe game with DHTML

What Exactly Is Dynamic HTML?

Simply put, Dynamic HTML uses normal HTML elements to create a Web page that relies on style sheets for element formatting, positioning, and scripting to *dynamically* change either HTML content, style, or positioning, without having to *re-download* the page from the server. Dynamic HTML isn't a "thing" by itself, but a collection of technologies working together to achieve interactive effects. So what can you do with DHTML? The possibilities are endless! Just to whet your appetite, here are a few of them:

- Move objects around the Web page
- Show or hide elements
- Create lists that expand or contract when you select an item
- Dynamically alter the color and size of Web content
- Provide drag-and-drop functionality similar to that used by modern graphical operating systems (such as Windows and Macintosh)

Dynamic HTML was born with the advent of the "fours." The World Wide Web Consortium developed HTML 4 and released the official Recommendation at about the same time Microsoft and Netscape released their competing Web browsers, Internet Explorer 4 and Navigator 4. There was a flurry of activity surrounding all this. HTML 4 promoted several new features to better integrate itself with Cascading Style Sheets and respond to user events. Microsoft and Netscape were both competing hard for market-share in the browser war, and the result of it all was a drive for something different: a level of user interactivity and "dynamism" in Web pages that previously was impossible without resorting to external programming. DHTML was born.

NEW TERM *Dynamic HTML* (DHTML) is a collection of Web technologies that increases the interactivity and dynamism of Web pages without resorting to external objects or programs.

For DHTML to work, it requires the following three key technologies supported by the Web browser:

- HTML
- Style sheets
- Scripting

It's obvious that you need to use HTML. Remember, however—HTML 4 has new ele-ments, such as div and span, and new attributes, such as id and style, that enable you to structure and format your content in ways that promote a tighter integration with style sheets and manipulation by scripting. The darker side of this is that even today, not all the leading manufacturers of Web browsers consistently implement HTML 4 in their Web browsers. This will be a common theme throughout this chapter.

Note
> The greatest challenge of Dynamic HTML is to overcome these inconsisten-cies—not just in HTML, but in all DHTML technologies—and create true, cross-browser dynamic Web pages. It *can* be done, but it takes more effort.

Style sheets are wonderful, once you know how to use them, and are a critical compo-nent of DHTML. Although DHTML technically isn't dependent on any one type of style sheet, the official W3C style sheet technology, Cascading Style Sheets (CSS), is the stan-dard. CSS level 2 (CSS2) enables you to format elements on your Web pages using prop-erties, such as font, color, and spacing, as well as positioning items on the Web page. To review CSS, refer to Day 10, "HTML and Style Sheets."

DHTML takes style to a new level. Rather than creating a style rule or positioning an element on the page and then forgetting about it, you can use DHTML to dynamically alter the visual style or position of your elements. As with HTML, there are problems with how Internet Explorer and Netscape Navigator implement CSS. Not only have neither *fully* implemented the specification, but each browser has implemented portions differently. Argh!

Finally, scripting is a sort of "glue" that holds together everything in DHTML. Scripting provides the dynamic nature of DHTML because scripts can run while a page loads, in response to a user action, or even when the user leaves your site.

Caution

If you've caught onto the pattern here, "inconsistent implementation across Web browsers," you should know that this makes referring to and relying on the "official" specification of any one technology dangerous. You should always read any browser-specific documentation you can find to ensure that the Web browsers you are targeting support what you are attempting to accomplish.

The scripting "lingua franca" of today is JavaScript. JavaScript was the first scripting language to be used with the Web, and currently enjoys the most widespread support across different Web browsers. Although you can create DHTML using other scripts, such as VBScript, I recommend always using JavaScript unless you are in a Microsoft-only environment (which I have yet to see in reality).

As you will see when we get to the DHTML examples, a large part of DHTML involves creating scripts that change elements' style, position, and perform other calculations to provide the "D" in DHTML. For this reason, I have included a short introduction to JavaScript, which you will read a bit later. Although you won't learn everything there is to know about JavaScript, you should at least be able to follow along with the examples.

Two final notes about what DHTML actually is. DHTML (the scripting part of it) relies on something called a *Document Object Model* (DOM) to identify, create, and manipulate objects in a Web page. For example, you have to be able to identify an element, such as an image, in order to manipulate it with a script. Likewise, you must be able to identify an element's style in order to change it. This is what the DOM does. It provides a bridge between the content of the Web page and scripts. Although the W3C currently is working on official DOM specifications, each Web browser has a unique DOM; therefore, the DOMs are covered in a separate section later in this chapter.

Finally, DHTML relies on *event handling* to track the actions of the Web browser and user. When the page loads, the onload event is triggered. Likewise, a when visitor clicks a button in a form, several events might be triggered that you, the DHTML author, can use to run scripts. As with everything else in DHTML, Microsoft Internet Explorer and

Netscape Navigator handle events in different fashion. Event handling is covered in more depth later on.

Learning JavaScript

JavaScript is a scripting language originally developed by Netscape and Sun Microsystems (the people who created Java), and was created to solve some of the shortcomings of HTML. Namely, HTML is a document *formatting* language not capable of performing "programming" tasks. Take the following HTML code, for example:

```
<img src="myImage.gif" height="100" width="300" />
```

In this case, the HTML code simply is telling the browser to display an image called myImage.gif on the page in an area 100 pixels high and 300 pixels wide. This is a pretty severe limitation when you think about it. Aside from hyperlinks and form controls, you can't manipulate information, data, objects, or respond to user events.

NEW TERM   *JavaScript* is a scripting language that allows you to write scripts, or small non-compiled programs, that are run by a Web browser from within a Web page.

Scripting languages, in general, and JavaScript, in particular, perform completely a different role than HTML. By their very nature, they are *programming* languages. This means that scripts can perform computations, manipulate objects, and respond to a wide variety of user events. Scripts, for example, perform tasks such as validating HTML form input, responding to mouse and keyboard actions, and dynamically change the position and style of HTML elements.

Unlike formal programming languages, such as C, C++, or Java, scripting languages are not compiled into machine-readable code prior to being executed. They are written in normal text and interpreted by a host rather than executed directly by a CPU. In the case of Web pages, the Web browser acts as the host and interprets scripts within (or referenced by) the Web page while it is loading.

Note   This is an important point worth repeating. Just as some older browsers cannot display many HTML 4 elements, not all browsers can interpret the latest version of JavaScript. Remember, it is the browser that is acting as the script host. You can't force a browser to run scripts it doesn't understand.

JavaScript Basics

Unfortunately, I can't teach you everything there is to know about JavaScript in such a short space. I will, however, try to give you an understanding of how JavaScript works so that you can look through the code in this lesson, and begin to understand what's being done.

Fundamentally, scripts are nothing but a series of statements that tell the script host (the Web browser) what to do. These statements can be simple commands setting variable values, such as the following:

```
var x = 14;
```

or more like the following complex multiline statements, that define functions:

```
function init() {
    if (x == 14) {
        alert(x);
    }
    else {
        alert("X doesn't equal 14");
    }
}
```

Notice that each statement ends in a semicolon (;) and that statements can be grouped together into blocks with curly braces {}. The preceding code uses braces to group statements into a function called init(). The if and else statements each use braces to contain the statements that apply to them.

You can include information within JavaScript scripts that will not be interpreted. These are called *comments*, and are used to explain portions of the script. You create single-line comments by using two forward slashes, //. You can place them at the beginning of a line, such as:

```
// This variable is used to hold temporary information
var x;
```

or you can place them at the end of a statement, such as:

```
var x; // Temporary variable
```

The script interpreter ignores everything after the double forward slashes, so be careful not to comment-out any important code!

You can use single-line comments to create a large comment block, such as:

```
// Script created on 9 Oct 99
// Copyright Sams Publishing
// All rights reserved
```

or use a special multiline comment. Multiline comments are created by entering a forward slash followed by an asterisk (/*) on the first line of the comment, and end with an asterisk and another forward slash (*/). The following example illustrates that type of multiline comment:

```
/* Script created on 9 Oct 99
   Copyright Sams Publishing
   All rights reserved */
```

Variables are one of the most convenient programming tools. They enable you to assign values to placeholders so that you can manipulate the data by referring to the placeholder. To declare a variable, all you need to do is enter var followed by the name of your placeholder, as in the following:

```
var myVariable;
```

> **Note**
>
> JavaScript is case-sensitive. This means that myVariable is different from myvariable and Myvariable.

If you want to declare a variable and immediately store a value in it, the code is a simple as this:

```
var myVariable = 1999;
```

JavaScript also contains operators that enable you to perform mathematical calculations and comparisons. Table 15.1 lists the most common operators and what they do.

Table 15.1   Common Computational and Comparative Operators

| Computational | | Comparative | |
Symbol	Description	Symbol	Description
+	Add	=	Assigns values
.	Subtract	==	Is equal to
*	Multiply	<	Less than
/	Divide	>	Greater than
++	Increment (+1)	<=	Less than or equal
--	Decrement (-1)	>=	Greater than or equal
		!=	Is not equal
		&&	Logical AND
		||	Logical OR

The following code, for example, declares three variables, assigns values to two, and then assigns the sum of the first two to the third:

```
var xPos = 142;
var yPos = 15;
var Pos;
Pos = xPos + yPos;
```

To increment or decrement a value, use those operators with the value or variable, as in the following:

```
Pos++;
```

This statement adds one to the current value of Pos.

To compare values, use the logical operators.

```
if (Pos == 150) {
    anotherFunction();
}
```

This brings me to my next point: *conditional branching*. The if statement is one of the most common conditional statements you can find in JavaScript. Use the if statement to compare one value to another (or perform a whole group of comparisons), and then, based on the result, take action. The previous code compared the variable Pos to 150. If Pos equals 150, then the code within the braces is executed. If Pos does not equal 150, the script continues on as if nothing had happened. If you want to try to catch all the results, use multiple if statements or include the else statement, as in the following code:

```
if ((Pos >= 150) && (Pos <=200)) {
    functionOne();
}
else {
    functionTwo();
}
```

This loop examines the variable Pos against two values: 150 and 200. If Pos is greater than or equal to 150 *and* less than or equal to 200 (in other words, if Pos is from 150–200), then the code branches to the function titled functionOne. If the logical comparison is not true, the else block is executed and functionTwo is called.

NEW TERM   *Conditional branching* creates two or more possible execution paths for a script to take. Conditional statements such as (X > Y) are used to test values and variables and determine the actual path.

When performing calculations or comparisons, parentheses group values or variables and determine the order in which they are interpreted. The following line of code forms a statement where Pos >= 150 and Pos <=200 are each interpreted first, and then the result of each is compared with the logical AND operator.

```
((Pos >= 150) && (Pos <= 200))
```

Likewise,

```
(((156 * 4 / 24) + 99) * 24)
```

15

is interpreted with the help of parentheses. In this case, 156 is multiplied by 4 and the result is divided by 24. That result is added to 99, and finally multiplied by 24. The final calculation results in 3000 (which, by completely accidental happenstance, is a nice round number).

> **Note**
>
> When confronted by multiple levels of parenthetical expressions, work from the inside out. You also should check to make sure that you always have the same number of left parentheses as you do right parentheses.

In addition to performing this task, you also use parentheses when creating a function or calling it from within the script. The parentheses contain parameters or arguments that the function uses to perform its task. The following code illustrates a simple function designed to create an alert box that displays the value of the user variable, which, in this case, is Laura.

```
var user = "Laura";
function alertUser(user) {
    alert(user);
}
```

To call the function, simply enter the function name with the parameter user enclosed in parentheses, as in the following:

```
alertUser(user);
```

Many functions do not have parameters, but they all must have the parentheses. For example, a sample init function listed here takes no parameters when called:

```
function init() {
    createImageArray();
    animateTitle();
}
```

This brings me to my next point: *functions*. Normally, scripts execute from top to bottom, in the order the statements are entered. Functions, however, break this flow and are blocks of code that are only executed when they are called from other parts of the script. Consider the example just listed. The init function stands apart from the script and does not execute until called. Therefore, when writing scripts, use functions to control the flow of execution and respond to unique events.

NEW TERM A *function* is a block of code that is set apart from the script's normal flow of execution. Functions run only when called from other parts of the script or HTML document.

If you haven't guessed by now, you can create functions by using the keyword `function`, followed by the function name. Remember to use the left and right parentheses to enclose any arguments, even if there are none. Following this, enter a left brace, and then input any statements you want the function to execute. To close the function, use a right brace.

You can include conditional statements, such as `if`, and loops within functions, like this:

```
function determinePosition() {
    if ((Pos >= 150) && (Pos <=200)) {
        functionOne();
    }
    else {
        functionTwo();
    }
}
```

Just make sure you have an equal number of opposing braces within the function. In the preceding listing, the `determinePosition` function has a set of braces at the top and bottom. Within the function, the `if` and `else` conditional statements each have a set of braces. It all adds up. There are three left braces and three right braces. If there weren't, you would receive an error when the script was executed.

Thus far, you've learned the basic syntax of JavaScript and some details of the language. Apart from adding a few values together, however, you really don't know how to do much. The missing link is, drum roll please, an *object*. Objects are simply collections of *properties* and *methods*. Think of them as containers that possess information, as well as the means to manipulate it.

NEW TERM   *Objects* are collections of properties and methods, holding information and the means to manipulate it.

Properties describe the object, and methods provide the means to manipulate it with your script. Suppose that you have an object called `Car`. Its properties might be the `color`, `year`, and `value`. You might have a method that calculates its current value based on the depreciation each year. To refer to the object, enter the object name followed by a period, and then include a property. This example sets the `Car` object's color to `blue`.

```
Car.color = "Blue";
```

To invoke a method, simply add the method after the object and property, as in the following code:

```
Car.value.calculate();
```

Because we're discussing scripting for the Web, most of the objects contain properties and methods that relate to the Web browser and HTML document. One of the most important objects is the document object. This object contains information about the HTML document loaded into the Web browser, has methods to respond to user events, and can perform other tasks.

Unfortunately, here's where it gets a bit more complicated. Each Web browser has defined a different set objects that may have different properties and methods. In addition, each browser has a set of *event handlers* that are used to respond to user actions, such as clicking the mouse or pressing a key.

> **Note**
>
> In Netscape Navigator, not all event handlers are available for all objects. You should consult Netscape's JavaScript documentation to see which events can be used for certain objects.

Because objects and events are somewhat problematic across the different browser versions, I will cover those subjects in more depth in following sections. First, however, examine how to integrate your scripts into HTML documents.

Integrating Scripts with HTML

JavaScript, of course, isn't HTML. They are entirely two different languages that perform completely different functions. You can't just throw script statements in your HTML document willy-nilly and expect the browser to automatically know what to do. The first thing you should do is specify a default scripting language in the head of the document, using the meta tag, employing the following statement:

```
<meta http-equiv="Content-Script-Type" content="text/javascript" />
```

Although using the meta tag to perform this function is optional, this statement ensures that the Web browser knows that you are using JavaScript, and, unless told differently, all scripts will be interpreted as such. That distinction is very important because you don't want to leave any doubt for the browser. Now on to including the scripts!

You can include JavaScript scripts in your HTML documents using any of the following three methods:

- Include inline scripts in response to intrinsic events
- Put scripts in the document head or body
- Link to external script files

Intrinsic events occur when something happens to the Web page. The body of the HTML document, for example, has an intrinsic event called onload that occurs when the document is loaded into the Web browser. These events are used as attributes to HTML

elements. The value of the attribute can be a script statement or a series of script statements. The following listing, for example, assigns the `onload` event to the `body` element,
and then executes a single statement that creates an alert box with the included text.

```
<body onload="alert('The page has loaded.')">
```

Note that inline script statements that need to use double quotation marks must use single quotation marks in this setting. The first double quotation mark begins the attribute
value, and the next one it runs across will terminate the value. If you were to mistakenly
enter the following code, the script would end at `alert(`, which obviously is something
you don't want.

```
<body onload="alert("The page has loaded.")">
```

> **Caution**
>
> When it comes to intrinsic events, don't be fooled by the official HTML spec-
> ification. Although the W3C lists a multitude of events that apply to certain
> elements, it is up to the Web browser to implement this functionality.
> Netscape Navigator in particular does not support intrinsic events "across
> the board" as Internet Explorer does. This fact makes DHTML harder when
> coding for Navigator.

You also can use multiple script statements inline when responding to an intrinsic event.
Consider the following code:

```
<body onload="var message = 'The page has loaded'; alert(message)">
```

I have two statements within this small script that respond to the `onload` event. The first
statement declares a variable and assigns a string to it. The second displays an alert box
that contains the message.

The second method for including scripts is to put them in the HTML document `head` or
`body`. To include a script, use the `script` element, and declare the type of script with the
`type` and/or the `language` attribute in the opening `script` tag. Both attributes perform
the same function in that they tell the browser which scripting language you are using.
Although `type` is the official standard, `language` is more commonly used. Because it
doesn't do any harm, I tend to include both.

```
<script type="text/javascript" language="javascript">
```

After the opening tag, enter any script statements you have created, and then close the
`script` element with an end tag.

```
<head>
<title>Sample Script</head>
    <meta http-equiv="Content-Script-Type" content="text/javascript" />
    <script type="text/javascript" language="javascript">
        var message="Hello World";
        alert(message);
    </script>
</head>
```

Although the previous script will run just fine in browsers that are "script compatible," it is common practice to comment out the script statements with HTML comment tags, as follows:

```
<script type="text/javascript" language="javascript">
<!-- Hide JavaScript from older browsers
    var message="Hello World";
    alert(message);
// stop hiding the script -->
</script>
```

Notice the last line of the script. I have included a JavaScript comment to ensure that the JavaScript interpreter does not think it is a line of script. If I ended the script with the following HTML comment, the browser would try to interpret it as JavaScript:

```
stop hiding -->
```

Another technique to ensure backward compatibility is to use the noscript element. This element enables you to include alternate content for browsers that don't support scripting. Begin with the opening noscript tag, and then enter your alternate content. Close the noscript element with an end tag, as in the following:

```
<script type="text/javascript" language="javascript">
<!-- Hide JavaScript from older browsers
    var message="Hello World";
    alert(message);
// stop hiding the script -->
</script>
<noscript>
    <p>You have a browser that is not compatible with scripting.</p>
</noscript>
```

As I stated earlier, you can include scripts in the document head or body. It is important to note that the order in which the scripts appear is the order that they execute. Therefore, a script that appears in the document head will run before one in the body. If you are using functions to control the flow of your script, you can effectively bypass this rule and control script execution based on how you intend it to work.

Finally, you can link to one or more external scripts (saved with a .js extension) by using the src attribute within the script element. The following example illustrates linking to two external scripts:

```
<script type="text/javascript" language="javascript" src="detect.js"></script>
<script type="text/javascript" language="javascript" src="animate.js"></script>
```

By linking to external scripts you can more easily manage common script routines that you use across multiple Web pages.

Now you know how to include scripts in your Web pages! To conclude this section, you should know that JavaScript is currently at version 1.3, but version 1.4 soon will arrive. Table 15.2 summarizes the JavaScript versions supported by Netscape Navigator and Microsoft Internet Explorer.

Table 15.2 JavaScript Versions Supported by Netscape Navigator and Microsoft Internet Explorer

JavaScript	Navigator	Internet Explorer
1.0	2.0*x*	3.0*x*
1.1	3.0*x*	4.0*x*
1.2	4.0-4.05	4.0*x*
1.3	4.06-4.61	5.0*x*
1.4	TBD	TBD

Note

Microsoft Internet Explorer technically does not interpret JavaScript, but a Microsoft script implementation that is based on JavaScript, called *JScript*, does. Don't let this confuse you! You should continue to write your scripts based on the JavaScript documentation.

Using Document Object Models

As mentioned earlier, Microsoft Internet Explorer and Netscape Navigator each have different document object models. Each object in the Web page (and many in the Web browser) contain different properties (that describe them), methods (that manipulate them), and event handlers (to respond to user actions). Next, you briefly will review each browser's model in order to arrive at some similarities.

Note

Fully realizing the capabilities of either DOM requires a depth of knowledge beyond the scope of this book. But, as with other Web-related code, you can learn a lot by cutting and pasting scripts and taking the time to study their results.

The Navigator DOM

Navigator's DOM is synonymous with the DOM presented in the official JavaScript documentation. This can be incredibly confusing when attempting to create cross-browser DHTML because while Internet Explorer interprets JavaScript, it does so in a different DOM context: its own. In other words, be careful when reading official JavaScript documentation. The information contained within applies only to Netscape Navigator.

Aside from a few top-level, predefined JavaScript objects, such as screen, the Navigator DOM is structured like a tree, with the topmost object called window. The window object represents the Web browser window or a frame within the browser. As such, the properties and events of the window object pertain to the Web browser.

Below the window object are several "sub-objects," with some of these branches branching themselves into more objects. The object directly under window that you are most interested in for your purposes today is the document object. The document object is created in Navigator by the HTML body tag, so you don't have to worry about creating it yourself.

Beneath the document object can be a plethora of different objects, each with its own set of properties and methods. Most of the objects you will use are HTML elements, such as images, style sheet objects, and form controls.

You continually will reference the document object and its descendants in DHTML, so it's important to learn how to reference them. When you call on an object in JavaScript, use dotted notation to refer to each object in the DOM hierarchy until you reach your destination. Following, for example, is how a reference to an image named myimage would appear:

```
document.myimage
```

To refer to the properties of the image, simply tack the property onto the end of that statement, as follows:

```
document.myimage.src
```

Perform a simple experiment. Create a Web page that has one image. (You can name it as I have, or use another name. Just be sure to substitute the correct value for the src attribute.) The image is located in the body of your HTML document. Just below the image is a script that will create an alert box that displays the width attribute of the image. For this example, it is important to place the script *after* the image, because the image needs to be loaded in order for the object to be created.

INPUT
```
<!DOCTYPE html PUBLIC "-//W3C//DTD XHTML 1.0 Transitional//EN"
"http://www.w3.org/TR/xhtml1/DTD/transitional.dtd">
<html>
<head>
<title>Netscape Navigator DOM Test</title>
<meta http-equiv="Content-Script-Type" content="text/javascript" />
</head>
<body>

<img id="barnimage" name="barnimage" src="barn.gif" height="100"
width="150" />

<script language="javascript" type="text/javascript">
<!-- Hide JavaScript
alert(document.barnimage.width);
// end hide JavaScript -->
</script>

</body>
</html>
```

Figure 15.1 shows the resulting alert box generated by Netscape Navigator. Notice that the image has yet to appear before the alert box is shown.

OUTPUT

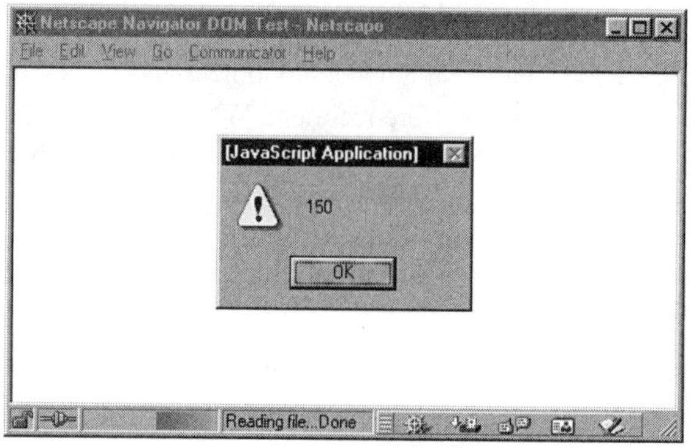

FIGURE 15.1

Accessing the properties of an image through JavaScript and Navigator's DOM.

Accessing other properties of the image is as easy as changing width to some another property, such as src.

To use a method of an object, simply use the method in place of the property, including any values that are required by the method. The following code, for example, uses the write method of the document object to write to the browser window:

```
document.write("Hello world!")
```

Some properties, such as the height of an image, are read-only. This means that you can view the value of the property; however, you cannot change it. Others, especially CSS properties (which are descendants of the object itself), are capable of being modified. To modify an object property, enter the object and property name as you normally would refer to it; however, include an equal sign, and then enter the new value. The following statement, for example, modifies the position of the image object `barnimage` to `150` pixels from the top of the window or previous element, depending on whether the image was positioned absolutely or relatively.

```
document.barnimage.top = "150"
```

One final point about the Navigator DOM is that the objects "under" an object are stored in an *array*. All image objects on a Web page, for example, are stored in the `document.images` property, as an array. The first image is stored in position `0`, with each image following the first. To access the first image in the array, use the following syntax:

```
document.images[0].width
```

Substituting this statement in the preceding image example, which created an alert box, would yield the same value: `150`.

The Internet Explorer DOM

The Internet Explorer (versions 4 and 5) DOM is similar to Navigator's DOM in that each browser creates objects with properties, methods, and events. The differences lie, however, in how they are organized and how you reference them in your scripts.

Internet Explorer has a `document` object much like Navigator's; however, underneath the `document` object, everything is contained in the `all` collection, which literally contains every HTML element on the Web page. When you need to reference an image in Internet Explorer, therefore, the statement would be as follows:

```
document.all.myimage
```

To access a property of method, add it to the end of the previous statement, just as you did with Navigator:

```
document.all.myimage.src
```

Style objects are treated differently in Internet Explorer. All references to style are handled by entering `.style` after the object name, and then entering the style property.

```
document.all.barnimage.style.top
```

You finish off the DOM discussion with the same image example for Internet Explorer that you used for Netscape Navigator.

INPUT

```
<!DOCTYPE html PUBLIC "-//W3C//DTD XHTML 1.0 Transitional//EN"
"http://www.w3.org/TR/xhtml1/DTD/transitional.dtd">
<html>
<head>
<title>Internet Explorer DOM Test</title>
<meta http-equiv="Content-Script-Type" content="text/javascript" />
</head>
<body>

<img id="barnimage" name="barnimage" src="barn.gif" height="100"
width="150" />

<script language="javascript" type="text/javascript">
<!-- Hide JavaScript
alert(document.all.barnimage.width);
// end hide JavaScript -->
</script>

</body>
</html>
```

Figure 15.2 shows the resulting alert box. Notice that in Internet Explorer, the image appears before the alert box is generated.

OUTPUT

FIGURE 15.2

Accessing the properties of an image through JavaScript and Internet Explorer's DOM.

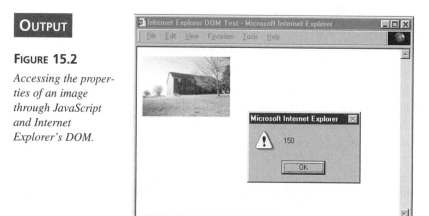

Handling Events

Events occur when the Web browser or user performs an action. The significance of events is that you can create scripts to respond to them. Unfortunately, there are wide differences in the ways Navigator and Internet Explorer track and detect events. In general, Navigator tends to be much more restrictive in the HTML elements that automatically trigger intrinsic events. You can assign many events to almost all elements in Internet Explorer.

> **Note** Because of the number of events and the differences in implementation, it is impossible to completely cover all contingencies in this book. For complete details, refer to Navigator- and Internet Explorer-specific documentation.

15

Another difference in event handling has to do with where the event is first detected, and which direction it travels (up or down) the document object hierarchy. Navigator uses a "trickle down" event model, whereby events are detected at the highest level in the document object model (the `window` object), and travel down the object model tree until an event handler responds to the event. Internet Explorer, not surprisingly, handles events in a completely opposite manner. Rather than trickling down, events in Internet Explorer "bubble up." The event first is detected by the element that generated the event (such as an image or `div` element). The event then moves up the document object chain, until handled or cancelled.

The practical upshot of this is that coding for events is pretty easy in Internet Explorer, but much more difficult in Navigator.

Coping with Reality: Cross-Browser DHTML Techniques

The majority of the chapter thus far has been devoted to understanding the technologies behind DHTML and how to use them separately. It's time to start creating real DHTML Web pages. As I have mentioned, the real challenge is creating DHTML so that you reach the largest possible audience within certain practical limitations. I say "practical" because true DHTML is not possible in any Web browser that doesn't implement scripting or style sheets, and impractical in those that suffer from partial or poor implementations. In other words, using DHTML, you'll never be able to reach 100 percent of all possible people.

The good news is that with a firm understanding of the differences between the leading Web browsers and some creative coding, you can create cross-browser DHTML Web pages that will perform some, or most, of the things you want, using one Web page.

The alternative is to create multiple versions of your Web page, targeted at the different "sects" of the Web browser market. I don't consider this a practical or tidy solution because you will end up multiplying your workload by two, three, four, or more times. Therefore, I will continue to focus on cross-browser DHTML in the sections that follow.

Sniffing for Browsers

The most critical task in creating cross-browser DHTML is detecting the Web browser that loads your page (commonly called *sniffing* for the Web browser). After you perform this task, you can route your scripts to execute functions or statements that are suited to a particular browser.

Don't worry about having to create this all on your own. Netscape has already undertaken this chore and published a comprehensive sniffer on its DevEdge Web site at `http://devedge.netscape.com/tech/dynhtml/index.html`. You can download the complete listing and use it in all your Web pages for free.

I'll use an abbreviated version in this chapter that only detects Netscape Navigator 4 and Microsoft Internet Explorer 4 and up. The following listing creates variables that parse the appropriate objects to return `true` or `false` values for the final variables: `is_nav4up` and `is_ie4up`.

```
// Trimmed down browser sniffer that
// detects Navigator 4+ and IE 4+.
// Reference is_nav4up and is_ie4up in other
// portions of the script
var agt = navigator.userAgent.toLowerCase();
var is_major = parseInt(navigator.appVersion);
var is_minor = parseFloat(navigator.appVersion);
var is_nav  = ((agt.indexOf('mozilla')!=-1) && (agt.indexOf('spoofer')==-1)
            && (agt.indexOf('compatible') == -1) && (agt.indexOf('opera')==-1)
            && (agt.indexOf('webtv')==-1));
var is_nav4up = (is_nav && (is_major >= 4));
var is_ie   = (agt.indexOf("msie") != -1);
var is_ie4up  = (is_ie  && (is_major >= 4));
```

To check for the existence of Netscape Navigator 4 and Microsoft Internet Explorer 4 and later versions, use the following script:

```
if (is_nav4up) {
    do something }
if (is_ie4up) {
    do something else }
```

You'll see that later as you perform some more scripting. The overall browser sniffer function exists solely to return the proper variables to you so that you can check in other portions of your script. By itself, it won't actually take any action.

The following example shows the browser sniffer in action. The body element of the Web page calls the doSniff function, which in turn, creates a variable called sniff and assigns it a string value to display, depending on the browser version it detects.

```
INPUT   <!DOCTYPE html PUBLIC "-//W3C//DTD XHTML 1.0 Transitional//EN"
        "http://www.w3.org/TR/xhtml1/DTD/transitional.dtd">

        <html>
        <head>
        <title>Browser Sniffing</title>
        <meta http-equiv="Content-Script-Type" content="text/javascript" />

        <script language="javascript" type="text/javascript">
        <!-- Hide JavaScript

        // Trimmed down browser sniffer that
        // detects Navigator 4+ and IE 4+.
        // Reference is_nav4up and is_ie4up in other
        // portions of the script
        var agt = navigator.userAgent.toLowerCase();
        var is_major = parseInt(navigator.appVersion);
        var is_minor = parseFloat(navigator.appVersion);
        var is_nav  = ((agt.indexOf('mozilla')!=-1) && (agt.indexOf('spoofer')==-
        1)
                    && (agt.indexOf('compatible') == -1) &&
        (agt.indexOf('opera')==-1)
                    && (agt.indexOf('webtv')==-1));
        var is_nav4up = (is_nav && (is_major >= 4));
        var is_ie   = (agt.indexOf("msie") != -1);
        var is_ie4up  = (is_ie  && (is_major >= 4));


        // Function to display the browser version
        function doSniff() {
            var sniff
            if (is_nav4up == true) {
               sniff = "Netscape Navigator 4+" }
            if (is_ie4up == true) {
               sniff = "Microsoft Internet Explorer 4+" }
            alert(sniff);
        }
        // end hide -->
        </script>
        </head>
        <body onload="doSniff()">
        </body>
        </html>
```

Figure 15.3 shows the result in Internet Explorer 5.

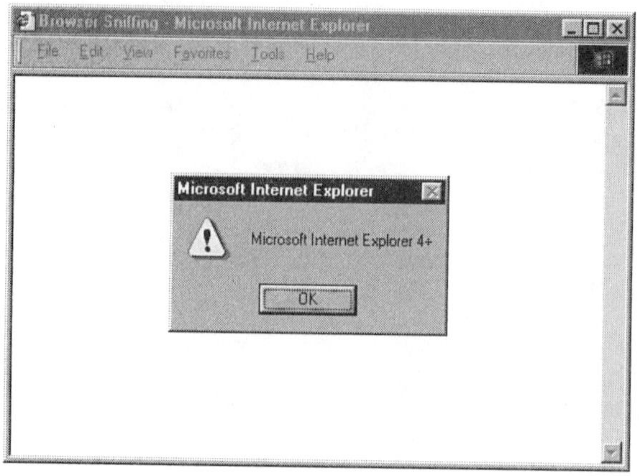

FIGURE 15.3

Sniffing for the Web browser detects the browser version.

Developing a Cross-Browser DOM Reference

Another useful tool to have is the means to automatically reference the correct DOM, depending on the browser. Rather than constantly having to refer to each document object model separately, set up a routing the creates cross-browser terminology. The following code does just that. It uses the objRef and styleRef variables to either hold null values (for Navigator) or .all and .style, respectively, for Internet Explorer. After sniffing for the browser, the variables are set accordingly.

```
// Object and Style Reference conventions
// for Navigator and IE. Use objRef and
// when referring to objects and both when
// accessing style properties.
var objRef, styleRef;
if (is_nav4up == true) {
   objRef = ""
   styleRef = ""
}
if (is_ie4up == true) {
   objRef = ".all"
   styleRef = ".style"
}
```

The following example creates a Web page that uses this logic. After sniffing for the browser, I've included the DOM reference code. Following that, there are two functions that create alert boxes to display the appropriate DOM information for Navigator or Internet Explorer. Within the body of the Web page, there are two div elements to position your text links. The links detect the onmouseover event and trigger the alert functions. Notice that the href attribute of the links is set to javascript:void(0). This is an easy way to use links to trigger functions, without having them link to anything.

INPUT

```
<!DOCTYPE html PUBLIC "-//W3C//DTD XHTML 1.0 Transitional//EN"
"http://www.w3.org/TR/xhtml1/DTD/transitional.dtd">

<html>
<head>
<title>Document Object Model References</title>
<meta http-equiv="Content-Script-Type" content="text/javascript" />

<script language="javascript" type="text/javascript">
<!-- Hide JavaScript

// Trimmed down browser sniffer that
// detects Navigator 4+ and IE 4+.
// Reference is_nav4up and is_ie4up in other
// portions of the script
var agt = navigator.userAgent.toLowerCase();
var is_major = parseInt(navigator.appVersion);
var is_minor = parseFloat(navigator.appVersion);
var is_nav  = ((agt.indexOf('mozilla')!=-1) && (agt.indexOf('spoofer')==-
1)
            && (agt.indexOf('compatible') == -1) &&
(agt.indexOf('opera')==-1)
            && (agt.indexOf('webtv')==-1));
var is_nav4up = (is_nav && (is_major >= 4));
var is_ie   = (agt.indexOf("msie") != -1);
var is_ie4up  = (is_ie  && (is_major >= 4));

// Object and Style Reference conventions
// for Navigator and IE. Use objRef and
// when referring to objects and both when
// accessing style properties.
var objRef, styleRef;
if (is_nav4up == true) {
   objRef = ""
   styleRef = ""
}
if (is_ie4up == true) {
   objRef = ".all"
   styleRef = ".style"
}


function alertstyle() {
   alert(eval("document" + objRef + ".div01" + styleRef + ".top"));
}

function alertobject() {
   alert(eval("document" + objRef + ".div02.id"));
}

// end hide JavaScript -->
```

```
</script>

<style type="text/css">
<!--
#div01 { position: absolute; }
#div02 { position: absolute; }
-->
</style>

</head>

<body>

<div id="div01" style="top: 50; left: 50;">
<a href="javascript:void(0)" onmouseover="alertstyle()">Style Alert</a>
</div>

<div id="div02" style="top: 100; left: 100;">
<a href="javascript:void(0)" onmouseover="alertobject()">Object Alert</a>
</div>

</body>
</html>
```

Figure 15.4 shows the result of your code. Notice that I have the cursor over the element that displays the style.

OUTPUT

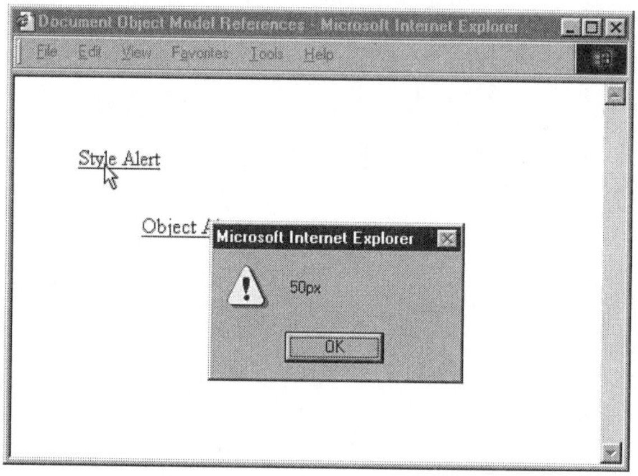

FIGURE 15.4

Using a cross-browser object DOM reference routine.

Without further ado, today's two exercises show you how to sniff for browsers and use that information in your scripts, create image rollovers, show and hide elements, expand menus, and other cross-browser DHTML techniques.

The overall goals of the two exercise are to show you how to perform the following tasks:

- Intertwine HTML, CSS, and JavaScript to achieve useful DHTML effects
- Ensure that your DHMTL pages are cross-browser compatible by checking the browser version, and then using that information in your scripts
- Give you a feel for one method of tackling DHTML
- Show practical examples of DHTML so that you can see the concepts in action, and use them as a foundation for further learning

Exercise 15.1: Creating Expandable Menus

In your first exercise, you will create a powerful, expandable menu Web page that relies on DHTML. When a user clicks an image next to a menu item, the menu will expand, showing submenus with additional content. When users click a menu item, the content will appear in a `div` element in the main area of the browser window. Note that you are not going to use the `table` or `frame` elements to provide structure. Instead, you'll use absolutely positioned `div` elements and modify their visibility. This exercise also uses `style` declarations in the `head` of the document.

First, create a template Web page with all the main structural elements in place and comments where you will add scripting, CSS, and HTML elements.

INPUT

```
<!DOCTYPE html PUBLIC "-//W3C//DTD XHTML 1.0 Transitional//EN"
"http://www.w3.org/TR/xhtml1/DTD/transitional.dtd">

<html>
<head>
<title>Ye old Brick House</title>
<meta http-equiv="Content-Script-Type" content="text/javascript" />

<!-- Most JavaScript will go here -->

<!-- CSS will go here -->

</head>
<body>

<!-- HTML will go here -->

</body>
</html>
```

Next, add the HTML that will form the content of the Web page. Structurally, I've named all top-level menus `toc100` and `toc200`. Each submenu is named according to the menu under which it falls. This makes keeping track of the organization much easier. I'm also using inline scripting to detect whether the element currently is visible, and switching the arrow image after the menu has been expanded.

Finally, I have included the content that will appear for each menu item. Don't worry about it all being visible. You'll set the `visibility` property to `hidden` in your style sheet section.

INPUT

```
<div id="title">
<img src="title.gif" height="100" width="500" />
</div>

<div id="toc0100">
<a href="javascript:void(0)" onclick="menuaction();
    if (show == 1) { document.menuimg.src = ea.src; return true }
    if (show == 0) { document.menuimg.src = ca.src; return true }">
<img id="menuimg" name="menuimg" src="expand.gif" width="10" height="10"
border="0" /></a>
History
</div>

<div id="toc0101">
<a href="javascript:void(0)" onclick="contentID='0101';
showcontent(0101)">The Early Days</a>
</div>

<div id="toc0102">
<a href="javascript:void(0)" onclick="contentID='0102';
showcontent(0101)">The Modern Era</a>
</div>

<div id="toc0200">
<a href="javascript:void(0)" onclick="contentID='0200';
showcontent(0101)">Pictures</a>
</div>

<div id="splash" align="center">
<img src="splash.jpg" height="206" width="300" />
</div>

<div id="content0101">
```

```
<p>This brick house was built in the 1800s. Originally part of a large
farm that consisted of several hundred acres, the house and barn now sit
on a 4 acre plot of land.</p>
</div>

<div id="content0102">
<p>There have been several modifications to the house, such as a
refurbished kitchen, but the exterior is largely as it was in the 1800s.
The barn, on the other hand, has been left unchanged.</p>
</div>

<div id="content0200">
<img src="house.jpg" height="93" width="150" />
<img src="barn.jpg" height="100" width="150" />
<img src="grounds.jpg" height="69" width="150" />
</div>
```

Next, add the CSS code in the head of the document. Use absolute positioning to place each menu item on the page, as well as the title graphic and splash screen. Some experimentation had to be done to figure out just where to place all the elements, but it didn't take too long. Notice that all the submenus and content initially are set to hidden. You'll use scripting to expand the menu and reposition all the elements so that they don't overlap (see Figure 15.5).

INPUT
```
<style type="text/css">
<!--
#title { position: absolute; top: 20; left: 50; }
#splash { position: absolute; top: 150; left: 200; visibility: visible; }
#toc0100 { position: absolute; top: 130; left: 20; visibility: visible; }
#toc0101 { position: absolute; top: 150; left: 50; visibility: hidden; }
#toc0102 { position: absolute; top: 170; left: 50; visibility: hidden; }
#toc0200 { position: absolute; top: 150; left: 20; visibility: visible; }
#content0101 { position: absolute; top: 150; left: 200; visibility:
hidden; }
#content0102 { position: absolute; top: 150; left: 200; visibility:
hidden; }
#content0200 { position: absolute; top: 150; left: 200; visibility:
hidden; }
-->
</style>
```

Now it's time to start scripting. Your first task is to create the global variables that will be used in the script.

OUTPUT

FIGURE 15.5

Expandable menus prior to adding the main script.

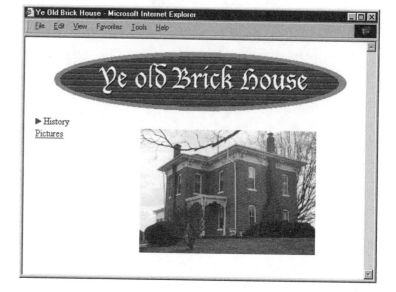

INPUT
```
<script language="javascript" type="text/javascript">
<!-- Hide JavaScript

// Global Variable declarations
// and image creation.
var ea = new Image(10,10); //ea for expand arrow
var ca = new Image(10,10); //ca for contract arrow
ea.src = "expand.gif";
ca.src = "contract.gif";
var show = 1;
var contentID;
```

Next, add the browser sniffer function.

INPUT
```
// Trimmed down browser sniffer that
// detects Navigator 4+ and IE 4+.
// Reference is_nav4up and is_ie4up in other
// portions of the script
var agt = navigator.userAgent.toLowerCase();
var is_major = parseInt(navigator.appVersion);
var is_minor = parseFloat(navigator.appVersion);
var is_nav  = ((agt.indexOf('mozilla')!=-1) && (agt.indexOf('spoofer')==-
1)
            && (agt.indexOf('compatible') == -1) &&
(agt.indexOf('opera')==-1)
            && (agt.indexOf('webtv')==-1));
var is_nav4up = (is_nav && (is_major >= 4));
var is_ie   = (agt.indexOf("msie") != -1);
var is_ie4up
```

▼   Next, add the cross-browser DOM referencing code.

INPUT

```
// Object and Style Reference conventions
// for Navigator and IE. Use objRef and
// when referring to objects and both when
// accessing style properties.
var objRef, styleRef;
if (is_nav4up == true) {   //for Nav these are blank
    objRef = ""
    styleRef = ""
}
if (is_ie4up == true) {  //for IE the are set
    objRef = ".all"
    styleRef = ".style"
}
```

Now to the functions that will do the work. The first function shows, hides, and repositions the menus. Notice that I'm using the DOM reference logic to create this function, without regard to the browser being used.

INPUT

```
// Function to reveal or hide
// sub-menus.
function menuaction() {
    if (show == 1) {
        eval("document" + objRef + ".toc0101" + styleRef + ".visibility =
'visible'");
        eval("document" + objRef + ".toc0102" + styleRef + ".visibility =
'visible'");
        eval("document" + objRef + ".toc0200" + styleRef + ".top =
'190'");
        show = 0;
        return true;
    }
    if (show == 0) {
        eval("document" + objRef + ".toc0101" + styleRef + ".visibility =
'hidden'");
        eval("document" + objRef + ".toc0102" + styleRef + ".visibility =
'hidden'");
        eval("document" + objRef + ".toc0200" + styleRef + ".top =
'150'");
        show = 1;
        return true;
    }
}
```

The next function shows the content. Here again, you need to recognize which elements first need to be hidden in order to clear the space for the content you want to display.

INPUT

```
// Function to hide other content layers
// and reveal the chosen layer.
function showcontent() {
```

▼

```
    if (contentID == "0101") {
        eval("document" + objRef + ".splash" + styleRef + ".visibility =
'hidden'");
        eval("document" + objRef + ".content0102" + styleRef +
".visibility = 'hidden'");
        eval("document" + objRef + ".content0200" + styleRef +
".visibility = 'hidden'");
        eval("document" + objRef + ".content0101" + styleRef +
".visibility = 'visible'");
    }
    if (contentID == "0102") {
        eval("document" + objRef + ".splash" + styleRef + ".visibility =
'hidden'");
        eval("document" + objRef + ".content0101" + styleRef +
".visibility = 'hidden'");
        eval("document" + objRef + ".content0200" + styleRef +
".visibility = 'hidden'");
        eval("document" + objRef + ".content0102" + styleRef +
".visibility = 'visible'");
    }
    if (contentID == "0200") {
        eval("document" + objRef + ".splash" + styleRef + ".visibility =
'hidden'");
        eval("document" + objRef + ".content0101" + styleRef +
".visibility = 'hidden'");
        eval("document" + objRef + ".content0102" + styleRef +
".visibility = 'hidden'");
        eval("document" + objRef + ".content0200" + styleRef +
".visibility = 'visible'");
    }
}
// end hiding -->
</script>
```

The final code listing is presented here:

INPUT

```
<!DOCTYPE html PUBLIC "-//W3C//DTD XHTML 1.0 Transitional//EN"
"http://www.w3.org/TR/xhtml1/DTD/transitional.dtd">

<html>
<head>
<title>Ye old Brick House</title>
<meta http-equiv="Content-Script-Type" content="text/javascript" />

<script language="javascript" type="text/javascript">
<!-- Hide JavaScript

// Global Variable declarations
// and image creation.
var ea = new Image(10,10); //ea for expand arrow
var ca = new Image(10,10); //ca for contract arrow
```

```
ea.src = "expand.gif";
ca.src = "contract.gif";
var show = 1;
var contentID;

// Trimmed down browser sniffer that
// detects Navigator 4+ and IE 4+.
// Reference is_nav4up and is_ie4up in other
// portions of the script
var agt = navigator.userAgent.toLowerCase();
var is_major = parseInt(navigator.appVersion);
var is_minor = parseFloat(navigator.appVersion);
var is_nav  = ((agt.indexOf('mozilla')!=-1) && (agt.indexOf('spoofer')==-
1)
            && (agt.indexOf('compatible') == -1) &&
(agt.indexOf('opera')==-1)
            && (agt.indexOf('webtv')==-1));
var is_nav4up = (is_nav && (is_major >= 4));
var is_ie   = (agt.indexOf("msie") != -1);
var is_ie4up  = (is_ie  && (is_major >= 4));

// Object and Style Reference conventions
// for Navigator and IE. Use objRef and
// when referring to objects and both when
// accessing style properties.
var objRef, styleRef;
if (is_nav4up == true) {    //for Nav these are blank
    objRef = ""
    styleRef = ""
}
if (is_ie4up == true) {  //for IE the are set
    objRef = ".all"
    styleRef = ".style"
}


// Function to reveal or hide
// sub-menus.
function menuaction() {
    if (show == 1) {
        eval("document" + objRef + ".toc0101" + styleRef + ".visibility =
'visible'");
        eval("document" + objRef + ".toc0102" + styleRef + ".visibility =
'visible'");
        eval("document" + objRef + ".toc0200" + styleRef + ".top =
'190'");
        show = 0;
        return true;
    }
    if (show == 0) {
```

```
        eval("document" + objRef + ".toc0101" + styleRef + ".visibility =
'hidden'");
        eval("document" + objRef + ".toc0102" + styleRef + ".visibility =
'hidden'");
        eval("document" + objRef + ".toc0200" + styleRef + ".top =
'150'");
        show = 1;
        return true;
    }
}

// function to hide other content layers
// and reveal the chosen layer.
function showcontent() {
    if (contentID == "0101") {
        eval("document" + objRef + ".splash" + styleRef + ".visibility =
'hidden'");
        eval("document" + objRef + ".content0102" + styleRef +
".visibility = 'hidden'");
        eval("document" + objRef + ".content0200" + styleRef +
".visibility = 'hidden'");
        eval("document" + objRef + ".content0101" + styleRef +
".visibility = 'visible'");
    }
    if (contentID == "0102") {
        eval("document" + objRef + ".splash" + styleRef + ".visibility =
'hidden'");
        eval("document" + objRef + ".content0101" + styleRef +
".visibility = 'hidden'");
        eval("document" + objRef + ".content0200" + styleRef +
".visibility = 'hidden'");
        eval("document" + objRef + ".content0102" + styleRef +
".visibility = 'visible'");
    }
    if (contentID == "0200") {
        eval("document" + objRef + ".splash" + styleRef + ".visibility =
'hidden'");
        eval("document" + objRef + ".content0101" + styleRef +
".visibility = 'hidden'");
        eval("document" + objRef + ".content0102" + styleRef +
".visibility = 'hidden'");
        eval("document" + objRef + ".content0200" + styleRef +
".visibility = 'visible'");
    }
}
// end hiding -->
</script>

<style type="text/css">
<!--
#title { position: absolute; top: 20; left: 50; }
```

```
#splash { position: absolute; top: 150; left: 200; visibility: visible; }
#toc0100 { position: absolute; top: 130; left: 20; visibility: visible; }
#toc0101 { position: absolute; top: 150; left: 50; visibility: hidden; }
#toc0102 { position: absolute; top: 170; left: 50; visibility: hidden; }
#toc0200 { position: absolute; top: 150; left: 20; visibility: visible; }
#content0101 { position: absolute; top: 150; left: 200; visibility:
hidden; }
#content0102 { position: absolute; top: 150; left: 200; visibility:
hidden; }
#content0200 { position: absolute; top: 150; left: 200; visibility:
hidden; }
-->
</style>
</head>

<body>

<div id="title">
<img src="title.gif" height="100" width="500" />
</div>

<div id="toc0100">
<a href="javascript:void(0)" onclick="menuaction();
    if (show == 1) { document.menuimg.src = ea.src; return true }
    if (show == 0) { document.menuimg.src = ca.src; return true }">
<img id="menuimg" name="menuimg" src="expand.gif" width="10" height="10"
border="0" /></a>
History
</div>

<div id="toc0101">
<a href="javascript:void(0)" onclick="contentID='0101';
showcontent(0101)">The Early Days</a>
</div>

<div id="toc0102">
<a href="javascript:void(0)" onclick="contentID='0102';
showcontent(0101)">The Modern Era</a>
</div>

<div id="toc0200">
<a href="javascript:void(0)" onclick="contentID='0200';
showcontent(0101)">Pictures</a>
</div>

<div id="splash" align="center">
<img src="splash.jpg" height="206" width="300" />
</div>

<div id="content0101">
```

15

```
<p>This brick house was built in the 1800s. Originally part of a large
farm that consisted of several hundred acres, the house and barn now sit
on a 4 acre plot of land.</p>
</div>

<div id="content0102">
<p>There have been several modifications to the house, such as a
refurbished kitchen, but the exterior is largely as it was in the 1800s.
The barn, on the other hand, has been left unchanged.</p>
</div>

<div id="content0200">
<img src="house.jpg" height="93" width="150" />
<img src="barn.jpg" height="100" width="150" />
<img src="grounds.jpg" height="69" width="150" />
</div>

</body>
</html>
```

This results in the Web page shown in Figures 15.6, where I have expanded the menu but
have not yet selected any content to be displayed.

OUTPUT

FIGURE 15.6

*Expandable menus in
Microsoft Internet
Explorer 5.*

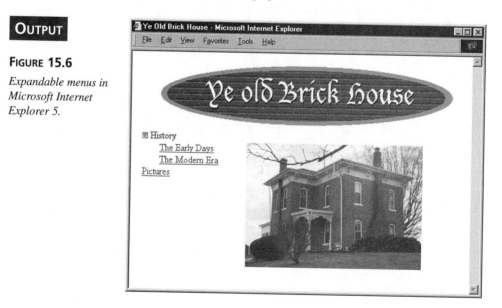

Figure 15.7 shows that I have selected a menu item. The content that was hidden now is
visible and displayed.

OUTPUT

FIGURE 15.7

Hidden content now revealed with DHTML.

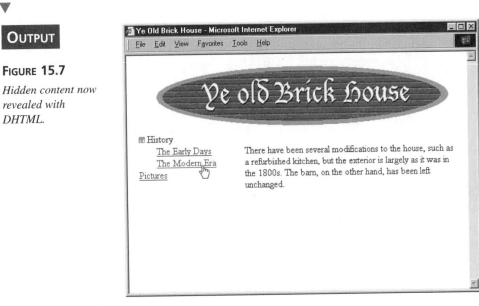

Figure 15.8 shows the same page in Netscape Navigator, revealing that it truly is cross-browser DHTML. I have expanded the menu but selected the bottom choice to display the pictures.

OUTPUT

FIGURE 15.8

Confirming cross-browser compatibility in Netscape Navigator 4.61.

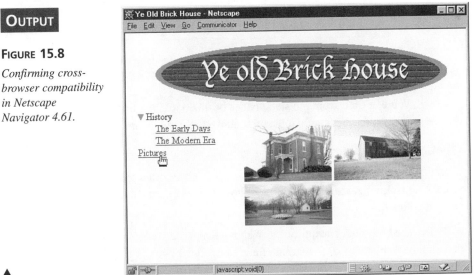

Exercise 15.2: Let's Play Tic-Tac-Toe

▲ To Do

The final exercise is a Web page that features an interactive tic-tac-toe game, created solely with DHTML. No additives or preservatives! The game and the Web page in which it resides use several handy DHTML techniques, such as browser sniffing, z-index ordering, element visibility, and animation. Figure 15.9 shows what you are trying to achieve.

FIGURE 15.9

Tic-tac-toe—created as a cross-browser DHTML Web page.

Title slides in from the top-left.

The game pieces are initially hidden, but appear when you click an "open" square.

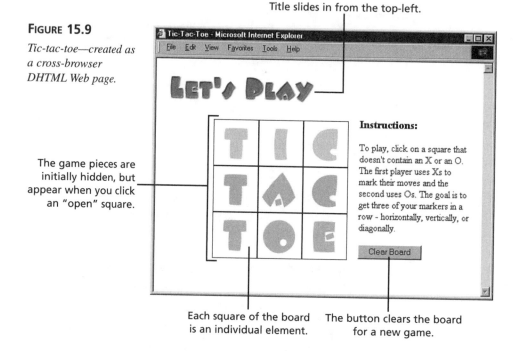

Each square of the board is an individual element.

The button clears the board for a new game.

Although you can't tell from the static pages of this book, the title actually slides in from off screen until it reaches its final position above the game board.

Creating the Graphics

Graphics are an important part of any Web page. Because this page centers on the very visual (but simple) game of tic-tac-toe, I chose to make them fun, lighthearted, simple, and yet colorful.

After I fleshed out the concept for the Web page and did some initial "trial" coding, I settled on a particular approach that, in effect, defined the game's graphics. My first thought was to create the game board as one large square, divided into nine boxes. After creating

▼

a board in this fashion, I discovered that it would be easier to create nine individual game

▼ board graphics that each that could be placed inside a `<div>` element. Because each graphic can be precisely placed using CSS, you can't really tell nine portions make up the overall board.

Note

> To create all the graphics for this Web page, I used a combination of Adobe Photoshop 5 and Adobe ImageReady. I realize that you may not have access to those programs, but there are other (less expensive) graphics packages available for you to use. The concepts of creating and optimizing the images essentially are the same, regardless of the application(s) you use.

To make the boards visually interesting, and by the odd coincidence that there are nine letters in tic-tac-toe, I chose to create each piece as a 77×77 pixel `.GIF` image and include a letter of the name of the game inside the individual pieces. I alternated the colors for the letters, with Tic being red, Tac set to black, and Toe as blue.

After this, I tinkered with the visibility of the text until I dimmed the letters to an appropriate background level. I didn't want them to be so powerful that they overshadowed the actual game pieces.

When all was said and done, I created nine `.GIF` files (shown in Figure 15.10), identically sized, and named them according to their position in the game board (such as `topleft.gif`, `centercenter.gif`, and so on).

FIGURE 15.10

All nine board images are "muted" so that they don't dominate the page.

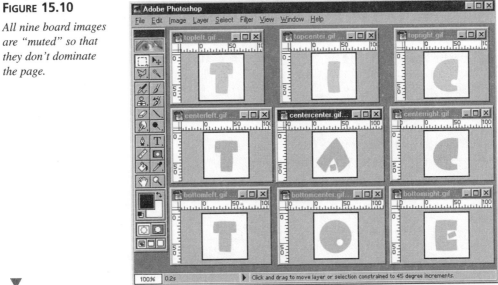

▼

▼ For the game pieces, I only needed to create two graphics: one X and one O. It is important to note that each of these also are 77×77 pixels and are not transparent. I didn't want any of the board to show through after a piece was "placed." Figure 15.11 shows the X and O game pieces in Photoshop.

FIGURE 15.11

The X and O game pieces.

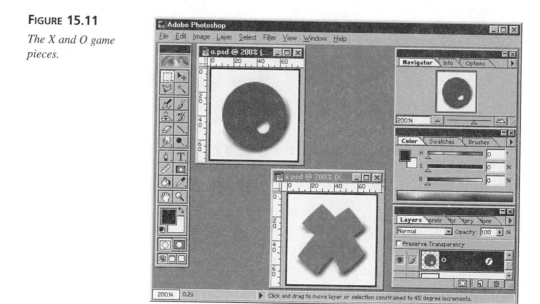

Finally, I created a title graphic, shown in Figure 15.12, that slides into position when the page loads. Rather than repeating "Tic-Tac-Toe," I chose to use "Let's Play" as the catch phrase.

The font I used to create all the text is Beesknees ITC, a stylish and somewhat whimsical font. For other types of text, I would choose something a bit easier to read, but this seems to fit perfectly.

Now that the graphics have been created, it's time to start coding.

Writing the HTML with a Dash of Style

▼ Begin by declaring the version of HTML you are using and then create the head and body of the document to form a shell.

FIGURE 15.12

The title graphic that slides into the page.

INPUT

```
<!DOCTYPE html PUBLIC "-//W3C//DTD XHTML 1.0 Transitional//EN"
"http://www.w3.org/TR/xhtml1/DTD/transitional.dtd">

<html>
<head>
<title>Tic-Tac-Toe</title>
<meta http-equiv="Content-Script-Type" content="text/javascript" />

<!-- Most JavaScript will go here -->

</head>
<body>

<!-- HTML will go here -->

</body>
</html>
```

At this point, you'll work inside the `body`. First, create the graphical title that you later will animate. Create a `div` and give it an `ID` so that you can manipulate it with the script you'll create later. Use absolute positioning to fix it on the Web page. Because you want the title to begin offscreen, assign negative values with the `left` and `top` style properties. The `z-index` property of `5` ensures that it will be on top of any other CSS layers. Inside the content of the `div` element, add the image using the `img` element, and then close the `div` element using the end `div` tag.

▼

```
<div id="titleimage"
    style="position: absolute;
              left: -100;
              top: -100;
              z-index: 5">
<img src="title.gif" height="57" width="254" />
</div>
```

That wasn't too hard, and if you understand it, you easily will be able to create the next elements of your game: the game board and game pieces.

The game board consists of nine individual div elements, each with its own image. I measured out all the dimensions in Photoshop to arrive at the proper coordinates for the top and left properties, and because you want the game board to be the lowest layer, assign each piece a z-index of 0. You also want to make sure that each square remains visible, so include the visibility property as well. Because you want an event to happen when a person clicks on the game board, use the onclick attribute of each div element to set a variable that defines the board's position and calls the update() function that will cause a game piece to be made visible on the board. As you look through the HTML that creates the board, notice that each square has a unique id, top and left properties. When the user clicks the mouse, the board sets the position variable to the correct position in the board. You'll use that later when you script the update() function.

```
<!-- begin game board divisions -->

<div id="topleft"
    style="position: absolute;
                  top: 100;
                  left: 100;
              z-index: 0;
          visibility: visible"
    onclick="position = 'topleft'; update();">
<img src="topleft.gif" height="77" width="77" />
</div>

<div id="topcenter"
    style="position: absolute;
                  top: 100;
                  left: 177;
              z-index: 0;
          visibility: visible"
    onclick="position = 'topcenter'; update();">
<img src="topcenter.gif" height="77" width="77" />
</div>
```

▼
```
<div id="topright"
```

```
        style="position: absolute;
                   top: 100;
                   left: 254;
                z-index: 0"
        onclick="position = 'topright'; update()">
<img src="topright.gif" height="77" width="77" />
</div>

<div id="centerleft"
        style="position: absolute;
                   top: 177;
                   left: 100;
                z-index: 0"
        onclick="position = 'centerleft'; update()">
<img src="centerleft.gif" height="77" width="77" />
</div>

<div id="centercenter"
        style="position: absolute;
                   top: 177;
                   left: 177;
                z-index: 0"
        onclick="position = 'centercenter'; update()">
<img src="centercenter.gif" height="77" width="77" />
</div>

<div id="centerright"
        style="position: absolute;
                   top: 177;
                   left: 254;
                z-index: 0"
        onclick="position = 'centerright'; update()">
<img src="centerright.gif" height="77" width="77" />
</div>

<div id="bottomleft"
        style="position: absolute;
                   top: 254;
                   left: 100;
                z-index: 0"
        onclick="position = 'bottomleft'; update()">
<img src="bottomleft.gif" height="77" width="77" />
</div>

<div id="bottomcenter"
        style="position: absolute;
                   top: 254;
                   left: 177;
                z-index: 0"
        onclick="position = 'bottomcenter'; update()">
<img src="bottomcenter.gif" height="77" width="77" />
```

▼

```
    </div>

    <div id="bottomright"
        style="position: absolute;
                      top: 254;
                     left: 254;
                  z-index: 0"
        onclick="position = 'bottomright'; update()">
    <img src="bottomright.gif" height="77" width="77" />
    </div>

    <!-- end game board divisions -->
```

Figure 15.13 shows your progress thus far.

OUTPUT

FIGURE 15.13

The positioned title (offscreen) and game board.

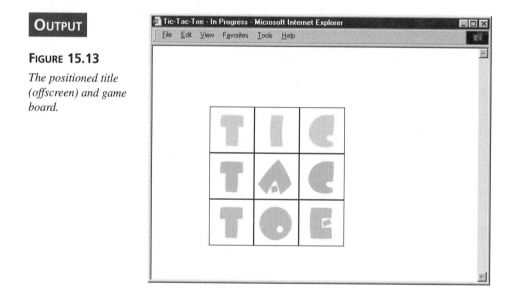

Now that the game board is finished, you can proceed to include each game piece. As a design decision, I thought it would be easiest to create both an X and O game piece that overlays every square on the board, but initially are hidden. When a person clicks the game board square, the script will determine on which side he or she is (X or O), and then make the appropriate graphic visible.

INPUT

```
    <!-- begin hidden o markers -->

    <div id="toplefto"
        style="position: absolute;
                      top: 100;
                     left: 100;
                  z-index: 3;
```

▼

15

```
                 visibility: hidden">
<img src="o.gif" height="77" width="77" />
</div>

<div id="topcentero"
    style="position: absolute;
                top: 100;
              left: 177;
           z-index: 3;
        visibility: hidden">
<img src="o.gif" height="77" width="77" />
</div>

<div id="toprighto"
    style="position: absolute;
                top: 100;
              left: 254;
           z-index: 3;
        visibility: hidden">
<img src="o.gif" height="77" width="77" />
</div>

<div id="centerlefto"
    style="position: absolute;
                top: 177;
              left: 100;
           z-index: 3;
        visibility: hidden">
<img src="o.gif" height="77" width="77" />
</div>

<div id="centercentero"
    style="position: absolute;
                top: 177;
              left: 177;
           z-index: 3;
        visibility: hidden">
<img src="o.gif" height="77" width="77" />
</div>

<div id="centerrighto"
    style="position: absolute;
                top: 177;
              left: 254;
           z-index: 3;
        visibility: hidden">
<img src="o.gif" height="77" width="77" />
</div>

<div id="bottomlefto"
    style="position: absolute;
```

```
                top: 254;
                left: 100;
            z-index: 3;
        visibility: hidden">
<img src="o.gif" height="77" width="77" />
</div>

<div id="bottomcentero"
    style="position: absolute;
                top: 254;
                left: 177;
            z-index: 3;
        visibility: hidden">
<img src="o.gif" height="77" width="77" />
</div>

<div id="bottomrighto"
    style="position: absolute;
                top: 254;
                left: 254;
            z-index: 3;
        visibility: hidden">
<img src="o.gif" height="77" width="77" />
</div>

<!-- end hidden o markers -->

<!-- begin hidden x markers -->

<div id="topleftx"
    style="position: absolute;
                top: 100;
                left: 100;
            z-index: 2;
        visibility: hidden">
<img src="x.gif" height="77" width="77" />
</div>

<div id="topcenterx"
    style="position: absolute;
                top: 100;
                left: 177;
            z-index: 2;
        visibility: hidden">
<img src="x.gif" height="77" width="77" />
</div>

<div id="toprightx"
    style="position: absolute;
                top: 100;
                left: 254;
```

```
                z-index: 2;
            visibility: hidden">
<img src="x.gif" height="77" width="77" />
</div>

<div id="centerleftx"
    style="position: absolute;
                top: 177;
                left: 100;
            z-index: 2;
            visibility: hidden">
<img src="x.gif" height="77" width="77" />
</div>

<div id="centercenterx"
    style="position: absolute;
                top: 177;
                left: 177;
            z-index: 2;
            visibility: hidden">
<img src="x.gif" height="77" width="77" />
</div>

<div id="centerrightx"
    style="position: absolute;
                top: 177;
                left: 254;
            z-index: 2;
            visibility: hidden">
<img src="x.gif" height="77" width="77" />
</div>

<div id="bottomleftx"
    style="position: absolute;
                top: 254;
                left: 100;
            z-index: 2;
            visibility: hidden">
<img src="X.gif" height="77" width="77" />
</div>

<div id="bottomcenterx"
    style="position: absolute;
                top: 254;
                left: 177;
            z-index: 2;
            visibility: hidden">
<img src="x.gif" height="77" width="77" />
</div>

<div id="bottomrightx"
```

▼

```
            style="position: absolute;
                        top: 254;
                       left: 254;
                    z-index: 2;
                 visibility: hidden">
<img src="x.gif" height="77" width="77" />
</div>

<!-- end hidden x markers -->
```

Whew, that was lengthy. Now it's time to include a few instructions so that people know how to play the game and clear the board. You will use the familiar div element again to include the instructions. You also will use a form that displays a *Clear Board* button.

INPUT

```
<div id="instructions"
    style="position: absolute;
                 top: 95;
                left: 350">
<h3>Instructions:</h3>
<p>To play, click on a square that doesn't contain an X or an O. The
first player uses Xs to mark their moves and the second uses Os. The goal
is to get three of your markers in a row - horizontally, vertically, or
diagonally.</p>

<form name="clearboard">
<input type="submit" value="Clear Board"
onclick="window.location.reload()" />
</form>
```

Figure 15.14 shows your progress.

OUTPUT

FIGURE 15.14

Adding instructions and a Clear Board button.

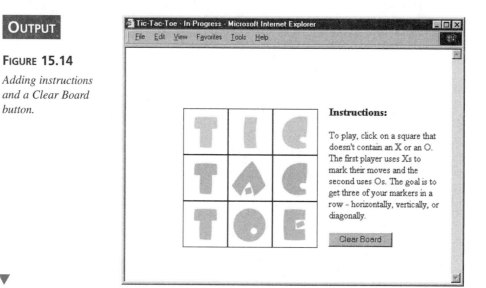

▼

▼ Because I want total control over the final appearance of the page, notice that I am again positioning this element absolutely. The form contains no `action` or `method` attributes because it only serves to create a submit button that calls the `window.location.reload()` function to reload the page.

JavaScripting Until the Wee Hours

Now that the Web page is built, you can begin to write the script that will do all the DHTML work!

First, you need to open the `script` element and create a few variables that will be used later. Note that immediately after the opening `script` tag, it is necessary to use an HTML comment element `<!--` to hide the code from nonscript browsers. At the end of the script, be sure to remember the closing comment tag, `-->`. JavaScript comments make use of two forward slashes (`//`).

INPUT

```
<script language="javascript" type="text/javascript">
<!-- Hide JavaScript

// Declaring a few variables
var player1 = "x";
var player2 = "o";
var currentplayer;
var position;
var yhop = 3;
var ygoal = 20;
var xhop = 3;
var xgoal = 20;
var delay = 1;
var xpos;
var ypos;
```

Next, you need to "sniff" for browsers. Because this Web page aims at being cross-browser compatible (to an extent), it is important to perform browser checking, popularly known as *sniffing*.

Rather than reinventing the wheel, I am using modified cross-browser code from Netscape that checks for the browser vendor, major and minor versions, platform, and many other items. Place this code in the `head` of your HTML document and wrap it in the `<script>` element.

INPUT

```
// Trimmed down browser sniffer that
// detects Navigator 4+ and IE 4+.
// Reference is_nav4up and is_ie4up in other
// portions of the script
var agt = navigator.userAgent.toLowerCase();
var is_major = parseInt(navigator.appVersion);
```

▼

```
var is_minor = parseFloat(navigator.appVersion);
var is_nav  = ((agt.indexOf('mozilla')!=-1) && (agt.indexOf('spoofer')==-
1)
                && (agt.indexOf('compatible') == -1) &&
(agt.indexOf('opera')==-1)
                && (agt.indexOf('webtv')==-1));
var is_nav4up = (is_nav && (is_major >= 4));
var is_ie  = (agt.indexOf("msie") != -1);
var is_ie4up = (is_ie  && (is_major >= 4));
```

To check for the existence of Netscape Navigator 4 and Microsoft Internet Explorer 4 and later versions, use the following script:

```
if (is_nav4up) {
    do something }
if (is_ie4up) {
    do something else }
```

The first function initializes the script and is called when the page is loaded in the browser. To be able to track which player is up next, set the currentplayer variable to player1, so that the first time a person clicks, he or she is known as player1.

The second part of this function tests to see whether the browser is Netscape Navigator and turns on event capturing for the mouse. This is important because Netscape does not recognize the onClick event in the div elements that make up the game board. Finally, call the slidetitle() function to animate the title graphic and bring it onto the Web page.

INPUT
```
// Initializes first player and
// begin event capturing for Netscape.
// Call from BODY element when loading page.
function init() {
    currentplayer = player1;
    if (is_nav4up == true ) {
        document.captureEvents(Event.CLICK | Event.MOUSEDOWN)
        document.onclick=updatenav
        document.onmousedown=updatenav
    }
    slidetitle();
}
```

The slidetitle() function checks to see which browser is present and animates the graphic accordingly. The only real difference is the way in which each browser calls the title image. Netscape uses document.titleimage and Internet Explorer uses document.all.titleimage.style. The if routines check to see that the left and top values for the title graphic don't equal the xgoal and ygoal variables declared earlier, which define the final position of the image. If neither property is equal to the ultimate position, you add the xhop and yhop values to the current position. These values determine how many pixels the image moves during each pass of this routine.

15

INPUT

```
// Slides the title graphic from offscreen.
function slidetitle() {
    if (is_nav4up == true ) {
        if ((parseInt(document.titleimage.left) != xgoal) ¦¦
            (parseInt(document.titleimage.top) != ygoal)) {
                document.titleimage.left = document.titleimage.left +
xhop;
                document.titleimage.top = document.titleimage.top + yhop;
                timeoutID = setTimeout("slidetitle()", delay); }
        }
    if (is_ie4up == true ) {
        if ((parseInt(document.all.titleimage.style.left) != xgoal) ¦¦
            (parseInt(document.all.titleimage.style.top) != ygoal)) {
                document.all.titleimage.style.left =
parseInt(document.all.titleimage.style.left) + xhop;
                document.all.titleimage.style.top =
parseInt(document.all.titleimage.style.top) + yhop;
                timeoutID = setTimeout("slidetitle()", delay); }
        }
    }
```

Because Netscape Navigator will not respond to the onclick event, it is necessary to create a separate routine to update the playing board when a user clicks on a square.

First, you obtain the position of the mouse cursor by using the e.pageX and e.pageY properties. You then perform a check to see which player currently is "up." The code within each player routine is identical, except that the X images are made visible for player 1 and the O images are made visible for player 2. The extensive position check is necessary to determine which square is clicked. Another odd point is that it also is necessary to check the visibility of the opposing marker in order to determine whether the square is "open." If the opposite maker is visible, no action occurs.

INPUT

```
// Updates when Navigator detects a mouse event.
// IE appears to ignore in favor of onClick.
function updatenav(e) {
    xpos = e.pageX;
    ypos = e.pageY;
    if (currentplayer == player1) {
        if (xpos >= 100 && xpos <= 176 && ypos >= 100 && ypos <= 176 &&
document.toplefto.visibility == "hide") {
                document.topleftx.visibility = "visible"; currentplayer =
player2;}
        if (xpos >= 177 && xpos <= 253 && ypos >= 100 && ypos <= 176 &&
document.topcentero.visibility == "hide") {
                document.topcenterx.visibility = "visible"; currentplayer =
player2;}
        if (xpos >= 254 && xpos <= 331 && ypos >= 100 && ypos <= 176 &&
document.toprighto.visibility == "hide") {
```

```
                document.toprightx.visibility = "visible"; currentplayer =
    player2;}
        if (xpos >= 100 && xpos <= 176 && ypos >= 177 && ypos <= 253 &&
    document.centerlefto.visibility == "hide") {
                document.centerleftx.visibility = "visible"; currentplayer =
    player2;}
        if (xpos >= 177 && xpos <= 253 && ypos >= 177 && ypos <= 253 &&
    document.centercentero.visibility == "hide") {
                document.centercenterx.visibility = "visible"; currentplayer
    = player2;}
        if (xpos >= 254 && xpos <= 331 && ypos >= 177 && ypos <= 253 &&
    document.centerrighto.visibility == "hide") {
                document.centerrightx.visibility = "visible"; currentplayer =
    player2;}
        if (xpos >= 100 && xpos <= 176 && ypos >= 254 && ypos <= 331 &&
    document.bottomlefto.visibility == "hide") {
                document.bottomleftx.visibility = "visible"; currentplayer =
    player2;}
        if (xpos >= 177 && xpos <= 253 && ypos >= 254 && ypos <= 331 &&
    document.bottomcentero.visibility == "hide") {
                document.bottomcenterx.visibility = "visible"; currentplayer
    = player2;}
        if (xpos >= 254 && xpos <= 331 && ypos >= 254 && ypos <= 331 &&
    document.bottomrighto.visibility == "hide") {
                document.bottomrightx.visibility = "visible"; currentplayer =
    player2;}
        }
        else {
            if (xpos >= 100 && xpos <= 176 && ypos >= 100 && ypos <= 176 &&
    document.topleftx.visibility == "hide") {
                document.toplefto.visibility = "show"; currentplayer =
    player1;}
        if (xpos >= 177 && xpos <= 253 && ypos >= 100 && ypos <= 176 &&
    document.topcenterx.visibility == "hide") {
                document.topcentero.visibility = "show"; currentplayer =
    player1;}
        if (xpos >= 254 && xpos <= 331 && ypos >= 100 && ypos <= 176 &&
    document.toprightx.visibility == "hide") {
                document.toprighto.visibility = "show"; currentplayer =
    player1;}
        if (xpos >= 100 && xpos <= 176 && ypos >= 177 && ypos <= 253 &&
    document.centerleftx.visibility == "hide") {
                document.centerlefto.visibility = "visible"; currentplayer =
    player1;}
        if (xpos >= 177 && xpos <= 253 && ypos >= 177 && ypos <= 253 &&
    document.centercenterx.visibility == "hide") {
                document.centercentero.visibility = "visible"; currentplayer
    = player1;}
        if (xpos >= 254 && xpos <= 331 && ypos >= 177 && ypos <= 253 &&
    document.centerrightx.visibility == "hide") {
                document.centerrighto.visibility = "visible"; currentplayer =
    player1;}
```

```
         if (xpos >= 100 && xpos <= 176 && ypos >= 254 && ypos <= 331 &&
document.bottomleftx.visibility == "hide") {
         document.bottomlefto.visibility = "visible"; currentplayer =
player1;}
         if (xpos >= 177 && xpos <= 253 && ypos >= 254 && ypos <= 331 &&
document.bottomcenterx.visibility == "hide") {
         document.bottomcentero.visibility = "visible"; currentplayer
= player1;}
         if (xpos >= 254 && xpos <= 331 && ypos >= 254 && ypos <= 331 &&
document.bottomrightx.visibility == "hide") {
         document.bottomrighto.visibility = "visible"; currentplayer =
player1;}
      }
   }
```

Next, you come to the function used by Internet Explorer to update the game board.
First, check to see who is the current player, set the marker type, and then reset the current player so that after a successful play occurs, the next player is up.

Next, evaluate each position and set the visibility property for the appropriate type
of marker. You do not need to perform any coordinate checks because this routine is
called by the specific game board location that is clicked.

INPUT

```
// Updates with the IE onClick event. Navigator
// ignores this event so no need to detect.
function update() {
    if (currentplayer == player1) {
        playermarker = "x";
        currentplayer = player2;
    }
    else {
        playermarker = "o";
        currentplayer = player1;
    }
    if (is_ie4up == true) {
        if (position == "topleft") {
            eval("document.all.topleft"+playermarker+
".style.visibility = 'visible'");}
        if (position == "topcenter") {
            eval("document.all.topcenter"+playermarker+
".style.visibility = 'visible'");}
        if (position == "topright") {
            eval("document.all.topright"+playermarker+
".style.visibility = 'visible'");}
        if (position == "centerleft") {
            eval("document.all.centerleft"+playermarker+
".style.visibility = 'visible'");}
        if (position == "centercenter") {
```

```
                       eval("document.all.centercenter"+playermarker+
        ".style.visibility = 'visible'");}
               if (position == "centerright") {
                       eval("document.all.centerright"+playermarker+
        ".style.visibility = 'visible'");}
               if (position == "bottomleft") {
                       eval("document.all.bottomleft"+playermarker+
        ".style.visibility = 'visible'");}
               if (position == "bottomcenter") {
                       eval("document.all.bottomcenter"+playermarker+
        ".style.visibility = 'visible'");}
               if (position == "bottomright") {
                       eval("document.all.bottomright"+playermarker+
        ".style.visibility = 'visible'");}
           }
        }
        //--> end hide JavaScript
        </script>
```

The final piece of the script appears in the HTML code itself. Be sure to call the `onload` function in the opening body tag, as in the following:

```
<body onload="init()">
```

The Finished Product

That was fairly intense. If it's not obvious by now, you really need to have a handle on all three DHTML technologies—HTML, CSS, and scripting—to make it work. Following is the final code listing:

```
<!DOCTYPE html PUBLIC "-//W3C//DTD XHTML 1.0 Transitional//EN"
"http://www.w3.org/TR/xhtml1/DTD/transitional.dtd">

<html>
<head>
<title>Tic-Tac-Toe</title>
<meta http-equiv="Content-Script-Type" content="text/javascript" />

<script language="javascript" type="text/javascript">
<!-- Hide JavaScript

// Declaring a few variables
var player1 = "x";
var player2 = "o";
var currentplayer;
var position;
var yhop = 3;
var ygoal = 20;
```

15

```
var xhop = 3;
var xgoal = 20;
var delay = 1;
var xpos;
var ypos;


// Trimmed down browser sniffer that
// detects Navigator 4+ and IE 4+.
// Reference is_nav4up and is_ie4up in other
// portions of the script
var agt = navigator.userAgent.toLowerCase();
var is_major = parseInt(navigator.appVersion);
var is_minor = parseFloat(navigator.appVersion);
var is_nav  = ((agt.indexOf('mozilla')!=-1) && (agt.indexOf('spoofer')==-1)
              && (agt.indexOf('compatible') == -1) && (agt.indexOf('opera')==-1)
              && (agt.indexOf('webtv')==-1));
var is_nav4up = (is_nav && (is_major >= 4));
var is_ie   = (agt.indexOf("msie") != -1);
var is_ie4up  = (is_ie  && (is_major >= 4));

// Initializes first player and
// begin event capturing for Netscape.
// Call from BODY element when loading page.
function init() {
    currentplayer = player1;
    if (is_nav4up == true ) {
        document.captureEvents(Event.CLICK ¦ Event.MOUSEDOWN)
        document.onclick=updatenav
        document.onmousedown=updatenav
    }
    slidetitle();
}


// Slides the title graphic from offscreen.
function slidetitle() {
    if (is_nav4up == true ) {
        if ((parseInt(document.titleimage.left) != xgoal) ¦¦
            (parseInt(document.titleimage.top) != ygoal)) {
                document.titleimage.left = document.titleimage.left + xhop;
                document.titleimage.top = document.titleimage.top + yhop;
                timeoutID = setTimeout("slidetitle()", delay); }
    }
    if (is_ie4up == true ) {
        if ((parseInt(document.all.titleimage.style.left) != xgoal) ¦¦
            (parseInt(document.all.titleimage.style.top) != ygoal)) {
```

```
                    document.all.titleimage.style.left =
parseInt(document.all.titleimage.style.left) + xhop;
                    document.all.titleimage.style.top =
parseInt(document.all.titleimage.style.top) + yhop;
                    timeoutID = setTimeout("slidetitle()", delay); }
    }
}

// Updates when Navigator detects a mouse event.
// IE appears to ignore in favor of onClick.
function updatenav(e) {
    xpos = e.pageX;
    ypos = e.pageY;
    if (currentplayer == player1) {
        if (xpos >= 100 && xpos <= 176 && ypos >= 100 && ypos <= 176 &&
document.toplefto.visibility == "hide") {
            document.topleftx.visibility = "visible"; currentplayer = player2;}
        if (xpos >= 177 && xpos <= 253 && ypos >= 100 && ypos <= 176 &&
document.topcentero.visibility == "hide") {
            document.topcenterx.visibility = "visible"; currentplayer =
player2;}
        if (xpos >= 254 && xpos <= 331 && ypos >= 100 && ypos <= 176 &&
document.toprighto.visibility == "hide") {
            document.toprightx.visibility = "visible"; currentplayer = player2;}
        if (xpos >= 100 && xpos <= 176 && ypos >= 177 && ypos <= 253 &&
document.centerlefto.visibility == "hide") {
            document.centerleftx.visibility = "visible"; currentplayer =
player2;}
        if (xpos >= 177 && xpos <= 253 && ypos >= 177 && ypos <= 253 &&
document.centercentero.visibility == "hide") {
            document.centercenterx.visibility = "visible"; currentplayer =
player2;}
        if (xpos >= 254 && xpos <= 331 && ypos >= 177 && ypos <= 253 &&
document.centerrighto.visibility == "hide") {
            document.centerrightx.visibility = "visible"; currentplayer =
player2;}
        if (xpos >= 100 && xpos <= 176 && ypos >= 254 && ypos <= 331 &&
document.bottomlefto.visibility == "hide") {
            document.bottomleftx.visibility = "visible"; currentplayer =
player2;}
        if (xpos >= 177 && xpos <= 253 && ypos >= 254 && ypos <= 331 &&
document.bottomcentero.visibility == "hide") {
            document.bottomcenterx.visibility = "visible"; currentplayer =
player2;}
        if (xpos >= 254 && xpos <= 331 && ypos >= 254 && ypos <= 331 &&
document.bottomrighto.visibility == "hide") {
            document.bottomrightx.visibility = "visible"; currentplayer =
player2;}
```

15

```
    }
    else {
        if (xpos >= 100 && xpos <= 176 && ypos >= 100 && ypos <= 176 &&
document.topleftx.visibility == "hide") {
            document.toplefto.visibility = "show"; currentplayer = player1;}
        if (xpos >= 177 && xpos <= 253 && ypos >= 100 && ypos <= 176 &&
document.topcenterx.visibility == "hide") {
            document.topcentero.visibility = "show"; currentplayer = player1;}
        if (xpos >= 254 && xpos <= 331 && ypos >= 100 && ypos <= 176 &&
document.toprightx.visibility == "hide") {
            document.toprighto.visibility = "show"; currentplayer = player1;}
        if (xpos >= 100 && xpos <= 176 && ypos >= 177 && ypos <= 253 &&
document.centerleftx.visibility == "hide") {
            document.centerlefto.visibility = "visible"; currentplayer =
player1;}
        if (xpos >= 177 && xpos <= 253 && ypos >= 177 && ypos <= 253 &&
document.centercenterx.visibility == "hide") {
            document.centercentero.visibility = "visible"; currentplayer =
player1;}
        if (xpos >= 254 && xpos <= 331 && ypos >= 177 && ypos <= 253 &&
document.centerrightx.visibility == "hide") {
            document.centerrighto.visibility = "visible"; currentplayer =
player1;}
        if (xpos >= 100 && xpos <= 176 && ypos >= 254 && ypos <= 331 &&
document.bottomleftx.visibility == "hide") {
            document.bottomlefto.visibility = "visible"; currentplayer =
player1;}
        if (xpos >= 177 && xpos <= 253 && ypos >= 254 && ypos <= 331 &&
document.bottomcenterx.visibility == "hide") {
            document.bottomcentero.visibility = "visible"; currentplayer =
player1;}
        if (xpos >= 254 && xpos <= 331 && ypos >= 254 && ypos <= 331 &&
document.bottomrightx.visibility == "hide") {
            document.bottomrighto.visibility = "visible"; currentplayer =
player1;}
    }
}


// Updates with the IE onClick event. Navigator
// ignores this event so no need to detect.
function update() {
    if (currentplayer == player1) {
        playermarker = "x";
        currentplayer = player2;
    }
    else {
        playermarker = "o";
```

```
            currentplayer = player1;
        }
        if (is_ie4up == true) {
            if (position == "topleft") {
                eval("document.all.topleft"+playermarker+".style.visibility =
'visible'");}
            if (position == "topcenter") {
                eval("document.all.topcenter"+playermarker+".style.visibility =
'visible'");}
            if (position == "topright") {
                eval("document.all.topright"+playermarker+".style.visibility =
'visible'");}
            if (position == "centerleft") {
                eval("document.all.centerleft"+playermarker+".style.visibility =
'visible'");}
            if (position == "centercenter") {
                eval("document.all.centercenter"+playermarker+".style.visibility =
'visible'");}
            if (position == "centerright") {
                eval("document.all.centerright"+playermarker+".style.visibility =
'visible'");}
            if (position == "bottomleft") {
                eval("document.all.bottomleft"+playermarker+".style.visibility =
'visible'");}
            if (position == "bottomcenter") {
                eval("document.all.bottomcenter"+playermarker+".style.visibility =
'visible'");}
            if (position == "bottomright") {
                eval("document.all.bottomright"+playermarker+".style.visibility =
'visible'");}
        }
}
//--> end hide JavaScript
</script>

</head>

<body onload="init()">

<div id="titleimage"
    style="position: absolute;
            left: -100;
            top: -100;
            z-index: 5">
<img src="title.gif" height="57" width="254" />
</div>

<!-- begin game board divisions -->
```

15

```
<div id="topleft"
    style="position: absolute;
                top: 100;
               left: 100;
            z-index: 0;
         visibility: visible"
    onclick="position = 'topleft'; update();">
<img src="topleft.gif" height="77" width="77" />
</div>

<div id="topcenter"
    style="position: absolute;
                top: 100;
               left: 177;
            z-index: 0;
         visibility: visible"
    onclick="position = 'topcenter'; update();">
<img src="topcenter.gif" height="77" width="77" />
</div>

<div id="topright"
    style="position: absolute;
                top: 100;
               left: 254;
            z-index: 0"
    onclick="position = 'topright'; update()">
<img src="topright.gif" height="77" width="77" />
</div>

<div id="centerleft"
    style="position: absolute;
                top: 177;
               left: 100;
            z-index: 0"
    onclick="position = 'centerleft'; update()">
<img src="centerleft.gif" height="77" width="77" />
</div>

<div id="centercenter"
    style="position: absolute;
                top: 177;
               left: 177;
            z-index: 0"
    onclick="position = 'centercenter'; update()">
<img src="centercenter.gif" height="77" width="77" />
</div>

<div id="centerright"
    style="position: absolute;
```

```
              top: 177;
              left: 254;
          z-index: 0"
    onclick="position = 'centerright'; update()">
<img src="centerright.gif" height="77" width="77" />
</div>

<div id="bottomleft"
    style="position: absolute;
              top: 254;
              left: 100;
          z-index: 0"
    onclick="position = 'bottomleft'; update()">
<img src="bottomleft.gif" height="77" width="77" />
</div>

<div id="bottomcenter"
    style="position: absolute;
              top: 254;
              left: 177;
          z-index: 0"
    onclick="position = 'bottomcenter'; update()">
<img src="bottomcenter.gif" height="77" width="77" />
</div>

<div id="bottomright"
    style="position: absolute;
              top: 254;
              left: 254;
          z-index: 0"
    onclick="position = 'bottomright'; update()">
<img src="bottomright.gif" height="77" width="77" />
</div>

<!-- end game board divisions -->

<!-- begin hidden o markers -->

<div id="toplefto"
    style="position: absolute;
              top: 100;
              left: 100;
          z-index: 3;
       visibility: hidden">
<img src="o.gif" height="77" width="77" />
</div>

<div id="topcentero"
    style="position: absolute;
```

```
                       top: 100;
                      left: 177;
                   z-index: 3;
              visibility: hidden">
<img src="o.gif" height="77" width="77" />
</div>

<div id="toprighto"
    style="position: absolute;
                      top: 100;
                     left: 254;
                   z-index: 3;
              visibility: hidden">
<img src="o.gif" height="77" width="77" />
</div>

<div id="centerlefto"
    style="position: absolute;
                      top: 177;
                     left: 100;
                   z-index: 3;
              visibility: hidden">
<img src="o.gif" height="77" width="77" />
</div>

<div id="centercentero"
    style="position: absolute;
                      top: 177;
                     left: 177;
                   z-index: 3;
              visibility: hidden">
<img src="o.gif" height="77" width="77" />
</div>

<div id="centerrighto"
    style="position: absolute;
                      top: 177;
                     left: 254;
                   z-index: 3;
              visibility: hidden">
<img src="o.gif" height="77" width="77" />
</div>

<div id="bottomlefto"
    style="position: absolute;
                      top: 254;
                     left: 100;
                   z-index: 3;
              visibility: hidden">
```

15

```
  <img src="o.gif" height="77" width="77" />
  </div>

  <div id="bottomcentero"
      style="position: absolute;
                 top: 254;
                 left: 177;
             z-index: 3;
         visibility: hidden">
  <img src="o.gif" height="77" width="77" />
  </div>

  <div id="bottomrighto"
      style="position: absolute;
                 top: 254;
                 left: 254;
             z-index: 3;
         visibility: hidden">
  <img src="o.gif" height="77" width="77" />
  </div>

  <!-- end hidden o markers -->

  <!-- begin hidden x markers -->

  <div id="topleftx"
      style="position: absolute;
                 top: 100;
                 left: 100;
             z-index: 2;
         visibility: hidden">
  <img src="x.gif" height="77" width="77" />
  </div>

  <div id="topcenterx"
      style="position: absolute;
                 top: 100;
                 left: 177;
             z-index: 2;
         visibility: hidden">
  <img src="x.gif" height="77" width="77" />
  </div>

  <div id="toprightx"
      style="position: absolute;
                 top: 100;
                 left: 254;
             z-index: 2;
         visibility: hidden">
  <img src="x.gif" height="77" width="77" />
  </div>
```

```
<div id="centerleftx"
    style="position: absolute;
                top: 177;
                left: 100;
            z-index: 2;
        visibility: hidden">
<img src="x.gif" height="77" width="77" />
</div>

<div id="centercenterx"
    style="position: absolute;
                top: 177;
                left: 177;
            z-index: 2;
        visibility: hidden">
<img src="x.gif" height="77" width="77" />
</div>

<div id="centerrightx"
    style="position: absolute;
                top: 177;
                left: 254;
            z-index: 2;
        visibility: hidden">
<img src="x.gif" height="77" width="77" />
</div>

<div id="bottomleftx"
    style="position: absolute;
                top: 254;
                left: 100;
            z-index: 2;
        visibility: hidden">
<img src="X.gif" height="77" width="77" />
</div>

<div id="bottomcenterx"
    style="position: absolute;
                top: 254;
                left: 177;
            z-index: 2;
        visibility: hidden">
<img src="x.gif" height="77" width="77" />
</div>

<div id="bottomrightx"
    style="position: absolute;
                top: 254;
                left: 254;
            z-index: 2;
```

15

```
                visibility: hidden">
<img src="x.gif" height="77" width="77" />
</div>

<!-- end hidden x markers -->

<div id="instructions"
    style="position: absolute;
                top: 95;
                left: 350">
<h3>Instructions:</h3>
<p>To play, click on a square that doesn't contain an X or an O. The first
player uses Xs to mark their moves and the second uses Os. The goal is to get
three of your markers in a row - horizontally, vertically, or diagonally.</p>

<form name="clearboard">
<input type="submit" value="Clear Board" onclick="window.location.reload()" />
</form>

</div>
</body>
</html>
```

The preceding code results (finally) in the Web page shown in Figures 15.15 and 15.16. Notice that although there are significant differences in the coding of the pages, in order to target Netscape Navigator and Internet Explorer, the pages look and, in fact, act identical in each browser. That's good!

OUTPUT

FIGURE 15.15

The final product in Microsoft Internet Explorer 5.

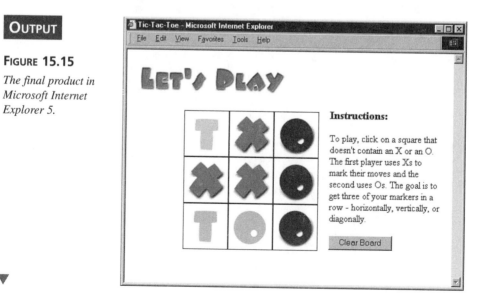

15

OUTPUT

FIGURE 15.16

*The same page
in Netscape
Navigator 4.61.*

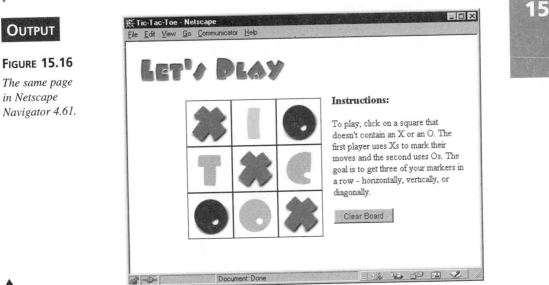

Continuing Your DHTML Education

I encourage you to visit both the Microsoft and Netscape Web sites devoted to DHTML.
Each offers an interesting perspective.

The Microsoft Web site (msdn.microsoft.com/workshop/author/default.asp) has a
ton of great information for using the DHTML capabilities unique to Internet Explorer 4
and 5.

Netscape appears to be leading the cross-browser compatibility charge and has extensive
articles and technical notes at devedge.netscape.com.

Other sites that have useful information include the following:

- WebReference Dynamic HTML Lab (www.webreference.com/dhtml/)—Contains
  examples and code ranging from drag-and-drop DHTML to expandable menus and
  outlines.
- Macromedia's Dynamic HTML Zone (www.dhtmlzone.com)—Offers DHTML articles, resources, and tutorials on a wide range on DHTML topics.
- Webmonkey (www.hotwired.com/webmonkey/dynamic_html/)—Provides an extensive section devoted to DHTML.

- Brainjar (www.brainjar.com)—Offers a library of JavaScript functions for adding DHTML to Web pages.
- The Dynamic Duo: Cross Browser Dynamic HTML (www.dansteinman.com/dynduo/index.html)—Provides extensive tutorials, projects, and sample code.

Summary

Today, you learned that Dynamic HTML is comprised of three technologies: HTML, style sheets, and scripting. Each one is important to DHTML and plays a distinct role. HTML provides the foundation for the Web page. Style sheets enable you to format and position elements to suit your taste. Scripting makes DHTML Dynamic.

Unfortunately, DHTML suffers from problems. Inconsistencies in how each Web browser implements the component technologies make coding cross-browser DHTML a challenge.

While this chapter offers a broad overview of DHTML and the technologies that make it up, it cannot hope to be an exhaustive tutorial for each element of DHTML.

Workshop

Today, you've learned how to use several different technologies—collectively known as Dynamic HTML—that will help you control the precise appearance of your Web pages and enable you to create pages that respond to user actions. The following workshop includes questions and a quiz about some of the most important topics discussed in this chapter.

Q&A

Q Is DHTML really worth the time and effort?

A Hmmm, that's a tough one. I'm very tempted to say "no," but you may need (or want) to create items that you can only achieve using DHTML. If you fall into that category, then yes, it will be worth it. If you find yourself spending all your time trying to create the ultimate DHTML Web page, but don't actually publish it, then you might want to go back to the basics and gradually work your way up to DHTML.

15

Q **There's so much information to learn. How do I do it?**

A First, start with HTML. Become an expert in it!

After that, you could take either of two approaches: master everything or learn only what you need.

The "master everything" approach leads you, in succession, from HTML to CSS, and then to JavaScript, moving on only when you are competent and comfortable with the technology at hand. After you master all three technologies, study how they interrelate and try your hand at DHTML.

The "learn only what you need" approach gets you started more quickly. Find a specific technique that you want to use, such as dynamically changing the visibility of an object, and learn how to do that. After you finish, go on to the next technique that you find interesting. You'll learn a little bit about all the technologies along the way, but will have DHTML to show for it almost immediately.

Q **Where is DHTML headed?**

A The W3C is working to develop a more standardized DOM, called *DOM Level 2*. Microsoft Internet Explorer 5 currently implements most of these ideas, and the next version of Netscape Navigator (5) hopes to do the same. The next official DOM promises to be quite a bit different from what is has been so far.

Q **What about Netscape's LAYER element and other browser-specific DHTML features?**

A As far as I'm concerned, cross-browser DHTML is where it's at if you're going to bother with DHTML at all. If you want to reach the most people (and offend the least), you should concentrate on creating Web pages that are (relatively) universal. I admit that these proprietary Web browser "features" can be very tempting, and that some of the effects are pretty neat; however, there's nothing more frustrating than spending weeks developing a cool DHTML Web page and finding out that most people can't even see it.

Quiz

1. Which three technologies make Dynamic HTML possible?

2. What is a Document Object Model?

3. Can you use VBScript or another scripting language to create DHTML?

4. What's the most important element of cross-browser DHTML?

Answers

1. HTML, style sheets, and scripting.

2. The "language" you use when you refer to scriptable objects on a Web page. Remember, Microsoft Internet Explorer and Netscape Navigator have different approaches to their DOMs; therefore, you need to use different statements to refer to the same object.

3. Yes, but you should know that VBScript isn't supported in Netscape Navigator without a special plug-in. Other scripting languages are even less supported. JavaScript is your best choice.

4. Undoubtedly, the browser sniffer function. This should accurately identify any Web browser that loads your page so that you can create alternate code for the ones you want to support.

Exercises

1. Improve on the tic-tac-toe game by creating the code necessary to make it a one-person game played against the computer.

2. Download one or more cross-browser DHTML APIs, and then integrate them into the tic-tac-toe game, creating different effects or using the APIs to replace the existing code.

PART 6

Designing Effective Web Pages

PART 6

DAY 16

Writing and Designing Web Pages: Dos and Don'ts

You won't learn about any HTML tags in this chapter or how to convert files from one strange file format to another. You're mostly done with the HTML part of Web page design. Next come the intangibles, the things that separate your pages from those of someone who just knows the tags and can fling text and graphics around and call it a site.

Armed with the information from the last five days, you could put this book down now and go off and merrily create Web pages to your heart's content. However, armed with both that information and what you'll learn today, you can create better Web pages. Do you need any more incentive to continue reading?

This chapter includes hints for creating well-written and well-designed Web pages, and it highlights dos and don'ts concerning the following:

- How to sort out the tangle of whether to use standard HTML 3.2 tags, newer HTML 4.0 tags, style sheets, HTML extensions, or a combination of two or more
- How to write your Web pages so that they can be easily scanned and read
- Issues concerning design and layout of your Web pages
- When and why you should create links
- How to use images effectively
- Other miscellaneous tidbits and hints

Using the HTML Extensions

In the past, before every browser developer was introducing its own new HTML tags, being a Web designer was easy. The only HTML tags you had to deal with were those from HTML 2.0, and the vast majority of the browsers on the Web could read your pages without a problem. Being a Web designer now is significantly more complicated. You have to work with the following several different types of Web page content:

- HTML 2.0 tags
- HTML 3.2 features such as tables, divisions, backgrounds, and color, which are supported by most, but not all, browsers
- HTML 4.0 and related features such as cascading style sheets, Dynamic HTML, and framesets
- XHTML 1.0, the proposed enhancement to HTML 4.0 that adds extensibility to HTML tags and prepares your Web pages for future Web requirements
- Plug-ins and other embedded objects, which use files and data that are external to the browser
- Browser-specific tags (from Netscape or Internet Explorer) that may or may not end up as part of the official HTML specification and whose support varies from browser to browser
- Other technologies (such as SMIL Boston, a synchronized multimedia language), proposed for future W3C specifications, that few to no browsers support

If you're finding all this information rather mind-boggling, you're not alone. Authors and developers just like you are trying to sort out the mess and make decisions based on how they want their pages to look. Cascading style sheets and Dynamic HTML do give you more flexibility with layout and content in HTML 4.0 and XHTML 1.0. Until more browsers support them, however, they limit the audience that can view your pages the way you want them to be viewed.

Choosing a strategy for using HTML is one of the more significant design decisions you'll make as you start creating Web pages. You might find it easier to look at the choices you have as a sort of continuum between the conservative and the progressive Web author (see Figure 16.1).

FIGURE 16.1

The Web author continuum.

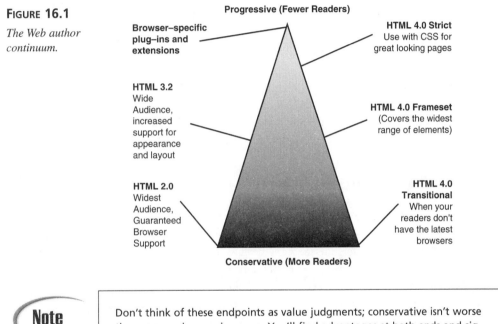

Progressive (Fewer Readers)

Browser–specific plug–ins and extensions

HTML 4.0 Strict
Use with CSS for great looking pages

HTML 3.2
Wide Audience, increased support for appearance and layout

HTML 4.0 Frameset
(Covers the widest range of elements)

HTML 2.0
Widest Audience, Guaranteed Browser Support

HTML 4.0 Transitional
When your readers don't have the latest browsers

Conservative (More Readers)

Note

Don't think of these endpoints as value judgments; conservative isn't worse than progressive, or vice versa. You'll find advantages at both ends and significant advantages in the middle.

Before the release of the HTML 4.0 standard, the continuum was a little bit more linear. The "old" continuum is depicted at the left side of the triangle in Figure 16.1.

The conservative Web developer stuck to older HTML 2.0 tags as defined by the standards. I'm not saying that the conservative Web developer is boring. You can create magnificent Web content with these older tags, and the advantage in using them is that the pages will be supported without a hitch by the greatest number of browsers. Your site reaches the widest possible audience by using this approach.

The middle-of-the-road Web developer added HTML 3.2 tags as defined by the standards. At that time, HTML 3.2 was where XHTML 1.0 is today. Although it was an accepted standard, Web developers had to wait for the browser world to catch up with the new standard. However, they were willing to take the risk that the majority of the people that visited their site would use at least one of the two major browsers, which by that time already supported the major HTML 3.2 tags.

The progressive Web developer, even today, wants the sort of control over layout that the more advanced tags have to offer and is willing to shut out a portion of the audience to get it. The progressive Web developer's pages are designed for a single browser (or at most two or three), tested only in a single browser, and might even have a big announcement on the pages that says These Pages Must Be Read Using Browser X. Using other browsers to read those pages may make the design unreadable or at least confusing—or it may be just fine.

To accommodate all these different scenarios, the HTML 4.0 and XHTML 1.0 definitions include three "flavors" of HTML, and the main differences between HTML 4.0 and XHTML 1.0 have been noted throughout this book. The three new style flavors are shown on the right side of the continuum in Figure 16.1, and are briefly described, as follows:

- **HTML 4.0 or XHTML 1.0 Transitional** is geared toward the conservative Web developer, who wants to support as many browsers as possible. It parallels those users who, in the older continuum, stuck to using HTML 2.0 tags. HTML 2.0 tags are still the bare-bones minimum that browsers are expected to support. Because HTML 3.2 browsers are seeing wider use, however, it is reasonably safe to consider the HTML 3.2 specification as the bottom line. The majority of the pages that you have created in this book fall into this category.

- **HTML 4.0 or XHTML 1.0 Frameset** is the recommended approach for Web developers who design their pages for HTML 3.2 browsers, but who also want to present their Web sites in framesets (which in the old continuum fell toward the progressive end of the spectrum). In my mind, this is today's middle-of-the-road approach. Although it supports more tags than the transitional approach, there are still many browsers in use that don't support frames.

- **HTML 4.0 or XHTML 1.0 Strict** is for the progressive Web developer who wants to design his or her pages purely by the HTML 4.0 or XHTML 1.0 specification. This means not using those tags that have been marked as "deprecated," but, instead, using cascading style sheets for document presentation.

Although the HTML 4.0 and XHTML 1.0 specifications are landmark efforts at satisfying every type of Web developer, there still exists that top point in the spectrum for the *really* progressive—those who continue to experiment with features that go above and beyond the formal specifications. As browser manufacturers continue to implement new and experimental features, the very progressive developers are eager to work with them. They support the latest and greatest versions of their favorite browsers and design pages using browser-specific tags.

The best position, in terms of choosing between interesting design and a wide audience, is probably a balance of the two. With some knowledge beforehand of the effects that HTML extensions will have on your pages, both in browsers that support them and those that don't, you can make slight modifications to your design that will enable you to take advantage of both sides. Your pages are still readable and useful in older browsers over a wider range of platforms, but they also can take advantage of the advanced features in the newer browsers. Today, this generally means adopting the HTML 3.2 or HTML 4.0 standard tags to achieve goals that are difficult or impossible with HTML 2.0, but at the same time being aware of their effect on browsers that don't yet support the full HTML 3.2 or 4.0 specification.

Throughout this book, I explain which tags are part of HTML 4.0 and which tags are available in which major browsers. I've also noted for each tag the alternatives you can use in cases in which a browser might not be able to view those tags. With this information in hand, you should be able to experiment with each tag in different browsers to see what the effect of each one is on your design.

The most important strategy I can suggest for using features that are more browser-specific, while still trying to retain compatibility with other browsers, is to test your files in those other browsers. Most browsers are freeware or shareware and available for downloading, so all you need to do is find and install them. By testing your pages, you can get an idea of how different browsers interpret different tags. Eventually, you'll get a feel for which features provide the most flexibility, which ones need special coding for alternatives in older or different browsers, and which tags can be used freely without complicating matters for other browsers.

Writing for Online Publication

Writing on the Web is no different from writing in the real world. Although the writing you do on the Web is not sealed in hard copy, it is still "published" and is still a reflection of you and your work. In fact, because your writing is online and therefore more transient to your readers, you'll have to follow the rules of good writing that much more closely because your readers will be less forgiving.

Because of the vast quantities of information available on the Web, your readers are not going to have much patience if your Web page is full of spelling errors or poorly organized. They are much more likely to give up after the first couple of sentences and move

16

on to someone else's page. After all, several million pages are available out there. No one has time to waste on bad pages.

I don't mean that you have to go out and become a professional writer to create a good Web page, but I'll give you a few hints for making your Web page easier to read and understand.

Write Clearly and Be Brief

Unless you're writing the Great American Web Novel, your readers are not going to visit your page to linger lovingly over your words. One of the best ways you can make the writing in your Web pages effective is to write as clearly and concisely as you possibly can, present your points, and then stop. Obscuring what you want to say with extra words just makes figuring out your point more difficult.

If you don't have a copy of Strunk and White's *The Elements of Style*, put down this book right now and go buy that book and read it. Then reread it, memorize it, inhale it, sleep with it under your pillow, show it to all your friends, quote it at parties, and make it your life. You'll find no better guide to the art of good, clear writing than *The Elements of Style*.

Organize Your Pages for Quick Scanning

Even if you write the clearest, briefest, most scintillating prose ever seen on the Web, chances are good your readers will not start at the top of your Web page and carefully read every word down to the bottom.

Scanning, in this context, is the first quick look your readers give to each page to get the general gist of the content. Depending on what your users want out of your pages, they may scan the parts that jump out at them (headings, links, other emphasized words), perhaps read a few contextual paragraphs, and then move on. By writing and organizing your pages for easy "scannability," you can help your readers get the information they need as fast as possible.

To improve the scannability of your Web pages, follow these guidelines:

- **Use headings to summarize topics**—Note how this book has headings and sub-headings. You can flip through quickly and find the portions that interest you. The same concept applies to Web pages.

- **Use lists**—Lists are wonderful for summarizing related items. Every time you find yourself saying something like "each widget has four elements" or "use the following steps to do this," the content after that phrase should be an ordered or unordered list.

- **Don't forget link menus**—As a form of list, link menus have all the advantages of lists for scannability, and they double as excellent navigation tools.
- **Don't bury important information in text**—If you have a point to make, make it close to the top of the page or at the beginning of a paragraph. Long paragraphs are harder to read and make gleaning the information more difficult. The further into the paragraph you put your point, the less likely anybody will read it.

Figure 16.2 shows the sort of writing technique that you should avoid.

16

FIGURE 16.2

DON'T: A Web page that is difficult to scan.

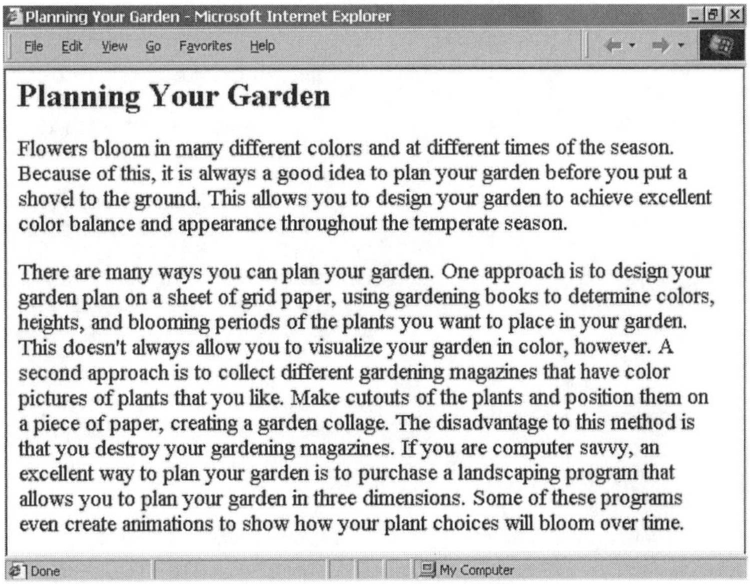

Planning Your Garden - Microsoft Internet Explorer

File   Edit   View   Go   Favorites   Help

Planning Your Garden

Flowers bloom in many different colors and at different times of the season. Because of this, it is always a good idea to plan your garden before you put a shovel to the ground. This allows you to design your garden to achieve excellent color balance and appearance throughout the temperate season.

There are many ways you can plan your garden. One approach is to design your garden plan on a sheet of grid paper, using gardening books to determine colors, heights, and blooming periods of the plants you want to place in your garden. This doesn't always allow you to visualize your garden in color, however. A second approach is to collect different gardening magazines that have color pictures of plants that you like. Make cutouts of the plants and position them on a piece of paper, creating a garden collage. The disadvantage to this method is that you destroy your gardening magazines. If you are computer savvy, an excellent way to plan your garden is to purchase a landscaping program that allows you to plan your garden in three dimensions. Some of these programs even create animations to show how your plant choices will bloom over time.

Done   My Computer

Because all the information on this page is in paragraph form, your readers have to read both paragraphs to find out what they want and where they want to go next.

How would you improve the example shown in Figure 16.2? Try rewriting this section so that readers can better find the main points from the text. Consider the following:

- These two paragraphs actually contain three discrete topics.
- The ways to plan the garden would make an excellent nested list.

Figure 16.3 shows what an improvement might look like.

FIGURE 16.3

DO: An improvement to the difficult-to-scan Web page.

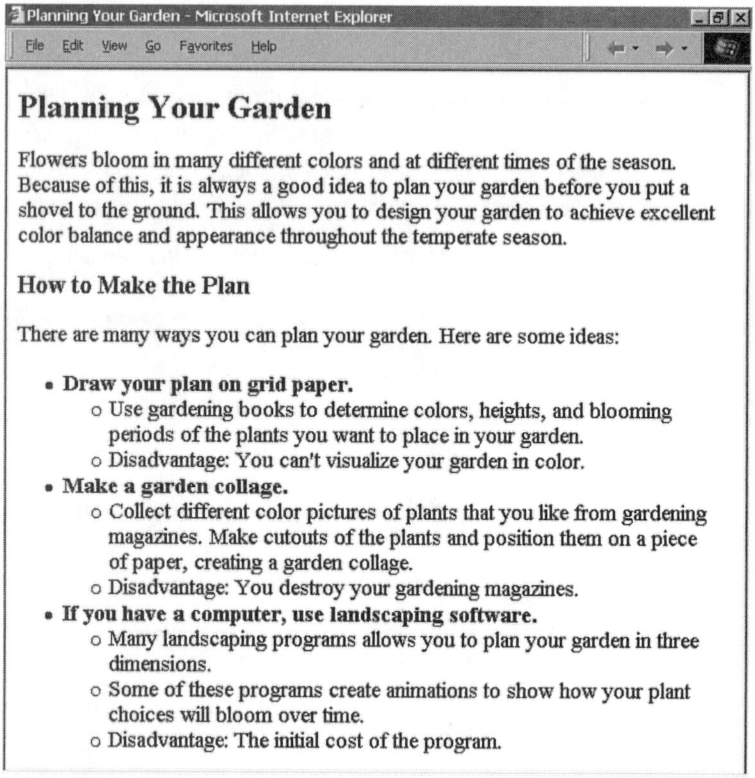

Make Each Page Stand on Its Own

As you write, keep in mind that your readers could jump into any of your Web pages from anywhere. For example, you can structure a page so that section four distinctly follows section three and has no other links to it. Then someone you don't even know might create a link to the page starting in or with section four. From then on, readers could very well find themselves on section four without even being aware that section three exists.

Be careful to write each page so that it stands on its own. The following guidelines will help:

* **Use descriptive titles**—The title should provide not only the direct subject of this page, but also its relationship to the rest of the pages in the site of which it is a part.

* **Provide a navigational link**—If a page depends on the one before it, provide a navigational link back to the page before it (and preferably also one up to the top level).

- **Avoid initial sentences like the following**—"You can get around these problems by…," "After you're done with that, do…," and "The advantages to this method are…." The information referred to by "these," "that," and "this" are off on some other page. If these sentences are the first words your readers see, they are going to be confused.

Be Careful with Emphasis

Use emphasis sparingly in your text. Paragraphs with a whole lot of boldface and italics or words in ALL CAPS are hard to read—whether you use them several times in a paragraph or if you emphasize long strings of text. The best emphasis is used only with small words (such as and, this, or but).

Link text also is a form of emphasis. Use single words or short phrases as link text. Do not use entire passages or paragraphs as links.

Figure 16.4 illustrates a particularly bad example of too much emphasis obscuring the rest of the text.

FIGURE 16.4

DON'T: Too much emphasis.

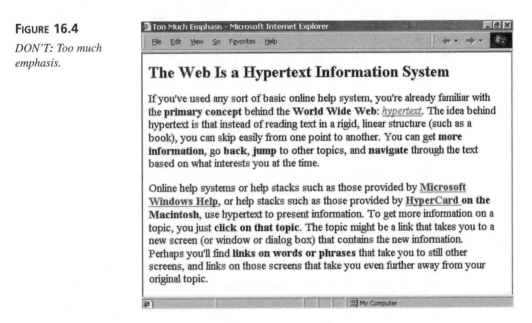

By removing some of the boldface and using less text for your links, you can considerably reduce the amount of distraction in the paragraph, as you can see in Figure 16.5.

The Web Is a Hypertext Information System

If you've used any sort of basic online help system, you're already familiar with the primary concept behind the World Wide Web: *hypertext*. The idea behind hypertext is that instead of reading text in a rigid, linear structure (such as a book), you can skip easily from one point to another. You can get more information, go back, jump to other topics, and navigate through the text based on what interests you at the time.

Online help systems or help stacks such as those provided by Microsoft Windows Help, or help stacks such as those provided by HyperCard on the Macintosh, use hypertext to present information. To get more information on a topic, you just click on that topic. The topic might be a link that takes you to a new screen (or window or dialog box) that contains the new information. Perhaps you'll find links on words or phrases that take you to still other screens, and links on those screens that take you even further away from your original topic.

Be especially careful of emphasis that moves or changes, such as marquees, blinking text, or animation, on your pages. Unless the animation is the primary focus of the page, use movement and sound sparingly to prevent distractions from the rest of your page.

Don't Use Browser-Specific Terminology

Avoid references in your text to specific features of specific browsers. For example, don't use the following wording:

- **Click Here**—What if your readers are using browsers without a mouse? A more generic phrase is "Select this link." (Of course, you should avoid the "here" syndrome in the first place, which neatly gets around this problem as well.)

- **To save this page, pull down the File menu and select Save**—Each browser has a different set of menus and different ways of accomplishing the same action. If at all possible, do not refer to specifics of browser operation in your Web pages.

- **Use the Back button to return to the previous page**—As in the preceding note, each browser has a different set of buttons and different methods for going back. If you want your readers to be able to go back to a previous page or to any specific page, link the pages.

Spell Check and Proofread Your Pages

Spell checking and proofreading may seem like obvious suggestions, but given the number of pages I have seen on the Web that have obviously not had either, this tip bears mentioning.

The process of designing a set of Web pages and making them available on the Web is like publishing a book, producing a magazine, or releasing a product. Publishing Web pages is, of course, considerably easier than publishing books, magazines, or other products, but just because the task is easy does not mean your product should be sloppy.

Thousands of people may be reading and exploring the content you provide. Spelling errors and bad grammar reflect badly on your work, on you, and on the content you're describing. Poor writing may be irritating enough that your readers won't bother to delve any deeper than your home page, even if the subject you're writing about is fascinating.

Proofread and spell check each of your Web pages. If possible, have someone else read them. Other people often can pick up errors that you, the writer, can't see. Even a simple edit can greatly improve many pages and make them easier to read and navigate.

Design and Page Layout

With the introduction of technologies such as style sheets and Dynamic HTML, people without a sense of design have been given even more opportunities to create a site that looks simply awful.

Probably the best rule to follow at all times as far as designing each Web page is this: *Keep the design as simple as possible.* Reduce the number of elements (images, headings, and rule lines) and make sure that the readers' eyes are drawn to the most important parts of the page first.

Keep this cardinal rule in mind as you read the next sections, which offer some other suggestions for basic design and layout of Web pages.

Use Headings as Headings

Headings often are rendered in graphical browsers in larger or bolder fonts. Therefore, using a heading tag to provide some sort of warning, note, or emphasis in regular text is often tempting (see Figure 16.6).

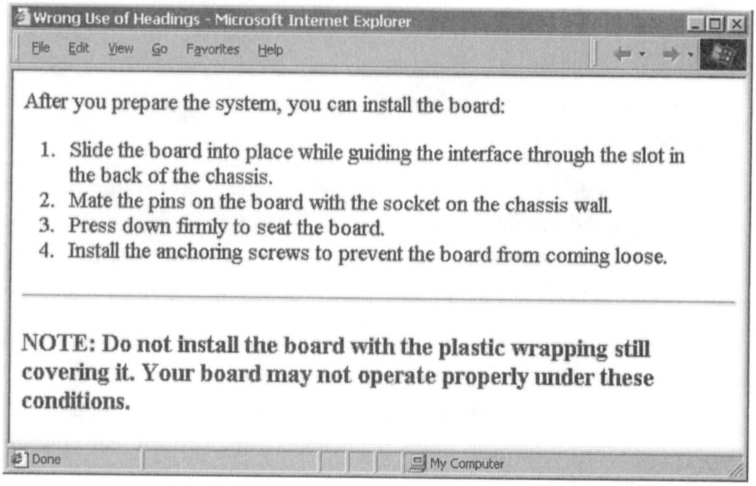

FIGURE 16.6

DON'T: The wrong way to use headings.

FIGURE 16.7

DO: An alternative to the wrong way to use headings.

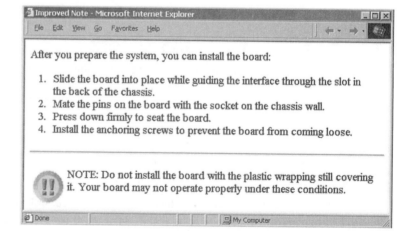

Headings work best when they're used as headings because they stand out from the text and signal the start of new topics. If you really want to emphasize a particular section of text, consider using a small image, a rule line, or some other method of emphasis instead. Figure 16.7 shows an example of the same text in Figure 16.6 with a different kind of visual emphasis.

Group Related Information Visually

Grouping related information within a page is a task for both writing and design. By grouping related information under headings, as I suggested in the "Writing for Online" section, you improve the scannability of that information. Visually separating each section from the others helps to make each section distinct and emphasizes the relatedness of the information.

If a Web page contains several sections of information, find a way to separate those sections visually—for example, with a heading, a rule line, or with tables, as shown in Figure 16.8.

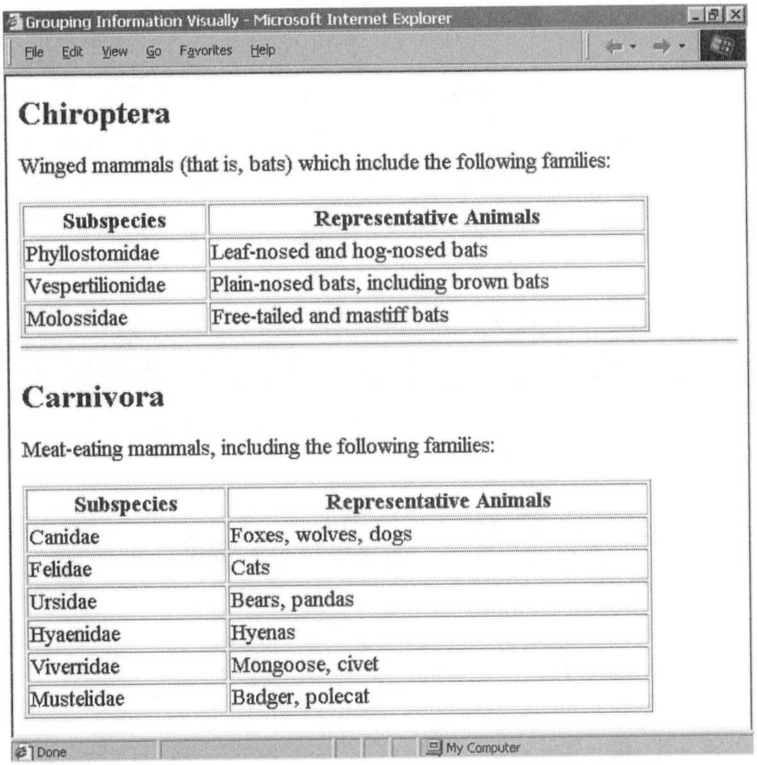

Chiroptera

Winged mammals (that is, bats) which include the following families:

Subspecies	Representative Animals
Phyllostomidae	Leaf-nosed and hog-nosed bats
Vespertilionidae	Plain-nosed bats, including brown bats
Molossidae	Free-tailed and mastiff bats

Carnivora

Meat-eating mammals, including the following families:

Subspecies	Representative Animals
Canidae	Foxes, wolves, dogs
Felidae	Cats
Ursidae	Bears, pandas
Hyaenidae	Hyenas
Viverridae	Mongoose, civet
Mustelidae	Badger, polecat

FIGURE 16.8

DO: Separate sections visually.

Use a Consistent Layout

When you're reading a book or a magazine, each page, each section, usually has the same layout. The page numbers are placed where you expect them, and the first word on each page starts in the same place.

The same sort of consistent layout works equally well in Web pages. A single "look and feel" for each page in your Web site is comforting to your readers. After two or three pages, they will know what the elements of each page are and where to find them. If you create a consistent design, your readers can find the information they need and navigate through your pages without having to stop at every page and try to find where elements are located.

Consistent layout can include the following:

- **Consistent page elements**—If you use second-level headings (`<h2>`) on one page to indicate major topics, use second-level headings for major topics on all your pages. If you have a heading and a rule line at the top of your page, use that same layout on all your pages.

- **Consistent forms of navigation**—Put your navigation menus in the same place on every page (usually the top or the bottom of the page), and use the same number of them. If you're going to use navigation icons, make sure you use the same icons in the same order for every page.

- **The use of external style sheets**—If you want to stick to pure HTML 4.0, you can create a master style sheet that defines background properties, text and link colors, font selections and sizes, margins, and more. The appearance of your pages maintains consistency throughout your site.

Using Links

Without links, Web pages would be really dull, and finding anything interesting on the Web would be close to impossible. The quality of your links, in many ways, can be as important as the writing and design of your actual pages. Here's some friendly advice on creating and using links.

Use Link Menus with Descriptive Text

As I've noted in this chapter and frequently in this book, using link menus is a great way of organizing your content and the links on a page. By organizing your links into lists or other menu-like structures, your readers can scan their options for the page quickly and easily.

Just organizing your links into menus, however, often isn't enough. When you arrange your links into menus, make sure that you aren't too short in your descriptions. Using menus of filenames or other marginally descriptive links in menus, like the menu shown in Figure 16.9, is tempting.

Well, this figure shows a menu of links, and the links are descriptive of the actual page to which they point, but they don't really describe the content of the page. How do readers know what's on the other side of the link, and how can they make decisions about whether they're interested in it from the limited information you've given them? Of these three links, only the last (`pesto-recipe.txt`) gives the readers a hint about what they will see when they jump to that file.

FIGURE 16.9

DON'T: A poor link menu.

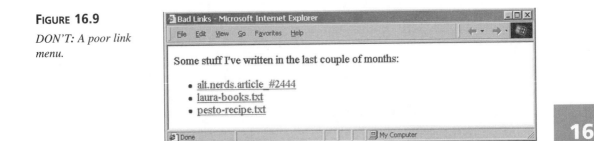

A better plan is either to provide some extra text describing the content of the file, as shown in Figure 16.10, or to avoid the filenames altogether (who cares?). Just describe the contents of the files in the menu, with the appropriate text highlighted, as shown in Figure 16.11.

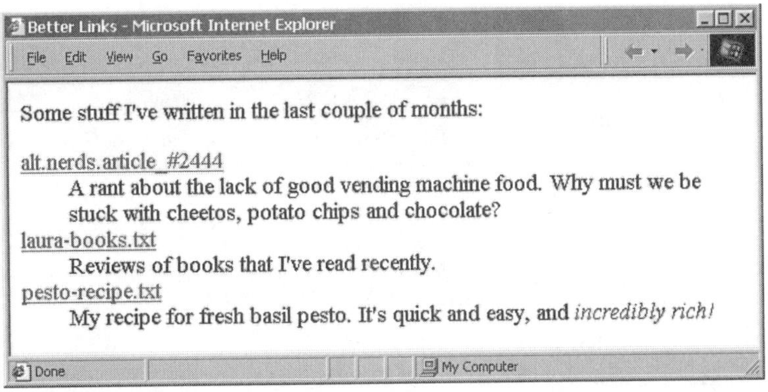

FIGURE 16.10

DO: A better link menu.

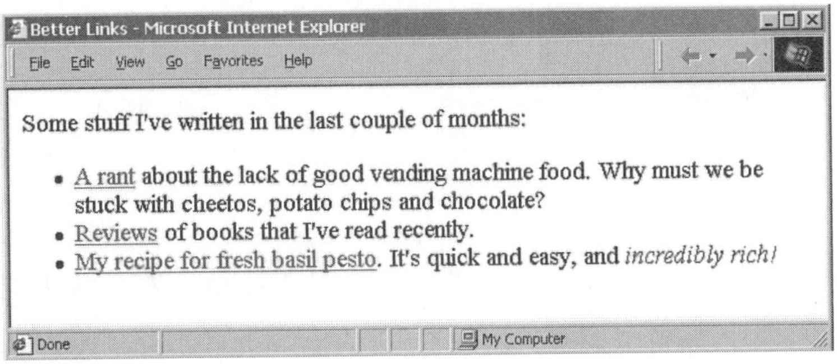

FIGURE 16.11

DO: Another better link menu.

Either one of these forms is better than the first; both give your readers more clues about what's on the other side of the link.

16

Use Links in Text

The best way to provide links in text is to first write the text without the links as if the text wasn't going to have links at all—for example, if you were writing it for hard copy. You then can highlight the appropriate words that will serve as the link text for links to other pages. Make sure that you don't interrupt the flow of the page when you include a link. The idea of using links in text is that the text should stand on its own. That way, the links provide additional or tangential information that your readers can choose to ignore or follow based on their own whims.

Figure 16.12 shows another example of using links in text. Here the text itself isn't overly relevant; it's just there to support the links. If you're using text just to describe links, consider using a link menu instead of a paragraph. Your readers can find the information they want more easily. Instead of having to read the entire paragraph, they can skim for the links that interest them.

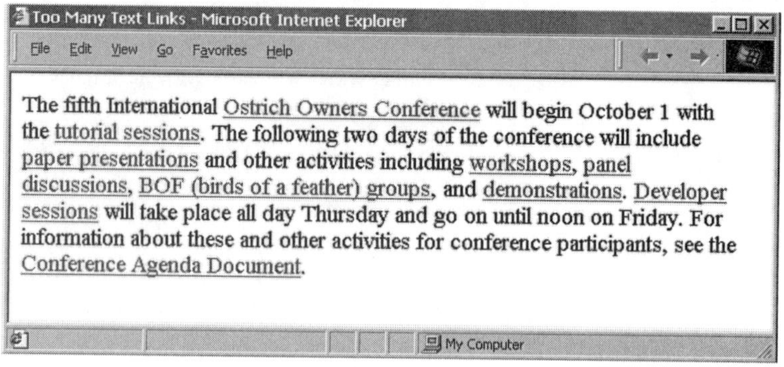

FIGURE 16.12

DON'T: Links in text that don't work well.

In Figure 16.13, you see one way to restructure the previous example. The most important items on the page are the name of the conference and the events and dates on which they occur. So you can restructure the page so that this information stands out on the page. As you can see in Figure 16.13, by presenting the events in a preformatted text table, the important information stands out from the rest.

Probably the easiest way to figure out whether you're creating links within text properly is to print out the formatted Web page from your browser. In hard copy, without hypertext, would the paragraph still make sense? If the page reads funny on paper, it'll read funny online as well. The revisions don't always have to be as different as they are shown in this example. Sometimes, simple rephrasing of sentences can often help enormously in making the text on your pages more readable and more usable both online and when printed.

FIGURE 16.13

DO: Restructuring the links in the text.

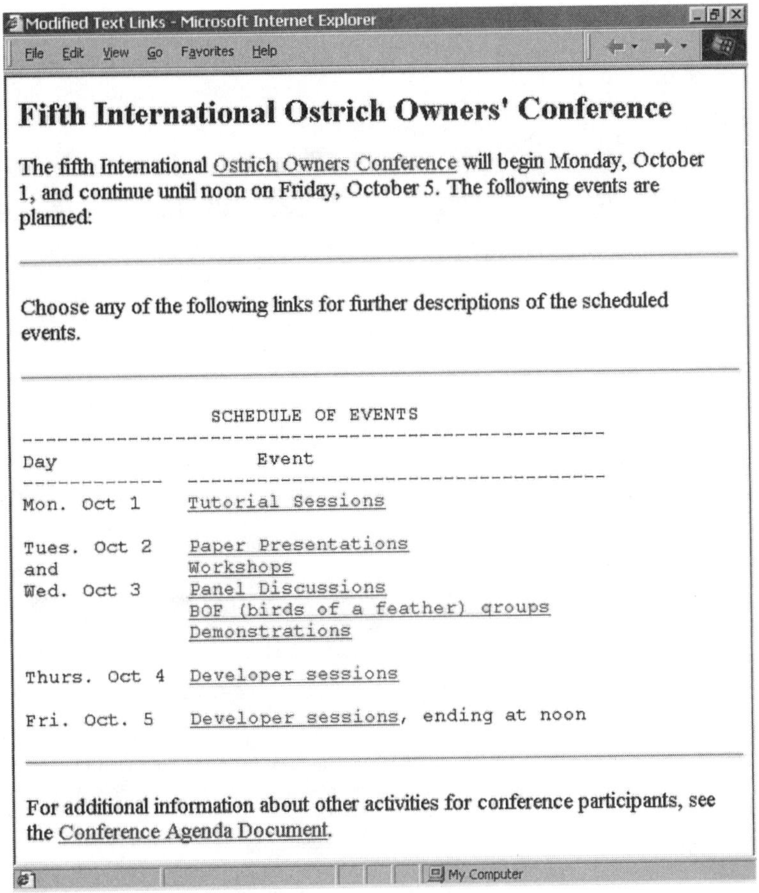

Avoid the Here Syndrome

A common mistake that many Web authors make in creating links in body text is using the *Here* syndrome. The Here syndrome is the tendency to create links with a single highlighted word (here) and to describe the link somewhere else in the text. Look at the following examples (with underlining indicating link text):

```
Information about ostrich socialization is contained here.

Select this link for a tutorial on the internal combustion engine.
```

Because links are highlighted on the Web page, the links visually pop out more than the surrounding text (or draw the eye, in graphic design lingo). Your readers will see the link first, before reading the text. Try creating links this way. Figure 16.14 shows a particularly heinous example of the Here syndrome. Close your eyes, open them quickly, pick a "here" at random, and then see how long it takes you to find out what the "here" is for.

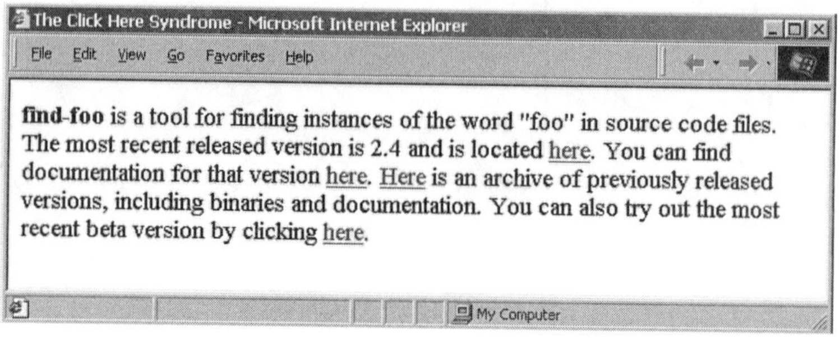

FIGURE **16.14**

DON'T: The Here syndrome.

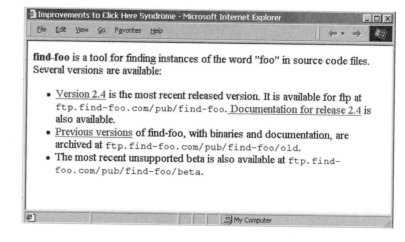

Now try the same exercise with a well-organized link menu of the same information, as shown in Figure 16.15.

FIGURE **16.15**

DO: The same page, reorganized.

Because "here" says nothing about what the link is used for, your poor readers have to search the text before and after the link itself to find out just what is supposed to be "here." In paragraphs that have many occurrences of "here" or other non-descriptive links, matching up the links with what they are supposed to link to becomes difficult, forcing your readers to work harder to figure out what you mean.

Instead of the following link:

```
Information about ostrich socialization is contained here.
```

a much better choice of wording would be something like this:

```
The Palo Alto Zoo has lots of information about ostrich socialization.
```

or

```
The Palo Alto Zoo has lots of information about ostrich socialization.
```

To Link or Not to Link

16

Just as with graphics, every time you create a link, consider why you're linking two pages or sections. Is the link useful? Will it give your readers more information or take them closer to their goal? Is the link relevant in some way to the current content?

Each link should serve a purpose. Link for relevant reasons. Just because you mention the word *coffee* deep in a page about some other topic, you don't have to link that word to the coffee home page. Creating such a link may seem cute, but if a link has no relevance to the current content, it just confuses your readers.

This section describes some of the categories of links that are useful in Web pages. If your links do not fall into one of these categories, consider the reasons why you're including them in your page.

Note   Thanks to Nathan Torkington for his "Taxonomy of Tags," published on the `www-talk` mailing list, which inspired this section.

Explicit navigation links indicate the specific paths readers can take through your Web pages: forward, back, up, home. These links are often indicated by navigation icons, as shown in Figure 16.16.

Implicit navigation links, shown in Figure 16.17, are different from explicit navigation links in that the link text implies, but does not directly indicate, navigation between pages. Link menus are the best example of this type of link; from the highlighting of the link text, it is apparent that you will get more information on this topic by selecting the link, but the text itself does not necessarily say so. Note the major difference between explicit and implicit navigation links: If you print a page containing both, you should no longer be able to pick out the implicit links.

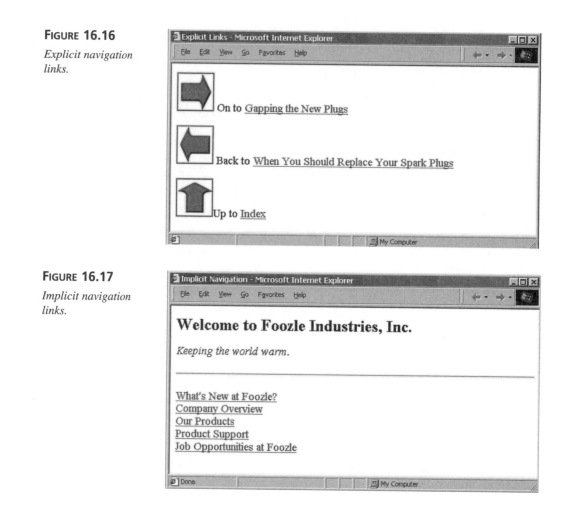

FIGURE 16.16

Explicit navigation links.

FIGURE 16.17

Implicit navigation links.

Implicit navigation links also can include table-of-contents-like structures or other overviews made up entirely of links.

Word or concept definitions make excellent links, particularly if you're creating large networks of pages that include glossaries. By linking the first instance of a word to its definition, you can explain the meaning of that word to readers who don't know what it means while not distracting those who do. Figure 16.18 shows an example of this type of link.

Finally, links to tangents and related information are valuable when the text content would distract from the main purpose of the page. Think of tangent links as footnotes or end notes in printed text (see Figure 16.19). They can refer to citations to other works or to additional information that is interesting but not necessarily directly relevant to the point you're trying to make.

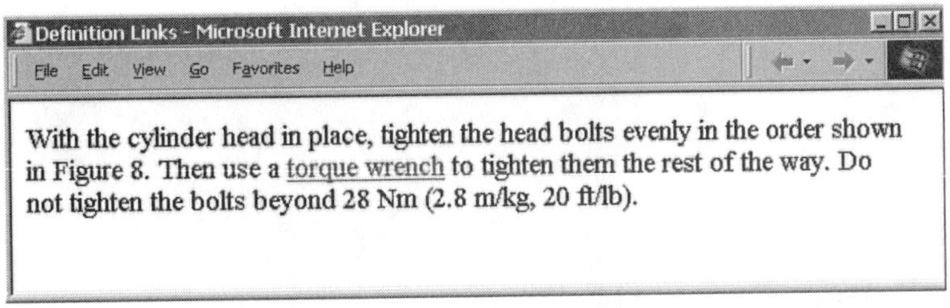

FIGURE 16.18

Definition links.

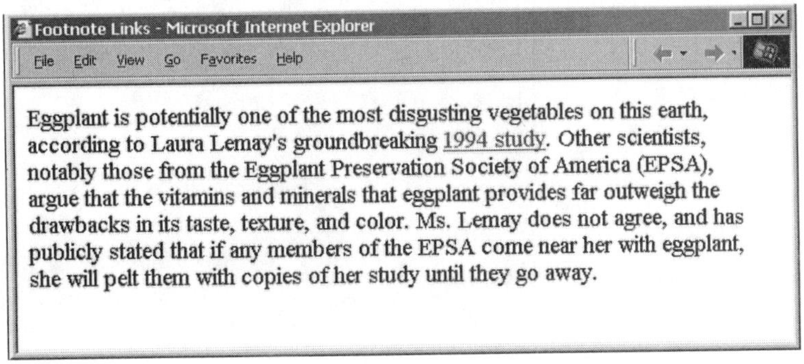

FIGURE 16.19

Footnote links.

16

Be careful that you don't get carried away with definitions and tangent links. You might create so many tangents that your readers spend so much time linking elsewhere that they can't follow the point of your original text. Resist the urge to link every time you possibly can, and link only to relevant tangents on your own text. Also, avoid duplicating the same tangent—for example, linking every instance of the letters *WWW* on your page to the WWW Consortium's home page. If you're linking twice or more to the same location on one page, consider removing most of the extra links. Your readers can select one of the other links if they're interested in the information.

Using Images

On Day 7, "Using Images, Color, and Backgrounds," you learned all about creating and using images in Web pages. This section summarizes many of the hints you learned in those chapters for using images.

Don't Overuse Images

Be careful about including a large number of images on your Web page. Besides the fact that each image adds to the amount of time it takes to load the page, including too many images on the same page can make your page look busy and cluttered and distract from the point you're trying to get across. Sometimes, people think that the more images they include on a page, the better it is. Figure 16.20 shows such an example.

FIGURE 16.20

DON'T: Too many
images.

Remember the hints I gave you in Day 7. Consider the reasons that you need to use each
image before you put it on the page. If an image doesn't directly contribute to the content, consider leaving it off.

Use Alternatives to Images

Of course, as soon as I mention images, I also have to mention that not all browsers can view those images. To make your pages accessible to the widest possible audience, you have to take the text-only browsers into account when you design your Web pages. The following two possible solutions can help:

- Use the `alt` attribute of the `<img>` tag to substitute appropriate text strings for the graphics automatically in text-only browsers (a requirement in XHTML 1.0). Use a descriptive label to substitute for the default `[image]` that appears in the place of each inline image.

- If providing a single-source page for both graphical and text-only browsers becomes too much work, and the result is not turning out to be acceptable, consider creating separate pages for each one: a page designed for the full-color, full-graphical browsers and a page designed for the text-only browsers. Then provide the option of choosing one or the other from your home page.

Keep Images Small

If you use images, keep in mind that each image is a separate network connection and takes time to load over a network, meaning that each image adds to the total time it takes to view a page. Try to reduce the number of images on a page, and keep your images small both in file size and in actual dimensions. In particular, keep the following hints in mind:

- A good rule of thumb for large images is that at a 28.8Kbps modem connection, your page will load at an average of 2K per second. The entire page (text and images) should not take more than 30 seconds to load; otherwise, you risk annoying your readers and having them move on without reading your page. This rule of thumb limits you to 60KB total for everything on your page. Strive to achieve that size by keeping your images small.

- For larger images, consider using thumbnails on your main page and then linking to the larger image rather than putting the larger image inline.

- Interlace your larger GIF files.

- Try the tests to see whether JPEG or GIF creates a smaller file for the type of image you're using.

- In GIF files, the fewer colors you use in the image, the smaller the image will be. You should try to use as few colors as possible to avoid problems with system-specific color allocation.

- You can reduce the physical size of your images by cropping them (using a smaller portion of the overall image) or by scaling (shrinking) the original image. When you scale the image, you might lose some of the detail from the original image.

- You can use the `width` and `height` attributes to scale the image to a larger size than the image actually is. These originally were Netscape-only extensions but are now a part of HTML 3.2. Note that the scaled result might not be what you expect. Test this procedure before trying it.

With some of the preceding suggestions in mind, take a second look at the images on the page. You *really* want to use all these different images on the page because you have your heart set on it. How can you put the page shown in Figure 16.20 on a diet, and improve its appearance?

As far as image sizes go, the graphic at the beginning of the page, which displays a logo for the site, could stand some size reduction. Being that it's basically just a banner and doesn't include any links on it, you can rework the graphic to be half as high. That cuts the download time for the graphic roughly in half.

Another problem that needs to be addressed is that the title of the page (in this case, the name of the site) doesn't appear anywhere as text on the page. Those who visit the site with graphics turned off won't know the name of the site! We need to add that to our improved version.

Those horizontal rules are a *big* problem. First, there are too many of them. Second, they overpower the banner image because they are so much wider. Third, they distract from the list of items because they create separation between them. So we'll reduce the quantity and the size of those images. More download time savings.

The bullets that appear before each list item are way too large. They could stand to be cut back to 50 percent of their size. As a rule, most bullets are kept to 30×30 pixels or less.

The bullets and text were centered on the page, making the list items look very disorganized. When you use images for bullets, there actually are several different approaches to doing so. You can make this an "official" bulleted list, using the `<ul>` tag, and use the `src` attribute to specify the bullet image. However, HTML 3.2 and earlier browsers will see standard bulleted lists instead of the images. Another alternative is to lay out the images and the list items in a borderless table. All the improvements I've suggested are shown in Figure 16.21.

FIGURE 16.21

DO: Better use of images.

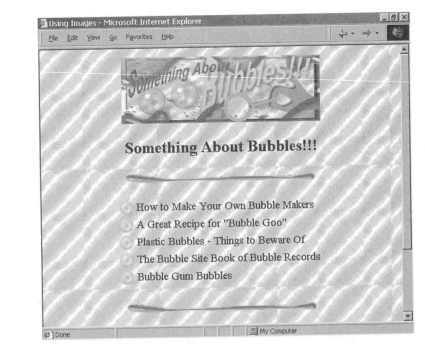

16

Watch Out for Display Assumptions

Many people create problems for their readers by making a couple of careless assumptions about other people's hardware. When you're developing Web pages, be kind and remember the following two guidelines:

- **Don't assume that everyone has screen or browser dimensions the same as yours.**

  Just because that huge GIF you created is wide enough to fit on your screen in your browser doesn't mean it'll fit someone else's. Coming across an image that is too wide is annoying because it requires the readers to resize their windows all the time or scroll sideways.

  To fit in the width of a majority of browsers' windows, try to keep the width of your images to fewer than 450 pixels.

- **Don't assume that everyone has full-color displays.**

  Test your images in resolutions other than full color. (You often can test in your image-editing program.) Many of your readers may have display systems that have only 16 colors, only grayscale, or just black and white. You may be surprised at the results: Colors drop out or dither strangely in grayscale or black and white, and the effect may not be what you intended.

Make sure your images are visible at all resolutions, or provide alternatives for high- and low-resolution images on the page itself.

Be Careful with Backgrounds and Link Colors

Using HTML extensions, you can use background colors and patterns and change the color of the text on your pages. Using this feature can be very tempting, but be very careful if you decide to do so. The capability to change the page and font colors and to provide fancy backdrops can cause you to quickly and easily make your pages entirely unreadable. Following are some hints for avoiding these problems:

- **Make sure you have enough contrast between the background and foreground (text) colors**—Low contrast can be hard to read. Also, light-colored text on a dark background is harder to read than dark text on a light background.

- **Avoid changing link colors at all**—Because your readers have attached semantic meanings to the default colors (blue means unfollowed, purple or red means followed), changing the colors can be very confusing.

- **Sometimes increasing the font size of all the text in your page using `<basefont>` can make it more readable on a background**—Both the background and the larger text will be missing in other browsers that don't support the Netscape tags.

- **If you're using a background pattern, make sure the pattern does not interfere with the text**—Some patterns may look interesting on their own but can make it difficult to read the text you put on top of them. Keep in mind that backgrounds are supposed to be in the background. Subtle patterns are always better than wild patterns. Remember, your readers are still visiting your pages for the content on them, not to marvel at your ability to create faux marble in your favorite image editor.

When in doubt, try asking a friend to look at your pages. Because you are familiar with the content and the text, you may not realize how hard your pages are to read. Someone who hasn't read them before will not have your biases and will be able to tell you that your colors are too close or that the pattern is interfering with the text. Of course, you'll have to find a friend who will be honest with you.

Other Good Habits and Hints

In this section, I've gathered several other miscellaneous hints and advice about good habits to get into when you're working with groups of Web pages. They include notes on how big to make each page in your site and how to sign your pages.

Link Back to Home

Consider including a link back to the top level or home page on every page of your site. Providing this link allows readers a quick escape from the depths of your content. Using a home link is much easier than trying to navigate backward through a hierarchy or trying to use the back facility of a browser.

Don't Split Topics Across Pages

Each Web page works best if it covers a single topic in its entirety. Don't split topics across pages; even if you link between them, the transition can be confusing. It will be even more confusing if someone jumps in on the second or third page and wonders what is going on.

If you think that one topic is becoming too large for a single page, consider reorganizing the content so that you can break up that topic into subtopics. This tip works especially well in hierarchical organizations. It allows you to determine exactly to what level of detail each "level" of the hierarchy should go, and exactly how big and complete each page should be.

Don't Create Too Many or Too Few Pages

There are no rules for how many pages you must have in your Web site, nor for how large each page should be. You can have one page or several thousand, depending on the amount of content you have and how you have organized it.

With this point in mind, you might decide to go to one extreme or to another, each of which has advantages and disadvantages. For example, say you put all your content in one big page and create links to sections within that page, as illustrated in Figure 16.22.

16

FIGURE 16.22

One big page.

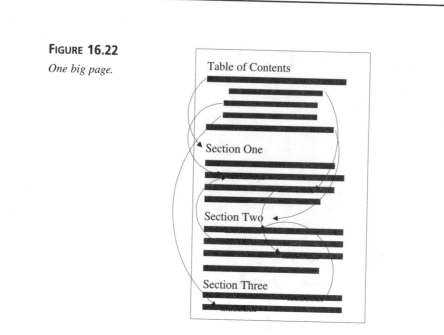

Advantages:

- One file is easier to maintain, and links within that file won't ever break if you move elements around or rename files.

- This file mirrors real-world document structure. If you're distributing documents both in hard copy and online, having a single document for both makes producing both easier.

Disadvantages:

- A large file takes a very long time to download, particularly over slow network connections and especially if the page includes a large number of graphics.

- Readers must scroll a lot to find what they want. Accessing particular bits of information can become tedious. Navigating at points other than at the top or bottom becomes close to impossible.

- The structure is overly rigid. A single page is inherently linear. Although readers can skip around within sections in the page, the structure still mirrors that of the printed page and doesn't take advantage of the flexibility of smaller pages linked in a non-linear fashion.

On the other extreme, you could create a whole bunch of little pages with links between them, as illustrated in Figure 16.23.

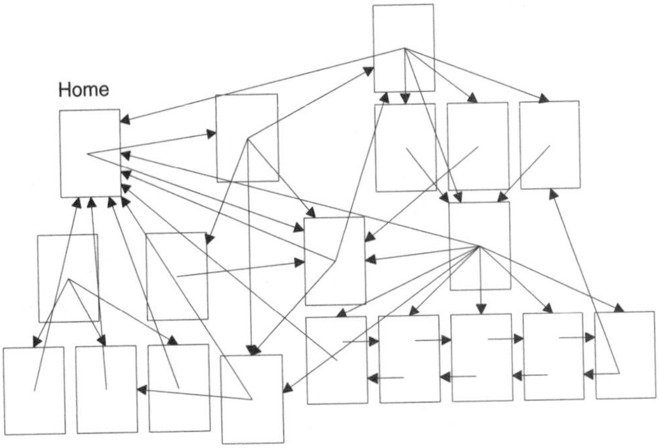

FIGURE 16.23

Many little pages.

Advantages:

- Smaller pages load very quickly.
- You often can fit the entire page on one screen, so the information in that page can be scanned very easily.

Disadvantages:

- Maintaining all those links will be a nightmare. Just adding some sort of navigational structure to that many pages may create thousands of links.
- If you have too many jumps between pages, the jumps may seem jarring. Continuity is difficult when your readers spend more time jumping than actually reading.

What is the solution? Often, the content you're describing will determine the size and number of pages you need, especially if you follow the one-topic-per-page suggestion. Testing your Web pages on a variety of platforms and network speeds will let you know whether a single page is too large. If you spend a lot of time scrolling around in it, or if it takes more time to load than you expected, your page may be too large.

Sign Your Pages

Each page should contain some sort of information at the bottom to act as the signature. I mention this tip briefly in Day 6, "More Text Formatting with HTML," as part of the description of the <address> tag; that particular tag was intended for just this purpose.

Consider putting the following useful information in the <address> tag on each page:

- Contact information for the person who created this Web page or the person responsible for it, colloquially known as the Webmaster. This information should include at least the person's name and preferably an email address.

- The status of the page. Is it complete? Is it a work-in-progress? Is it intentionally left blank?

- The date this page was last revised. This information is particularly important for pages that change often. Include a date on each page so that people know how old it is.

- Copyright or trademark information, if it applies.

- The URL of this page. Including a printed URL of a page that is found at that same URL may seem a bit like overkill, but what happens if someone prints out the page and loses any other reference to it in the stack of papers on her desk? Where did it come from? (I've lost URLs many times and often wished for a URL to be typed on the document itself.)

Figure 16.24 shows a nice example of an address block.

FIGURE 16.24

An sample address.

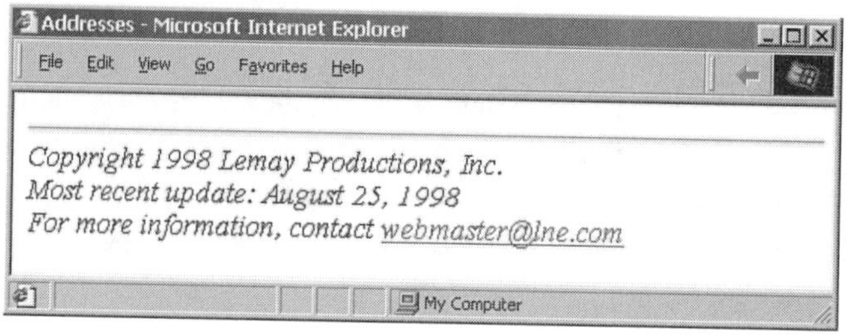

```
Copyright 1998 Lemay Productions, Inc.
Most recent update: August 25, 1998
For more information, contact webmaster@lne.com
```

A nice touch to include on your Web page is to link a Mailto URL to the text containing the email address of the Webmaster, as in the following:

```
<address>
Laura Lemay <a href="mailto:lemay@lne.com">lemay@lne.com</A>
</address>
```

This way, the readers of the page who have browsers that support the Mailto URL can simply select the link and send mail to the relevant person responsible for the page without having to retype the address into their mail programs.

Note

Linking Mailto URLs will work only in browsers that support Mailto URLs. Even in browsers that don't accept them, the link text will appear as usual, so there's no harm in including the link.

Finally, if you don't want to clutter each page with a lot of personal contact or boilerplate copyright information, a simple solution is to create a separate page for the extra information and then link the signature to that page. Here's an example:

```
<address>
<a href="copyright.html">Copyright</a> and
<a href="webmaster.html">contact</a> information is available.
</address>
```

Provide Non-Hypertext Versions of Hypertext Pages

16

Although the Web provides a way to create pages in new and exciting ways, some readers still like to read text offline, on the bus, or at the breakfast table. These kinds of readers have real problems with hypertext pages because after you start using hypertext to organize a document, it becomes difficult to tell your browser to "print the whole thing"—the browser knows only the boundaries of individual pages.

If you're using the Web to publish anything that might be readable and usable outside the Web, consider also creating a single text or PostScript version. You then can make it available as an external document for downloading. This way, your readers can both browse the document online and, if they want to, print it out for reading offline. You can even link the location of the hard-copy document to the start of the hypertext version, like the following:

```
A <a href="ftp://myhome.com/pub/mydir/myfile.ps">PostScript version</a> of
this document is available via ftp at myhome.com in the directory /pub/mydir/
myfile.ps.
```

Of course, a handy cross-reference for the hard-copy version would be to provide the URL for the hypertext version, as follows:

```
This document is also available on hypertext form on
the World Wide Web at the URL:
http://myhome.com/pub/mydir/myfile.index.html.
```

Summary

The main dos and don'ts for Web page design from this chapter are as follows:

- Do understand the differences between HTML 2.0, HTML 3.2, and the different flavors of HTML 4.0 and XHTML 1.0. Decide which design strategy to follow while using them.
- Do provide alternatives, if at all possible, if you use non-standard HTML tags.
- Do test your pages in multiple browsers.
- Do write your pages clearly and concisely.

- Do organize the text of your page so that your readers can scan for important information.

- Don't write Web pages that are dependent on pages before or after them in the structure. Do write context-independent pages.

- Don't overuse emphasis (such as boldface, italic, all caps, link text, blink, or marquees). Do use emphasis sparingly and only when absolutely necessary.

- Don't use terminology specific to any one browser (click here, use the back button, and so on).

- Do spell check and proofread your pages.

- Don't use heading tags to provide emphasis.

- Do group related information both semantically (through the organization of the content) and visually (through the use of headings or by separating sections with rule lines).

- Do use a consistent layout across all your pages.

- Do use link menus to organize your links for quick scanning, and do use descriptive links.

- Don't fall victim to the Here syndrome with your links.

- Do have good reasons for using links. Don't link to irrelevant material.

- Don't link repeatedly to the same site on the same page.

- Do keep your layout simple.

- Don't clutter the page with a large number of pretty but unnecessary images.

- Do provide alternatives to images for text-only browsers.

- Do try to keep your images small so that they load faster over the network.

- Do be careful with backgrounds and colored text so that you do not make your pages flashy but unreadable.

- Do always provide a link back to your home page.

- Do match topics with pages.

- Don't split individual topics across pages.

- Do provide a signature block or link to contact information at the bottom of each page.

- Do provide single-page, non-hypertext versions of linear documents.

Workshop

Put on your thinking cap again, because it's time for another review. The questions, quiz, and exercises in this chapter will help get you in the frame of mind where you think about the items that you should (or should not) include on your pages.

Q&A

16

Q **I've seen statistics on the Web that say the majority of people on the Web are using Netscape and Internet Explorer. Why should I continue designing my pages for other browsers and testing my pages in other browsers when most of the world is using one of these two browsers anyhow?**

A You can design your pages explicitly for Netscape, Internet Explorer, or both if you want to; your pages are your pages, and the decision is yours. But, given how easily you can make small modifications that allow your pages to be viewed and read in other browsers without losing much of the design, why lock out the remainder of your audience for the sake of a few tags? Remember, with estimates of the size of the Web growing all the time, that minority of readers could very well be a million people or more.

Q **I'm converting existing documents into Web pages. These documents are very text-heavy and are intended to be read from start to finish instead of being quickly scanned. I can't restructure or redesign the content to better follow the guidelines you've suggested in this chapter—that's not my job. What can I do?**

A Some content is going to be structured this way, particularly when you're converting a document written for paper to online. Ideally, you would be able to rewrite and restructure for the online site, but realistically you often cannot do anything with the content other than throw it online.

All is not lost, however. You can still improve the overall presentation of these documents by providing reasonable indexes to the content (summaries, tables of contents pages, subject indexes, and so on), and by including standard navigation links back out of the text-heavy pages. In other words, you can create an easily navigable framework around the documents themselves, which can go a long way toward improving content that is otherwise difficult to read online.

Q **I have a standard signature block that contains my name and email address, revision information for the page, and a couple of lines of copyright information that my company's lawyers insisted on. It's a little imposing, particularly on small pages, where the signature is bigger than the page itself!**

A If your company's lawyers agree, consider putting all your contact and copyright information on a separate page and then linking it on every page rather than duplicating it every time. This way, your pages won't be overwhelmed by the legal stuff, and if the signature changes, you won't have to change it on every single page.

Quiz

1. What are the three "flavors" of HTML 4.0 and XHTML 1.0, and which of the three accommodates the widest range of users?

2. What are some ways you can your pages organize your pages so that readers can scan them more easily?

3. True or false: headings are a good thing to use when you want information to stand out because the text is large and bold.

4. True or false: you can reduce the download time of an image by using the `width` and `height` attributes of the `<img>` tag to scale the image down.

5. What are the advantages and disadvantages of creating one big Web page versus several smaller ones?

Answers

1. The three "flavors" of HTML 4.0 and XHTML 1.0 are *Transitional* (for the widest range of users, and designed to accommodate those who are using older browsers), *Frameset* (which includes all tags in the Transitional specification, plus those for framesets), and *Strict* (for those who want to stick to pure HTML 4.0 or XHTML 1.0 tags and attributes).

2. You can use headings to summarize topics, use lists to organize and display information, use link menus for navigation, and separate important information from long paragraphs.

3. False. You should use headings as headings. You can emphasize text on pages in other ways, or use a graphic to draw attention to an important point.

4. A trick question—when you use the `width` and `height` attribute to make a large image appear smaller on your page, it may reduce the dimensions of the file, but it will not decrease the download time. You still download the same image, but the browser just fits that large image into a smaller space.

5. The advantages of creating one large page are that one file is easier to maintain, links won't break, and it mirrors real-world document structure. The disadvantages are that it will have a longer download time, readers have to scroll a lot, and the structure is rigid and too linear.

Exercises

1. Try your hand at reworking the example shown in Figure 16.2. Organize the information into a definition list or into a table. Make it easy for the reader to scan for the important points in the page.

2. Try the same with the example shown in Figure 16.4. How can you arrange the information on that page so that it is easier to find the important points and links on the page?

16

DAY 17

Examples of Good and Bad Web Design

In this chapter, you'll walk through some simple examples of pages and sites that you might find out on the Web. (Actually, you won't find these particular pages out on the Web; I developed these examples specifically for this chapter.) Each of these Web sites is either typical of the kind of information being provided on the Web today or shows some unique method for solving problems you might run into while developing your own sites. In particular, you'll explore the following Web sites:

- A company profile for Foozle Industries, a company that specializes in sweaters and knitted products
- An encyclopedia of motorcycles, with images, sounds, and other media clips
- A catalog for a small nursery, in which you can both browse and order herbs, spices, and aromatic vegetables

In each example, I note some of the more interesting features of the page as well as some of the issues you might want to consider as you develop your own pages and sites.

The code and images for these examples are included on the book's Web support site
(see the inside back cover for details).

Example One: A Company Profile

Foozle Industries, Inc. makes a wide variety of knitted clothing and blankets for all occasions. Customers visiting the Foozle Industries Web site would first be presented with the Foozle Industries home page (see Figure 17.1). Overall, the Web author has decided to use Cascading Style Sheets to format the appearance of the Web pages.

In addition to the consistency that the author achieved with style sheets, there are other items that appear the same from page to page. Each of the main pages in the site includes a small but attractive banner that displays the title of each of the main pages. Also, the bottom of each page includes a navigation bar, copyright information, and an email address to contact for questions or comments about the site.

FIGURE 17.1

*Foozle Industries
home page.*

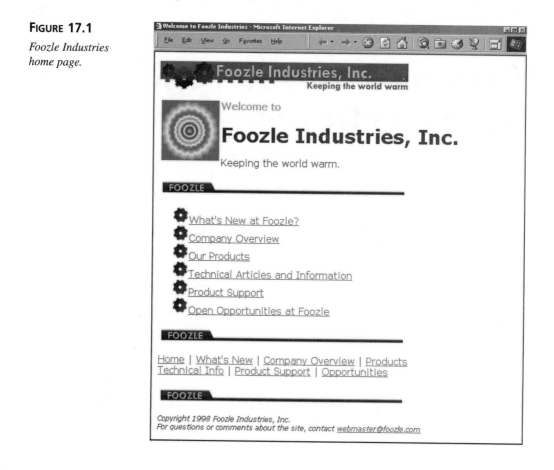

From this simple but nonpretentious home page, the customer has several choices of pages to visit on Foozle's Web site, arranged in a link menu. I won't describe all of them in this section, but I'll mention just a few that provide interesting features.

What's New at Foozle?

Selecting the What's New link takes you, appropriately, to the What's New page (see Figure 17.2). This is the first link on the home page and the second (after the Home link) in the navigation bar.

FIGURE 17.2

The Foozle What's New page.

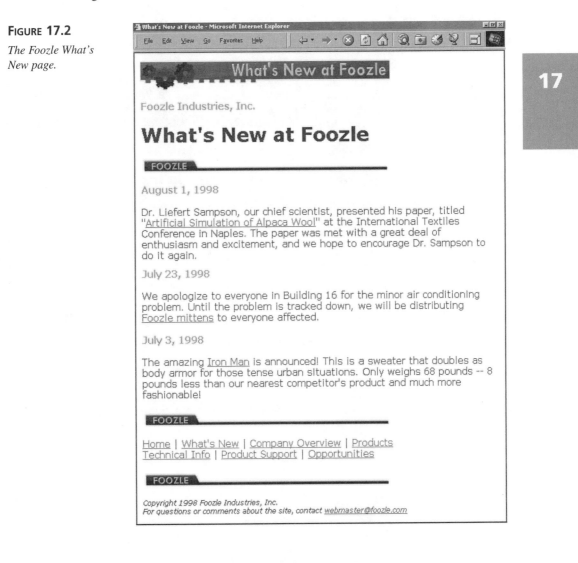

17

Organized in reverse chronological order (from the most recent event backwards), the What's New page contains information about interesting things going on at Foozle Industries, both inside and outside the company. This page is useful for announcing new products to customers on the Web, or just providing information about the site, the company, or other Foozle information. What's New pages, in general, are useful for sites that are visited repeatedly and frequently, as they enable your readers to find the new information on your site quickly and easily without having to search for it.

In this What's New page, the topmost item in the list of new things is a note about a paper presented by the Foozle chief scientist at a conference in Naples. That item has a link attached to it, implying that the paper itself is on the other side of that link, and, sure enough, it is (see Figure 17.3).

FIGURE 17.3

All about Foozle Alpaca wool.

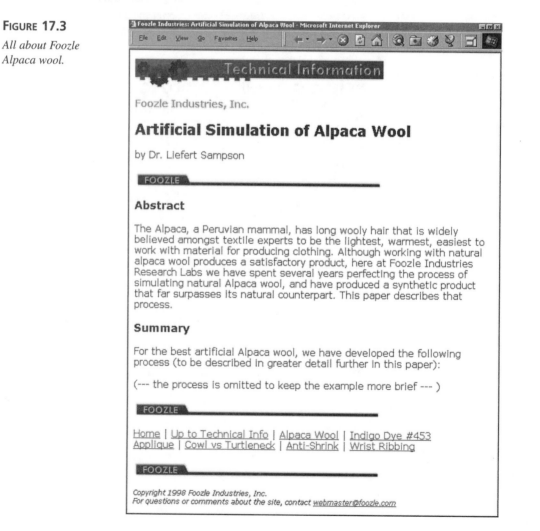

Alpaca wool is fascinating, but where do you go from here? The links at the bottom of the page are different here than they are on the main level page. Here, the reader has several new navigation choices. He or she can go to the Foozle home page (through the Home link), up to the Technical Info page (through the Technical Info link), or sideways to any of the other technical papers, the titles of which are briefly shown in the navigation bar. This same navigation bar appears on all the technical papers within this section, allowing for easy navigation between them.

You've visited the home page already, so now go on to the Technical Information page.

Technical Information

The Technical Information section of the Foozle Web site provides a list of the papers Foozle has published describing technical issues surrounding the making of sweaters (see Figure 17.4). (You didn't know there were any, did you?) Each link in the list takes you to the paper it describes.

From here, you can move down in the hierarchy and read any of the papers, or choose any of the other main pages in the Web through links in the navigation bar. You then would have the choice of exploring the other portions of the Web site: the What's New page, the Company Overview, the product descriptions, or the listing of open opportunities.

The Company Overview

The Company Overview page provides a list of links to other pages that display more information about the company. If you so choose, you can learn more about what the company does, its mission, its company history, and the location of the company headquarters. This page appears in Figure 17.5.

The Foozle Products Page

Choosing the next link in the navigation bar, you come to the Foozle Products page. Here, you can link to catalog sheets (similar to those shown in the Shopping Catalog example that appears later in this chapter). This is the perfect place to provide pictures, descriptions, and pricing information for all the products that the company makes. The Products page is shown in Figure 17.6.

17

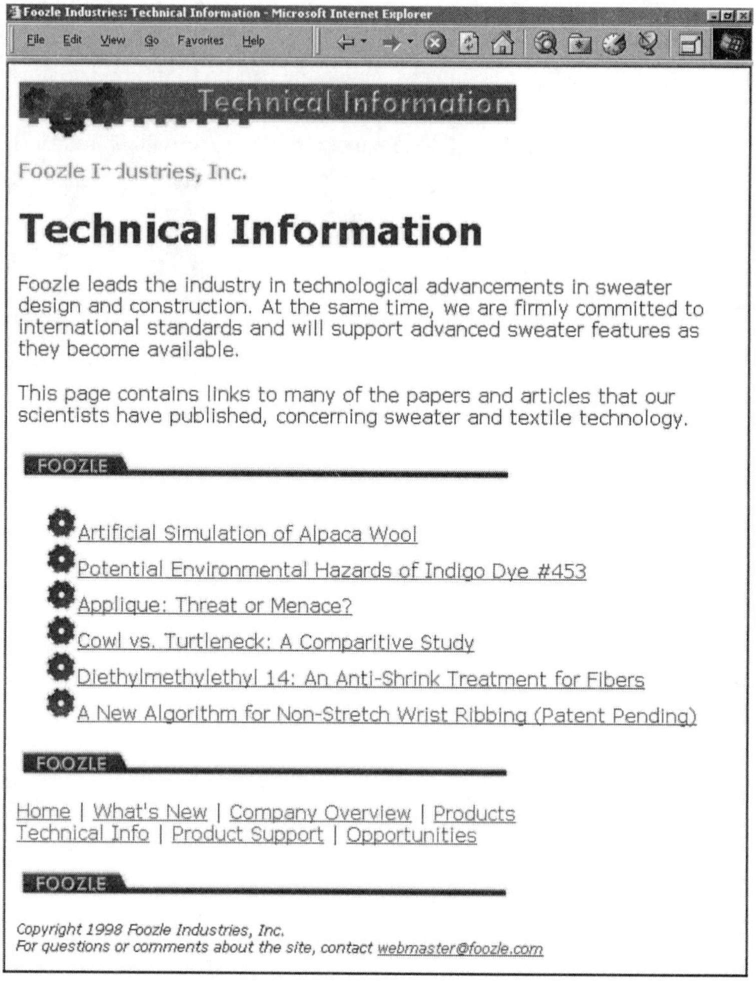

FIGURE 17.4

*The Technical
Information section.*

Technical Information

Foozle Industries, Inc.

Technical Information

Foozle leads the industry in technological advancements in sweater design and construction. At the same time, we are firmly committed to international standards and will support advanced sweater features as they become available.

This page contains links to many of the papers and articles that our scientists have published, concerning sweater and textile technology.

FOOZLE

- Artificial Simulation of Alpaca Wool
- Potential Environmental Hazards of Indigo Dye #453
- Applique: Threat or Menace?
- Cowl vs. Turtleneck: A Comparitive Study
- Diethylmethylethyl 14: An Anti-Shrink Treatment for Fibers
- A New Algorithm for Non-Stretch Wrist Ribbing (Patent Pending)

FOOZLE

Home | What's New | Company Overview | Products
Technical Info | Product Support | Opportunities

FOOZLE

Copyright 1998 Foozle Industries, Inc.
For questions or comments about the site, contact webmaster@foozle.com

FIGURE 17.5

The Company Overview page.

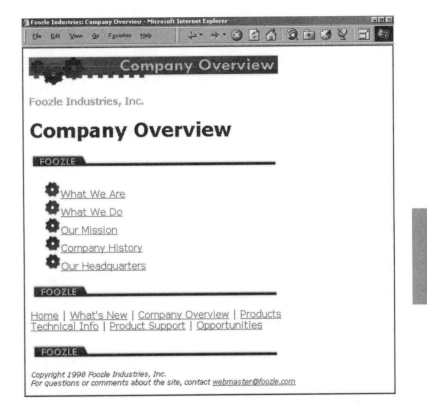

The Product Support Page

Even users of sweaters and knitted products have to be supported. A customer could have many questions about the use and care of his Foozle product, so Foozle has appropriately provided a place for customers to obtain this information. In Figure 17.7, you see the Product Support page, which provides a list of frequently asked questions about Foozle products. If the customer's question isn't answered on the page, the customer email address of the support department is provided on the page.

From here, you can move down in the hierarchy and read any of the papers, or select any of the other main pages in the Web site.

FIGURE 17.6

The Foozle Products page.

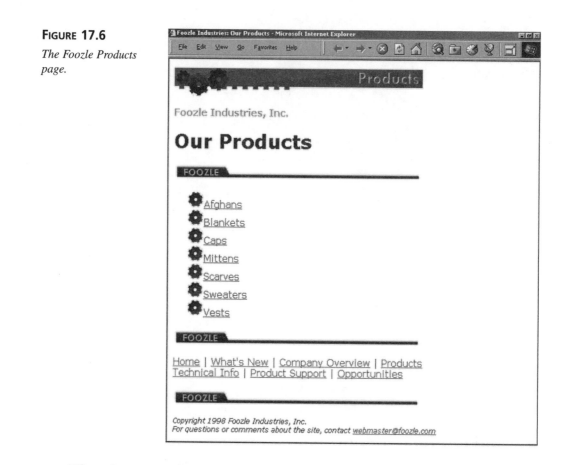

The Open Opportunities Page

A progressive company, such as Foozle, is constantly looking for talented individuals to work for its company and welcomes inquiries and resumes, even when there are no openings available. Figure 17.8 displays a page that lists open opportunities (when they are available), and provides contact information for those who are seeking employment with the company.

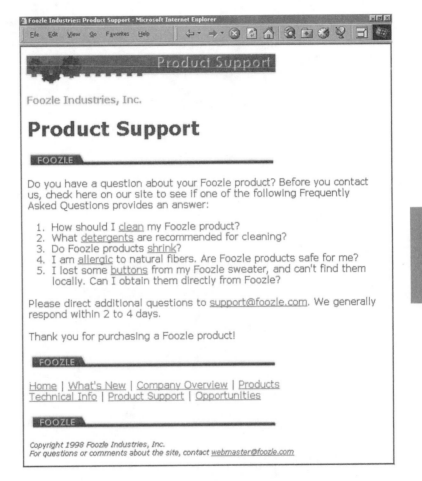

FIGURE 17.7

*The Product Support
page.*

17

Features of This Web Site and Issues for Development

This Web site for a simple company profile is quite straightforward in terms of design; the structure is a simple hierarchy, with link menus for navigation to the appropriate pages. You also can include the navigation bar at the top of the page; or even both at the top and the bottom of the page in the event that the reader does not read the entire page. Expanding the navigation system is a simple matter of adding "limbs" to the hierarchy by adding new links to the top-level page.

FIGURE 17.8

*The Open
Opportunities page.*

Note, however, the path you took through the few pages in this Web site. In a classic hierarchy, you visit each "limb" in turn, exploring downward, and then creeping back up levels to visit new pages. Remember the link between the What's New page and the paper on Alpaca wool? This link caused you to move sideways from one limb (the What's New page) to another (the Technical Papers section). By providing a different navigation bar that enables you to navigate home, up, or sideways to other technical papers, you can easily find your way back to any of the major sections in the Web.

In this example, of course, given its simplicity, there is little confusion. If a hierarchy is much more complicated than this, with multiple levels and sub-trees, however, having links that cross hierarchical boundaries enables you to break out of the structure and that can be confusing. After a few lateral links, it can become difficult to figure out where you are in the hierarchy. This is a common problem with most hypertext systems, and often is referred to as *getting lost in hyperspace*.

Few really good solutions exist to the problem of getting lost. A current solution is to provide framesets that simplify navigation in sites that are more complex; however, even those must be designed with care. Too many frames not only adds to the confusion, but also makes it difficult to read pages at lower resolutions. I prefer to avoid the problem by trying not to create too many lateral links across a hierarchy. If you stick with the rigid structure of the hierarchy and provide only navigational links, readers can usually figure out where they are. If not, they usually have only two main choices: Move back up in the hierarchy to a known point, or drill deeper into the hierarchy for more detailed information.

17

Example Two: A Multimedia Encyclopedia

The Multimedia Encyclopedia of Motorcycles is a set of Web pages that provides extensive information about motorcycles and their manufacturers. In addition to text information about each motorcycle maker, the multimedia encyclopedia includes photographs, sounds (engine noises!), and video for many of the motorcycles listed.

The index is organized alphabetically, one page per letter or group of letters (`a.html`, `b.html`, `c.html`, `d.html`, `efg.html`, and so on.) To help navigate into the body of the encyclopedia, the home page for this site is an overview page.

The Overview Page

The overview page is the main entry point into the body of the encyclopedia (see Figure 17.9).

This page provides two main ways to get into the encyclopedia: by selecting the first letter of the marque, or by selecting the name of one of the specific marques mentioned in the list itself.

Note

A *marque* is a fancy term used by motorcycle and sports car fanatics to refer to manufacturers of a vehicle.

FIGURE 17.9

The Motorcycle Encyclopedia overview page.

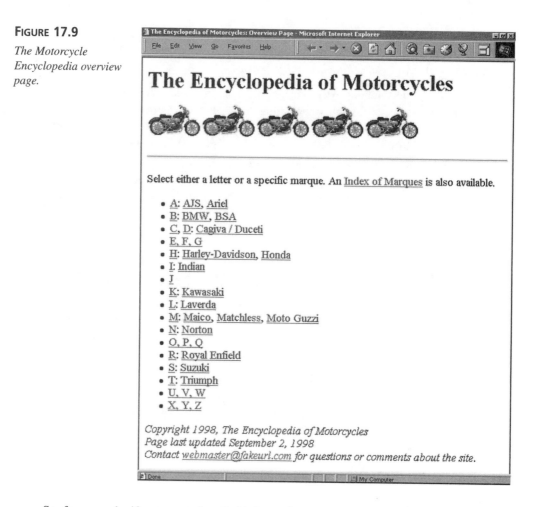

So, for example, if you wanted to find information about the Norton motorcycle company, you could select N, for Norton, and then from there scroll down to the appropriate link in the N page. Because Norton is one of the major manufacturers listed next to the N link on the Overview page, however, you could select that link instead, and go straight to the Norton page.

The Norton Page

Each individual page contains an entry for each of the marques. If the reader has chosen a specific manufacturer, the link points directly to that specific page (for example, the page for Norton, shown in Figure 17.10). Each marque page contains information about the manufacturer and the various motorcycles they have produced over the years.

The Encyclopedia of Motorcycles: Norton - Microsoft Internet Explorer
The Encyclopedia of Motorcycles
Overview | Index of Marques
Norton
The Norton company began in 1902 when James Lansdowne Norton put a French Clement engine into a frame of his own design. In 1907 Norton designed his own engine and competed on it in the TT races of 1909-1911.
Although Norton himself died in 1925, the company's 350cc and 500cc single-cylinder motorcycles went on to win several TT races in the 20's and 30's. Norton met further success in the late 40's due to the development of the 500cc Dominator Twin engine.
The Dominator slowly increased in capacity throughout the 50's and 60's -- from 500cc to 600, 650, and finally 750cc. The Vandervell family acquired the company from Norton, and it later changed hands to AMC, who also owned Matchless and AJS. Following this, the company was acquired by the Manganese Bronze Holding Company, who focused on the 750cc version of the Dominator and renamed it the Atlas.
The Norton Commando was released in 1967, with a new frame that promised to cut down on vibration. The Commando, in 750cc and 850cc models, was to become the flagship model of the Norton Motorcycle Company for ten years.
In the mid-70's the Norton Company ran into financial trouble, and was merged with the Triumph/BSA company to form NVT (Norton-Villers-Triumph). Since then, the company has struggled along under several different owners. Other than an interesting foray into motorcycles powered by Wankel rotary engines, the company has produced few motorcycles.
Norton Media
The following media files are available on Norton products. Where multiple links appear beneath a description, they are different versions of the same file. Select a version that is compatible with your browser.
Line drawing of the 1926 490cc OHV Engine
(49K GIF File)
850 Commando
(46K JPEG File)
(120K GIF File)
850 Commando Engine
(350K AU Sound File)
(479K WAV File)
3D Rotational Rendering of a Norton Motorcycle
(289KB Animated GIF)
(194KB Windows AVI)
(190KB Quick Time Video)
(151KB MPEG-1 Video)
Norton Manx winning a race in 1938
(768K Quicktime Video)
Copyright 1998, The Encyclopedia of Motorcycles
Page last updated September 2, 1998
Contact webmaster@fakeurl.com for questions or comments about the site.

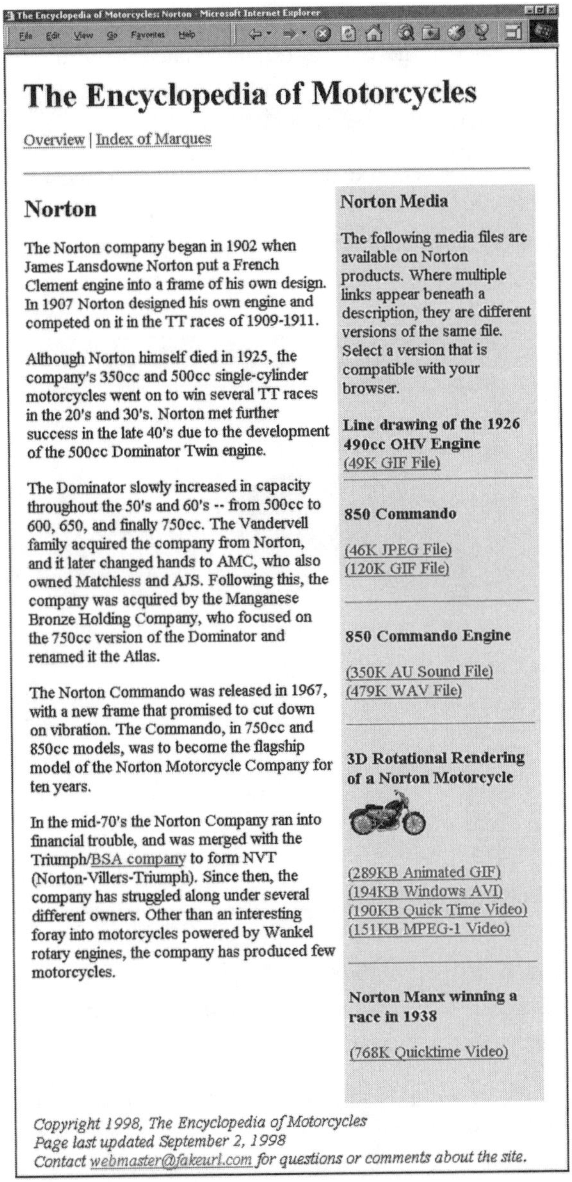

FIGURE 17.10
Entry for Norton.

So where are the pictures? This was supposed to be a multimedia encyclopedia, wasn't it? In addition to the text describing Norton itself, which is displayed in the left side of a table, the page also includes a list of external media files. The media list is included in the right side of the table. Because the background color of the cell that includes these links is colored differently, the media links are visually isolated from the text on the page, making it clear that these are extra, but related, features about the Norton company. The media section includes images of various motorcycles, sound clips of how they sound, and film of famous riders on their Nortons.

Each media file is described in text and contains links to those files so that you can download them if you choose. Selecting the link that displays a 3D rotational rendering of a Norton motorcycle in animated GIF format, for example, accesses the animated GIF file displayed in Figure 17.11.

FIGURE 17.11

A 3D rendering of a Norton motorcycle.

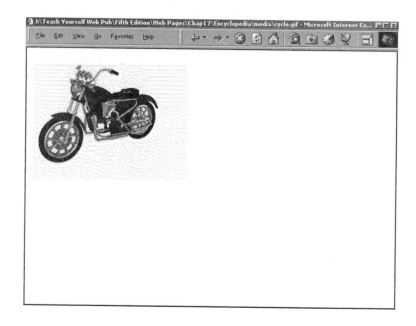

Note also that in each point in the text where another manufacturer is mentioned, that manufacturer is linked to its own entry. Selecting the word BSA in the last paragraph on the Norton page, for example, takes you to the entry for BSA (see Figure 17.12).

In this way, the reader can jump from link to link and manufacturer to manufacturer, exploring the information the encyclopedia contains based on what interests him or her. After he or she is done exploring, however, getting back to a known point is always important. For just this purpose, each entry in the encyclopedia contains a Back to Overview link. The duplication of this link in each entry means that the reader never has to scroll far in order to find the line.

FIGURE **17.12**

Entry for BSA.

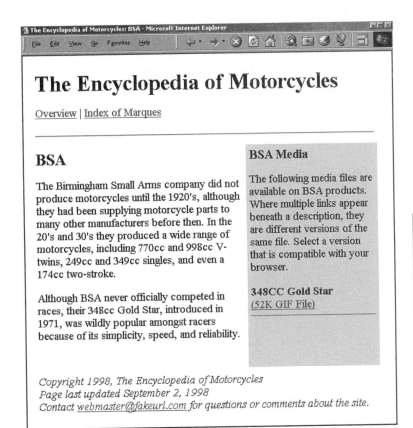

The Index of Marques is shown in the browser window:

The Encyclopedia of Motorcycles

Overview | Index of Marques

BSA

The Birmingham Small Arms company did not produce motorcycles until the 1920's, although they had been supplying motorcycle parts to many other manufacturers before then. In the 20's and 30's they produced a wide range of motorcycles, including 770cc and 998cc V-twins, 249cc and 349cc singles, and even a 174cc two-stroke.

Although BSA never officially competed in races, their 348cc Gold Star, introduced in 1971, was wildly popular amongst racers because of its simplicity, speed, and reliability.

BSA Media

The following media files are available on BSA products. Where multiple links appear beneath a description, they are different versions of the same file. Select a version that is compatible with your browser.

348CC Gold Star
(52K GIF File)

Copyright 1998, The Encyclopedia of Motorcycles
Page last updated September 2, 1998
Contact webmaster@fakeurl.com for questions or comments about the site.

The Index of Marques

Back on the main overview page, there's one more feature I'd like to point out: The overview also contains a link to an Index of Marques, an alphabetical listing of all the manufacturers of motorcycles mentioned in the encyclopedia (see Figure 17.13).

Each name in the index is, as you might expect, a link to the entry for that manufacturer in the encyclopedia itself, providing yet another way to quickly navigate into the alphabetic listings. An additional enhancement to the index appears near the top of the page. The Jump To list of links enables the reader to quickly access the marques that begin with a specific letter, rather than having to scroll through the entire index. By selecting, the "O" section in the Jump To links, for example, the reader jumps to the "O" anchor on the page. Another link, at the end of the "O" section (similar to that shown at the end of the "A" section in Figure 17.13) takes the reader back to the top of the page, where he or she can choose another letter.

FIGURE 17.13

The Index of Marques.

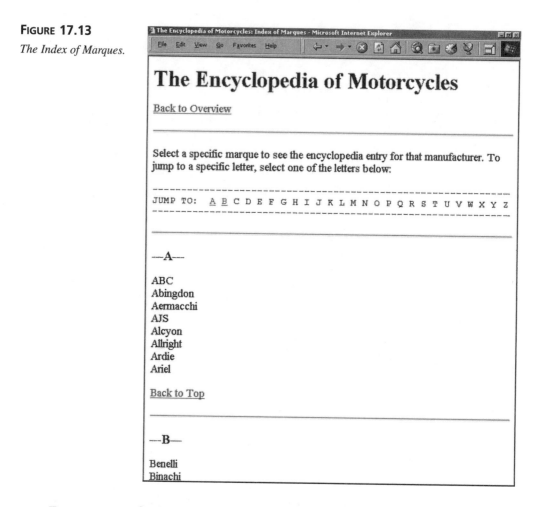

Features of This Web Site and Issues for Development

Probably the best feature of the design of this encyclopedia is the overview page. In many cases, an online encyclopedia of this sort would provide links to each letter in the alphabet and leave it at that. If you wanted to check out Norton motorcycles, you would select the link for "N" and then scroll down to the entry for Norton. By providing links to some of the more popular motorcycle makers on the overview page itself, the author of this Web page provides a simple, quick reference that shortens the scrolling time and takes its readers directly to where they want to be.

The addition of the Index of Marques also is a nice touch, as it enables readers to jump directly to the entry of a particular manufacturer's name, to reduce the amount of scrolling required to find the entry they want. Again, it's the same content in the encyclopedia. The overview page simply provides several different ways to find the information for which readers might be looking.

The encyclopedia itself is structured in a loosely based Web pattern, making it possible for readers to jump in just about anywhere and then follow cross-references and graze through the available information, uncovering connections between motorcycles and marques and motorcycle history that might be difficult to uncover in a traditional paper encyclopedia. Also, by providing all the media files external to the pages themselves, the author of this Web site not only allows the encyclopedia to be used equally well by those who view images when they browse the Web and those who don't, but also keeps each page small so it can load quickly over the Internet.

Finally, note that every marque page (such as the Norton and BSA pages shown in Figures 17.10 and 17.12) has a link back to the Overview page and to the Index of Marques. If there were more than these links, they would clutter the page and look ugly. But because the only explicit navigation choices are back to the Overview or to the Index of Marques, including these two links enables the reader to quickly and easily get back out of the encyclopedia. He or she does not have to scroll to the top or the bottom of the document, as would be the case in a more conventional organization.

The biggest issue with developing a Web site of this kind is in setup and maintenance. Depending on the amount of material you have to put online, the task of arranging it all presents immediate challenges (do you use exactly 26 files, one for each letter of the alphabet, or do you feature one manufacturer per page?) Perhaps, as a compromise, you can combine the marques that have a little bit of information (such as the BSA page) on a letter page (b.html), and feature the more prominent marques, like Norton, on a page of their own.

In any case, creating the links for all the cross-references and all the external media can be daunting indeed. Fortunately, a site of this sort does not have to be updated very often, so after the initial work is done, the maintenance is not all that difficult. To add new information, you simply put it in the appropriate spot, create new links to and from the new information, and there you are.

Example Three: A Shopping Catalog

Anna's Herb and Spice Garden is a commercial nursery specializing in growing and shipping herbs, spices, and aromatic vegetables for the discerning gardener and chef. It offers more than 120 species of plants, as well as books and other related items. Figure 17.14 shows the home page for Anna's Herb and Spice Garden.

Anna, too, has used Cascading Style Sheets to provide background colors and text and link colors for her Web site. Her company name appears within the title of each Web page, and also appears in graphic form with a logo image at the top of each page. Anna has decided to place links to the main pages in her Web near the top of the page. This doesn't force the reader to scroll through the entire page to navigate elsewhere. The navigation bar provides links to the pages that are most-used by readers: the Home page, the Browse Catalog page, How to Order, and the Order Form.

FIGURE 17.14

Anna's Herb and Spice Garden home page.

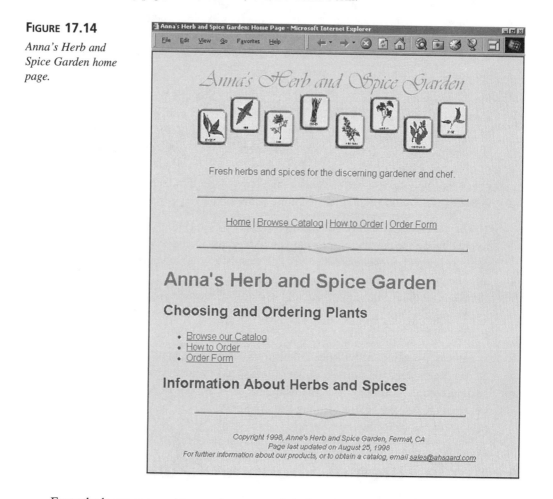

From the home page, customers have several choices: browse the catalog, get information about ordering, and actually order the plants or other products they have chosen.

Browsing the Catalog

Selecting the Browse Our Catalog link takes customers to another menu page, where they have several choices for how they want to browse the catalog (see Figure 17.15).

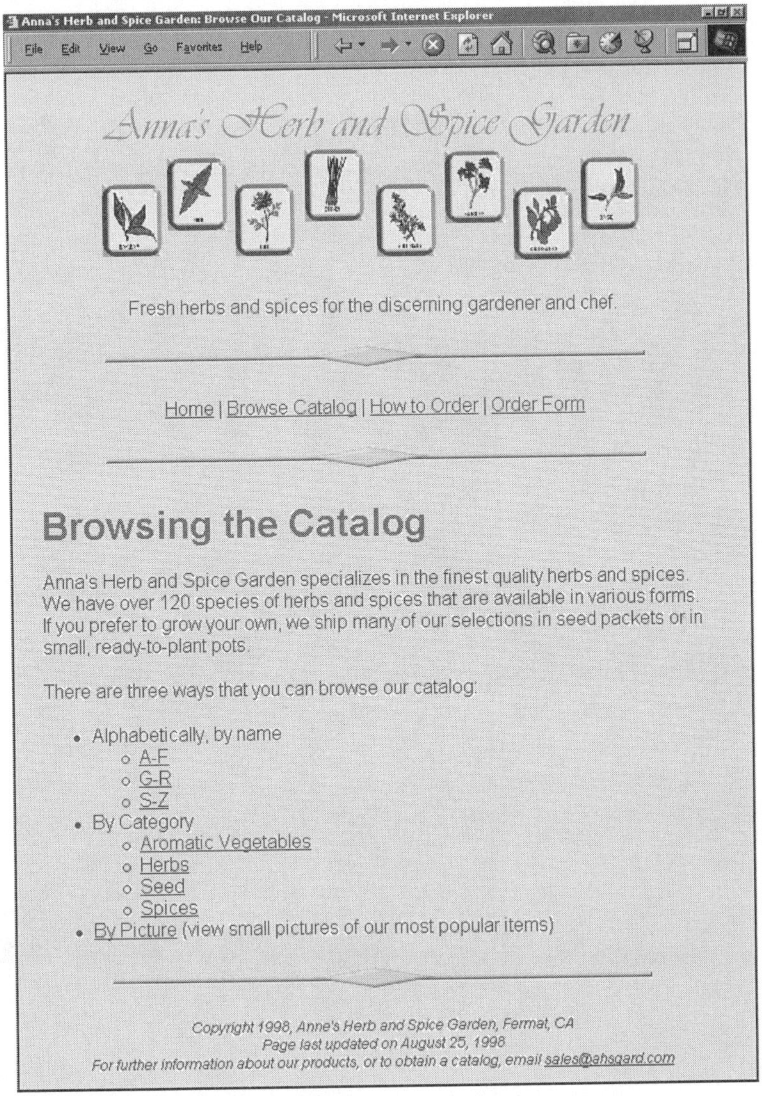

FIGURE 17.15

How to browse the catalog.

By providing several different views of the catalog, the author is serving many different kinds of customers. For those who know about herbs and spices and who just want to look up a specific variety, the alphabetic index is most appropriate. Those who know they would like some fresh herb plants for their gardens but are not sure which kinds of herbs they want, for example, can browse by the Herb category. Finally, those who don't really know or care about the names but would like something that looks nice can use the photo gallery.

The alphabetical links (A–F, G–R, S–Z) take customers to an alphabetical listing of the plants available for purchase. Figure 17.16 shows a sample listing from the alphabetical catalog. In this case, the A–F page is displayed.

FIGURE 17.16

The Catalog, A–F alphabetical link.

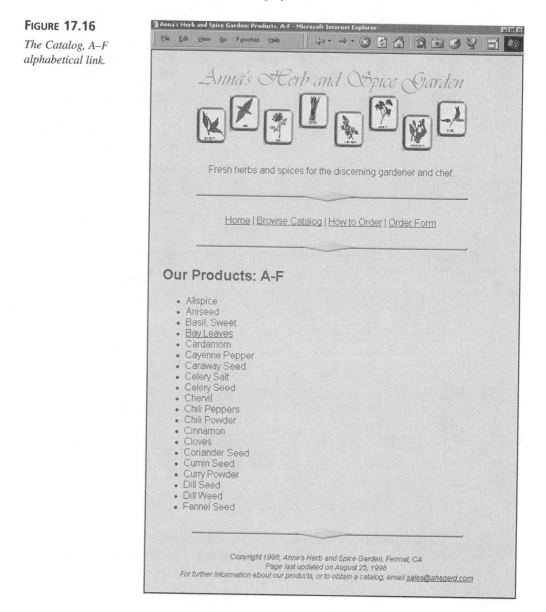

I haven't completed all the links on this page, but assume that each of the links takes the reader to a page that displays more information about a particular herb, spice, or aromatic vegetable. If the reader chooses the link to learn more about Bay Leaves (which is completed on the page shown in Figure 17.16), he or she is directed to a page that describes the product in more detail. An example is shown in Figure 17.17.

FIGURE **17.17**

A product page.

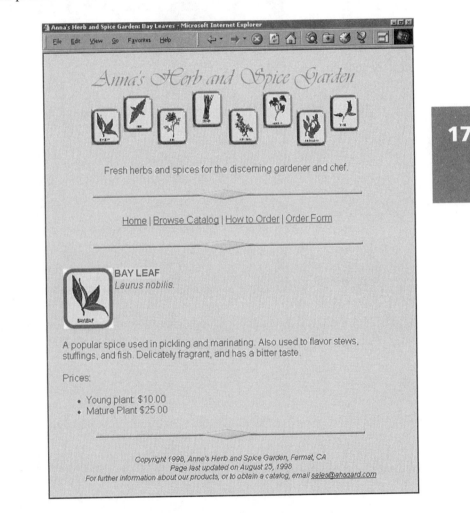

Each product page displays a small photograph of the plant (here shown as line art images for representation). Next to the photo are the English and Latin or scientific names of the herb. Following that is a brief description of the typical uses of each herb, a description of its taste, and other information that might be noteworthy. Finally, a bulleted list displays the ways the reader can order the plant and the prices of each.

The second view of the catalog (accessible from the Browsing the Catalog page shown in Figure 17.15) is the category view. Selecting one of the links in the By Category section of the Browse the Catalog page takes the reader to yet another page of menus. In this case, if the reader selects the Herb category, the page shown in Figure 17.18 appears.

FIGURE **17.18**

A category view.

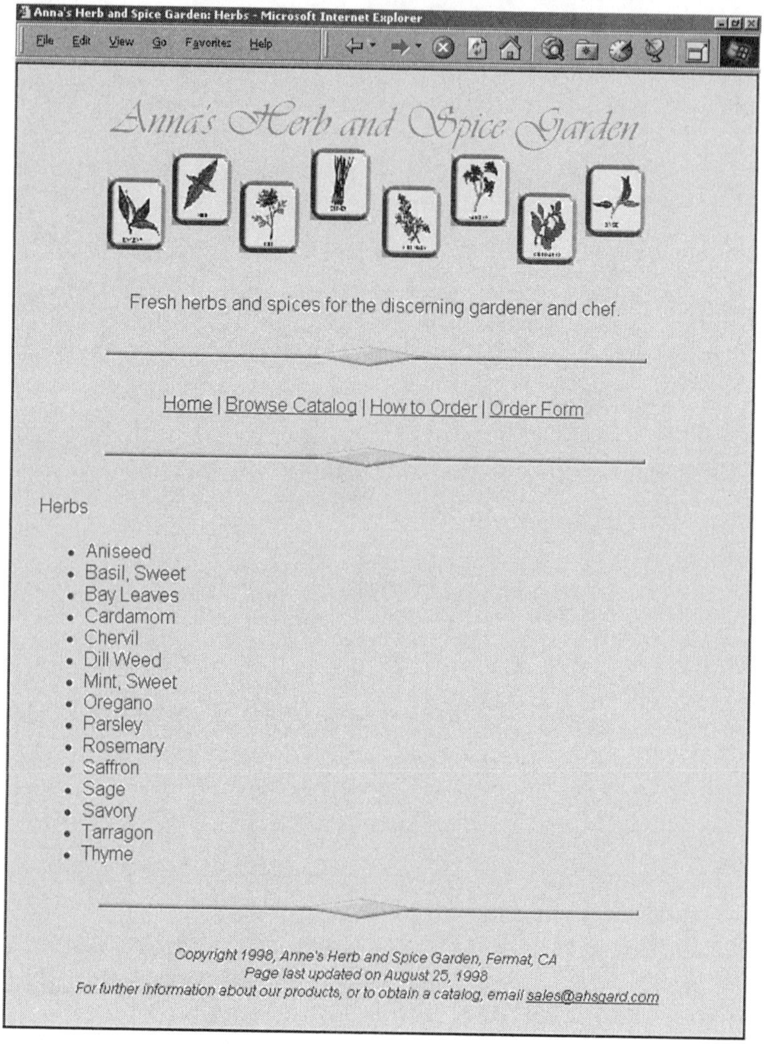

Anna's Herb and Spice Garden: Herbs - Microsoft Internet Explorer

File   Edit   View   Go   Favorites   Help

Anna's Herb and Spice Garden

Fresh herbs and spices for the discerning gardener and chef.

Home | Browse Catalog | How to Order | Order Form

Herbs

- Aniseed
- Basil, Sweet
- Bay Leaves
- Cardamom
- Chervil
- Dill Weed
- Mint, Sweet
- Oregano
- Parsley
- Rosemary
- Saffron
- Sage
- Savory
- Tarragon
- Thyme

Copyright 1998, Anne's Herb and Spice Garden, Fermat, CA
Page last updated on August 25, 1998
For further information about our products, or to obtain a catalog, email sales@ahsgard.com

Selecting the Herbs category takes customers to a listing of the available herbs. Again, I have not completed all the links on this page, but each link takes the reader to a specific product page, such as the one shown in Figure 17.17. From the category index, customers can go back to the Browse Catalog page. Here, there's one more way to view the catalog: the photo gallery.

The photo gallery enables customers to browse many of the plants available at the nursery by looking at pictures of them, rather than having to know their scientific names. If a customer wants to find a plant that he or she saw in someone else's garden, but can't remember its name, for example, this is the ideal place to browse. This feature is obviously available only to graphical browsers but provides an excellent way to browse for interesting cacti.

The photo gallery page (shown in Figure 17.19) is organized as a series of icons, with each small picture of the plant linking to a larger JPEG equivalent. The text description of each picture also takes you back to the appropriate entry in the main catalog.

Ordering

After customers finish browsing the catalog, and they have an idea of the plants they want to order, they can jump to the Anna's Herb and Spice Garden How to Order page and find out how to place their order.

The page for ordering is just some simple text (see Figure 17.20): information about where to call or send checks, tables for shipping costs, notes on when the nursery will ship plants, and so on.

In the section on ordering by mail, there is a link to an order form. You can create the order form in several different ways. If you don't want to get into the bother of creating forms and writing form handlers, you can create a simple text file that includes an order form. Customers can download or display the order form in their browsers, as shown in Figure 17.21. They then can print it out, fill in the blanks, and send it to the nursery.

There are other ways that you can provide external versions of this document as well. For example, you can provide a postscript file, an Adobe Acrobat Reader file (which uses a .PDF extension), or even specific word processor formats, such as Microsoft Word or Word Perfect. Simply store the files on your Web site as you would any other page, and include a link to that file on your Web page. The reader will be prompted to download the page if he does not have a viewer or helper application that can display the document as a Web page.

FIGURE 17.19

The Photo Gallery page.

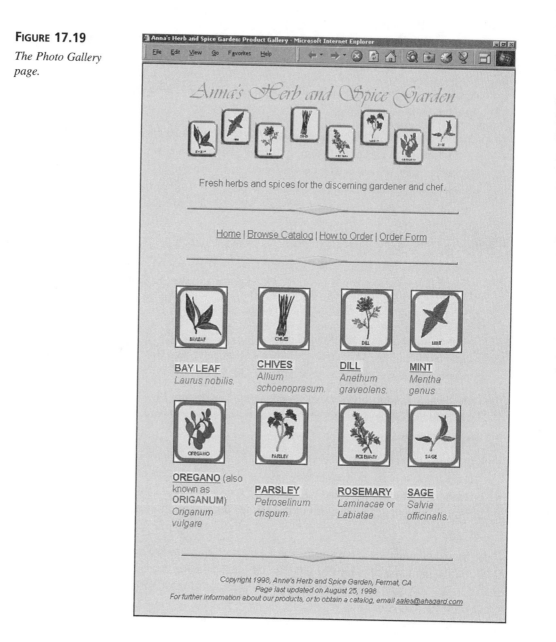

FIGURE 17.20

Ordering plants.

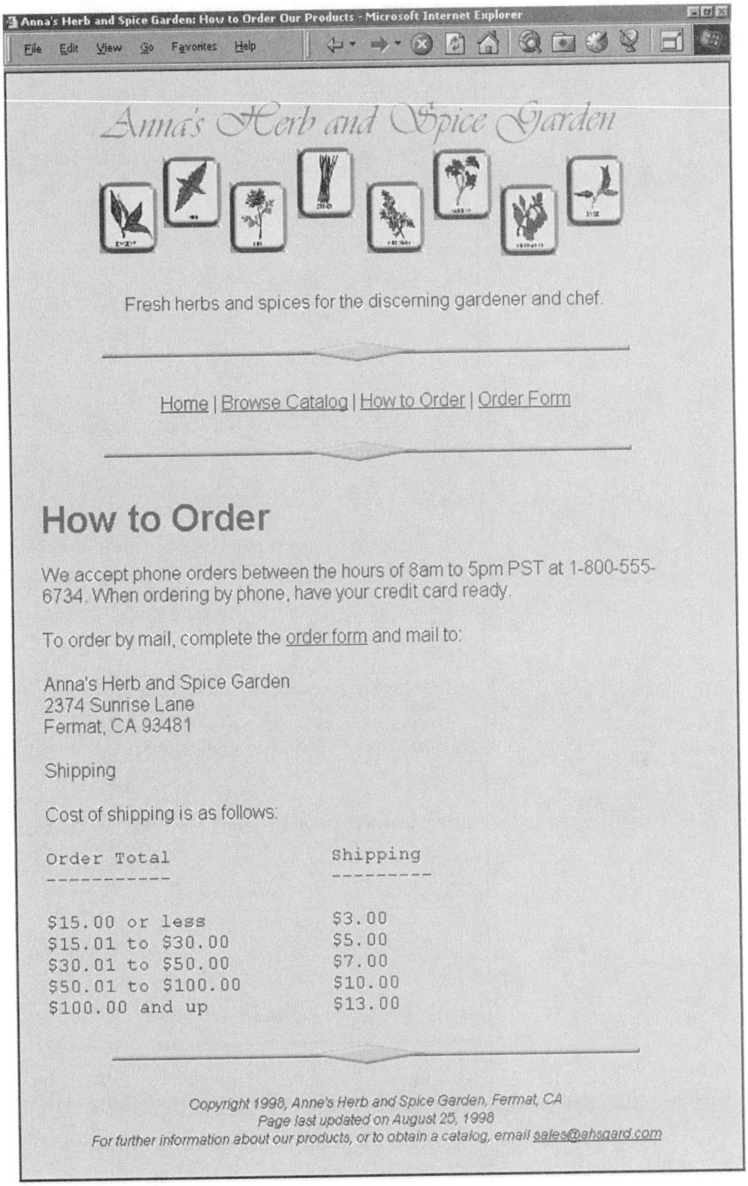

Anna's Herb and Spice Garden: How to Order Our Products - Microsoft Internet Explorer

File   Edit   View   Go   Favorites   Help

Anna's Herb and Spice Garden

Fresh herbs and spices for the discerning gardener and chef.

Home | Browse Catalog | How to Order | Order Form

How to Order

We accept phone orders between the hours of 8am to 5pm PST at 1-800-555-6734. When ordering by phone, have your credit card ready.

To order by mail, complete the order form and mail to:

Anna's Herb and Spice Garden
2374 Sunrise Lane
Fermat, CA 93481

Shipping

Cost of shipping is as follows:

```
Order Total              Shipping
------------             ---------

$15.00 or less           $3.00
$15.01 to $30.00         $5.00
$30.01 to $50.00         $7.00
$50.01 to $100.00        $10.00
$100.00 and up           $13.00
```

Copyright 1998, Anne's Herb and Spice Garden, Fermat, CA
Page last updated on August 25, 1998
For further information about our products, or to obtain a catalog, email sales@ahsgard.com

17

FIGURE 17.21

The text order form.

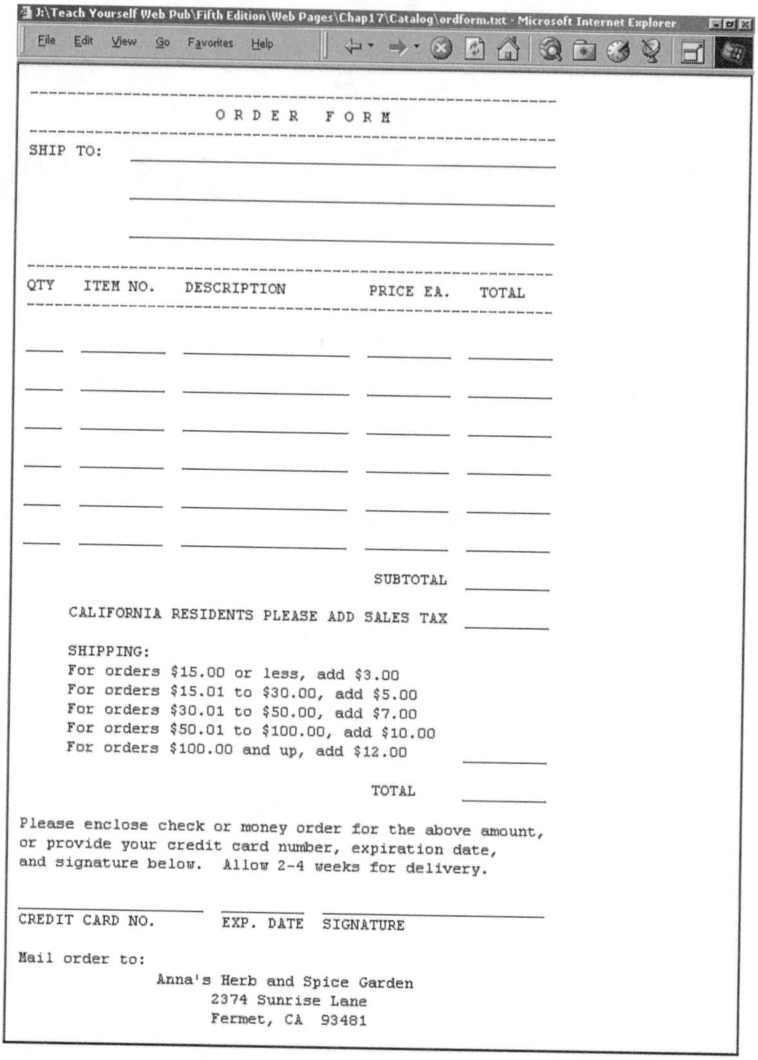

```
 J:\Teach Yourself Web Pub\Fifth Edition\Web Pages\Chap17\Catalog\ordform.txt - Microsoft Internet Explorer
 File   Edit   View   Go   Favorites   Help

----------------------------------------------------------------
                         O R D E R    F O R M
----------------------------------------------------------------
SHIP TO:        _____

                _____

                _____


----------------------------------------------------------------
QTY   ITEM NO.   DESCRIPTION        PRICE EA.   TOTAL
----------------------------------------------------------------

___   _____   _____       _____   _____

___   _____   _____       _____   _____

___   _____   _____       _____   _____

___   _____   _____       _____   _____

___   _____   _____       _____   _____

___   _____   _____       _____   _____

                                  SUBTOTAL   _____

     CALIFORNIA RESIDENTS PLEASE ADD SALES TAX   _____

     SHIPPING:
     For orders $15.00 or less, add $3.00
     For orders $15.01 to $30.00, add $5.00
     For orders $30.01 to $50.00, add $7.00
     For orders $50.01 to $100.00, add $10.00
     For orders $100.00 and up, add $12.00      _____

                                  TOTAL      _____

Please enclose check or money order for the above amount,
or provide your credit card number, expiration date,
and signature below.  Allow 2-4 weeks for delivery.

_____   _____ _____
CREDIT CARD NO.             EXP. DATE  SIGNATURE

Mail order to:
             Anna's Herb and Spice Garden
                 2374 Sunrise Lane
                 Fermet, CA  93481
```

You also can design an online order form, an example of which is shown in Figure 17.22. This approach may not be as straightforward as it seems, as there are several things you'll need to consider:

- If you are accepting online orders, consider that many customers are very wary of entering their credit card information online due to security reasons. The best alternative here is to include your online catalog on a secure server that protects the information entered by the customer.

- If your catalog is not placed on a secure server, be sure to inform customers of this and provide alternate methods to place an order. Include a phone number to call, or use a text order form similar to the one shown in Figure 17.21. This way, they can use more traditional means to place their orders.

- Another alternative is to include everything *but* the credit card information on the online order form. After you receive an order from a customer, you can send an email confirmation that it was received. Include in the message an order reference number, as well as a phone number that the customer can call to provide the billing information.

- When a customer submits an order, do you want to automatically add the online orders to a dynamic database? This is entirely possible, but requires advanced Web programming and familiarity with database structures and other techniques that haven't been discussed in this book.

Returning to Anna's Herb and Spice Garden site, note that the third bullet on the Anna's Herb and Spice Garden home page is a direct link to the order form file. It's provided here so that repeat customers won't have to take the added step of going back to the ordering, shipping, and payment page again.

Features of This Web Site and Issues for Development

In any online shopping service, the goals are to allow the reader to browse the items for sale and then to order those items. Within the browsing goal, there are several subgoals. What if the reader wants a particular item? Can it be found quickly and easily? What if someone just wants to look through the items for sale until he or she finds something interesting?

These two goals for browsing the online inventory may seem to conflict, but in this particular example, they've been handled especially well through the use of multiple views on the content of the catalog. The multiple views do provide a level of indirection (an extra menu between the top-level page and the contents of the catalog itself), but that small step provides a branching in the hierarchy structure that helps each different type of customer accomplish his or her goals.

I've intentionally left some holes in this site, however, to demonstrate ways you can improve on the navigation. Catalog browsing, for example, could be enhanced by adding a different menu to each of the ways you can view the catalog. Consider the first site example you saw in this chapter, where the main page had a navigation bar that linked to all the main pages in the Web (refer to Figure 17.1). When you navigated to the Technical Information subsection, however, you had another navigation bar that linked between the technical papers (refer to Figure 17.3). A similar system would greatly enhance Anna's catalog.

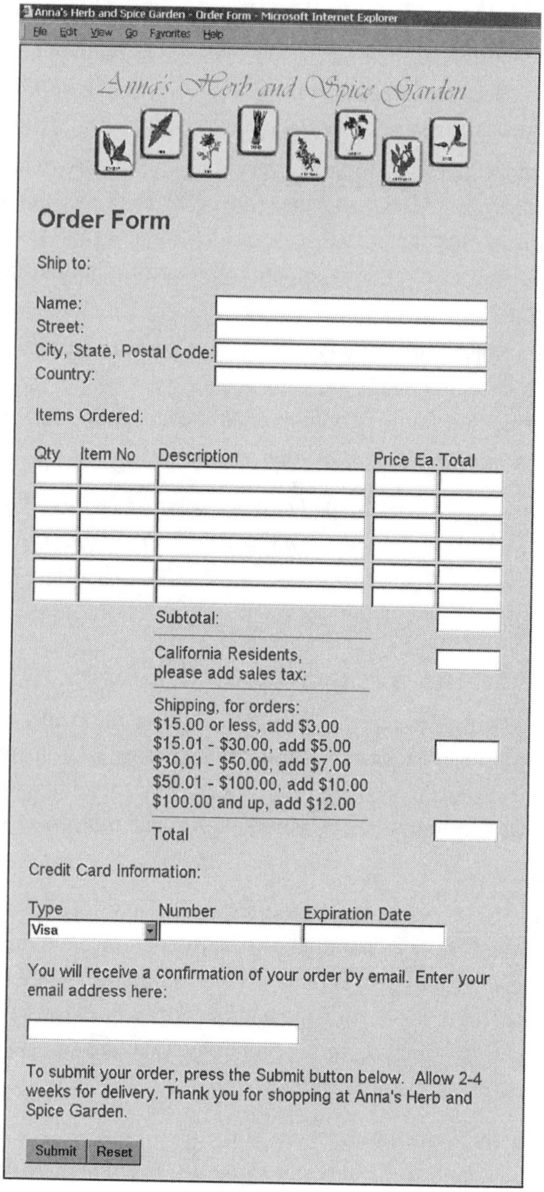

FIGURE 17.22

An online order form.

Additionally, the most *important* thing that Anna wants to accomplish on her site is to increase sales. How can she improve on the navigation for that? The best way is to provide a link to the How to Order page, or to the Order Form, or both, on any page that displays product information. If readers come across the Bay Leaf page shown in Figure 17.17, and decide that is *just* the plant them, for example, they might forget that the How to Order page takes them right to the order form. Place a link to the order form right beneath the pricing information on the page. One click, and you have a customer.

Probably the hardest part of building and maintaining a set of Web pages of this sort is maintaining the catalog itself, particularly if items need to be added or removed, or if prices change frequently. If the nursery had only one catalog view (the alphabetical one), this would not be so bad, as you could make changes directly to the catalog files. With additional views and the links between them, however, maintenance of the catalog becomes significantly more difficult.

Ideally, this sort of information could be stored in a database rather than as individual HTML files. Databases are designed to handle information like this and to be able to generate different views on request. But how do you hook up the database with the Web pages?

17

Given enough programming skill (and familiarity with databases), you could create a program to do database queries from a Web page, and return a neatly formatted list of items. Then, on the Web page, when someone requests the alphabetical listing, he or she would get an automatically generated list that was as up-to-date as the database was. But to do this, you'll need a database that can talk to your Web server, which, depending on the system on which your Web server runs, may or may not be technically feasible. You also need the programming skill to make it work, using advanced Web technologies such as CGI, Java, JavaScript, VBScript, Dynamic HTML, or other approaches. Unfortunately, these are topics that can get quite involved and go beyond the scope of this book. Refer to *Sams Teach Yourself Java 2 Platform in 21 Days* by Laura Lemay, *Sams Teach Yourself JavaScript 1.3 in 24 Hours* by Michael Moncour, and *Java 2 Platform Unleashed* by Jamie Jaworski for more information.

An alternative solution is to keep the data in the database and then periodically dump it to text and format it in HTML. The primary difficulty with that solution, of course, is how much work it would take to do the conversion each time while still preserving the cross-references to the other pages. Could the process be automated, and how much setup and daily maintenance would that involve?

With this type of application, these are the kind of questions and technical challenges you may have to deal with if you create Web sites. Sometimes the problem involves more than designing, writing, and formatting information on the screen.

Summary

I've presented only a few ideas for using and structuring Web pages here; the variations on these themes are unlimited for the Web pages you will design.

Probably the best way to find examples of the sort of Web pages you might want to design and how to organize them is to go out on the Web and browse what's out there. While you're browsing, in addition to examining the layout and design of individual pages and the content they describe, keep an eye out for the structures people have used to organize their pages, and try to guess why they might have chosen that organization. ("They didn't think about it" is a common reason for many poorly organized Web pages, unfortunately.) Critique other people's Web pages with an eye for their structure and design. Is it easy to navigate them? Did you get lost? Can you easily get back to a known page from any other location in their site? If you had a goal in mind for this site, did you achieve that goal, and if not, how would you have reorganized it?

Learning from other people's mistakes and seeing how other people have solved difficult problems can help you make your own Web pages better.

Workshop

Hopefully, today, you've learned several different things that will help you improve the appearance and functionality of your Web pages. The following workshop includes questions and a quiz about some of the most important topics discussed in this chapter.

Q&A

Q These Web sites are really cool. What are their URLs?

A As I noted at the beginning of this chapter, the Web sites I've described here are mockups of potential Web sites that could exist (and the mockups are on the Web support site for this book). Although many of the designs and organizations that I have created here were inspired by existing Web pages, these pages do not actually exist on the Web.

Q The examples here used some sort of hierarchical organization. Are hierarchies that common, and do I have to use them? Can't I do something different?

A Hierarchies are extremely common on the Web, but that doesn't mean that they're bad. Hierarchies are an excellent way of organizing your content, especially when the information you're presenting lends itself to a hierarchical organization.

You can certainly do something different to organize your site. You might, for example, prefer to use framesets, as discussed in Day 12, "Frames and Linked Windows." The simplicity of hierarchies, however, allows them to be easily structured, easily navigated, and easily maintained. Why make more trouble for yourself and for your readers by trying to force a complicated structure on otherwise simple information?

Quiz

1. What are some ways that you can help readers find their way around your Web site easier?

2. What can you do to help prevent your readers from getting lost in your Web site?

3. When developing a site that includes a lot of information, such as an online encyclopedia, what is the biggest issue in development?

4. What are the advantages of providing multiple ways of browsing through an online shopping catalog?

5. When you are using the Web to take orders for products, what is one of the primary concerns in obtaining those orders over the Web?

Answers

1. Provide navigation bars that link to each of the main pages in your Web. Different navigation bars can be designed for sub-levels in the Web. For consistency, it usually is best to locate the navigation bars in the same location on each page. Navigation bars can be located at the top, bottom, or left sides of a Web page (the most common areas). Frequently Asked Questions pages, What's New pages, and Table of Contents pages also are handy ways to provide links to the pages on your site.

2. In general, try to stick with a rigid hierarchical structure and avoid using lateral links that cross the hierarchy. This helps readers keep track of where they are in your Web site.

3. The biggest issue in developing a Web site that is rich with information is in setup and maintenance. Deciding how to best organize and arrange the information is the most difficult, and creating all the cross-reference links to pages and media also is time consuming. Because most of the information contained in an online encyclopedia is unlikely to change much, however, the maintenance to a site like this will not be very high.

4. Arranging online shopping catalogs to display products in several different categories (such as by product type, product number, product appearance, and so on) helps readers find your products easier. The most logical place to start is to organize your products by category. If your products are well known to customers, they may appreciate the advantage of searching by product name or product number. Others like to search by appearance of a product (for example, by color or size).

5. The main issue in obtaining orders over the Web is how to deal with security issues. Many customers do not like to provide their credit information online. Be sure to provide alternative means to obtain orders, and try to locate your order forms on a secure server.

Exercises

1. Using the Encyclopedia of Motorcycles as a guide, plan or create a frameset with two or three frames. How would you create an interface that navigates readers from section to section easily?

2. You also can apply some of the navigation and design tips that you learned in this chapter to personal home pages. Foozle Industries provides some good examples of navigation bars and linking pages. The Encyclopedia of Motorcycles provides good tips for linking topics of interest together and providing pictures or other media as descriptions. You can easily use these as guides in developing personal Web pages.

Designing for the Real World

In previous lessons, you learned some pointers about what you should (or should not) do when you plan your Web site and design your pages. You also learned some pointers about what makes a good (or bad) Web site. There is still another important factor that you should take under consideration, and that is how to design your pages for the "real world."

You've already learned that the real world consists of many different users with many different computer systems that use many different browsers. One of the things we haven't yet addressed, however, is the many different user preferences and experience levels that the visitors to your site will have. By anticipating the needs of the real world, you can better judge how you should design your pages. In this chapter, you'll learn some ways that you can anticipate these needs, as well as the following:

- Things to consider when you try to determine the preferences of your audience
- How to add features that will be helpful to new users

- Various methods that help users find their way around your site
- HTML code that displays the same Web page in each of the XHTML 1.0 specifications (Transitional, Frameset, and Strict)

What Is the Real World Anyway?

You are probably most familiar with surfing the Internet while using a computer that runs on a specific operating system, such as Windows 95 or 98, Windows NT, Macintosh, or another similar operating system. For all intents and purposes, you think you have a pretty good idea of what Web pages look like to everyone.

Hopefully, as you've learned throughout this book, you realize now that the view you typically see on the Web isn't the view that everyone else sees. The real world has many different computers, with many different operating systems. Even if you try to design your pages for the most common operating system, and the most common browsers, however, there is another factor that you can't anticipate: *user preference*. Consider the following family for an example:

- Bill is a top-level executive at a Fortune 100 company. His company has its own intranet. Most everyone in the company uses the same operating system and the same browser. Bill is used to seeing the Internet in a certain way—mostly text, with a smattering of images here and there to stress informational points—a lean and mean Web with very little multimedia and a lot of information. He finds all the extra "glitz" annoying and inconvenient to download, so he turns off the images and sound.

- Bill's wife, Susan, has never used a computer before, but she's always wanted to learn. She's a genealogist by hobby and has learned that the Internet holds many resources for genealogists. She also wants to publish her family history on the Web. When she and her husband power up their new home computer for the first time, she's thrilled. But soon, she's asking questions such as, "Can we fit more on the screen? Those letters are bit too small...can we make them larger? Where are the pictures? How come you have the music turned off...it says that there is sound on this page!" Already, she wants to see the Internet much differently than her husband is used to seeing it.

- Bill and Susan have a son, Tom, who's in high school. He's an avid gamer and wants to see effects—*glitz, media*! He pumps up the volume as loud as he can and pushes the capacities of their new computer to the max. He also thinks "Browser X" is better than "Browser Y" because all his friends use it for online virtual reality gaming. He wants to design a Web site that provides hints, tips, and tricks for one of his favorite online games.

- Tom's older sister, Jill, is an art major in college, studying to be a commercial artist. She has a keen interest in sculpture and photography. She plans to use the new computer for homework assignments, so she'll be looking at the Web with a keen visual interest. She wants to view her pages in true-color, in the highest resolution possible.

- Then there are the senior members of the family—Susan's aging parents—who have recently moved in with the family after years of living in a very small rural town. Their experience with computers is minimal—they've only seen them in stores and were afraid to touch them for fear of breaking them. To them, computers are a complete mystery that they find absolutely amazing. So they want to learn. They share Susan's genealogical interest, but Dad's eyes don't see quite as well as they used to. He needs a special browser so that he can hear the text as well as see it.

All these people are using the same computer, and the same operating system, to view the Web. In all cases but one (young Tom), they also are using the same browser. The example, however, illustrates some of the other things that you need to think about when you design your Web: the needs of the users themselves. These needs fall into different areas, some of which are easier to accommodate than others. Here are some of the considerations you see from the previous example.

18

Considering User Experience Level

You see varied levels of experience in our fictitious family. Although it is true that everyone is keenly interested in the Web, some of them have never seen a Web browser before. So, when you design your site, you should consider that the people who visit your site might have varying levels of experience and browsing requirements.

Will the topics that you discuss on your site be of interest to people with different levels of experience? If so, you might want to build in some features that help them find their way around easier. In Day 17, "Examples of Good and Bad Web Design," you learned some tips about designing navigation systems that can help prevent people from getting lost in cyberspace. That's a good start, but maybe it's not such a bad idea to include a page on your Web site that describes your navigation system in more detail.

Figure 18.1 shows the top portion of a page that helps readers learn more about your site. Links at the beginning of the page take the reader to several different sections on the page. The sections are titled About the Site, The Navigation System, Browser Recommendations, and Other Files You Might Need. Each of these sections, in turn, links to pages that provide a more detailed description of the contents of the site.

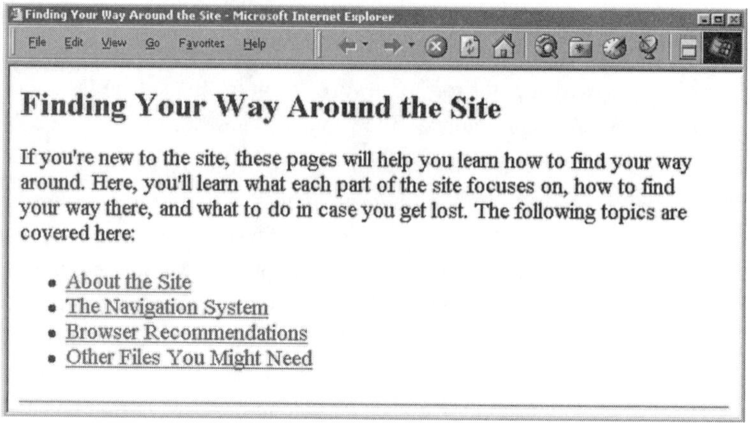

FIGURE **18.1**

*A page that helps
readers find their way
around the site.*

List Pages That Provide Descriptions of Your Site

The About the Site section provides links to pages that will help the reader quickly review the contents of your Web site or learn what has been added since his or her last visit. Figure 18.2 shows an example of a simple link menu for this instance. Following are some good examples to include and link to in this category:

- A What's New page that lists and links to recent additions to your site
- A Table of Contents page that lists the page title and an optional brief description of each page on your Web site
- A Frequently Asked Questions page that lists questions you have received from visitors, as well as answers to them

These pages are the most common types of pages that are used to help readers learn more about your site, but you might come up with additional ideas more particular to your topic. If so, it's a good idea to list the pages that will be most helpful to your readers.

Describe Your Navigation System

Navigation systems vary from site to site, and they are not always easy for a new Web user to understand. Typically, navigation systems fall into one of three areas: simple text navigation systems, image navigation systems, or frameset navigation systems. If you think your navigation system might need explanation, provide descriptions or links to help the reader learn how to use it. Figure 18.3 shows an example of a link menu that takes the reader to pages that describe various navigation systems on a Web site.

FIGURE 18.2

Link to pages that help the reader learn about the contents of your Web site.

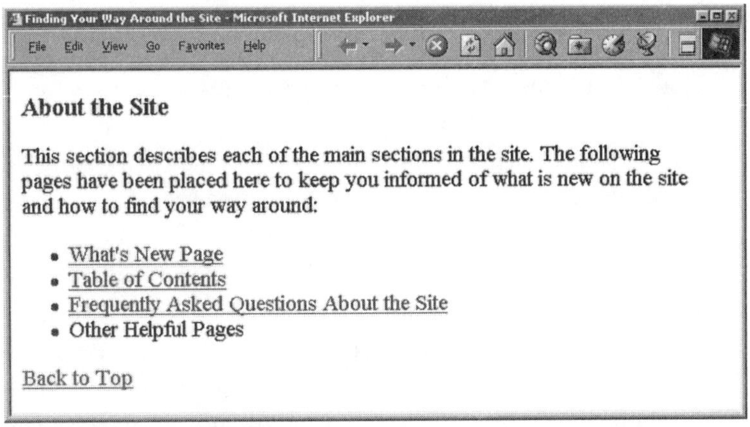

FIGURE 18.3

Describe your navigation system.

18

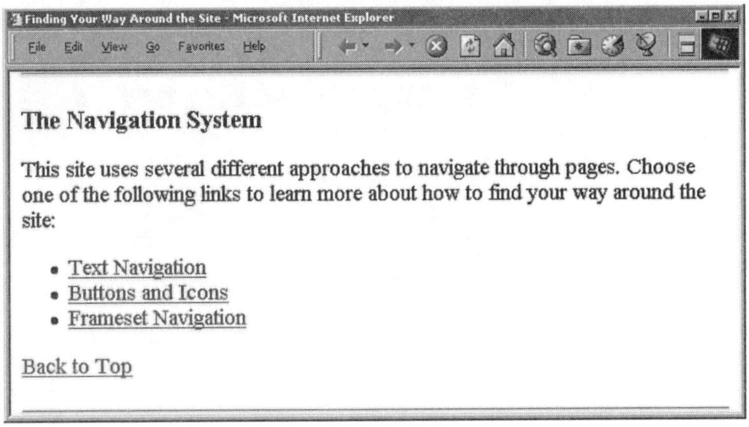

When you describe your navigation system, try to make the descriptions easy to understand. Suppose that your text navigation bar looks like the following example, and that it appears on all of the main pages in the Web site:

```
Home ¦ Contents ¦ FAQ ¦ What's New ¦ Email ¦ Guest Book ¦ Links
```

This menu bar might be self-explanatory to those who have visited your site before, but to someone new to your site or to the Web, it might not make a lot of sense. The following descriptions might be helpful to new users:

- **Home**—"Use the Home link to return to the Home page on this Web site."
- **Contents**—"The Table of Contents page provides links to all the pages on the Web site. If you are new to the site, this is a good place to start."

- **FAQ**—Someone new to the Internet might not know what FAQ means, so an explanation is necessary. How about something like, "The FAQ (Frequently Asked Questions) page lists some of the questions that we have received from visitors, along with their answers."

- **Email**—Here's another link that could use clarification. Does this link take the reader to email that you've actually received, or is it a link that sends email to you? A description such as, "Use the Email link to send questions or comments about this site to our Webmaster," tells the reader exactly what you want to use this link for.

When you use images and icons as navigation, the icons aren't always easy to identify. Perhaps you recall the Rainy Day Distractions example that you saw in Day 12, "Frames and Linked Windows." To refresh your memory, the frameset is shown in Figure 18.4. The left frame includes images and icons for navigation, and the bottom frame displays an equivalent text navigation bar.

FIGURE 18.4

Using images, icons, and frameset navigation.

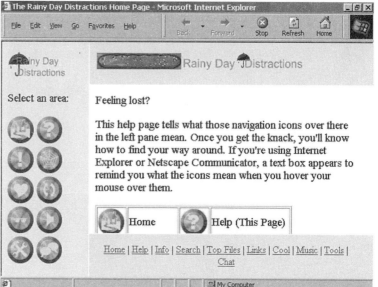

In some cases, it isn't really obvious what the icons on the navigation buttons stand for. The page in the Main frame displays a brief description of each icon, but more description probably is necessary for new users. Here, you can place each icon next to a description that is similar to those I described for the text navigation bar.

Framesets are sometimes very difficult for new readers to understand. A brief How To page that describes your frameset can be very useful for a new reader. One way to describe your frameset is to provide a small screen shot of it on a Web page, similar to that shown in Figure 18.5. Identify each of the frames in your frameset by a name that the reader can easily remember (Left, Top, Main, and Bottom, for example) and place descriptions of the purpose of each one on the same page. For example, you might describe the frames in Figure 18.5 as follows:

- Use the icons in the Left frame to select the pages that you want to view in the larger Main frame. If you don't remember what the icons mean, select the question mark icon (?) for Help, or use the text navigation bar in the Bottom frame.

- The Top frame in the frameset displays our site logo at all times, so that you'll remember where you are.

- The Main frame displays all the pages you choose from the Left or Bottom frames. Also, when you select a link that appears on a page in the Main frame, the page to which you link also will appear in the Main frame.

- The text links in the Bottom frame serve the same function as the icons in the Left frame. These links are provided for those who do not see images in their browsers, or those who prefer to use text links.

18

FIGURE **18.5**

Describing a frameset.

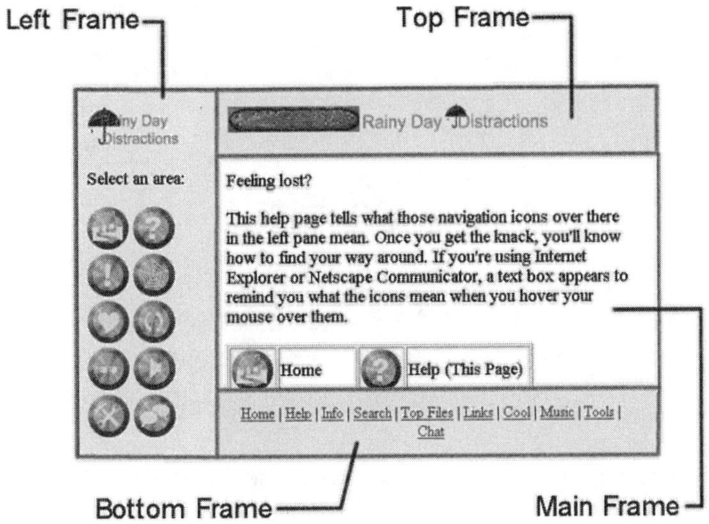

Left Frame

Top Frame

Bottom Frame

Main Frame

Add Browser Recommendations

Another item that is very helpful for new visitors is to indicate the browsers for which you designed the site. Figure 18.6 displays a simple example of how you can achieve this.

Here, the reader learns that the site was designed for HTML 3.2 and later browsers that support framesets (the HTML 4.0 Frameset specification). A list informs the reader of the browsers that you used to test the site and provides links to download those browsers. Finally, the Web author wants to know whether users of other browsers are experiencing problems. An email address is provided so that the Web author can learn about problems that appear in browsers she was unable to test.

FIGURE 18.6

Adding browser recommendations.

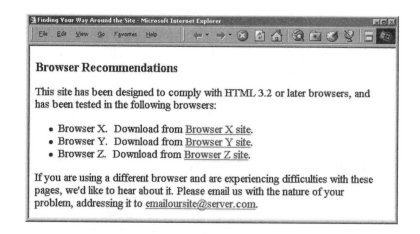

List Other Necessary Files

Aside from browser recommendations, you also should inform users of special plug-ins or other files that she might need to download. If you have files on your site that are not in HTML format (such as compressed files, Word processing documents, images other than GIF or JPG, and so on), you should inform the reader that she may need a special viewer. List the viewers or external applications that she may need.

An example of a link menu for external files is shown in Figure 18.7. Here, the Web author lists some of the external applications that might be needed to view or use some of the files included on the site. The fictitious site includes several Adobe Acrobat Reader (.PDF) and Zip-compressed (.ZIP) files that appear on several different pages. By including links to all the necessary readers and external applications on one page (such as Adobe Acrobat Reader and WinZip, for example), the reader quickly learns about the files that are necessary to use the site to full advantage.

FIGURE 18.7

Listing other files that might be necessary.

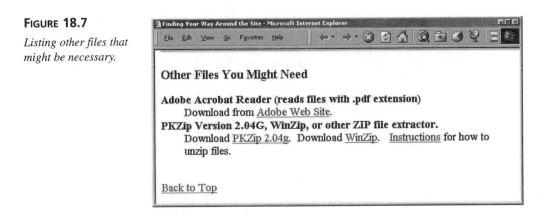

Determining User Preference

In addition to the various levels of experience that readers have, it also is guaranteed that everyone has their own preferences for how they'll want to view your Web pages. How do you please them all? The truth is, you can't. But, you *can* give it your best shot. Part of good Web design is to anticipate what readers want to see on your site. This becomes more difficult when the topics you discuss on your Web site are of interest to a wider audience.

You'll notice that each person in our fictitious family has a need to see the Web differently. Sometimes this is due to interests, but other times it's because of special needs. Therein lies the key to anticipating what you'll need on your Web pages.

A topic such as "Timing the Sparkplugs on your 300cc Motorcycle Engine" is of interest to a more select audience. The topic will attract those who are interested in motorcycles—more selectively, those who want to repair their own motorcycles. It can be relatively easy to anticipate the types of things these readers would like to see on your site. Step-by-step instructions can guide them through each process, while images or multimedia can display techniques that are difficult to describe by text alone.

"The Seven Wonders of the Ancient World," on the other hand, could attract students of all ages, as well as their teachers. Archaeologists, historians, and others with an interest in ancient history also might visit the site. Now you have a wider audience, a wider age range, and a wider range of educational levels. It won't be quite as easy to build a site that will please them all.

18

In cases such as this, it might help to narrow your focus a bit. One way is to design your site for a specific user group, such as the following:

- **Elementary school students and their teachers**—This site requires a very basic navigation system that is easy to follow. Content should be basic and very easy to read. Bright, colorful images and animations can help keep the attention of young readers.

- **High school students and their teachers**—You can use a slightly more advanced navigation system. Multimedia and the latest in Web technologies might keep these students coming back for more.

- **College students and their professors**—A higher level of content is necessary, whereas multimedia may be less importance. An online encyclopedia format might be a good approach here.

- **Professional researchers and historians**—This type of site probably will require pages that are heavier in text content than media.

It's not always possible to define user groups for your Web site. In these cases, start with your *own* preferences. Survey other sites that include content similar to what you want to put on your Web site. As you browse through the sites, ask yourself what you hope to see there. Is the information displayed well? Is there enough help or assistance on the site? Does the site have too much or too little media? If you have a friend or two who is willing to do the survey along with you, it helps to have additional feedback before you start your own site. Take notes and incorporate any ideas that come up into your Web pages.

After you design some initial pages, ask friends, family members, and associates to browse through your site and pick it apart. Keep in mind that when you ask others for constructive criticism, you might not hear things that you want to hear; however, this process is important, because you'll often get many new ideas on how to improve your site even more.

Deciding on an HTML 4.0 or XHTML 1.0 Approach

In earlier chapters, you learned about the various flavors of HTML 4.0 and XHTML 1.0 and how each of them is geared toward users of older or newer browsers. These flavors are the following:

- **HTML 4.0 or XHTML 1.0 Transitional**—For those who want to provide support for older browsers

- **HTML 4.0 or XHTML 1.0 Frameset**—For those who want to use frameset navigation in addition to supporting the tags found in HTML 4.0 Transitional
- **HTML 4.0 or XHTML 1.0 Strict**—For those who want to develop pages that strictly adhere to the HTML 4.0 or XHTML 1.0 specification by not using deprecated elements or attributes

HTML 4.0 and XHTML 1.0 Transitional

If you expect that your readers will use a wide variety of different browsers, it probably is to your advantage to design your Web pages around the HTML 4.0 or XHTML 1.0 Transitional specification. By doing so, you provide backward compatibility with older browsers. The Transitional specification provides the flexibility to use tags that are deprecated in the strict HTML 4.0 specification. Therefore, if you want to use presentational commands that were introduced in HTML 3.2 (such as the center or align attributes for alignment or bgcolor and color attributes for background and foreground colors), you can do so.

Take, for example, the Halloween House of Terror page that you created in Day 7, "Using Images, Color, and Backgrounds." Here, the page has undergone yet another face-lift, as shown in the following code and figure. This page uses HTML 3.2-compatible tags to display the presentation and appearance of the page. Fonts, colors, and alignment are formatted with tags that have been deprecated in the Strict specification.

The deprecated tags and attributes are shown in italics in the following code example. In addition, a table is used to create a staggered layout of links, descriptions, and images on the page. Figure 18.8 shows the result of the following code as it is displayed in Internet Explorer:

INPUT

```
<!DOCTYPE html PUBLIC "-//W3C//DTD XHTML 1.0 Transitional//EN"
"http://www.w3.org/TR/xhtml1/DTD/transitional.dtd"><html>
<head>
<title>Welcome to the Halloween House of Terror</title>
</head>
<body bgcolor="#ff9933" link="#990000">
<h1 align="center">
    <font face="Arial, sans-serif">
    The Halloween House of Terror!!</font></h1>
<div align="center">
    <p>
        <img src="skel05.gif" alt="skel05.gif" width="140" height="100" />
        <img src="skel07.gif" alt="skel07.gif" width="140" height="100" />
        <img src="skel06.gif" alt="skel06.gif" width="140" height="100" />
    </p>
</div>
<hr />
<p>
```

18

```
<font face="Arial, sans-serif">
      Voted the most frightening haunted house three years in a row, the
      <font color="#cc0000"><b>Halloween House of Terror</b></font>
      provides the ultimate in Halloween thrills. Over 20 rooms of
thrills and
      excitement to make your blood run cold and your
      hair stand on end!
   </font>
</p>
<hr />
<p><font face="Arial, sans-serif">
      Don't take our word for it ... preview some images of what awaits!
   </font>
</p>
<div align="center">
   <table border="0" width="75%" cellspacing="5" cellpadding="5">
     <tr>
        <td width="30%">
           <font face="Arial, sans-serif">
           <img src="skel01.gif" alt="skel01.gif" width="140"
height="100" />
           </font>
        </td>
        <td width="40%" bgcolor="#CC0000"> <font face="Arial, sans-serif">
      Watch out for Esmerelda. You never know what she has in her
cauldron.
        </font> </td>
        <th width="30%" bgcolor="#FF6600"> <b><font face="Arial, sans-
serif">
        <a href="entry.gif">The Entry Way</a> </font></b> </th>
     </tr>
     <tr>
        <th width="30%" bgcolor="#FF6600"> <b><font face="Arial, sans-
serif">
        <a href="bedroom.gif">The Master Bedroom</a> </font></b> </th>
        <td width="40%" bgcolor="#CC0000"> <font face="Arial, sans-serif">
        Don't open the closet door, whatever you do!</font></td>
          <td width="30%">
             <font face="Arial, sans-serif">
             <img src="skel02.gif" alt="skel02.gif" width="140"
height="100" />
             </font>
          </td>
       </tr>
       <tr>
          <td width="30%">
             <font face="Arial, sans-serif">
             <img src="skel03.gif" alt="skel03.gif" width="140"
height="100" />
             </font></td>
```

```
        <td width="40%" bgcolor="#CC0000"> <font face="Arial, sans-serif">
        More than a few innocents have been cast in chains for eons. They
just
        aren't the same anymore.</font></td>
        <th width="30%" bgcolor="#FF6600"><b> <font face="Arial, sans-
serif">
        <a href="galley.gif">The Galley</a></font></b></th>
      </tr>
      <tr>
        <th width="30%" bgcolor="#FF6600"> <b><font face="Arial, sans-
serif">
        <a href="dungeon.gif">The Dungeon</a> </font> </b></th>
        <td width="40%" bgcolor="#CC0000"> <font face="Arial, sans-serif">
        Better listen to the tour guides, or you'll get lost! </font>
</td>
        <td width="30%">
        <font face="Arial, sans-serif">
        <img src="skel04.gif" alt="skel04.gif" width="140" height="100"
/>
        </font></td>
      </tr>
    </table>
</div>
<hr />
<p><font face="Arial, sans-serif"> The
    <font color="#cc0000">Halloween House of Terror</font>
    is open from October 20 to November 1st, with a gala celebration
    on Halloween night. Our hours are: </font></p>
<ul>
    <li>
        <font face="Arial, sans-serif">
        Mon-Fri 5PM-midnight</font>
    </li>
    <li>
        <font face="Arial, sans-serif">
        Sat &amp; Sun 5PM-3AM</font>
    </li>
    <li>
        <font face="Arial, sans-serif">
        Halloween Night (31-Oct): 3PM-???</font></li>
</ul>
<p align="center">
<font face="Arial, sans-serif"> The
    <font color="#cc0000">Halloween House of Terror</font>
    is located at:<br />
    The Old Waterfall Shopping Center<br />
    1020 Mirabella Ave<br />
    Springfield, CA 94532</font></p>
</body>
</html>
```

18

OUTPUT

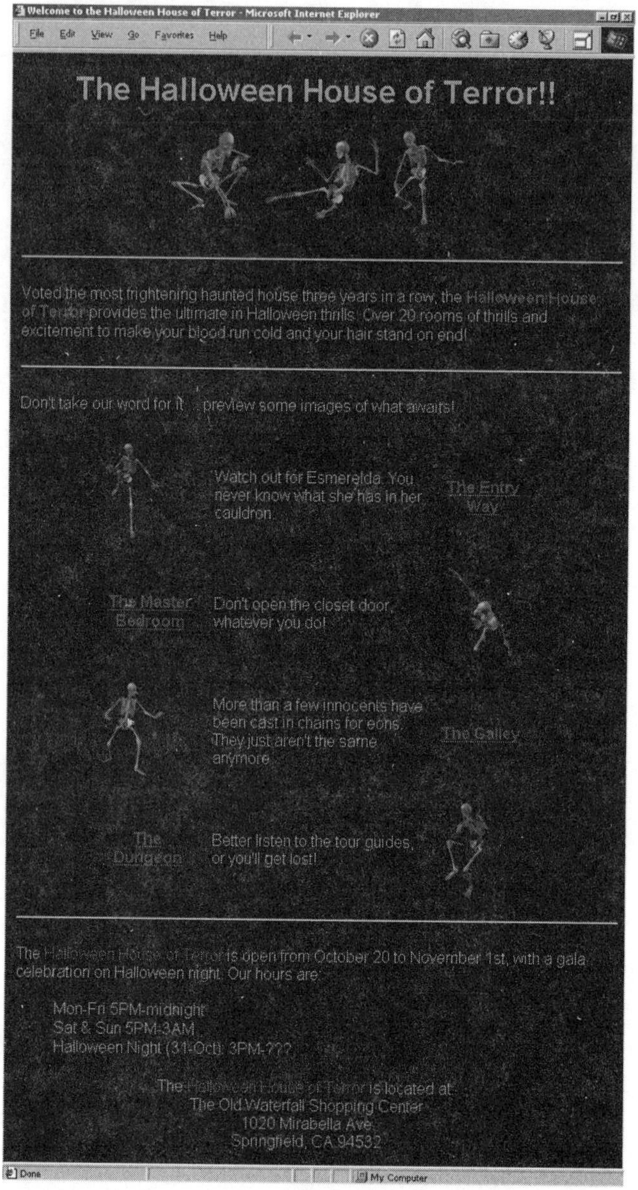

FIGURE 18.8
An example of HTML 4.0 Transitional code in Internet Explorer.

HTML 4.0 and XHTML 1.0 Framesets

If you prefer to use a frameset to navigate through your site, the most logical choice is the HTML 4.0 or XHTML 1.0 Frameset specification. Here, you can use all the tags and attributes that are "legal" in the HTML 4.0 or XHTML 1.0 Transitional specification. In addition, you can utilize all tags and attributes that pertain to framesets and frames.

The key to good frameset design is to create as few frames as possible while making the navigation system easy to understand. The hard decision, however, is to determine for which resolution you want to design your frameset because the browser is divided into multiple sections. The more frames you create in the frameset, the smaller each page will be in each frame.

In Figure 18.9, the Halloween House of Terror Web page has been converted to a frameset. The main frame displays exactly the same page as you saw in Figure 18.8; however, the links in the left frame take the reader to the pictures and descriptions of each room in the haunted house. By adding the links in the left frame, the reader no longer has to use his browse button to take a small virtual tour through the haunted house, so the navigation is greatly simplified.

The code for the frameset divides the browser window into two frames: `left` and `right`. The `navigation.html` page loads into the left frame, and the main page (`main.html`) loads into the right frame. The code for the frameset looks like the following:

```
<!DOCTYPE html PUBLIC "-//W3C//DTD XHTML 1.0 Frameset//EN"
"http://www.w3.org/TR/xhtml1/DTD/frameset.dtd">
<html>
<head>
<title>Halloween House of Terror Frameset</title>
</head>
<frameset cols="170,*">
  <frame name="left" src="navigation.html" />
  <frame name="right" src="main.html" />
  <noframes>
  <body>
  <p> ... insert noframes content here ... </p>
  </body>
  </noframes>
</frameset>
</html>
```

The code for the left frame in the frameset (navigation.html) displays each page in the right frame when the user selects one of the image links (as defined by the `<target="right">` tag). Each image link displays alternate text when the user hovers his mouse over the button, or when images are turned off in the browser. The code for the left frame looks like the following:

```
<!DOCTYPE html PUBLIC "-//W3C//DTD XHTML 1.0 Transitional//EN"
"http://www.w3.org/TR/xhtml1/DTD/transitional.dtd">
<html>
<head>
```

18

```
<title>The Halloween House of Terror</title>
<base target="right" />
</head>
<body bgcolor="#ff9933" text="#000000">
<p><font face="Arial">The Halloween<br />
House of<br />
Terror</font></p>
<p><a href="main.html" target="right">
   <img src="button01.gif" alt="Home" width="125" height="50" />
   </a></p>
<p><a href="entry.html" target="right">
   <img src="button02.gif" alt="The Entry Way" width="125" height="50" />
   </a></p>
<p><a href="bedroom.html" target="right">
   <img src="button03.gif" alt="The Master Bedroom" width="125" height="50" />
   </a></p>
<p><a href="galley.html" target="right">
   <img src="button04.gif" alt="The Galley" width="125" height="50" />
   </a></p>
<p><a href="dungeon.html" target="right">
   <img src="button05.gif" alt="The Dungeon" width="125" height="50" />
   </a></p>
<p><a href="location.html" target="right">
   <img src="button06.gif" alt="Hours and Location" width="125" height="50" />
   </a></p>
</body>
</html>
```

FIGURE 18.9

An example of HTML 4.0 Frameset code in Internet Explorer.

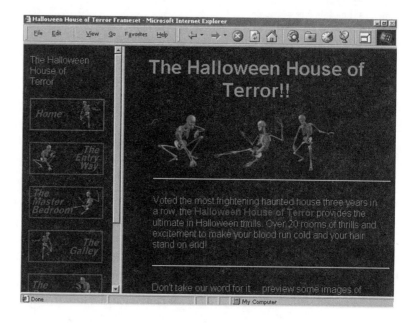

HTML 4.0 and XHTML 1.0 Strict

The Transitional and Frameset specifications enable you to provide support for older browsers (anything earlier than either Netscape Navigator 4.0 or Microsoft Internet Explorer 4.0). The HTML 4.0 or XHTML 1.0 Strict specification, however, allows for a wider range of display options through the use of Cascading Style Sheets (CSS), as well as other Web technologies that you've learned in this book. With the introduction of new types of Web browsing hardware, there will be an increasing need in the near future to use the Strict specification. One drawback to using HTML 4.0 or XHTML 1.0 Strict at the present time, however, is that there may be a wait before the majority of users visit your site with compatible browsers.

To comply with the HTML 4.0 or XHTML 1.0 Strict specification, you must avoid using any HTML tags and attributes marked as *deprecated*. Instead, use Cascading Style Sheets or other methods, such as Dynamic HTML, to implement page presentation.

If you are willing to shut out a portion of your audience now, there are several advantages to using the HTML 4.0 or XHTML 1.0 Strict specification. As you learned in Day 10, "XHTML and Style Sheets," you have greater control of page layout and appearance by using CSS technology. In many ways, you can lay out your pages much the same as if you were using a page layout program or word processing program. Another advantage is that Cascading Style Sheets level 2 (or CSS2 for short) incorporates additional features for non-visual browsers. This means that you can design pages that can be browsed by those who are visually impaired, or who have other special needs.

The following code example illustrates how you can implement the page shown in Figure 18.8 into the XHTML 1.0 Strict specification. In this example, the Halloween House of Terror uses embedded style sheet properties and values to format the text and images on the page. The colors for the text, links, and table cells are defined in the style section at the beginning of the page. Margins are added to the top, bottom, left, and right of the Web page. Also, rather than using standard bullets, the bulleted list at the bottom of the page displays image bullets as defined by the style sheet. The result of the following code is shown in Figure 18.10 in Internet Explorer.

INPUT

```
<!DOCTYPE html PUBLIC "-//W3C//DTD XHTML 1.0 Strict//EN"
"http://www.w3.org/TR/xhtml1/DTD/strict.dtd">
<html>
<head>
<title>Welcome to the Halloween House of Terror</title>
<style type="text/css">
<!-
body { background-color: #ff9933;
        color: #000000;
```

18

```
                    font-family: Arial, sans-serif;
                    font-size: 12pt;
                    margin-left: 20px;
                    margin-right: 20px;
                    margin-top: 10px;
                    margin-bottom: 10px }
         a:link{ color: #990000 }
         a:visited{ color: #CC00CC }
         a:active{ color: #CC0000 }
         h1{ font-family: Arial, sans-serif;
              font-size: 24pt }
         table { text-align: center }
         th { background-color: #ff6600;
             color: #000000;
             font-family: Arial, sans-serif;
             font-size: 12pt;
             font-weight: bold }
         td { color: #000000;
             font-family: Arial, sans-serif;
             font-size: 12pt }
         td.red { background-color: #cc0000 }
         ul { list-style-image: url("bullet.gif") }
         .bloodred { color:#CC0000 }
         .bloodredbold { color: #CC0000; font-weight: bold }
         .center { text-align: center }
         -->
         </style>
         </head>
         <body>
         <h1 class="center">The Halloween House of Terror!!</h1>
         <div class="center">
         <dl>
         <dd>
         <img src="skel05.gif" alt="skel05.gif" width="140" height="100" />
         <img src="skel07.gif" alt="skel07.gif" width="140" height="100" />
         <img src="skel06.gif" alt="skel06.gif" width="140" height="100" />
         </dd>
         </dl>
         </div>
         <hr />
         <p>Voted the most frightening haunted house three years in a row,
         the <span class="bloodredbold">Halloween House of Terror</span>
         provides the ultimate in Halloween thrills. Over 20 rooms of
         thrills and excitement to make your blood run cold and your hair
         stand on end!</p>
         <hr />
         <p>Don't take our word for it ... preview some images of what
         awaits!</p>
```

```
<table border="0" summary="House of Terror" width="75%" cellspacing="5"
cellpadding="5">
<tr>
<td>
<img src="skel01.gif" alt="skel01.gif width="140" height="100" />
</td>
<td class="red">Watch out for Esmerelda. You never
know what she has in her cauldron.</td>
<th><a href="code/entry.gif">The Entry Way</a></th>
</tr>
<tr>
<th><a href="code/bedroom.gif">The Master Bedroom</a></th>
<td class="red">Don't open the closet door, whatever
you do!</td>
    <td>
    <img src="skel02.gif" alt="skel02.gif" width="140" height="100"
/></td>
</tr>
<tr>
    <td><img src="skel03.gif" alt="skel03.gif" width="140" height="100"
/></td>
<td class="red">More than a few innocents have been
cast in chains for eons. They just aren't the same anymore.</td>
<th><a href="code/galley.gif">The Galley</a></th>
</tr>
<tr>
<th><a href="code/dungeon.gif">The Dungeon</a></th>
<td class="red">Better listen to the tour guides, or
you'll get lost!</td>
    <td><img src="skel04.gif" alt="skel04.gif" width="140" height="100"
/></td>
</tr>
</table>
<hr />
<p>The <span class="bloodred">Halloween House of Terror</span> is
open from October 20 to November 1st, with a gala celebration on
Halloween night. Our hours are:</p>
<ul>
<li>Mon-Fri 5PM-midnight</li>
<li>Sat &amp; Sun 5PM-3AM</li>
<li>Halloween Night (31-Oct): 3PM-???</li>
</ul>
<p class="center">The <span class="bloodred">Halloween House of
Terror</span> is located at:<br />
The Old Waterfall Shopping Center<br />
1020 Mirabella Ave<br />
Springfield, CA 94532</p>
</body>
</html>
```

18

OUTPUT

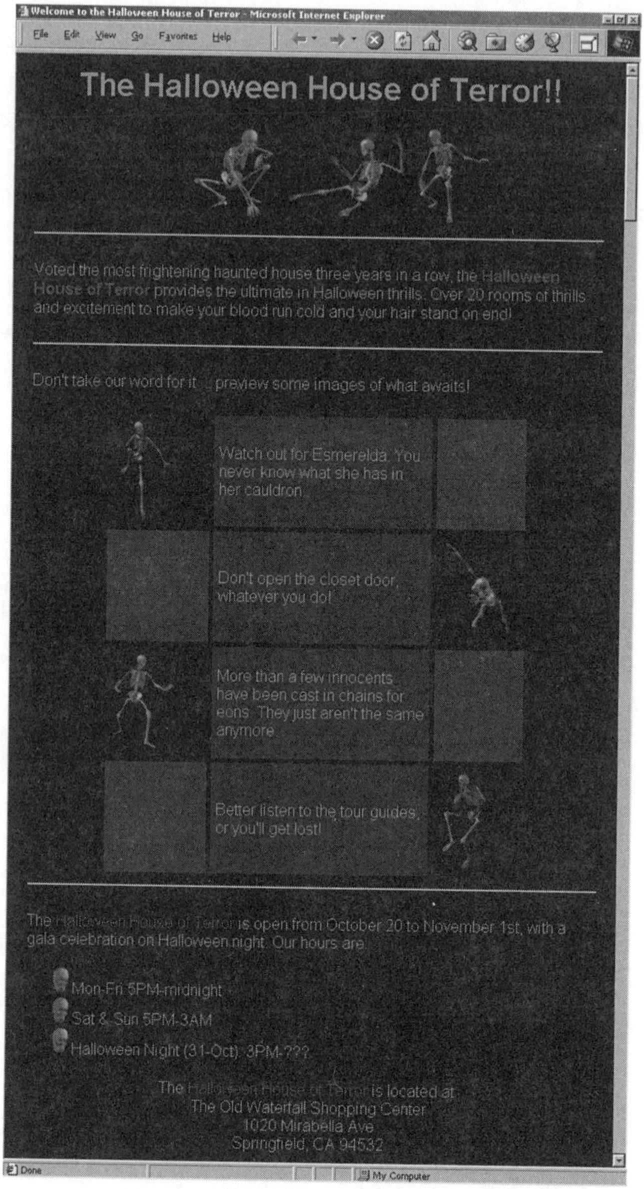

FIGURE 18.10

An example of HTML 4.0 Strict code in Internet Explorer.

Summary

HTML 4.0 and XHTML 1.0 each accommodate the needs of many by providing three different approaches to Web site design. Hopefully, you now realize that the needs of your readers also can affect the approach you use in your Web site design. The key is to anticipate the needs of the readers and to try to address their needs as broadly as possible. Not every site has to be filled with media that implements the latest and greatest Web technologies. On the other hand, certain topics almost demand higher levels of page design. Listen to the needs of your readers when you design your pages, and you'll keep them coming back.

Workshop

As if you haven't had enough already, here's a refresher course. As always, there are questions, a quiz, and exercises that will help you remember some of the most important points.

Q&A

Q Feedback from visitors to my site varies a lot. Some want my pages to use less media, while others want more. Is there an easy way to satisfy both of them?

A You've already learned that you can provide links to external media files. This is the best approach to take for readers that want to see less media, because they won't see the media unless they select a link to display the file.

You also can use advanced scripting methods (such as JavaScript or VBScript) to detect which browsers your readers are using. After the browser type is determined, the script can automatically direct readers to pages that are compatible with that browser. This requires additional design time on your part. Not only do you have to write script to accomplish this, but you also might need to create several different versions of your Web pages. If you don't want to detect browser types automatically, you also can use links on your home page to direct the readers to the types of pages they want to view. Simply use the home page as a gateway to your "plain and simple site" or to your "media-intensive site" and enable the reader to make the decision.

Q I use a lot of external files on my Web site, and they can be downloaded from several different pages. Wouldn't it be more efficient to include a link to the correct readers or viewers on the pages on which the external files appear?

A Although it is much easier for the reader to download an external file and the appropriate reader or helper application from the same page, it might be more difficult for you to maintain your pages when the URLs for the helper applications change. A good compromise is to include a Download page on your Web site that includes links to all helper applications that the reader will need. When the user downloads the external file that you have provided on the site, he or she can then navigate to your Download page. From there, the reader can download the helper application that is needed to view the file.

Quiz

1. What are some of the ways that real-world user needs vary?

2. What are some important things to include on your site that will help those who are new to computers or the Internet?

3. How does the use of the HTML 4.0 or XHTML 1.0 Transitional specification help you accommodate the needs of more individuals?

4. True or false: it's better to have a lot of frames in a frameset because you can keep more information in the browser window at the same time.

5. What are the advantages and disadvantages of using HTML 4.0 or XHTML 1.0 Strict to fulfill the needs of your readers?

Answers

1. Users will have different levels of experience. Browser preferences will vary. Some want to see a lot of media, while others prefer no media at all. Some prefer images and media that are interactive, while others prefer simpler pictures that demonstrate a process or technique on how to do something. Other preferences are more specific to the interests of the readers.

2. Include pages on your site that help the reader find the information he or she is looking for. Also include pages that describe how the users find their way around the site.

3. HTML 4.0 or XHTML 1.0 Transitional is designed to be backward compatible with older browsers. It enables you to use tags and attributes that are deprecated in the Strict specification.

4. False. Too many frames can be confusing for new users and also display pages in areas that will be too small to be useful when they are viewed at lower resolutions.

5. The disadvantage to using HTML 4.0 or XHTML 1.0 Strict is that there will be a wait until the majority of readers are using browsers that are fully compliant. The advantages are that HTML 4.0 and XHTML 1.0 Strict provide support for special presentational capabilities, such as those who are not using visual browsers.

Exercises

1. Design a simple navigation system for a Web site and describe it in a manner that seems to make sense to you. Then, ask others to review your descriptions and verify that your explanations are clear to them.

2. Make a list of the topics that you want to discuss on your Web site. Go through the list a second time and see if you can anticipate the types of people that will be interested in those topics. Finally, review the list a third time and list the special needs that you might need to consider for each type of user group.

PART 7

Going Live on the Web

DAY 19

Putting Your Site Online

For the past six days, you've been creating and testing your Web pages on your local machine with your own browser. You may not even have had a network connection attached to your machine. At this point, you most likely have a Web site put together with a well-organized structure and with a reasonable number of meaningful images (each with carefully chosen alt text). You've also written your text with wit and care, used only relative links, and tested it extensively on your own system.

Now, on the last day of the week, you're finally ready to publish your site, to put it all online so that other people on the Web can see it and link their pages to yours. In this chapter and the next, you'll learn everything you need to get started publishing the work you've done, how to let people know it's there, and how to keep it fine-tuned after it's online.

Today you'll learn about the following topics:

- What a Web server does and why you need one
- Where you can find a Web server on which to put your site
- How to install your Web site
- How to find out your URL
- How to test and troubleshoot your Web pages

What Does a Web Server Do?

To publish Web pages, you'll need a Web server. The Web server is a program that sits on a machine on the Internet, waiting for a Web browser to connect to it and make a request for a file. After a request comes over the wire, the server locates and sends the file back to the browser. The process is as easy as that.

Web servers and Web browsers communicate by using the *Hypertext Transfer Protocol* (HTTP), a special language created specifically for the request and transfer of hypertext documents over the Web. Because of this use, Web servers often are called HTTPD servers.

Note

> The *D* in *HTTPD* stands for *daemon*. Daemon is a UNIX term for a program that sits in the background and waits for requests. When this program receives a request, it wakes up, processes the request, and then goes back to sleep. You don't have to work in UNIX for a program to act like a daemon, so Web servers on any platform are still called HTTPDs. Most of the time, I call them Web servers.

Other Things Web Servers Do

Although the Web server's primary purpose is to answer requests from browsers, a Web server is responsible for several other tasks. You'll learn about some of them today.

File and Media Types

In Day 13, "Multimedia: Adding Sounds, Videos, and More," you learned about content-types and how browsers and servers use file extensions to determine the types of files. Servers are responsible for telling the browsers the kind of content files contain. You can configure a Web server to send different kinds of media or to handle new and different files and extensions. In "Questions to Ask Your Webmaster" later in this chapter, you'll learn about some of the important questions you should ask your Web presence provider or webmaster before you publish your pages.

File Management

The Web server also is responsible for very rudimentary file management—mostly in determining where to find a file and keeping track of where it's gone. If a browser requests a file that doesn't exist, the Web server sends back the page with the 404: File Not Found message. You also can configure servers to create aliases for files (the same file but accessed with a different name). Aliases redirect files to different locations (automatically pointing the browser to a new URL for files that have moved) and return a default file or a directory listing if a browser requests a URL ending with a directory name.

Finally, servers keep log files for information on how many times each file on the site has been accessed, including the site that accessed it, the date, and, in some servers, the type of browser and the URL of the page from which they came.

CGI Scripts, Programs, and Forms Processing

One of the more interesting (and more complex) tasks that a server can perform is to run external programs on the server machine based on input readers provide from their browsers. These special programs most often are called CGI scripts and are the basis for creating interactive forms. CGI scripts also are sometimes used to process clickable server-side imagemaps, which you learned about in Day 9, "Creating and Using Imagemaps." You also can use CGI scripts to connect a Web server with a database or other information system on the server side.

CGI scripting is an older method of handling forms. Today, there are solutions that don't require server-side processing. Among them are scripting languages such as VBScript and JavaScript. Unfortunately, these are topics that go beyond the scope of this book.

Server-Side File Processing

Some servers can process files before they send them along to the browsers. On a simple level are server-side includes, which can insert a date or a chunk of boilerplate text into each page, or run a program. Many of the access counters you see on pages are run in this way. You also can use server-side processing in much more sophisticated ways to modify files on-the-fly for different browsers or to execute small bits of scripting code.

Authentication and Security

Some Web sites require you to register for their services and make you log in using a name and password every time you visit their sites. This process, called *authentication* (or *password protection*), is a feature most Web servers now include. By using authentication, you can set up users and passwords, and you can restrict access to certain files and directories. You also can restrict access to files or to an entire site based on site names or IP addresses—for example, to prevent anyone outside your company from viewing files that are intended for internal use.

NEW TERM   *Authentication*, or password protection, is the capability to protect files or directories on your Web server so that they require your readers to enter names and passwords before the files can be viewed.

19

For security, some servers now provide a mechanism for secure connections and transactions by using Netscape's SSL protocol. *SSL* (short for *Secure Socket Layer*) provides authentication of the server (to prove that the server is who it says it is) and an encrypted connection between the browser and the server so that sensitive information between the two is kept secret.

Locating a Web Server

Before you can put your Web site on the Web, you'll need to find a Web server that you can use. Depending on how you get your access to the Internet, locating a Web server may be really easy or not quite so easy.

Using a Web Server Provided by Your School or Work

If you get your Internet connection through school or work, that organization most likely will allow you to publish Web pages on its own Web server. Given that these organizations usually have fast connections to the Internet and people to administer the site for you, this situation is ideal if you have it.

If you're in this situation, you'll have to ask your system administrator, computer consultant, Webmaster, or network provider whether a Web server is available, and, if so, what the procedures are for getting your pages installed. You'll learn more about what to ask later in this chapter.

Using a Commercial Internet or Web Service

You may pay for your Internet access through an Internet service provider (ISP), an IPP (Internet presence provider), or a commercial online service. Many of them also allow you to publish your Web pages using that service, although doing so may cost you extra. The service might have restrictions on the kinds of pages you can publish, or whether (if at all) you can run CGI scripts or other server-side processing. Ask your provider's help line or participate in online groups or conferences related to Internet services to see how others have set up Web publishing.

In the last few years, several organizations that provide nothing but Web publishing services have popped up. These services, most commonly known as Web presence providers, usually provide you with some method for transferring your files to their sites (usually FTP), and they provide the disk space and the network connections for access to your files. They also have professional site administrators on site to make sure the servers are running well all the time.

Generally, you are charged a flat monthly rate, with some additional cost if you use a large amount of disk space or if you have especially popular pages that take up a lot of network bandwidth. Some services even allow CGI scripts for forms and server-side imagemaps and will provide consulting to help you set them up; a few will even set up their server with your own hostname so that it looks as though you've got your own server running on the Web. These features can make using commercial Web sites an especially attractive option.

Most commercial Internet providers provide your Web space in a subdirectory on their server, and your URL might be something like `http://www.ispname.net/~youraccountname`. You also can obtain a virtual domain account through an Internet service provider or Web hosting service, a very reasonably priced option nowadays.

To set up a virtual domain account, you will need to register your domain name with InterNIC. The initial cost to register and acquire your domain name and IP address can be as low as $70 for two years. Thereafter, an annual fee keeps your domain name active. For all intents and purposes, a virtual domain account appears to the outside world as if you are running a Web site on your own server. Your site will have an address such as `http://www.mygreatsite.com/`.

Many ISPs and Web presence providers assist you with registering your domain name with InterNIC. You also can register your domain directly with Network Solutions—the private company that currently administers InterNIC registrations in the United States—at `www.networksolutions.com/`.

> **Note**
>
> The Ultimate Web Host List at `http://webhostlist.internetlist.com/` is a good resource for finding and evaluating Web hosting services. Appendix A, "Sources for Further Information," includes a section of links that display additional lists of Web providers.

19

Note that unlike your main Internet service provider, which you generally want located in your city or somewhere close to minimize phone bills, services that publish Web pages can be located anywhere on the Internet. Therefore, you can shop for the least expensive prices and best services without having to worry about geographical location.

Setting Up Your Own Server

If you are really courageous and want the ultimate in Web publishing, running your own Web site is the way to go. If you run your own site, you can publish as much as you want and include any kind of content you want. You'll also be able to use forms; CGI scripts;

plug-ins; advanced Web technologies, such as channels and netcasting; imagemaps; and many other special options. Other Web publishing services might not let you use these kinds of features; however, running a server is definitely not for everyone. The cost, maintenance time, and technical background required to run your own server can be daunting and requires a level of expertise that the average user might not possess.

Organizing and Installing Your HTML Files

After you have access to a Web server, you can publish the Web site you've labored so hard to create. Before you actually move it into place on your server, however, it's important to organize your files. You also should have a good idea of what goes where so that you don't lose files or so your links don't break in the process.

Questions to Ask Your Webmaster

The *Webmaster* is the person who runs your Web server; this person also may be your system administrator, help desk administrator, or network administrator. Before you can publish your files, you should learn several facts from the Webmaster about how the server is set up. The following list of questions also will help you later in this book when you're ready to figure out what you can and cannot do with your server:

- **Where on the server will I put my files?** In many cases, your Webmaster can create a special directory for you. Know where that directory is and how to gain access to it.

  In some other cases, particularly on UNIX machines, you might be able to just create a special directory in your home directory and store your files there. If that's the case, your Webmaster will tell you the name of the directory.

- **What is the URL of my top-level directory?** This URL may be different from the actual pathname to your files.

- **What is the name of the system's default index file?** This file is loaded by default when a URL ends with a directory name. Usually, it is `index.html` or `index.htm`; however, it sometimes may be `default.html`, `Homepage.html`, and so on.

- **Can I run CGI or other types of scripts?** Depending on your server, the answer to this question may be a flat-out "no," or you may be limited to certain programs and capabilities.

- **Do you support special plug-ins or file types?** If your site is designed to handle special types of media (Real Audio, Shockwave or Shockwave Flash, or other similar plug-ins or Web enhancements), your Webmaster may need to configure the server to accommodate those file types. Check to see if the server can handle special types of media before you create them.

- **Do you support FrontPage Server Extensions?** Microsoft FrontPage, a very popular Web authoring tool for the Windows platform (and for the Macintosh platform as well), enables you to develop advanced Web pages that incorporate forms and other advanced features. To utilize many of these advanced features, however, the Web server must have the FrontPage Server Extensions installed on it. If you are interested in using FrontPage to design advanced pages, be sure to ask your ISP whether they support the Server Extensions.

- **Does my site have limitations on what or how much I can put up?** Some sites restrict pages to specific content (for example, only work-related pages) or allow you only a few pages on the system. They might prevent more than a certain number of people from accessing your pages at once or may have other restrictions on what sort of publishing you can perform. Make sure that you understand the limitations of the system and that you can work within these limitations.

- **Is there a limit to the amount of bandwidth that my visitors can download?** This is somewhat related to the preceding question. Your provider might not place a limit on the number of pages you put on your site, but you might be charged extra if you exceed a certain amount of bandwidth per month. So, before you place 10MB worth of content on a Web site and load your pages with dozens of fat graphics, sound files, and video clips, ask your Web provider whether you have a bandwidth limit. The bandwidth usually relates to the amount of downloads that you see on your site (each time a page is accessed or a file is downloaded).

- **Do you provide any canned scripts that I can use for my Web pages?** If you aren't keen on writing your own scripts to add advanced features on your pages, check with your service provider to see whether they provide any that might be of assistance. Many ISPs, for example, provide scripts that enable you to put page counters on your home page. Others might provide access to form processing scripts as well.

Keeping Your Files Organized Using Directories

Probably the easiest way to organize each of your sites is to include all the files for the site in a single directory. If you have many extra files—for your images, for example—you can put them in a subdirectory to that main directory. Your goal is to contain all your files in a single place rather than scatter them around on your disk. After you contain your files, you can set all your links in your files to be relative to that one directory. If you follow these hints, you stand the best chance of being able to move the directory around to different servers without breaking the links.

19

Having a Default Index File and Correct Filenames

Web servers usually have a default index file that's loaded when a URL ends with a directory name rather than a filename. In the preceding section, you learned that one of the questions you should ask your Webmaster is, "What is the name of this default file?" For most Web servers, this file usually is called `index.html` (`index.htm` for DOS). Your home page, or top-level index, for each site should be called by this name so that the server knows which page to send as the default page. Each subdirectory, in turn, if it contains any HTML files, also should have a default file. If you use this default filename, the URL to that page will be shorter because you don't have to include the actual filename. So, for example, your URL might be `http://www.myserver.com/www/` rather than `http://www.myserver.com/www/index.html`.

Each file also should have an appropriate extension indicating the type of file it is so that the server can map it to the appropriate file type. If you've been following along in the book so far, all your files already should have this special extension, so you should not have any problems. Table 19.1 reminds you of the list of the common file extensions that you should be using for your files and media.

Table 19.1 Common File Types and Extensions

Format	Extension
HTML	`.html, .htm`
ASCII Text	`.txt`
PostScript	`.ps`
GIF	`.gif`
JPEG	`.jpg, .jpeg`
AU Audio	`.au`
WAV Audio	`.wav`
MPEG Audio	`.mp2, .mp3`
MPEG Video	`.mpeg, .mpg`
QuickTime Video	`.mov`
AVI Video	`.avi`

If you're using special media in your Web site that is not part of this list, you might need to specially configure your server to handle this file type. You'll learn more about this issue later in this chapter.

Installing Your Files

Got everything organized? Then all that's left is to move everything into place on the server. After the server can access your files, you're officially published on the Web. That's all there is to putting your pages online.

Where, however, is the appropriate spot on the server? You should ask your Webmaster for this information. You also should find out how to get to that special spot on the server, whether it's simply copying files, using FTP to put them on the server, or using some other method.

Moving Files Between Systems

If you're using a Web server that has been set up by someone else, you usually will have to move your Web files from your system to theirs using FTP, Zmodem transfer, or some other method. Although the HTML markup within your files is completely cross-platform, moving the actual files from one type of system to another sometimes has its catches. In particular, be careful to do the following:

- **Transfer all files as binary**—Your FTP or file-upload program may give you an option to transfer files in binary or text mode (or may give you even different options altogether). Always transfer everything—all your HTML files, images, and media—in binary format (even the files that are indeed text; you can transfer a text file in binary mode without any problems).

  If you're working on a Macintosh, your transfer program most likely will give you many options with names such as MacBinary, AppleDouble, or other strange names. Avoid all of them. The option you want is *flat binary* or *raw data*. If you transfer files in any other format, they may not work when they get to the other side.

- **Watch out for filename restrictions**—If you're moving your files to or from DOS systems, you'll have to watch out for the dreaded 8.3—the DOS rule that says filenames must be only eight characters long with three-character extensions. If your server is a PC, and you've been writing your files on some other system, you may have to rename your files and the links to them to have the right file-naming conventions. (Moving files you've created on a PC to some other system usually is not a problem.)

  Also, watch out if you're moving files from a Macintosh to other systems; make sure that your filenames do not have spaces or other funny characters in them. Keep your filenames as short as possible, use only letters and numbers, and you'll be fine.

19

- **Watch out for upper- or lowercase sensitivity**—Some operating systems and file management programs show filenames in all lowercase (such as myfile.html). In reality, however, DOS-based filenames might be in all caps (such as MYFILE.HTML). If the code in your Web pages contains lowercase links to these files (as is usually the case), you'll experience broken links when you transfer your Web pages to a server that uses case-sensitive URLs (such as UNIX servers). Double-check the case sensitivity in your files after you transfer them to your site.

- **Be aware of carriage returns and line feeds**—Different systems use different methods for ending a line; the Macintosh uses carriage returns, UNIX uses line feeds, and DOS uses both. When you move files from one system to another, most of the time the end-of-line characters will be converted appropriately, but sometimes they won't. The characters not converting can result in your file coming out double-spaced or all on one single line on the system to which it was moved.

Most of the time, this failure to convert doesn't matter because browsers ignore spurious returns or line feeds in your HTML files. The existence or absence of either one is not terribly important. Where it might be an issue is in sections of text you've marked up with <pre>; you may find that your well-formatted text that worked so well on one platform doesn't come out well formatted after it's been moved.

If you do have end-of-line problems, you have a couple of options for how to proceed. Many text editors enable you to save ASCII files in a format for another platform. If you know the platform to which you're moving, you can prepare your files for that platform before moving them. If you're moving to a UNIX system, small filters for converting line feeds called dos2unix and unix2dos may be available on the UNIX or DOS systems. And, finally, you can convert Macintosh files to UNIX-style files by using the following command line on UNIX:

```
tr '\015' '\012' < oldfile.html > newfile.html
```

In this example, oldfile.html is the original file with end-of-line problems, and newfile.html is the name of the new file.

Remote Management Tools

New tools enable you to manage and update the contents of your pages remotely on a remote Web server. Foremost among them are tools from Netscape and Microsoft.

Microsoft's FrontPage is a Web development tool aimed at small- to medium-sized Web sites. FrontPage provides a WYSIWYG page editor, a site manager for managing document trees and links, as well as a variety of server extensions that can be used with a variety of servers, ranging from Windows-based Microsoft and Netscape servers to UNIX servers.

These extensions allow Webmasters to include a variety of features in their sites, including interactive discussion groups and other interactive features. These extensions also enable you to use FrontPage to upload files into place on the server as you make changes in the content of your site. FrontPage enables you to publish your Web site to a remote server, regardless of whether it has the FrontPage Server Extensions installed.

Similarly, Netscape's LiveWire includes a tool called SiteManager that enables you to upload new content to a remote server. Unlike FrontPage, however, LiveWire is really designed for use with Netscape's FastTrack and Enterprise Web servers. LiveWire provides a server-side scripting language using JavaScript that works only with the Netscape servers. Still, the SiteManager tool can be used to manage document trees and links for any site and can be used to upload content via FTP to a server.

Other site development and management tools, such as Fusion from NetObjects (www.netobjects.com) or Macromedia Dreamweaver (www.macromedia.com), provide the capability to develop offline and then update content on a remote server.

What's My URL?

At this point, you have a server, your Web pages are installed and ready to go, and you just need to tell people that your site exists. All you need now is a URL.

If you're using a commercial Web server or a server that someone else administers, you might be able to find out easily what your URL is by asking the administrator. (In fact, you were supposed to ask your Webmaster this question, as noted previously.) Otherwise, you'll have to figure it out yourself. Luckily, determining your URL isn't very hard.

As noted in Day 5, "All About Links," URLs are made of three parts: the protocol, the hostname, and the path to the file. To determine each of these parts, answer the following questions:

- **What am I using to serve the files?** If you're using a real Web server, your protocol is http. If you're using FTP or Gopher, the protocol is ftp and gopher, respectively. (Isn't this easy?)

- **What's the name of my server?** This is the network name of the machine on which your Web server is located, typically beginning with www, such as www.mysite.com. If the name doesn't start with www, don't worry; having this name doesn't affect whether people can get to your files. Note that the name you'll use is the fully qualified hostname—that is, the name that people elsewhere on the Web would use to get to your Web server, which may not be the same name you use to get to your Web server. This name usually will have several parts and end with .com, .edu, or the code for your country (for example, .uk, .fr, and so on).

19

With some SLIP or PPP connections, you might not even have a network name, just a number, such as 192.123.45.67. You can use it as the network name.

If the server has been installed on a port other than 80, you'll need to know this number, too. Your Webmaster will know this information.

- **What's the path to my home page?** The path to your home page most often begins at the root of the directory where Web pages are stored (part of your server configuration), which may or may not be the top level of your file system. If you've put files into the directory /home/www/files/myfiles, for example, your pathname in the URL might just be /myfiles. This is a server-configuration question, so if you can't figure out the answer, you might have to ask your server administrator.

  If your Web server has been set up so that you can use your home directory to store Web pages, you can use the UNIX convention of the tilde (~) to refer to the Web pages in your home directory. You don't have to include the name of the directory you created in the URL itself. If I have the Web page home.html in a directory called public_html in my home directory (lemay), for example, the path to that file in the URL would be /~lemay/home.html.

After you know the answers to the three preceding questions, you can construct a URL. Remember from Day 5 that a URL looks like the following:

```
protocol://machinename.com:port/path
```

You should be able to plug your values for each of these elements into the appropriate places in the URL structure, as in the following examples:

```
http://www.mymachine.com/www/tutorials/index.html
ftp://ftp.netcom.com/pub/le/lemay/index.html
http://www.commercialweb.com:8080/~lemay/index.html
```

Test, Test, and Test Again

Now that your Web pages are available on the Internet, you can take the opportunity to test them on as many platforms using as many browsers as you possibly can. Only after you've seen how your documents look on different platforms will you realize how important it is to design documents that can look good on as many platforms and browsers as possible.

Try looking at your pages now. You might be surprised at the results. In Day 21, "Testing, Revising, and Maintaining Your Web Site," you'll learn how to fix some of the errors that you might find after your site is published on a remote server. We'll touch base on a few of the more common problems in this chapter.

Troubleshooting

What happens if you upload all your files to the server, try to display your home page in your browser, and something goes wrong? Here's the first place to look.

Can't Access the Server

If your browser can't even get to your server, this problem most likely is not one that you can fix. Make sure that you have the right server name and that it's a complete hostname (usually ending in `.com`, `.edu`, `.net`, or some other common ending name). Make sure that you haven't mistyped your URL and that you're using the right protocol. If your Webmaster told you that your URL included a port number, make sure that you're including that port number in the URL after the hostname.

Also make sure that your network connection is working. Can you get to other Web servers? Can you get to the top-level home page for the site itself?

If none of these ideas solve the problem, perhaps your server is down or not responding. Call your Webmaster to find out whether he or she can help.

Can't Access Files

What if all your files are showing up as `Not Found` or `Forbidden`? First, check your URL. If you're using a URL with a directory name at the end, try using an actual file-name at the end and see whether this trick works. Double-check the path to your files; remember that the path in the URL might be different from the path on the actual disk. Also, keep in mind that uppercase and lowercase are significant. If your file is `MyFile.html`, make sure you're not trying `myfile.html` or `Myfile.html`.

If the URL appears to be correct, the next thing to check is file permissions. On UNIX systems, all your directories should be world-executable, and all your files should be world-readable. You can ensure that all the permissions are correct by using the following commands:

```
chmod 755 filename
chmod 755 directoryname
```

Can't Access Images

You can get to your HTML files just fine, but all your images are coming up as icons or broken icons. First, make sure the references to your images are correct. If you've used relative pathnames, you should not have this problem. If you've used full pathnames or file URLs, the references to your images may very well have broken when you moved the files to the server. (I warned you...)

19

In some browsers, notably Netscape, if you select an image with the right mouse button (hold down the button on a Macintosh mouse), you'll get a pop-up menu. Choose the View This Image menu item to try to load the image directly, which will give you the URL of the image where the browser thinks it's supposed to be (which may not be where *you* think it's supposed to be). You often can track down strange relative pathname problems this way.

If the references all look good and the images worked just fine on your local system, the only other place a problem could have occurred is in transferring the files from one system to another. As mentioned earlier in this chapter, make sure you transfer all your image files in binary format. If you're on a Macintosh, make sure you transfer the files as raw data or just data. Don't try to use MacBinary or AppleDouble format; otherwise, you'll get problems on the other side.

Links Don't Work

If your HTML and image files are working just fine, but your links don't work, you most likely used pathnames for those links that applied only to your local system. For example, you used absolute pathnames or file URLs to refer to the files to which you're linking. As mentioned for images, if you used relative pathnames and avoided file URLs, you should not have a problem.

Files Are Displaying Incorrectly

Suppose that you've got an HTML file or a file in some media format that displays or links just fine on your local system. After you upload the file to the server and try to view it, the browser gives you gobbledygook; for example, it displays the HTML code itself instead of the HTML file, or it tries to display an image or media file as text.

This problem could happen in two cases. The first is a situation in which you're not using the right file extensions for your files. Make sure that you're using one of the right file extensions with the right uppercase and lowercase.

In the second case in which this problem could happen, your server is misconfigured to handle your files. If you're working on a DOS system where all your HTML files have extensions of `.htm`, for example, your server may not understand that `.htm` is an HTML file. (Most modern servers do, but some older ones don't.) You also might be using a newer form of media that your server doesn't understand. In either case, your server may be using some default content-type for your files (usually `text/plain`), which your browser then tries to handle (and doesn't often succeed).

To fix this problem, you'll have to configure your server to handle the file extensions for the media with which you're working. If you're working with someone else's server, you'll have to contact your Webmaster and have him or her set up the server correctly. Your Webmaster will need two types of information to make this change: the file extensions you're using and the content-type you want him or her to return. If you don't know the content-type you want, refer to the listing of the most popular types in Appendix E, "MIME Types and File Extensions."

Summary

In this chapter, you've reached the final point in creating a Web site: publishing your work to the World Wide Web at large through the use of a Web server, either installed by you or available from a network provider. Here, you learned what a Web server does and how to get one, how to organize your files and install them on the server, and how to find your URL and use it to test your pages.

Workshop

From here on, everything you'll learn is icing on an already-substantial cake. You'll simply be adding more features (interactivity, forms) to the site you already have available on the Web. Congratulations! Have some ice cream.

Q&A

Q I have my pages published at an ISP I really like; my URL is something like `http://www.thebestisp.com/users/mypages/`. Instead of this URL, I'd like to have my own hostname—something like `http://www.mypages.com/`. How can I do this?

A You have two choices. The easiest way is to ask your ISP if it allows you to have your own domain name. Many ISPs have a method for setting up your domain so that you can still use their services and work with them—only your URL changes. Note that having your own hostname may cost more money, but if you really must have that URL, then this may be the way to go. Many Web hosting services have plans starting as low as $20 a month for this type of service, and it currently costs $70 to register your domain for two years.

The other option is to set up your own server with your own domain name. This option could be significantly more expensive than working with an ISP, and it requires at least some background in basic network administration. You'll learn all about this process in Chapter 20, "Letting People Know It's There."

19

Q I created all my image files on a Macintosh, uploaded them to my UNIX server by using the Fetch FTP program, tested it all, and it works fine. Now, however, I'm getting email from people saying that none of my images are working. What's going on here?

A Usually, when you upload the files using Fetch, you can choose from a pull-down menu where the default is MacBinary. Make sure you change that to Raw Data.

MacBinary files work well when they're viewed on a Macintosh. In addition, because I assume that you're using a Macintosh to test your site, they'll work fine; however, they won't work on any other system. To ensure that your images work across platforms, upload them as Raw Data.

Q I created my files on a DOS system, using the .htm extension, like you told me to earlier in the book. Now I've published my files on a UNIX system provided by my employer. The problem now is that when I try to get to my pages by using my browser, I get the HTML code for those pages—not the formatted result! It all worked on my system at home. What went wrong?

A Some older servers will have this problem. Your server has not been set up to believe that files with an .htm extension are actually HTML files, so they send them as the default content-type (text/plain) instead. Then, when your browser reads one of your files from a server, it reads that content-type and assumes that you have a text file, so your server is messing up everything.

You can fix this problem in several ways. By far, the best way to fix it is to tell your Webmaster to change the server configuration so that .htm files are sent as HTML—usually a very simple step that will magically cause all your files to work properly from then on.

If you can't find your Webmaster, or for some strange reason he or she will not make this change, your only other option is to change all your filenames after you upload them to the UNIX system. Note that you'll have to change all the links within those files as well. (Finding a way to convince your Webmaster to fix this problem would be a *much* better solution.)

Quiz

1. What is the basic function of a Web server?

2. Name some ways that you can obtain an Internet connection.

3. What is a default index file, and what is the advantage of using them in all directories?

4. What should you be aware of when uploading your files to your Internet site?

5. What are some things that you should check immediately after you upload your Web pages?

Answers

1. A Web server is a program that sits on a machine on the Internet (or intranet). It determines where to find files and keeps track of where the files are going.

2. You can obtain Internet connections through school or work, from commercial Internet or Web services, or you can set up your own Web server.

3. The default index file is loaded when a URL ends with a directory name rather than a filename. Typical examples of default index files are `index.html`, `index.htm`, or `default.htm`. If you use default filenames, you can use a URL such as `http://www.mysite.com/` rather than `http://www.mysite.com/index.html` to get to the home page in the directory.

4. Transfer all your files in binary format, watch for filename restrictions, watch out for upper- or lowercase sensitivity, and watch for carriage returns and line feeds.

5. Check to see that your browser can reach your Web pages on the server, that you can access the files on your Web site, and that your links and images work as you expect them to. After you determine that everything appears the way you think it should, have friends and family test your pages in other browsers.

Exercises

1. Start shopping and considering where you want to store your Web site. Call two or more places to determine what benefits you will get if you locate your Web pages on their server.

2. Upload and test a practice page (even if it's a simple or blank page that you'll add content to later) to learn the process. You might work out a few kinks this way before you actually upload all your hard work on the Web.

19

DAY 20

Letting People Know It's There

The "Build it, and they will come" motto from the movie *Field of Dreams* notwithstanding, people won't simply start to visit your site of their own accord after you've put it online. In fact, with probably millions of sites online already, and some of these holding thousands of documents, it's highly unlikely that anyone could ever stumble across your site by accident. So, how do you entice people to come to your site? What is the best way to cause people to flock to your site? This chapter helps you learn some of the ways to generate interest in your site, including the following:

- Methods for advertising your site
- Getting your site listed on the major Web directories
- Listing your site with the major Web indexes
- Using Usenet to announce your site
- Using business cards, letterheads, and brochures
- Locating more directories and related Web pages
- How to use log files and counters to find out who's viewing your pages

Registering and Advertising Your Web Pages

To get people to visit your Web site, you need to advertise its existence in as many ways as possible. After all, the higher the visibility, the greater the prospect of your site receiving a large number of hits.

NEW TERM *Hits* is a Web-speak term for the number of visits your Web site receives. This term does not differentiate between people, but instead is simply a record of the number of times a copy of your Web page has been downloaded.

There are many ways that you can promote your site. You can list your site on major Web directories and indexes, announce it in newsgroups, list your URL on business cards, and so much more. The following sections describe each method of approach.

World Wide Web Site Listings

When many people first start working with the World Wide Web, they find it hard to understand that there are other people out there, on numerous other Web sites, who are just *itching* for the chance to include a hyperlink to other Web pages as part of their own lists. What new people find even *harder* to understand is that, for the most part, no cost is involved.

There is a simple reason for the existence of so many of these apparently philanthropic individuals. When the World Wide Web was young and fresh, the best way for a person to promote the existence of his site was by approaching other Web developers and asking them to list his site on their pages. In return for this favor, this person also would list their sites on his pages. Over time, this process has been refined somewhat, but today, many sites still are happy to include a link to your site. In fact, don't be surprised if you occasionally receive email from someone asking to be included in your list of sites.

This cooperative nature is a strikingly unique feature of the World Wide Web. Rather than competing for visitors with other similar sites, most Web pages actually *include* lists of their competitors.

Unfortunately, however, a problem still exists with just exchanging hyperlink references with other sites. As was originally the case, people still need to be able to locate a single site as a starting point. To this end, some sort of global Internet directory was needed. Currently, no single site on the World Wide Web can be regarded as the Internet directory, but a few major directories and libraries come very close.

Yahoo!

By far, the most well-known directory of Web sites is the Yahoo! site (see Figure 20.1), created by David File and Jerry Yang, at www.yahoo.com/. This site started in April 1994 as a small, private list of David's and Jerry's favorite Web sites. Since then, it has become a highly regarded catalog and index of Web sites and is now its own company.

FIGURE 20.1

Yahoo!

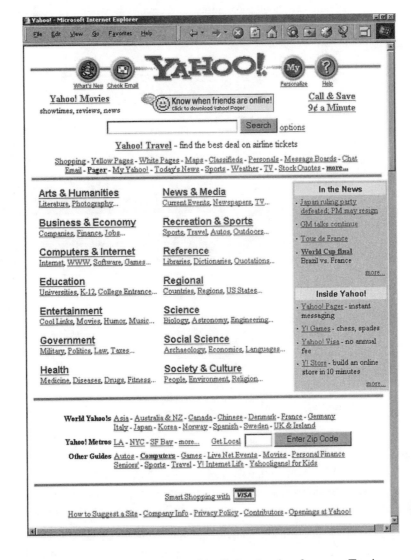

Yahoo! uses an elegant, multilevel catalog to organize all the sites it references. To view the contents of any level of the catalog, you select the major category hyperlink that most closely represents the information you are interested in and then follow the chain of associated pages to a list of related Web sites, like the one shown in Figure 20.2. Following is the full URL of this page:

```
http://dir.yahoo.com/Computers_and_Internet/Internet/World_Wide_Web/Announcement
_Services/
```

You definitely should take a look at the page shown in Figure 20.2. It contains a list of Announcement Services and related Web pages that can help you spread the word about your new Web site.

FIGURE 20.2

The Announcement Services category in Yahoo!.

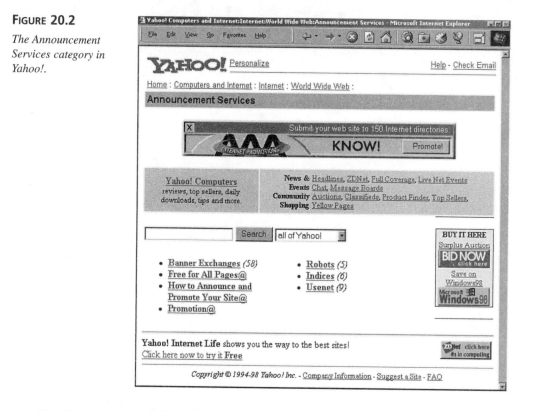

To add your site to the list maintained by Yahoo!, return to the Yahoo! home page at www.yahoo.com and select the category appropriate to your site. Work your way down the catalog through any subcategories until you locate a list of sites similar to your own.

Suppose that you've created a site that discusses Camel Racing. You navigate your way down through the Recreation links, which then leads to Sports, which then has a category called Camel Racing. Yes, there really is a category like this, and following is its URL:

```
http://dir.yahoo.com/Recreation/Sports/Camel_Racing/
```

If you scroll down to the bottom of this page, you see a link that says "How to Suggest a Site." Click this link to display the Suggest a Site page shown in Figure 20.3

(`http://docs.yahoo.com/info/suggest/`). This page provides complete instructions and takes you through the steps of adding your site to Yahoo!. The process currently involves filling out information on four screens of pages, and the forms are very easy to understand.

FIGURE 20.3

The Suggest a Site page on Yahoo!.

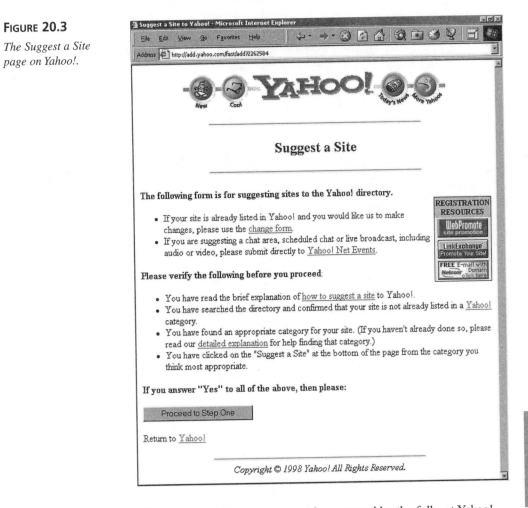

After you submit your site suggestion, your request is processed by the folks at Yahoo!. Soon, you'll find your site listed among the other Camel Racing pages!

The World Wide Web Virtual Library

The World Wide Web (W3) Virtual Library, located at `http://vlib.org/Overview.html`, is another very popular online catalog. Unlike Yahoo!, which is operated by a single group of people, the W3 Virtual Library is a distributed effort. As such, the contents of each category are maintained by different people (all volunteers) and sometimes housed on different computers all over the world.

The World Wide Web Virtual Library is somewhat more selective about the sites that it includes on its pages. Not every site will become listed here; however, if you have a top notch site, you should give them a try. To submit your URL for inclusion in a category of the Virtual Library, you need to send an email request to the person that maintains it. One way to obtain a list of the email addresses for each maintainer, or VLibrarian (short for virtual librarian), is to point your Web browser to `http://conbio.rice.edu/vl/database/output.cfm`. The first page, shown in Figure 20.4, displays the first 25 categories and also contains a link to the VLibrarian's email address. This is the person who you contact to have your site reviewed for inclusion in the virtual library.

FIGURE 20.4

The World Wide Web Virtual Library.

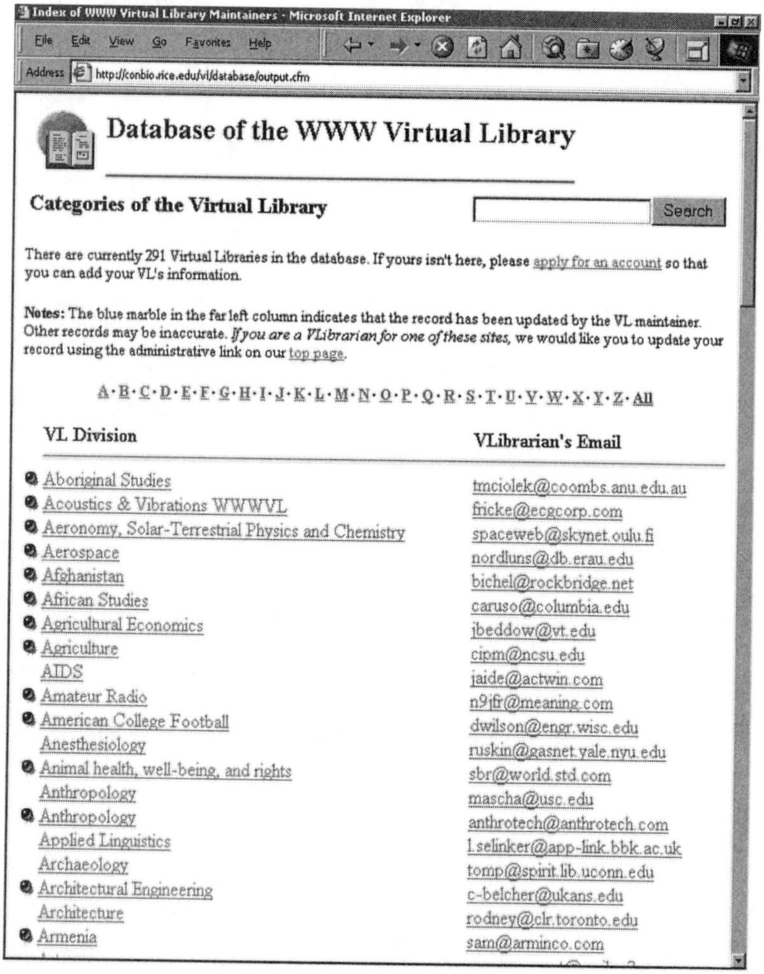

Yellow Pages Listings

Another popular method of promoting your site is by registering it with the growing number of Yellow Pages directories that have begun to spring up on the World Wide Web. You can best think of these sites as the electronic equivalent of your local telephone Yellow Pages directory.

As a rule, Yellow Pages sites are designed specially for commercial and business Web users who want to advertise their services and expertise. For this reason, most of the Yellow Pages sites offer both free and paid advertising space, with the paid listings including graphics, corporate logos, and advanced layout features. A free listing, on the other hand, tends to be little more than a hyperlink and a short comment. When you're starting out, free advertising is, without a doubt, the best advertising. Of the Yellow Pages sites currently in operation, the GTE Superpages is one of the most popular.

The GTE Superpages home page at www.superpages.com/ is shown in Figure 20.5. This home page gives you access to two separate Yellow Pages-type directories: one for business information gleaned from actual United States Yellow Pages information (which includes businesses without actual Web sites) and one specifically for businesses with Web sites. Both are organized into categories, and both listings enable you to search for specific business names and locations.

Private Directories

In addition to the broad mainstream Web directories, many private directories on the World Wide Web cater to more specific needs. Some of these directories deal with single issues, whereas others are devoted to areas such as online commerce, education, business, and entertainment.

The best way to locate most of these directories is to use an Internet search tool such as Lycos (www.lycos.com/) or WebCrawler (www.webcrawler.com/). Alternatively, most of these directories will already be listed in such places as Yahoo! and the W3 Virtual library, so a few minutes spent visiting relative catalogs at these sites normally is very beneficial.

20

FIGURE 20.5

The GTE Superpages home page.

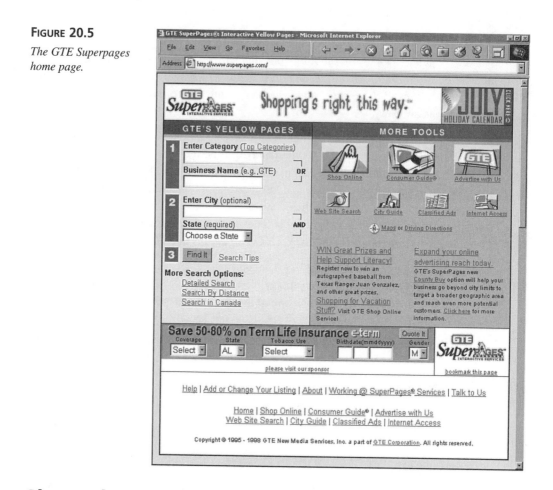

Site Indexes and Search Engines

After you list your new site on the major directories and maybe a few smaller directories, you next need to turn your attention to the indexing and search tools. The following are the names and URLs of the most popular of these:

Alta Vista	`www.altavista.com/`
Excite	`www.excite.com/`
HotBot	`www.hotbot.com/`
Infoseek	`http://infoseek.go.com/`
Lycos	`www.lycos.com/`
Snap.com	`www.snap.com/`

Unlike directories, which contain a hierarchical list of Web sites that have been submitted for inclusion to the directory, these indexes have search engines (sometimes called *spiders*) that prowl the Web and store information about every page and site they find. The indexes then store a database of sites that you can search by using a form.

After you publish your site on the Web and other people link to your site, chances are that a search engine eventually will get around to finding and exploring your site. However, you can tell these indexes ahead of time that your site exists and get your site indexed much faster. Each of these search engines provides a mechanism that enables you to submit your site for inclusion as part of its index. You'll take a look at a few of these search engines in this section.

AltaVista

One of the most popular and fastest Web indexes is Compaq's AltaVista index at `www.altavista.com/`. AltaVista indexes a good portion of the Web but stands out by having an extremely fast search engine. So, the process of looking up specific search terms on the Web is quick and thorough.

You can submit your page to AltaVista using the form at `www.altavista.digital.com/av/content/addurl.htm`, as shown in Figure 20.6.

Excite

Excite became known as a search engine and index of the Internet because it offered a unique capability: to search by concept rather than simply by keyword. The software that Excite uses to do this attempts to use a particular algorithm to extract meaning from your concept phrase to find relevant documents. Excite is on the Web at `www.excite.com/`, and you can submit pages at `www.excite.com/info/add_url/`.

HotBot

A search engine that has recently grown in popularity on the Web is HotBot, which you can find at `www.hotbot.com/`. From this search page, shown in Figure 20.7, readers can browse sites by category, view different collections of sites, shop online, and also view sites by geographical region. Shopping bots also enable readers to find online shopping sites of interest.

20

To add a page to HotBot, point your browser to `www.hotbot.com/addurl.asp`.

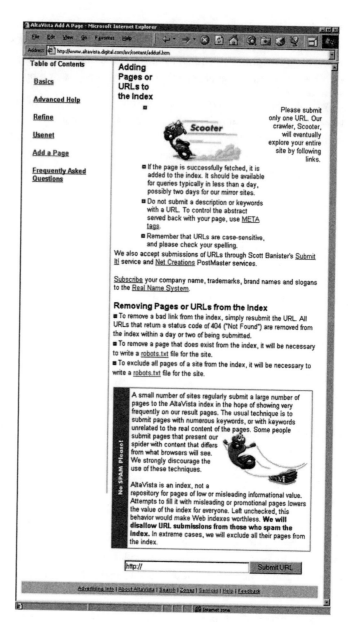

FIGURE 20.7

HotBot's home page.

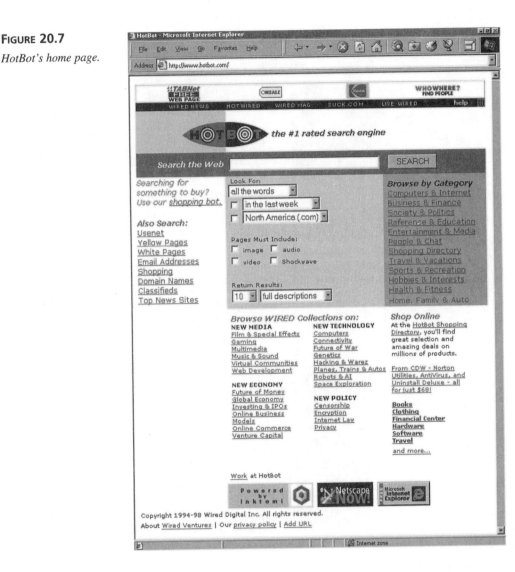

20

Lycos

Lycos was one of the earliest search engines and still claims to have the largest overall coverage of the Web. Lycos is located at www.lycos.com/. To add your page to Lycos, as shown in Figure 20.8, point your browser to www.lycos.com/addasite.html. For each page you submit, you must include the URL and your email address.

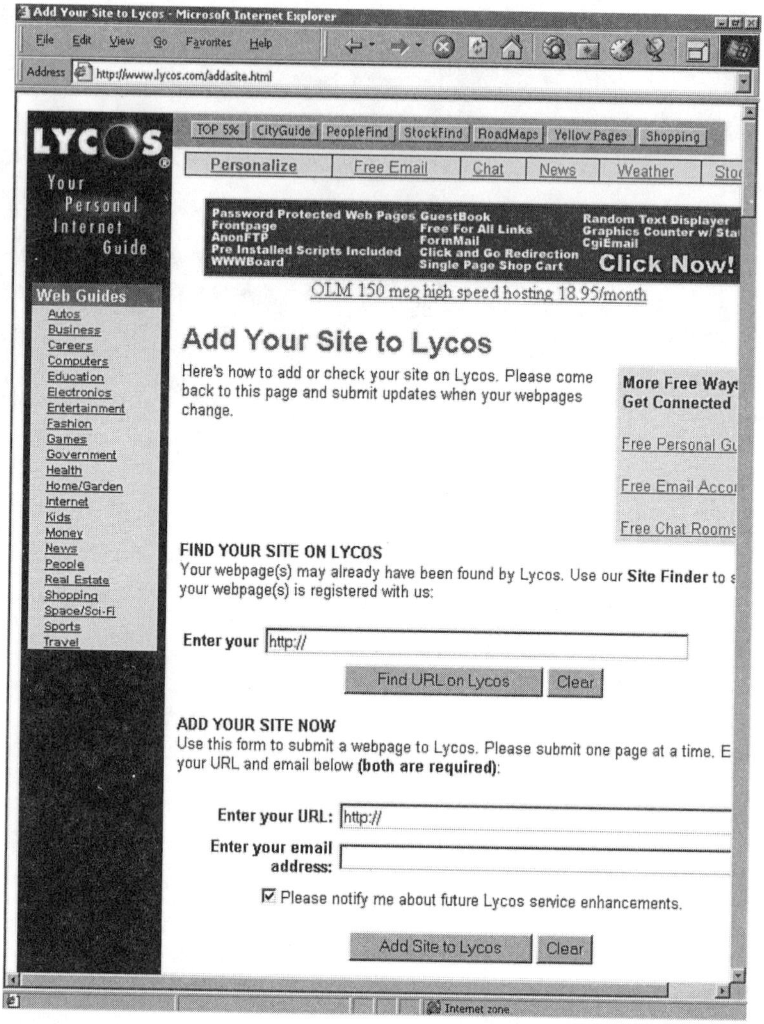

FIGURE 20.8

Lycos's registration page.

Infoseek

Back in 1995, *PC Computing* magazine voted Infoseek, shown in Figure 20.9 and located at http://infoseek.go.com/, the Most Valuable Internet Tool, and the service has expanded considerably since then. Like Lycos, Infoseek is a Web indexing tool, but what makes it even more powerful is its capability to search through many kinds of additional services and databases in addition to the World Wide Web. Such functionality, however, does come at a cost—only the Web search engine can be used without charge.

FIGURE 20.9

Infoseek.

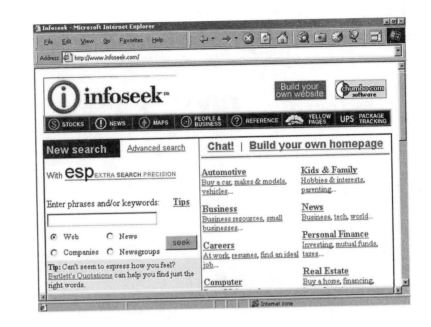

Submission Tools

Besides the search tools already covered, there are many others that offer differing capabilities. You'll need to make a separate submission to each to ensure that your site is indexed.

Rather than listing the URLs and details for each of these sites, I will turn this discussion to two special Web pages that take much of the drudgery out of submitting Web sites to search indexes and directories.

PostMaster2

The PostMaster2 site, shown in Figure 20.10 and located at www.netcreations.com/ postmaster/index.html, is an all-in-one submission page that asks you to complete all the details required for about two dozen Web indexes and directories. It includes many of the search engines I've already discussed. The submission form at www.netcreations. com/postmaster/registration/try.html, which takes some time to complete, enables you to try out the PostMaster service for free. After you complete the form, PostMaster2 submits your information to all these sites at once, so you don't have to go to each one individually.

FIGURE 20.10

PostMaster2.

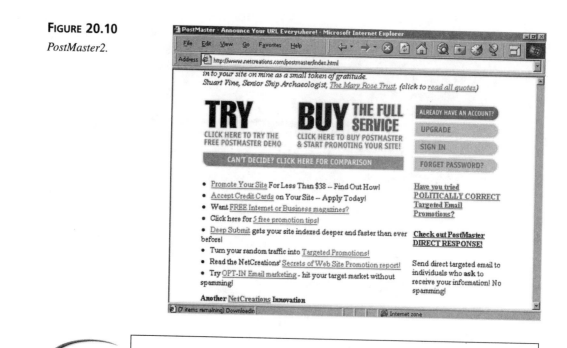

> **Note** PostMaster2 also offers a commercial version of its submission system that delivers announcements about your new site to more than 400 magazines, journals, and other periodicals, in addition to all the sites included in the free version. Using the commercial version, however, is an expensive exercise.

Submit It!

The Submit It! service, provided by Scott Banister, is a lot like PostMaster in that it also helps you submit your URL to different directories and search indexes. It supports just about all the same services, but it is set apart in the way in which you submit your information. Figure 20.11 shows only a portion of all the search indexes and directories currently supported by Submit It!. To view the list in its entirety, point your browser to www.submit-it.com/subcats.htm.

Submit It! doesn't ask you to complete one enormous page, something that many people find daunting. Instead, after you've filled out some general information, you select only the sites to which you want to submit an entry and then perform each submission one site at a time.

To learn more about Submit It!, point your Web browser to www.submit-it.com/.

FIGURE 20.11

Submit It!

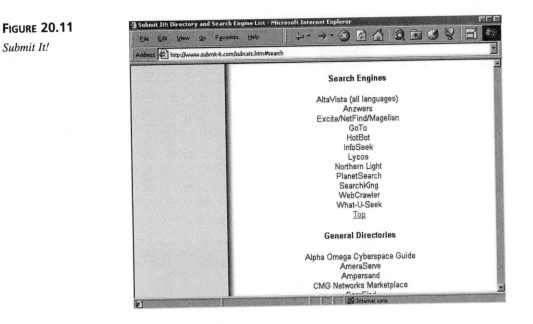

Announce Your Site Using Usenet

The World Wide Web is not the only place on the Internet that you can announce the launch of your new Web site. Many people make use of a small set of Usenet newsgroups that are designed especially for making announcements. To locate these newsgroups, look for newsgroup names that end with .announce. (Refer to the documentation that came with your Usenet newsreader for information about how to find these newsgroups.)

One newsgroup is even devoted just to World Wide Web-related announcements. This newsgroup, named comp.infosystems.www.announce, is shown in Figure 20.12. If your browser supports reading Usenet news, and you've configured it to point to your new server, you can view articles submitted to this newsgroup—and add your own announcements—by entering the following URL into the Document URL field:

news:comp.infosystems.www.announce

One post in particular to look for in comp.infosystems.www.announce is an excellent FAQ called "FAQ: How to Announce Your New Web Site." This FAQ contains an up-to-date list of all the best and most profitable means of promoting your Web site. If you can't locate the FAQ in this newsgroup (as shown in Figure 20.12), you can view an online version at http://ep.com/faq/webannounce.html.

20

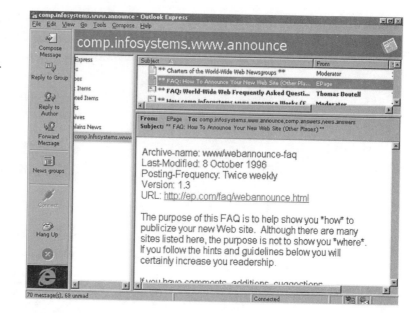

Figure 20.12

The comp.
infosystems.www.
announce *newsgroup.*

Note

comp.infosystems.www.announce is a moderated newsgroup. As such, any submissions you make to it are approved by a moderator before they appear in the newsgroup listing. To ensure that your announcement is approved, you should read the charter document that outlines the announcement process. You can read this document by pointing your Web browser to www.sangfroid.com/charter.html.

Web Rings

A relatively new way to advertise and promote your site on the Web is to include yourself in one or more *Web rings*. A Web ring is a collection of sites that focuses on a specific topic of interest. The main gateway to an immense collection of Web rings, covering just about any topic you can imagine, is the Web Ring home page, located at www.webring.com/ (see Figure 20.13).

The concept behind a Web ring is simple. To join one or more of these Web rings, you submit your URL to a ringmaster that is in charge of the ring. In turn, you are asked to include some code (and sometimes some images) on a prominent page in your site. Most often, this is your home page, or a page that is dedicated to displaying the Web rings to which you belong.

FIGURE 20.13

The Web Ring home page.

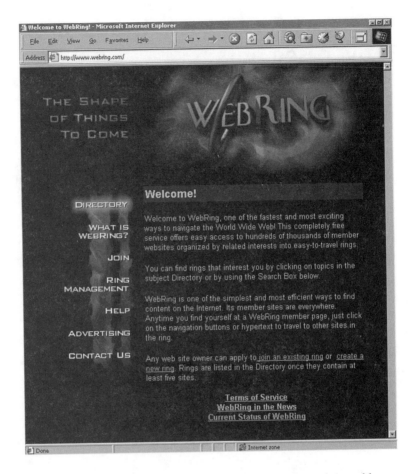

The code that you place on your page provides a simple navigation system that enables users to navigate to and from other sites in the Web ring. This way, readers can focus their Web browsing session on Web sites that share a common interest or goal.

Web rings have seen phenomenal growth since the beginning of 1998, and it looks as though the growth isn't slacking down a bit. This definitely is a good way to attract many readers who are interested in the same topics that you cover on your Web sites.

For further information on how to join or start a Web ring, check out Web Ring's Join page at www.webring.com/join.html.

20

Business Cards, Letterheads, Brochures, and Advertisements

Although the Internet is a wonderful place to promote your new Web site, many people fail to consider other great advertising methods.

Most businesses spend a considerable amount of money each year producing business cards, letterheads, and other promotional material. Only recently, however, have they started to print their email addresses and Web site URLs on them. With tens of millions of people on the Internet in the United States alone, chances are that many of your customers are already on the Internet or will be within a few years.

By printing your email address and home page URL on all your correspondence and promotional material, you can reach an entirely new group of potential site visitors. And who knows, maybe you'll even pick up new clients by spending time explaining to people what all your new address information means.

The bottom line with the promotion of your Web site is lateral thinking. You need to use every tool at your disposal if you want to have a successful and active site.

Finding Out Who's Viewing Your Web Pages

Welcome to being happily published. At this point, you've got your pages up on the Web and ready to be viewed, you've advertised and publicized your site to the world, and people are (hopefully) flocking to your site in droves. Or are they? How can you tell? You can find out in a number of ways, including using log files and access counters.

Log Files

The best way to figure out how often your pages are being seen and by whom is to see whether you can get access to your server's log files. The server keeps track of all this information and, depending on how busy the server is, may keep this information around for weeks or even months. Many commercial Web publishing providers have a mechanism for you to view your own Web logs or to get statistics about how many people are accessing your pages and from where. Ask your Webmaster for help.

If you do get access to the raw log files, you'll most likely see a whole lot of lines that look something like the following. (I've broken this one up onto two lines so that it fits on the page.)

```
vide-gate.coventry.ac.uk - - [17/Apr/1996:12:36:51 -0700]
   "GET /index.html HTTP/1.0" 200 8916
```

What does this information mean? This is the standard look and feel for most log files. The first part of the line is the site that accessed the file. (In this case, it was a site from the United Kingdom.) The two dashes are used for authentication. (If you have login names and passwords set up, the username of the person who logged in and the group that person belonged to will appear here.) The date and time the page was accessed appear inside the brackets. The next part is the actual filename that was accessed; here it's the index.html at the top level of the server. The GET part is the actual HTTP command the browser used; you usually see GET here. Finally, the last two numbers are the HTTP status code and the number of bytes transferred. The status code can be one of many things: 200 means the file was found and transferred correctly; 404 means the file was not found (yes, it's the same status code you get in error pages in your browser). Finally, the number of bytes transferred usually will be the same number of bytes in your actual file; if it's a smaller number, the reader interrupted the load in the middle.

Access Counters

If you don't have access to your server's log files for whatever reason, and you'd like to know at least how many people are looking at your Web pages, you can install an access counter on your page. You've probably seen counters several times in your Web browsing; they look like odometers or little meters that say "Since July 15, 1900, this page has been accessed 5,456,234,432 times."

Many Web counters are available; however, most of them require you to install something on your server, or that you configure server-side includes on them. A few, including the following sites, provide access counters that don't require server setup (but may cost you some money).

The Web counter at www.digits.com/ is easy to set up and very popular. If you have a site without a lot of hits (fewer than 1,000 a day), the counter service is free. Otherwise, you'll need to be part of the commercial plan, with the access counter costing $30 and up.

After you sign up for the digits.com counter service, you'll get an URL that you include on your pages as part of an <img> tag. Then, when your page is hit, the browser retrieves that URL at digits.com's server, which generates a new odometer image for you.

Table 20.1 lists some free counter services.

20

Table 20.1   Access Counter Services

Name	URL
XOOMCounter	www.pagecount.com/
Jcount	www.jcount.com/
WebTracker	www.fxweb.holowww.com/tracker/
LiveCounter	www.chami.com/counter/classic/

Summary

In this chapter, you've learned the many ways that you can advertise and promote your site, and also how to use log files to keep track of the number of visitors to your site. At last, you're on the Web and people are coming to visit. There is yet one more important topic to learn, and that is how to keep your site up-to-date and current. You'll learn this in the next chapter.

Workshop

As always, we wrap up the chapter with a few questions, a quiz, and exercises. Here are some pointers and refreshers on how to promote your Web site.

Q&A

Q There are so many of those search engines! Do I have to add my URL to all of them?

A No, you don't have to, but think of the (vastly overused) analogy of the Internet as a superhighway. When you're driving down a real highway, think of the clutter of billboards that are clamoring for your attention. How many of them do you really notice? You seem to remember the ones you see most frequently. Listing your pages on multiple search engines is much like travelling down different roads and listing makes your URL more visible to others.

Q What about sending my URL to tons of newsgroups all at once? Is that a good way to advertise my site?

A Well, yes and no. Most people that frequent newsgroups don't take too kindly to spamming (slamming the same message or URL across dozens upon dozens of newsgroups at once). It really is proper Web etiquette to use discretion when you post your URL to a newsgroup. Perhaps if you plan ahead and post your URL politely and discretely to a small handful of related newsgroups at once, it won't be so bad. It's a little more work on your part to do it this way, but you'll make fewer enemies, for sure.

Q **In regard to the Web rings, what if I can't find a suitable place for the code that they want me to place on my home page? What alternatives do I have?**

A It depends on the Web ring and the person who runs it. Each Web ring has a list of instructions that tell you how to add the code to your pages. Some of them are very particular about where you place them (for example, they must be on your home page), while others let you place them on a prominent page in your site. Others give you the option to include graphics or just create text-only mention of the Web rings.

If your ringleader allows you to place the Web ring code on a page other than your home page, be sure to provide a link to your Web ring page on your home page. A simple text link such as "For a listing of the Web rings to which this site belongs, please visit my Web Ring page." That should do it!

Quiz

1. Name some of the ways that you can promote your Web site.

2. What is the definition of a hit?

3. What are the advantages of using an all-in-one submission page to promote your site?

4. What's one rule to follow when you promote your site on newsgroups?

Answers

1. Some ways you can promote your site are major Web directories and indexes, announcements in newsgroups, listings on business cards, and Web rings on the World Wide Web.

2. Hits are the number of times that a copy of your Web page has been downloaded.

3. An all-in-one submission page enables you to submit your URL to several different site promotion areas and Web robots at once. Some provide a small number of submissions for free, and a larger number of submissions for an additional fee.

4. The main rule of thumb is not to blindly spam your URL to multiple newsgroups at the same time. It's good Web etiquette to be polite and post your URL selectively. Better yet, post your URL to newsgroups in which you actually participate.

20

Exercises

1. Visit some of the all-in-one submission pages listed in this chapter to obtain a list of the sites in which you want to promote your Web pages. Review each of the choices to see whether there are special requirements for listing your page.

2. Design a new business card or brochure that advertises your company and your Web site.

DAY 21

Testing, Revising, and Maintaining Your Web Site

After you closely read all the preceding chapters of this book, you went out and created your own Web site. You included a pile of pages linked together in a meaningful way, a smattering of images, and a form or two. You then added tables and image alignment, converted several images to JPEG, added some really cool video clips of you and your cat, and set up a script that rings a bell every time someone clicks on a link. Cascading style sheets give all these nifty pages a nice, uniform appearance. Dynamic HTML layers graphics over images and text and really adds spice to your site. You think it's pretty cool. In fact, you think your pages can't get much cooler than this. You're finally done.

I have bad news. You're not done yet. You have to think about two more aspects now: testing what you've got and maintaining what you will have.

Testing is making sure that your Web site works—not just from the technical side (Are you writing correct HTML? Do all your links work?), but also from the usability side (Can people find what they need to find on your pages?). In addition, you'll want to make sure that your site is readable in multiple browsers, especially if you're using some of the more recent tags you learned about.

Even after you test everything and it all works right, you're still not done. Almost as soon as you publish the initial site, you'll want to add stuff to it and change what's already there to keep the site interesting and up-to-date. Trust me on this point. On the Web, where the very technology is changing, a Web site is never really done. Some pages are just less likely to change than others.

After you're done with this chapter, you'll know all about the following topics:

- Integrity testing, which is making sure that your Web pages will actually work
- Usability testing, including making sure that your pages are being used in the way you expect and that your goals for the site are being met
- Adding pages to your site or making revisions to it without breaking what is already there

Integrity Testing

Integrity testing has nothing to do with you or whether you cheated on your taxes. Integrity testing is simply making sure that the pages you've just put together work properly—that they display without errors and that all your links point to real locations. This type of testing doesn't say anything about whether your pages are useful or whether people can use them, just that they're technically correct. The following are the three steps to integrity testing:

1. Make sure that you've created correct HTML.
2. Test the look of your pages in multiple browsers.
3. Make sure that your links work (both initially and several months down the road).

Validating Your HTML

The first step is to make sure you've written correct HTML: that all your tags have the proper closing tags, that you haven't overlapped any tags, or used tags inside other tags that don't work.

That, however, is what reviewing your page in different browsers should accomplish, isn't it? Well, not really. Browsers are designed to try to work around problems in the HTML files they're parsing, to assume that they know what you were trying to do in the first place, and to display something if they can't figure out what you were trying to do. (Remember the example of how tables looked in a browser that didn't accept tables? In that example, the browser tried its very best to determine what you were trying to do.) Some browsers are more lenient than others in the HTML they accept. A page with errors might work fine in one browser and not work at all in another.

HTML has only one true definition, however, and it is defined by the HTML specification. Some browsers can play fast and loose with the HTML you give them. If you write correct HTML in the first place, however, your pages are guaranteed to work without errors in all browsers that support the version of HTML in which you're writing.

Note

Actually, to be technically correct, the one true definition of HTML is defined by what is called the HTML *DTD*, or *Document Type Definition*. HTML is defined by a language called SGML, a larger language for defining other markup languages. The DTD is an SGML definition of a language, so the HTML DTD is the strict technical definition of what HTML looks like.

How can you make sure that you're writing correct HTML? If you've been following the rules and examples I wrote about in earlier chapters, you've been writing correct HTML. Everyone, however, forgets closing tags, puts tags in the wrong places, or drops the closing quotation marks from the end of an `href`. (I do that all the time, and it breaks quite a few browsers.) The best way to find out whether your pages are correct is to run them through an *HTML validator*.

Note

Many HTML editors now provide limited validation of HTML code. In the case of programs such as HoTMetaL Pro from Softquad, these programs can even prevent you from creating documents that violate the editor's internal validator. With most editors, however, the validation is limited and incomplete. On top of that, many editors not only allow you to produce incorrect HTML, but even generate incorrect HTML for you. For this reason, using another HTML validator is a good idea.

HTML validators are written to check HTML and only HTML. The validators don't care what your pages look like—just that you're writing your HTML to the current HTML specification. Some validators check against older and newer HTML specifications. Newer validators check your code against one of the three "flavors" of HTML 4.0 or XHTML 1.0 (Strict, Frameset, or Transitional).

In terms of writing portable HTML and HTML that can be read by future generations of authoring tools, it probably is a good idea to make sure that you're writing correct

21

HTML. You don't want to end up hand-fixing thousands of pages when the ultimate HTML authoring tool appears, and you discover that it can't read anything you've already done.

Even if you're writing correct HTML, you should test your pages in multiple browsers to ensure that you haven't made any strange design decisions. Using a validator doesn't get you off the hook when designing.

So, how do you run these HTML validators? Several are available on the Web, either for downloading and running locally on your own system, or as Web pages in which you can enter your URLs into a form. The validator then tests them over the network. I like two in particular: W3C's HTML validation service and Neil Bowers' Weblint.

> **Note**
>
> As with all Web sites, these services change all the time, supporting new features and changing their appearance. Although they may look different from the examples in this book by the time you look at them, the examples should give you a strong idea of how these services work.

In the next section, I demonstrate a couple of online validators you can use on the Web.

There are also standalone HTML validators that you can use on your own computer. One such validator for the Windows 95/NT platform is CSE 3310 HTML Validator. This standalone HTML validator helps you find and correct several different HTML problems, such as misspelled or invalid tags, attributes and values, character entities, missing quotes, missing closing tags, incorrect tag placement and nesting, and more. You can learn more about this validator at the CSE 3310 home page at `www.htmlvalidator.com/`. You also can download a free trial lite version at `www.htmlvalidator.com/htmldownload.html`.

Weblint

The Weblint program is a general HTML checker. In addition to ensuring that your syntax is correct, it also checks for some of the more common mistakes, such as mismatched closing tags, `title` outside `head`, multiple elements that should appear only once, and so on. It also points out other hints; for example, have you included `alt` text in your `<img>` tags? Its output is considerably friendlier than other HTML validators, but it is less picky about true HTML compliance. (In fact, it might complain about more recent tags, such as tables and other extended HTML additions.)

Figure 21.1 shows the Weblint page at `www.unipress.com/cgi-bin/WWWeblint`. In particular, it shows the form you can use to submit pages for checking.

FIGURE 21.1

Weblint HTML checker.

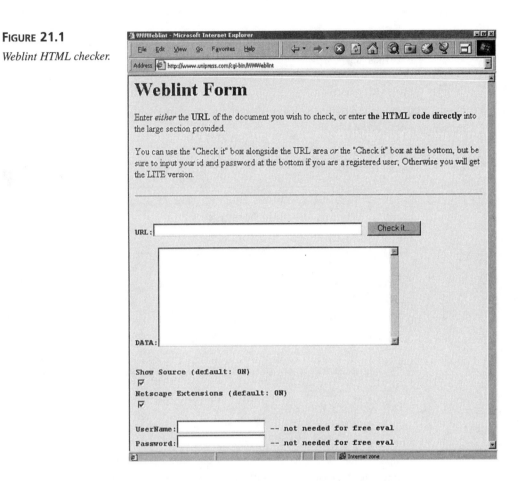

The Weblint page enables you to check your HTML code either by entering an existing URL to a page that you have published on the Internet, or by typing or pasting code into the data box. For a quick example of what Weblint can tell you about your HTML code, take the following code example and type it into the DATA field. I mistakenly left off the <p> tag at the beginning of the paragraph, but remembered to use the </p> tag, as follows:

```
<!DOCTYPE html PUBLIC "-//W3C//DTD XHTML 1.0 Transitional//EN"
"http://www.w3.org/TR/xhtml1/DTD/transitional.dtd">
<html>
<head>
<title>Validating HTML Code</title>
</head>
<body>
```

21

```
Every once in a while I get the urge to be funny. Luckily for
   those around me it usually passes in a few minutes. But sometimes
   I write things down.</p>
</body>
</html>
```

Figure 21.2 shows the output of a sample test I did with the same page that produced the missing <p> tag error.

FIGURE 21.2

Weblint output.

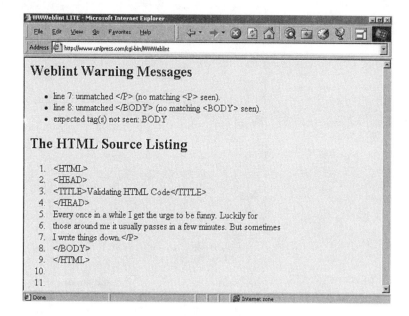

Interestingly enough, Weblint pointed out that I was missing opening <head>, <title> and <body> tags. It did not report the fact that I had a </p> without a corresponding <p>.

Weblint is no longer a free service. Subscriptions are now available for $9.95 for six months, or $16.95 per year; however, you can try a free evaluation in which only the first 2,048 bytes of your documents will be validated. (Note that this will generate some fake errors because of missing tags in the remainder of longer documents.)

The W3C HTML Validation Service

While several validators that help you check HTML 4.0 code exist, there are few that are XHTML 1.0 compliant. The best source to validate your pages, however, is the W3C HTML Validation Service, which you can find at `http://validator.w3.org/`. This is a free validation service that enables you to check your HTML code against various DTDs (document type definitions.) In addition to the various incarnations of "official" HTML (including HTML 4.01 and XHTML 1.0), the W3C validator also enables you to check for Netscape and Internet Explorer-specific code. You can find a complete list of the DTDs this validator checks against at `http://validator.w3.org/sgml-lib/catalog`.

To use this validation service, enter in the Location field the URL of the Web page you want to validate, as shown in Figure 21.3. (Note that at press time, there was no option to paste snippets of code into an online form).

FIGURE 21.3

The W3C HTML Validation Service validation form.

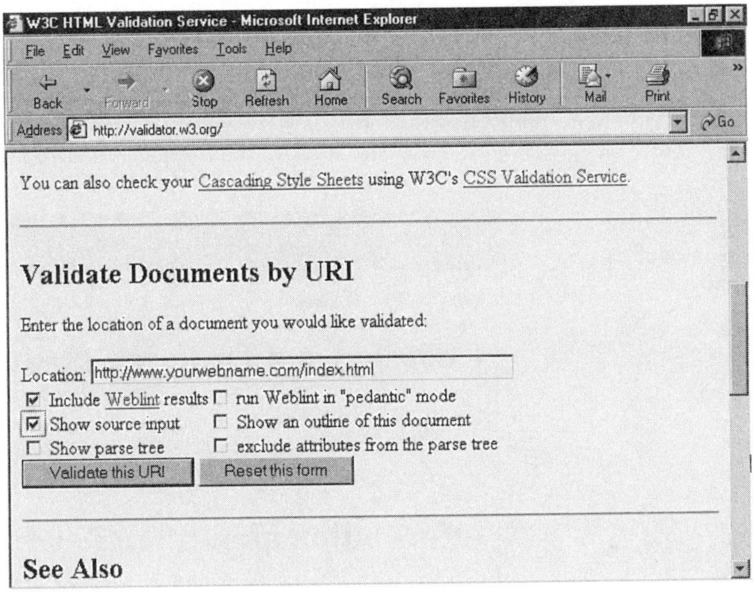

After you enter the URL of your Web page, you can select one or more of the following options:

- Include Weblint results—If you check this option, the W3C validator will include Weblint results in your code validation. The Weblint explanations are a bit more user-friendly and can assist you in repairing your code more easily.

- Run Weblint in "pedantic" (very strict) mode—If you check this option, the W3C validator will test your pages against the most strict compliance available with Weblint.

- Show source input—This option includes a listing of the source code that the validator checked. This is helpful in determining exactly where errors appear in your code, as the source code listing includes line numbers associated with the validation errors returned by the validator.

- Show an outline of this document—If headings appear on your page, this option returns an outline of your Web page document. It is helpful in determining whether

21

your Web page structure follows standard outline procedures (such as H2 beneath H1, H3 beneath H2, and so on).

- Show parse tree—This option is still under construction at press time. The parse tree helps you determine the structure of the HTML tags in your document.
- Exclude attributes from the parse tree—If you choose this option, attributes will be eliminated from the parse tree, which may help you read it more clearly.

To Do

Exercise 21.1: Validating a Sample Page

Just to show the kinds of errors that the W3C Validation Service and Weblint pick up, put together the following sample file with some errors in it that you might commonly make. This example is Susan's Cactus Gardens home page, as shown in Figure 21.4.

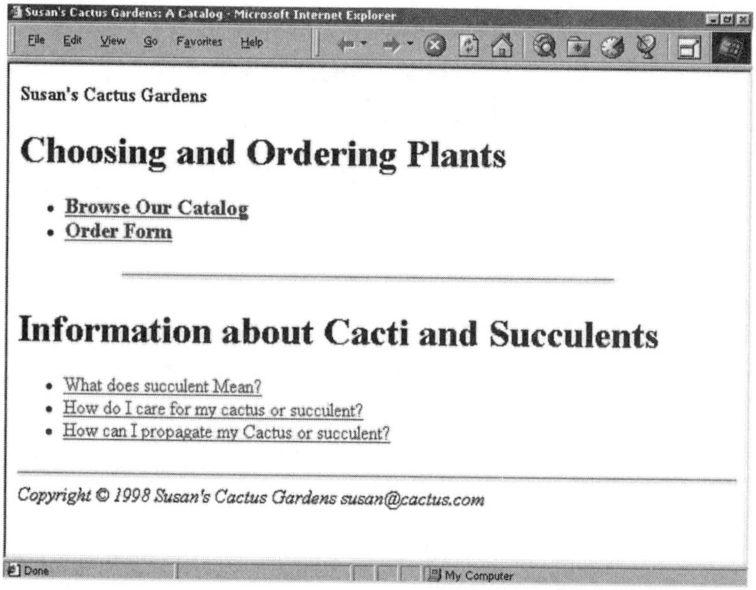

FIGURE 21.4

Susan's Cactus Gardens.

In Internet Explorer, the page looks and behaves relatively fine. The following code that was used is riddled with errors, however. See whether you can find them here before you run it through a validator.

```
<!DOCTYPE html PUBLIC "-//W3C//DTD XHTML 1.0 Transitional//EN"
"http://www.w3.org/TR/xhtml1/DTD/transitional.dtd">
<html>
<head>
<title>Susan's Cactus Gardens:  A Catalog</title>
<head>
<body>
```

```
<strong>Susan's Cactus Gardens</strong>
<h1>Choosing and Ordering Plants</h3>
<ul>
<h3>
<li><a href="browse.html">Browse Our Catalog
<li><a href="order.html>How To Order</a>
<li><a href="form.html">Order Form</a>
</ul>
</h3>
<hr width=70% align=center>
<h1>Information about Cacti and Succulents</h1>
<ul>
<li><a href="succulent.html">What does succulent mean?</a>
<li><a href="caring.html">How do I care for my cactus or succulent?</a>
<li><a href="propogation.html">How can I propagate my Cactus or
succulent?</a>
</ul>
<hr>
<address>Copyright &copy; 1999 Susan's Cactus Gardens
susan@cactus.com</address>
```

Now, publish this page on to the Internet, and jot down its URL. Go to the W3C HTML Validation Service at `http://validator.w3.org/` and enter the URL of your "bad" Web page into the Location field of the form. Check the Include Weblint Results and Show Source Input options (these will help you decipher the errors), and then click the Validate URI button. What returns shortly thereafter is a Results page that looks (in part) like the page shown in Figure 21.5.

FIGURE 21.5

The W3C HTML Validation Service's response to the file with errors.

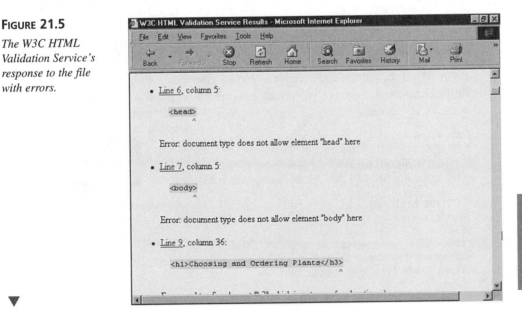

21

▼ Start with the errors reported by Weblint, since their descriptions are less cryptic than those that the W3C HTML Validation Service returns. If you scroll down to the Weblint results section, you see that Weblint reports the following errors for lines 6 and 7:

```
line 6: <HEAD> must immediately follow <HTML>
line 6: tag <HEAD> should only appear once. I saw one on line 4!
line 6: <HEAD> cannot appear in the HEAD element.
line 7: <BODY> must immediately follow </HEAD>
line 7: <BODY cannot appear in the HEAD element.
```

The following shows lines 1 through 7 again.

```
<!DOCTYPE html PUBLIC "-//W3C//DTD XHTML 1.0 Transitional//EN"
"http://www.w3.org/TR/xhtml1/DTD/transitional.dtd">
<html>
<head>
<title>Susan's Cactus Gardens:  A Catalog</title>
<head>
<body>
```

The <head> tag on the sixth line should be </head>. Some browsers have difficulties with the body of the document if you forget to close the head, so make sure to fix this problem.

After you fix this error, many of the other errors in the list from Weblint that refer to *X* cannot appear in the head element should disappear.

The next error that Weblint reports is for line 9, as follows:

```
line 9: malformed heading - open tag is <h1>, but closing is </H3>
```

This one's easy to figure out. The author accidentally closed an h1 with an h3. The opening and closing tags should match, so change the </h3> to <h1>.

The results from Weblint don't show an obvious comment for line 10. Near the end of the Weblint results, however, you do see an error message that sheds some clues about a problem, as follows:

```
line 0: no closing </UL> seen for <UL> on line 10
```

If you look at line 15, you do see a closing </ul> tag. So, what is the problem? Take another look at lines 10 through 16, and you'll notice that the <ul> and <h3> tags are not properly nested, as follows:

```
<ul>
<h3>
<li><a href="browse.html">Browse Our Catalog
<li><a href="order.html>How To Order</a>
<li><a href="form.html">Order Form</a>
</ul>
</h3>
```
▼

▼ If you reverse the order of the opening <ul> and <h3> tags, the Weblint error message should disappear. The revised code appears as follows:

```
<h3>
<ul>
<li><a href="browse.html">Browse Our Catalog
<li><a href="order.html>How To Order</a>
<li><a href="form.html">Order Form</a>
</ul>
</h3>
```

Continuing with the problems shown in the preceding unordered list, another error indicates an odd number of quotation marks in line 13:

```
line 13:odd number of quotes in element <a href="order.html>
line 13:value for attribute HREF ("order.html) of element A should
  be quoted (i.e. HREF=""order.html")
```

Note that the filename order.html has no closing quotation mark. This code will work in older versions of Netscape or Internet Explorer, but not in too many other browsers, and it's one of the most common errors. The corrected code should appear as follows:

```
<li><a href="order.html">How To Order</a>
```

Lines 13 and 14 contain the next errors:

```
line 13: <a> cannot be nested-</A> not yet seen for <A> on line 12.
line 14: <a> cannot be nested-</A> not yet seen for <A> on line 12.
```

Actually, this error is on line 12:

```
<li><a href="browse.html">Browse Our Catalog
```

No </a> tag appears at the end of this line, which explains the complaint. You can't put an <a> tag inside another <a> tag, so Weblint gets confused. (Several instances of this error occur in the report.) Always remember to close all <a> tags at the end of the link text. Correcting this error also will eliminate the error associated with line 18, which tells you that <a> should be inside <h1> rather than <h1> inside <a>. It also corrects the errors for lines 20 through 22, which read that <a> cannot be nested—</a> not yet seen for <a> on line 12.

Continuing down the error list, Weblint complains quite a bit about line 17, as follows:

```
line 17: attribute "WIDTH" for <hr> is extended markup.
line 17: value for attribute WIDTH (70%) of element HR should be quoted
  (i.e. WIDTH="70%")
line 17: attribute "ALIGN" for <hr> is extended markup.
line 17: illegal value for WIDTH attribute of hr (70%).
```

21

Extended markup tags usually are browser-specific; however, they also can't point to tags
▼ that have been deprecated in the strict HTML definition. When Weblint complains about

▼ tags being extended markup, compare the same lines to the results you see in the W3C
HTML Validation service. If you are using the HTML 4.0 or XHTML 1.0 Transitional
specification, which allows the use of extended markup tags, the choice is up to you as to
whether you want to keep the troublesome areas in your code. If you are designing your
pages for the HTML 4.0 or XHTML 1.0 specification, however, extended markup tags
can alert you to code you might have to approach in a different manner. In the case of the
width attribute, this can be handled with the use of CSS properties.

Should you decide to keep the width attribute for the <hr> tag, remember to enclose the
attribute values in quotes. Although Weblint didn't complain about the center value of
the align attribute, you also should enclose it in quotes. The corrected code for line 17
should appear as follows:

```
<hr width="70%" align="center">
```

The last of the errors are all similar and refer to missing closing tags:

```
line 0: No closing </HTML> seen for <HTML> on line 1.
line 0: No closing </HEAD> seen for <HEAD> on line 2.
line 0: No closing </HEAD> seen for <HEAD> on line 4.
line 0: No closing </BODY> seen for <BODY> on line 5.
line 0: No closing </UL> seen for <UL> on line 8.
line 0: No closing </H3> seen for <H3> on line 9.
line 0: No closing </A> seen for <A> on line 10.
```

A quick check shows that </body> and </html> are missing from the end of the file,
which clears up that problem. Changing the second <head> to </head> and the </h3> to
</h1> clears up these errors as well.

What about the next two, however? Weblint complains that <ul> and <h3> don't have
closing tags, but there they are at the end of the list. Look at the order in which they
appear. The author overlapped the ul and h3 tags, closing the ul before closing the h3.
By simply reversing the order of the tags, you can fix these two errors.

The last error is that missing </a> tag, which you've already fixed.

All right, you've made the first pass in Weblint, and you've corrected the code. The following code example shows the revised code as it now should appear:

```
<!DOCTYPE html PUBLIC "-//W3C//DTD XHTML 1.0 Transitional//EN"
"http://www.w3.org/TR/xhtml1/DTD/transitional.dtd">
<html>
<head>
<title>Susan's Cactus Gardens:  A Catalog</title>
</head>
<body>
<strong>Susan's Cactus Gardens</strong>
<h1>Choosing and Ordering Plants</h1>
```

```
<h3>
<ul>
<li><a href="browse.html">Browse Our Catalog</a>
<li><a href="order.html">How To Order</a>
<li><a href="form.html">Order Form</a>
</ul>
</h3>
<hr width="70%" align="center">
<h1>Information about Cacti and Succulents</h1>
<ul>
<li><a href="succulent.html">What does succulent mean?</a>
<li><a href="caring.html">How do I care for my cactus or succulent?</a>
<li><a href="propogation.html">How can I propagate my Cactus or succulent?</a>
</ul>
<hr>
<address>Copyright &copy; 1999 Susan's Cactus Gardens
susan@cactus.com</address>
</body>
</html>
```

Now make another test of the page. As you can see in Figure 21.6, the W3C HTML Validation Service still shows some errors. In fact, there are quite a few.

FIGURE 21.6

The W3C HTML Validation Service result of the revised page.

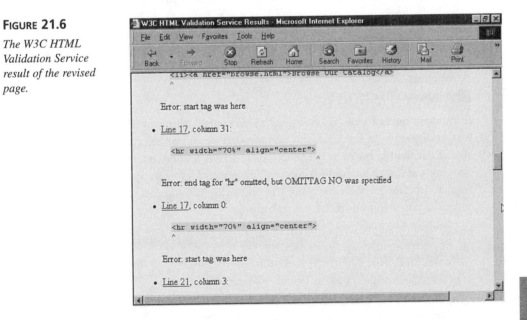

At press time, Weblint did not report errors that related to XHTML 1.0, whereas you will find these errors noted in the W3C HTML Validation Service section. To reduce the number of errors that you see in relation to XHTML 1.0, take a quick first pass, and

21

▼ make sure that all your tags are properly closed. In particular, notice that in the code that
preceded Figure 21.6, six `<li>` tags are not closed. These items appear on lines 12
through 14, and lines 20 through 22. They should be closed as follows:

```
<li><a href="browse.html">Browse Our Catalog</a></li>
<li><a href="order.html">How To Order</a></li>
<li><a href="form.html">Order Form</a></li>

<li><a href="succulent.html">What does succulent mean?</a></li>
<li><a href="caring.html">How do I care for my cactus or succulent?</a></li>
<li><a href="propogation.html">How can I propagate my Cactus or
succulent?</a></li>
```

In addition, lines 17 and 24 have `<hr>` tags that need to be closed, as follows:

```
<hr width="70%" align="center" />

<hr />
```

Congratulations! The cactus page is now HTML-compliant, and it only took two programs!

This example, of course, is extreme. Most of the time, your pages won't have nearly as
many problems as this one. (In addition, if you're using an HTML editor, many of these
mistakes might never show up.) Keep in mind that Internet Explorer blithely skipped
over all these errors without so much as a peep. Are all the browsers that read your files
▲ going to be this accepting?

Browser Testing

As noted before, all that HTML validators do is make sure your HTML is correct. They
won't tell you anything about your design. After you finish the validation tests, you still
should test your pages in as many browsers as you can find to ensure that the design is
working and that you haven't done anything that looks fine in one browser but awful in
another. Because most browsers are free and easily downloaded, you should be able to
collect at least two or three for your platform.

Ideally, you should at least test each of your pages in the following browsers:

- Netscape or Microsoft, with images enabled and with images turned off
- Another browser, such as Opera or Mosaic
- A text-based browser, such as Lynx

By using these browsers, you should get an idea of how different browsers will view
your pages. If you use Netscape or Microsoft extensions in your pages, you might want
to test the pages in both Netscape and Microsoft Internet Explorer to ensure that things
look right with both browsers.

Verifying Your Links

The third and final test is to make sure that your links work. The most obvious way to do so, of course, is to sit with a browser and follow them yourself. This approach might be fine for small sites, but with large sites, checking links can be a long and tedious task. Also, after you check links the first time, the sites you've linked to might move or rename their pages. Because the Web is always changing, even if your pages stay constant, your links still might break.

By checking the error logs that your server keeps, you can find out about some broken links on your own pages, which you might have caused when moving things around. These logs note the pages that cannot be found: both the missing page and the page that contains the link to that page. For a link to appear in the error logs, someone must have already tried to follow the link—and failed. Catching the broken link before one of your readers tries it would be a better plan.

Using an automatic link checker, which is a tool that ranges over your pages and ensures that the links in the pages point to real files or real sites elsewhere on the Web, is the best way to check for broken links. Several link checkers are available, including more general-purpose Web spiders (programs that go from link to link, searching the Web). These can be made to test your own local documents. Be careful, however, that the link checkers don't go berserk and start crawling other people's sites in addition to your own. Check out MOMspider at `www.ics.uci.edu/WebSoft/MOMspider/` to see a good example of an automatic link checker.

If you are developing a very large site, validating manually all your links can be out of the question. Fortunately, many Web development programs now come with utilities that maintain and verify that all links on your pages work properly. Microsoft FrontPage is one such program that enables you to check and validate internal and external links on your pages.

You also can use a standalone link checker, such as Tetranet Software's LinkBot, which helps you validate and maintain all links on your Web pages. This program checks for broken anchors, missing image attributes, and a whole lot more. For more information on this program, visit the Tetranet home page at `http://tetranetsoftware.com/`.

Usability Testing

21

Usability testing ensures that your documents are usable, even after you have tested them for simple technical correctness. You can put up a set of Web pages easily, but are your readers going to be able to find what they need? Is your organization satisfying the goals you originally planned for your pages? Do people get confused easily when they explore your site, or frustrated because it's difficult to navigate?

Usability testing is a concept that many industries have been using for years. The theory behind usability testing is that the designers who are creating the product (be it a software application, a VCR, a car, or so on) cannot determine whether the product is easy to use because they are too closely involved in the project. They know how the product is designed, so, of course, they know how to use it. The only way to determine the ease of use of a product is to watch those who have never seen it before as they use it and note the troublesome places. Then, based on the feedback, you can make changes to the product, retest it, make more changes, and so on.

Web sites are excellent examples of products that benefit from usability testing. Even getting a friend to look at your pages might teach you a lot about how you've organized your site and whether people who are not familiar with the structure you've created can find their way around.

Following are some tasks you might want your testers to try on your pages:

- Ask your testers to browse your pages, with no particular goal in mind, and watch where they go. What parts interest them first? What paths do they take through the site? Which pages do they stop to read, and which pages do they skip?

- Ask your testers to find a particular topic or page, preferably one buried deep within your site. Can they find it? What path do they take to find it? How long does it take them to find it? How frustrated do they get while trying to find it?

- Ask your testers for suggestions. Everyone has opinions on other people's Web pages, but the viewers probably won't send you mail, even if you ask them. Ask your testers how they would change your Web pages to make them better.

Sit with your testers and take notes. The results might surprise you and give you new ideas for organizing your pages.

Examining Your Logs

Another method of usability testing your documents after you publish them on the Web is to track your server logs. Your Web server or provider keeps logs of each hit on your page (each time a browser retrieves that document) and where it came from. Examining your Web logs can teach you the following interesting facts:

- The most popular pages, which might not be the pages you expect. You might want to make it easier to find those pages from the topmost page in the site.

- The patterns people use to explore your pages; that is, the order in which they read them.

- Common spelling errors people make when trying to access your pages. Files that were looked for but not found will appear in your error files (usually contained in the same directory as the log files). Using symbolic links or aliases, you might be able to circumvent some of these problems if they occur frequently.

Updating and Adding Pages to Your Site

Even after you publish your pages and test them extensively both for integrity and usability, your site isn't done. In fact, I could argue that your site is never done. Even if you manage to make your site as usable as it could possibly be, you can always think of new information and new pages to add, updates to make, new advances in HTML that must be experimented with, and so on.

So how do you maintain Web sites? Easy. You create new pages and link them to the old pages, right? Well, maybe. Before you do, however, read this section for hints on the best way to proceed.

Adding New Content

I'd like to start this section with a story.

In San Jose, California, is a tourist attraction called the Winchester Mystery House, which originally was owned by Sarah Winchester, heiress to the Winchester Arms Company fortune. The story goes that after the deaths of her husband and daughter, she was told by a spiritualist that the spirits of the men who had died from Winchester guns were haunting her. The spiritualist advised her to begin building rooms onto the farmhouse in order to appease the spirits, which she did.

The result was that all the new additions built onto the existing house were added with no plan for making them livable or even logical—as long as the work never stopped. The house now has over 160 rooms, stairways that lead nowhere, doors that open into walls, secret passageways, and a floor plan that is nearly impossible to navigate without a map.

Some Web sites look a lot like this mystery house. They might have begun with a well-planned, organized, and usable structure, but as more pages were added, the structure began to break down. The original goals of the site become lost, and eventually result in a mess of interlinked pages in which readers easily get lost and find it impossible to locate what they need (see Figure 21.7).

21

FIGURE 21.7

A confused set of Web pages.

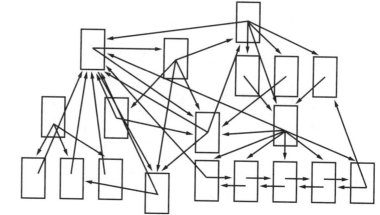

Avoid the Winchester Mystery House school of Web page design. When you add new pages to an existing site, keep the following hints in mind:

- **Stick to your structure**—If you've followed the hints so far, you should have a basic structure to your site, such as a hierarchy or a linear structure. Most of the time, adding new material to an existing structure is easy; the new material can go in a logical place. As you add pages, try to maintain the original structure.

- **Focus on your goals**—Keep your original goals in mind when you add new content. If the new content distracts from or interferes with these goals, consider not adding it, or downplay its existence. If your goals have changed, you might want to revise your entire site rather than just tacking on new material.

- **Add branches if necessary**—Sometimes, the easiest way to add new material, particularly to a hierarchy, is to add an entirely new subsite rather than try to add the content. If the new content you're adding can be made into its own site, consider adding it that way.

Revising Your Structure

You sometimes might find that your site has grown to the point that the original structure no longer works, or that because your goals have changed, the original organization makes it difficult to access the new material. Maybe you didn't use an organized structure to begin with, and now you realize that you need one.

Web sites are organic things, and it's likely that if you frequently modify your site, you'll need to revise your original plan or structure. You often can find ways to modify parts of the site so that the new material fits in and the overall site hangs together.

It sometimes helps to return to your original plan for the site (you did create one, didn't you?) and first revise it before arbitrarily adding to and modifying the site. In particular, try the following suggestions:

- **List the goals of your site**—List how people are going to use the site and how you want it to be perceived. Compare these new goals to the original goals. If they are different, look at ways in which you can modify your current structure so that you can still achieve your new goals.
- **Modify your list of topics**—Modifying usually is the most difficult part of altering your Web site because that might involve taking pieces from other topics and rearranging the information. Try to keep track of the old and new topics; this will help you when you actually start editing pages.
- **Consider changing your structure if it is not working**—If you started with a simple Web structure that now is too complex to navigate easily, consider imposing a more rigid structure on that site. If you currently have a very shallow hierarchy (very few levels but many options on the topmost page), consider giving it more balance by using more levels and fewer options.

After your new plan is in place, you usually can identify areas in which moving pages or contents of pages can help make the site easier to use. Keep your new plan in mind as you make your changes and take your time. If you try to introduce too many changes at once, you run the risk of breaking links and losing track of the changes you make. If you previously had performed usability testing on your pages, remember to take into account those results as well.

Summary

Planning, writing, testing, and maintaining are the four horsemen of Web page design. You learned about planning and writing, which entail developing a structure, creating your pages, linking them together, and then refining what you have—all throughout this book. In this chapter, you learned about the other half of the process—the half that continues even after you've published everything and people are flocking to your site.

Testing ensures that your pages work correctly. You initially might have performed some rudimentary evaluations by viewing your pages in more than one browser, trying out your links, and ensuring that all your CGI scripts were installed and called from the right place. In this chapter, however, you learned how to perform real testing—integrity testing with HTML validators and automatic link checkers, and usability testing to determine whether people actually find your pages useful.

21

Maintenance takes place when you add new stuff to your site and then evaluate and modify it to ensure that the site still flows and functions well, despite the new information. Performing maintenance prevents your foundational planning from going to waste by ensuring that the new information does not obscure the original information. In addition, maintenance sometimes requires you to develop a new site structure as well as create a new set of pages. Today, you learned how to perform maintenance and properly revise your Web pages.

Now you are done—at least until it's time to change everything again. You've learned quite a lot this week, and now you are ready to build your own Web sites. The most important thing to remember while doing this is to have fun and enjoy it.

Workshop

Here you are, at the end of the book, armed with a wealth of information about creating, presenting, and publishing your Web pages on the World Wide Web. The final workshop contains some questions about HTML validation and also includes a quiz and exercises that will refresh your memory on some of the items that you've learned throughout the book.

Q&A

Q I still don't understand why HTML validation is important. I test my pages in many browsers. Why should I go through all this extra work to make them truly HTML-compliant? Why does it matter?

A Look at the situation this way. Imagine that, sometime next year, Web Company Z comes out with a super-hot HTML authoring tool that will enable you to create Web pages quickly and easily, link them together, build hierarchies that you can move around visually, and do all the really nifty stuff that in the past has always been difficult. In addition, this tool will read your old HTML files so that you don't have to write everything from scratch.

"Great," you say. You purchase the program and try to open and edit your HTML files with it; however, your HTML files contain errors. The errors never appeared in the browsers; nonetheless, errors they remain. Because the authoring tool is more strict than browsers about what it can read (and it has to be with this nifty front end), you are unable to read in all your original files without first modifying them—manually. Introducing errors while manually modifying files can result in more time spent correcting the mistakes than writing the pages in the first place.

Q Do I have to run all my files through both the W3C Validator and Weblint? That's an awful lot of work.

A You don't have to do both if you don't have the time or the inclination, but I can't really recommend one over the other because both provide different capabilities that are equally important. Weblint points out the most obvious errors in your pages and performs other nifty tasks, such as pointing out missing `alt` text. The W3C validator is more complete but also more strict. While it points out structural errors in your document, the error messages are extremely cryptic and difficult to understand.

If you download these programs and run them locally, keep in mind that checking a whole directory full of files won't take very much time. Additionally, when you get the hang of writing good HTML code, you'll make fewer errors. In light of this, perhaps using both programs wouldn't be that much of a hassle.

Quiz

1. True or false: HTML is the only language you'll ever need to learn to create Web pages.

2. What are some ways you can reduce the size of Web pages that are very media-intensive (those that contain a large number of graphics and multimedia elements)?

3. What are some important things to remember when you design Web pages that use framesets?

4. True or false: If all my links work on my local computer, I don't have to test them again after I upload them to my remote Web site.

5. List some things that can improve the readability of your Web pages.

Answers

1. This might have been true in the earlier days of the Web, but may not be the case any longer. While you can create Web pages that use only HTML tags, you'll need to learn additional technologies, such as Cascading Style Sheets (refer to Day 10, "XHTML and Style Sheets"), JavaScript and Dynamic HTML (refer to Day 15, "Using Dynamic HTML"), and others to implement state-of-the-art Web pages that feature advanced positioning and presentation.

2. Reduce the dimensional size of the graphics or animations. You also can reduce the size of the images by compressing them (using JPG images), or by reducing the number of colors in the palette (for GIF images). If all else fails, provide a small thumbnail of your image, or of one of the frames in the animation, and let the reader elect to download or view it. For further information, review Day 7 "Using Images, Color, and Backgrounds."

21

3. When using framesets, don't split the browser screen into too many frames. It can be confusing to your readers, and there may not be enough room to display your pages adequately at lower resolutions. Next, if any of the pages contain links to pages on other sites, remember to use `target="_top"` so that the reader breaks out of your frameset to navigate to the other site. If your framed pages contain graphics, size them smaller so that they fit within the framed pages at lower resolutions. Also, be sure to include some content within the `<noframes>` element so that readers who are not using frame-compatible browsers can still access the content on your site. For further information, review Day 12, "Frames and Linked Windows."

4. False. Several things can cause links to break when you transfer your Web pages to a remote server. For further information, review Day 19, "Putting Your Site Online."

5. Try not to use too many inline hyperlinks—use lists and tables to organize them so that they stand out more. Avoid the use of really long paragraphs, if possible. Use headings as headings, not to stress important points. Don't overuse emphasis (italics and bold text), as it can be distracting. Use animated graphics strategically to draw attention to important information on your Web pages. For further information, review Day 16, "Writing and Designing Web Pages: Dos and Don'ts," and Day 17, "Examples of Good and Bad Web Design."

Exercises

1. As you near the end of the book, the logical exercise at this point (if you haven't started already) is to begin your own Web site. Start by using tags with which you are comfortable. Add graphics, links, and tables when you're ready. As your knowledge progresses, try some of the more advanced features, such as frames, Cascading Style Sheets, Dynamic HTML, and other HTML extensions.

2. Publish your Web pages on the World Wide Web, as outlined in Day 19. Test your pages and then spread the word about your site. Remember, the beauty of the World Wide Web is that your pages aren't cast in stone. You can modify, delete, or add to your Web site any time you choose.

Part 8

Appendixes

APPENDIX A

Sources for Further Information

Haven't had enough yet? In this appendix, you'll find the URLs for all kinds of information about the World Wide Web, HTML, developing Web presentations, and locations of tools to help you write HTML documents. With this list, you should be able to find just about anything you need on the Web.

Note

Some of the URLs in this section refer to FTP sites. Some of these sites might be very busy during business hours, and you might not be able to immediately access the files. Try again during non-prime hours.

Also, some of these sites, for mysterious reasons, might be accessible through an FTP program, but not through Web browsers. If you are consistently getting refused from these sites using a browser, and you have access to an FTP program, try that program instead.

The sites are divided into the following categories and listed in alphabetical order under each category:

Access Counters

Browsers

Collections of HTML and WWW Development Information

Forms and Imagemaps

HTML Editors and Converters

HTML Validators, Link Checkers, and Simple Spiders

Java, JavaScript, and Embedded Objects

Log File Parsers

Other

Servers and Server Administration

Sound and Video

Specifications for HTML, HTTP, and URLs

The Common Gateway Interface (CGI) and CGI Scripting

The Future of HTML and the Web

Tools and Information for Images

Web Providers

WWW Indexes and Search Engines

Access Counters

Access counters without server programs
http://www.digits.com/

Digits for use in access counters
http://www.digitmania.holowww.com/

Page Count
http://www.pagecount.com/

Jcount
http://www.jcount.com/

WebTracker
http://www.fxweb.holowww.com/tracker/

LiveCounter
http://www.chami.com/prog/lc/

A

Yahoo!'s list of access counters

http://dir.yahoo.com/Computers_and_Internet/Internet/World_Wide_Web/
Programming/Access_Counters/

Browsers

Amaya (X)

http://www.w3.org/Amaya/

Emacs-W3 (for Emacs)

http://www.cs.indiana.edu/elisp/w3/docs.html

Internet Explorer

http://www.microsoft.com/windows/ie/default.htm

Lynx (UNIX and DOS)

http://www.cc.ukans.edu/about_lynx/

Netscape Communicator (X, Windows, Macintosh) Download Page

http://home.netscape.com/computing/download/index.html

Collections of HTML and Web Development Information

CNET Builder.com

http://home.cnet.com/category/0-3880.html

The home of the WWW Consortium

http://www.w3.org/

The HTML Writer's Guild

http://www.hwg.org/

The Virtual Library

http://www.wdvl.com/

The World Wide Web FAQ

http://www.boutell.com/faq/

Yahoo!'s WWW section

http://dir.yahoo.com/Computers_and_Internet/Internet/World_Wide_Web/

MSDN (Microsoft Developer's Network) Online

http://msdn.microsoft.com/default.asp

Forms and Imagemaps

Carlos' forms tutorial
http://robot0.ge.uiuc.edu/~carlosp/cs317/cft.html

HotSpots (a Windows imagemap tool)
http://www.1automata.com/hotspots/index.html

Mapedit: A tool for Windows and X11 for creating imagemap map files
http://www.boutell.com/mapedit/

The original NCSA forms documentation
http://hoohoo.ncsa.uiuc.edu/cgi/forms.html

Imaptool (Linux/X-Windows imagemap tool)
http://www.saunalahti.fi/~uucee/ownprojects/

LiveImage (Windows-based imagemap tool)
http://www.mediatec.com/

Poor Person's Image Mapper (Web-based imagemap creation system)
http://zenith.berkeley.edu/~seidel/ClrHlpr/imagemap.html

Yahoo! forms list
http://www.yahoo.com/Computers_and_Internet/Internet/World_Wide_Web/Programming/Forms/

HTML Editors and Converters

A great list of editors
http://www.yahoo.com/Computers_and_Internet/Software/Internet/World_Wide_Web/HTML_Editors/

Homesite
http://www1.allaire.com/Products/HomeSite/

HotDog (Windows)
http://www.sausage.com

HoTMetaL Pro (Windows, Macintosh, UNIX)
http://www.sq.com

HTML Assistant Pro (Windows)
http://www.brooknorth.com/download/

HTML Transit
http://www.infoaccess.com

Microsoft FrontPage (Windows, Macintosh)
http://www.microsoft.com/frontpage/

HTML Validators, Link Checkers, and Simple Spiders

Weblint
http://www.unipress.com/cgi-bin/WWWeblint

Yahoo!'s List of HTML Validation and HTML Checkers
http://www.yahoo.com/Computers_and_Internet/Information_and_Documentation/
Data_Formats/HTML/Validation_and_Checkers

Yahoo!'s List of Web Spiders and Robots
http://www.yahoo.com/Computers_and_Internet/Internet/World_Wide_Web/Search
ing_the_Web/Robots__Spiders__etc__Documentation/

Java, JavaScript, and Embedded Objects

Gamelan (An index of Java applets)
http://www.developer.com/directories/pages/dir.java.html

JavaScript Developer Central
http://developer.netscape.com/tech/javascript/index.html

Java Developer Central
http://developer.netscape.com/tech/java/index.html

Sun's Java home page
http://www.javasoft.com/

Yahoo! Java directory
http://www.yahoo.com/Computers_and_Internet/Programming_Languages/Java/

Log File Parsers

Wusage
http://www.boutell.com/wusage/

Yahoo!'s List
http://www.yahoo.com/Computers_and_Internet/Software/Internet/World_Wide_W
eb/Servers/Log_Analysis_Tools/

Other

Tim Berners-Lee's style guide

http://www.w3.org/hypertext/WWW/Provider/Style/Overview.html

The Yale HyperText style guide

http://info.med.yale.edu/caim/manual/index.html

Servers and Server Administration

Access control in NCSA HTTPD

http://hoohoo.ncsa.uiuc.edu/docs/setup/access/Overview.html
http://hoohoo.ncsa.uiuc.edu/docs/tutorials/user.html
http://hoohoo.ncsa.uiuc.edu/docs/setup/admin/UserManagement.html

Apache (UNIX)

http://www.apache.org/

JigSaw Server (Java)

http://www.w3.org/Jigsaw/

Current list of official MIME types

ftp://ftp.isi.edu/in-notes/iana/assignments/media-types/media-types

MacHTTP and WebStar (Macintosh)

http://www.starnine.com/

Microsoft Internet Information Server (Windows NT)

http://www.microsoft.com/ntserver/web/default.asp

Netscape's Web servers (UNIX, Windows NT)

http://home.netscape.com/comprod/server_central

O'Reilly webSite (Windows 95/NT)

http://website.ora.com/

Sound and Video

Audio Applications (commercial, bundled, shareware) for SGI Systems

http://reality.sgi.com/employees/cook/audio.apps/

AVI-Quick (Macintosh converter for AVI to QuickTime)
SoundHack (sound editor for Macintosh)
Sound Machine (sound capture/converter/editor for Macintosh)

A

SoundAPP (Macintosh sound converter)
Sparkle (MPEG player and converter for Macintosh)
WAVany (Windows sound converter)
WHAM (Windows sound converter)
`http://www.shareware.com/SW/Search/Quick/` (search for the program and platform you're interested in)

FastPlayer (Macintosh QuickTime player and "flattener")
`ftp://ftp.ncsa.uiuc.edu/Mosaic/Mac/Helpers/fast-player-110.hqx`

The Internet Underground Music Archive (IUMA)
`http://www.iuma.com/`

Yahoo!'s video information
`http://www.yahoo.com/Computers_and_Internet/Multimedia/Video/`

Yahoo!'s sound information
`http://www.yahoo.com/Computers/Multimedia/Sound/`

Specifications for HTML, HTTP, and URLs

Frames
`http://home.netscape.com/assist/net_sites/frames.html`

The HTTP specification (as defined in 1992)
`http://www.w3.org/hypertext/WWW/Protocols/HTTP/HTTP2.html`

The HTML Level 2 specification
`http://www.w3.org/hypertext/WWW/MarkUp/html-spec/index.html`

The HTML 3.2 draft specification
`http://www.w3.org/MarkUp/Wilbur/`

The HTML 4.0 specification
`http://www.w3.org/TR/1998/REC-html40-19980424/`

The XHTML 1.0 Draft specification
`http://www.w3.org/TR/1999/xhtml-modularization-19990406/`

Information about HTTP
`http://www.w3.org/pub/WWW/Protocols/`

Pointers to URL, URN, and URI information and specifications
`http://www.w3.org/hypertext/WWW/Addressing/Addressing.html`

The Common Gateway Interface (CGI) and CGI Scripting

An archive of CGI Programs at NCSA

ftp://ftp.ncsa.uiuc.edu/Web/httpd/Unix/ncsa_httpd/cgi

The CGI specification

http://hoohoo.ncsa.uiuc.edu/cgi/interface.html

cgi-lib.pl (A Perl library to manage CGI and Forms)

http://www.bio.cam.ac.uk/cgi-lib/

The original NCSA CGI documentation

http://hoohoo.ncsa.uiuc.edu/cgi/

Un-CGI (A program to decode form input)

http://www.hyperion.com/~koreth/uncgi.html

The Future of HTML and the Web

Adobe Acrobat

http://www.adobe.com/prodindex/acrobat/main.html

SSL information

http://www.netscape.com/info/security-doc.html

Cascading Style Sheets overview

http://www.w3.org/Style/

JavaScript Style Sheets

http://developer.netscape.com/docs/technote/dynhtml/css/css.htm

Web security overview

http://www.w3.org/Security/Overview.html

Yahoo!'s list on security, encryption, and authentication

http://www.yahoo.com/Computers_and_Internet/Security_and_Encryption/

Tools and Information for Images

Anthony's Icon Library

http://www.cit.gu.edu.au/~anthony/icons/index.html

Barry's Clip Art Server

http://www.barrysclipart.com/

GIF Converter for Macintosh
Graphic Converter for Macintosh
LView Pro for Windows
Transparency for Macintosh
http://www.shareware.com/SW/Search/Quick/ (search for the program and platform you're interested in)

giftrans
ftp://ftp.rz.uni-karlsruhe.de/pub/net/www/tools/giftrans.c

Internet Bag Lady
http://www.dumpsterdive.com

Yahoo!'s clip art list
http://dir.yahoo.com/Computers_and_Internet/Graphics/Clip_Art/

Yahoo!'s GIF list
http://dir.yahoo.com/Computers_and_Internet/Graphics/Data_Formats/GIF/

Yahoo!'s PNG List
http://dir.yahoo.com/Computers_and_Internet/Graphics/Data_Formats/
PNG__Portable_Network_Graphics_/

Yahoo!'s icons list
http://dir.yahoo.com/Arts/Design_Arts/Graphic_Design/
Web_Page_Design_and_Layout/Graphics/Icons/

Web Providers

Yahoo's List of Web Hosting Services
http://dir.yahoo.com/Business_and_Economy/Companies/Internet_Services/
Web_Services/Hosting/

Yahoo's List of Directories of Internet Access Providers
http://dir.yahoo.com/Business_and_Economy/Companies/Internet_Services/
Access_Providers/Directories/

The List (Worldwide list of Internet Providers)
http://thelist.internet.com/

Web Indexes and Search Engines

AltaVista
http://www.altavista.com/

Excite

http://www.excite.com

HotBot

http://www.hotbot.com

Lycos

http://www.lycos.com/

Web Crawler

http://www.webcrawler.com/

Yahoo!

http://www.yahoo.com/

InfoSeek

http://www.infoseek.com/

APPENDIX B

HTML 4.0 Quick Reference

This appendix provides a quick reference to the elements and attributes of the HTML 4.0 language, as specified by the World Wide Web Consortium. It is based on the information provided in the *HTML 4.0 Specification*, Revised 24-Apr-1998 (most current version at press time). The latest version of this document can be found at www.w3.org/TR/REC-html40/.

To make the information readily accessible, this appendix organizes HTML elements by their function in the following order:

- **Structure**

  bdo, body, Comments, div, !DOCTYPE, h1...h6, head, hr, html, meta, span, title

- **Text Phrases and Paragraphs**

  acronym, address, blockquote, br, cite, code, del, dfn, em, ins, kbd, p, pre, q, samp, strong, sub, sup, var

- **Text Formatting Elements**

  b, basefont, big, font, i, s, small, strike, tt, u

- **Lists**

  dd, dl, dt, li, menu, ol, ul

- **Links**

  a, base, link

- **Tables**

  caption, col, colgroup, table, tbody, td, tfoot, th, thead, tr

- **Frames**

  frame, frameset, iframe, noframes

- **Embedded content**

  applet, area, img, map, object, param

- **Style**

  style

- **Forms**

  button, fieldset, form, input, isindex, label, legend, option, select, textarea

- **Scripts**

  script, noscript

Within each section, the elements are listed alphabetically and the following information is presented:

- Usage—A general description of the element.
- Start/End Tag—Indicates whether these tags are required, optional, or illegal. Differences between HTML and XHTML are noted.
- Attributes—Lists the attributes of the element with a short description of its effect.
- Deprecated—Lists deprecated attributes, attributes that are still supported in HTML 4.0 and in most browsers, but that are in the process of being phased out in favor of newer techniques, such as style sheets.
- Empty—Indicates whether the element can be empty.
- Notes—Relates any special considerations when using the element and indicates whether the element is new, deprecated, or obsolete.

Common Attributes and Events

The HTML 4.0 specification includes several attributes that apply to a significant number of elements. These are referred to as %coreattrs, %i18n, and %events throughout this appendix and are explained in the following section.

%coreattrs

Four attributes are abbreviated as %coreattrs in the following sections. They are as follows:

- id="..."   A global identifier
- class="..."   A list of classes separated by spaces
- style="..."   Style information
- title="..."   Provides more information for a specific element, as opposed to the title element, which entitles the entire Web page

%i18n

Two attributes for internationalization (i18n) are abbreviated as %i18n:

- lang="..."   The language identifier
- dir="..."   The text direction (ltr, rtl)

%events

The following intrinsic events are abbreviated %events:

- onclick="..."   A pointing device (such as a mouse) was single-clicked.
- ondblclick="..."   A pointing device (such as a mouse) was double-clicked.
- onmousedown="..."   A mouse button was clicked and held down.
- onmouseup="..."   A mouse button that was clicked and held down was released.
- onmouseover="..."   A mouse moved the cursor over an object.
- onmousemove="..."   The mouse was moved.
- onmouseout="..."   A mouse moved the cursor off an object.
- onkeypress="..."   A key was pressed and released.
- onkeydown="..."   A key was pressed and held down.
- onkeyup="..."   A key that was pressed has been released.

Structure

HTML relies upon several elements to provide structure to a document (as opposed to structuring the text within), as well as provide information that is used by the browser or search engines.

<bdo>...</bdo>

Usage	The bidirectional algorithm element is used to selectively turn off the default text direction. Default text direction is left to right, but can be changed (to render Hebrew text from right to left, for example).
Start/End Tag	Required/Required.
Attributes	`lang="..."` The language of the document.
	`dir="..."` The text direction (`ltr`, `rtl`).
Empty	No.
Notes	The `dir` attribute is mandatory.

<body>...</body>

Usage	Contains the content of the document.
Start/End Tag	Optional/Optional (HTML); Required/Required (XHTML 1.0).
Attributes	`%coreattrs, %i18n, %events`
	`onload="..."` Intrinsic event triggered when the document loads.
	`onunload="..."` intrinsic event triggered when document unloads.
Deprecated	The following presentational attributes are deprecated in favor of setting these values with style sheets.
	`background="..."` URL for the background image.
	`bgcolor="..."` Sets background color.
	`text="..."` Text color.
	`link="..."` Link color.
	`vlink="..."` Visited link color.
	`alink="..."` Active link color.
Empty	No.
Notes	There can be only one `body`, and it must follow the `head`. The body element can be replaced by a `frameset` element.

Comments `<!-- ... -->`

Usage	Inserts notes or scripts that are not displayed by the browser.
Start/End Tag	Required/Required.
Attributes	None.
Empty	Yes.
Notes	Comments are not restricted to one line and can be any length. The end tag is not required to be on the same line as the start tag.

B

`<div>...</div>`

Usage	Division element is used to add structure to a block of text.
Start/End Tag	Required/Required.
Attributes	%coreattrs, %i18n, %events.
Deprecated	The align attribute is deprecated in favor of controlling alignment through style sheets. align="..." Controls alignment (left, center, right, justify).
Empty	No.
Notes	Cannot be used within a P element.

`<!DOCTYPE...>`

Usage	Version information appears on the first line of an HTML document and is a Standard Generalized Markup Language (SGML) declaration rather than an element.
Notes	Optional in HTML documents, but required in XHTML 1.0.

`<h1>...</h1>` through `<h6>...</h6>`

Usage	The six headings (h1 is the uppermost, or most important) are used in the body to structure information in a hierarchical fashion.
Start/End Tag	Required/Required.

Attributes	%coreattrs, %i18n, %events.
Deprecated	The align attribute is deprecated in favor of control-ling alignment through style sheets.
	align="..." Controls alignment (left, center, right, justify).
Empty	No.
Notes	Visual browsers will display the size of the headings in relation to their importance, with h1 being the largest and h6 the smallest.

\<head>...\</head>

Usage	This is the document header and contains other ele-ments that provide information to users and search engines.
Start/End Tag	Optional/Optional (HTML); Required/Required (XHTML 1.0).
Attributes	%i18n.
	profile="..." URL specifying the location of meta data.
Empty	No.
Notes	There can be only one head per document. It must fol-low the opening html tag and precede the body.

\<hr>

Usage	Horizontal rules are used to separate sections of a Web page.
Start/End Tag	Required/Illegal - See Note for XHTML 1.0 Requirements.
Attributes	%coreattrs, %events.
Deprecated	align="..." Controls alignment (left, center, right, justify).
	noshade="..." Displays the rule as a solid color.
	size="..." The size of the rule.
	width="..." The width of the rule.
Empty	Yes.

Notes	In XHTML 1.0, this tag should take the XML form of `<hr />` to ensure compatibility with older browsers.

`<html>...</html>`

Usage	The `html` element contains the entire document.
Start/End Tag	Optional/Optional (HTML); Required/Required (XHTML 1.0).
Attributes	`%i18n`.
Deprecated	`version="..."` URL of the document type definition specifying the HTML version used to create the document.
Empty	No.
Notes	The version information is duplicated in the `<!DOC-TYPE...>` declaration and therefore is not essential.

`<meta>`

Usage	Provides information about the document.
Start/End Tag	Required/Illegal (see note for XHTML 1.0 requirements).
Attributes	`%i18n`.
	`http-equiv="..."` HTTP response header name.
	`name="..."` Name of the meta information.
	`content="..."` Content of the meta information.
	`scheme="..."` Assigns a scheme to interpret the meta data.
Empty	Yes.
Notes	In XHTML 1.0, this tag should take the XML form of `<meta />` to ensure compatibility with older browsers.

`<span>...</span>`

Usage	Organizes the document by defining a span of text.
Start/End Tag	Required/Required.
Attributes	`%coreattrs, %i18n, %events`.
Empty	No.

`<title>...</title>`

Usage	This is the name you give your Web page. The `title` element is located in the `head` element and is displayed in the browser window title bar.
Start/End Tag	Required/Required.
Attributes	`%i18n`.
Empty	No.
Notes	Only one title allowed per document.

Text Phrases and Paragraphs

You can structure text phrases (or blocks) to suit a specific purpose, such as creating a paragraph. This should not be confused with modifying the formatting of the text.

`<acronym>...</acronym>`

Usage	Defines acronyms.
Start/End Tag	Required/Required.
Attributes	`%coreattrs, %i18n, %events`.
Empty	No.

`<address>...</address>`

Usage	Provides a special format for author or contact information.
Start/End Tag	Required/Required.
Attributes	`%coreattrs, %i18n, %events`.
Empty	No.
Notes	The `br` element is commonly used inside the `address` element to break the lines of an address.

`<blockquote>...</blockquote>`

Usage	Displays long quotations.
Start/End Tag	Required/Required.
Attributes	`%coreattrs, %i18n, %events`.
	`cite="..."` The URL of the quoted text.
Empty	No.

B

`<br>`

Usage	Forces a line break.
Start/End Tag	Required/Illegal (see note for XHTML 1.0 requirements).
Attributes	`%coreattrs`, `%i18n`, `%events`.
Deprecated	`clear="..."` Sets the location where next line begins after a floating object (`none`, `left`, `right`, `all`).
Empty	Yes.
Notes	In XHTML 1.0, this tag should take the XML form of ` ` to ensure compatibility with older browsers.

`<cite>...</cite>`

Usage	Cites a reference.
Start/End Tag	Required/Required.
Attributes	`%coreattrs`, `%i18n`, `%events`.
Empty	No.

`<code>...</code>`

Usage	Identifies a code fragment for display.
Start/End Tag	Required/Required.
Attributes	`%coreattrs`, `%i18n`, `%events`.
Empty	No.

`<del>...</del>`

Usage	Shows text as having been deleted from the document since the last change.
Start/End Tag	Required/Required.
Attributes	`%coreattrs`, `%i18n`, `%events`.
	`cite="..."` The URL of the source document.
	`datetime="..."` Indicates the date and time of the change.
Empty	No.
Notes	New element in HTML 4.0.

`<dfn>...</dfn>`

Usage	Defines an enclosed term.
Start/End Tag	Required/Required.
Attributes	%coreattrs, %i18n, %events.
Empty	No.

`<em>...</em>`

Usage	Emphasized text.
Start/End Tag	Required/Required.
Attributes	%coreattrs, %i18n, %events.
Empty	No.

`<ins>...</ins>`

Usage	Shows text as having been inserted in the document since the last change.
Start/End Tag	Required/Required.
Attributes	%coreattrs, %i18n, %events.
	cite="..." The URL of the source document.
	datetime="..." Indicates the date and time of the change.
Empty	No.
Notes	New element in HTML 4.0.

`<kbd>...</kbd>`

Usage	Indicates text a user would type.
Start/End Tag	Required/Required.
Attributes	%coreattrs, %i18n, %events.
Empty	No.

`<p>...</p>`

Usage	Defines a paragraph.
Start/End Tag	Required/Optional (HTML); Required/Required (XHTML 1.0).

Attributes	%coreattrs, %i18n, %events.
Deprecated	align="..." Controls alignment (left, center, right, justify).
Empty	No.

`<pre>...</pre>`

Usage	Displays preformatted text.
Start/End Tag	Required/Required.
Attributes	%coreattrs, %i18n, %events.
Deprecated	width="..." The width of the formatted text.
Empty	No.

`<q>...</q>`

Usage	Displays short quotations that do not require paragraph breaks.
Start/End Tag	Required/Required.
Attributes	%coreattrs, %i18n, %events.
	cite="..." The URL of the quoted text.
Empty	No.
Notes	New element in HTML 4.0.

`<samp>...</samp>`

Usage	Identifies sample output.
Start/End Tag	Required/Required.
Attributes	%coreattrs, %i18n, %events.
Empty	No.

`<strong>...</strong>`

Usage	Stronger emphasis.
Start/End Tag	Required/Required.
Attributes	%coreattrs, %i18n, %events.
Empty	No.

B

_{...\}

Usage	Creates subscript.
Start/End Tag	Required/Required.
Attributes	%coreattrs, %i18n, %events.
Empty	No.

\^{...\}

Usage	Creates superscript.
Start/End Tag	Required/Required.
Attributes	%coreattrs, %i18n, %events.
Empty	No.

\<var>...\</var>

Usage	A variable.
Start/End Tag	Required/Required.
Attributes	%coreattrs, %i18n, %events.
Empty	No.

Text Formatting Elements

Text characteristics such as the size, weight, and style can be modified by using these elements, but the HTML 4.0 specification encourages you to use style sheets instead.

\...\

Usage	Bold text.
Start/End Tag	Required/Required.
Attributes	%coreattrs, %i18n, %events.
Empty	No.

\<basefont>

Usage	Sets the base font size.
Start/End Tag	Required/Illegal (see note for XHTML 1.0 requirements).
Deprecated	size="..." The font size (1 through 7 or relative, that is, +3).

color="..."   The font color.

face="..."   The font type.

Empty	Yes.
Notes	Deprecated in favor of style sheets. In XHTML 1.0, this tag should take the XML form of `<basefont />` to ensure compatibility with older browsers.

B

`<big>...</big>`

Usage	Large text.
Start/End Tag	Required/Required.
Attributes	%coreattrs, %i18n, %events.
Empty	No.

`<font>...</font>`

Usage	Changes the font size and color.
Start/End Tag	Required/Required.
Deprecated	size="..." The font size (1 through 7 or relative, that is, +3).
	color="..." The font color.
	face="..." The font type.
Empty	No.
Notes	Deprecated in favor of style sheets.

`<i>...</i>`

Usage	Italicized text.
Start/End Tag	Required/Required.
Attributes	%coreattrs, %i18n, %events.
Empty	No.

`<s>...</s>`

Usage	Strikethrough text.
Start/End Tag	Required/Required.
Attributes	%coreattrs, %i18n, %events.
Empty	No.
Notes	Deprecated in favor of style sheets.

`<small>...</small>`

Usage	Small text.
Start/End Tag	Required/Required.
Attributes	%coreattrs, %i18n, %events.
Empty	No.

`<strike>...</strike>`

Usage	Strikethrough text.
Start/End Tag	Required/Required.
Attributes	%coreattrs, %i18n, %events.
Empty	No.
Notes	Deprecated in favor of style sheets.

`<tt>...</tt>`

Usage	Teletype (or monospaced) text.
Start/End Tag	Required/Required.
Attributes	%coreattrs, %i18n, %events.
Empty	No.

`<u>...</u>`

Usage	Underlined text.
Start/End Tag	Required/Required.
Attributes	%coreattrs, %i18n, %events.
Empty	No.
Notes	Deprecated in favor of style sheets.

Lists

You can organize text into a more structured outline by creating lists. Lists can be nested.

`<dd>...</dd>`

Usage	The definition description used in a dl (definition list) element.
Start/End Tag	Required/Optional (HTML); Required/Required (XHTML 1.0).

Attributes	%coreattrs, %i18n, %events.
Empty	No.
Notes	Can contain block-level content, such as the <p> element.

<dir>...</dir>

Usage	Creates a multicolumn directory list.
Start/End Tag	Required/Required.
Attributes	%coreattrs, %i18n, %events.
Deprecated	compact Compacts the displayed list.
Empty	No.
Notes	Must contain at least one list item. This element is deprecated in favor of the ul (unordered list) element.

<dl>...</dl>

Usage	Creates a definition list.
Start/End Tag	Required/Required.
Attributes	%coreattrs, %i18n, %events.
Deprecated	compact Compacts the displayed list.
Empty	No.
Notes	Must contain at least one <dt> or <dd> element in any order.

<dt>...</dt>

Usage	The definition term (or label) used within a dl (definition list) element.
Start/End Tag	Required/Optional (HTML); Required/Required (XHTML 1.0).
Attributes	%coreattrs, %i18n, %events.
Empty	No.
Notes	Must contained text (which can be modified by text markup elements).

<li>...</li>

| Usage | Defines a list item within a list. |

Start/End Tag	Required/Optional (HTML); Required/Required (XHTML 1.0).
Attributes	`%coreattrs, %i18n, %events`.
Deprecated	`type="..."` Changes the numbering style (`1, a, A, i, I`), ordered lists, or bullet style (`disc, square, circle`) in unordered lists.
	`value="..."` Sets the numbering to the given integer, beginning with the current list item.
Empty	No.

`<menu>...</menu>`

Usage	Creates a single-column menu list.
Start/End Tag	Required/Required.
Attributes	`%coreattrs, %i18n, %events`.
Deprecated	`compact` Compacts the displayed list.
Empty	No.
Notes	Must contain at least one list item. This element is deprecated in favor of the `ul` (unordered list) element.

`<ol>...</ol>`

Usage	Creates an ordered list.
Start/End Tag	Required/Required.
Attributes	`%coreattrs, %i18n, %events`.
Deprecated	`compact` Compacts the displayed list.
	`start="..."` Sets the starting number to the chosen integer.
	`type="..."` Sets the numbering style (`1, a, A, i, I`).
Empty	No.
Notes	Must contain at least one list item.

`<ul>...</ul>`

Usage	Creates an unordered list.
Start/End Tag	Required/Required.
Attributes	`%coreattrs, %i18n, %events`.

Deprecated	`compact` Compacts the displayed list.
	`type="..."` Sets the bullet style (`disc`, `square`, `circle`).
Empty	No.
Notes	Must contain at least one list item.

B

Links

Hyperlinking is fundamental to HTML. These elements enable you to link to other documents.

`<a>...</a>`

Usage	Used to define links and anchors.
Start/End Tag	Required/Required.
Attributes	`%coreattrs`, `%i18n`, `%events`.
	`charset="..."` Character encoding of the resource.
	`name="..."` Defines an anchor.
	`href="..."` The URL of the linked resource.
	`target="..."` Determines where the resource will be displayed (user-defined name, `_blank` (in a new unnamed window), `_parent` (in the immediate parent frameset), `_self` (in the same frame as the current document), or `_top` (in a full browser window that removes the frameset completely).
	`rel="..."` Forward link types.
	`rev="..."` Reverse link types.
	`accesskey="..."` Assigns a hotkey to this element.
	`shape="..."` Enables you to define client-side imagemaps using defined shapes (`default`, `rect`, `circle`, `poly`).
	`coords="..."` Sets the size of the shape using pixel or percentage lengths.
	`tabindex="..."` Sets the tabbing order between elements with a defined `tabindex`.
Empty	No.

\<base>

Usage	All other URLs in the document are resolved against this location.
Start/End Tag	Required/Illegal (see note for XHTML 1.0 requirements).
Attributes	`href="..."` The URL of the linked resource.
	`target="..."` Determines where the resource will be displayed (user-defined name, `_blank`, `_parent`, `_self`, `_top`).
Empty	Yes.
Notes	Located in the document `head`. In XHTML 1.0, this tag should take the XML form of `<base />` to ensure compatibility with older browsers.

\<link>

Usage	Defines the relationship between a link and a resource.
Start/End Tag	Required/Illegal (see note for XHTML 1.0 requirements).
Attributes	`%coreattrs, %i18n, %events`.
	`href="..."` The URL of the resource.
	`rel="..."` The forward link types.
	`rev="..."` The reverse link types.
	`type="..."` The Internet content type.
	`media="..."` Defines the destination medium (`screen`, `print`, `projection`, `braille`, `speech`, `all`).
	`target="..."` Determines where the resource will be displayed (user-defined name, `_blank`, `_parent`, `_self`, `_top`).
Empty	Yes.
Notes	Located in the document `head`. In XHTML 1.0, this tag should take the XML form of `<link />` to ensure compatibility with older browsers.

Tables

Tables are meant to display data in a tabular format. Tables are widely used for page layout purposes, but with the advent of style sheets, this is being discouraged by the HTML 4.0 specification.

`<caption>...</caption>`

Usage	Displays a table caption.
Start/End Tag	Required/Required.
Attributes	`%coreattrs, %i18n, %events.`
Deprecated	`align="..."` Controls alignment (`left`, `center`, `right`, `justify`).
Empty	No.
Notes	Optional.

`<col>`

Usage	Groups columns within column groups in order to share attribute values.
Start/End Tag	Required/Illegal (see note for XHTML 1.0 requirements).
Attributes	`%coreattrs, %i18n, %events.` `span="..."` The number of columns the group contains. `width="..."` The column width as a percentage, pixel value, or minimum value. `align="..."` Horizontally aligns the contents of cells (`left`, `center`, `right`, `justify`, `char`). `char="..."` Sets a character on which the column aligns. `charoff="..."` Offset to the first alignment character on a line. `valign="..."` Vertically aligns the contents of a cell (`top`, `middle`, `bottom`, `baseline`).
Empty	Yes.
Notes	In XHTML 1.0, this tag should take the XML form of `<col />` to ensure compatibility with older browsers.

B

`<colgroup>...</colgroup>`

Usage	Defines two or more columns as a group.
Start/End Tag	Required/Optional (HTML); Required/Required (XHTML 1.0).
Attributes	`%coreattrs, %i18n, %events`.
	`span="..."` The number of columns in a group.
	`width="..."` The width of the columns.
	`align="..."` Horizontally aligns the contents of cells (`left, center, right, justify, char`).
	`char="..."` Sets a character on which the column aligns.
	`charoff="..."` Offset to the first alignment character on a line.
	`valign="..."` Vertically aligns the contents of a cell (`top, middle, bottom, baseline`).
Empty	No.

`<table>...</table>`

Usage	Creates a table.
Start/End Tag	Required/Required.
Attributes	`%coreattrs, %i18n, %events`.
	`width="..."` Table width.
	`cols="..."` The number of columns.
	`border="..."` The width in pixels of a border around the table.
	`frame="..."` Sets the visible sides of a table (`void, above, below, hsides, lhs, rhs, vsides, box, border`).
	`rules="..."` Sets the visible rules within a table (`none, groups, rows, cols, all`).
	`cellspacing="..."` Spacing between cells.
	`cellpadding="..."` Spacing in cells.
Deprecated	`align="..."` Controls alignment (`left, center, right, justify`).
	`bgcolor="..."` Sets the background color.
Empty	No.

<tbody>...</tbody>

Usage	Defines the table body.
Start/End Tag	Optional/Optional (HTML); Required/Required (XHTML 1.0).
Attributes	%coreattrs, %i18n, %events.
	align="..." Horizontally aligns the contents of cells (left, center, right, justify, char).
	char="..." Sets a character on which the column aligns.
	charoff="..." Offset to the first alignment character on a line.
	valign="..." Vertically aligns the contents of cells (top, middle, bottom, baseline).
Empty	No.

<td>...</td>

Usage	Defines a cell's contents.
Start/End Tag	Required/Optional (HTML); Required/Required (XHTML 1.0).
Attributes	%coreattrs, %i18n, %events.
	axis="..." Abbreviated name.
	axes="..." axis names listing row and column headers pertaining to the cell.
	rowspan="..." The number of rows spanned by a cell.
	colspan="..." The number of columns spanned by a cell.
	align="..." Horizontally aligns the contents of cells (left, center, right, justify, char).
	char="..." Sets a character on which the column aligns.
	charoff="..." Offset to the first alignment character on a line.
	valign="..." Vertically aligns the contents of cells (top, middle, bottom, baseline).

B

Deprecated	`nowrap="..."` Turns off text wrapping in a cell.
	`bgcolor="..."` Sets the background color.
	`height="..."` Sets the height of the cell.
	`width="..."` Sets the width of the cell.
Empty	No.

`<tfoot>...</tfoot>`

Usage	Defines the table footer.
Start/End Tag	Required/Optional (HTML); Required/Required (XHTML 1.0).
Attributes	`%coreattrs, %i18n, %events`.
	`align="..."` Horizontally aligns the contents of cells (`left, center, right, justify, char`).
	`char="..."` Sets a character on which the column aligns.
	`charoff="..."` Offset to the first alignment character on a line.
	`valign="..."` Vertically aligns the contents of cells (`top, middle, bottom, baseline`).
Empty	No.

`<th>...</th>`

Usage	Defines the cell contents of the table header.
Start/End Tag	Required/Optional (HTML); Required/Required (XHTML 1.0).
Attributes	`%coreattrs, %i18n, %events`.
	`axis="..."` Abbreviated name.
	`axes="..."` axis names listing row and column headers pertaining to the cell.
	`rowspan="..."` The number of rows spanned by a cell.
	`colspan="..."` The number of columns spanned by a cell.
	`align="..."` Horizontally aligns the contents of cells (`left, center, right, justify, char`).

B

	`char="..."` Sets a character on which the column aligns.
	`charoff="..."` Offset to the first alignment character on a line.
	`valign="..."` Vertically aligns the contents of cells (`top`, `middle`, `bottom`, `baseline`).
Deprecated	`nowrap="..."` Turns off text wrapping in a cell.
	`bgcolor="..."` Sets the background color.
	`height="..."` Sets the height of the cell.
	`width="..."` Sets the width of the cell.
Empty	No.

`<thead>...</thead>`

Usage	Defines the table header.
Start/End Tag	Required/Optional (HTML); Required/Required (XHTML 1.0).
Attributes	`%coreattrs, %i18n, %events.`
	`align="..."` Horizontally aligns the contents of cells (`left`, `center`, `right`, `justify`, `char`).
	`char="..."` Sets a character on which the column aligns.
	`charoff="..."` Offset to the first alignment character on a line.
	`valign="..."` Vertically aligns the contents of cells (`top`, `middle`, `bottom`, `baseline`).
Empty	No.

`<tr>...</tr>`

Usage	Defines a row of table cells.
Start/End Tag	Required/Optional (HTML); Required/Required (XHTML 1.0).
Attributes	`%coreattrs, %i18n, %events.`
	`align="..."` Horizontally aligns the contents of cells (`left`, `center`, `right`, `justify`, `char`).

char="..."   Sets a character on which the column aligns.

charoff="..."   Offset to the first alignment character on a line.

valign="..."   Vertically aligns the contents of cells (top, middle, bottom, baseline).

Deprecated	bgcolor="..." Sets the background color.
Empty	No.

Frames

Frames create new "panels" in the Web browser window that are used to display content from different source documents.

`<frame>`

Usage	Defines a frame.
Start/End Tag	Required/Illegal (see note for XHTML 1.0 requirements).
Attributes	name="..." The name of a frame.
	src="..." The source to be displayed in a frame.
	frameborder="..." Toggles the border between frames (0, 1).
	marginwidth="..." Sets the space between the frame border and content.
	marginheight="..." Sets the space between the frame border and content.
	noresize Disables sizing.
	scrolling="..." Determines scrollbar presence (auto, yes, no).
Empty	Yes.
Notes	In XHTML 1.0, this tag should take the XML form of <frame /> to ensure compatibility with older browsers.

`<frameset>...</frameset>`

Usage	Defines the layout of frames within a window.
Start/End Tag	Required/Required.
Attributes	`rows="..."` The number of rows.
	`cols="..."` The number of columns.
	`onload="..."` The intrinsic event triggered when the document loads.
	`onunload="..."` The intrinsic event triggered when the document unloads.
Empty	No.
Notes	Framesets can be nested.

B

`<iframe>...</iframe>`

Usage	Creates an inline frame.
Start/End Tag	Required/Required.
Attributes	`name="..."` The name of the frame.
	`src="..."` The source to be displayed in a frame.
	`frameborder="..."` Toggles the border between frames (0, 1).
	`marginwidth="..."` Sets the space between the frame border and content.
	`marginheight="..."` Sets the space between the frame border and content.
	`scrolling="..."` Determines scrollbar presence (auto, yes, no).
	`height="..."` Height.
	`width="..."` Width.
Deprecated	`align="..."` Controls alignment (left, center, right, justify).
Empty	No.

`<noframes>...</noframes>`

Usage	Alternative content when frames are not supported.
Start/End Tag	Required/Required.

Attributes	None.
Empty	No.

Embedded Content

Also called *inclusions*, embedded content applies to Java applets, imagemaps, and other multimedia or programmatic content that is placed in a Web page to provide additional functionality.

`<applet>...</applet>`

Usage	Includes a Java applet.
Start/End Tag	Required/Required.
Deprecated	`align="..."` Controls alignment (`left`, `center`, `right`, `justify`).
	`alt="..."` Displays text while loading.
	`archive="..."` Identifies the resources to be pre-loaded.
	`code="..."` The applet class file.
	`codebase="..."` The URL base for the applet.
	`height="..."` The width of the displayed applet.
	`hspace="..."` The horizontal space separating the image from other content.
	`name="..."` The name of the applet.
	`object="..."` The serialized applet file.
	`vspace="..."` The vertical space separating the image from other content.
	`width="..."` The height of the displayed applet.
Empty	No.
Notes	Applet is deprecated in favor of the `object` element.

`<area>`

Usage	Defines links and anchors.
Start/End Tag	Required/Illegal (see note for XHTML 1.0 requirements).

Attributes	`shape="..."` Enables you to define client-side imagemaps using defined shapes (`default`, `rect`, `circle`, `poly`).
	`coords="..."` Sets the size of the shape using pixel or percentage lengths.
	`href="..."` The URL of the linked resource.
	`target="..."` Determines where the resource will be displayed (user-defined name, `_blank`, `_parent`, `_self`, `_top`).
	`nohref="..."` Indicates that the region has no action.
	`alt="..."` Displays alternative text.
	`tabindex="..."` Sets the tabbing order between elements with a defined `tabindex`.
Empty	Yes.
Notes	In XHTML 1.0, this tag should take the XML form of `<area />` to ensure compatibility with older browsers.

`<img>`

Usage	Includes an image in the document.
Start/End Tag	Required/Illegal (see note for XHTML 1.0 requirements).
Attributes	`%coreattrs`, `%i18n`, `%events`.
	`src="..."` The URL of the image.
	`alt="..."` Alternative text to display.
	`height="..."` The height of the image.
	`width="..."` The width of the image.
	`usemap="..."` The URL to a client-side imagemap.
	`ismap` Identifies a server-side imagemap.
Deprecated	`align="..."` Controls alignment (`left`, `center`, `right`, `justify`).
	`border="..."` Border width.
	`hspace="..."` The horizontal space separating the image from other content.

B

vspace="..." The vertical space separating the image from other content.

Empty	Yes.
Notes	In XHTML 1.0, this tag should take the XML form of <img /> to ensure compatibility with older browsers.

<map>...</map>

Usage	When used with the area element, creates a client-side imagemap.
Start/End Tag	Required/Required.
Attributes	%coreattrs.
	name="..." The name of the imagemap to be created.
Empty	No.

<object>...</object>

Usage	Includes an object.
Start/End Tag	Required/Required.
Attributes	%coreattrs, %i18n, %events.

declare A flag that makes the current object definition a declaration only.

classid="..." The URL of the object's location.

codebase="..." The URL for resolving URLs specified by other attributes.

data="..." The URL to the object's data.

type="..." The Internet content type for data.

codetype="..." The Internet content type for the code.

standby="..." Show message while loading.

height="..." The height of the object.

width="..." The width of the object.

usemap="..." The URL to an imagemap.

shapes= Enables you to define areas to search for hyperlinks if the object is an image.

name="..." The URL to submit as part of a form.

	`tabindex="..."` Sets the tabbing order between elements with a defined `tabindex`.
Deprecated	`align="..."` Controls alignment (`left`, `center`, `right`, `justify`).
	`border="..."` Displays the border around an object.
	`hspace="..."` The space between the sides of the object and other page content.
	`vspace="..."` The space between the top and bottom of the object and other page content.
Empty	No.

`<param>`

Usage	Initializes an object.
Start/End Tag	Required/Illegal (see note for XHTML 1.0 requirements).
Attributes	`name="..."` Defines the parameter name.
	`value="..."` The value of the object parameter.
	`valuetype="..."` Defines the value type (`data`, `ref`, `object`).
	`type="..."` The Internet media type.
Empty	Yes.
Notes	In XHTML 1.0, this tag should take the XML form of `<param />` to ensure compatibility with older browsers.

Style

Style sheets (both inline and external) are incorporated into an HTML document through the use of the `style` element.

`<style>...</style>`

Usage	Creates an internal style sheet.
Start/End Tag	Required/Required.
Attributes	`%i18n`.
	`type="..."` The Internet content type.

media="..." Defines the destination medium (screen, print, projection, braille, speech, all).

title="..." The title of the style.

| Empty | No. |
| Notes | Located in the head element. |

Forms

Forms create an interface for the user to select options and submit data back to the Web server.

<button>...</button>

Usage	Creates a button.
Start/End Tag	Required/Required.
Attributes	%coreattrs, %i18n, %events.

name="..." The button name.

value="..."   The value of the button.

type="..."   The button type (button, submit, reset).

disabled="..." Sets the button state to disabled.

tabindex="..."   Sets the tabbing order between elements with a defined tabindex.

onfocus="..."   The event that occurs when the element receives focus.

onblur="..."   The event that occurs when the element loses focus.

| Empty | No. |

<fieldset>...</fieldset>

Usage	Groups related controls.
Start/End Tag	Required/Required.
Attributes	%coreattrs, %i18n, %events.
Empty	No.

<form>...</form>

Usage	Creates a form that holds controls for user input.
Start/End Tag	Required/Required.
Attributes	%coreattrs, %i18n, %events.

action="..."   The URL for the server action.

enctype="..."   Specifies the MIME (Internet media type).

onsubmit="..."   The intrinsic event that occurs when the form is submitted.

onreset="..."   The intrinsic event that occurs when the form is reset.

target="..."   Determines where the resource will be displayed (user-defined name, _blank, _parent, _self, _top).

accept-charset="..."   The list of character encodings.

method="..."   The HTTP method (post or get).

Empty	No.

<input>

Usage	Defines controls used in forms.
Start/End Tag	Required/Illegal (see note for XHTML 1.0 requirements).
Attributes	%coreattrs, %i18n, %events.

type="..."   The type of input control (text, password, checkbox, radio, submit, reset, file, hidden, image, button).

name="..."   The name of the control (required except for submit and reset).

value="..."   The initial value of the control (required for radio and checkboxes).

checked="..."   Sets the radio buttons to a checked state.

disabled="..."   Disables the control.

readonly="..."   For text password types.

B

`size="..."` The width of the control in pixels except for text and password controls, which are specified in number of characters.

`maxlength="..."` The maximum number of characters that can be entered.

`src="..."` The URL to an image control type.

`alt="..."` An alternative text description.

`usemap="..."` The URL to a client-side imagemap.

`tabindex="..."` Sets the tabbing order between elements with a defined `tabindex`.

`onfocus="..."` The event that occurs when the element receives focus.

`onblur="..."` The event that occurs when the element loses focus.

`onselect="..."` Intrinsic event that occurs when the control is selected.

`onchange="..."` Intrinsic event that occurs when the control is changed.

`accept="..."` File types allowed for upload.

Deprecated	`align="..."` Controls alignment (`left`, `center`, `right`, `justify`).
Empty	Yes.
Notes	In XHTML 1.0, this tag should take the XML form of `<input />` to ensure compatibility with older browsers.

`<isindex>`

Usage	Prompts the user for input.
Start/End Tag	Required/Illegal (see note for XHTML 1.0 requirements).
Attributes	`%coreattrs`, `%i18n`.
Deprecated	`prompt="..."` Provides a prompt string for the input field.
Empty	Yes.

| Notes | In XHTML 1.0, this tag should take the XML form of `<isindex />` to ensure compatibility with older browsers. |

B

`<label>`...`</label>`

Usage	Labels a control.
Start/End Tag	Required/Required.
Attributes	`%coreattrs`, `%i18n`, `%events`.
	`for="..."` Associates a label with an identified control.
	`disabled="..."` Disables a control.
	`accesskey="..."` Assigns a hotkey to this element.
	`onfocus="..."` The event that occurs when the element receives focus.
	`onblur="..."` The event that occurs when the element loses focus.
Empty	No.

`<legend>`...`</legend>`

Usage	Assigns a caption to a `fieldset`.
Start/End Tag	Required/Required.
Attributes	`%coreattrs`, `%i18n`, `%events`.
	`accesskey="..."` Assigns a hotkey to this element.
Deprecated	`align="..."` Controls alignment (`left`, `center`, `right`, `justify`).
Empty	No.

`<option>`...`</option>`

Usage	Specifies choices in a `select` element.
Start/End Tag	Required/Optional (HTML); Required/Required (XHTML 1.0).
Attributes	`%coreattrs`, `%i18n`, `%events`.
	`selected="..."` Specifies whether the option is selected.
	`disabled="..."` Disables control.

value="..."   The value submitted if a control is submitted.

Empty   No.

<select>...</select>

Usage   Creates choices for the user to select.

Start/End Tag   Required/Required.

Attributes   %coreattrs, %i18n, %events.

name="..."   The name of the element.

size="..."   The width in number of rows.

multiple   Allows multiple selections.

disabled="..."   Disables the control.

tabindex="..."   Sets the tabbing order between elements with a defined tabindex.

onfocus="..."   The event that occurs when the element receives focus.

onblur="..."   The event that occurs when the element loses focus.

onselect="..."   Intrinsic event that occurs when the
control is selected.

onchange="..."   Intrinsic event that occurs when the
control is changed.

Empty   No.

<textarea>...</textarea>

Usage   Creates an area for user input with multiple lines.

Start/End Tag   Required/Required.

Attributes   %coreattrs, %i18n, %events.

name="..."   The name of the control.

rows="..."   The width in number of rows.

cols="..."   The height in number of columns.

disabled="..."   Disables the control.

readonly="..."   Sets the displayed text to read-only
status.

tabindex="..."   Sets the tabbing order between elements with a defined `tabindex`.

`onfocus="..."` The event that occurs when the element receives focus.

`onblur="..."` The event that occurs when the element loses focus.

`onselect="..."` Intrinsic event that occurs when the control is selected.

`onchange="..."` Intrinsic event that occurs when the control is changed.

Empty	No.
Notes	Text to be displayed is placed within the start and end tags.

Scripts

Scripting language is made available to process data and perform other dynamic events through the `script` element.

`<script>...</script>`

Usage	Contains client-side scripts that are executed by the browser.
Start/End Tag	Required/Required.
Attributes	`type="..."` Script language Internet content type.
	`src="..."` The URL for the external script.
Deprecated	`language="..."` The scripting language, deprecated in favor of the `type` attribute.
Empty	No.
Notes	You can set the default scripting language in the `meta` element.

`<noscript>...</noscript>`

Usage	Provides alternative content for browsers unable to execute a script.
Start/End Tag	Required/Required.
Attributes	None.
Empty	No.

Character Entities

Table B.1 contains the possible numeric and character entities for the ISO-Latin-1 (ISO8859-1) character set. Where possible, the character is shown.

Note

Not all browsers can display all characters, and some browsers may even display different characters from those that appear in the table. Newer browsers seem to have a better track record for handling character entities, but be sure and test your HTML files extensively with multiple browsers if you intend to use these entities.

Table B.1 ISO-Latin-1 Character Set

Character	Numeric Entity	Character Entity (if any)	Description
	&#00;–&#08;		Unused
	&#09;		Horizontal tab
	&#10;		Line feed
	&#11;–&#31;		Unused
	&#32;		Space
!	&#33;		Exclamation mark
"	&#34;	&quot;	Quotation mark
#	&#35;		Number sign
$	&#36;		Dollar sign
%	&#37;		Percent sign
&	&#38;	&amp;	Ampersand
'	&#39;		Apostrophe
(	&#40;		Left parenthesis
)	&#41;		Right parenthesis
*	&#42;		Asterisk
+	&#43;		Plus sign
,	&#44;		Comma
-	&#45;		Hyphen
.	&#46;		Period (fullstop)
/	&#47;		Solidus (slash)
0–9	0–9		Digits 0–9

Character	Numeric Entity	Character Entity (if any)	Description
:	&#58;		Colon
;	&#59;		Semicolon
<	&#60;	&lt;	Less than
=	&#61;		Equals sign
>	&#62;	&gt;	Greater than
?	&#63;		Question mark
@	&#64;		Commercial at
A–Z	A–Z		Letters A–Z
[	&#91;		Left square bracket
\	&#92;		Reverse solidus (backslash)
]	&#93;		Right square bracket
^	&#94;		Caret
_	&#95;		Horizontal bar
`	&#96;		Grave accent
a–z	a–z		Letters a–z
{	&#123;		Left curly brace
|	|		Vertical bar
}	&#125;		Right curly brace
~	&#126;		Tilde
	&#127;–Ÿ		Unused
			Non-breaking space
¡	&#161;	&iexcl;	Inverted exclamation
¢	&#162;	&cent;	Cent sign
£	&#163;	&pound;	Pound sterling
¤	&#164;	&curren;	General currency sign
¥	&#165;	&yen;	Yen sign
¦	&#166;	¦ or &brkbar;	Broken vertical bar
§	&#167;	&sect;	Section sign
¨	&#168;	¨ or ¨	Umlaut (dieresis)
©	&#169;	&copy;	Copyright

continues

Table B.1 continued

Character	Numeric Entity	Character Entity (if any)	Description
ª	`&#170;`	`&ordf;`	Feminine ordinal
‹	`&#171;`	`&laqo;`	Left angle quote, guillemet left
¬	`&#172;`	`&not;`	Not sign
	`&#173;`	`&shy;`	Soft hyphen
®	`&#174;`	`&reg;`	Registered trademark
¯	`&#175;`	`&macr;` or `&hibar;`	Macron accent
°	`&#176;`	`&deg;`	Degree sign
±	`&#177;`	`&plusmn;`	Plus or minus
²	`&#178;`	`&sup2;`	Superscript two
³	`&#179;`	`&sup3;`	Superscript three
´	`&#180;`	`&acute;`	Acute accent
	`&#181;`	`&micro;`	Micro sign
¶	`&#182;`	`&para;`	Paragraph sign
·	`&#183;`	`&middot;`	Middle dot
¸	`&#184;`	`&cedil;`	Cedilla
¹	`&#185;`	`&sup1;`	Superscript one
º	`&#186;`	`&ordm;`	Masculine ordinal
›	`&#187;`	`&raquo;`	Right angle quote, guillemet right
1/4	`&#188;`	`&fraq14;`	Fraction one-fourth
1/2	`&#189;`	`&fraq12;`	Fraction one-half
3/4	`&#190;`	`&fraq34;`	Fraction three-fourths
¿	`&#191;`	`&iquest;`	Inverted question mark
À	`&#192;`	`&Agrave;`	Capital A, grave accent
Á	`&#193;`	`&Aacute;`	Capital A, acute accent
Â	`&#194;`	`&Acirc;`	Capital A, circumflex accent
Ã	`&#195;`	`&Atilde;`	Capital A, tilde
Ä	`&#196;`	`&Auml;`	Capital A, dieresis or umlaut mark
Å	`&#197;`	`&Aring;`	Capital A, ring
Æ	`&#198;`	`&AElig;`	Capital AE dipthong (ligature)
Ç	`&#199;`	`&Ccedil;`	Capital C, cedilla
È	`&#200;`	`&Egrave;`	Capital E, grave accent

Character	Numeric Entity	Character Entity (if any)	Description
É	&#201;	&Eacute;	Capital E, acute accent
Ê	&#202;	&Ecirc;	Capital E, circumflex accent
Ë	&#203;	&Euml;	Capital E, dieresis or umlaut mark
Ì	&#204;	&Igrave;	Capital I, grave accent
Í	&#205;	&Iacute;	Capital I, acute accent
Î	&#206;	&Icirc;	Capital I, circumflex accent
Ï	&#207;	&Iuml;	Capital I, dieresis or umlaut mark
Ð	&#208;	Ð or Đ	Capital Eth, Icelandic
Ñ	&#209;	&Ntilde;	Capital N, tilde
Ò	&#210;	&Ograve;	Capital O, grave accent
Ó	&#211;	&Oacute;	Capital O, acute accent
Ô	&#212;	&Ocirc;	Capital O, circumflex accent
Õ	&#213;	&Otilde;	Capital O, tilde
Ö	&#214;	&Ouml;	Capital O, dieresis or umlaut mark
∞	&#215;	&times;	Multiply sign
Ø	&#216;	&Oslash;	Capital O, slash
Ù	&#217;	&Ugrave;	Capital U, grave accent
Ú	&#218;	&Uacute;	Capital U, acute accent
Û	&#219;	&Ucirc;	Capital U, circumflex accent
Ü	&#220;	&Uuml;	Capital U, dieresis or umlaut mark
¥Y	&#221;	&Yacute;	Capital Y, acute accent
Þ	&#222;	&THORN;	Capital THORN, Icelandic
ﬞ	&#223;	&szlig;	Small sharp s, German (sz ligature)
à	&#224;	&agrave;	Small a, grave accent
á	&#225;	&aacute;	Small a, acute accent
â	&#226;	&acirc;	Small a, circumflex accent
ã	&#227;	&atilde;	Small a, tilde
ä	&#228;	&auml;	Small a, dieresis or umlaut mark
å	&#229;	&aring;	Small a, ring
æ	&#230;	&aelig;	Small ae dipthong (ligature)

continues

Table B.1   continued

Character	Numeric Entity	Character Entity (if any)	Description
ç	ç	ç	Small c, cedilla
è	è	è	Small e, grave accent
é	é	é	Small e, acute accent
ê	ê	ê	Small e, circumflex accent
ë	ë	ë	Small e, dieresis or umlaut mark
ì	ì	ì	Small i, grave accent
í	í	í	Small i, acute accent
î	î	î	Small i, circumflex accent
ï	ï	ï	Small i, dieresis or umlaut mark
ð	ð	ð	Small eth, Icelandic
ñ	ñ	ñ	Small n, tilde
ò	ò	ò	Small o, grave accent
ó	ó	ó	Small o, acute accent
ô	ô	ô	Small o, circumflex accent
õ	õ	õ	Small o, tilde
ö	ö	ö	Small o, dieresis or umlaut mark
÷	÷	÷	Division sign
ø	ø	ø	Small o, slash
ù	ù	ù	Small u, grave accent
ú	ú	ú	Small u, acute accent
û	û	û	Small u, circumflex accent
ü	ü	ü	Small u, dieresis or umlaut mark
´y	ý	ý	Small y, acute accent
þ	þ	þ	Small thorn, Icelandic
ÿ	ÿ	ÿ	Small y, dieresis or umlaut mark

APPENDIX **C**

Cascading Style Sheet (CSS) Quick Reference

Cascading Style Sheets allow for advanced placement and rendering of text and graphics on your pages. You can apply text, images, and multimedia to your Web pages with great precision. This appendix provides a quick reference to CSS1, as well as those properties and values that are included in the CSS2 recommendation dated May 12, 1998. This is the most current version of this document at press time.

Note

This appendix is based on the information provided in the Cascading Style Sheets, Level 2 W3C recommendation dated May 12, 1998, which can be found at http://www.w3.org/TR/ REC-CSS2/.

To make the information readily accessible, this appendix organizes CSS properties in the following order:

- Block-level properties
- Background and color properties
- Box model properties
- Font properties
- List properties
- Text properties
- Visual effects properties
- Aural style sheet properties
- Generated content/automatic numbering properties
- Paged media properties
- User interface properties
- Cascading Style Sheet units

How to Use This Appendix

Each property contains information presented in the following order:

- Usage—A description of the property
- CSS1 values—Legal CSS1 values and syntax
- CSS2 values—Legal CSS2 values and syntax
- Initial—The initial value
- Applies to—Elements to which the property applies
- Inherited—Whether the property is inherited
- Notes—Additional information

Deciphering CSS values is an exercise that requires patience and a strict adherence to the rules of logic. As you refer to the values for each property listed in this appendix, you should use the following scheme to understand them.

Values of different types are differentiated as follows:

- **Keyword values**—Keywords are identifiers, such as red, auto, normal, and inherit. They do not have quotation marks.
- **Basic data types**—These values, such as <number> and <length>, are contained within angled brackets to indicate the data type of the actual value used in a style statement. It is important to note that this refers to the data type and is not the actual value. The basic data types are described at the end of this appendix.

- **Shorthand reference**—Values that are enclosed in angled brackets and single quotation marks, such as `<'background-color'>` within the `background` property, indicate a shorthand method for setting the desired value. The values identified in `background-color` are available for use in the `background` property. If you choose to set the background color for the document body, for example, you can choose to do so by using either `body { background: red }` or `body { background-color: red }`.
- **Pre-defined data types**—Values within angled brackets without quotes, such as `<border-width>` within the `'border-top-width'` property, are similar to the basic data types but contain predefined values. The available values for `<border-width>`, for example, are `thin`, `thick`, `medium`, and `<length>`.

When more than one value is available, they are arranged according to the following rules:

- **Adjacent words**—Several adjacent words indicate all values must be used but can be in any order.
- **Values separated by bars "¦"**—The bar separates two or more alternatives, only one of which can occur.
- **Values separated by double-bars "¦¦"**—The double bar separates two or more options, of which one or more must occur in any order.
- **Brackets "[]"**—Brackets group the values into statements that are evaluated much like a mathematical expression.

When evaluating the values listed in this appendix, the order of precedence is that adjacent values take priority over those separated by double bars and then single bars.

In addition to this, special modifiers may follow each value or group of values. These are the following:

- *** (asterisk)**—The preceding type, word, or group occurs zero or more times
- **+ (plus)**—The preceding type, word, or group occurs one or more times
- **? (question mark)**—The preceding type, word, or group is optional
- **{} (curly braces)**—Surrounding a pair of numbers, such as {1,2}, indicates the preceding type, word, or group occurs at least once and at most twice

Block-Level Properties

Block-level elements are those that are formatted visually as blocks. A paragraph or a list, for example, is a block.

bottom, left, right, top

Usage	Specifies how far a box's bottom, left, right, or top content edge is offset from the respective bottom, left, right or top of the box's containing block.
CSS2 Values	`<length>` | `<percentage>` | `auto` | `inherit`
Initial	`auto`
Applies to	All elements.
Inherited	No.
Notes	Percentage refers to height of containing block.

direction

Usage	Specifies the direction of inline box flow, embedded text direction, column layout, and content overflow.
CSS1 Values	`ltr` | `rtl`
CSS2 Values	`inherit`
Initial	`ltr`
Applies to	All elements.
Inherited	Yes.
Notes	See `unicode-bidi` for further properties that relate to embedded text direction.

display

Usage	Specifies how the contents of a block are to be generated.
CSS1 Values	`inline` | `block` | `list-item`
CSS2 Values	`run-in` | `compact` | `marker` | `table` | `inline-table` | `table-row-group` | `table-column-group` | `table-header-group` | `table-footer-group` | `table-row` | `table-cell` | `table-caption` | `none` | `inherit`
Initial	`inline`
Applies to	All elements.
Inherited	No.

float

Usage	Specifies whether a box should float to the left, right, or not at all.
CSS1 Values	none | left | right
CSS2 Values	inherit
Initial	none
Applies to	Elements that are not positioned absolutely.
Inherited	No.

position

Usage	Determines which CSS2 positioning algorithms are used to calculate the coordinates of a box.
CSS2 Values	static | <relative> | <absolute> | fixed | inherit
Initial	static
Applies to	All elements except generated content.
Inherited	No.

unicode-bidi

Usage	Opens a new level of embedding with respect to the bidirectional algorithm when elements with reversed writing direction are embedded more than one level deep.
CSS2 Values	normal | embed | bidi-override | inherit
Initial	normal
Applies to	All elements.
Inherited	No.

z-index

Usage	Specifies the stack level of the box and whether the box establishes a local stacking context.
CSS2 Values	auto | <integer> | inherit
Initial	auto
Applies to	Elements that generate absolutely and relatively-positioned boxes.
Inherited	No.

Background and Color Properties

Where HTML enables you to specify background and color properties for text, link, and background on a global basis in the document head, CSS includes similar properties that enable you to customize colors for individual elements. The following properties are those that affect foreground and background colors of page elements.

background

Usage	Shorthand property for setting the individual background properties at the same place in the style sheet.
CSS1 Values	[<'background-color'> || <'background-image'> || <'background-repeat'> || <'background-attachment'> || <'background-position'>]
CSS2 Values	inherit
Initial	Not defined.
Applies to	All elements.
Inherited	No.

background-attachment

Usage	If a background image is specified, this property specifies whether it is fixed in the viewport or scrolls along with the document.
CSS1 Values	scroll	fixed
CSS2 Values	inherit
Initial	scroll
Applies to	All elements.
Inherited	No.

background-color

Usage	Sets the background color of an element.
CSS1 Values	<color>	transparent
CSS2 Values	inherit
Initial	transparent
Applies to	All elements.
Inherited	No.

background-image

Usage	Sets the background image of an element.
CSS1 Values	`<uri>` | `none`
CSS2 Values	`inherit`
Initial	`none`
Applies to	All elements.
Inherited	No.
Notes	Authors also should specify a background color that will be used when the image is unavailable.

background-position

Usage	Specifies the initial position of the background image, if one is specified.
CSS1 Values	`[[<percentage> | <length>](1,2) | [top | center | bottom] || [left | center | right]]`
CSS2 Values	`inherit`
Initial	0% 0%.
Applies to	Block-level and replaced elements.
Inherited	No.

background-repeat

Usage	Specifies whether an image is repeated (tiled) and how, if a background image is specified.
CSS1 Values	`repeat-x | repeat-y | repeat | no-repeat`
CSS2 Values	`inherit`
Initial	`repeat`
Applies to	All elements.
Inherited	No.

color

Usage	Describes the foreground color of an element's text content.
CSS1 Values	`<color>`
CSS2 Values	`inherit`

C

Initial	Depends on browser.
Applies to	All elements.
Inherited	Yes.

Box Model Properties

Each page element in the document tree is contained within a rectangular box and laid out according to a visual formatting model. The following elements affect an element's box.

border

Usage	A shorthand property for setting the same width, color, and style on all four borders of an element.
CSS1 Values	['border-width' || 'border-style' | <color>]
CSS2 Values	inherit
Initial	Not defined for shorthand properties.
Applies to	All elements.
Inherited	No.
Notes	This property accepts only one value. To set different values for each side of the border, use the border-width, border-style, or border-color properties.

border-bottom, border-left, border-right, border-top

Usage	Shorthand properties for setting the width, style, and color of an element's bottom, left, right, or top border (respectively).
CSS1 Values	['border-bottom-width' || 'border-style' || <color>]
	['border-left-width' || 'border-style' || <color>]
	['border-right-width' || 'border-style' || <color>]
	['border-top-width' || 'border-style' || <color>]
CSS2 Values	inherit
Initial	Not defined.
Applies to	All elements.
Inherited	No.

border-color

Usage	Sets the color of the four borders.
CSS1 Values	`<color> (1,4)	transparent`
CSS2 Values	`inherit`
Initial	The value of the `<color>` property.
Applies to	All elements.
Inherited	No.
Notes	This property accepts up to four values, as follows:
	One value: Sets all four border colors
	Two values: First value for top and bottom; second value for right and left
	Three values: First value for top; second value for right and left; third value for bottom
	Four values: Top, right, bottom, and left respectively

border-bottom-color, border-left-color, border-right-color, border-top-color

Usage	Specifies the colors of a box's border.
CSS1 Values	`<color>`
CSS2 Values	`inherit`
Initial	The value of the `<color>` property.
Applies to	All elements.
Inherited	No.

border-style

Usage	Sets the style of the four borders.
CSS1 Values	`none	dotted	dashed	solid	double	groove	ridge	inset	outset`
CSS2 Values	`inherit`
Initial	`none`
Applies to	All elements.
Inherited	No.
Notes	This property can have from one to four values (see notes under `border-color` for explanation). If no

C

value is specified, the color of the element itself will take its place.

`border-bottom-style, border-left-style, border-right-style, border-top-style`

Usage	Sets the style of a specific border (bottom, left, right, or top).
Values	Same as `border-style`.
Initial	`none`
Applies to	All elements.
Inherited	No.

`border-width`

Usage	A shorthand property for setting `border-width-top`, `border-width-right`, `border-width-bottom`, and `border-width-left` at the same place in the style sheet.
CSS1 Values	`[thin	medium	thick]` | `<length>`
CSS2 Values	`inherit`
Initial	Not defined.
Applies to	All elements.
Inherited	No.
Notes	This property accepts up to four values (see notes under `border-color` for explanation).

`border-bottom-width, border-left-width, border-right-width, border-top-width`

Usage	Sets the width of an element's bottom, left, right, or top border (respectively).
CSS1 Values	`[thin	medium	thick]` | `<length>`
CSS2 Values	`inherit`
Initial	`medium`
Applies to	All elements.
Inherited	No.

clear

Usage	Indicates which sides of an element's box or boxes may not be adjacent to an earlier floating box.
CSS1 Values	none | left | right | both
CSS2 Values	inherit
Initial	none
Applies to	Block-level elements.
Inherited	No.

height, width

Usage	Specifies the content height or width of a box.
CSS1 Values	<length> | auto
CSS2 Values	<percentage> | inherit
Initial	auto
Applies to	All elements but non-replaced inline elements and table columns; also does not apply to column groups (for height) or row groups (for width).
Inherited	No.

margin

Usage	Shorthand property for setting margin-top, margin-right, margin-bottom and margin-left at the same place in the style sheet.
CSS1 Values	<length> | <percentage> | auto
CSS2 Values	inherit
Initial	Not defined (shorthand property).
Applies to	All elements.
Inherited	No.

margin-bottom, margin-left, margin-right, margin-top

Usage	Sets the bottom, left, right, and top margins of a box (respectively).
CSS1 Values	<length> | <percentage> | auto
CSS2 Values	inherit

Initial	0
Applies to	All elements.
Inherited	No.

`max-height, max-width`

Usage	Constrains the height and width of a block to a maximum value.
CSS2 Values	`<length>` | `<percentage>` | `inherit`
Initial	100%
Applies to	All elements.
Inherited	No.
Notes	Percentages refer to the height of the containing block.

`min-height, min-width`

Usage	Constrains the height and width of a block to a minimum value.
CSS2 Values	`<length>` | `<percentage>` | `inherit`
Initial	0
Applies to	All elements.
Inherited	No.
Notes	Percentages refer to the height of the containing block.

`padding`

Usage	Shorthand property that sets `padding-top`, `padding-right`, `padding-bottom` and `padding-left` at the same place in the style sheet.
CSS1 Values	`<length>` | `<percentage>`
CSS2 Values	`inherit`
Initial	Not defined.
Applies to	All elements.
Inherited	No.

`padding-top`, `padding-right`, `padding-bottom`, `padding-left`

Usage	Specifies the width of the padding area of a box's top, right, bottom, and left sides.
CSS1 Values	`<length>` | `<percentage>`
CSS2 Values	`inherit`
Initial	0
Applies to	All elements.
Inherited	No.
Notes	Values cannot be negative. Percentage values refer to the width of the containing block.

Font Properties

Far more powerful than the font tags and attributes found in HTML 4.0, Cascading Style Sheets enable you to affect many additional elements of a font. CSS1 font properties assume that the font is resident on the client's system and specify alternative fonts through other properties. The properties proposed in CSS2 go beyond that, enabling authors to actually describe the fonts they want to use, and increases the capability for browsers to select fonts when the font the author specified is not available.

`font`

Usage	A shorthand property for setting `font-style`, `font-variant`, `font-weight`, `font-size`, `line-height`, and `font-family` at the same place in the style sheet.
CSS1 Values	`[['font-style' || 'font-variant' || 'font-weight']?` `'font-size' [/'line-height']? font-family`
CSS2 Values	`caption` | `icon` | `menu` | `message-box` | `small-caption` | `status-bar` | `inherit`
Initial	See individual properties.
Applies to	All elements.
Inherited	Yes.
Notes	Percentages allowed on `font-size` and `line-height`. For backward compatibility, set `font-stretch` and `font-size-adjust` by using their respective individual properties.

font-family

Usage	Specifies a list of font family names and generic family names.
CSS1 Values	`[[<family-name> | <generic-family> [,]*` `[<family-name> ¦ <generic-family>],`
CSS2 Values	`inherit`
Initial	Depends on browser.
Applies to	All elements.
Inherited	Yes.
Notes	`<family-name>` displays a font family of choice (Arial, Helvetica, or Bookman, for example). `<generic-family>` assigns one of five generic family names: `serif`, `sans-serif`, `cursive`, `fantasy`, or `monospace`.

font-size

Usage	Describes the size of the font when set solid.
CSS1 Values	`<absolute-size> | <relative-size> | <length> | <percentage>`
CSS2 Values	`inherit`
Initial	`medium`
Applies to	All elements.
Inherited	The computed value is inherited.
Notes	Percentages can be used relative to the parent element's font size.

font-size-adjust

Usage	Enables authors to specify a z-value for an element that preserves the x-height of the first choice substitute font.
CSS2 Values	`<number> | none | inherit`
Initial	`none`
Applies to	All elements.
Inherited	Yes.
Notes	Percentages can be used relative to the parent element's font size.

font-stretch

Usage	Specifies between normal, condensed, and extended faces within a font family.
CSS2 Values	`normal` | `wider` | `narrower` | `ultra-condensed` | `extra-condensed` | `condensed` | `semi-condensed` | `semi-expanded` | `expanded` | `extra-expanded` | `ultra-expanded` | `inherit`
Initial	`normal`
Applies to	All elements.
Inherited	Yes.

font-style

Usage	Requests normal (roman or upright), italic, and oblique faces within a font family.
CSS1 Values	`normal` | `italic` | `oblique`
CSS2 Values	`inherit`
Initial	`normal`
Applies to	All elements.
Inherited	Yes.

font-variant

Usage	Specifies a font that is not labeled as a small-caps font (`normal`) or one that is labeled as a small-caps font (`small-caps`).
CSS1 Values	`normal` | `small-caps`
CSS2 Values	`inherit`
Initial	`normal`
Applies to	All elements.
Inherited	Yes.

font-weight

Usage	Specifies the weight of the font.
CSS1 Values	`normal` ¦ `bold` ¦ `bolder` ¦ `lighter` ¦ `100` ¦ `200` ¦ `300` ¦ `400` ¦ `500` ¦ `600` ¦ `700` ¦ `800` ¦ `900`

C

CSS2 Values	`inherit`
Initial	`normal`
Applies to	All elements.
Inherited	Yes.
Notes	Values 100 through 900 form an ordered sequence. Each number indicates a weight that is at least as dark as its predecessor. Normal is equal to a weight of 400, while bold is equal to a weight of 700.

List Properties

When an element is assigned a `display` value of `list-item`, the element's content is contained in a box, and an optional marker box can be specified. The marker defines the image, glyph, or number that is used to identify the list item. The following properties affect list items and markers.

list-style

Usage	Shorthand notation for setting `list-style-type`, `list-style-image` and `list-style-position` at the same place in the style sheet.
CSS1 Values	[`'list-style-type'` ‖ `'list-style-position'` ‖ `'list-style-image'`]
CSS2 Values	`inherit`
Initial	Not defined.
Applies to	Elements with `display` property set to `list-item`.
Inherited	Yes.

list-style-image

Usage	Sets the image that will be used as the list item marker.
CSS1 Values	`<uri>` | `none`
CSS2 Values	`inherit`
Initial	`none`
Applies to	Elements with `display` property set to `list-item`.
Inherited	Yes.

list-style-position

Usage	Specifies the position of the marker box with respect to the line item content box.
CSS1 Values	inside | outside
CSS2 Values	inherit
Initial	outside
Applies to	Elements with display property set to list-item.
Inherited	Yes.

list-style-type

Usage	Specifies the appearance of the list item marker when list-style-image is set to none.
CSS1 Values	disc | circle | square | decimal | lower-roman | upper-roman | lower-alpha | upper-alpha | none
CSS2 Values	leading-zero | western-decimal | lower-greek | lower-latin | upper-latin | hebrew | armenian | georgian | cjk-ideographic | hiragana | katakana | hiragana-iroha | katakana-iroha | inherit
Initial	disc
Applies to	Elements with display property set to list-item.
Inherited	Yes.

Text Properties

The following properties affect the visual presentation of characters, spaces, words, and paragraphs.

letter-spacing

Usage	Specifies the spacing behavior between text characters.
CSS1 Values	normal | <length>
CSS2 Values	inherit
Initial	normal
Applies to	All elements.
Inherited	Yes.

line-height

Usage	Specifies the minimal height of each inline box.
CSS1 Values	`normal	number	<length>	<percentage>`
CSS2 Values	`inherit`
Initial	`normal`
Applies to	All elements.
Inherited	Yes.

text-align

Usage	Describes how a block of text is aligned.
CSS1 Values	`left	right	center	justify`
CSS2 Values	`<string>	inherit`
Initial	Depends on browser and writing direction.
Applies to	Block-level elements.
Inherited	Yes.

text-decoration

Usage	Describes decorations that are added to the text of an element.
CSS1 Values	`none	underline	overline	line-through	blink`
CSS2 Values	`inherit`
Initial	`none`
Applies to	All elements.
Inherited	No.

text-indent

Usage	Specifies the indentation of the first line of text in a block.
CSS1 Values	`<length>	<percentage>`
CSS2 Values	`inherit`
Initial	0
Applies to	Block-level elements.
Inherited	Yes.

text-shadow

Usage	Accepts a comma-separated list of shadow effects to be applied to the text of an element.
CSS2 Values	none | <color> | <length> | inherit
Initial	none
Applies to	All elements.
Inherited	No.
Notes	You also can use text shadows with :first-letter and :first-line pseudo-elements.

text-transform

Usage	Controls the capitalization of an element's text.
CSS1 Values	capitalize | uppercase | lowercase | none
CSS2 Values	inherit
Initial	none
Applies to	All elements.
Inherited	Yes.

vertical-align

Usage	Affects the vertical positioning of the boxes generated by an inline-level element.
Values	baseline | sub | super | top | texttop | middle | bottom | text-bottom | sub | <percentage>
CSS2 Values	inherit
Initial	baseline
Applies to	Inline-level and table-cell elements.
Inherited	No.

white-space

Usage	Specifies how whitespace inside the element is handled.
CSS1 Values	normal | pre | nowrap
CSS2 Values	inherit
Initial	normal

C

| Applies to | Block-level elements. |
| Inherited | Yes. |

word-spacing

Usage	Specifies the spacing behavior between words.
Values	normal | <length>
CSS2 Values	inherit
Initial	normal
Applies to	All elements.
Inherited	Yes.

Visual Effects Properties

The following properties affect visual rendering of an element.

clip

Usage	Defines which portion of an element's rendered content is visible.
CSS2 Values	<shape> | auto | inherit
Initial	auto
Applies to	Block-level and replaced elements.
Inherited	No.

overflow

Usage	Specifies whether the contents of a block-level element are clipped when they overflow the element's box.
CSS2 Values	visible | hidden | scroll | auto | inherit
Initial	visible
Applies to	Block-level and replaced elements.
Inherited	No.

visibility

| Usage | Specifies whether the boxes generated by an element are rendered. |

CSS2 Values	`visible	hidden	collapse	inherit`
Initial	`inherit`
Applies to	All elements.
Inherited	No.

Aural Style Sheet Properties

Aural style sheets, a proposed media type for CSS2, are primarily used for the blind and visually-impaired communities. Page contents are read to the user. The aural style sheet "canvas" uses dimensional space to render sounds in specified sequences as page elements are displayed and selected.

azimuth

Usage	Enablesyou to position a sound. Designed for spatial audio, which requires binaural headphones or five-speaker home theater systems.
CSS2 Values	`<angle>	[[left-side	far-left	left	center-left	center	center-right	right	far-right	right-side] || behind]| leftwards	rightwards	inherit`
Initial	`center`
Applies to	All elements.
Inherited	Yes.

cue

Usage	Shorthand property for `cue-before` and `cue-after`. Plays a sound before or after an element is rendered.
CSS2 Values	`cue-before	cue-after	inherit`
Initial	Not defined (shorthand property).
Applies to	All elements.
Inherited	No.

cue-after, cue-before

Usage	Plays a sound after (`cue-after`) or before (`cue-before`) an element is rendered.

CSS2 Values	`<uri>` | `none` | `inherit`
Initial	`none`
Applies to	All elements.
Inherited	No.

elevation

Usage	Enables you to position the angle of a sound. For use with spatial audio (binaural headphones or five-speaker home theater setups required).
CSS2 Values	`<angle>` | `below` | `level` | `above` | `higher` | `lower` | `inherit`
Initial	`level`
Applies to	All elements.
Inherited	Yes.

pause

Usage	A shorthand property for setting `pause-before` and `pause-after` in the same location in the style sheet.
CSS2 Values	`<time>` | `<percentage>` | `inherit`
Initial	Depends on browser.
Applies to	All elements.
Inherited	No.

pause-after, pause-before

Usage	Specifies a pause to be observed before or after speaking an element's content.
CSS2 Values	`<time>` | `<percentage>` | `inherit`
Initial	Depends on browser.
Applies to	All elements.
Inherited	No.

pitch

| Usage | Specifies the average pitch (frequency) of the speaking voice. |

CSS2 Values	`<frequency>` | `x-low` | `low` | `medium` | `high` | `x-high` | `inherit`
Initial	`medium`
Applies to	All elements.
Inherited	Yes.
Notes	Average pitch for the standard male voice is around 120hZ; for the female voice, it is around 210hZ.

pitch-range

Usage	Specifies variation in average pitch. Used to vary inflection and add animation to the voice.
CSS2 Values	`<number>` | `inherit`
Initial	50
Applies to	All elements.
Inherited	Yes.

play-during

Usage	Specifies a sound to be played as a background while an element's content is spoken.
CSS2 Values	`<uri>` | `mix?` | `repeat?` | `auto` | `none` | `inherit`
Initial	`auto`
Applies to	All elements.
Inherited	No.

richness

Usage	Specifies the richness, or brightness, of the speaking voice.
CSS2 Values	`<number>` | `inherit`
Initial	50
Applies to	All elements.
Inherited	Yes.

speak

Usage	Specifies whether text will be rendered aurally, and in what manner.

CSS2 Values	normal	none	spell-out	inherit
Initial	normal
Applies to	All elements.
Inherited	Yes.

speak-header

Usage	Specifies whether table headers are spoken before every cell, or only before a cell when it is associated with a different header than a previous cell.
CSS2 Values	once	always	inherit
Initial	once
Applies to	Elements that have header information.
Inherited	Yes.

speak-numeral

Usage	Speaks numbers as individual digits (100 is spoken as "one zero zero", or as a continuous full number (100 is spoken as "one hundred").
CSS2 Values	digits	continuous	inherit
Initial	continuous
Applies to	All elements.
Inherited	Yes.

speak-punctuation

Usage	Speaks punctuation literally (period, comma, and so on) or naturally as various pauses.
CSS2 Values	code	none	inherit
Initial	none
Applies to	All elements.
Inherited	Yes.

speech-rate

| Usage | Specifies the speaking rate of the voice. |

CSS2 Values	`<number>` | `x-slow` | `slow` | `medium` | `fast` | `x-fast` | `faster` | `slower` | `inherit`
Initial	`medium`
Applies to	All elements.
Inherited	Yes.

stress

Usage	Specifies the height of "local peaks" in the intonation of a voice. Controls the amount of inflection within stress markers.
CSS2 Values	`<number>` | `inherit`
Initial	50
Applies to	All elements.
Inherited	Yes.
Notes	A companion to the `pitch-range` property.

voice-family

Usage	Specifies a comma-separated list of voice family names.
CSS2 Values	`<specific-voice>` | `<generic-voice>` | `inherit`
Initial	Depends on browser.
Applies to	All elements.
Inherited	Yes.

volume

Usage	Specifies the median volume of a waveform. Ranges from 0 (minimum audible volume level) to 100 (maximum comfortable level).
CSS2 Values	`<number>` | `<percentage>` | `silent` | `x-soft` | `soft` | `medium` | `loud` | `x-loud` | `inherit`
Initial	`medium`
Applies to	All elements.
Inherited	Yes.
Notes	Silent renders no sound at all. x-soft = 0, soft = 25, medium = 50, loud = 75, and x-loud = 100.

C

Generated Content/Automatic Numbering Properties

CSS2 introduces properties and values that enable authors to render content automatically (for example, numbered lists can be generated automatically). Authors specify style and location of generated content with `:before` and `:after` pseudo-elements that indicate the page elements before and after which content is generated automatically.

content

Usage	Used with `:before` and `:after` pseudo-elements to generate content in a document.
CSS2 Values	`<string>` | `<uri>` | `<counter>` | `attr(X)` | `open-quote` | `close-quote` | `no-open-quote` | `no-close-quote` | `inherit`
Initial	`empty string`
Applies to	`:before` and `:after` pseudo-elements.
Inherited	All.

counter-increment

Usage	Accepts one or more names of counters (identifiers), each one optionally followed by an integer. The integer indicates the amount of increment for every occurrence of the element.
CSS2 Values	`<identifier>` | `<integer>` | `none` | `inherit`
Initial	`none`
Applies to	All elements.
Inherited	No.

counter-reset

Usage	Contains a list of one or more names of counters. The integer gives the value that the counter is set to on each occurrence of the element.
CSS2 Values	`<identifier>` | `<integer>` | `none` | `inherit`
Initial	`none`
Applies to	All elements.
Inherited	No.

marker-offset

Usage	Specifies the distance between the nearest border edges of a marker box and its associated principal box.
CSS2 Values	`<length>` | `auto` | `inherit`
Initial	`auto`
Applies to	Elements with `display` property set to `marker`.
Inherited	No.

quotes

Usage	Specifies quotation marks for embedded quotations.
CSS2 Values	`<string>` | `<string>+` | `none` | `inherit`
Initial	Depends on browser.
Applies to	All elements.
Inherited	Yes.

C

Paged Media Properties

Normally, a Web page appears as a continuous page. CSS2 introduces the concept of paged media, which is designed to split a document into one or more discrete pages for display on paper, transparencies, computer screens, and so on. Page size, margins, page breaks, widows, and orphans can all be set with the following properties and values.

marks

Usage	Specifies whether cross marks, crop marks, or both should be rendered just outside the page box. Used in high-quality printing.
CSS2 Values	`crop` | `cross` | `none` | `inherit`
Initial	`none`
Applies to	Page context.
Inherited	N/A.

orphans

Usage	Specifies the minimum number of lines of a paragraph that must be left at the bottom of a page.

CSS2 Values	`<integer>` I `inherit`
Initial	2
Applies to	Block-level elements.
Inherited	Yes.

page

Usage	Used to specify a particular type of page where an element should be displayed.
CSS2 Values	`<identifier>` `:left` I `:right` I `auto`
Initial	`auto`
Applies to	Block-level elements.
Inherited	Yes.
Notes	By adding `:left` or `:right`, the element can be forced to fall on a left or right page.

page-break-after, page-break-before

Usage	Specifies page breaks before the following element or after the preceding element.
CSS2 Values	`auto` I `always` I `avoid` I `left` I `right` I `inherit`
Initial	`auto`
Applies to	Block-level elements.
Inherited	No.

page-break-inside

Usage	Forces a page break inside the parent element.
CSS2 Values	`avoid` I `auto` I `inherit`
Initial	`auto`
Applies to	Block-level elements.
Inherited	Yes.

size

Usage	Specifies the size and orientation of a page box.
CSS2 Values	`<length>` I `auto` I `portrait` I `landscape` I `inherit`
Initial	`auto`

Applies to	Page context.
Inherited	N/A.

widows

Usage	Specifies the minimum number of lines of a paragraph that must be left at the top of a page.
CSS2 Values	`<integer>	inherit`
Initial	2
Applies to	Block-level elements.
Inherited	Yes.

Table Properties

The CSS table model is based on the HTML 4.0 table model, which consists of tables, captions, rows, row groups, columns, column groups, and cells. In CSS2, tables can be rendered visually and aurally. Authors can specify how headers and data will be spoken through attributes defined previously under "Aural Page Properties."

border-collapse

Usage	Selects a table's border model.
CSS2 Values	`collapse	separate	inherit`
Initial	`collapse`
Applies to	Table and inline table elements.
Inherited	Yes.

border-spacing

Usage	In separated borders model, specifies the distance that separates the adjacent cell borders.
CSS2 Values	`<length>	<length> ?	inherit`
Initial	0
Applies to	Table and inline table elements.
Inherited	Yes.

caption-side

Usage	Specifies the position of the caption box with respect to the table box.
CSS2 Values	top | bottom | left | right | inherit
Initial	top
Applies to	Table caption elements.
Inherited	Yes.

column-span, row-span

Usage	Specifies the number of columns or rows (respectively) spanned by a cell.
CSS2 Values	<integer> | inherit
Initial	1
Applies to	Table-cell, table-column, and table-column-group elements (column-span); table-cell elements (row-span).
Inherited	No.

empty-cells

Usage	In separated tables model, specifies how borders around cells that have no visible content are rendered.
CSS2 Values	borders | no-borders | inherit
Initial	borders
Applies to	Table cell elements.
Inherited	Yes.

table-layout

Usage	Controls the algorithm used to lay out the table cells.
CSS2 Values	auto | fixed | inherit
Initial	auto
Applies to	Table and inline table elements.
Inherited	No.
Notes	Fixed table layout depends on the width of the table and its columns. Auto table layout depends on the contents of the cells.

User Interface Properties

User interface properties enable customization of cursor appearance, color preferences, font preferences, and dynamic outlines.

cursor

Usage	Specifies the type of cursor which displays for a pointing device.
CSS2 Values	`<uri>` | `auto` | `crosshair` | `default` | `pointer` | `move` | `e-resize` | `ne-resize` | `nw-resize` | `n-resize` | `se-resize` | `sw-resize` | `s-resize` | `w-resize` | `text` | `wait` | `help` | `inherit`
Initial	`auto`
Applies to	All elements.
Inherited	Yes.

outline

Usage	Shorthand property for setting `outline-color`, `outline-style`, and `outline-width`.
CSS2 Values	`outline-color` | `outline-style` | `outline-width` | `inherit`
Initial	See individual properties.
Applies to	All elements.
Inherited	No.
Notes	Similar to `border` property, creates an outline around visual objects such as buttons, active form fields, image maps, and so on. Using `outline` property rather than `border` property does not cause reflow when displaying or suppressing the outline. Outlines also can be non-rectangular.

outline-color

Usage	Specifies the color of the outline.
CSS2 Values	`<color>` | `invert` | `inherit`
Initial	`invert`
Applies to	All elements.
Inherited	No.

outline-style

Usage	Specifies the style of the outline.
CSS2 Values	same as <border-style>	inherit
Initial	none
Applies to	All elements.
Inherited	No.

outline-width

Usage	Specifies the width of the outline.
CSS2 Values	same as <border-width>	inherit
Initial	medium
Applies to	All elements.
Inherited	No.

Cascading Style Sheet Units

Several Cascading Style Sheet attributes use standard units to define measurements, styles, colors, and other identifiers. Throughout this appendix, unit measurements have been enclosed within angle brackets (< >). The following section lists the values associated with each unit type.

<absolute-size>

Absolute sizes refer to font sizes computed and kept by the user's browser. The following values are from smallest to largest:

```
xx-small
x-small
small
medium
large
x-large
xx-large
```

<angle>

Angle values are used with aural style sheets. Their format is an optional sign character (+ or -) immediately followed by a number. The following are angle units:

deg	degrees
grad	grads
rad	radians

`<border-style>`

These properties specify the type of line that surrounds a box's border. The `border-style` value type can take one of the following:

none	Forces border width to zero
dotted	A series of dots
dashed	A series of short line segments
solid	A single line segment
double	Two solid lines, with the sum of the two lines and the space between them equaling the value of `border-width`
groove	Renders a border that looks as though it is carved into the canvas
ridge	Renders a border that looks as though it is coming out of the canvas
inset	Renders a border that looks like the entire box is embedded into the canvas
outset	Renders a border that looks like the entire box is coming out of the canvas

`<border-width>`

The `border-width` property sets the width of the border area. It can take one of the following values:

thin	A thin border
medium	A medium border
thick	A thick border
`<length>`	An explicit value (cannot be negative)

`<color>`

Colors can be defined by keyword (as defined in HTML 4.0) or by a numerical RGB specification. Following are the accepted formats:

C

Keyword:	aqua | black | blue | fuchsia | gray | green | lime | maroon | navy | olive | purple | red | silver | teal | white | yellow
#rgb	example for Blue: { color: #00f }
#rrggbb	example for Blue: { color: #0000ff }
rgb (integer range)	example for Blue: { color: rgb(0,0,255) }
rgb (float range)	example for Blue: { color: rgb(0%, 0%, 100%) }

<family-name>

Fonts can be specified by the name of a font family of choice. Examples of this are Arial, Times New Roman, Helvetica, Baskerville, and so on. Font family names that contain whitespace (tabs, line feeds, carriage returns, form feeds, and so on) should be quoted.

<frequency>

Frequency identifiers are used with aural style sheets. The format is a number immediately followed by one of the following identifiers:

Hz	Hertz
kHz	Kilohertz

<generic-family>

Authors are encouraged to use generic font family names as a last alternative, in case a user does not have a specified font on his or her system. Generic font family names are keywords and must not be enclosed in quotes. The following are examples of each:

serif	Times New Roman, MS Georgia, Garamond
sans-serif	Arial, Helvetica, Futura, Gill Sans
cursive	Zapf-Chancery, Caflisch Script
fantasy	Critter, Cottonwood
monospace	Courier, MS Courier New, Prestige

<generic-voice>

Generic voices are the aural equivalent of generic font family names (see preceding) and are used in conjunction with <voice-family>. The following are possible generic voice values:

```
male

female

child
```

<integer>

An integer consists of one or more digits (0 through 9). It may be preceded by a - or a + to indicate the sign. See also <number>.

Lengths are specified by an optional sign character (+ or -) immediately followed by a number with or without a decimal point, immediately followed by one of the following unit identifiers:

Relative values:

em	The font size of the relevant font
ex	The x-height of the relevant font
px	Pixels, relative to the viewing device

Absolute values:

pt	Points (1/72nd of an inch)
in	Inches
cm	Centimeters
mm	Millimeters
pc	Picas (12 points, or 1/6 of an inch)

<number>

A number can consist of an integer, or it can be zero or more digits, followed by a dot (.), followed by one or more digits. Numbers may be preceded by a - or a + to indicate the sign. See also <integer>.

<percentage>

Percentage values are always relative to another value, such as a length. The format is an optional sign character (+ or -), immediately followed by a number, immediately followed by %.

<relative-size>

Relative sizes are interpreted relative to the font size of the parent element. The following are possible values:

larger

smaller

`<shape>`

In CSS2, the only valid shape value is `rect(<top> <right> <bottom> <left>`, where the latter four descriptors specify offsets from the respective sides of the box.

`<specific-voice>`

Specific voice values are the aural style sheet equivalent of font-family. Values are specific names of a voice (for example: teacher, comedian, preacher, and so on).

`<time>`

Time units are used with aural style sheets. Their format is a number immediately followed by one of the following identifiers:

ms	Milliseconds
s	Seconds

`<uri>`

URI (Uniform Resource Indicator) values are used to designate addresses of page elements such as images.

The format of a URI is `url` (followed by optional whitespace, followed by an optional single quote or double quotation mark, followed by the URI itself, followed by an optional single or double quote, followed by optional whitespace). To clarify, here is an example of the proper syntax:

```
body { background: url ("http://www.foo.com/images/background.gif" }
```

APPENDIX D

Colors by Name and Hexadecimal Value

Table D.1 contains a list of all the color names recognized by Navigator 2.0 and Internet Explorer 3.0 (and later versions of both browsers, of course) and also includes their corresponding Hexadecimal (Hex) Triplet values. To see all these colors correctly, you must have a 256-color or better video card and the appropriate video drivers installed. Also, depending on the operating system and computer platform you are running, some colors may not appear exactly as you expect them to.

TABLE D.1 Color Values and HEX Triplet Equivalents

Color Name	HEX Triplet	Color Name	HEX Triplet
aliceblue	#f0f8ff	azure	#f0ffff
antiquewhite	#faebd7	beige	#f5f5dc
aqua	#00ffff	bisque	#ffe4c4
aquamarine	#7fffd4	black	#000000

continues

TABLE D.1   continued

Color Name	HEX Triplet	Color Name	HEX Triplet
blanchedalmond	#ffebcd	dimgray	#696969
blue	#0000ff	dodgerblue	#1e90ff
blueviolet	#8a2be2	firebrick	#b22222
brown	#a52a2a	floralwhite	#fffaf0
burlywood	#deb887	forestgreen	#228b22
cadetblue	#5f9ea0	fuchsia	#ff00ff
chartreuse	#7fff00	gainsboro	#dcdcdc
chocolate	#d2691e	ghostwhite	#f8f8ff
coral	#ff7f50	gold	#ffd700
cornflowerblue	#6495ed	goldenrod	#daa520
cornsilk	#fff8dc	gray	#808080
crimson	#dc143c	green	#008000
cyan	#00ffff	greenyellow	#adff2f
darkblue	#00008b	honeydew	#f0fff0
darkcyan	#008b8b	hotpink	#ff69b4
darkgoldenrod	#b8860b	indianred	#cd5c5c
darkgray	#a9a9a9	indigo	#4b0082
darkgreen	#006400	ivory	#fffff0
darkkhaki	#bdb76b	khaki	#f0e68c
darkmagenta	#8b008b	lavender	#e6e6fa
darkolivegreen	#556b2f	lavenderblush	#fff0f5
darkorange	#ff8c00	lemonchiffon	#fffacd
darkorchid	#9932cc	lightblue	#add8e6
darkred	#8b0000	lightcoral	#f08080
darksalmon	#e9967a	lightcyan	#e0ffff
darkseagreen	#8fbc8f	lightgoldenrodyellow	#fafad2
darkslateblue	#483D8b	lightgreen	#90ee90
darkslategray	#2f4f4f	lightgrey	#d3d3d3
darkturquoise	#00ced1	lightpink	#ffb6c1
darkviolet	#9400d3	lightsalmon	#ffa07a
deeppink	#ff1493	lightseagreen	#20b2aa
deepskyblue	#00bfff	lightskyblue	#87cefa

Color Name	HEX Triplet	Color Name	HEX Triplet
lightslategray	#778899	peachpuff	#ffdab9
lightsteelblue	#b0c4de	peru	#cd853f
lightyellow	#ffffe0	pink	#ffc0cb
lime	#00ff00	plum	#dda0dd
limegreen	#32cd32	powderblue	#b0e0e6
linen	#faf0e6	purple	#800080
magenta	#ff00ff	red	#ff0000
maroon	#800000	rosybrown	#bc8f8f
mediumaquamarine	#66cdaa	royalblue	#4169e1
mediumblue	#0000cd	saddlebrown	#8b4513
mediumorchid	#ba55d3	salmon	#fa8072
mediumpurple	#9370db	sandybrown	#f4a460
mediumseagreen	#3cb371	seagreen	#2e8b57
mediumslateblue	#7b68ee	seashell	#fff5ee
mediumspringgreen	#00fa9a	sienna	#a0522d
mediumturquoise	#48d1cc	silver	#c0c0c0
mediumvioletred	#c71585	skyblue	#87ceeb
midnightblue	#191970	slateblue	#6a5acd
mintcream	#f5fffa	slategray	#708090
mistyrose	#ffe4e1	snow	#fffafa
navajowhite	#ffdead	springgreen	#00ff7f
navy	#000080	steelblue	#4682b4
oldlace	#fdf5e6	tan	#d2b48c
olive	#808000	teal	#008080
olivedrab	#6b8e23	thistle	#d8bfd8
orange	#ffa500	tomato	#ff6347
orangered	#ff4500	turquoise	#40e0d0
orchid	#da70d6	violet	#ee82ee
palegoldenrod	#eee8aA	wheat	#f5deb3
palegreen	#98fb98	white	#ffffff
paleturquoise	#afeeee	whitesmoke	#f5f5f5
palevioletred	#db7093	yellow	#ffff00
papayawhip	#ffefd5	yellowgreen	#9acd32

D

APPENDIX E

MIME Types and File Extensions

Table E.1 lists some the file extensions and MIME content types supported by many popular Web servers. If your server does not list an extension for a particular content type, or if the type you want to use is not listed at all, you will have to add support for that type to your server configuration.

TABLE E.1 MIME Types and HTTPD Support

MIME Type	File What It Is (If Noted)	Extensions
application/acad	AutoCAD Drawing files	dwg, DWG
application/arj		arj
application/clariscad	ClarisCAD files	CCAD
application/drafting	MATRA Prelude drafting	DRW
application/dxf	DXF (AutoCAD)	dxf, DXF

continues

TABLE E.1 continued

MIME Type	File What It Is (If Noted)	Extensions
application/excel	Microsoft Excel	xl
application/i-deas	SDRC I-DEAS files	unv, UNV
application/iges	IGES graphics format	igs, iges, IGS, IGES
application/mac-binhex40	Macintosh BinHex format	hqx
application/msword	Microsoft Word	word, w6w, doc
application/mswrite	Microsoft Write	wri
application/octet-stream	Uninterpreted binary	bin
application/oda		oda
application/pdf	PDF (Adobe Acrobat)	pdf
application/postscript	PostScript	ai, PS, ps, eps
application/pro_eng	PTC Pro/ENGINEER	prt, PRT, part
application/rtf	Rich Text Format	rtf
application/set	SET (French CAD standard)	set, SET
application/sla	Stereolithography	stl, STL
application/solids	MATRA Prelude Solids	SOL
application/STEP	ISO-10303 STEP data files	stp, STP, step, STEP
application/vda	VDA-FS Surface data	vda, VDA
application/x-csh	C-shell script	csh
application/x-director	Macromedia Director	dir, dcr, dxr
application/x-dvi	TeX DVI	dvi
application/x-gzip	GNU Zip	gz, gzip
application/x-mif	FrameMaker MIF Format	mif
application/x-hdf	NCSA HDF Data File	hdf
application/x-latex	LaTeX source	latex
application/x-netcdf	Unidata netCDF	nc,cdf
application/x-sh	Bourne shell script	sh
application/x-stuffit	Stuffit Archive	sit
application/x-tcl	TCL script	tcl
application/x-tex	TeX source	tex
application/x-texinfo	Texinfo (Emacs)	texinfo,texi
application/x-troff	Troff	t, tr, roff
application/x-troff-man	Troff with MAN macros	man

MIME Type	What It Is (If Noted)	File Extensions
application/x-troff-me	Troff with ME macros	me
application/x-troff-ms	Troff with MS macros	ms
application/x-wais-source	WAIS source	src
application/x-bcpio	Old binary CPIO	bcpio
application/x-cpio	POSIX CPIO	cpio
application/x-gtar	GNU tar	gtar
application/x-shar	Shell archive	shar
application/x-sv4cpio	SVR4 CPIO	sv4cpio
application/x-sv4crc	SVR4 CPIO with CRC	sv4crc
application/x-tar	4.3BSD tar format	tar
application/x-ustar	POSIX tar format	ustar
application/x-winhelp	Windows Help	hlp
application/zip	ZIP archive	zip
audio/basic	Basic audio (usually μ-law)	au, snd
audio/x-aiff	AIFF audio	aif, aiff, aifc
audio/x-mpeg.mp3	MP3 audio	mp3
audio/x-mpegurl	URL resource of MP3 Audio	m3u, mp3url
audio/x-pn-realaudio	RealAudio	ra, ram
audio/x-pn-realaudio-plugin	RealAudio (plug-in)	rpm
audio/x-wav	Windows WAVE audio	wav
image/gif	GIF image	gif
image/ief	Image Exchange Format	ief
image/jpeg	JPEG image	jpg, JPG, JPE, jpe, JPEG, jpeg
image/pict	Macintosh PICT	pict
image/tiff	TIFF image	tiff, tif
image/x-cmu-raster	CMU raster	ras
image/x-portable-anymap	PBM Anymap format	pnm
image/x-portable-bitmap	PBM Bitmap format	pbm
image/x-portable-graymap	PBM Graymap format	pgm
image/x-portable-pixmap	PBM Pixmap format	ppm
image/x-rgb	RGB Image	rgb

E

continues

TABLE E.1   continued

MIME Type	File What It Is (If Noted)	Extensions
image/x-xbitmap	X Bitmap	xbm
image/x-xpixmap	X Pixmap	xpm
image/x-xwindowdump	X Windows dump (xwd) format	xwd
multipart/x-zip	PKZIP Archive	zip
multipart/x-gzip	GNU ZIP Archive	gzip
text/html	HTML	html, htm
text/plain	Plain text	txt, g, h, C, cc, hh, m, f90
text/richtext	MIME Richtext	rtx
text/tab-separated-values	Text with tab-separated values	tsv
text/x-setext	Struct enhanced text	etx
video/mpeg	MPEG video	mpeg, mpg, MPG, MPE, mpe, MPEG, mpeg
video/quicktime	QuickTime Video	qt, mov
video/msvideo	Microsoft Windows Video	avi
video/x-sgi-movie	SGI Movieplayer format	movie
x-world/x-vrml	VRML Worlds	wrl

INDEX

Q - R